CULTURE WARS

AN ENCYCLOPEDIA OF
ISSUES, VIEWPOINTS, AND VOICES

Volume 2

Roger Chapman, Editor

M.E.Sharpe
Armonk, New York
London, England

M.E. Sharpe, Inc.
80 Business Park Drive
Armonk, NY 10504

© 2010 by M.E. Sharpe, Inc.

Cover photos (clockwise from upper left) provided by Getty Images and the following: Katja Heinemann; Terry Ashe/Time & Life Pictures; Mark Leffingwell/AFP; Michael Springer; Karen Bleier/AFP.

Library of Congress Cataloging-in-Publication Data

Culture wars : an encyclopedia of issues, viewpoints, and voices / Roger Chapman, editor.
    p. cm.
  Includes bibliographical references and index.
   ISBN 978-0-7656-1761-3 (hardcover : alk. paper)
   1. Culture conflict—Encyclopedias. 2. Politics and culture—Encyclopedias. 3. Social problems—Encyclopedias. 4. Social conflict—Encyclopedias. 5. Ethnic conflict—Encyclopedias.
I. Chapman, Roger.

HM1121.C85 2010
306.0973′03—dc22   2009011925

Printed and bound in the United States

The paper used in this publication meets the minimum requirements of American National Standard for Information Sciences—Permanence of Paper for Printed Library Materials,
ANSI Z 39.48.1984.

CW (c) 10 9 8 7 6 5 4 3 2 1

Publisher: Myron E. Sharpe
Vice President and Director of New Product Development: Donna Sanzone
Vice President and Production Director: Carmen Chetti
Executive Development Editor: Jeff Hacker
Project Manager: Angela Piliouras
Program Coordinator: Cathleen Prisco
Assistant Editor: Alison Morretta
Text Design and Cover Design: Jesse Sanchez
Typesetter: Nancy Connick

Contents

CULTURE WARS

Volume 2

MacKinnon, Catharine

Catharine MacKinnon, feminist legal theorist, attorney, law professor, and author, helped shape American legal theory pertaining to sexual discrimination by broadening the definition to include sexual harassment. She has also campaigned against pornography, linking it to male aggression and dominance toward women. Her positions and active lobbying for changes in American law propelled her into the culture wars, and she has often faced opposition from the left and the right.

She was born Catharine Alice MacKinnon on October 7, 1946, in Minneapolis, Minnesota, and raised in an upper-middle-class home. Her father, George E. MacKinnon, was a federal judge, U.S. Representative (R-MN), and adviser to the presidential campaigns of Dwight Eisenhower and Richard M. Nixon. Educated at Smith College (BA, 1969), Yale Law School (JD, 1977), and Yale University (PhD, political science, 1987), MacKinnon has been a professor at the University of Michigan Law School since 1990. She was also a visiting professor at the University of Chicago (1980–1982, 1984–1988). Her books include *Sexual Harassment of Working Women: A Case of Sex Discrimination* (1979), *Toward a Feminist Theory of the State* (1989), *Only Words* (1993), *Are Women Human?* (1998), and *Sex Equality* (2001).

Best known for her militant antipornography activism, MacKinnon rejects pornography because it exemplifies and reproduces male domination, which she argues is the defining characteristic of American society. She has argued that pornography constitutes a violation of women's civil rights. She rejects the legal framework of obscenity and community standards in U.S. pornography law, viewing such distinctions as legal disguises for the male viewpoint. Pornography laws, she argues, thus work to ensure the availability of pornography for men, while rendering women's subordination invisible. Working with the radical feminist and antipornography advocate Andrea Dworkin in 1983, MacKinnon drafted a civil rights ordinance that defined pornography as "the graphic sexually explicit subordination of women through pictures and/or words." The ordinance was briefly adopted in Minneapolis and Indianapolis but was later ruled unconstitutional.

Ever controversial, MacKinnon has faced opposition from every side of the political spectrum. The mainstream left has argued that her antipornography statute violates free speech guarantees under the First Amendment to the Constitution. Like legal scholar Richard Posner and *Playboy* founder Hugh Hefner, many liberals believe that pornography should not be censored.

Conservatives argue that MacKinnon's assertions regarding male domination are untrue. Where she sees oppression, many conservatives see contentment and social order. They reject her claims of gender hierarchy, describing instead natural sexual differences and the mutual compatibility of complementary gender roles. Like MacKinnon, however, many conservatives reject pornography, albeit on different grounds—they believe it is immoral (often from a religious perspective).

MacKinnon has also faced opposition from some feminists who see her views as dangerously aligned with the Religious Right. The problem is not pornography, some of her critics argue, but "sexual oppression," which stigmatizes not only pornographers and pornography consumers but other "sexual minorities" like prostitutes, sadomasochists, homosexuals, transsexuals, and fetishists. They argue that sex is a realm of potential freedom for women, and that pornography produced by and for women can be an important feminist act.

C. Heike Schotten

See also: Dworkin, Andrea; Feminism, Second-Wave; Feminism, Third-Wave; Flynt, Larry; Hefner, Hugh; Pornography; Religious Right.

Further Reading
Califia, Pat. *Public Sex: The Culture of Radical Sex*. San Francisco: Cleis, 2000.

MacKinnon, Catharine, and Andrea Dworkin, eds. *In Harm's Way: The Pornography Civil Rights Hearings*. Cambridge, MA: Harvard University Press, 1998.

Posner, Richard. *Overcoming Law*. Cambridge, MA: Harvard University Press, 1995.

Rubin, Gayle. "Thinking Sex: Notes for a Radical Theory for the Politics of Sexuality." In *Pleasure and Danger: Exploring Female Sexuality*, ed. Carole Vance, 267–319. Boston: Routledge, 1984.

Madonna

The singer, songwriter, and dancer Madonna, widely known as the "Queen of Pop," released eighteen albums from 1983 to 2008, selling more than 200 million copies worldwide—believed to be the most ever by any female recording artist. A film actress, producer, and children's author as well as a pop music icon, Madonna is well known for generating controversy with the sexual, political, and religious imagery in her music and video recordings and her live performances.

She was born Madonna Louise Veronica Ciccone on August 16, 1958, in Bay City, Michigan, and raised in a Catholic family in the suburbs of Detroit. She left college and moved to New York in 1978 to pursue a dancing career and began singing with a rock band

The Catholic-born pop superstar Madonna has raised the hackles of church groups, cultural conservatives, and parental organizations, among others, with her irreverent lyrics and sexually explicit performances. *(Frank Micelotta/ Getty Images)*

called the Breakfast Club. Her career took off in the early 1980s after she signed a recording contract. Her debut album, *Madonna* (1983), produced Top 10 hits that established her as a star. She also began her pioneering work in music videos, appearing in elaborate, often sexually explicit productions that helped make her a multimedia pop-culture star. Her song lyrics, music videos, live performances, and publications all pushed conventional boundaries of decency. At the First Annual MTV Video Music Awards, she performed "Like a Virgin" (1984) wearing a wedding dress while writhing on stage, simulating masturbation, shocking viewers and incensing critics. The Who's That Girl Tour (1987) featured Madonna in fishnet stockings and a corset with gold-tipped conical breasts.

Madonna's 1986 song "Papa Don't Preach" raised new issues by addressing teenage pregnancy and abortion. Conservatives interpreted the line "But I made up my mind, I'm keeping my baby" to mean that Madonna advocated a pro-life stance. Opponents of abortion were

disappointed, however, when she did not speak out publicly for their cause. Others, including women's organizations and parents, criticized the singer for promoting teenage pregnancy.

With the release of her music video "Like a Prayer" (1989), new controversy erupted because of the mix of Catholic imagery and eroticism. At one point in the video, Madonna appears to be making out with Jesus. The Pope openly condemned this video, and Pepsi canceled its Madonna television commercial.

Madonna's book *Sex* (1992), an instant best-seller, featured a collection of hardcore sexual fantasies, poems, and photos; Madonna was depicted acting out sexual fantasies, including sadomasochism. She stirred further controversy the following year with the explicit sexual overtones and her irreverent behavior as a dominatrix in The Girlie Show world tour. A marked change in behavior began to be seen with the release of her album *Bedtime Stories* (1994) and her Golden Globe–winning performance in the film *Evita* (1996), but Madonna's calm demeanor proved fleeting.

At the MTV Video Music Awards in 1998, Madonna angered Hindus when she sported facial markings considered holy during her performance of "Ray of Light." Her eighth album, *Music* (2000), debuted at number one on the Billboard Charts and led to more raised eyebrows. The music video for "What It Feels Like for a Girl" (2000), directed by her husband, Guy Ritchie, contained so much explicit violence that both MTV and VH1 banned the video after only one airing. In the video, Madonna went on a rampage of violence, including ramming a car into a group of people, shooting a water pistol at police, and running the car into a lightpost.

In 2003, Madonna released another controversial album, *American Life*. The video to the title track contained graphic scenes of war and finished with Madonna throwing a grenade in the lap of a George W. Bush look-alike. She pulled the video but still earned a reputation as unpatriotic and anti-American. Later that same year, the singer caused a stir by French kissing Britney Spears and Christina Aguilera on stage during the MTM Video Music Awards program.

Madonna's Confessions tour led to another controversy with the Catholic Church. She performed "Live to Tell" (2006) while hanging on a cross with a crown of thorns on her head. The act outraged Catholics, and there were calls for Madonna's excommunication. The concert also received criticism from the Russian Orthodox Church and the Federation of Jewish Communities of Russia, adding more entries to the list of groups disenchanted with the singer's use of religious symbolism.

In 2008, Madonna was inducted into the Rock and Roll Hall of Fame, released the album *Hard Candy*, signed a $100 million deal with the concert promoter Live Nation, and agreed to provide a divorce settlement of between $76 million and $92 million to actor Guy Ritchie (earlier she had divorced actor Sean Penn).

Margaret Dykes

See also: Abortion; Catholic Church; National Organization for Women; Penn, Sean; Pornography; Race; Rock and Roll; Rodman, Dennis.

Further Reading

Bego, Mark. *Madonna: Blonde Ambition.* New York: Harmony Books, 1992.

Benson, Carol, and Allan Metz, eds. *The Madonna Companion: Two Decades of Commentary.* New York: Shirmer Books, 1999.

Guilbert, Georges-Claude. *Madonna as Postmodern Myth: How One Star's Self-Construction Rewrites Sex, Gender, Hollywood, and the American Dream.* Jefferson, NC: McFarland, 2002.

Madonna Official Web site. www.madonna.com.

Paglia, Camille. "Mercurial Girl." *Rolling Stone,* May 18, 2006.

Mailer, Norman

The author of more than thirty books, Norman Mailer was a social commentator and cultural provocateur as well as one of America's most prominent literary figures in the latter half of the twentieth century. Remembered for his New Journalism writings, which blended fiction and nonfiction, Mailer chronicled the counterculture and the New Left as a participant observer. Many of his writings are infused with a philosophy of Manichean dualism, a binary construct of reality: good and evil, "hip" and "square," and the like. A self-described "left conservative," Mailer regarded American society as a battleground between what is natural and artificial. He was "left" in that he favored "hipsters" and radicals, viewing them as existentialists fighting against conformity and "technological fascism." He was "conservative" in that he favored primitivism, famously asserting that technology (including birth control), plastic, and cancer all are related to the unnatural and inauthentic modern lifestyle. Mailer's writings from the 1950s through the 1970s marked his major participation in the culture wars.

Norman Kingsley Mailer was born on January 31, 1923, in Long Branch, New Jersey, and grew up in Brooklyn, New York. After graduating from Harvard University (SB, aeronautical engineering, 1943), he was drafted into the army and served in the Pacific Theater during World War II. When the war was over, he attended the Sorbonne in Paris and published *The Naked and the Dead* (1946), a bleak, hyper-real war novel, suggesting that the defeat of fascism came at the price of adopting some of its ways. Mailer became instantly famous and went on to practice a hipster lifestyle. He co-founded the alternative Greenwich Village weekly newspaper the *Village Voice* (1955) and used it to experiment with essay writing. He twice ran unsuccessfully for mayor of New York City (1960 and 1969), the first time shortly after stabbing his second wife while in a drunken state. (He had six marriages.) From 1984 to 1986, he served as the president of PEN (Poets, Playwrights, Editors, Essayists, and Novelists). Mailer died on November 10, 2007.

One of Mailer's early controversies was the publication of "The White Negro" (1957), an essay in *Dissent* that romanticized the black male as the prototype of the hipster. Mailer suggested that black Americans are truly liberated, including sexually, because they are not part of mainstream society. The black novelist James Baldwin, in his *Esquire* essay "The Black Boy Looks at the White Boy" (1961), accused Mailer of reducing the American Negro male to "a kind of walking phallic symbol." The Beat novelist Jack Kerouac objected to Mailer for linking hipsters with violent psychopaths. Indeed, Mailer connected the bravery of criminals with the counterculture in general. In an infamous passage of "The White Negro"—which Norman Podhoretz deplored as "the most morally gruesome"—Mailer praises hypothetical hoodlums who would be daring enough to "beat in the brains" of a candy-store owner.

In the essay collection *Advertisements for Myself* (1959), Mailer categorized himself as a major writer with the potential of changing American culture. "The way to save your work and reach many more readers is to advertise yourself," he wrote, explaining why he sought the public spotlight, which some regarded as a bald rationalization of the author's egotism. Mailer explained that, in his mind, he had been running for president for the past decade, adding, "I am imprisoned with a perception which will settle for nothing less than making a revolution in the consciousness of our time." By the 1970s, he would have less grandiose ambitions, concluding that novelists had lost their stature in society.

In the meantime, he joined in the political clamor of his day. On invitation of the Students for a Democratic Society (SDS), Mailer spoke at the University of California at Berkeley during the spring of 1965. Addressing the student crowd, he ridiculed President Lyndon Johnson and the Vietnam War, arguing that rational debate was pointless and that the only way to end the war was to engage in outrageous forms of protest. He later wrote *Why Are We in Vietnam?* (1967), a novel about a manly bear hunt in Alaska that uses the word "Vietnam" only once (on the last page), but serves as an allegory of the U.S. intervention in Southeast Asia. This was followed by his most acclaimed nonfiction work, the Pulitzer Prize–winning *Armies of the Night* (1968), an account of the 1967 antiwar march on the Pentagon, including his arrest, and a probing study of the New Left. In this work, what he called "history as a novel, the novel as history," Mailer refers to himself in the third person as "the Novelist," "the Ruminator," "the General," and "the Historian."

Also in 1968, he produced *Miami and the Siege of Chicago*, a work covering the two party conventions but focusing heavily on the antiwar violence in Chicago that year at the Democratic National Convention. That event, in Mailer's view, represented the Democratic Party turning against its working-class base.

In response to feminist attacks against him, Mailer wrote *The Prisoner of Sex* (1971), in which he specifically targets Kate Millett, the author of *Sexual Politics: A Manifesto of Revolution* (1970). Millett, he contends, had taken male authors out of context in deconstructing their "gender bias." In Mailer's view, biology constitutes at least half of a woman's destiny, and feminist ideology has certain totalitarian aspects. Although his retort was strong and mean-spirited, referring to Millet as "Kate-baby" and "laboratory assistant Kate," Mailer is credited with being the first major male writer to seriously address the women's liberation movement.

Mailer ended the 1970s with *The Executioner's Song* (1979), about the murder and robbery spree of Gary Gilmore and his subsequent death by firing squad in Utah. This work, billed as "a true-life novel," won Mailer his second Pulitzer Prize and provoked a national debate on capital punishment. Mailer, however, was more interested in the relativism of good and evil. He explored how each character in the story, which he initially entitled *American Virtue*, had a different concept of virtue. Mailer regarded Gilmore as "a monster who killed two people, but not totally a monster." Later, Mailer was blamed for his role in the paroling of Jack Henry Abbott, the author of a collection of prison letters to Mailer entitled *In the Belly of the Beast* (1981), who, weeks after being released, fatally stabbed a waiter.

Roger Chapman

See also: Counterculture; Democratic Party; Feminism, Third-Wave; Generations and Generational Conflict; Gilmore, Gary; Kerouac, Jack; Millett, Kate; New Journalism; New Left; Students for a Democratic Society; Vietnam War; War Protesters.

Further Reading

Dearborn, Mary V. *Mailer: A Biography.* Boston: Houghton Mifflin, 1999.

Lennon, J. Michael. *Conversations with Norman Mailer.* Oxford: University Press of Mississippi, 1988.

———. *Critical Essays on Norman Mailer.* Boston: G.K. Hall, 1986.

Wenke, Joseph. *Mailer's America.* Hanover, NH: University Press of New England, 1987.

Malcolm X

The black nationalist Malcolm X shocked mainstream America during the 1950s and 1960s with his angry rhetoric against perceived social injustices experienced by African Americans. He also criticized blacks for their self-loathing, which he attributed to "brainwashing" on the part of the "white devils." A critic of the Reverend Martin Luther King, Jr., and his nonviolent resistance against segregation, Malcolm X advocated violent self-defense. Renewed interest in this controversial figure followed the release of Spike Lee's biographical film, *Malcolm X* (1992).

The son of a Baptist minister who was an adherent of Marcus Garvey's Back to Africa movement, Malcolm X was born Malcolm Little on May 19, 1925, in Omaha, Nebraska. In 1929, the family moved to Lansing, Michigan, where the father died two years later under mysterious circumstances; Malcolm later blamed white supremacists. Following his mother's admittance to a mental institution, Malcolm and his siblings were placed in foster homes. He moved to Boston at age sixteen, then drifted to Harlem in New York City, and returned to Boston, where he got involved in drug-related activity and ended up incarcerated for burglary (1946–1952).

During his imprisonment, Malcolm converted to Islam as a member of Elijah Muhammad's Nation of Islam, or Black Muslim movement. Shortly after his release, having taken the name of "X" and discarded the "slave name" Little, he was appointed the assistant minister to Muslim Temple Number One in Detroit. He went on to establish mosques in Boston and Philadelphia, and by 1963 had become the leading spokesman and national minister of the Black Muslim movement. Later that year, however, following the assassination of President John F. Kennedy, he was censured by Elijah Muhammad for comments about "chickens coming home to roost."

In 1964, disenchanted with his mentor, who was embroiled in a sex scandal, Malcolm left the Nation to form the Organization of Afro-American Unity. At this juncture, he changed his name to El-Hajj Malik El-Shabazz, believing it more akin to his adopted religion and African ancestry. Following a pilgrimage to Mecca that year, he returned to the United States with a broader vision, one more hopeful of racial harmony. On February 21, 1965, Malcolm was gunned down in Harlem, New York, while giving a speech. (A week earlier his home had been firebombed.) The three assassins were members of the Nation of Islam.

What many regard as the quintessential or defining speech by Malcolm X, delivered in Cleveland, Ohio, on April 3, 1964, is titled "The Ballot or the Bullet." In a call for unity among the 22 million "Africans who are in America," Malcolm chastised listeners to "wake up" and realize that "it's got to be the ballot or the bullet." Referring to the filibuster then taking place in the Senate against the Civil Rights Act of 1964, he charged a "segregationist conspiracy" led by Democrats who officially speak in favor of civil rights but do not expel from their party the Dixiecrats (the southern Democrats) impeding progress for black rights. If the government cannot provide protection to blacks, he argued, then "it's time for Negroes to defend themselves."

Roger Chapman

See also: Afrocentrism; Civil Rights Movement; Haley, Alex; King, Martin Luther, Jr.; Lee, Spike; Muslim Americans; Nation of Islam; White Supremacists.

Further Reading

Collins, Rodnell, and Ella Coll. *Malcolm X: The Man Behind the Myth.* New York: HarperCollins, 1997.

Conyers, James L., and Andrew P. Smallwood. *Malcolm X: A Historical Reader.* Durham, NC: Carolina Academic Press, 2008.

Malcolm X, with Alex Haley. *The Autobiography of Malcolm X.* New York: Ballantine Books, 1965, 1992.

Tyner, James A. *The Geography of Malcolm X: Black Radicalism and the Remaking of American Space.* New York: Routledge, 2006.

Wilson, August. "The Legacy of Malcolm X." *Life,* December 1992.

Manson, Marilyn

Controversial rock musician Marilyn Manson, born Brian Hugh Warner, legally changed his name to the one that he used in his performing group, combining the names of film star Marilyn Monroe and cult figure Charles Manson to reflect the dark genre of "shock rock." Conservative, pro-family, and Christian groups have blamed Marilyn Manson's music and stagecraft for negative youth trends such as teen suicide, drug use, and school shootings.

Born in Canton, Ohio, on January 5, 1969, he began attending Heritage Christian School in Canton in 1974 but later transferred to the public school system, taking with him a negative view of the Christian religion that would later be expressed in his music. In 1989, while living in Fort Lauderdale, Florida, he formed the Goth band Marilyn Manson and the Spooky Kids. He has produced nearly a dozen albums, including *Portrait of the American Family* (1994), *Antichrist Superstar* (1996), *Holy Wood (In the Shadow of the Valley of Death)* (2000), and *The Golden Age of Grotesque* (2003). He has also appeared on television and in films, including Michael Moore's *Bowling for Columbine* (2002).

In the tradition of shock rock, Manson has been known to startle audiences by appearing at concerts dressed in knee-high black boots, women's clothing, black eyeliner and lipstick, white foundation makeup, and bizarre contact lenses. Stage props have included fire, animals, cages, raw chicken parts, and chainsaws—and he has been known to expose himself during performances. In 1994, he was arrested in Jacksonville, Florida, for performing naked during the group's "American Family Tour." Consistent with another stage antic—tearing apart Bibles—Manson became an honorary ordained reverend in the Church of Satan in 1988.

While Manson's detractors have focused on the pornographic and Satanist themes in his music and performances, others have hailed him as a champion of free speech because he pushes the bounds of the First Amendment. Groups such as the American Civil Liberties Union (ACLU), Music Industry Coalition (Mass MIC), Rock Out Censorship (ROC), and Parents for Rock and Rap have taken up the cause of defending Manson and his right to free expression. Others have dismissed Manson as simply the latest shock rocker in the tradition of early heavy metal bands such as Alice Cooper and Kiss, who used outrageous stage theatrics to sell more albums.

Manson's infamy grew in the wake of the 1999 Columbine High School shootings in Littleton, Colorado, when it was learned that the two assailants had been influenced by his music. In response, Manson had a letter printed in *Rolling Stone* magazine, stating that American society and not his music is to be blamed for the killings. Despite the controversy, he has maintained a large cult following, consisting largely of suburban teens who dress in black attire and wear black makeup.

David J. Childs

See also: American Civil Liberties Union; Censorship; Family Values; Fundamentalism, Religious; Gun Control; Moore, Michael; Rock and Roll; School Shootings.

Further Reading

Marilyn Manson Web site. www.marilynmanson.com.

Manson, Marilyn, and Neil Strauss. *The Long Hard Road Out of Hell.* New York: Regan Books, 1999.

Rogers, Kalen. *Marilyn Manson: The Unauthorized Biography.* New York: Omnibus, 1997.

Mapplethorpe, Robert

Robert Mapplethorpe was an acclaimed American artist whose provocative black-and-white photographs generated intensive debates over the nature of obscenity and the role of the state in funding and censoring works of art. Though well known in artistic circles before his death in March 1989, Mapplethorpe made national headlines later that year when conservative senator Jesse Helms (R-NC) brought the artist's photographs to the floor of the U.S. Senate in an attempt to introduce content restrictions on grants provided through the National Endowment for the Arts (NEA). Helms's campaign resulted in record attendance at Mapplethorpe's exhibitions, a dramatic increase in the value of the photographer's work, and reduced budgets and a climate of defensiveness at the NEA.

Mapplethorpe, born on November 4, 1946, in Floral Park, New York, left home at the age of sixteen to pursue a career in fine arts. After receiving a BFA from the Pratt Institute in Brooklyn in 1970, he began constructing images that combined magazine photographs, painting, and found objects. He later took up photography, producing a number of self-portraits, images of celebrities such as Andy Warhol, Richard Gere, and Deborah Harry, a series of photographs of bodybuilder Lisa Lyons, album covers for New Wave rockers Patti Smith and Television, and floral still lifes. It was Mapplethorpe's frank depictions of homoerotic and sadomasochistic themes, however, that would garner the most notoriety among political and religious conservatives. He died in Boston of complications from AIDS on March 9, 1989.

Mapplethorpe's work entered the culture wars after the Institute of Contemporary Art in Philadelphia received a $30,000 grant from the NEA to organize an exhibition of his photography entitled *The Perfect Moment*. The exhibit opened without controversy in the fall of 1988, and then traveled to Chicago in February of the following year. However, shortly before it was to have opened at the Corcoran Gallery of Art in Washington, D.C., in June, Helms obtained a catalog of the exhibit. The senator, already alarmed over NEA support for an exhibit featuring Andres Serrano's *Piss Christ* (which depicted a crucifix submerged in a jar of urine), convinced the Senate to pass legislation that banned federal funding for works of art considered obscene. Helms's actions drew praise from conservative organizations such as the American Family Association and Citizens for Community Values, and fierce condemnation from arts groups, liberals, and free-speech advocates.

The Corcoran Gallery, meanwhile, canceled its planned showing of *The Perfect Moment*, a decision that led to widespread protest and an eventual apology from the gallery. When the exhibit opened at the Contemporary Art Center in Cincinnati in 1990, gallery officials were indicted for pandering obscenity, though they were later acquitted. Following the 1994 Republican takeover of Congress, the NEA suffered a budget reduction of about 40 percent as a result of the Mapplethorpe controversy and associated issues.

Robert Teigrob

See also: AIDS; Alexander, Jane; Censorship; Gays in Popular Culture; Helms, Jesse; National Endowment for the Arts; National Endowment for the Humanities; Pornography; Serrano, Andres; Warhol, Andy; Wildmon, Donald.

Further Reading

Mapplethorpe, Robert. *Mapplethorpe.* New York: Random House, 1992.

McLeod, Douglas, and Jill Mackenzie. "Print Media and Public Reaction to the Controversy over NEA Funding for Robert Mapplethorpe's 'The Perfect Moment' Exhibit." *Journalism and Mass Communication Quarterly* 75:2 (Summer 1998): 278–91.

Morrisroe, Patricia. *Robert Mapplethorpe: A Biography.* New York: Papermac, 1995.

Marriage Names

The 1970s brought a change in the custom in which a bride automatically forfeited her maiden name upon marriage and took the surname of her husband. At the time, some businesses refused to issue credit cards to women under their own names, instead issuing cards that read, for example, Mrs. John Smith. After the feminist movement of the late 1960s and 1970s, however, a variety of options became more culturally acceptable for marriage names, not only for women but for men as well.

Although a seemingly innocuous personal choice, the issue of marriage names sparked considerable debate in America. Many conservatives and religious leaders argued that a woman who does not take her husband's name is not committed to her role as a wife and that a man who does not insist that his wife take his surname is weak.

Women who chose to retain their maiden name, however, argued that adopting their husband's name would be tantamount to enslaving themselves and forgoing individual rights. Many professional women who had built careers before marriage preferred to keep their names. These same women might choose to take their husband's name when placed in a public role—as Hillary Rodham did when her husband, Bill Clinton, ran for governor of Arkansas.

The practices of retaining one's maiden name, taking a spouse's surname, hyphenating both surnames, or combining the two surnames into a new name are all acceptable in American culture today. In fact, the trend for a man to take on his wife's surname or for both husband and wife to take both surnames is increasing. However, when faced with children's surnames, many couples continue the tradition of using the husband's surname in order to avoid confusion with the schools and other social situations. Some women who choose this option argue that there is little difference between carrying their husband's last name and carrying their father's.

The marriage name issue has been more controversial in the United States than in other countries that have prescribed rules about surnames. In France, for instance, women maintain their birth name for all legal documents but use their husband's surname in social situations. In Spain, Latin America, and China, women usually maintain their birth name after marriage. In America, couples now have a myriad of choices as to marriage names.

Tanya Hedges Duroy

See also: Clinton, Bill; Clinton, Hillary; Ferraro, Geraldine; Feminism, Second-Wave; Ms.

Further Reading

Forbes, Gordon B., Leah E. Adams-Curtis, Kay B. White, and Nicole R. Hamm. "Perceptions of Married Women and Married Men with Hyphenated Surnames." *Sex Roles: A Journal of Research* (March 2002): 167–75.

Johnson, David R., and Laurie K. Scheuble. "Women's Marital Naming in Two Generations: A National Study." *Journal of Marriage and Family* 57 (1995): 724–32.

Scheuble, Laurie K., and David R. Johnson. "Married Women's Situational Use of Last Names: An Empirical Study." *Sex Roles: A Journal of Research* (July 2005): 143–51.

Marxism

The ghost of Karl Marx continues to hover over arguments between the left and right in America, particularly when the debate focuses on economic disparities. Between the end of World War II in 1945 and the end of the Cold War in 1991, the conflict between the two superpowers, the United States and the Soviet Union, was generally understood as a contest between communism (or Marxism) and capitalism. Although the end of the Cold War was widely attributed in the democratic West to the inherent weakness of communism, Marx's criticisms of the effects of capitalism remain potent for many on the left.

Marxism is a political and economic theory that originated in the nineteenth century with such writings by Karl Marx as *Das Kapital* (*Capital*, 1867–1894) and *The Communist Manifesto* (1848), written with Friedrich Engels. Focusing on economic relationships, Marx regarded class as the primary political interest motivating human activity and leading to political conflict. According to classic Marxist theory, the system of capitalism inevitably causes exploitation and thereby contains the seeds of its own destruction. Marx argued that capitalism produces alienation; people as workers are forced into a wage system that exploits their labor and robs them of control over their own lives—leading ultimately to worldwide revolution. Although Marx predicted that capitalism would collapse because of its own "internal logic," communist systems based on Marxism have repeatedly failed.

In the United States, Marxism has been primarily an academic theory, with only limited effective political action, while opposition to Marxist ideas is an almost obligatory rallying cry for both major political parties. At the beginning of the twenty-first century, Marxism does not pose a serious threat to American power, but it remains a much demonized ideology in the United States, particularly among conservatives, because of conditions in and relations with holdover communist states such as Cuba and North Korea. Marxism has also been part of a great debate on the left, including feminists, civil rights supporters, and other political activists, as some liberals seek to analyze and resist the forces of globalization.

The popular discourse of the Cold War convinced many in the United States that Marxism is the exact opposite of American capitalist democracy. Although the communist movement once had a limited foothold in American society, primarily with the labor movement, by the 1950s there was little or no tolerance for members or sympathizers of the Communist Party of the United States of America (CPUSA). During the "Red Scare" of that decade, it was dangerous for anyone to maintain any affiliation with the CPUSA or related organizations, known as "communist fronts." Such individuals, including teachers, government bureaucrats, unionists, writers, and filmmakers, were sniffed out and fired, blacklisted, or imprisoned—whether they were actual members, erstwhile sympathizers, or just opponents of what they regarded as a "witch hunt."

"Red baiting" remained a common political tactic even as the 1960s ushered in a period of radicalism. President Lyndon B. Johnson's reluctance to pull U.S. forces out of Vietnam was motivated in part by a fear of being seen as "soft on communism." President Richard M. Nixon, only because he for years had garnered a strong anticommunist reputation, was later able to withdraw U.S. troops from Vietnam and establish ties with communist China. Ronald Reagan, who as a Hollywood actor had testified as a friendly witness before the House Committee on Un-American Activities, emphasized his strong anticommunist views on the campaign trail, and as president he called the Soviet Union "an evil empire."

In other countries, however, and for academics in the United States, Marxism has remained an intellectual and political force. Contemporary Marxist scholars use the perspective of class struggle in considering such phenomena as mass culture and how it masks the effects of capitalism, anticolonial struggles in the Third World, and globalization. Marxist ideas have also been reflected in the antisweatshop movement, global unionization movement, protests against the World Trade Organization, and liberation theology in Latin America. Some international leaders, particularly in the Third World, have turned to Marxist theory in critiquing American hegemony.

While Marxism remains a powerful source of ideas for the political left, its emphasis on economic power and class identity has embroiled the theory and its advocates in struggles within the left. Marxists have long criticized what they call the fragmentation caused by various groups on the left, arguing that feminists, civil rights advocates, and gay rights activists have divided the left and distracted it from the primary struggle against capitalism.

Claire E. Rasmussen

See also: Battle of Seattle; Cold War; Communists and Communism; Cuba; Feminism, Second-Wave; Gay Rights Movement; Globalization; McCarthyism; New Left; Race; Soviet Union and Russia; Vietnam War; Wealth Gap.

Further Reading

Brzezinski, Zbigniew. *The Grand Failure: The Birth and Death of Communism in the Twentieth Century.* New York: Collier, 1989.

Elster, Jon. *Making Sense of Marx.* Cambridge, MA: Cambridge University Press, 1985.

Joseph, Jonathan. *Marxism and Social Theory.* New York: Palgrave Macmillan, 2006.

Kolakowski, Leszek. *Main Currents of Marxism: The Founders, the Golden Age, the Breakdown.* New York: W.W. Norton, 2008.

Walker, David M., and Daniel Gray. *Historical Dictionary of Marxism.* Lanham, MD: Scarecrow Press, 2007.

McCain, John

A prominent Republican U.S. senator from Arizona, John McCain has stood out as an enigmatic figure during the increasing political polarization of the culture wars. Although a self-avowed conservative, McCain has often held political and social positions that attract moderates and independents while simultaneously putting him at odds with the Religious Right and the base of his own party. He won the Republican nomination for president of the United States in 2008 but was defeated by Democrat Barack Obama on Election Day.

The son of a high-ranking American naval officer, John Sydney McCain III was born in the Panama Canal Zone on August 29, 1936. After graduating from the U.S. Naval Academy (1958), he became a navy pilot and was shot down over North Vietnam in October 1967. As a prisoner of war in Hanoi (1967–1973), he suffered torture and other violations of human rights. McCain retired from the military in 1981, moved to Arizona, and entered politics, first serving in the House of Representatives (1983–1987) and then succeeding Barry Goldwater in the Senate (1987–present).

In Washington, McCain quickly earned a reputation as a maverick, although his political career was jeopardized in 1989 when he was investigated as one of the Keating Five, a group of senators accused of improperly shielding a corrupt savings-and-loan executive. In the end, McCain was cleared of any illegality but criticized for acting with poor judgment.

McCain adopted a variety of positions at odds with hardcore conservatives. He urged normalization of U.S.-Vietnamese relations as he worked on resolving the Vietnam MIA-POW issue. He favored sanctions on South Africa's apartheid regime, federal support for fetal tissue research, and a moderate approach to environmental issues. He went before conservative antigay groups and spoke about tolerance. He also, however, supported every aspect of the Republican Contract with America and voted to impeach President Bill Clinton. The Republican Party, he maintained, was large enough to include "different voices in honorable disputes."

That belief was tested during his bid for the Republican presidential nomination in 2000. Pushing his reformist agenda and touting the need for the McCain-Feingold campaign finance reform bill, opposed by the vast majority of Republican incumbents, McCain said the legislation was needed because trial lawyers control Democrats and the insurance companies Republicans. His campaign bus, christened the Straight Talk Express, symbolized his desire to court moderates. Winning a surprisingly large victory over George W. Bush in the New Hampshire primary, McCain experienced a bitter contest a few weeks later in South Carolina.

Bush started the South Carolina campaign with a speech at ultra-conservative Bob Jones University, prompting religious conservatives like Pat Robertson to quickly line up against McCain. A vicious negative campaign by Bush and a series of semi-official smear campaigns ensured the defeat of McCain, who decried Robertson and Jerry Falwell as "agents of intolerance." After losing the majority of the primaries on Super Tuesday, McCain suspended his campaign and eventually gave Bush a half-hearted endorsement. Later, he was more enthusiastic backing Bush's reelection.

During Bush's second term McCain, thinking about another presidential run, began reaching out to social conservatives while trying to retain the support of moderates. Thus, McCain voted against a constitutional amendment banning same-sex marriage, but worked to stop same-sex marriage bills in Arizona; voted against Bush's initial tax cuts, but later voted to make them permanent; and put himself at odds with Republicans over some gun control measures and the handling of enemy combatants, but endorsed the teaching of Intelligent Design.

McCain's 2008 primary campaign was a hard-fought affair among Republicans, but it ended much sooner than the drawn-out battle among Democrats that eventually saw Barack Obama beat Hillary Clinton for the nomination. McCain won the GOP nomination in spite of heavy early opposition from many on the right, including influential radio commentator Rush Limbaugh, who during the primaries said he would prefer a Democrat over McCain. Many political observers felt that conservative Republican primary voters split their allegiance among other candidates, helping McCain win the nomination.

Hoping in part to energize the conservative Republican base and to attract women voters who might have resented Obama not choosing Hillary Clinton as his running mate, McCain chose Sarah Palin, the governor of Alaska and a newcomer to national politics, as his vice presidential candidate. Many conservatives applauded the choice, with William Kristol calling her "fantastic." Others, including a columnist for the conservative and influential *National Review*, worried about Palin's record and performance during the campaign, felt that she was "out of her league," and urged her to bow out. During the campaign, Palin energized many conservative rallies, but her support among the general public fell quickly. By late October, after a series of disastrous interviews with news networks and being skewered by late-night comedians, a *Wall Street Journal*/NBC News poll found that 55 percent of Americans felt she was not qualified to be president.

McCain lost to Obama in the general election, garnering almost 46 percent of the popular vote and only 173 of the 538 Electoral College votes. Besides losing the traditional swing states of Ohio and Florida, McCain narrowly lost the red states of Virginia, North Carolina, and Indiana. The campaign was often sidetracked by extraneous issues, but in the end, the massive public rejection of the Bush presidency and the details of the growing economic crisis that came to light that fall helped to secure Obama's victory. After the election, the Republican Party and right-wing conservatives began a series of public and private deliberations to determine the future course of the party.

John Day Tully

See also: Bob Jones University; Campaign Finance Reform; Clinton Impeachment; Contract with America; Creationism and Intelligent Design; Gay Rights Movement; Palin, Sarah; Religious Right; Republican Party; Same-Sex Marriage; Vietnam War.

Further Reading

Alexander, Paul. *Man of the People: The Life of John McCain.* Hoboken, NJ: John Wiley & Sons, 2003.

Drew, Elizabeth. *Citizen McCain.* New York: Simon & Schuster, 2002.

McCain, John, with Mark Salter. *Faith of My Fathers: A Family Memoir.* New York: Random House, 2008.

———. *Worth the Fighting For: A Memoir.* New York: Random House, 2002.

Schecter, Cliff. *The Real McCain: Why Conservatives Don't Trust Him—and Why Independents Shouldn't.* Sausalito, CA: PoliPointPress, 2008.

Welch, Matt. *McCain: The Myth of a Maverick.* New York: Palgrave Macmillan, 2007.

McCarthy, Eugene

Enigmatic and often unpredictable, U.S. Senator Eugene McCarthy (D-MN) attracted national attention in 1968 when he carried the banner for antiwar forces by challenging President Lyndon B. Johnson in that year's first Democratic primary. His stunning showing in New Hampshire (42 percent of the vote to Johnson's 49 percent) rested on the work of a legion of students who got "Clean for Gene" and waged a door-to-door campaign. McCarthy's White House bid altered the political landscape: Johnson withdrew from the presidential campaign, and Robert F. Kennedy declared his candidacy.

Temperamentally conservative and introspective, McCarthy did not fit the pattern of a 1960s political activist. His Vietnam stance during the New Hampshire campaign was vague, and he attracted more votes from those who thought Johnson was insufficiently hawkish than from those who wanted immediate withdrawal. On the other hand, he proposed radical solutions for some of the nation's pressing social and economic issues.

Born on March 29, 1916, in Watkins, Minnesota, Eugene Joseph McCarthy grew up in a deeply religious Catholic household. He attended St. John's University (BA, 1935) and the University of Minnesota (MA, 1941), taught public school, and was briefly a Benedictine novice (1942–1943). His deep belief in Catholic social activism soon led him into politics. In 1948, the Democratic Farmer Labor Party nominated him to oppose the Republican incumbent of Minnesota's Fourth Congressional District. He won the election and served five terms in the U.S. House of Representatives (1949–1958), followed by two terms in the U.S. Senate (1959–1971). Despite a generally unimpressive legislative record, he was well regarded by congressional colleagues, though many were surprised by his decision to challenge Johnson in 1968.

After the New Hampshire results, the race for the Democratic nomination became a three-way contest among McCarthy, Kennedy (who soon emerged as the front runner), and Vice President Hubert Humphrey. Kennedy's assassination in June left McCarthy dispirited and unfocused, his campaign lagging. He remained aloof after Humphrey was nominated, giving the vice president only a lukewarm, last-minute endorsement. McCarthy retired from the Senate in 1971, a decision he seemed later to regret.

In retirement, McCarthy taught, lectured, and wrote poetry, political commentary, and other works. He tried more than once to restart his political career, occasionally renewing old political connections or acting on old grudges, seeking the Democratic presidential nomination in 1972 and running an ill-fated independent campaign for president in 1976. He died on December 10, 2005, remembered primarily for his major role in the political drama of 1968.

Gary L. Bailey

See also: Catholic Church; Cronkite, Walter; Democratic Party; Johnson, Lyndon B.; Kennedy Family; Vietnam War; War Protesters.

Further Reading

LaFeber, Walter. *The Deadly Bet: LBJ, Vietnam, and the 1968 Election*. Lanham, MD: Rowman and Littlefield, 2005.

Larner, Jeremy. *Nobody Knows: Reflections on the McCarthy Campaign of 1968*. New York: Macmillan, 1969.

McCarthy, Eugene J. *First Things First: New Priorities for America*. New York: New American Library, 1968.

Rising, George. *Clean for Gene: Eugene McCarthy's 1968 Presidential Campaign*. Westport, CT: Greenwood, 1997.

Sandbrook, Dominic. *Eugene McCarthy: The Rise and Fall of Postwar American Liberalism*. New York: Alfred A. Knopf, 2004.

McCarthy, Joseph

In the culture wars, the name Joseph McCarthy is associated with the 1950s Red Scare and political witch hunts referred to as McCarthyism. As a Republican U.S. senator from Wisconsin, McCarthy staked his political reputation on fighting communist subversion in the U.S. government, but in the end he was censured by his Senate colleagues for the manner in which he conducted that attack. Although most historians and political commentators remember McCarthy for publicly accusing individuals of disloyalty by making use of hearsay and insubstantial evidence for the purpose of political grandstanding, leaving ruined careers in his wake, over the years some conservative revisionists have defended his memory in a quest to rehabilitate his public image. While most observers regard him as a demagogue, a passionate few argue that he was the victim of a liberal media.

Born into a large Catholic family on November 14, 1908, near Grand Chute, Wisconsin, Joseph Raymond McCarthy grew up poor on a farm. Later, he obtained a law degree at Marquette University (LLB, 1935), took up the practice of law, and sought to launch a political career. Although unsuccessful in campaigning as a Democrat for Shawano County district attorney (1936), he later won a nonpartisan race for the state's tenth judicial circuit court (1939). Following a stint as a Marine Corps intelligence officer in the Pacific during World War II, he won a U.S. senate seat after narrowly defeating the progressive Robert M. La Follette, Jr., in the 1946 Republican primary. He was elected to a second term in 1952. McCarthy died on May 2, 1957, in Bethesda, Maryland, from liver failure due to alcoholism.

McCarthy's notoriety began on February 9, 1950, during an address to a Republican women's club in Wheeling, West Virginia, in which he made the accusation that many in the U.S. State Department were communists or communist sympathizers. After an investigation by the Tydings Committee, headed by Senator Millard Tydings (D-MD), McCarthy's charges were dismissed as groundless—although some Republicans denounced the Democratic-controlled proceedings as a whitewash. Tydings later that year lost his reelection race during a campaign in which McCarthy passed out fliers with a photograph of the Maryland legislator juxtaposed with one of Earl Browder, the head of the Communist Party of the United States. Meanwhile, on June 1, 1950, with McCarthy clearly in mind, freshman senator Margaret Chase Smith (R-MA) delivered her "Declaration of Conscience" speech on the Senate floor, arguing that those who "shout the loudest about Americanism" ignore "some of the principles of Americanism" when they convert the Senate into "a forum of hate" and violate the Constitution by using the tactic of "trial by accusation."

As chair of the Permanent Subcommittee on Investigations, under the Senate Committee on Governmental Operations, McCarthy continued to make headlines as he hunted for communists in various parts of the government, including the Voice of America, the U.S. Information Libraries, the Government Printing Office, and the Army Signal Corps. His tactics were called into question by the renowned television journalist Edward R. Murrow in "Report on Senator McCarthy," a *See It Now* program aired on March 9, 1954. The following month, the Senate began holding the Army-McCarthy hearings to investigate McCarthy's allegations of communist espionage in the army and the countercharge that the senator had sought preferential treatment from the army for one of his committee staff members who had been drafted. McCarthy's rude and ruthless manner and constant interruptions during the televised proceedings shocked many of the 20 million viewers, adding drama and poignancy to the moment when army counsel Joseph Welch pointedly asked McCarthy: "Have you no sense of decency, sir, at long last?" A public backlash against McCarthy ensued, including a spirited recall drive in Wisconsin. The senator's detractors began wearing "Joe Must Go" and "McCarthy for Fuehrer" buttons. As the army hearings were winding down in June, Senator Ralph Flanders (VT-R) introduced a resolution to censure McCarthy, and on December 2, 1954, the Senate voted 65–22 to condemn McCarthy for actions "contrary to senatorial traditions."

During the 1960s, the Senator Joseph R. McCarthy Educational Foundation, founded by members of the John Birch Society in Appleton, Wisconsin, began a campaign to address "the lies by politicians, educators and members of the news media" about the late senator. The founders began hosting annual graveside services and remembrance dinners, and called for a commemorative McCarthy postage stamp and a national holiday in his honor. In the same town, from January 2002 to January 2004, the Outagamie Museum offered the nation's first exhibit on McCarthy, using a purposefully ambiguous title: "Joseph McCarthy: A Modern Tragedy."

In perhaps what was the first major defense of

McCarthyism, the conservative activist William F. Buckley (with his brother-in-law L. Brent Bozell) published *McCarthy and His Enemies: The Record and Its Meaning* (1954), arguing that McCarthy's anticommunism was "a movement around which men of goodwill and stern morality can close ranks." John A. Stormer, a member of the John Birch Society, followed with the best-seller *None Dare Call It Treason* (1964), a work supportive of McCarthy in that it warned that the United States was losing the Cold War because of communist subversion in American society. Medford Evans, also a member of the John Birch Society, wrote *The Assassination of Joe McCarthy* (1970); and years later his son, M. Stanton Evans, a writer for the *National Review*, published *Blacklisted by History: The Untold Story of Senator Joe McCarthy and His Fight Against America's Enemies* (2007). In *Joseph McCarthy: Reexamining the Legacy of America's Most Hated Senator* (2000), Arthur Herman, a one-time staffer at the Smithsonian Institution, argues that McCarthy was simply guilty of "making a good point badly." These works attempt to vindicate McCarthy by suggesting that though he made "mistakes," the danger of communism was real and something liberals generally refuse to acknowledge. In *Treason: Liberal Treachery from the Cold War to the War on Terrorism* (2003), the conservative pundit Ann Coulter asserts that "McCarthy's crusade" benefited the country by making it a "disgrace" to be a communist.

Roger Chapman

See also: Buckley, William F., Jr.; Cold War; Communists and Communism; Coulter, Ann; John Birch Society; La Follette, Robert, Jr.; Marxism; McCarthyism; Murrow, Edward R.; Republican Party; Revisionist History; Taft, Robert A.

Further Reading

Cunningham, Jesse G., and Laura K. Egendorf, eds. *The McCarthy Hearings*. San Diego, CA: Greenhaven Press, 2003.

Evans, M. Stanton. *Blacklisted by History: The Untold Story of Joseph McCarthy and His Fight Against America's Enemies*. New York: Crown Forum, 2007.

Oshinsky, David M. *A Conspiracy So Immense: The World of Joe McCarthy*. New York: Oxford University Press, 2005.

Schrecker, Ellen. *Many Are the Crimes: McCarthyism in America*. New York: Little, Brown, 1998.

Thelen, David P., and Esther S. Thelen. "Joe Must Go: The Movement to Recall Senator Joseph R. McCarthy." *Wisconsin Magazine of History* 49:3 (1965–1966): 185–209.

McCarthyism

The term "McCarthyism" was coined by cartoonist Herbert Block (Herblock) in the March 29, 1950, edition of the *Washington Post* to refer to the campaign to root out alleged communists from American institutions. Not many were amused, however, during the anticommunist crusade of the 1950s as personified by the grandstanding of U.S. senator Joseph R. McCarthy (R-WI). McCarthy quickly became a symbol for the myriad efforts by American politicians and self-proclaimed patriots to outdo each other in exposing and ruining communists and other suspicious groups, policies, and lifestyles. It was generally believed that the "containment" of Soviet advances abroad—the mandate of the "cold war" inaugurated by President Harry Truman in March 1947—necessitated similar vigilance at home. The term "McCarthyism" continues to circulate today in the political rhetoric of the culture wars, referring to the kind of fear tactics, unsupported accusations, and demagoguery employed during the Red Scare.

The "Brown Scare" and Formation of HUAC

In light of the fascist takeover in several European countries during the 1920s and 1930s, Americans had begun to wonder whether such a thing might happen in their country, making conditions ripe for a "Brown Scare" (a reference to the brown shirts worn by Nazi storm troopers). Threats to democratic ideals seemed evident, given the appearance of the German-American Bund, the Silver Shirts, and other pro-Nazi groups. Although none of these organizations appeared ready to lead a fascist revolution in America, several politicians, President Franklin Roosevelt among them, chose to play on public fears. The political advantages became evident, for instance, when the America First Committee, a broad coalition of pacifists opposed to the U.S. military buildup and aid to Great Britain, was cast as a union of Nazi sympathizers—Roosevelt even had the FBI illegally tap the phones of its leaders. Progressive Wisconsin Senator Robert La Follette, Jr., upset many conservatives when he used his congressional probe, set up to investigate violations of the National Labor Relations Act (1935), to paint anti-union industrialists as an equivalent danger to New Deal community rebuilding.

In this context, the House Committee on Un-American Activities (HUAC) was made permanent in 1938. The body had been created by liberal Democrats in 1934 to investigate the success of fascist propaganda. Conservative Texas Democrat Martin Dies, who chaired HUAC from 1937 to 1944, made exaggerated, unsubstantiated claims about the extent and scope of American fascism like his liberal predecessors. Under Dies's leadership, HUAC also began to target the radical and liberal left. It used the specter of communist infiltration as a means to dismantle New Deal agencies conservatives had long opposed, including the Federal Theatre Project (FTP), which was shut down in June 1939 after HUAC interrogation. With the 1946 Republican takeover of Congress, Dies's successors looked to work more aggressively in exposing communism in America. Freshmen

"I HAVE HERE IN MY HAND ----"

DOCTORED PHOTO

FAKED LETTER

In a 1954 Herblock cartoon during the Army-McCarthy hearings, Senator Joe McCarthy holds a "doctored photo" and "faked letter" that he claimed were FBI documents. *(A 1954 Herblock Cartoon, copyright by The Herb Block Foundation)*

senators Richard Nixon (R-CA) and Joseph McCarthy (who ousted La Follette) would join in this task.

"Red Scare" Politics and Culture

After the demise of the Soviet Union in the early 1990s, U.S. access to Soviet archives and the Venona surveillance project (secret U.S. eavesdropping on Soviet communications during and after World War II) suggest that Americans had more cause to dread "red" subversion than "brown." While official Communist Party numbers in the United States peaked around 100,000 in 1939, members were loyal to the Soviet Union. In turn, they were used to recruit and plant spies in key government agencies. During the 1930s "Popular Front" supporters, trying to ground socialism in American domestic policies, had become an important and visible wing of the New Deal coalition. By some estimates, 10 million American workers belonged to unions with communist leadership in 1947.

The second Red Scare (the first took place during World War I) began to coalesce when HUAC launched an investigation of Hollywood in 1946. Committee members targeted a broad political spectrum of entertainers for accusations of disloyalty—although it was true that nine of the Hollywood Ten charged with contempt for refusing to testify had been members of the Communist Party. HUAC Republicans felt vindicated when, after having lambasted New Deal Democrats for harboring Soviet spies, they received testimony from former Krem-

lin operative turned anticommunist journalist Whittaker Chambers that such had been the case. Chambers named Harvard-educated New Dealer Alger Hiss, who convincingly refuted the charges before HUAC, leading Truman to condemn the committee's partisanship. Chambers then came out with copies of State Department documents that Hiss had reportedly passed to him. Hiss went to prison for perjury, and Democrats were perceived as being "soft on communism." With the help of the liberal anticommunist think tank Americans for Democratic Action (ADA), Republicans went on to drive Popular Front liberals out of prominence.

The transformation of anticommunism into a mass cultural panic was further aided by the revelation of espionage activity that passed on atomic secrets to the Soviet Union—e.g., the cases of Klaus Fuchs (a former Manhattan Project scientist) and Julius and Ethel Rosenberg. Congress added to HUAC the Senate Internal Security Committee and the Senate Permanent Subcommittee on Investigations, which together considered over one hundred cases between 1949 and 1954. The Smith Act (1940), originally targeting fascist plots to overthrow the U.S. federal government, was used to prosecute twelve Communist Party leaders in 1948. This antisubversion law was strengthened by the Internal Security or McCarran Act (1950) and the Communist Control Act (1954). The FBI and Loyalty Review Boards, as part of Truman's Loyalty Program (1947), would investigate millions of federal employees well into the 1950s, resulting in thousands of resignations and dismissals but no formal charges of espionage. In addition, a number of teachers and lawyers were fired without explanation after the FBI began leaking confidential findings to employers. In 1947, U.S. attorney general Tom Clark added to his initial "list" of pro-German and pro-Japanese groups up to 154 communist and "front" organizations. The Taft-Hartley Act (1946), along with widely circulated publications such as *Red Channels* (1950) put out by former FBI agents, empowered citizens to ensure that communists and "fellow travelers" would no longer serve in labor unions, Hollywood, or television.

McCarthy's Rise and Fall

The "scare" aspect of the anticommunist campaign was directly attributable to the rhetoric and tactics of Senator Joseph McCarthy beginning in the early 1950s. Having watched from behind as fellow Republican Richard Nixon led the initial congressional charge against Soviet penetration, McCarthy was provoked by the unexpected fall of China to communists in 1949 to launch a broader campaign. In a Lincoln Day speech in February 1950, he claimed to have compiled a list of 205 known communists then working for the U.S. State Department. Some of these names were of individuals who had failed to pass security screenings in 1946, mostly for reasons other than ties to the Communist Party, as the Democratic-controlled (Millard) Tydings Committee later established. This committee unwittingly gave McCarthy a platform to spin more stories of communist destruction of the American way of life. Still seeking revenge for the profiling of political conservatives as Nazis during World War II, McCarthy and Republicans found the post-Hiss Democratic administration an easy target. Before long, television cameras would be capturing McCarthy's complaints that President Truman, secretary of state Dean Acheson, and former secretary of state George Marshall had more or less orchestrated China's "enslavement."

Winning the chairmanship of the Subcommittee on Investigations in 1953, McCarthy became an even more polarizing figure. He was a crystallizing center for popular opposition to New Deal planning, public health programs, the United Nations, and homosexuals (even though his top aide was bisexual). A 1954 poll suggested that 50 percent of Americans had a favorable opinion of the senator. He especially found friends among fellow Catholics, including William F. Buckley, Jr., editor of the *National Review* and an early voice of the conservative resurgence. All the same, the liberal ADA painted McCarthy as a reckless, self-interested demagogue. Members of his own party, like Maine senator Margaret Chase Smith, publicly condemned McCarthy's "character assassinations" as unbecoming of the country he claimed to defend. In *The Crucible* (1952), blacklisted playwright Arthur Miller revisited the seventeenth-century Salem witch hunts to insinuate the similarly irrational essence of McCarthyism. "We must not confuse dissent with disloyalty," concluded CBS newscaster Edward R. Murrow in his 1954 *See It Now* indictment of the senator.

The backlash against McCarthy in 1954 signaled a temporary halt to McCarthyism. Having been united by anticommunism but then divided by McCarthy, Democrats and Republicans once again united when McCarthy turned on Eisenhower appointees and various military personnel. The televised Army-McCarthy hearings in April were the senator's final undoing. During a dramatic episode, after McCarthy revealed that an assistant investigative attorney years earlier had been a fleeting member of the leftist National Lawyers' Guild, attorney for the army Joseph Welch asked him, "Have you no sense of decency, sir, at long last?" Thinking he did not, the Senate voted overwhelmingly to censure him in December. McCarthy died of cirrhosis of the liver in 1957.

McCarthyism Continued

In a renewed interest in civil liberties, a series of U.S. Supreme Court cases in 1957 and 1958 curbed the anticommunist powers of Congress and the White House. Also, in 1962, the blacklisting of entertainers came to an end—one of the Hollywood Ten (screenwriter Dalton

Trumbo) even received screen credit for *Exodus* (1960) and *Spartacus* (1960). Nonetheless, the federal government did not cease its campaign against perceived political subversion. For example, in 1956, the FBI began its Counter Intelligence Program (COINTELPRO) to disrupt the Communist Party, which by that time had only about 3,000 members. By the 1960s, COINTELPRO agents were infiltrating, intimidating, and sometimes attacking protest groups, mostly leftist ones, such as the Students for a Democratic Society (SDS) and the Black Panthers. In 1974, President Richard Nixon, who earlier had politically benefited by exploiting the fear of communism, resigned from office in order to avoid impeachment for his abuse of executive power in the Watergate scandal.

During the 1980s, media watchdog and political conservative Reed Irvine, began Accuracy in Academia (AIA), enlisting student volunteers to anonymously monitor class lectures on college campuses and report "liberal bias." This type of surveillance of academia later became the forte of neoconservatives, including David Horowitz and Daniel Pipes, who founded organizations such as Students for Academic Freedom and Campus Watch. These organizations named names of professors thought to be biased and misleading, and the Internet became a tool for singling out liberal professors. Horowitz also published a book entitled *The Professors: The 101 Most Dangerous Academics in America* (2006). All of this, opponents have argued, amounts to a campaign in the spirit of McCarthyism.

Indeed, it is difficult to peruse political blogs and not find occasional references to McCarthyism. Some opponents of drug testing, for example, refer to the practice as "chemical McCarthyism"; others critical of health checks for obesity refer to that idea as "medical McCarthyism." To characterize any public policy or proposal as McCarthyism—whether it be zero-tolerance law enforcement, proposals for a national ID card, antismoking restrictions, or virtually any perceived form of "Big Brother" monitoring—is to suggest that it is sinister, unfair, a threat to individual freedom, and driven by ulterior motives.

Some civil libertarians castigated President George W. Bush for his response to terrorism following the attacks of September 11, arguing that he took advantage of public fear to advance his conservative agenda while unfairly portraying his opponents as "soft on terrorism." The USA PATRIOT Act (2001), which Bush persuaded Congress to pass, was quickly characterized by critics as being in the tradition of the Smith and McCarran Acts because of perceived harm to civil and academic freedoms in the name of national security. In response to such charges, conservative pundit Ann Coulter wrote *Treason* (2003), accusing liberals of trying to impede counterterrorism efforts by resorting to unfair comparisons to McCarthyism. This did not stop film actor George Clooney from offering a tribute to Edward R. Murrow in the film *Good Night, and Good Luck* (2005), which some reviewers interpreted as a kind of editorial that praised one who directly opposed McCarthy in order to speak out against the post-9/11 political climate.

Mark Edwards

See also: Academic Freedom; Chambers, Whittaker; Cold War; Communists and Communism; Hiss, Alger; Hollywood Ten; Horowitz, David; Irvine, Reed; Labor Unions; McCarthy, Joseph; Murrow, Edward R.; Neoconservatism; Nixon, Richard; USA PATRIOT Act.

Further Reading

Cole, David. "The New McCarthyism: Repeating History in the War on Terrorism." *Harvard Civil Rights–Civil Liberties Law Review* 38 (Winter 2003): 1–30.

Fried, Richard M. *Nightmare in Red: The McCarthy Era in Perspective.* New York: Oxford University Press, 1990.

Haynes, John E. *Red Scare or Red Menace? American Communism and Anticommunism in the Cold War Era.* Chicago: Ivan R. Dee, 1996.

Heale, M.J. *McCarthy's Americans: Red Scare Politics in State and Nation, 1935–1965.* Athens: University of Georgia Press, 1998.

Herman, Arthur. *Joseph McCarthy: Reexamining the Life and Legacy of America's Most Hated Senator.* New York: Free Press, 2003.

Schrecker, Ellen. *Many Are the Crimes: McCarthyism in America.* Boston: Little, Brown, 1990.

McCloskey, Deirdre

After nearly three decades as a respected male economist and academic, Donald N. McCloskey underwent sex reassignment surgery in 1996, took the name Deirdre N. McCloskey, and subsequently began writing from a feminist perspective. Born on September 11, 1942, in Ann Arbor, Michigan, McCloskey attended Harvard University (BA, 1964; PhD, 1970), and built a reputation by arguing that economists rely unduly on statistics and mathematical formulas, that persuasion and rhetoric play a central role in human decision making, and that the field of economics is more art than science. McCloskey has held teaching positions at the University of Chicago (1968–1980), University of Iowa (1980–1999), and University of Illinois at Chicago (since 1999).

In November 1995, at age fifty-three, McCloskey informed colleagues of the decision to become a woman, reportedly prompting the department chair at the University of Iowa to express deadpan relief that at least it was not something as drastic as renouncing capitalism for socialism. After the sex-change surgery and a sabbatical at Erasmus University in Rotterdam, the Netherlands, McCloskey published *The Vices of Economists, The Virtues of the Bourgeoisie* (1997), a work that criticizes economists, especially male ones, for relying on theory and statistics

that fail to explain many aspects of human behavior. Although there are numerous references to gender in this work, the economist was a founding member of the International Association for Feminist Economics prior to the sex-change operations, suggesting some continuity of thought regardless of gender identity.

McCloskey's memoir *Crossing* (1999) explains the decision behind the sex-change operation and the subsequent ramifications, including a divorce after thirty years of marriage and other family problems. Laura A. McCloskey, a psychology professor at the University of Arizona and sister of the economist, tried to get her brother committed to a mental hospital, an action that was subsequently condemned in a resolution passed by the Social Science History Association. Deirdre McCloskey's academic Web site has included personal references about her transgender experience, as well as links to GenderPAC (Gender Public Advocacy Coalition) and the International Foundation for Gender Education.

Critics have charged McCloskey with perpetuating stereotypes about women. The economist claimed, for example, that changing genders made her gentler and more caring and that her teaching style became more affirming and less rude toward students. Her enthusiastic discussions on makeup and female friendship have led some women to wonder whether she is acting out womanhood from an unenlightened male perspective. Perhaps more controversial in the long run will be McCloskey's academic work, such as *The Bourgeois Virtues: Ethics for an Age of Commerce* (2006), which maintains that capitalism is both morally good and good for morality.

Roger Chapman

See also: Feminism, Second-Wave; Feminism, Third-Wave; Jorgensen, Christine; Transgender Movement; Women's Studies.

Further Reading

Balak, Benjamin. *McCloskey's Rhetoric: Discourse Ethics in Economics.* New York: Routledge, 2006.

McCloskey, Deirdre. *Crossing: A Memoir.* Chicago: University of Chicago Press, 1999.

Ryan, Alan. "Is Capitalism Good for You?" *New York Review of Books*, December 21, 2006.

Wilson, Robin. "Leading Economist Stuns Field by Deciding to Become a Woman." *Chronicle of Higher Education*, February 16, 1996.

McGovern, George

An anti–Cold War Democrat, the U.S. senator and 1972 presidential candidate George McGovern of South Dakota called for reducing military spending in order to expand social programs. His defeat at the hands of incumbent Richard Nixon in 1972 represented a signal event in the culture wars because a major candidate had sought the White House—only to lose overwhelmingly—by rejecting a centrist campaign strategy for one that sought to build a coalition around minorities, women, and youth. Some suggested that McGovern's campaign staff resembled the cast for *Hair*, the 1969 Broadway musical about the counterculture. In the end, McGovern received only 37.5 percent of the popular vote and the Electoral College votes of only Massachusetts and the District of Columbia. The hit country-and-western single "Uneasy Rider" (1973) by Charlie Daniels features a humorous stanza in which a southern redneck is falsely accused of having voted for McGovern.

The son of a Methodist minister, George Stanley McGovern was born in Avon, South Dakota, on July 19, 1922. Following service as a bomber pilot in World War II (1943–1945) and finishing a degree at Dakota Wesleyan University (BA, 1946), McGovern pursued his interest in the social gospel while working as a student minister and attending Garrett Theological Seminary in Evanston, Illinois (1946–1947). He later studied history at Northwestern University (MA, 1949; PhD, 1953), taught at Dakota Wesleyan (1949–1953), and ended up as the executive secretary of the South Dakota

The landslide defeat of 1972 Democratic candidate George McGovern (right) became associated, in some circles, with liberal lost causes and defeatist foreign policy. Running mate Thomas Eagleton (left) withdrew after disclosures of electroshock treatment for depression. *(Anthony Korody/ Getty Images)*

Democratic Party (1953–1956). From there he launched a political career, serving in the U.S. House of Representatives (1957–1961) and the U.S. Senate (1963–1981), in between directing the Food for Peace program under the Kennedy administration (1961–1962).

As a legislator, McGovern supported President Lyndon Johnson's Great Society program, civil rights reforms, school busing, increased federal spending for entitlement programs, and the nuclear test ban. One of the first senators to oppose the Vietnam War, which he characterized as a "terrible cancer eating away the soul of the nation," McGovern futilely attempted to end the conflict by utilizing the power of the legislative branch. In May 1970, he sponsored with Mark O. Hatfield (R-OR) a Senate amendment to cut off war funding; the measure was defeated by a 62–29 vote. The following year, McGovern offered a similar amendment that failed 55–39; and in 1972, his amendment for a troop withdrawal was defeated 52–44. As a presidential candidate, McGovern campaigned primarily on the promise to end the war in ninety days and to grant amnesty to draft evaders.

The Democratic nomination of McGovern for president was a consequence of the 1968 election, in which Nixon defeated Vice President Hubert Humphrey. Later, McGovern wrote an essay for *Harper's Magazine*, "The Lessons of 1968" (January 1970), in which he called on the Democratic Party to reform its platform as well as its method of selecting its standard bearer in order to be more representative of women, minorities, and young people. Under the new rules drafted by the McGovern-Fraser Commission—McGovern shared the task with Representative Donald M. Fraser of Minnesota—state central committees were no longer permitted to select the delegates to the national convention, but were required to hold open primaries or caucuses. This shifted power from the party bosses to rank-and-file Democrats, enabling a candidate such as McGovern, one of the most liberal of the party, to emerge as the nominee. After the presidency of Jimmy Carter (1977–1981), who likewise had been a political outsider, national party leaders instituted counter-reform measures for regaining some control. Still later, with the influence of Bill Clinton, the Democratic Party shifted more to the right to undo the McGovern legacy.

It could be argued that McGovern's loss was a combination of factors, not all ideological. Nixon's campaign benefited from the May 1972 shooting of George Wallace, a segregationist whose withdrawal from the race as a third-party candidate ensured that the Republican vote would not be split. In addition, McGovern made mistakes during the campaign that gave voters the impression that he was indecisive and untrustworthy. For example, after it became known that his running mate, Senator Thomas F. Eagleton of Missouri, had suffered depression and been treated with electric shock therapy, McGovern held a press conference and said he supported Eagleton "1,000 percent"—only to replace him later with R. Sargent Shiver, Jr. McGovern also backpedaled on a proposal for a guaranteed income after Republicans ridiculed it as a handout for people unwilling to work. As the McGovern campaign suffered the "dirty tricks" that were part of the Watergate conspiracy, it was being openly opposed by Democrats for Nixon, an organization spearheaded by the former Texas governor John Connally, who opposed isolationist foreign policy. Ultimately, Nixon undermined McGovern's key issue by convincing voters that the war was winding down.

In 1980, the year Ronald Reagan was elected president, McGovern lost his Senate seat to James Abdnor, a Republican candidate heavily funded by abortion opponents. In 1984, McGovern was briefly a candidate for the party's presidential nomination, promoting national health care and promising to decrease the military budget. Later, as U.S. ambassador to the United Nations Food and Agricultural Agencies in Rome, Italy (1998–2001), he promoted genetically modified food. McGovern has written a number of books, including *A Time of War, A Time of Peace* (1968), *The Third Freedom: Ending Hunger in Our Time* (2001), and *The Essential America: Our Founders and the Liberal Tradition* (2004). He was awarded the Presidential Medal of Freedom in 2000.

In the 2000s, McGovern voiced criticism of George W. Bush, rating him as the worst president in American history, including Nixon. "On just about every level I can think of, Bush's actions are more impeachable than were those of Nixon," he argued. McGovern drew parallels between the Iraq War and the Vietnam War, stating that "in both cases we went to war with a country that was no threat to us." In April 2007, Vice President Dick Cheney suggested that the Democratic Party, in urging an American withdrawal from Iraq, was adopting the same losing platform offered by McGovern in 1972.

Roger Chapman

See also: Civil Rights Movement; Cold War; Counterculture; Democratic Party; Great Society; Nixon, Richard; United Nations; Vietnam War; Wallace, George; Watergate; Wounded Knee Incident.

Further Reading

Anson, Robert Sam. *McGovern: A Biography.* New York: Holt, Rinehart & Winston, 1972.

Brinkley, Douglas. "George McGovern." *Rolling Stone*, May 3, 2007.

Dougherty, Richard. *Goodbye, Mr. Christian: A Personal Account of McGovern's Rise and Fall.* Garden City, NJ: Doubleday, 1973.

Leo, John. "The New McGovernites." *U.S. News & World Report*, November 7, 2005.

McGovern, George S. *Grassroots: The Autobiography of George McGovern.* New York: Random House, 1977.

McIntire, Carl

The fundamentalist radio preacher and ministry founder Carl McIntire became known in postwar America for objecting to conservative evangelical efforts to "modernize." Most notably, he rejected the evangelical preacher Billy Graham for his willingness to coordinate his Crusades with nonevangelical churches and for his openness to preaching before racially mixed audiences. Incapable of political compromise or strategic coalition building, McIntire could never join the ranks of Jerry Falwell or Tim LaHaye as an effective player in the New Christian Right, but he did fight the Federal Communications Commission (FCC) over his radio station for many years, protest the policies of the National Council of Churches (NCC), and make high-profile attacks against the Reverend Martin Luther King, Jr., and other civil rights activists, thereby emerging as a controversial and highly charged symbol of old-school American fundamentalism.

Born in Ypsilanti, Michigan, on May 17, 1906, Carl Curtis McIntire attended Southeastern State Teachers College in Durant, Oklahoma (1923–1926), Park College in Parkville, Missouri (BA, 1927), Princeton Theological Seminary (1928–1929), and Westminster Theological Seminary (ThB, 1931). Ordained in 1931 as a minister of the Presbyterian Church, he was stripped of his ordination five years later for his strident criticism of the church's "liberal" missionary activities. In 1937, McIntire's congregation in Collingswood, New Jersey, began identifying itself as the Bible Presbyterian Church. That same year, he established Faith Theological Seminary in Wilmington, Delaware, whose early graduates included the evangelical pastor and author Francis Schaeffer. McIntire went on to found the American Council of Christian Churches (1941) and the International Council of Christian Churches (1948) as alternatives to the NCC and the World Council of Churches, ecumenical Protestant organizations he condemned as "apostate" and hopelessly liberal.

For decades, McIntire disseminated his religious and political views in the newspaper *Christian Beacon* (beginning in 1936) and a daily radio program, *The Twentieth Century Reformation Hour* (beginning in 1955). At its peak in the late 1960s, the half-hour radio show aired on more than 600 stations, including McIntire's own WXUR, based in Media, Pennsylvania. In 1968, after years of fielding complaints from citizens offended by the program's right-wing, racist orientation, the FCC moved to revoke McIntire's broadcasting license for flagrant violation of the Fairness Doctrine. McIntire appealed the case, but the

FCC's decision was upheld in the 1972 federal District Court case of *Brandywine v. Mainline Radio.*

An exceptional showman, McIntire first came to national media attention in 1953 when, along with fellow fundamentalist broadcaster Billy James Hargis, he unleashed thousands of Bible messages attached to balloons from West Germany over the Iron Curtain. McIntire also briefly ran a floating pirate radio station off the New Jersey coast (after first posing with eye patch and pirate hat for photographers on shore); held several "Victory in Vietnam" rallies in Washington, D.C., in the early 1970s; and played table tennis in front of the White House to protest Nixon's "Ping Pong diplomacy" with China in 1971. If his political efforts were largely ineffective, McIntire was, nonetheless, an accomplished culture warrior when it came to finding publicity for his right-wing causes. He died on March 19, 2002, in Voorhees, New Jersey.

Heather Hendershot

See also: Cold War; Federal Communications Commission; Fundamentalism, Religious; Graham, Billy; Hargis, Billy; LaHaye, Tim, and Beverly LaHaye; Religious Right; Schaeffer, Francis; Vietnam War; World Council of Churches.

Further Reading

Fea, John. "Carl McIntire: From Fundamentalist Presbyterian to Presbyterian Fundamentalist." *American Presbyterian* 72:4 (Winter 1994): 253–68.

Forster, Arnold, and Benjamin R. Epstein. *Danger on the Right: The Attitudes, Personnel and Influence of the Radical Right and Extreme Conservatives.* New York: Random House, 1964.

Hendershot, Heather. "God's Angriest Man: Carl McIntire, Cold War Fundamentalism, and Right-Wing Radio." *American Quarterly* 59:2 (June 2007): 373–96.

Jorstad, Erling. *The Politics of Doomsday: Fundamentalists of the Far Right.* Nashville and New York: Abingdon Press, 1970.

McLuhan, Marshall

A controversial and highly influential Canadian media theorist, Marshall McLuhan coined the term "global village" and famously stated that "the medium is the message" (and later, "the medium is the massage"), arguing that the impact of electronic communications is greater than the actual information being transmitted. Many academics viewed him as an intellectual charlatan; dubbed his provocative aphorisms "McLuhanisms"; and complained that his ideas on technological determinism were mere assertions, not supported by empirical data. The novelist Tom Wolfe, on the other hand, considered McLuhan in the same league as Newton, Darwin, Freud, Einstein, and Pavlov.

Herbert Marshall McLuhan was born on July 21, 1911, in Edmonton, Alberta, Canada. He studied English at the University of Manitoba (BA, 1932; MA, 1934) and Cambridge University (BA, 1936; MA, 1939; and PhD, 1942), although he originally sought to be an engineer. McLuhan taught at the University of Wisconsin, Madison (1936–1937), University of St. Louis (1937–1944), and Assumption University in Windsor, Ontario (1944–1946), before moving to the University of Toronto, where he taught for more than three decades (1946–1979). In 1963, he established the Centre for Culture and Technology at the University of Toronto for studying "the psychic and social consequences of technologies and media." McLuhan's many published works include *The Mechanical Bride: Folklore of Industrial Man* (1951), *The Gutenberg Galaxy: The Making of Typographic Man* (1962), and *Understanding Media: The Extensions of Man* (1964). He also co-authored *The Medium Is the Massage: An Inventory of Effects* (1967), *From Cliché to Archetype* (1970), and *City as Classroom* (1977). He died in Toronto on December 31, 1980.

McLuhan divided human history into broad periods on the basis of communications developments: the tribal age, the print age, and the electronic age. The tribal age, he argued, depended on speech, sound, nonlinear thinking, and direct human connection for obtaining information. The printing press ushered in the second age, characterized by importance of the eye and linear thinking but less need for immediate tribal contact because one could read in private. The electronic age, beginning with the wireless telegraph and continuing with radio and television, was viewed by McLuhan as a return to instantaneous communication that would foster retribalization and ultimately lead to a "global village." He regarded TV as an acoustic medium, not a visual one, requiring nonlinear thinking. The electronic age, he warned, would change how people think and render less important the culture of print. These changes, which McLuhan regarded as inevitable, were not personally pleasing to him. As he said in a 1970 interview, "Only madmen would use radio and TV if they knew the consequences."

In fact, McLuhan blamed television for the decline in student test scores and literacy, declaring a print-based educational system with its linear thinking incompatible with the electronic age. Contrary to conventional wisdom, McLuhan did not regard watching television as a passive activity, but thought of TV as a "cool" medium requiring viewer involvement for filling in details. McLuhan also linked electric media with rock and roll and drugs. "One turns on his consciousness through drugs," he said during a 1969 interview, "just as he opens up all his senses to a total depth involvement by turning on the TV dial." McLuhan also observed that television would change political debate, giving the edge to candidates, like John F. Kennedy, who possess "cool, low-definition qualities." The cool medium of television made long, protracted wars such as Vietnam less possible, he argued, because viewers will lose patience.

Roger Chapman

See also: Canada; Counterculture; Education Reform; Kennedy Family; Leary, Timothy; Medved, Michael; Postmodernism; Rock and Roll; Vietnam War; War on Drugs; Wolfe, Tom.

Further Reading

McLuhan, Eric, and Frank Zingrone, eds. *Essential McLuhan.* New York: BasicBooks/HarperCollins, 1995.

Meyrowitz, Joshua. *No Sense of Place: The Impact of Electronic Media on Social Behavior.* New York: Oxford University Press, 1985.

Moss, George, and Linda M. Morra. *At the Speed of Light There Is Only Illumination: A Reappraisal of Marshall McLuhan.* Ottawa: University of Ottawa Press, 2004.

Postman, Neil. *Amusing Ourselves to Death: Public Discourse in the Age of Show Business.* New York: Penguin, 1985.

McVeigh, Timothy

Before the al-Qaeda attacks of September 11, 2001, the worst act of terrorism ever committed on American soil was the April 19, 1995, truck bombing of the Alfred P. Murrah Federal Building in Oklahoma City. The bombing was planned and carried out by Timothy McVeigh, a twenty-six-year-old U.S. Army veteran with ties to domestic right-wing extremist groups.

Born on April 22, 1968, in Lockport, New York, Timothy James McVeigh grew up in a Catholic, middle-class family and was introduced to firearms by his grandfather. After a blizzard in 1977, the young man became interested in survivalist training; his personal ideology was an amalgamation of what he read in comic books, *Soldier of Fortune* magazine, and the writings of the militia movement and Ku Klux Klan. According to psychiatrists who examined him before trial, he had harbored fantasies of being a hero since his childhood.

McVeigh enlisted in the army in May 1988 and participated in the 1991 Persian Gulf War, earning a bronze star and a combat infantry badge. While attending basic training, he befriended Terry Nichols and Michael J. Fortier, who would later be implicated in the Oklahoma City bombing. Although he intended to reenlist, McVeigh left the military in December 1991 after failing the Special Forces qualifications course. His return to civilian life was marked by a restless bitterness. Much of his time was spent attending gun shows and mixing with elements of the militia movement.

The bombing of the federal building was revenge for the April 19, 1993, federal assault on the compound of the Branch Davidians, a Seventh-Day Adventist cult, near Waco, Texas, that left eighty-two dead. The Waco tragedy angered McVeigh because it started out as a federal investigation of firearms violations. Earlier he had read *The Turner Diaries* (1978), a terrorist novel by William Pierce, a white supremacist, in which the main character, Earl Turner, uses a truck bomb to blow up the FBI headquarters in Washington as a protest over stricter gun laws. McVeigh decided to turn fiction into reality. His bomb, in the form of a Ryder rental truck containing sixteen 55-gallon drums packed with 4,800 pounds (2,182 kilos) of ammonium nitrate fertilizer mixed with liquid nitromethane, demolished the building, left 168 dead, and injured more than 400 others. Among the dead and injured were children who attended a day-care center on the second floor of the building. Afterward, borrowing a Pentagon euphemism from the Gulf War, McVeigh dismissed the children's deaths as "collateral damage." He never expressed remorse, explaining that Harry Truman did not apologize for dropping the atomic bombs on Japan, a decision that also killed children.

On June 2, 1997, McVeigh was found guilty of eleven counts of murder and conspiracy, and the jury recommended the death penalty. Appeals of the verdict and sentence were unsuccessful, and on June 11, 2001, McVeigh was executed by lethal injection at the federal penitentiary in Terre Haute, Indiana. (Terry Nichols was convicted for his role in the incident in December 1997 and sentenced to life in prison; Michael Fortier, who testified against both McVeigh and Nichols, received a twelve-year sentence.) After McVeigh's execution, conspiracy theories lingered. Some demolition experts argue that a single bomb could not have caused so much damage. The writer Gore Vidal and others suggested that there may have been a Muslim terrorist connection, with McVeigh serving as the "useful idiot." Many agree that McVeigh, influenced by the antigovernment rhetoric of right-wing ideologues and the paranoia of the militia movement, saw himself as a freedom fighter and not a terrorist.

Roger Chapman

See also: Capital Punishment; Comic Books; Conspiracy Theories; Gun Control; Hiroshima and Nagasaki; Militia Movement; Muslim Americans; September 11; Vidal, Gore; Vigilantism; Waco Siege; White Supremacists.

Further Reading

Hoffman, David. *The Oklahoma City Bombing and the Politics of Terror.* Venice, CA: Feral House, 1998.

Michel, Lou, and Dan Herbeck. *American Terrorist: Timothy McVeigh and the Oklahoma City Bombing.* New York: Regan Books, 2001.

Vidal, Gore. *Perpetual War for Perpetual Peace: How We Got to Be So Hated.* New York: Thunder's Mouth Press / Nation Books, 2002.

Mead, Margaret

Perhaps the twentieth century's most famous social anthropologist, Margaret Mead stirred controversy with pioneering work that contrasted human social relations in traditional and Western societies, as exemplified in her initial book, *Coming of Age in Samoa* (1928), and later summary works, *Sex and Temperament in Three Primitive Societies* (1935) and *Male and Female* (1949). Mead argued from research of isolated Pacific Island societies that child-rearing ideals, sex roles, marriage, sexual behavior, the nature of moral authority, and other social arrangements vary from culture to culture, and none is based on universal absolutes. Her conclusions infuriated social conservatives, who held her partly responsible for the excesses of the sexual revolution.

Born in Philadelphia on December 16, 1901, Mead studied psychology at Bernard College (BA, 1923) and anthropology at Columbia University (MA, 1924; PhD, 1929). Her major fieldwork was conducted in Samoa (1925–1926), New Guinea (beginning in 1928), and Bali (1930s and 1950s). Long affiliated with the American Museum of Natural History in New York (1926–1969), Mead also taught at a number of universities, including Stanford, Harvard, and Yale. She died on November 15, 1978.

Traditionalists viewed Mead's rejection of biodeterminism (the view that immutable biological differences largely dictate gender and social roles) as attacks on religion and society. Conservative commentators argued that her popularizing of "the fantasies of sexual progressives" contributed to the practice of casual sex, a higher rate of divorce, and an increase in abortion in America. The anthropologist Derek Freeman went so far as to characterize Mead's Samoan ethnography as a "hoaxing," but that critique, in turn, was criticized by the American Anthropological Association as "unscientific" and "misleading." The dispute, which is ongoing, is referred to as the "Mead-Freeman controversy."

Mead also seeded controversy over generational conflict, the consequence of perhaps her most visionary work, *Culture and Commitment: A Study of the Generation Gap* (1970, updated 1978), which disputed the primacy of adult authority over children. The eighty-page treatise crowns her career with a radical hypothesis: rapid demographic, social, and technological changes in modern society were rendering traditional adult values and authority obsolete. Mead argued that the older generation must adopt imaginative ways of understanding contemporary society and global change in order to effectively raise children for a future in which "there are no guides." Parents who try to direct modern children with "simple assertions" such as, "Because it is *right* to do so, because *God* says so, or because *I* say so" (emphasis hers), must yield to "a world in which conflicting points of view, rather than orthodoxies, are prevalent and accessible." Instead of "anger and bitterness" at "the discovery that what they had hoped for no longer exists for their children," Mead concluded, adults must embrace "consciously, delightedly, and industriously rearing unknown children for an unknown world."

Mike Males

See also: Abortion; Family Values; Generations and Generational Conflict; Kinsey, Alfred; Race; Sexual Revolution.

Further Reading

Freeman, Derek. *The Fateful Hoaxing of Margaret Mead: A Historical Analysis of Her Samoan Researches.* Boulder, CO: Westview Press, 1999.

Gewertz, Deborah, and Frederick Errington. "We Think, Therefore They Are? On Occidentalizing the World." In *Cultures of United States Imperialism*, ed. Amy Kaplan and Donald E. Pease, 635–55. Durham, NC: Duke University Press, 1993.

Mark, Joan T. *Margaret Mead, Anthropologist: Coming of Age in America.* New York: Oxford University Press, 1998.

Shankman, Paul. "Culture, Biology, and Evolution: The Mead–Freeman Controversy Revisited." *Journal of Youth and Adolescence*, 29:5 (2000): 539–56.

Media Bias

The claim of bias in the American media is a common refrain in the rhetoric of the culture wars. The expectation that news reporting should be neutral and objective developed in the United States in the nineteenth and early twentieth centuries. The question of whether the media should be, or even can be, unbiased has been intensely debated in recent decades. It is worth noting that accusations of media bias, while typically directed against political bias in news reporting, have also been directed against everything from sitcoms to cartoon strips to Hollywood films.

Right-wing critics of the media tend to identify journalists as the source of media bias. The rise in criticism of journalists as liberal elitists has coincided with the growing voice of populist conservatism in the United States. One formative event in this development was Reed Irvine's founding of the influential conservative watchdog organization Accuracy in Media (AIM) in 1969. That same year, Vice President Spiro T. Agnew described the media as home to "nattering nabobs of negativism." More recently, conservative commentators Rush Limbaugh, Bill O'Reilly, Ann Coulter, and others have repeated the criticism. According to Coulter in *How to Talk to a Liberal* (2004), the typical journalist has only one standard: "Will this story promote the left-wing agenda?" Bernard Goldberg's best-selling *Bias* (2002) argues that the personal views of journalists are overwhelmingly liberal, and that this gives a liberal shape to their news

The Fox News Channel was launched in 1996 with the purpose of correcting the liberal bias perceived in mainstream television networks. Despite its slogan of "Fair and Balanced," Fox has been accused by liberals and media watchdog groups of disseminating explicitly conservative opinion. *(Katja Heinemann/Aurora/Getty Images)*

stories. Goldberg further contends that the media denigrate and marginalize religious belief and are to the left of mainstream America on topics such as abortion, the death penalty, and homosexuality. Conservatives argue that they have succeeded in attracting attention—and adherents—to their view because they reflect the perception of the broader American public.

Critics on the left have a different argument about media bias. Left-wing critics of the media tend to focus on the effects of economic power, especially the influence of corporate ownership and funding of the media. Eric Alterman's *What Liberal Media?* (2003), a critical response to Bernard Goldberg, argues that while there is some merit to the charge that the media are liberal on social issues, there is clear conservative bias in the media when it comes to economic issues. Noam Chomsky and Edward S. Herman argue in *Manufacturing Consent* (1988) that various systemic features of the media work to muffle or prevent the publication of stories that would harm the interests of major corporations. They argue that the dependence of mainstream media on advertising dollars limits the degree to which the media can criticize corporations. They also stress that major media outlets are themselves part of corporations—NBC, for example, is owned by General Electric.

Progressives argue that the idea of a liberal media is a conservative myth used to pressure journalists not to run stories that threaten those in power. One important institutional development for left-of-center media criticism was the founding of Fairness and Accuracy in Reporting (FAIR), a media watchdog organization, in 1986. The visibility of left-wing criticism of mainstream media has

grown considerably since 2000, with documentaries such as *Bowling for Columbine* (2002), *Fahrenheit 9/11* (2004), and *Outfoxed* (2004) receiving significant attention.

The form of media most commonly held under scrutiny is television news. Many conservative commentators hold that the nightly news shows of the Big Three networks (ABC, CBS, and NBC) display a strong liberal bias. Longtime CBS news anchor Dan Rather in particular was criticized by the right. The network most frequently singled out for criticism by liberal commentators is the Fox News Channel. Various other forms of media—e.g., National Public Radio, the *New York Times*, talk radio, and a wide assortment of other outlets—have been criticized as biased by those on the left and the right.

The topic of media bias raises philosophical issues often associated with postmodernism. One central question concerns the language of objectivity and value-neutrality that has become part of the self-image of serious journalism and whether news coverage can ever be "merely" factual, in view of the fact that values are involved in selecting facts to report. Thus, disputes over media coverage concern not only whether what is reported is true but the question of which information reaches the screen or newspapers. One influential concept of bias-free reporting is the idea of showing a variety of perspectives on any given issue. This concept, taken to an extreme, means giving equal time to all sides of an issue regardless of the truth or credibility of the positions in question. Many of the devices of television news, especially those aimed at persuading the viewer of the authority, impartiality, and objectivity of the broadcast, have been parodied by such popular television programs as *The Daily Show* and *The Colbert Report*.

One important development in relation to media bias is the growth of narrowcasting—media aimed at a specific, homogeneous demographic group. Narrowcasting has encouraged news reporting that is both more willingly and more explicitly partisan and, as a result, has contributed to cultural polarization.

Daniel Callcut

See also: Chomsky, Noam; Coulter, Ann; Irvine, Reed; Moore, Michael; Murdoch, Rupert; National Public Radio; New Journalism; *New York Times, The*; Postmodernism; Public Broadcasting Service; Rather, Dan; Stewart, Jon; Talk Radio.

Further Reading

Adkins-Covert, Twanya J., and Philo C. Wasburn. *Media Bias? A Comparative Study of* Time, Newsweek, *the* National Review, *and the* Progressive, *1975–2000.* Lanham, MD: Lexington Books, 2009.

Alterman, Eric. *What Liberal Media? The Truth About Bias and the News.* New York: Basic Books, 2004.

Chomsky, Noam, and Edward S. Herman. *Manufacturing Consent: The Political Economy of the Mass Media.* New York: Pantheon Books, 1988.

Goldberg, Bernard. *Bias: A CBS Insider Exposes How the Media Distort the News.* Washington, DC: Regnery, 2002.

Kallen, Stuart A., ed. *Media Bias.* San Diego, CA: Greenhaven Press, 2004.

Streissguth, Thomas. *Media Bias.* New York: Marshall Cavendish Benchmark, 2007.

Medical Malpractice

"Medical malpractice" is a legal term that refers to negligent treatment, or failure to take appropriate action, on the part of a doctor or other medical practitioner that causes harm to a patient.

An often rancorous partisan debate in the culture wars, the issue of malpractice suits has been labeled a "crisis" by the American Medical Association (AMA). In 1975, *Newsweek* magazine concurred, declaring malpractice "medicine's most serious crisis." From 1960 to the mid-1980s, the frequency of medical malpractice claims in America rose from 1 to 17.5 per every 100 physicians. During the same period, plaintiff awards in major cities such as Chicago and San Francisco rose from $50,000 to $1.2 million. In addition to the specific repercussions for the medical community, insurance companies, and the overall cost of health care, the debate on medical malpractice has touched on larger issues of tort reform.

According to the U.S. Department of Justice, in 2001 there were a total of 1,156 medical malpractice trials, including claims of permanent injury (67 percent) and death (33 percent). The overall success rate for plaintiffs was 27 percent, with a median award in jury trials of $431,000—up 50 percent from $287,000 just five years earlier. From 1992 to 2001, between 1 and 4 percent of successful plaintiff winners also received punitive damages, averaging about $250,000 per litigation. Many other cases were settled out of court.

The AMA began earnestly addressing medical malpractice during the 1950s with the aim of reducing lawsuits by improving medical care, most notably by reforming hospital procedures and prompting standardization of medical records. (Of all malpractice suits at the time, 70 percent arose from incidents at hospitals.) Since surveys during that period found that most doctors did not consider medical malpractice lawsuits a major problem, AMA leadership began making them a topic of discussion in its *Journal of the American Medical Association.*

By the 1960s, the AMA shifted its focus of attack to the legal system, blaming the surge in malpractice lawsuits on lawyers and plaintiffs. During this period, rules pertaining to the statutes of limitations had been liberalized in favor of injured patients (that is, allowing a longer filing period for a malpractice claim since resulting health repercussions are not always initially known). Although there was a rise in the number of malpractice suits, it paralleled the increase in the number of physicians. The average award for medical malpractice in 1964 was $5,000, but several highly publicized cases gave successful plaintiffs windfalls of $100,000 or more. Malpractice suddenly became a high-profile public issue, covered in the mainstream press and made the subject of federal government inquiry. In November 1969, a subcommittee of the Senate Committee on Executive Reorganization issued a 1,060-page report on medical malpractice that asserted, albeit with no statistical support, "Most malpractice suits are the direct result of injuries suffered by patients during medical treatment or surgery. The majority have proved justifiable." Critics questioned the claim of justifiability when 90 percent of malpractice cases that went to court were won by physician defendants.

Citing the high cost of medical malpractice insurance, political conservatives generally favor reform measures to cap the amount of damages a person can receive for a medical mistake and to penalize and deter those who file "frivolous" suits. Malpractice claims, usually initiated in state courts, have been blamed in part for the spiraling cost of health care and for the trend toward "defensive medicine" to shield doctors from potential liability. In 1975, California passed a law capping noneconomic damages at $250,000; by the mid-1980s, several other states passed similar caps. From the mid-1970s to the beginning of the twenty-first century, it should be noted, personal-injury suits in America, including medical malpractice claims, have remained flat on a nationwide basis, while lawsuits against other businesses have more than tripled.

Liberal advocacy groups such as Ralph Nader's Public Citizen charge that the medical malpractice "crisis" is propaganda advanced by medical, pharmaceutical, and insurance lobbyists who seek legislative protection to shield their clients from accountability. According to a number of reports, the dramatic rise in medical malpractice insurance rates in the mid-1970s, mid-1980s, and late 1990s were the consequence of insurance underwriting and investment cycles (relating to interest rates and market-based investments) and had little to do with any rise in malpractice awards.

In 2003, hospitals, doctors, and other health professionals paid $11 billion for malpractice insurance, a sum representing less than 1 percent of the total $1.5 trillion national health care cost. That same year, $27 billion was spent on automobile liability, $57 billion on workers' compensation insurance premiums, and $5 billion for product liability insurance. Of the 900,000 practicing physicians in the United States that year, the average premium was $12,000 per doctor. However, the premiums do vary significantly from state to state—for example, doctors in Florida typically pay seventeen times more for malpractice insurance than doctors in Minnesota.

Also, premium rates are typically higher for obstetrics and gynecology than for other medical specialties. States that have passed strict tort caps have not seen dramatic decreases in the cost of malpractice premiums. In California, doctors experienced a reduction in the cost of premiums after voters in 1988 approved Proposition 103, which regulated insurers and mandated policyholder refunds.

Critics of the AMA's campaign against malpractice suits emphasize that the primary problem is medical malpractice itself. The California Medical Insurance Feasibility Study of the mid-1970s, conducted by the California Hospital Association and the California Medical Association, found that doctors and hospitals in that state were responsible for injuring 140,000 patients, leading to 14,000 deaths, in 1974. Of the total number of injured, 24,000 were considered a consequence of medical malpractice. In the mid-1980s, Harvard University conducted a study on medical injuries in New York, concluding that there had been 27,000 injuries from medical malpractice in 1984. Harvard did another study in 1992, this time in Utah and Colorado, reaching similar results as in California and New York—that is, that the number of injuries from medical malpractice is far greater than the number of lawsuits filed for medical malpractice. In California, only one lawsuit was filed for every ten malpractice injuries; in New York, the ratio was one lawsuit for every seven malpractice injuries; and in Utah and Colorado, the ratio was one for every six. According to a November 1999 report issued by the U.S. Academy of Sciences, entitled *To Err Is Human*, 98,000 people die from medical mistakes each year in the United States, more than the number killed in automobile and work-related accidents.

Roger Chapman

See also: Health Care; Nader, Ralph; Tort Reform.

Further Reading

Baker, Tom. *The Medical Malpractice Myth.* Chicago: University of Chicago Press, 2005.

Danzon, Patricia A. *Medical Malpractice: Theory, Evidence, and Public Policy.* Cambridge, MA: Harvard University Press, 1985.

Hogan, Neal C. *Unhealed Wounds: Medical Malpractice in the Twentieth Century.* New York: LFB Scholarly, 2003.

Sloan, Frank A., et al. *Suing for Medical Malpractice.* Chicago: University of Chicago Press, 1993.

Weiler, Paul C. *Medical Malpractice on Trial.* Cambridge, MA: Harvard University Press, 1991.

Medical Marijuana

Advocates of medical marijuana argue that the main ingredient of the drug (THC, or tetrahydrocannabinol) is useful for treating nausea caused by chemotherapy in connection with cancer treatment, loss of appetite associated with AIDS, eye pain due to glaucoma, and spasms and seizures triggered by multiple sclerosis. Opponents of medical marijuana, suspecting that the attributed medicinal benefits have been exaggerated, note that cannabis has never been screened for efficacy and safety by the Food and Drug Administration (FDA). Furthermore, skeptics argue, smoking marijuana for the "benefit" of THC is questionable since it could be more safely delivered by pill, suppository, or nasal inhaler. Generally, political conservatives view medical marijuana as a purposeful step toward complete legalization of the drug.

In contradiction of federal law, voters in a number of states have approved by wide margins ballot items allowing the possession and use of marijuana for medical treatment—Proposition 215 in California (1996); Proposition 200 in Arizona (1996); Question 8 in Alaska (1998); Measure 67 in Oregon (1998); Question 9 in Nevada (1998); Question 2 in Maine (1999); Amendment 20 in Colorado (2000); Initiative 148 in Montana (2004); and Proposal 1 in Michigan (2008). The District of Columbia approved a medical marijuana referendum in 1998, but Congress, exercising its oversight of the federal city, overturned the law. State legislatures have passed legislation permitting medical marijuana in Hawaii (2000), Maryland (2003), Rhode Island (2006), and New Mexico (2007). The General Assembly of Rhode Island overrode the veto of Governor Donald Carcieri, a Republican who argued that the law would only lead to more marijuana being sold on the streets. Robert Ehrlich, the governor of Maryland, was the first Republican elected official to approve such a measure.

Tod H. Mikuriya, a California physician, was instrumental in getting his state to be the first to pass a medical-marijuana referendum, but colleagues criticized him for allowing his advocacy to cloud his professional judgment. In 2004, the California medical board fined Mikuriya $75,000 and placed him on probation for writing marijuana prescriptions for sixteen individuals without conducting appropriate physical examinations. By the time of his death in 2007, he had reportedly prescribed marijuana to some 9,000 individuals. The founder of the California Cannabis Research Medical Center (and its subgroup the Society of Cannabis Clinicians), Mikuriya openly admitted to routinely smoking marijuana with his morning coffee.

As pharmacies have refused to sell medical marijuana, such prescriptions have instead been filled by "cannabis buyers' clubs" that are listed as medical distributors. Many of these clubs have been raided by the U.S. Drug Enforcement Administration. In the case of *U.S. v. Oakland Cannabis Buyers' Cooperative* (2001), the U.S. Supreme Court ruled against the distributors, stating that "medical necessity" is not a legal defense against violation of federal law. In *Gonzalez v. Raich* (2005), the high court ruled 6–3 that the federal Controlled Substances Act, which outlaws the possession and distribution of marijuana, preempts state laws authorizing medical marijuana. Many political conservatives who generally prefer states' rights over the power of the federal government make an exception when it comes to drug policies.

Roger Chapman

See also: Food and Drug Administration; War on Drugs.

Further Reading

Ferraiolo, Kathleen. "From Killer Weed to Popular Medicine: The Evolution of American Drug Control Policy, 1937–2000." *Journal of Policy History* 19:2 (2007): 147–79.

Marijuana Policy Project. *State-by-State Medical Marijuana Laws: How to Remove the Threat of Arrest.* Washington, DC: Marijuana Policy Project, 2007.

Minamide, Elaine. *Medical Marijuana.* Detroit, MI: Greenhaven Press, 2007.

Medved, Michael

An Orthodox Jew and liberal turned conservative, Michael Medved has participated in the culture wars as film critic, author, and radio talk show host. He came to public prominence with *What Really Happened to the Class of '65?* (1976), a best-selling book co-authored with David Wallechinsky. Adapted into an NBC television series (1978), the book is a probing assessment of the counterculture generation, specifically the alumni of California's Palisades High School who had been featured in *Time* magazine.

Medved was born on October 3, 1948, in Philadelphia and grew up in San Diego and Los Angeles, California. After graduating from Palisades High School, he studied American history at Yale University (BA, 1969), where he also briefly studied law (1969–1970). This was followed by a creative writing program at California State University, San Francisco (MFA, 1974). Early jobs included teaching at a Hebrew school in New Haven, Connecticut (1969–1970), working as a speechwriter for various Democratic candidates (1970–1972), and writing for an advertising agency in Oakland, California (1972–1974). Other early writings include *The Shadow Presidents: The Secret History of the Chief Executives and Their Top Aides* (1979) and *Hospital: The Hidden Lives of a Medical Center Staff* (1983).

For years a film critic for the Public Broadcasting Service (co-host of *Sneak Previews*, 1985–1996) and the *New York Post* (1993–1996), Medved emerged as a popular voice for social conservatives, including the Religious Right. After guest hosting for Rush Limbaugh's radio talk show, Medved began his own syndicated program in 1996, broadcasting at KVI-AM out of Seattle. His autobiography, *Right Turns: Unconventional Lessons from a Controversial Life* (2005), provides some detail on his political about-face, from campaigning for Robert Kennedy to supporting Ronald Reagan. Daniel Lapin, an Orthodox rabbi and affiliate of the Religious Right, was Medved's mentor.

Sounding much like the media theorist Marshall McLuhan, Medved has suggested that the medium of television, regardless of the programming, is its own message and one that erodes the values of the viewer. The counterculture generation, he continues, while it grew up watching such wholesome programs as *The Mickey Mouse Club* (1955–1959), *Father Knows Best* (1954–1960), and *Leave It to Beaver* (1957–1963), nonetheless failed to mature into responsible adulthood. According to Medved, those who watch television to excess are prone to be impatient, self-pitying, and superficial.

Despite such theorization, Medved has devoted much of his career to critiquing the content of films and television shows. In *Hollywood vs. America: Popular Culture and the War on Traditional Values* (1992), he asserts that the values of Tinsel Town—which are belittling to religion and the sanctity of marriage and family—are out of sync with mainstream American values. He also contends that it would be more financially profitable for Hollywood to make more G-rated films and fewer R-rated ones. Although long concerned about violence in films, Medved defended Mel Gibson's *Passion of the Christ* (2004). Earlier, he collaborated with younger brother Harry in writing several whimsical works—beginning with *Golden Turkey Awards* (1980)—that rated the all-time "worst" films.

Roger Chapman

See also: Counterculture; Gibson, Mel; Kennedy Family; Lapin, Daniel; Limbaugh, Rush; McLuhan, Marshall; Reagan, Ronald; Religious Right.

Further Reading

Catanzaro, Michael J. "Michael Medved." *Human Events*, February 20, 1998.

Medved, Michael. "The Demand Side of Television." In *Building a Healthy Culture: Strategies for an American Renaissance*, ed. Don Eberly, 416–23. Grand Rapids, MI: William B. Eerdmans, 2001.

———. *Hollywood vs. America: Popular Culture and the War on Traditional Values.* New York: HarperCollins, 1992.

Michael Medved Web site. www.michaelmedved.com.

"The Thorn in Hollywood's Side." *Christianity Today*, April 27, 1992.

Men's Movement

The men's movement that developed in America in the 1970s, which sought to promote social and cultural changes that centered on understandings of manhood, gender relations, and family life, was not a unified coalition. The numerous groups clustered under this heading outlined a variety of issues and recommendations for social change. Scholars have generally viewed the men's movement as a response to the feminist movement of the 1970s. In general, the men's movement attempted to define masculinity and assert the importance of the roles of men in American society.

Reactions to Second-Wave Feminism

A "men's liberation movement" developed in the early 1970s alongside second-wave feminism. Applying feminist insights, its leaders concluded that contemporary understandings of gender roles were detrimental to men as well as to women. Although members of the men's liberation movement frequently saw themselves as allies of feminism, some in the feminist movement believed that men's liberation had the potential to undermine the radical potential of feminism by focusing on individuals rather than on the institutional structures of power that fostered women's oppression.

As the men's liberation movement waned in the late 1970s, the "men's rights movement" began to assert that feminist ideologies were damaging to men and that the male had become the victim. The men's rights movement, building on feminist notions of gender roles, posited that the constraints of masculinity were more stringent and potentially damaging to men than notions of femininity were to women. Some advocates argued that men were the true victims of sexual harassment, pornography, false accusations of rape, and media bias. The "father's rights movement" of the late 1980s argued in favor of men's right to custody in cases of divorce, the elimination of alimony and child-support arrangements, and greater control in cases where a partner is considering abortion.

Consequently, the men's rights movement had important political ramifications. Most activists were white, middle-class males who felt threatened by what they viewed as a culture of entitlement for women and minorities. Such men tended to move to the right politically, thereby exacerbating the gender gap in the American electorate.

The Mythopoetic Movement

The leaders of the "mythopoetic men's movement" drew on myths and fairy tales to create gendered archetypes and encouraged men to analyze these stories in order to achieve personal insights. They argued that industrialization and modernization, rather than feminism, had a deleterious effect on American men and masculinity. Robert Bly in his best-seller *Iron John* (1980), one of the movement's seminal texts, argues that pre-industrial societies were characterized by rituals through which

fathers initiated their sons into manhood, but the Industrial Revolution feminized men by separating them from their fathers, leaving them to learn the meanings of masculinity from their mothers. Bly calls on men to embark on a "spiritual journey" through which they can discover their "deep masculine" natures. The attempts of participants in the mythopoetic men's movement to recapture a pre-industrial masculinity often took the form of appropriations of Native American and non-Western cultures. Men traveled to remote locations to take part in retreats that often involved Native American rituals, drumming, chanting, and an emphasis on notions of warriorhood. Mythopoetic leaders also touted the potential for such retreats to promote male bonding, an activity that they viewed as critical to men's development in the absence of meaningful relationships between fathers and sons.

Although some critics, including journalist Susan Faludi in *Backlash* (1991), argued that the mythopoetic men's movement was a reaction against feminism, Bly and others maintained that the movement developed without reference to feminism—that it was about men rather than women. Leaders of the movement articulated a belief in essential differences between men and women; "deep" masculinity was portrayed as a timeless and unchanging phenomenon, although individual agency played a role in gender construction. Bly suggested that there were parallels between feminists and mythopoets, as both groups struggled against a society and culture that circumscribed their self-definitions and their day-to-day activities. However, the mythopoetic men's movement was largely anti-intellectual and apolitical; its members focused on spirituality rather than on analysis of their activities. Critics claimed that, like the men's liberation movement, it ignored institutions and power structures that worked to men's benefit.

Return to Traditional Roles

The Promise Keepers of the mid-1990s represented a more conscious effort to work against the changes brought about by feminism. The Promise Keepers aimed for a reassertion of masculinity and a return to men's leadership in families. The movement was deeply rooted in conservative Christianity; one of its goals was the "remasculinization" of images of Jesus Christ. Their call for a return to traditional gender and family roles was premised on a belief in God-given biological characteristics, dictating that women are best suited to childrearing and other domestic duties, while men are meant to be breadwinners and community and family leaders. The Promise Keepers have drawn criticism for their apparently antigay and antifeminist agenda. Most Promise Keepers are middle-class, white, Protestant men, but the group has made efforts to reach across racial lines. Such efforts have generally been stymied, however, by the differing priorities of members of other ethnic and racial groups, particularly African-American men.

The Million Man March, organized in October 1995 by Nation of Islam leader Louis Farrakhan, was based on a declaration that black men intended to confront the crisis they perceived in black communities and families. The movement's emphasis on the need for men to assume leadership roles echoed the ideas of the Promise Keepers, but participants used a language of gender equality that went beyond the framework of the Promise Keepers.

While participants in the various men's movements have articulated a shared sense that Americans must reexamine and redefine masculinity, there has not been a unified approach to achieving that end.

Charlotte Cahill

See also: Evangelicalism; Farrakhan, Louis; Feminism, Second-Wave; Feminism, Third-Wave; Gay Rights Movement; Million Man March; Promise Keepers; Victimhood; Women's Studies.

Further Reading

Claussen, Dane S., ed. *The Promise Keepers: Essays on Masculinity and Christianity.* Jefferson, NC: McFarland, 2000.

Griswold, Robert L. *Fatherhood in America: A History.* New York: Basic Books, 1993.

Hagan, Kay Leigh, ed. *Women Respond to the Men's Movement.* San Francisco: Pandora, 1992.

Kimmel, Michael. *Manhood in America: A Cultural History.* New York: Free Press, 1996.

Magnuson, Eric Paul. *Changing Men, Transforming Culture: Inside the Men's Movement.* Boulder, CO: Paradigm Publishers, 2007.

Messner, Michael A. *Politics of Masculinities: Men in Movements.* Thousand Oaks, CA: Sage, 1997.

Mexico

Given that Mexico and the United States share a common border and yet are vastly different in terms of political and social traditions, religion, and economic development, it was perhaps inevitable that Mexico would become a major battleground topic in America's culture wars.

The dominant issue during the 1990s was free trade, in the context of the North American Free Trade Agreement (NAFTA), signed by the United States, Mexico, and Canada in 1992 and taking effect on January 1, 1994. Under the provisions of the agreement, goods and services would be exchanged freely, without tariffs, between the participating nations. Initially, support for NAFTA came from liberals, who maintained that increasing trade would lead to more jobs and more rapid economic growth in Mexico; conservative opponents argued that untold numbers of American workers would lose their jobs as production moved across the border, where labor was cheaper. Subsequently, however, liberals came to express disillusionment with NAFTA (and globalization in general) because of its negative impact on small farmers and businesses as American products flooded the market and Wal-Mart stores displaced local *tiendas*.

The controversy over illegal immigration from Mexico has been another ongoing debate in the culture wars, heightened by the September 11, 2001, terrorist attacks and the resulting wave of xenophobia. Many liberals and some conservatives have emphasized the economic plight of impoverished Mexicans who travel to the United States in search of work, as well as the benefits of cheap labor to American businesses. Some have called for amnesty or other legal mechanism to allow undocumented immigrants to obtain American citizenship. Most conservatives, however, view illegal aliens as lawbreakers who should be deported. Many Americans characterize illegal aliens from Mexico as invaders who smuggle drugs, take jobs from American workers, and enjoy social and medical services without paying taxes. Although liberals applaud the multiculturalism that Mexicans and other Latin Americans have brought to the United States, conservatives warn of "Mexifornia" (an overrunning of the state of California by Mexicans) and the threat of unchecked immigration to America's Anglo-Protestant cultural and political identity. The movement to make English the official language of the United States is a response to the perceived cultural threat posed by the influx of Hispanics.

The conservative camp of the culture wars has pushed for the completion of a wall at the southern border of the United States to prevent illegal aliens from turning America into another Third World nation. Such a wall, it is further argued, would strengthen America's homeland security and serve as a protection against terrorism and drug smuggling. During the summer of 2005, to highlight dissatisfaction with the open border, civilian vigilante volunteers of the Minuteman Project patrolled the frontier between Mexico and Arizona to deter illegal crossings. The opposing camp maintains that the two countries must recognize their interdependence and work together to resolve the economic problems, such as unemployment and low wages, that lead so many Mexicans to cross the border into the United States.

Sue Davis

See also: Bush Family; Canada; Clinton, Bill; English as the Official Language; Globalization; Illegal Immigrants; Immigration Policy; Migrant Labor; September 11; Vigilantism; Wal-Mart; War on Drugs.

Further Reading

Cooper, Marc. "High Noon on the Border." *Nation*, June 6, 2005.

Dominguez, Jorge I., and Rafael Fernandez de Castro. *United States and Mexico: Between Partnership and Conflict*. New York: Routledge, 2001.

Hanson, Victor Davis. "Frank Talk About 'Mexifornia.'" *Imprimis*, November 2003.

Huntington, Samuel P. *Who Are We? The Challenges to America's National Identity*. New York: Simon & Schuster, 2004.

Preston, Julia, and Samuel Dillon. *Opening Mexico: The Making of a Democracy*. New York: Farrar, Straus, and Giroux, 2004.

Microsoft

In 1998, the U.S. Department of Justice, under President Bill Clinton, initiated an antitrust lawsuit against Microsoft, the world's largest computer software company and the maker of the Windows computer operating system. The suit alleged that Microsoft, headquartered in Redmond, Washington, and run by founder and CEO Bill Gates, had become a monopoly, illegally stifling competition and innovation. The public debate on the case focused on the rights of producers versus those of consumers. Gates maintained that what was good for Microsoft was good for computer and Internet users, but hackers who disagreed fought back by releasing computer viruses aimed at crippling Microsoft systems.

The ubiquitous personal computer (PC) is only a few decades old. The first IBM PC became available in 1981. Foreseeing the personal computer's potential far more clearly than his former bosses at "Big Blue," who remained wedded to the mainframe, Gates shipped the initial copies of his Windows operating system in 1985. Windows 3.0, the first truly user-friendly version of Microsoft's product, was released on May 22, 1990, and quickly became the industry standard, a position Gates's company solidified five years later when it introduced Windows 95.

Windows 95 was launched one week after Netscape, a tiny start-up company headquartered in Mountain View, California, went public. At the leading edge of what would become the dot-com boom (and subsequent bust), Netscape's stock offering was wildly successful, as investors flocked to buy shares in the company that had acquired the rights to Mosaic, a browser for connecting to sites on the World Wide Web. Beginning in 1993, when Mosaic had only twelve users, Netscape transformed Mosaic into Navigator, the first "killer application" of the PC age. Two years later, Netscape's browser completely dominated the market.

Whether the release of Windows 95 was timed deliberately or not, 1995 marked the start of the "browser wars" and Microsoft's protracted encounters with the an-titrust authorities of the United States and the European Union. The browser wars spilled over into the culture wars, as Microsoft's products came under attack by some members of the "open-source community," endorsers of the idea that the code for operating personal computers and the software applications running on them should be freely available to all. Resentful of Microsoft's market dominance, hackers engaged in a campaign to disable Windows-based PCs by distributing viruses and worms over the Internet that exploited vulnerabilities in the operating system's security defenses.

Although Microsoft had been the subject of a Federal Trade Commission investigation into the provisions of licensing agreements with PC manufacturers in the early 1990s, Windows 95 drew the battle lines more sharply. That version of Microsoft's operating system was bundled with the first edition of the company's own Web browser, Internet Explorer, intended to compete directly with Netscape Navigator. Because Internet Explorer was included with Windows 95 at no charge and given a prominent place on PC desktops, Netscape complained to the Department of Justice that Microsoft was engaged in an unlawful attempt to drive it from the market.

Joined by the attorneys general of twenty states and the District of Columbia, the Justice Department sued Microsoft in May 1998, charging that the company had monopolized the market for PC operating systems and had used its monopoly unlawfully in a variety of ways. Chief among the charges was that Microsoft had introduced Internet Explorer to prevent Navigator from becoming an alternative to Windows as a platform for running software applications.

The federal judge who presided over the Microsoft case, Thomas Penfield Jackson, ultimately ruled in the government's favor. Since Windows was preloaded on 90 percent of the new PCs shipped in the United States, and Microsoft's large market share had created a barrier to entry by manufacturers of rival operating systems because most software applications were written for Windows, the judge concluded that the company possessed monopoly power. On June 28, 2001, Judge Jackson ordered Microsoft, within ninety days, to break itself into two separate firms, one devoted to operating systems and the other to software applications. That remedy was overturned on appeal, however, and the case eventually was settled in early 2003 on terms that preserved Microsoft's organizational structure but imposed various restrictions on its business practices.

As it turned out, Internet Explorer's share of the browser market reached 85 percent by 2006, while Netscape, after its purchase by America Online, lost its position completely. However, open-source applications took off: Linux, the operating system written by Linus Torvalds, steadily attracted users, as did the Web browser Firefox and e-mail client Thunderbird, both distributed at no charge by Mozilla.org. None of these developments were anticipated by Judge Jackson, who also excluded Apple's MacIntosh operating system from the market he determined Microsoft to have monopolized.

Microsoft's legal troubles were far from over. In March 2004, the European Commission, concerned, among other things, about the competitive effects of Microsoft's bundling Media Player with later versions of Windows, found that Microsoft had abused its dominance of the operating system market and fined the company half a billion euros. With the support of George W. Bush's Justice Department, Microsoft appealed the commission's fine. As Gates announced in 2006 that he was stepping down as the company's CEO in order to devote more time to his philanthropic work with the Bill and Melinda Gates Foundation, EU Antitrust Commissioner Neelie Kroes threatened to levy more fines on Microsoft for failing to comply with the commission's 2004 order.

William F. Shughart II

See also: Internet.

Further Reading

Auletta, Ken. *World War 3.0 and Its Enemies.* New York: Random House, 2001.

Heilemann, John. *Pride Before the Fall: The Trials of Bill Gates and the End of the Microsoft Era.* New York: HarperCollins, 2001.

Liebowitz, Stan J., and Stephen E. Margolis. *Winners, Losers, and Microsoft: Competition and Antitrust in High Technology.* Oakland, CA: Independent Institute, 1999.

McKenzie, Richard B., and William F. Shughart II. "Is Microsoft a Monopolist?" *Independent Review* 3:2 (1998): 165–97.

Rubinfeld, Daniel L. "Maintenance of Monopoly: *U.S. v. Microsoft* (2001)." In *The Antitrust Revolution: Economics, Competition, and Policy,* 4th ed., ed. John E. Kwoka, Jr., and Lawrence J. White, 476–501. New York: Oxford University Press, 2004.

Migrant Labor

Disagreements about migrant labor have been a constant in America's culture wars. The migrant stream, which often originates in Mexico and south Texas, creates not only transnational and ethnic exchange but also cultural conflict. This interethnic exchange illustrates the increasing social diversity of the United States since the 1940s.

A 1942 agreement between the U.S. and Mexican governments created the Bracero Program, through which Mexican nationals legally entered the United States to work in agriculture. The program was originally intended to prop up U.S. industries threatened by labor shortages during World War II, but farm own-

ers quickly recognized the utility of cheap, compliant Mexican labor, which, after the braceros arrived at their intended destinations, remained largely unregulated. Braceros, who lived together in labor camps that were often only rudimentary places to eat and sleep, worked under temporary contracts. They often came to agreement with farm owners that they would work at the same farm in subsequent harvest seasons, returning legally through the Bracero Program or otherwise.

By 1945, an estimated 50,000 braceros were working on American farms at any given time. Another 75,000 worked in the railroad industry under a separate program. Farm owners became so reliant on this pool of cheap labor that, although the program was intended to end with the conclusion of the war, many states continued importing braceros as late as 1964.

César Chávez and NFWA

As large agribusinesses consolidated control of farm ownership in the mid-twentieth century, working conditions for migrant workers—who lacked protection by federal labor or collective bargaining law—steadily worsened. A young man working in Los Angeles in the early 1950s, César Chávez, took notice of the migrant workers' plight and in 1962 began the National Farm Workers' Association (NFWA), which organized California's largely Mexican-American (Chicano) and Filipino farm workers into a formidable labor force. Previous attempts at organizing migrant workers had failed, but Chávez exuded a personal magnetism, due in large part to his devout Catholicism and his commitment to nonviolent social protest, which appealed to many workers. Thus, a cultural revolution had begun.

Meanwhile, on Thanksgiving Day in 1960, television journalist Edward R. Murrow broadcast a documentary called *Harvest of Shame*, which revealed the poor living and working conditions faced by migrants. Thus, when Chávez launched the now-famous grape strike and boycott from the union's headquarters in Delano, California, it did not take long for it to garner nationwide attention. After a highly publicized 300-mile march from Delano to Sacramento in spring 1966, Chávez announced a nationwide boycott of table grapes. Support groups formed to assist the workers in cities across the nation, and the boycott finally broke the will of most California growers in July 1970, when many agreed to sign collective bargaining agreements with the union.

The victory proved only temporary. When most of the contracts expired in 1973, the majority of California growers signed with the Teamster's Union, and a bitter struggle between the two labor organizations ensued. It was in the 1970s that the farm workers' movement began to disintegrate. Chávez ran afoul of many Chicano movement leaders when he issued public proclamations critical of illegal immigrants. Several union leaders became disillusioned with Chávez's leadership. Antonio Orendain, the union's original secretary-treasurer, broke away and formed the Texas Farm Worker's Union in the Río Grande Valley in 1975. By the 1980s, the NFWA had lost much of its force, though Chávez remains a celebrated hero in the Mexican-American struggle for civil rights. His legacy survives not only in the United Farm Workers (formerly NFWA) but also in the spirit of farm labor organizations like the Coalition of Immokalee Workers, a Florida-based group that led a protracted nonviolent boycott against the fast-food chain Taco Bell in the late 1990s and early 2000s. In September 2004, the Farm Labor Organizing Committee, resorting to Chávez-style boycotting, succeeded in unionizing most of the guest workers who harvest crops in North Carolina.

Post-9/11 Politics

In addition to the many Mexicans in border cities who have "green cards" allowing them to commute daily across the border to work for U.S. employers, millions of illegal immigrants cross the border yearly in search of work.

Since the terrorist attacks on September 11, 2001, the issue of illegal immigration has become deeply politicized, as many fear that fundamentalist Islamic terrorists will take advantage of the relatively porous U.S.-Mexican border to enter the United States. This fear led to the formation of the Minuteman Project, a volunteer group that patrols the border and assists the U.S. Border Patrol in capturing illegal immigrants. Some high-profile conservatives, such as media commentator Pat Buchanan, argued that President George W. Bush's inability to address the "border problem" made the Minutemen an unfortunate necessity. Liberals, however, criticize the Minutemen for their abuse and harassment of immigrants.

Although most Mexicans who cross the border illegally do so to participate in the U.S. workforce as well as consume goods made in the United States, many conservative lawmakers have proposed increasingly stiff penalties on illegal immigrants and the businesses that employ them. In protests during spring 2006, hundreds of thousands of ethnic Mexicans took to the streets in cities such as Dallas and Los Angeles. Illegal immigration and the future of migrant labor will be hotly debated for years to come.

Timothy Paul Bowman

See also: Chávez, César; Hispanic Americans; Illegal Immigrants; Immigration Policy; Labor Unions; Mexico; Militia Movement; Murrow, Edward R.; September 11; Vigilantism.

Further Reading

Acuña, Rodolfo. *Occupied America: A History of Chicanos.* 5th ed. New York: Longman, 2004.

Gamboa, Erasmo. *Mexican Labor and World War II: Braceros in the Pacific Northwest, 1942–1947.* Austin: University of Texas Press, 1990.

Gómez-Quiñones, Juan. *Chicano Politics: Reality and Promise, 1940–1990.* Albuquerque: University of New Mexico Press, 1990.

Herzog, Lawrence A. *Where North Meets South: Cities, Space, and Politics on the U.S.-Mexico Border.* Austin: University of Texas, Center for Mexican American Studies, 1990.

Militia Movement

The militia movement is a loosely organized network of paramilitary groups in the United States, most prominent in the early to mid-1990s but still active in the early twenty-first century. Militia members typically oppose gun control legislation, believing that the Second Amendment to the U.S. Constitution protects individuals' right to bear arms and that an armed citizenry is a crucial bulwark of liberty. Members also tend to distrust the federal government and fear that the United States is in danger of losing its sovereignty to a tyrannical "New World Order," possibly to be ushered in by the United Nations.

While militia rhetoric frequently includes calls for violent action, members do not consider themselves enemies of the United States. Rather, they see themselves as the true heirs of the nation's founders in a country where most citizens no longer understand the meaning of liberty. They also embrace an account of the American Revolution that largely credits small groups of citizen soldiers with winning the nation's independence.

The militia movement is commonly associated with the Patriot movement, a broader social movement that includes gun advocates, tax protesters, survivalists, "sovereign citizenship" proponents, some white supremacist groups, some abortion opponents, and "Wise Use" militants who generally oppose environmental legislation such as the Endangered Species Act as infringements on property rights. The feature that distinguishes militias from other groups involved in the Patriot movement is their commitment to armed paramilitary groups. Militia members hold that such organizations are authorized by the Second Amendment and statutes that define most male (and some female) adults as members of the "unorganized militia."

Critics of the militia movement contend that it is a hotbed of racism and anti-Semitism and that its members embrace a faulty interpretation of the Constitution. Also, militias are criticized for teaching an inaccurate account of the American Revolution by exaggerating the effectiveness of militias in that struggle while ignoring the role of a professionalized Continental Army and assistance from France in securing independence.

Although militia leaders have generally avoided explicitly racist appeals, critics note that many militia leaders have previously been members of white supremacist organizations such as Aryan Nations, Posse Comitatus, the Ku Klux Klan, and a variety of Christian Identity groups, and that many militias have adopted these groups' organizational structures and tactics. According to the Southern Poverty Law Center, militia leaders have minimized racist rhetoric in order to broaden their appeal but without abandoning the underlying belief system. Critics also note parallels between conspiratorial accounts of the coming New World Order and earlier, explicitly anti-Semitic conspiracy theories.

The militia movement is part of a long history of paramilitary organizations in the United States and has intellectual precursors such as the John Birch Society's critique of internationalism. Militia leaders transferred their conspiracy theories to the federal government after President George H.W. Bush, on the eve of the 1991 Persian Gulf War, announced a new world order, followed shortly thereafter by the demise of the Soviet Union and the emergence of the United States as the world's sole superpower. Gun control legislation as well as federal assaults against citizens at Ruby Ridge, Idaho, and Waco, Texas, confirmed in the minds of militia leaders fears of "Big Brother" operating out of Washington.

The Ruby Ridge incident in August 1992 involved an effort to arrest fugitive white supremacist Randy Weaver on weapons charges. Weaver's son and wife were killed in the incident, as was a U.S. marshal. Before Weaver's surrender, the standoff generated national attention and drew a crowd of outraged antigovernment protesters to the site. Similarly, a federal assault on the Branch Davidian compound in Waco, Texas, which ended on April 19, 1993, with at least seventy-five deaths, also provoked outrage. The federal government, in its quest to enforce gun control, was seen as repressive and willing to commit murder. Militia members were also troubled by the passage of the Brady Bill (1993), which imposed a five-day waiting period for the purchase of handguns, and a ban on assault rifles (1994).

In response to the events at Ruby Ridge, a group met in October 1992 at Estes Park, Colorado, for a meeting called the Rocky Mountain Rendezvous. There Larry Pratt, leader of the group Gun Owners of America, declared conventional political efforts to be ineffective and called for the formation of small, armed groups to resist federal oppression. In February 1994, the Militia of Montana was founded by John, David, and Randy Trochmann, friends of Randy Weaver. This group distributed instructions on how to form a militia group. Among the groups using these instructions was the Michigan Militia, established by Baptist minister and gun store owner Norman Olson and real estate agent Ray Southwell in April 1994; it quickly became the largest militia organization in the United States, with as many as 7,000 members.

Between 1994 and 1996, more than 400 militia groups were active in the United States. Estimates of total membership vary from 20,000 to 300,000. The movement began to decline after the bombing of the Alfred P. Murrah Federal Building in Oklahoma City on April 19, 1995, although the effect was not immediate. Although Timothy McVeigh, who was eventually executed for the bombing, was not a militia member, he had attended a Michigan Militia meeting and came to be associated with the movement in the public's mind. In 1996, there was an eighty-one-day standoff between law enforcement officials and a group called the Montana Freemen, and in 1997 there was a seven-day confrontation with a group called the Republic of Texas; both ended peacefully after negotiations. After the terrorist attacks of September 11, 2001, a distinct decline followed in the militia movement—the number of known groups fell below 200—with no significant resurgence.

Thomas C. Ellington

See also: Conspiracy Theories; Founding Fathers; Globalization; Gun Control; McVeigh, Timothy; Montana Freemen; Revisionist History; Ruby Ridge Incident; United Nations; Vigilantism; Waco Siege; White Supremacists.

Further Reading

Chermak, Steven M. *Searching for a Demon: The Media Construction of the Militia Movement*. Boston: Northeastern University Press, 2002.

Crothers, Lane. *Rage on the Right: The American Militia Movement from Ruby Ridge to Homeland Security*. New York: Rowman and Littlefield, 2003.

Dees, Morris, with James Corcoran. *Gathering Storm: America's Militia Threat*. New York: HarperCollins, 1996.

Michael, George. *Confronting Right-Wing Extremism in the U.S.A.* New York: Routledge, 2003.

Mulloy, D.J. *American Extremism: History, Politics, and the Militia Movement*. New York: Routledge, 2004.

Milk, Harvey

Elected in 1977 to the San Francisco board of supervisors, Harvey Milk was the first openly gay politician to hold office in a major American city. His assassination the following year by a political rival and the light prison sentence for the perpetrator (seven years and eight months) triggered a riot by gays and lesbians in San Francisco. In tape recordings, voicing a premonition of an early violent death, Milk expressed hope that "hundreds will step forward, so that gay doctors come out, the gay lawyers, gay judges, gay bankers, gay architects. I hope that every professional gay would just say 'Enough.'"

Harvey Bernard Milk was born on May 22, 1930, in Woodmere, New York. After graduating from New York

State Teachers College at Albany (1951) and completing a tour in the U.S. Navy (honorably discharged in 1955), he worked as an insurance salesman and financial analyst in New York, maintaining politically conservative views, even campaigning for Barry Goldwater during the 1964 presidential election. Over time, influenced by his participation in theater productions, he joined the counterculture movement and relocated to San Francisco in 1972. There he opened a camera shop in Castro, the city's main gay district, and emerged as a leader of the growing gay community.

Founding the Castro Valley Association, Milk represented local merchants in dealing with municipal government. Known as the "mayor of Castro Street," he began to politically organize from his place of business, launching a voter registration drive. After losing three close races, Milk was finally elected to the city's board of supervisors in 1977. Less than a year into his term, on November 27, 1978, he was shot and killed, while standing next to Mayor George Moscone, by a former city supervisor named Dan White. The murder was revenge for Milk and Moscone's refusal to reinstate White to the board; he had formally resigned and then changed his mind.

Although Milk wanted to be known as a "politician who happens to be gay" rather than a "gay politician"—he supported local unions, all minority groups, small businessmen against big business and the political "machines" of both parties, and worked to save neighborhoods from commercial development—the cause of gay rights was his abiding passion. In an era when being gay was considered a psychological perversity and many cities still had antihomosexual statutes on the books, Milk called on all gays to come out of the closet and assert their gay pride. He thought that if every homosexual, from bus drivers to doctors, refused to hide their sexual orientation, society would stop thinking of gays as sexual deviants. In the 1970s, however, there was still widespread opposition to gays and homosexuality—from Anita Bryant's referendum drive in Florida to repeal an ordinance prohibiting discrimination based on sexual orientation to John Briggs's Proposition 6 in California, which would have prohibited any advocate of homosexuality from teaching in the public schools. During his brief tenure as a city supervisor, Milk faced Briggs, a state senator, in a televised debate on the proposition—which was decisively voted down by Californians in November 1978, just weeks before Milk's assassination.

E. Michael Young

See also: Bryant, Anita; Counterculture; Gay Rights Movement; Goldwater, Barry; Outing; Penn, Sean.

Further Reading

Shilts, Randy. *The Mayor of Castro Street: The Life and Times of Harvey Milk.* New York: St. Martin's Press, 1982.

Millett, Kate

A feminist activist, artist, and cultural and literary critic, Kate Millett is known primarily as the author of *Sexual Politics: A Manifesto for Revolution* (1970), a revised PhD outline that became an unlikely best-seller, landed Millett on the cover of *Time* magazine and provided the modern women's liberation movement with its theoretical underpinnings. The book's main thesis is that gender roles are socially constructed, imposed by a male-dominated society in order to subordinate women.

Katharyn Murray Millett was born on September 14, 1934, to an Irish Catholic family in St. Paul, Minnesota. She studied literature at the University of Minnesota (BA, 1956), St. Hilda's College at Oxford University (MA, 1958), and Columbia University (PhD, 1970). As an activist, Millett joined the National Organization for Women and chaired its Education Committee (1965–1968), but she was also involved in the civil rights movement, including the Congress of Racial Equality. She has taught at numerous institutions of higher learning, including Wasada University in Tokyo, Barnard College, Bryn Mawr College, and California State University, Sacramento.

Sexual Politics indicts romance, the family as a political unit, and monogamous marriage, and it critiques the literary canon through such writers as

A leading theoretician of second-wave feminism, Kate Millett rose to prominence and gave impetus to the movement with the publication of her first book, *Sexual Politics*, in 1970. *(Fred W. McDarrah/Getty Images)*

D.H. Lawrence, Henry Miller, Charlotte Brontë, and Norman Mailer. The manifesto inspired Mailer's *The Prisoner of Sex* (1971), in which he argues that males also have a sensitive side. The publication of *Sexual Politics* placed Millett at the forefront of second-wave feminism along with Betty Freidan, Gloria Steinem, and Germaine Greer. Other books by Millett followed, focusing on contemporary world events and autobiographical experiences to analyze the intersection of interpersonal relationships and larger cultural attitudes and ideologies.

Millett's other works include *The Prostitution Papers* (1973), a defense of prostitute rights; *Flying* (1974), an autobiography that expresses discomfort with her celebrity role as feminist spokesperson; *Sita* (1977), an account of her affair with a woman; *The Basement* (1979), an examination of female-adolescent brutality; *Going to Iran* (1982), a report on her brief trip promoting Muslim women's rights; *The Loony Bin Trip* (1990), a memoir in which she discusses her mental breakdown; *The Politics of Cruelty* (1994), a treatise on patriarchal state-sanctioned violence and torture; *A.D.: A Memoir* (1995), a reflection on her severed relationship with an aunt over her deception involving lesbianism; and *Mother Millett* (2001), an indictment on the institutionalization of the elderly through the story of the illness and death of Millett's mother.

Millett has faced criticism from conservatives and liberal feminists. While married to Japanese sculptor Fumio Yoshimura for many years, she was also openly in relationships with women. Millett's bisexuality, along with her reluctance to be cast as a "leader" of what was a large, grassroots movement, prompted "mainstream" feminists to look elsewhere for a representative voice, while gay rights activists admonished her for not coming out earlier. Culture critics such as Camille Paglia read Millett's work as overly bitter and out of touch with a third-wave feminism that has moved beyond casting women as victims of patriarchy.

Rebecca Nicholson-Weir

See also: Civil Rights Movement; Family Values; Feminism, Second-Wave; Feminism, Third-Wave; Friedan, Betty; Gay Rights Movement; Lesbians; Mailer, Norman; National Organization for Women; Outing; Sex Offenders; Steinem, Gloria; Victimhood.

Further Reading

Millett, Kate. *Sexual Politics*. Urbana: University of Illinois Press, 2000.

Moi, Toril. *Sexual Textual Politics: Feminist Literary Theory*. New York: Routledge, 1985.

Paglia, Camille. *Sexual Personae: Art and Decadence from Nefertiti to Emily Dickinson*. New Haven, CT: Yale University Press, 1990.

Million Man March

One of the largest peaceful demonstrations ever held on the National Mall in Washington, D.C., the Million Man March took place on October 16, 1995, led by the controversial leader of the Nation of Islam, Louis Farrakhan. The purpose of the event, as conceived at the African American Leadership Summit in June 1994, was to inspire and unite the black male community.

The Million Man March brought together hundreds of thousands of black men—estimates varied significantly—from more than 400 cities across America for "a day of atonement, reconciliation, and responsibility." Participants gathered to hear prominent social activists and writers, such as Farrakhan, Jesse Jackson, Dick Gregory, Rosa Parks, and Maya Angelou, call for an end to racism, white supremacy, violence, substance abuse, crime, and underemployment. The day-long program, heralding the return of collective and peaceful civil rights actions, was reminiscent of the 1963 March on Washington led by the Reverend Martin Luther King, Jr. Numerous organizations, including the National Black United Front, All African People's Revolutionary Party, and Union Temple Baptist Church, pledged to continue the struggle for civil rights. Blacks were encouraged to register to vote, join local African-American organizations, and become strong community activists. Farrakhan called for nothing less than the political, economic, and spiritual empowerment of African-American males.

The Million Man March brought the discussion of discrimination back into the mainstream media and pitted conservative commentators against the more radical black press. Although it was generally considered a success, the march was marred by controversy. When the U.S. Park Police estimated the crowd at only 400,000, Farrakhan and other activists threatened to sue the National Park Service for attempting to undermine the significance of the movement. Some black feminists and scholars, namely Angela Davis and Marcia Gillespie, took issue with the male focus of the event. Some mainstream African-American organizations, including the National Association for the Advancement of Colored People (NAACP), refused to endorse the event due to the radical and politically incorrect nature of some of Farrakhan's teachings.

The black press faulted the rightist press for focusing too heavily on Farrakhan's notoriety. Although planners repeatedly urged journalists to "separate the message from the messenger," Farrakhan's controversial character remained a prominent feature of the mainstream media coverage. As he promoted the event by speaking about self-determination and moral and spiritual improvement, Farrakhan undermined any potential broad appeal by simultaneously issuing anti-Semitic, sexist, and black supremacist statements. Consequently, his comments deterred many conservative Republicans from fully endorsing the march.

Despite such controversies, the Million Man March presented a more positive image of African-American manhood to contrast with the negative media images fueled by the O.J. Simpson murder trial, which ended on October 3, 1995. The event inspired the Millions More Movement, which became heavily involved in administering aid to the victims of Hurricane Katrina (2005), and the Million Mom March for gun control in 1999.

Kelly L. Mitchell

See also: Angelou, Maya; Civil Rights Movement; Farrakhan, Louis; Hurricane Katrina; Jackson, Jesse; King, Martin Luther, Jr.; Malcolm X; Men's Movement; Nation of Islam; National Association for the Advancement of Colored People; O.J. Simpson Trial; Parks, Rosa.

Further Reading

Alex-Assensoh, Yvette M., and Lawrence J. Hanks, eds. *Black and Multiracial Politics in America.* New York: New York University Press, 2000.

Clatterbaugh, Kenneth C. *Contemporary Perspectives on Masculinity: Men, Women, and Politics in Modern Society.* Boulder, CO: Westview Press, 1997.

Madhubati, Haki R., and Maulana Karenga. *Million Man March / Day of Absence: A Commemorative Anthology.* Chicago: Third World Press, 1996.

Miranda Rights

As a consequence of the U.S. Supreme Court's landmark decision in the case of *Miranda v. Arizona* (1966), law enforcement officials in America are required to verbally communicate an individual's "Miranda rights" to anyone questioned while in police custody. Miranda warnings consist of notification of the individual's right to refuse to answer interrogative questions, a warning that any answers may be used by prosecutors at trial, and a guarantee upon request of the assistance of counsel during questioning.

Inasmuch as issues of crime and punishment are central to ideological tensions in American society, liberals and conservatives disagree bitterly as to the impact of the Miranda case on crime-control policy and the jurisprudential foundations of this key limitation on police authority. Disputes about the applicability of Miranda rights occur whenever a criminal defendant during a trial challenges the admissibility of a verbal statement made while in police custody. In short, the assertion of a violation of Miranda rights centers on either an involuntary confession or a denial of legal counsel during police questioning. For conservatives, Miranda rights unduly "handcuff" police officers in the fight against crime.

Furthermore, since evidence can be thrown out in court if it is determined that the defendant's Miranda rights had been denied, conservatives argue that the "rights of criminals" allow loopholes for lawbreakers to escape justice. Liberals, on the other hand, see Miranda rights as safeguarding individual civil liberties against the strong arm of the government.

Two years prior to the Miranda decision, the Supreme Court's ruling in *Escobedo v. Illinois* (1964) established the basic framework for evaluating right-to-counsel claims. In that case, the high court held that denying a criminal suspect access to an attorney in the context of custodial interrogation violates the right-to-counsel provision of the Sixth Amendment and the due process clause of the Fourteenth Amendment. Furthermore, the *Escobedo* ruling announced a key implication of the Sixth Amendment's language—at the moment police investigative efforts are trained on a particular individual, a right to counsel goes into effect and remains during all subsequent police procedures.

Miranda, importantly, is distinct from the *Escobedo* case in at least two ways. First, Miranda rights were created to give meaning to the Fifth Amendment's self-incrimination clause requiring that "No person shall . . . be compelled in any criminal case to be a witness against himself." Second, Miranda rights dictate that police allow persons held in custody access to an attorney, at the government's expense if necessary, during all periods of interrogation. Moreover, the *Miranda* ruling was an extension of the *Escobedo* principle to persons who are not the sole focus of a police investigation yet are subject to custodial interrogation.

The *Miranda* decision established a heightened standard against which courts measure the admissibility at trial of a confession rendered during police custody. Prior to the mid-1960s, judicial rulings in state courts on the admissibility of confessions turned on various applications of the due process clause of the Fourteenth Amendment. Consequently, the adoption of the *Escobedo* rules and, especially, the exacting *Miranda* rules were of revolutionary impact in the arenas of street-level police work and the nation's courtrooms—settings where civil liberties and law enforcement activities often collide.

Today, conservatives cite *Miranda* as an example of the unchecked liberal jurisprudence of the Warren Court, an impediment to effective law enforcement, and a decision with no foundation in constitutional text that ultimately empowers criminals. Supporters of the *Miranda* decision argue that such warnings are demanded by the Constitution's Fifth Amendment, address the pragmatic goal of enhancing the reliability of confessions, and, perhaps ironically, ease prosecutors' efforts to turn arrests into convictions.

In 2000, much to the disappointment of the Warren Court's detractors, the Supreme Court in *Dickerson v. U.S.*, reaffirmed the central role of Miranda rights in the American system of criminal justice. Rejecting conservatives' invitation to review custodial confessions solely according to subjective measures of voluntariness, Chief Justice William Rehnquist's opinion for the Court referred to the essential holding in *Miranda* as "part of our national culture."

Beyond technical constitutional claims, liberals continue to advance two positions that, if correct, effectively undermine Miranda's critics. First, supporters of *Miranda* maintain that a large percentage of arrestees waive their Miranda rights and speak freely with police interrogators. Second, proponents of Miranda rights, particularly the American Civil Liberties Union (ACLU), point to scientific studies indicating that it is highly unusual for criminal defendants to successfully challenge a conviction on the grounds of a Miranda rights violation. Though conducted prior to the announcement of the Court's decision in *Dickerson*, an interview with ACLU legal director Steven Shapiro on PBS's *NewsHour with Jim Lehrer* in January 2000 captured the left's perennial and most persuasive response to Miranda's critics. "If anything," Shapiro explained, "it makes it easier to admit confessions at trial, as long as police obey the rules."

Exhaustively debated for more than forty years, the subject of Miranda rights fuels a key ideological divide in American society. On opposite sides of the divide are two distinct cultural forces—one defined by a liberal ideology and supportive of limitations on the power of the state, the other conservative and suspicious of policies expanding the rights of persons accused of criminal wrongdoing. Though opposed, these positions are traceable to broader, persistent tensions among Americans on the issues of crime and punishment.

Bradley Best

See also: American Civil Liberties Union; Judicial Wars; Police Abuse; Rehnquist, William H.; Right to Counsel; Warren, Earl.

Further Reading

Cassel, Paul G., and Richard Fowles. "Handcuffing the Cops? A Thirty Year Perspective on Miranda's Harmful Effects on Law Enforcement." *Stanford Law Review* 50 (1998): 1055–145.

Leo, Richard A. "Inside the Interrogation Room." *Journal of Criminal Law and Criminology* 86:2 (1996): 266–303.

Samaha, Joel. *Criminal Procedure.* 4th ed. Belmont, CA: Wadsworth, 1999.

Shulhofer, Richard J. "Reconsidering Miranda." *University of Chicago Law Review* 54 (1987): 435–61.

Stewart, Gary L. *Miranda: The Story of America's Right to Remain Silent.* Tuscon: University of Arizona Press, 2004.

Mondale, Walter

When he ran for president in 1984, Walter ("Fritz") Mondale, a former U.S. senator (D-MN) and vice president to Jimmy Carter, was defeated by Ronald Reagan, who won a second term as president and lay claim to a conservative political realignment. Mondale was unable to resurrect a New Deal coalition that could bridge the generational and ideological gaps of the Democratic Party.

Walter Frederick Mondale was born on January 5, 1928, in Ceylon, Minnesota. He attended the University of Minnesota, studying political science (BA, 1951) and law (LLB, 1956), in between completing a hitch in the U.S. Army. As a student, he helped manage Hubert Humphrey's first successful bid for the U.S. Senate (1948). Mondale's subsequent political career was rich and varied: Minnesota attorney general (1960–1964); U.S. senator (1964–1976); vice president (1977–1981); chair of the National Democratic Institute for International Affairs (1986–1993); U.S. ambassador to Japan (1993–1996); and U.S. special envoy to Indonesia (1998). After Senator Paul Wellstone's sudden death in 2002, Mondale made an unsuccessful attempt to win that seat for the Democrats.

Greatly influenced by his father's liberal populism, Mondale as state attorney general emphasized consumer protection and civil rights, earning a reputation as a "people's lawyer." He took over Humphrey's seat in the Senate after his mentor became Lyndon B. Johnson's vice president in 1964. Senator Mondale supported Johnson's Great Society programs and pushed for such later progressive initiatives as a $2 billion child-care program that President Richard M. Nixon vetoed in 1971.

As Jimmy Carter's vice president, Mondale redefined the role of an office long considered unimportant. The staffs of the president and vice president were integrated for the first time, and Mondale became the first vice president to have an office in the West Wing of the White House, near the Oval Office. He met regularly with President Carter, had access to the same information, and was not sidelined with "busy work." However, he proved unable to meaningfully shape the Carter presidency, as the administration's policies were different from those of the New Deal and Great Society liberalism. With the emergence of "Reagan Democrats," many voters deserted the Carter-Mondale ticket in 1980, electing Ronald Reagan to his first term as president.

In 1984, Mondale was the Democratic presidential standard bearer. His selection of U.S. Representative Geraldine Ferraro (D-NY) as a running mate, the first female candidate for vice president, showed his willingness to include new elements of the Democratic coalition. But Reagan, running as a moderate conservative, drew support from many Democrats, and Mondale, facing the reality of inflation, openly stated during the campaign that if elected he would increase taxes. When the votes were tallied, Mondale carried only his home state and the District of Columbia.

Diane Benedic

See also: Adler, Mortimer J.; Carter, Jimmy; Democratic Party; Ferraro, Geraldine; Great Society; Humphrey, Hubert H.; Johnson, Lyndon B.; New Deal; Nixon, Richard; Reagan, Ronald; Republican Party; Wellstone, Paul.

Further Reading

Gillon, Steven M. *The Democrats' Dilemma: Walter F. Mondale and the Liberal Legacy.* New York: Columbia University Press, 1992.

Lewis, Finlay. *Mondale: Portrait of an American Politician.* New York: Harper and Row, 1980.

Montana Freemen

A white-supremacist group founded in 1992, the Montana Freemen (sometimes referred to as the Christian Freemen) rejected federal authority, asserting that the U.S. government based on the Constitution is illegal. Influenced by other right-wing militia and survivalist groups, including Posse Comitatus and Christian Identity, the Freemen were secessionists who refused to pay taxes and maintained that members of "the white race" are Israelites and subject only to the laws of the Bible (what they call "common law").

The Freemen movement, based near the northeastern Montana town of Jordan, achieved notoriety in the mid-1990s for attempting to defraud banks and businesses of billions of dollars by writing bogus checks and money orders. They placed fraudulent liens on the assets of other individuals, especially public officials, to obtain collateral for carrying out illegal banking schemes. Freemen leaders were known for hosting workshops on how to engage in bank fraud, rationalizing it as legitimate activity against an "illegal" system. However, one prominent militia leader, Charles Duke of the Patriot movement, publicly dismissed the Freemen as "nothing but criminals."

In September 1995, the Montana Freemen "established" their own government, Justus [*sic*] Township, a 960-acre (390-hectare) compound consisting of four ranches in Garfield County about 100 miles (160 kilometers) northeast of Billings. The settlement attracted some individuals who had lost farms or ranches to foreclosures and sheriff auctions, but the group remained small in number. In May 1996, Leroy M. Schweitzer, Daniel Petersen, and eight other Freemen were indicted for trying to harm the national banking system. In June 1996, after an eighty-one-day standoff with 633 federal agents, the remaining sixteen of twenty-six Montana Freemen surrendered without firing a shot, ending one of the longest armed sieges in U.S. history. Federal agents

were criticized for being overly patient with the Freemen, but the FBI was determined not to repeat the mistakes of Waco and Ruby Ridge, two earlier standoffs with other extremists that ended with lost lives. The federal government spent $7.5 million in apprehending the Freemen.

Later, in federal court, it was determined that the Montana Freemen wrote 3,432 bogus checks totaling $15.5 billion. Although less than 1 percent of the checks cleared, the group was able to accumulate $144,000 in cash, along with an assortment of money orders and gold and silver coins. After two federal trials, the main leaders of the Freemen received prison sentences. In March 1999, Schweitzer, the Freemen's founder, was sentenced to twenty-two-and-a-half years in prison.

In other cases, individuals associated with the Freemen movement have been implicated in various criminal conspiracies, including a plan to bomb a mosque near Denver in 1999. A group in Michigan that included a former member of the Montana Freemen was convicted in December 2001 of issuing $550 million of counterfeit U.S. Treasury checks.

Roger Chapman

See also: Aryan Nations; Militia Movement; Ruby Ridge Incident; Waco Siege; White Supremacists.

Further Reading

Barkun, Michael. *Religion and the Racist Right: The Origins of the Christian Identity Movement.* Rev. ed. Chapel Hill: University of North Carolina Press, 1997.

Jakes, Dale, Connie Jakes, and Clint Richmond. *False Prophets: The Firsthand Account of a Husband-Wife Team Working for the FBI and Living in Deepest Cover with the Montana Freemen.* Los Angeles: Dove Books, 1998.

Shannan, J. Patrick. *The Montana Freemen: The Untold Story.* Jackson, MS: Center for Historical Analysis, 1996.

Moore, Michael

Film producer and writer Michael Moore has achieved fame and fortune in the culture wars for a highly politicized series of documentary films that are unabashedly liberal and populist in both perspective and audience appeal. Relying on ambush interviews, news and archival footage, animation, satire, and comedy, Moore has taken on the interests of corporate America and the federal government (especially Republican administrations) on issues including industrial unemployment, gun culture, the war in Iraq, and health care. Opponents charge him with manipulating facts, distorting the sequence of events, and editing videotape to create false impressions. He has also been criticized for owning stock in some of the companies he has vilified in his productions.

The son of a General Motors factory worker, Michael Francis Moore was born on April 23, 1954, in Davison,

Populist documentary filmmaker Michael Moore (left) joins a fellow liberal foot soldier in the culture wars, comedian-turned-politician Al Franken, at the 2004 Democratic National Convention in Boston. *(Mario Tama/Getty Images)*

Michigan, a suburb of Flint. He attended Catholic schools until the age of fourteen and at one point considered becoming a priest. In 1972, at age eighteen, he was elected to the Davison County School Board. Ironically, he failed to complete his freshman year at the University of Michigan–Flint, dropping out to work in local radio and journalism. He began hosting a public radio program called *Radio Free Flint* and founded an alternative newspaper called the *Flint Voice* (later renamed the *Michigan Voice*). By 1985, Moore was a commentator at National Public Radio. Later, he was dismissed after a few months as an editor of the left-wing magazine *Mother Jones* (1986), but he used the windfall from an out-of-court settlement to start Dog Eat Dog Films, a documentary film production company.

Moore's films include *Roger & Me* (1989), about the decision of General Motors to close its factory in Flint, Michigan; *Bowling for Columbine* (2002), about the culture of guns and violence in America, in the wake of the 1999 student shootings at Columbine High School in Littleton, Colorado; *Fahrenheit 9/11* (2004), about President George W. Bush in wake of the September 11 terrorist attacks and the decision to go to war against Iraq; and *Sicko* (2007), about the nation's failing health care system. In addition to his films, Moore has written several books, including *Downsize This! Random Threats from Unarmed America* (1997), about corporate crime and the effects of corporate downsizing on working-class families; *Stupid White Men, and Other Sorry Excuses for the State of the Nation* (2002), about conservative politics during the Bush presidency; and *Dude, Where's My Country?* (2003), which Moore called "a book of political humor" (and used at the expense of political conservatives).

In *Fahrenheit 9/11*, perhaps his most controversial and popular film, Moore suggests that the Bush administration's invasion of Iraq was launched on behalf of the American oil industry, while portraying military recruitment efforts as exploitation of the economically disadvantaged. Moore grossed about $200 million worldwide from the release of the film, but his primary goal of thwarting Bush's 2004 reelection bid failed. In fact, according to some critics, the film's confrontational style led to a voter backlash that helped Bush defeat Democratic opponent John Kerry in 2004. Months prior to the election, the singer Linda Ronstadt was booed off the stage in Las Vegas after praising Moore and the film. Conservatives that year produced three film rebuttals to *Fahrenheit 9/11*, including *Michael Moore Hates America*, *Celsius 41.11: The Temperature at Which the Brain . . . Begins to Die*, and *FahrenHYPE 9/11*.

Jessie Swigger and Roger Chapman

See also: Bush Family; Election of 2000; Gun Control; Health Care; Kerry, John; School Shootings; September 11.

Further Reading

Larner, Jesse. *Forgive Us Our Sins: Michael Moore and the Future of the Left.* Hoboken, NJ: John Wiley & Sons, 2006.

Palash, Dave, and Christopher Hitchens. *The Real Michael Moore: A Critical Biography.* New York: Touchstone Books, 2008.

Rapoport, Roger. *Citizen Moore: The Life and Times of an American Iconoclast.* Muskegon, MI: RDR Books, 2007.

Schweizer, Peter. *Do As I Say (Not As I Do): Profiles in Liberal Hypocrisy.* New York: Doubleday, 2005.

Toplin, Robert Brent. *Michael Moore's Fahrenheit 9/11: How One Film Divided a Nation.* Lawrence: University Press of Kansas, 2006.

Moore, Roy S.

A former chief justice of Alabama (2001–2003), Roy Stewart Moore is best known for defying a federal court order in August 2003 to remove a monument of the Ten Commandments from the rotunda of the state Supreme Court building in Montgomery—an act of defiance for which he was removed from office.

Moore was born on February 11, 1947, in Gadsden, Alabama. Upon graduating from the U.S. Military Academy (1969), he served as a second lieutenant in Germany and then in Vietnam, where he commanded a military police unit. Following graduation at the University of Alabama School of Law (JD, 1977) and passing the bar exam, Moore served as deputy district attorney for Etowah County and then worked in private practice. In 1992, Governor Guy Hunt appointed Moore to finish out the term of a county circuit judge who died in office. Two years later, Moore defeated a Democratic challenger to win election to a full six-year term.

It was in this position that Moore first gained significant public notice, as the American Civil Liberties Union (ACLU) challenged his practice of beginning court sessions with prayer and his posting of the Ten Commandments in the courtroom. The ACLU filed suit against Moore in 1995, and the State of Alabama in turn filed suit on his behalf. The ACLU claim was eventually dismissed due to a lack of standing by the plaintiffs.

Moore was elected chief justice of Alabama in 2000, having campaigned as the "Ten Commandments Judge." On the night of July 31, 2001, Moore had a 2.5-ton granite monument of the Ten Commandments installed in the rotunda of the Supreme Court building, while a crew from Coral Ridge Ministries videotaped the installation. Moore unveiled the monument the next morning and a number of groups, including the ACLU, responded by filing suit in federal court. The monument, they argued, amounted to a state endorsement of the Judeo-Christian deity and was thus a violation of the First Amendment's Establishment Clause. The Ten Commandments, Moore countered, represent the moral foundation of American law, adding that his display was protected by the First Amendment's Free Exercise Clause and was in harmony with the Alabama Constitution's acknowledgment of God's sovereignty.

The federal district court rejected Moore's position and ordered him to remove the monument, and this ruling was upheld on appeal. Moore refused to comply, however, calling it an illegal order that he was duty-bound to disobey. On November 13, 2003, as a consequence of his refusal to comply with a federal court order, the Alabama Court of the Judiciary removed Moore from office. In 2006, Moore failed to win the Republican primary for the Alabama governorship.

Thomas C. Ellington

See also: American Civil Liberties Union; American Civil Religion; Church and State; Coulter, Ann; Fundamentalism, Religious; Religious Right; Ten Commandments.

Further Reading

Coulter, Ann. "Man of the Year: Roy Moore." *Human Events*, December 22, 2003.

Davis, Derek H. "Religion and the Abuse of Judicial Power." *Journal of Church and State* 39:2 (Spring 1997): 203–14.

Green, Joshua. "Roy and His Rock." *Atlantic Monthly*, October 2005.

Moore, Roy, with John Perry. *So Help Me God: The Ten Commandments, Judicial Tyranny, and the Battle for Religious Freedom*. Nashville, TN: Broadman and Holman, 2005.

Moral Majority

The Moral Majority was a conservative political organization founded in 1979 by the Reverend Jerry Falwell, a fundamentalist Baptist preacher and television evangelist based in Lynchburg, Virginia. Part of the Religious Right, the Moral Majority helped pave the way for a new level of participation and influence in American politics on the part of evangelicals.

In its early years the Moral Majority claimed rapid growth, reporting 7 million members by 1983, though most observers believe that figure to be inflated. For instance, when the Moral Majority was at its peak in the early 1980s, some 750,000 people received copies of the group's newspaper while direct-mail solicitations returned an average of only 10,000 contributions.

The organization claimed to represent Christian Americans disheartened by the secular turn in American culture and politics. Falwell repeatedly argued that America faced certain peril if it were to abandon its Judeo-Christian heritage. The Moral Majority advocated positions that were largely cultural in nature and domestic in focus. It opposed abortion and supported school prayer. It was against sex education in public schools, arguing that knowledge of contraceptives would encourage young, unmarried people to be sexually promiscuous. The group criticized entitlement programs for the poor, linking welfare to the rise of children born out of wedlock. Deeming free enterprise as biblical, the group generally regarded welfare programs as socialistic.

To a lesser degree, the Moral Majority also advanced certain foreign policy positions. The primacy of premillennial dispensationalism in fundamentalist thought, which holds that the reconstitution of Israel signals the end times, led the group to support policies favorable to the modern state of Israel. Indeed, the organization endorsed Ronald Reagan's 1980 candidacy for president in large part because President Jimmy Carter had affirmed the Palestinian right to a homeland. The group also supported President Reagan's efforts to defeat leftist guerrillas in Central America, wishing to curtail any potential establishment of an atheistic communist society.

In addition to being the object of scorn by liberals, the Moral Majority was attacked by moderates and even members of the political right, including the syndicated columnist James J. Kilpatrick. Many detractors accused the Moral Majority of seeking to establish an American theocracy. As evidence, they pointed to the group's support of policies said to undermine the separation of church and state. Detractors also viewed the Moral Majority as bigoted and intolerant, noting the group's depiction of the AIDS epidemic as divine retribution for sinful lifestyles and Falwell's vigorous support of the South African apartheid regime.

In January 1986, Falwell announced that he was closing the Moral Majority and replacing it with the Liberty Foundation. The organization's decline has been attributed to a number of factors, including competition from other Christian advocacy groups vying for financial contributions from evangelicals; the group's shifting focus on issues not directly related to moral concerns; and Falwell's controversial statements that repelled moderate and mainstream believers. The Liberty Foundation folded in 1989 and was superseded by Pat Robertson's Christian Coalition.

Although the Moral Majority was relatively short-lived, its formation and ascendancy was emblematic of the growing participation of evangelicals in politics. Many of the issues the Moral Majority advocated remain on the conservative political agenda, and some have been addressed through legislation. A number of states, for example, have restricted access to abortion and also passed laws permitting moments of silence (for prayer purposes) in schools.

Carolyn Gallaher

See also: Abortion; AIDS; Carter, Jimmy; Evangelicalism; Falwell, Jerry; Fundamentalism, Religious; Israel; Premillennial Dispensationalism; Religious Right; School Prayer; Sex Education.

Further Reading

Fitzgerald, Frances. *Cities on a Hill.* New York: Touchstone, 1987.

Snowball, David. *Continuity and Change in the Rhetoric of the Moral Majority.* New York: Praeger, 1991.

Webber, Robert. *The Moral Majority: Right or Wrong?* Westchester, IL: Cornerstone Books, 1981.

Moral Relativism

See Relativism, Moral

Morgan, Robin

A feminist activist, lesbian, writer, and editor, Robin Morgan has been a major figure in promoting radical feminism, an ideology that links all social oppression to patriarchy. In 1967, she was a co-founder of the short-lived New York Radical Women and its political wing, Women's International Terrorist Conspiracy from Hell (WITCH). The following year, she was the principal organizer of the first protest against the Miss America beauty pageant. In 1979, she helped establish Women Against Pornography, arguing that pornography is the theory of the practice of rape. Morgan has also compiled and edited anthologies that advance radical feminism at the national level, *Sisterhood Is Powerful: An Anthology of Writings from the Women's Liberation Movement* (1970); at the international level (including the Third World), *Sisterhood Is Global: The International Women's Movement Anthology* (1984); and into the twenty-first century, *Sisterhood Is Forever: The Women's Anthology for a New Millennium* (2003). While some have criticized her for being antimale, dogmatic, and loose with facts, others praise her for voicing a universal female rage.

Robin Evonne Morgan was born on January 29, 1941, in Lake Worth, Florida, and grew up in Mount Vernon, New York. She had her own radio show, called Little Robin Morgan, at the age of four, and became something of a child star on the 1950s television series Mama. After studying literature and writing at Columbia University (no degree, 1956–1959), she worked as a freelance book editor and agent in New York City. She had her first poems published in the early 1960s and contributed articles and essays to a number of counterculture publications of the period. In the early 1970s she began contributing to *Ms. Magazine*, which she later edited (1990–1993). Over the years, Morgan has played important roles in the founding of women's aid organizations, and in 1984 she co-founded the Sisterhood Is Global Institute, a think tank. In 2007, she was named Humanist Heroine of the year by the American Humanist Association.

During the1968 Miss America pageant in Atlantic City, New Jersey, Morgan led a group of about one hundred feminists in a widely publicized "guerrilla theater" demonstration, in which participants crowned a sheep as the pageant winner and tossed "instruments of torture to women"—bras, high-heeled shoes, and copies of *Playboy* magazine—into a designated Freedom Trash Can. In her public statement, titled "No More Miss America!" Morgan compared the contest to the judging of animals at the 4-H Club county fair, only more commercialized. She criticized the pageant for choosing only white women as Miss America, for its role as cheerleader for U.S. troops in the Vietnam War, and for imposing "Madonna-Whore" expectations on American women.

Morgan was an early feminist critic of the New Left, arguing that it was controlled by a male hierarchy disinterested in women's issues—a topic of her famous essay, "Goodbye to All That" (1970). In addition to advocating female separatism in the struggle for gender equality, she has made multiculturalism an aspect of feminism. In *The Anatomy of Freedom: Feminism, Physics, and Global Politics* (1982), Morgan links feminism with the holistic movement, and in *The Demon Lover: On the Sexuality of Terrorism* (1989), she argues that terrorism is the logical consequence of patriarchy. She has chronicled her personal development as a feminist in *Going Too Far: The Personal Documents of a Feminist* (1977); *The Word of a Woman: Feminist Dispatches 1968–1992* (1992); and an autobiography, *Saturday's Child: A Memoir* (2001). Morgan has further explored feminism in her creative works, most notably her first volume of poetry, *Monster* (1972).

Roger Chapman

See also: Beauty Pageants; Feminism, Second-Wave; Feminism, Third-Wave; Hefner, Hugh; Lesbians; Ms.; Multiculturalism and Ethnic Studies; New Left; Pornography; Vietnam War; Women's Studies.

Further Reading

Jay, Karla. "What Ever Happened to Baby Robin?" *Lambda Book Report*, June 2001.

Morgan, Robin. "No More Miss America!" In *The Radical Reader*, ed. Timothy Patrick McCarthy and John McMillan, 425–27. New York: The New Press, 2003.

———, ed. *Sisterhood Is Powerful: An Anthology of Writings from the Women's Liberation Movement.* New York: Random House, 1970.

Willis, Pat. "Robin Morgan, 2007 Humanist Heroine." *Humanist*, November–December 2007.

Morrison, Toni

The writings of novelist, children's author, essayist, and playwright Toni Morrison, the first African American to win the Nobel Prize in Literature (1993), address issues of history, identity, race, and gender from a black feminist perspective, asking readers to engage in "rememory" (remembering what has been forgotten). The subjects explored in her work—from slavery and its legacies to race relations to the O.J. Simpson trial—have made Morrison an active participant in the culture wars.

Born Chloë Anthony Wofford on February 18, 1931, in Lorain, Ohio, she was the first woman in her family to attend college, studying at Howard University (BA, 1953) and Cornell University (MA, 1955). She taught at Texas Southern University (1955–1957), Howard University (1957–1964), the State University of New York at Purchase (1971–1972), Yale University (1976–1977), the State University of New York at Albany (1984–1987), and Princeton University (1989–2006). In 1964, she became an editor at Random House. In 1970, she made her debut as a novelist.

Morrison's novels—*The Bluest Eye* (1969), *Sula* (1973), *Song of Solomon* (1977), *Tar Baby* (1981), *Beloved* (1987), *Jazz* (1992), *Paradise* (1998), *Love* (2003), *A Mercy* (2008)—largely draw on the African-American lore she heard growing up in a family with roots in the South. Her play *Dreaming Emmett* (1986) focuses on the murder of fourteen-year-old Emmett Till in Mississippi in 1955. Black elites rallied around her work, and when *Beloved* failed to win the 1987 National Book Award, such prominent figures as Henry Louis Gates, Jr., Maya Angelou, Alice Walker, and others praised Morrison in an open letter to the *New York Times*. The novel did win the Pulitzer Prize (1988) and was made into a movie by Oprah Winfrey (1998). The Nobel Prize committee cited Morrison's *Beloved* and other novels for their "visionary force and poetic import."

As an editor at Random House from 1964 to 1983, Morrison helped shape the canon of African-American literature, reaching out to other black authors such as Toni Cade Bambara, June Jordan, and Gayl Jones. She saw biographies of Muhammad Ali and Huey P. Newton get published and helped produce *The Black Book* (1974), a scrapbook of black hidden history.

Morrison caused a stir in 1998 when she referred to President Bill Clinton as the "first black president." Her participation in the culture wars, however, has been mostly at the academic level through her nonfiction books. In *Race-ing Justice, En-gendering Power: Essays on Anita Hill, Clarence Thomas, and the Construction of Social Reality* (1992), she focuses on the 1991 scandal surrounding allegations of sexual harassment against U.S. Supreme Court nominee Clarence Thomas. With Claudia Brodsky Lacour, she edited *Birth of a Nation'hood: Gaze, Script, and Spectacle in the O.J. Simpson Case* (1997), examining the O.J. Simpson murder trial, which Morrison believes was correctly judged by the jury. Her *Playing in the Dark: Whiteness and the Literary Imagination* (1992) analyzes the "black character" in white literature, arguing that black characters serve as "metaphorical shortcuts" pertaining to what is dreaded and desired.

Kirk Richardson

See also: Angelou, Maya; Clinton, Bill; Feminism, Second-Wave; Great Books; Hill, Anita; Literature, Film, and Drama; O.J. Simpson Trial; Race; Thomas, Clarence; Till, Emmett.

Further Reading

Bloom, Harold. *Toni Morrison*. Broomall, PA: Chelsea House, 2000.

Fulz, Lucille P. *Toni Morrison: Playing with Difference*. Urbana: University of Illinois Press, 2003.

Gillespie, Carmen. *Critical Companion to Toni Morrison: A Literary Reference to Her Life and Work*. New York: Facts On File, 2008.

Peach, Linden. *Toni Morrison*. New York: St. Martin's Press, 2000.

Mothers Against Drunk Driving

Founded in 1980, Mothers Against Drunk Driving (MADD) is a nationwide grassroots organization that has lobbied successfully for tougher law enforcement against drunk driving. Widely viewed as an effective "do-gooder" organization that has helped reverse societal complacency toward drunk driving, MADD has nonetheless drawn criticism from those who think its positions are repressive.

Originally known as Mothers Against Drunk Drivers, MADD was started in California by Candy Lightner in reaction to the death of her thirteen-year-old daughter, Cari, a victim of a hit-and-run motorist who was drunk at the time and who had a record of repeated drunk-driving offenses. Back then about half of the 45,000 annual traffic fatalities in the United States were linked to drunk driving. In 1980, Lightner compelled California governor Jerry Brown to form a state commission to study the problem of drunk driving. Two years later, she persuaded President Ronald Reagan to do the same at the national level. Lightner served on both commissions, and her cause was further boosted by the 1983 airing of *Mothers Against Drunk Drivers: The Candy Lightner Story*, an NBC television movie. By 1985, MADD had 320 chapters in forty-seven states.

With its headquarters in Hurst, Texas, MADD pushed for (1) reducing the trend for plea bargaining in which drunk-driving charges are dropped in exchange for admissions of lesser offenses; (2) imposing mandatory jail time, higher fines, and longer periods of driver license suspension/revocation for drunk driving; (3) lowering the legal limit for motorist blood alcohol count (BAC); (4) utilizing drunk-driving countermeasures such as random sobriety checkpoints at police roadblocks; and (5) raising the nation's legal drinking age.

The National Minimum Drinking Age Act of 1984, heavily lobbied for by MADD, raised the drinking age from eighteen to twenty-one. This was controversial because it meant that a young person old enough to vote or serve in the military would be denied the right to drink alcohol. According to MADD, 50,000 American teenagers had died in alcohol-related crashes from 1974 to 1984, roughly equivalent to the number of Americans killed in the Vietnam War. Dismissing the argument that age eighteen represents adulthood, Lightner answered, "There are different age limits for different levels of responsibility: thirty-five for President, thirty for Senator, twenty-three for FBI agent. We just don't feel that kids at eighteen, many of whom are just learning how to drive, should be allowed to drink too." President Reagan, who regarded the bill as a violation of states' rights, reluctantly signed it into law.

In 1985, following reports questioning Lightner's financial management of MADD, the organization's executive committee voted to sideline her. Relations further deteriorated between MADD and its founder when, in 1994, Lightner became a lobbyist for the American Beverage Association, representing the alcohol industry. She also sided against MADD's campaign to lower the national BAC limit from .10 to .08, arguing that existing laws simply needed to be enforced. In a 2002 interview with the *Washington Times*, Lightner characterized MADD as turning "neo-prohibitionist," adding, "I didn't start MADD to deal with alcohol . . . [but] to deal with the issue of drunk driving."

In 2008, much to the chagrin of MADD, 130 college presidents called for lowering the drinking age in order to reduce campus surreptitious drinking, which they said is linked to binge drinking. Those in favor of keeping the drinking age at twenty-one noted the 11 percent decline in alcohol-related deaths of young people since the passage of the 1984 law.

Roger Chapman

See also: Automobile Safety; Reagan, Ronald.

Further Reading

Jacobs, James B. *Drunk Driving: An American Dilemma*. Chicago: University of Chicago Press, 1989.

Liebschutz, Sarah F. "The National Minimum Drinking-Age Law." *Publius* 15:3 (Summer 1985): 39–51.

Mothers Against Drunk Driving Web site. www.madd.org.

Reinarman, Craig. "The Societal Construction of an Alcohol Problem: The Case of Mothers Against Drunk Drivers and Societal Control in the 1980s." *Theory and Society* 17:1 (January 1988): 91–120.

Sadoff, Mickey. *Get MADD Again, America!* Irving, TX: Mothers Against Drunk Driving, 1991.

Motion Picture Association of America

Established in 1922, the Motion Picture Association of America (MPAA) is a nonprofit trade organization that serves as the advocate of the U.S. film, home video, and television industries. Originally called the Motion Pictures Producers and Distributors Association, it was formed to promote the interests of the major movie studios and to safeguard against government intervention. The latter concern grew out of the U.S. Supreme Court's decision in *Mutual Film Corporation v. Industrial Commission of Ohio* (1915), which affirmed the right of states to establish film censorship boards. Much of the MPAA's involvement in the culture wars stems from its film rating system, the voluntary industry standard.

The MPAA instituted its Production Code in 1930 in response to increasing public complaints about film content. The guidelines, which some regarded as an attempt to censor the industry, were created out of fear that local authorities would ban the showing of films that they deemed immoral. This concern was enhanced when the Catholic Legion of Decency (CLD) declared a boycott of films it considered indecent. The Code mandated that films, prior to public release, receive a certificate from the MPAA.

In the 1960s, filmmakers asserted that the Production Code was stifling their creativity, and movies began to be released without the MPAA certificate. Attempts by the CLD or other groups to boycott productions no longer represented a serious threat, and the MPAA responded by creating its "Suggested for Mature Audiences" rating in 1966. Due to its perceived lack of stringency the Production Code was abolished in 1967.

The following year, after meeting with government representatives and the National Association of Theater Owners in response to public outrage about the content of certain films, the MPAA adopted a new ratings system. The initial designations were G, M, R, and X. The purpose was to rate the content of a movie to provide the public with guidance as to specific elements: violence, sexuality, and harsh language. Later, the MPAA refined the ratings to include the now-familiar G (General Audiences), PG (Parental Guidance Suggested), PG-13 (Parents Strongly Cautioned), R (Restricted; viewer must be age 17 or accompanied by a parent or guardian), and NC-17 (No One Under 17 Admitted).

The MPAA rating system has been the object of diverse and ongoing complaints. Some filmmakers find that the system has had the unintended effect of forcing studios to change film content, as filmmakers consciously make alterations to obtain a particular rating for commercial purposes. In addition, independent distributors sometimes believe that their films are rated unfairly. They point to major studio productions that contain more violence, sex, and strong language than many of their films but receive a less-restrictive rating.

According to a study by the Harvard School of Public Health in 2004, the standards used to determine movie ratings have been steadily declining. The result, according to the study, has been a significantly greater degree of sex, violence, and strong language in films between 1992 and 2003. Other groups, including the Conference of Catholic Bishops, an offshoot of CLD, have also noticed the trend, resurrecting concerns about film content.

The independent documentary *This Film Is Not Yet Rated* (2005) explores the widespread inconsistencies in the MPAA's approach to film ratings; in the book *The Movie Ratings Game* (1972), Stephen Farber confronts the issue from an insider's perspective. Despite criticism of the ratings system, many believe that it has generally benefited filmmakers more than it has hurt them. As the concerns grow on both sides of the issue, the MPAA and its ratings system no doubt will remain controversial.

James W. Stoutenborough

See also: Catholic Church; Censorship; Comic Books; Literature, Film, and Drama; Record Warning Labels; Zappa, Frank.

Further Reading

Bernstein, Matthew. *Controlling Hollywood: Censorship and Regulation in the Studio Era.* New Brunswick, NJ: Rutgers University Press, 1999.

Black, Gregory D. *The Catholic Crusade Against the Movies, 1940–1975.* Cambridge, UK: Cambridge University Press, 1998.

Farber, Stephen. *The Movie Ratings Game.* Washington, DC: Public Affairs Press, 1972.

Lewis, Jon. *Hollywood v. Hard Core: How the Struggle over Censorship Saved the Modern Film Industry.* New York: New York University Press, 2000.

Motion Picture Association of America Web site. www.mpaa.org.

Moynihan, Daniel Patrick

Daniel Patrick Moynihan was a U.S. senator (D-NY) and sociologist whose ideas on poverty and race relations in America generated considerable controversy. Born in Tulsa, Oklahoma, on March 16, 1927, he was raised in an impoverished neighborhood in New York City and served in the U.S. Navy during World War II. He attended Tufts University (BA, 1948; MA, 1949; PhD, 1961) and held various positions in New York state government during the 1950s. In 1961, President John F. Kennedy appointed him assistant secretary of labor, in which capacity he quickly emerged as a key figure in President Lyndon B. Johnson's War on Poverty.

Perhaps most controversial among Moynihan's extensive writings was his 1965 report "The Negro Family: The Case for National Action." In it, he argued that the "deterioration of the Negro family," particularly in urban areas, was responsible for the gap in incomes and living standards between African Americans and other Americans, and that these circumstances were impeding the progress of the civil rights movement. The Moynihan Report, as it was popularly known, further suggested that policymakers should rely more heavily on the research and methodologies of social scientists. Critics of the report charged that it blamed the victim rather than the cause of the problem, provided an excuse for inaction on the critical issues of race and poverty, and drew attention away from the real sources of these problems, but the Moynihan Report did mark a change in government approaches as policymakers moved away from their focus on legal issues and considered broader questions about African-American communities.

Amid growing tensions with President Johnson, Moynihan resigned from the Department of Labor and in 1966 became a professor at Harvard University. The debate over the Moynihan Report caused him to question his commitment to liberalism, and in time he would become identified with the neoconservative movement. He returned to Washington in 1968 to serve in the Nixon administration as assistant to the president for urban affairs. Moynihan again became the center of controversy in 1970, after writing a memo to the president in which he outlined the significant gains in income and education level in the African-American community, contended that racial politics in America had become too highly charged to be constructive, and suggested that the "issue of race could benefit from a period of 'benign neglect.'" Critics cited the memo as evidence that Moynihan did not care about the problems of African Americans.

Moynihan served as U.S. ambassador to India from 1971 to 1973 and as U.S. representative to the United Nations from 1975 to 1976. He used the latter position to promote the growth of liberal democracy around the globe. Although he was highly popular at home, he drew criticism from abroad for his relentless defense of

American interests. Moynihan was elected to four terms in the U.S. Senate (1977–2001), where he became chair of the Finance Committee and cemented his reputation as a political maverick. Ever unpredictable, he was willing to criticize politicians and policies without regard for party loyalties. Although he supported the neoconservative push for a muscular Cold War foreign policy, Moynihan was also deeply concerned about human rights and criticized the Reagan administration's policies in Latin America. Elected as a Democrat, he worked toward welfare reform and opposed President Bill Clinton's health care proposals. Moynihan was awarded the Presidential Medal of Freedom in 2000. He died on March 26, 2003.

Charlotte Cahill

See also: Affirmative Action; Civil Rights Movement; Clinton, Hillary; Family Values; Great Society; Johnson, Lyndon B.; Kennedy Family; Neoconservatism; United Nations; War on Poverty; Wealth Gap.

Further Reading

Ehrman, John. *The Rise of Neoconservatism: Intellectuals and Foreign Affairs, 1945–1994.* New Haven, CT: Yale University Press, 1995.

Glazer, Nathan, and Daniel Patrick Moynihan. *Beyond the Melting Pot: The Negroes, Puerto Ricans, Jews, Italians, and Irish of New York City.* Cambridge, MA: MIT Press, 1963.

Katzmann, Robert A., ed. *Daniel Patrick Moynihan: The Intellectual in Public Life.* Baltimore: Johns Hopkins University Press, 2004.

Rainwater, Lee, and William L. Yancey. *The Moynihan Report and the Politics of Controversy.* Cambridge, MA: MIT Press, 1967.

Schoen, Douglas. *Pat.* New York: Harper and Row, 1979.

Ms.

An alternative to "Miss" and "Mrs.," the honorific "Ms." (pronounced *Miz*) promotes gender equality by providing women the female equivalent of "Mr.," rendering marital status irrelevant in how one is addressed. During the 1970s, after Ms. emerged as a trademark of the women's liberation movement, critics characterized it as "contrived" and "man-hating." Feminists regarded the term as empowering because it defined a woman as an individual in her own right. With the trend of more brides retaining their maiden names (by 2000 that represented about 20 percent of college-educated women), Ms. became a more convenient designation as well.

As early as 1952, the National Office Management Association recommended the designator Ms. to simplify recordkeeping and the drafting of correspondence. The term was consequently introduced in secretarial manuals, which drew the attention of feminists during the 1960s. In March 1970, the National Organization of Women (NOW) formally adopted Ms. as the appropriate title for any woman. The designation also inspired the name of a new feminist periodical, the influential *Ms. Magazine.* Founded in 1972 by Gloria Steinem, *Ms.* stood out as a different kind of women's magazine, one that was countercultural and independent, dismissing notions of beauty and domesticity and declaring a woman as having an identity not defined by her relationship to a man.

Also in 1972, Congresswoman Bella Abzug (D-NY) introduced legislation that would have restricted the federal government from using Mrs. or Miss in correspondence or records. Although her bill did not pass, the U.S. Treasury Department and the Government Printing Office subsequently authorized the use of Ms. Also in 1972, feminists lobbied the *New York Times* to officially adopt Ms. for identifying women in news articles and editorials; the editors refused. In March 1974, women activists began what would be twelve years of random picketing outside the *Times*'s office in protest of the continued use of Miss and Mrs.

The *Times* began questioning its policy on Ms. after Congresswoman Geraldine Ferraro of New York emerged as the Democrat's vice presidential candidate in 1984. The influential political columnist and language expert William Safire suggested that since Ferraro, married to John Zaccaro, had kept her maiden name, it was not technically correct to refer to her as "Mrs. Ferraro." On the other hand, he pointed out, identifying her as "Miss Ferraro" was likewise inaccurate. Thus, Safire concluded, it made sense to call her Ms. Ferraro. Ironically, although the candidate preferred to be addressed as "Congresswoman" or "Ms.," during the campaign, she continued to use the conventional "Mrs." for private matters. On June 19, 1986, the editors of the paper announced, "The *Times* believes that 'Ms.' has become a part of the language and is changing its policy."

As Ms. became assimilated in everyday speech as a courtesy title, the term was largely rendered apolitical. Some have concluded that this is because the feminist values of the 1970s have been adopted as mainstream. True or not, polls conducted over the years have indicated a lingering stereotype that women who use Ms. are more likely to be masculine, divorced, or less than ideal wives and mothers. The original *Ms. Magazine* ceased publication in 1989 but was resurrected the following year as a bimonthly, in smaller format, and without advertising.

Roger Chapman

See also: Feminism, Second-Wave; Feminism, Third-Wave; Ferraro, Geraldine; Gender-Inclusive Language; Marriage Names; Morgan, Robin; National Organization for Women; *New York Times, The*; Steinem, Gloria.

Further Reading

Atkins-Sayre, Wendy. "Naming Women: The Emergence of 'Ms.' as a Liberatory Title." *Women and Language* 28:1 (2005): 8–16.

Crawford, Mary, Amy C. Stark, and Catherine Hackett Renner. "The Meaning of Ms." *Psychology of Women Quarterly* 22 (1998): 197–208.

Farrell, Amy Erdman. *Yours in Sisterhood:* Ms. Magazine *and the Promise of Popular Feminism*. Chapel Hill: University of North Carolina Press, 1998.

Multicultural Conservatism

"Multicultural conservatism" is a term coined by political historian Angela D. Dillard in her book *Guess Who's Coming to Dinner Now?* (2001), an examination of conservative African Americans, Latinos, homosexuals, and members of other minority groups that usually align with the political left. Although members of ethnic or other minority groups, these conservatives typically reject the communal associations of multiculturalism and "identity politics." Instead, they call for politics based on individualism, and they tend to support conservative positions on family values and free markets.

Exemplars of multicultural conservatism include Bruce Bawer, Linda Chavez, Dinesh D'Souza, Alan Keyes, Richard Rodriguez, Phyllis Schlafly, Thomas Sowell, Andrew Sullivan, Clarence Thomas, and Condoleezza Rice, and organizations such as the Lincoln Institute for Research and Education, Independent Women's Forum, and Log Cabin Republicans. Multicultural conservatives also have close ties with the mainstream conservative movement, working within such larger conservative organizations as the Heritage Foundation, American Enterprise Institute, and Hoover Institution.

Multicultural conservatism is often associated with the rise of neoliberalism and the prominence of neoconservatives and the Religious Right within the Republican Party. Its adherents share the neoliberal aversion to government intervention in market policy and support low taxes, and at the same time they oppose what they see as the trend of secular humanism in American culture and its detrimental effects on traditional families, gender roles, and morality.

It is their staunch opposition to affirmative action and other policies they perceive as giving preferential treatment based on race, ethnicity, gender, or sexuality that place multicultural conservatives in the center of public consciousness—and often controversy. Multicultural conservatives see the elimination of legalized discrimination occasioned by the civil rights movement as sufficient to create equal opportunities for minorities and women. Critical of the identity politics of the "civil rights establishment," multicultural conservatives view preferential social policies as an inversion of the goals of the civil rights movement. They advocate race-blind policies and often criticize minorities and homosexuals as lacking self-reliance and clinging to deviant or pathological beliefs, values, and institutions. Instead of attributing social or economic disparities to racism, sexism, or homophobia, multicultural conservatives often cite cultural deficiencies or individual inadequacies as explanations for the problems of minorities and women. They argue that policies promoting preferential treatment for women and minorities fuel a victim mentality in those social groups.

Multicultural conservatives have faced occasional marginalization from the right and have complained that the mainstream conservative movement needs to increase its outreach efforts toward women and minorities. Critics on the left point out that some multicultural conservatives who oppose policies such as affirmative action have gained prominence within the conservative movement simply by virtue of their minority status. Critics of multicultural conservatives cite polling and public opinion data to suggest that their views are not representative of minorities and women generally. Ironically, such attacks have sometimes led multicultural conservatives to position themselves as misunderstood and victimized minorities within their own social groups.

Corey Fields

See also: Affirmative Action; Civil Rights Movement; D'Souza, Dinesh; Family Values; Heritage Foundation; Neoconservatism; Religious Right; Schlafly, Phyllis; Secular Humanism; Sowell, Thomas; Thomas, Clarence; Victimhood.

Further Reading

Dillard, Angela D. *Guess Who's Coming to Dinner Now? Multicultural Conservatism in America*. New York: New York University Press, 2001.

Multiculturalism and Ethnic Studies

Multiculturalism has been a contentious topic of the culture wars because it emphasizes pluralism over common heritage, challenging traditional views of Americanism. Instead of focusing on the nation as a whole, multiculturalists consider culture and history through the prisms of race, ethnicity, class, gender, and even sexual orientation. The view is that the United States is too vast and complicated to have one grand narrative, but rather it is a nation of many different groups with unique stories. Critics argue that multiculturalism undermines national unity, hinders integration, taints scholarship, distorts the past by making "fringe" history the central focus, instills victimhood status on minorities, dismisses individualism by relegating each person to a group, and imposes political correctness. Advocates of multiculturalism argue that it acknowledges America's diversity; shows how the nation is richer and more expansive than its stock Anglo-Protestant heritage; opens space for other viewpoints to be presented and seriously examined; and fosters tolerance, understanding, and democracy.

The debate on multiculturalism centers on two competing metaphors—the melting pot versus the salad bowl. The former emphasizes homogeneity, viewing America as composed of immigrants from all over the world, who are absorbed into the nation, acculturated as one people in accordance with the motto inscribed on the Great Seal of the United States, *E Pluribus Unum* (out of many, one), as if all were put into one pot and made into an American stew. The latter emphasizes diversity, viewing America as one nation composed of many ethnic groups, like different ingredients made into a tossed salad, in which each kind of vegetable remains distinct, although each shares a common bowl and perhaps some dressing (made from constitutional principles and concepts of equal opportunity) adds some common flavoring.

A movement began in the late 1960s to incorporate multiculturalism into higher education by introducing programs of ethnic studies. This developed out of a student protest movement at the University of California at Berkeley and San Francisco State College in 1968. The protesters, who formed a group called the Third World Liberation Front, demanded separate academic programs to focus on African Americans, Asian Americans, Hispanics, and American Indians.

The argument for ethnic studies programs was that the academic curriculum of the university was biased from a Eurocentric perspective, ignoring the history and culture of other ethnicities. By February 1969, after weeks of student violence, Governor Ronald Reagan called out the National Guard. Calm was not restored, however, until the following month, after both campuses opened ethnic studies programs.

The Berkeley program started out offering thirty-four courses and had a student enrollment of 990. In 1983, Berkeley was the first institution to offer a doctoral program in ethnic studies. Two years later there were 500 black studies programs on the nation's college campuses. In 1974 there were 200 ethnic studies programs. By the 1980s there was a resurgence of ethnic studies at schools across the nation. Beginning with San Diego State College in 1970, programs in women's studies were introduced, operating on the rationale that the general curriculum is patriarchal. By 1975 there were 112 women's studies programs across the country. Sexual diversity studies or sexuality studies programs, commonly known as LGBTQ (lesbian, gay, bisexual, transgender/transsexual, and queer) studies, were also founded. The City College of San Francisco established the first department of gay, lesbian, and bisexual studies, which began with a gay literature class in 1978.

Opposition to ethnic studies has centered on pedagogical issues. Some argue that these programs, by being ghettoized, unwittingly marginalize the study of minorities. It would have been far more effective, critics suggest, to integrate ethnic studies into the "regular" curriculum. The general trend has been that whites avoid ethnic studies, men avoid women's studies, and heterosexuals avoid LGBTQ studies, meaning that these special programs have a narrow audience. With such awareness, some schools, including Bowling Green State University beginning in 1991, have mandated diversity courses as part of graduation requirements. The trend of required ethnic studies has often been at the expense of the Western humanities, including its emphasis on the cultural canon or "great books." Trading the great books for ethnic studies has been disheartening to social conservatives, who believe that the traditional values enshrined in the canon have historically been the basis of America's greatness and cultural unity.

Roger Chapman

See also: Civil Rights Movement; Diversity Training; Gay Rights Movement; Great Books; Hispanic Americans; Multicultural Conservatism; Muslim Americans; National Endowment for the Humanities; Political Correctness; Race; Transgender Movement; Women's Studies.

Further Reading

Bernstein, Richard. *Dictatorship of Virtue: Multiculturalism and the Battle for America's Future.* New York: Random House, 1994.

Foster, Lawrence, and Patricia Susan Herzog. *Defending Diversity: Contemporary Philosophical Perspectives on Pluralism and Multiculturalism.* Amherst: University of Massachusetts Press, 1994.

Goldberg, David Theo. *Multiculturalism: A Critical Reader.* Cambridge, MA: Blackwell, 1994.

Huntington, Samuel P. *Who Are We? The Challenges to American National Identity.* New York: Simon & Schuster, 2004.

Schoem, David Louis. *Multicultural Teaching in the University.* Westport, CT: Praeger, 1993.

Wood, Peter. *Diversity: The Invention of a Concept.* San Francisco: Encounter Books, 2003.

Mumford, Lewis

A social philosopher, architectural critic, urban planner, and educator, the broadly influential Lewis Mumford is remembered especially for his warnings about the spiritual consequences of modernity and the dehumanizing aspects of technology.

Born in Flushing, New York, on October 19, 1895,

Mumford studied at the New School for Social Research (beginning in 1912), as well as City College of New York and Columbia University, but he never obtained a degree. After serving in the U.S. Navy (1917–1918), he worked as associate editor of the *Sociological Review* and then became a freelance writer. He is the author of more than thirty books, including *The Study of Utopias* (1922), *The Culture of the Cities* (1938), *The Condition of Man* (1944), *The Conduct of Life* (1951), *The City in History* (1961), *The Myth of the Machine* (1967–1970), and *The Pentagon of Power* (1971). He was the architectural critic for the *New Yorker* magazine for more than thirty years and, beginning in 1929, taught at such institutions as Dartmouth, Stanford University, the Massachusetts Institute of Technology, and the University of California, Berkeley.

Many of Mumford's writings on literature, cities, and architecture address the problems of modernity associated with the dehumanizing aspects of technology. Although he had once been optimistic about the assertion of the human spirit through technological advancements, he later changed his mind and warned about "technics," the interweaving of high-tech innovation with the social fabric such that the goals and processes of technology take on a life of their own. He coined the term "megatechnics" to describe the constant, unrestricted expansion and replacement that robs manufactured artifacts of their quality and durability while creating the need for higher levels of consumption, advertising, credit, and depersonalization. In *The Pentagon of Power*, he cites New York City's newly constructed World Trade Center as an example of "purposeless gigantism" and "technological exhibitionism" that threatens to dominate humanity.

Mumford's humanism and emphasis on the social aspects of urban development were in direct opposition to popular notions of progress and betterment of the human condition in the twentieth century. While some critics see Mumford as antitechnology, his views are more complex—he differentiated technology used to solve human problems from oppressive technology existing for its own sake. In 1964, he was awarded the Presidential Medal of Freedom. Mumford died on January 26, 1990, in Amenia, New York.

Cynthia J. Miller

See also: Literature, Film, and Drama; Mailer, Norman; Nuclear Age; Postmodernism; Science Wars.

Further Reading
Miller, Donald L., ed. *The Lewis Mumford Reader.* Athens: University of Georgia Press, 1995.
Mumford, Lewis. *Sketches from Life: The Autobiography of Lewis Mumford.* New York: Dial Press, 1982.
Stunkel, Kenneth R. *Understanding Lewis Mumford: A Guide for the Perplexed.* Lewistown, NY: Edwin Mellen Press, 2004.
Wojtowicz, Robert. *Sidewalk Critic: Lewis Mumford's Writings on New York.* Princeton, NJ: Princeton Architectural Press, 2000.

Murdoch, Rupert

As chief executive of News Corporation—whose holdings include major newspapers, magazines, film studios, television stations, and other assets in the United States, United Kingdom, Australia, and elsewhere—Rupert Murdoch is one of the most powerful figures in world media. His U.S. media enterprises, in particular Fox News, have heightened the culture wars by promoting a politically conservative agenda.

He was born Keith Rupert Murdoch on March 11, 1931, in Australia, where his father was an influential newspaper executive. After attending Oxford University (MA, 1953), he returned to Australia to take over his father's newspaper business, which he christened News Corporation. Over the next decade, Murdoch acquired a string of newspapers throughout Australia, and in 1964 he founded the country's first national paper, the *Australian*. Murdoch's goals of acquiring outlets in other types of media were restricted by Australia's cross-media ownership laws, however, and his newspapers often carried editorials demanding advantageous changes to those laws.

Murdoch moved to Great Britain in the mid-1960s and became a major force in newspapers there as well, acquiring the nation's leading paper, the *Times*, in 1981. But he was best known for his tabloid newspapers, particularly the *Sun* in London, which featured topless models. In 1986 and 1987, he revolutionized the newspaper business in the UK by moving printing and production in-house to avoid the British printers' unions.

By the mid-1970s, Murdoch was breaking into American media ownership, first acquiring the *San Antonio News* in 1973 and the *New York Post* in 1976, while founding the supermarket tabloid the *National Star* in 1974. He became a naturalized U.S. citizen in 1985 in order to satisfy a legal requirement that only Americans could own television stations. The following year, he founded the Fox television network, and in 1996 the twenty-four-hour cable station Fox News. He also founded the right-wing *Weekly Standard* magazine. By the beginning of the new millennium, Murdoch had expanded his holdings into satellite TV and the Internet. In 2004, he moved News Corporation's base from Australia to the United States, apparently to take advantage of America's more relaxed cross-media ownership laws. In 2007, the same year Fox Business Channel was launched, Murdoch spent over $5 billion acquiring the *Wall Street Journal*.

Murdoch has aroused controversy with the purportedly conservative bias of reporting in his diverse media holdings. The most noteworthy incident occurred in

November 2000, when Fox News called the presidential election in favor of George W. Bush before the votes had been accurately counted in Florida. The Robert Greenwald documentary *Outfoxed: Rupert Murdoch's War on Journalism* (2005) provocatively showcases the conservative tilt of Fox News.

Some commentators suggest, however, that Murdoch's politics are more complex than a simple favoritism for the right wing, as he tends to support policies that further his business interests and profitability. Events or political developments that may negatively affect Murdoch's profits are rarely reported by his news outlets, but his newspapers are infamous for giving glowing reviews of books and movies produced by his other companies.

Benjamin W. Cramer

See also: China; Election of 2000; Federal Communications Commission; Labor Unions; Media Bias; Neoconservatism; O'Reilly, Bill; Pornography; Republican Party; *Weekly Standard, The.*

Further Reading

Chenoweth, Neil. *Rupert Murdoch: The Untold Story of the World's Greatest Media Wizard.* New York: Crown Business, 2001.

Kitty, Alexandra. *Outfoxed: Rupert Murdoch's War on Journalism.* New York: Disinformation, 2005.

Page, Bruce. *The Murdoch Archipelago.* New York: Simon & Schuster, 2003.

Tuccille, Jerome. *Rupert Murdoch: Creator of a Worldwide Media Empire.* Washington, DC: Beard Books, 2003.

Wolff, Michael. *The Man Who Owns the News: Inside the Secret World of Rupert Murdoch.* New York: Doubleday, 2008.

Murrow, Edward R.

A pioneer of radio journalism and television news for the Columbia Broadcasting System (CBS), Edward R. Murrow rose to prominence with his World War II broadcasts from Europe and made his mark in the culture wars by criticizing Senator Joseph McCarthy (R-WI) on the air in March 1954. In turn, critics of Murrow castigated his news analysis as editorial opinion and labeled his station "the Red network."

Egbert Roscoe Murrow was born of Quaker parents on April 24, 1908, near Polecat Creek, North Carolina. He grew up in the state of Washington and graduated from Washington State College (BA, 1930). Elected president of the National Student Federation of America (1929), he later served as assistant director of the Institute of International Education (1932–1937). Murrow joined CBS radio in 1935 and two years later moved to London as director of European operations. With his signature opening, "This is London," Murrow broadcast live reports of the events leading up to World War II and, with the

help of a crack reporting team known as "Murrow's boys," the progress of the war until its conclusion in 1945. Later, it was argued by at least one writer that Murrow's broadcasts drew America into the war.

After returning to the United States, Murrow continued working for CBS, making the transition to the new medium of television beginning in 1950. He served as host of various programs, including the issues-oriented series *See It Now*. After leaving CBS in 1961, Murrow served under President John F. Kennedy as director of the United States Information Agency (1961–1963). In 1964, he was awarded the Presidential Medal of Freedom. Murrow died of lung cancer on April 27, 1965.

Prior to challenging the veracity and methods of Senator McCarthy, Murrow spoke out critically against the House Committee on Un-American Activities (HUAC), stating in an October 1947 broadcast, "The right of dissent . . . is surely fundamental to the existence of a democratic society. That's the right that went first in every nation that stumbled down the trail of totalitarianism." *See It Now*, which Murrow co-produced with Fred W. Friendly, offered four hard-hitting broadcasts that were critical of the Red Scare and McCarthyism: "The Case of Milo Radulovich" (October 20, 1953), "An Argument in Indianapolis" (November 24, 1953), "Report on Senator McCarthy" (March 9, 1954), and "Annie Lee Moss Before the McCarthy Committee" (March 16, 1954).

The exposé on Radulovich—an Air Force Reserve lieutenant facing dismissal because, although declared "loyal," he was classified as a "security risk" due to his father's and sister's alleged radical politics—raised the

Edward R. Murrow of CBS News, seen here during election night coverage in 1952, became a paragon for subsequent generations of television reporters and investigative journalists. His great legacy in the culture wars was confronting McCarthyism. *(CBS Photo Archive/Getty Images)*

issue of guilt by association. The Indianapolis story focused on the American Legion's attempt to block the formation of a local chapter of the American Civil Liberties Union, raising the issue of the right of assembly. The report on McCarthy presented the senator "in his own words and pictures," exposing his half-truths and unaccountability. The segment on Moss, a Pentagon cafeteria worker accused of having communist ties, raised the issue of due process of law. A subsequent viewer poll revealed strong agreement with Murrow about McCarthy. Murrow's opposition to McCarthyism was the subject of the Hollywood film *Good Night, and Good Luck* (2005).

Murrow's legacy, however, was about more than confronting the Red Scare. His influence is evident in the long-running CBS program *60 Minutes* and other investigative "news magazine" shows, which borrowed the format of *Harvest of Shame* (1960), Murrow's exposé on the plight of migrant workers. A critic of television and its increasing commercialism, Murrow advanced the concept of noncommercial broadcasting that helped lay the foundation for the Public Broadcasting Service. Many prominent journalists credit Murrow with inspiring them to strive for excellence in their reporting.

Roger Chapman

See also: American Civil Liberties Union; Communists and Communism; McCarthy, Joseph; McCarthyism; Media Bias; Migrant Labor; National Public Radio; Public Broadcasting Service.

Further Reading

Edwards, Bob. *Edward R. Murrow and the Birth of Broadcast Journalism.* Hoboken, NJ: John Wiley & Sons, 2004.

Kendrick, Alexander. *Prime Time: The Life of Edward R. Murrow.* Boston: Little, Brown, 1969.

Ranville, Michael. *To Strike a King: The Turning Point in the McCarthy Witch-Hunts.* Troy, MI: Momentum Books, 1997.

Rosteck, Thomas. *See It Now Confronts McCarthyism: Television Documentary and the Politics of Representation.* Tuscaloosa: University of Alabama Press, 1994.

Seib, Philip M. *Broadcasts from the Blitz: How Edward R. Murrow Helped Lead America into War.* Washington, DC: Potomac, 2007.

Muslim Americans

Muslim Americans, who by conservative estimates numbered 2.35 million in 2008, are part of the multicultural phenomenon of the United States. The growth of Islam in the country is largely due to the influx of immigrants from Muslim countries since 1965, spurred by the reform of federal immigration policies that relaxed restrictions on the influx of non-Europeans. To-

day, however, approximately 35 percent of Muslims in the United States are native born. Since the majority religion among native-born Americans is Christianity, with Protestantism perceived as a dominant influence in American culture, Muslim Americans have lived in relative obscurity, though subjected to occasional misunderstanding and mistrust. After the terrorist attacks of September 11, 2001, such tensions have been heightened.

Muslims have lived in North America since the era of transatlantic slavery. In the early twentieth century, a series of Middle Eastern Muslim families migrated to the United States, establishing several sizable Islamic communities in places such as Cedar Rapids, Iowa; Detroit, Michigan; and Sacramento, California. By century's end, the majority of native-born Muslims were African American, with the remaining number composed of children of immigrants and converts from other backgrounds. In the United States, Muslims from the majority Sunni and minority Shi'ite sects generally have enjoyed peaceful, cooperative relations. A 2006 survey of Muslim registered voters found that 12 percent identified themselves as Shi'ite, 36 percent as Sunni, and 40 percent as "just a Muslim." Of the more than 1,200 mosques across the United States in 2008, more than one-third were located in California (227) or New York (240). Most foreign-born Muslims are from the Middle East or North Africa, followed closely by Eastern Europe, and then Asia. There are few differences in earnings and educational levels between Muslims and their non-Muslim neighbors in the United States, in contrast to France, Germany, and England, where Muslims are 20 percent more likely to live in poverty.

Among the several branches of Islam in African-American communities is the Nation of Islam, founded in 1931 by Wallace Fard in Detroit. This religious movement is noted for contextualizing Islamic teachings to the political concerns of blacks living in a white-dominated society. Fard's assistant, Elijah Muhammad, was more radical, calling on African Americans to renounce Christianity, which he characterized as the religion of the "white oppressor." This message resonated with Malcolm Little, who after finishing a prison sentence in the early 1950s changed his name to Malcolm X (in order to discard his Christian slave name) and went on to propel the growth of the Nation of Islam through his dynamic oratory. Malcolm X's message focused on separatism and economic self-help, in contrast to the goal of integration then being promoted by the Christian-inspired civil rights movement. He eventually gravitated toward Sunni Islam, as did most Nation of Islam followers. In New York, the minister Louis Farrakhan kept the Nation of Islam alive, often attracting controversy with his fiery rhetoric, including statements considered to be anti-Semitic.

Since the terrorist attacks of September 11, most

Muslim Americans have reported a feeling of oppression, convinced they are under federal surveillance. There have also been occasional reports of random violence and hate crimes against Muslims, including vandalism and attacks on mosques. The case of the "American Taliban," twenty-year-old John Walker Lindh, who was captured in Afghanistan in the winter of 2001, heightened official concern that Muslim centers in the United States were potential incubators for "homegrown terrorism." Lindh, a white middle-class Californian who had converted to Islam after reading *The Autobiography of Malcolm X* (1965), was persuaded to participate in a jihad in Afghanistan after studying Arabic in Yemen and Pakistan. Although he apologized for his actions (while having no connection with the September 11 attacks), Lindh was sentenced to twenty years in prison. California Muslims in 2007 were alarmed following disclosure of a counterterrorism effort by the Los Angeles Police Department to "map" Islamic enclaves in Los Angeles, but the ensuing outcry over "racial profiling" brought a halt to that undertaking. On the opposite coast, Mohammad Qatanani, a Palestinian who for a dozen years had served as imam of the Islamic Center of Passaic County, New Jersey, faced deportation proceedings in 2008 for not reporting on a green-card application his detainment several decades prior in Israel.

Within the Muslim American community, cultural conflicts over the interpretation of Islam have been on the rise, often led by the younger American-born descendents of Muslim immigrants in opposition to the foreign-born imams. (Only 15 percent of American mosques are led by American-born imams.) Gender equality has been a divisive issue. The American-born journalist Asra Nomani, for example, refused to follow her mosque's proscriptions that women must enter through the back door and pray behind the men—a controversy she publicly aired in her autobiographical work *Standing Alone in Mecca* (2005). Many such controversies over Islamic customs have arisen in the Muslim Student Associations, founded in 1963. Ingrid Mattson, director of the Islamic chaplaincy program at Hartford Seminary in Connecticut, broke a gender barrier in 2006 when she became the first female president (as well as convert) of the Islamic Society of North America, the largest Muslim organization in the United States.

In 2006, Keith Ellison, an African American, became the first Muslim elected to the U.S. Congress. A member of Minnesota's Democratic-Farmer-Labor Party, Ellison later drew national attention, much of it negative, for taking his oath of office while placing his hand on the Koran, using a copy that once belonged to President Thomas Jefferson. Among the critics of this act was Congressman Virgil Goode, Jr. (R-VA), who expressed alarm over the growth of Islam in the United States, attributing it to "illegal immigration" and diversity visas for Middle Eastern immigrants. The Council on American-Islamic Relations requested an apology, but

Goode refused. Islamaphobic literature also targeted the Democratic presidential candidate Barack Obama by suggesting that he is a closeted Muslim, a smear parodied in a controversial *New Yorker* magazine cartoon cover (July 21, 2008) that portrays Obama as a flag-burning Muslim in Arabian dress and his wife, Michelle, as a gun-toting black nationalist.

Susan Pearce

See also: Ali, Muhammad; Farrakhan, Louis; Fundamentalism, Religious; Haley, Alex; Malcolm X; Montana Freemen; Nation of Islam; Obama, Barack; Saudi Arabia; September 11.

Further Reading

Barrett, Paul M. *American Islam: The Struggle for the Soul of a Religion.* New York: Farrar, Straus, and Giroux, 2007.
Curtis, Edward, ed. *The Columbia Sourcebook of Muslims in the United States.* New York: Columbia University Press, 2008.
Haddad, Yvonne Yazbeck, ed. *Muslims of America.* New York: Oxford University Press, 1993.
Kukis, Mark. *"My Heart Became Attached": The Strange Journey of John Walker Lindh.* Washington, DC: Brassey's, 2003.
Nomani, Asra Q. *Standing Alone in Mecca: An American Woman's Struggle for the Soul of Islam.* New York: HarperSanFrancisco, 2005.
Walker, Dennis. *Islam and the Search for African-American Nationhood: Elijah Muhammad, Louis Farrakhan, and the Nation of Islam.* Atlanta, GA: Clarity Press, 2005.

My Lai Massacre

My Lai-4, a hamlet located about 100 miles (160 kilometers) southeast of Saigon, was the site of a notorious American war crime during the Vietnam War. On March 16, 1968, between 400 and 500 unarmed Vietnamese civilians, including women and children, were massacred during a search-and-destroy mission by U.S. Army infantrymen. In November 1969, the American investigative reporter Seymour M. Hersh broke the story, which won him a Pulitzer Prize.

Interpreting My Lai has been a polarizing issue of the culture wars, prompting debate on national virtue. For skeptics of American exceptionalism, including the view that the United States serves as a moral beacon to the rest of the world, My Lai reveals a national "heart of darkness." For others, My Lai simply represents "a tragic aberration." Motion picture director Oliver Stone, himself a Vietnam veteran, used My Lai as the basis for a pivotal scene in his Academy Award–winning film *Platoon* (1986). Later, during the Iraq War, some commentators compared the American abuse of prisoners at Abu Ghraib prison to the degeneracy of My Lai.

The My Lai killings were carried out by members of the 11th Infantry Brigade, specifically Charlie Company of the 1st Battalion, 20th Infantry. Frustration and fear, as well as poor command, were said to be contributing factors to the moral lapse. In the Quang Ngai province where the village was situated, U.S. forces suffered many casualties at the hands of Vietcong who operated in and around the hamlets. In the two months preceding the massacre, nearly one-third of Charlie Company, headed by Captain Ernest Medina, had been killed or wounded. The locals, feigning lack of knowledge about the Vietcong, seldom cooperated with the Americans. After a sweep through the area turned up nothing, Lieutenant William L. Calley, Jr., the leader of 1st Platoon, ordered all villagers rounded up and killed. After witnessing the events from the air, Hugh C. Thompson, Jr., an army helicopter pilot, landed and directly confronted Calley. Thompson went on to evacuate some wounded civilians and later reported what he saw to his superiors. The incident was covered up, however, and the deaths that day were officially reported as Vietcong fatalities.

A year later, Ronald L. Ridenhour, a discharged Vietnam veteran, wrote of the massacre to Congressman Mo Udall (D-AZ). In his letter, dated March 29, 1969, Ridenhour emphasized the importance of "principles of justice and the equality of every man, however humble" and urged "a widespread and public investigation on this matter." Of the twenty-five men subsequently indicted by the military for murder, conspiracy, and/or perjury, charges were dropped for all but four. Medina and Calley were charged with murder, and their superiors, Colonel Oran K. Henderson and Major General Samuel Koster, were charged with dereliction of duty and cover-up. Only Calley was convicted. On March 29, 1971, a military jury declared him guilty of the premeditated murder of twenty-two civilians. According to a 1971 *Newsweek* magazine poll, 79 percent of Americans disapproved of the court-martial finding against Calley, largely viewing him as a scapegoat. Half of the respondents believed that My Lai represented a "common" event in Vietnam, while 24 percent classified it as "isolated." Lieutenant Calley was originally sentenced to life in prison, later reduced to twenty years; he was paroled in 1974.

In *RN: The Memoirs of Richard Nixon* (1978), the former president viewed My Lai as "inexcusable" but complained that many critics "were not really interested in the moral questions raised by the Calley case, as they were interested in using it to make political attacks against the Vietnam war." In *People of the Lie* (1983), the noted psychiatrist M. Scott Peck characterizes the My Lai incident as an example of "group evil" and the initial cover-up as "a gigantic group lie."

Although decades passed, other My Lai–like atrocities of the Vietnam War eventually came to light. In 2003, the *Toledo Blade* published a series of articles detailing the killing of civilians, prisoner abuse, and corpse mutilations over a seven-month period in 1967 by a "Tiger Force" platoon of the 101st Airborne Division operating in the Quang Ngai province (the same region as My Lai). Lieutenant Colonel Anthony B. Herbert was relieved of his battalion command in 1969 after reporting a series of war crimes by the U.S. Army's 173rd Airborne Brigade; internal military documents declassified in 1994 (and discovered by a researcher in 2006) confirmed his allegations of prisoner abuse and revealed that he was punished for being a whistleblower. In 2001, Bob Kerrey, a former U.S. senator (D-NE) and Congressional Medal of Honor recipient, admitted to killing women and children during a 1969 U.S. Navy SEAL mission in the Mekong Delta, stating, "I have not been able to justify what we did . . . morally."

Roger Chapman

See also: Abu Ghraib and Gitmo; American Exceptionalism; Cold War; Human Rights; Nixon, Richard; Stone, Oliver; Vietnam Veterans Against the War; Vietnam War; War Protesters; Whistleblowers.

Further Reading

Bilton, Michael, and Kevin Sim. *Four Hours in My Lai.* New York: Viking, 1992.

Herbert, Anthony B., with James T. Wooten. *Soldier.* New York: Dell, 1973.

Hersh, Seymour. *Cover-Up.* New York: Vintage Books, 1973.

Olson, James S., and Randy Roberts. *My Lai: A Brief History with Documents.* Boston and New York: Bedford/St. Martin's, 1998.

Sherman, Scott. "The Other My Lai." *Nation*, March 1, 2004.

Nader, Ralph

As a consumerist and citizens' advocate, Ralph Nader has long fought for tougher federal regulations to address automobile safety, work hazards, air and water pollution, tainted meat, food additives, product labeling, whistleblower protection, public access to government records, and so on. Conservatives and libertarians have faulted Nader for demonizing corporations while promoting the growth of government bureaucracy. Some critics have also denigrated Nader as a self-appointed gadfly, although over the years he has had an extensive base of support, albeit a liberal one. Up until the 2000 presidential election Nader was generally esteemed by progressives and even moderate Democrats, but that relationship soured after his third-party candidacy was blamed for facilitating George W. Bush's defeat of Al Gore. Since then many of his once former supporters have vilified Nader as a political curmudgeon and ideological purist.

The son of Lebanese immigrants, Ralph Nader was born on February 27, 1934, in Winsted, Connecticut. He studied government and economics at Princeton University (BA, 1955) and attended Harvard Law School (LLB, 1958). After graduation he served as a cook in the U.S. Army (1959), traveled overseas (1959–1961), taught history and government at the University of Hartford (1961–1963), and worked on the staff of Assistant Secretary of Labor Daniel Patrick Moynihan (1964). He then gained national attention with the publication of *Unsafe at Any Speed: The Designed-In Dangers of the American Automobile* (1965). After a short stint teaching law at Princeton University (1967–1968), Nader began his public advocacy work, founding the Center for the Study of Responsive Law (1969) as well as other public-interest groups, and serving as director of Public Citizen (1971–1980). On four occasions Nader ran for president of the United States as a third-party candidate (1996, 2000, 2004, and 2008).

Haunted by an accident scene he came across in which a little girl in the car crash had been decapitated by a glove-box door, Nader during his last year of law school wrote an essay entitled "American Cars: Designed for Death," which appeared in the *Harvard Law Record*. The following year he expanded on that topic in the *Nation* magazine with the article "The Safe Car You Can't Buy." That led to the publication of *Unsafe at Any Speed*, which critiqued the design hazards of the Chevrolet Corvair and indicted the Detroit auto executives for callous disregard of automobile safety at a time when there were 50,000 annual traffic fatalities. In response to the public outcry

generated by Nader's best-seller, Congress in 1966 conducted hearings on auto safety, requesting the author's testimony. This led to the passage of the National Traffic and Motor Vehicle Safety Act (1966), which established the Highway Traffic Safety Administration and mandated seat belts and safety glass in windshields.

General Motors had sought to discredit Nader, hiring private detectives to investigate his past, tap his phones, and entrap him with prostitutes. When this failed scheme came to light, federal lawmakers became ever more convinced to pass automobile safety legislation. Nader sued the company for violating his privacy and in 1970 accepted an out-of-court settlement of $284,000, using much of the proceeds for seed money in establishing consumerist organizations, such as the Public Interest Research Group (PIRG). Nader was a reformer, not a revolutionary, and his approach was to emphasize research and reporting as opposed to demonstrations and civil disobedience. Young people joined Nader's cause, establishing PIRG chapters on many college campuses and developing a network nicknamed "Nader's Raiders." Public Citizen, Nader's umbrella organization, has been credited with being a driving force behind the establishment of the Occupational Safety and Health Administration (1970), the Environmental Protection Agency (1970), and the Consumer Product Safety Commission (1972).

Nader's public influence, however, was already waning by the time of the Reagan Revolution of the 1980s. This period was characterized by the undermining of the federal agencies and regulations that Nader's organizations had fought to establish. Heading the regulatory bodies were political appointees who saw their role as curtailing government while aiding commerce. The succeeding decade continued to be disappointing for Nader as President Bill Clinton charted a centrist course, virtually ignoring the progressive wing of the Democratic Party. At a time when Nader was expressing concern that multinational corporations were violating worker rights and environmental protections with impunity, Clinton led the United States in accepting the North American Free Trade Agreement (1993) and joining the World Trade Organization (1994).

During the 1970s Nader had turned down invitations to run for president as a third-party candidate, but his attitude changed by the 1990s as he came to regard the Democratic Party as having become "Demopublican." He was a "none of the above" presidential candidate in the 1992 New Hampshire primary, but his first major run for president occurred four years later as a Green Party candidate tallying a mere 0.7 percent of the popular vote. In 2000, he increased his showing to 2.7 percent of the national total, in the process gathering 97,421 votes in Florida, where the election was ultimately decided by only 537 votes. Certain Nader had thrown the election to the Republicans, the normally staid Michael Dukakis at the time stated that he would "strangle the guy with my bare hands." In his account of the 2000 election, *Crashing the Party* (2002), Nader further alienated Democrats by indicating no remorse. Nader's 2004 and 2008 presidential bids as a Reform Party candidate generated scant public support.

Roger Chapman

See also: Automobile Safety; Clinton, Bill; Democratic Party; Election of 2000; Environmental Movement; Freedom of Information Act; Genetically Modified Foods; Globalization; Occupational Safety; Third Parties; Whistleblowers.

Further Reading

Burt, Dan M. *Abuse of Trust: A Report on Ralph Nader's Network.* Washington, DC: Regnery Gateway, 1982.

Marcello, Patricia Cronin. *Ralph Nader: A Biography.* Westport, CT: Greenwood Press, 2004.

Martin, Justin. *Nader: Crusader, Spoiler, Icon.* Cambridge, MA: Perseus, 2002.

Nader, Ralph. *Crashing the Party: Taking on the Corporate Government in an Age of Surrender.* New York: Thomas Dunne Books/St. Martin's Press, 2002.

———. *The Ralph Nader Reader.* New York: Seven Stories Press, 2000.

Young, Charles M. "Crashing the Party." *Rolling Stone*, September 14, 2000.

Nation, The

The oldest weekly magazine in the United States (founded in 1865), the *Nation* is known for independent but generally leftist, often dissenting, views on government, society, and culture. Although circulation increased from 20,000 (1970s) to more than 173,000 (2004), the magazine has often faced financial crises, forcing negotiations between strong-minded editors and wealthy publishers.

In pieces by the likes of Wendell Phillips Garrison, Edward Godkin, Charles Eliot Norton, Henry James, and W.E.B. Du Bois to those by Martin Luther King, Jr., Hunter S. Thompson, Edward Said, Susan Sontag, Gore Vidal, Barbara Ehrenreich, Katha Pollitt, Eric Alterman, Lani Guinier, Jonathan Schell, and Mumia Abu-Jamal, the *Nation* has commented forcefully on presidential impeachments, wars, and the persistent issues of race, class, and gender. It also has fostered controversy within its own pages among editors, columnists, and correspondents. Vital interests in international affairs (especially the Middle East), environmentalism, and the arts round out the *Nation*'s critiques of changing American culture.

In the 1950s, when the magazine was facing declining circulation and constant conflict with Joseph McCarthy (New York City schools banned the magazine), West Coast correspondent Carey McWilliams assumed a central editorial role. Famous for his defense of migrant workers, McWilliams revitalized the publication with contributions from intellectuals like C. Wright Mills, Marxist historians, and new foreign commentators while creating dialogues between traditional leftists and emergent New Left voices. During his tenure as editor from 1950 to 1975, the magazine, in editorials and articles, called for mercy for Julius and Ethel Rosenberg, despite their conviction for passing atomic secrets to the Soviet Union; expressed disapproval over Levittown policies denying the sale of homes to blacks; deplored CIA activities in Cuba; endorsed the March on Washington in 1963; condemned California governor Ronald Reagan for suggesting that a "bloodbath" might be necessary for ending campus violence; and criticized the U.S. bombing campaign in the Vietnam War.

Before becoming the publisher in 1995, Victor Navasky, editor from 1978 to 1994, steered the magazine through financial and political crises alongside other liberals including Paul Newman and E.L. Doctorow. The Nation Institute, founded in 1966, offers programs, internships, and awards for creative citizenship. Cruises, local conversation groups, and unique personal ads also cement the *Nation*'s reputation as both a human and media community of influence and liberal dissent.

Under Navasky's successor, Katrina vanden Heuvel, the magazine adamantly opposed the U.S. invasion of Iraq and broke the Valerie Plame leak story (pertaining to the U.S. decision to invade Iraq) in 2003. The *Nation* ran articles on corruption, mismanagement, and environmental issues throughout the presidency of George W. Bush, without excusing the perceived weakness or "cowardice" among Democrats and other opposition factions. Meanwhile, right-wing critics charged both the magazine and its contributors with being anti-American.

Gary W. McDonogh

See also: Bush Family; Du Bois, W.E.B.; Ehrenreich, Barbara; King, Martin Luther, Jr.; McCarthyism; Migrant Labor; New Left; Niebuhr, Reinhold; Rosenberg, Julius, and Ethel Rosenberg; Said, Edward; Thompson, Hunter S.; Vidal, Gore.

Further Reading

Horowitz, Irving Louis. "Shaping the *Nation* Magazine." *Sewanee Review* 113:4 (Fall 2005): 648–54.

McWilliams, Carey. *The Education of Carey McWilliams.* New York: Simon & Schuster, 1979.

Nation Web site. www.thenation.com.

Navasky, Victor. *A Matter of Opinion.* New York: Farrar, Straus, and Giroux, 2005.

Navasky, Victor, and Katrina vanden Heuvel, eds. *The Best of the* Nation: *Selections From the Independent Magazine of Politics and Culture.* New York: Thunder's Mouth Press, 2000.

Nation of Islam

The Nation of Islam, a black separatist organization whose members are known as Black Muslims, was founded by Wallace D. Fard in the early 1930s and grew under the leadership of Elijah Muhammad from the 1930s until his death in 1975. During the early 1960s, its most visible spokesperson was Malcolm X. The original organization was transformed into a more orthodox movement of Sunni Islam under Elijah Muhammad's son, Wallace D. Muhammad. Resisting these changes, a splinter group led by Louis Farrakhan formed in the 1970s and retained the principles and name of the original organization. The two groups reconciled in 2000. In both forms, the Nation of Islam has rejected the integrationist doctrine of the civil rights movement, stressing black self-sufficiency and discipline, and the "evils" of white, "racist" America.

The Nation of Islam drew its inspiration from nineteenth-century Pan-Africanism and the African nationalism proclaimed by Marcus Garvey in the early twentieth century. The Black Muslim movement owes its origin to Fard, or Fard Muhammad, a door-to-door silk peddler who hawked his wares and ideology in Depression-era Detroit. There he established the first Temple of Islam, its educational arms—the University of Islam and the Muslim Girls Training Class—and a paramilitary unit called the Fruit of Islam. Fard taught that American blacks are the descendents of a virtuous race of gods, members of the primordial tribe of Shabazz, and that, in rebellion against Allah, an evil renegade scientist called Yakub formed white people ("blue-eyed devils") through genetic manipulation. Although whites have taken over the world, Fard explained, their 6,000-year reign expired in 1914, and the return of Allah in the person of Fard marks the process of resurrection of black people from a state of mental death.

Elijah Poole, the son of a Baptist preacher, became Fard's prophet and messenger, Elijah Muhammad, and led the movement after Fard's disappearance in 1934. Muhammad was imprisoned for over three years during World War II on draft evasion charges, and jails and prisons became important recruiting grounds for the Nation of Islam. Its teachings offered an explanation for the racism and exploitation experienced by black inmates, also giving them the dignity, hope, and discipline needed to straighten out their lives.

The most famous prison convert was Malcolm Little, renamed Malcolm X by Elijah Muhammad. Malcolm quickly established himself as the group's foremost proselytizer and organizer of the 1960s. As minister of the Boston temple, he recruited Louis Walcott, later renamed Louis Farrakhan. Along with such groups as the Black Panther Party, the Black Muslims became media representatives of black nationalist rejection of white American values. In contrast, the media portrayed the nonviolent civil rights movement of Martin Luther King, Jr., as moderate, peaceful, and Christian.

Relations between Malcolm X and Elijah Muhammad became strained in the early 1960s. Malcolm objected to Muhammad's extramarital relations with his secretaries. Muhammad officially silenced Malcolm following the latter's statement that the assassination of President John F. Kennedy had been "a case of the chickens coming home to roost." Further, Malcolm's pilgrimage to Mecca convinced him that according to Islam, white people were not inherently evil. When Malcolm broke with the organization in 1964, he was vilified in the Nation of Islam's newspaper, *Muhammad Speaks*. On February 21, 1965, assassins from the Newark mosque murdered Malcolm X at the Audubon Ballroom in Harlem.

Malcolm X was not the only antagonist from within the Nation of Islam. Elijah's seventh son, Wallace D. Muhammad, had grown estranged from his father. During a three-year imprisonment, Wallace had studied traditional Sunni Islamic teachings and rejected key Nation of Islam doctrines, such as his father's quasi-divine status as prophet and messenger of Allah, and the deity of Wallace Fard. Despite a series of expulsions from and returns to the fold, Wallace was anointed as the new leader of the Nation of Islam upon the death of his father in 1975 and quickly began transforming the group into an orthodox Muslim organization. He reinterpreted Fard and Elijah's doctrines as masterful teachings designed to prepare black Americans for the truth of traditional Islam. He changed his name to Warith Deen Muhammad and moved the organization away from its radical anti-Americanism and racial separatism. The organization was renamed the World Community of al-Islam in the West (and later the American Muslim Mission). Warith's transition to the mainstream was signaled by his invitation to offer the prayer of invocation before the U.S. Senate in 1992.

The rapid transformation of the Nation of Islam led to membership losses, the revelation of grave financial problems, and the formation of a number of splinter organizations. Most significant was the resurrected Nation of Islam under Louis Farrakhan, whose supporters point to anecdotal evidence suggesting that he was Elijah's true choice as successor. In November 1977, Farrakhan openly announced that he would reestablish the Nation of Islam in a form faithful to Elijah Muhammad's teachings. Farrakhan maintained the original rhetoric of racial separatism and moral uplift and demonstrated the appeal of the new Nation of Islam to ghetto culture, drawing gang members and rap musicians into its orbit.

Farrakhan supported the campaign of Jesse Jackson for nomination as the 1984 Democratic presidential candidate. When news reports revealed that Jackson had made anti-Jewish remarks, Farrakhan came to the candidate's defense, referring to Judaism as a "dirty" religion. Farrakhan's anti-Semitism was thereafter emphasized by the media. But the success of the 1995 Million Man March, a rally of black men in Washington, D.C., to foster black unity, self-respect, and personal responsibility, more strongly established the Nation of Islam as a voice for the concerns of the African-American community at large.

Since the 1980s, however, the Nation of Islam has been the only widely acknowledged black separatist voice in public discourse.

Steve Young

See also: Afrocentrism; Anti-Semitism; Black Panther Party; Civil Rights Movement; Farrakhan, Louis; Jackson, Jesse; King, Martin Luther, Jr.; Malcolm X; Million Man March; Muslim Americans; Race.

Further Reading

Marsh, Clifton E. *From Black Muslims to Muslims: The Resurrection, Transformation, and Change of the Lost-Found Nation of Islam in America, 1930–1995.* Lanham, MD: Scarecrow, 1996.

Ogbar, Jeffrey O.G. *Black Power: Radical Politics and African American Identity.* Baltimore: Johns Hopkins University Press, 2004.

Turner, Richard Brent. *Islam in the African-American Experience.* Bloomington: Indiana University Press, 2003.

Walker, Dennis. *Islam and the Search for African-American Nationhood: Elijah Muhammad, Louis Farrakhan, and the Nation of Islam.* Atlanta, GA: Clarity Press, 2005.

National Association for the Advancement of Colored People

Founded in 1905 by a group of black intellectuals led by W.E.B. Du Bois, the National Association for the Advancement of Colored People (NAACP)—now the oldest and largest U.S. civil rights organization—has been at the forefront of the culture wars in its long struggle to destroy the sociopolitical underpinnings of racial discrimination. As an activist organization, the NAACP directs legal and social campaigns designed to help African Americans and other marginalized groups by promoting racial equality, securing justice in the courts, fostering suffrage, and advancing education and employment opportunities.

After World War II ended, the NAACP, which in 1945 had a membership of 450,000 (including 150,000 in its chapters in the South), worked to dismantle Jim Crow laws throughout the South and end school desegregation. White southerners viewed the growing NAACP rolls and the corresponding militancy of NAACP members as direct threats to the long-standing racial order of the South. NAACP spokespersons were typically characterized as outside radicals who, unaware of southern customs, were upsetting the amicable relations that blacks and whites had established since Emancipation.

During the 1950s, the NAACP won some major victories. Its Legal Defense Fund, under the direction of Thurgood Marshall, challenged the long-standing doctrine of "separate but equal" and convinced the U.S. Supreme Court in *Brown v. Board of Education* (1954) that racial segregation in schools is a violation of the Equal Protection Clause of the Constitution's Fourteenth Amendment. The following year, Rosa Parks, a local NAACP leader, initiated the Montgomery (Alabama) Bus Boycott, sparking the modern civil rights movement. NAACP headquarters, local branches, and associated youth councils worked alongside other organizations during this period to challenge and eradicate Jim Crow as a formal legal impediment to black equality.

By the 1960s, numerous activists in the civil rights movement began to question the NAACP's tactics. Younger activists, wishing for speedier results, regarded the NAACP as overly cautious and conservative. They called into question the association's tendency toward legal activism, economic boycotts, and political coalition building, arguing that such methods were too indirect and nonthreatening to white supremacy. Indeed, protest policies were largely shaped by the middle- and upper-class status of the organization's older leadership, while the younger radicals who were willing to confront Jim Crow head-on by staging sit-ins accused their seniors of being complacent and acquiescent. The young radicals of the sixties found NAACP officials' willingness to work with local, state, and federal government to bring about change as a sign that their elders had "sold out" to the establishment. Black nationalist leaders such as the Nation of Islam's Malcolm X made similar complaints, chiding the NAACP and other civil rights organizations' belief in civil disobedience as ineffective in battling virulent racists.

Cold War politics presented further complications for the NAACP. Opponents charged the association with communist influences and infiltration during the height of McCarthyism. NAACP leaders were forced into silence when outspoken socialists such as Paul Robeson and W.E.B. Du Bois (who had long since left the organization) were targeted in communist witch hunts. The labeling of virtually all civil rights activists as potential or actual communists hindered the NAACP's aggressiveness, thus reinforcing the young black activists' impression that the association had lost its radical edge.

Nonetheless, the cornerstones of the NAACP's agenda—legal advocacy and legislative lobbying—led to significant courtroom and congressional victories. As the NAACP Legal Defense Fund continued to win key cases after *Brown*, the NAACP's office in Washington, D.C., headed by Clarence Mitchell, Jr., helped secure passage of the monumental Civil Rights Acts of 1964, 1965, and 1968.

Despite the gains in racial equality that stemmed directly from the efforts of the organization, the prestige of the NAACP declined. The loss of influence was exacerbated by widely publicized internal conflicts and the overwhelming persistence of black poverty and unemployment, de facto segregation, job discrimination, police brutality, and the failures of school desegregation. By the 1970s and 1980s, such social problems seemed insurmountable under the conservative ideologies and policies of President Ronald Reagan. As government funding for social programs was severely reduced, blighted urban spaces and their residents found little protection in the NAACP.

During the 1990s, as the organization faced financial problems, two of its leading officials were accused of fiscal improprieties. The NAACP rebounded, however, reestablishing its financial integrity and activist agenda under the leadership of Kweisi Mfume, a former U.S. representative (D-MD). The Legal Defense Fund continued to be active, offering legal support for the University of Michigan affirmative action cases that were heard by the Supreme Court in 2003. Meanwhile, the NAACP focused its energies on economic development and educational opportunities for black youth. It has openly opposed school vouchers, arguing that "school choice" programs will not result in quality education for all children but will lead to increased educational apartheid. The organization also redirected its attention to gun control legislation, women's and gay rights, racial profiling, and black political participation as well as the issue of voting disfranchisement.

The NAACP was directly involved in investigating alleged voting improprieties in the 2000 presidential election, placing it at odds with President George W. Bush. From 2001 to 2005, Bush refused to address the annual meeting of the NAACP, becoming the first president since Herbert Hoover to snub the invitation, and accused the association of being overly harsh and critical. In 2004, the Internal Revenue Service began an investigation of the NAACP's tax-exempt status as a result of a speech given by the group's chair, Julian Bond, in which he openly criticized the president. Subsequently, Bush met with NAACP leaders and addressed the 2006 NAACP national meeting. Despite the challenges and changing sociopolitical tides throughout its existence, the NAACP finds itself at the core of the nation's culture wars in the twenty-first century.

Robert S. Smith

See also: Affirmative Action; Black Panther Party; Black Radical Congress; *Brown v. Board of Education* (1954); Busing, School; Civil Rights Movement; Du Bois, W.E.B.; McCarthyism; Nation of Islam; Parks, Rosa; School Vouchers; Voting Rights Act.

Further Reading

Berg, Manfred. *"The Ticket to Freedom": The NAACP and the Struggle for Black Political Participation.* Gainesville: University Press of Florida, 2005.

Cortner, Richard C. *A Mob Intent on Death: The NAACP and the Arkansas Riot Cases.* Middletown, CT: Wesleyan University Press, 1988.

Greenberg, Jack. *Crusaders in the Courts: How a Dedicated Band of Lawyers Fought for the Civil Rights Revolution.* New York: Basic Books, 1994.

Kellogg, Charles F. *NAACP: A History of the National Association for the Advancement of Colored People.* Baltimore: Johns Hopkins University Press, 1967.

Tushnet, Mark V. *The NAACP's Legal Strategy Against Segregated Education, 1925–1950.* Chapel Hill: University of North Carolina Press, 1987.

Vose, Clement E. *Caucasians Only: The Supreme Court, the NAACP, and the Restrictive Covenant Cases.* Berkeley: University of California Press, 1959.

Zangrando, Robert L. *The NAACP Crusade Against Lynching, 1909–1950.* Philadelphia: Temple University Press, 1980.

National Endowment for the Arts

The National Endowment for the Arts (NEA) is an independent federal agency that provides grants in support of the visual, literary, and performing arts. A lightning rod in the culture wars, the NEA has long been opposed by political conservatives who think government funding of the arts is a bad idea in general. During the late 1980s and early 1990s, the NEA came under attack for sponsoring what critics regarded as "offensive" art.

The NEA is a legacy of President Lyndon B. Johnson's Great Society. It was established in September 1965 as part of the National Foundation on the Arts and Humanities, with the mission "to foster the excellence, diversity and vitality of the arts in the United States and to broaden public access to the arts." With that mandate, the NEA in its first forty years awarded more than 120,000 grants totaling $3.9 billion and has been a major force in the establishment of regional arts organizations, including theater, ballet, and opera companies, symphony orchestras, and museums. As annual funding of the NEA grew over the years—from $2.8 million at its inception to a peak of $175.9 million in 1992—fiscal conservatives bristled over what they called "cultural welfare." Proponents of public funding of the arts, however, emphasize the economic benefits. In the first decade of the twenty-first century, they point out, the arts contributed $37 billion annually to the national economy, returning $3.5 billion in taxes. NEA supporters also note that federal grants to the arts are more than matched by donations from the private sector.

From New Deal to Great Society

Federal funding of the arts originated with President Franklin Roosevelt's Works Progress Administration (WPA). Although that New Deal program ended in 1943, various members of Congress in subsequent years floated bills for establishing a national arts program. Since some WPA projects, including public murals and plays, had been leftist in political orientation, conservatives were ambivalent about reviving arts funding. The Cold War eventually became a rationale for a federal arts program because of the desire to contrast American values, most notably freedom of expression, with those of the totalitarian Soviet Union. President Harry Truman in 1951 requested a report on the national arts, which was released two years later during the Eisenhower administration. In the meantime, art funds were appropriated for cultural presentations overseas. In 1955, Eisenhower recommended a Federal Advisory Committee on the Arts, but stressed that it should not dispense grants.

During the Kennedy administration, a commissioned report by August Heckscher, director of the Twentieth Century Fund, recommended the creation of an Advisory Arts Council and the establishment of a National Arts Foundation for issuing federal grants to private organizations and state arts councils. In June 1963, acting on the Heckscher report, President Kennedy issued an executive order for establishing a national council on the arts. The federal government, Kennedy argued, "surely has a significant part to play in helping establish the conditions in which art can flourish." If government can encourage science, he added, likewise it ought to encourage the arts. Although Kennedy's assassination in November 1963 halted momentum for the council he proposed, Congress in mid-1964 approved the National Council of the Arts, albeit without funding for grants. In 1965, Johnson followed up with legislation that would fund both the arts and the humanities. The Republican Policy Committee opposed the bill, arguing that the arts and humanities were already "thriving" and would continue to do so provided the "deadening hand of federal bureaucracy" was kept away. Over such objections, the NEA, with Roger Stevens as founding chairman (1965–1969), was established.

From Nixon to Reagan

To the surprise of many, the NEA budget under the Nixon and Ford administrations expanded by 1,400 percent. With Nancy Hanks as chair (1969–1977), the NEA budget grew from $8.2 million in 1970 to $123 million in 1978, leading critics to suggest that Nixon had used the NEA to help soften his public image. By 1974, however, conservative senator Jesse Helms (R-NC) was calling into question a $15,000 NEA grant to "a person named Erica Jong so that she could produce a reportedly filthy, obscene book called *Fear of Flying*." Prior to that, there had been criticism of writer George Plimpton, another individual grant recipient, for the kinds of material he was compiling in a series of literary anthologies—one short story with a graphic sex scene was, at the urging of Hanks, excised from the third volume.

The NEA during the Carter administration was stirred by a populism-elitism controversy. With Livingston L. Biddle, Jr., as chair (1977–1981), the NEA "decentralized" art funding by allocating half its grants to traditional American arts. This led to the establishment of the Folk Arts Program (1978) and the National Heritage Fellowships (1980), which came largely at the expense of programs geared to Western European classical arts. Critics accused Carter of politicizing the NEA by having funds spread around geographically, arguing that projects of higher artistic merit were being passed over. Carter supporters disagreed, charging that the Ivy League elitists of cosmopolitan New York, Boston, Chicago, and Los Angeles were just sulking. During the 1980 presidential campaign, Republican candidate Ronald Reagan pledged that he would end the politicization of the arts.

When Reagan entered the White House, his goal was to replace the NEA with a privatized corporation divested of public funding. Friend and fellow actor Charlton Heston was appointed co-chair of a task force to study public funding of the arts, but to Reagan's chagrin, the commission stopped short of recommending the abolition of the NEA. During his first year as president, Reagan reduced arts funding from $158.7 million to $143.4 million—considerably less than his original proposal to slash the NEA budget by 51 percent. The tenure of NEA chair Francis S.M. "Frank" Hodsoll (1981–1989) brought a 28 percent increase in challenge monies, an effort to increase private giving.

Under Reagan, interestingly, the pomp and pageantry of the NEA was expanded with the establishment of the annual National Medal of Arts (for outstanding artists) and the Presidential Design Awards (for federal projects). In 1985, the National Academy Awards presented the NEA with its own award, a special citation for twenty years of support of the arts. By 1989, the final year of Reagan's second term, the NEA budget had grown to $169 million. That same year, *Newsweek* columnist Robert Samuelson called the NEA "a highbrow pork barrel."

The Helms Amendment

Fiscal conservatives were in a conundrum because their desire to eliminate the NEA was kept in check by the elites who often supported conservative candidates but at the same time were major benefactors of the arts. This constituency, generally representative of the corporate sector, came to view the NEA as an essential partner in the arts. By the late 1980s and early 1990s, critics of the NEA, generally conservative Republicans, began shifting their arguments from fiscal concerns to moral ones, focusing attention on "offensive" art that had been funded by tax dollars.

In 1984, Congressman Mario Biaggi (D-NY) protested a NEA-sponsored production of Verdi's *Rigoletto* because of references to the Italian Mafia. Biaggi proposed an amendment to the NEA funding bill prohibiting grant recipients from using their work to "denigrate any ethnic, racial, religious or minority group"; the amendment was not passed. The following year, Texas Republican congressmen Dick Armey, Tom DeLay, and Steve Bartlett protested the NEA's sponsorship of "pornographic" poetry. The trio introduced an amendment to limit future arts funding to projects of "significant literary, scholarly, cultural or artistic merit" that are "reflective of exceptional taste." This amendment was passed.

The NEA under President George H.W. Bush faced a political crisis in 1989. Outrage was directed against Andres Serrano's *Piss Christ* (1987), a photograph of a plastic crucifix immersed in yellow urine. The artist had been a recipient of a $15,000 subgrant from the Southeastern Center for Contemporary Art in Winston-Salem, North Carolina, which had received its funding from the NEA. Around the same time, homoerotic photographs by Robert Mapplethorpe, part of a retrospective collection titled *Robert Mapplethorpe: The Perfect Moment*, were on a travel exhibit sponsored by the University of Pennsylvania's Institute of Contemporary Art, made possible by a $30,000 NEA grant. The fact that Mapplethorpe, a homosexual artist, had recently died of AIDS, only added to the drama.

Numerous members of Congress condemned the Serrano photograph, most notably Senator Alphonse D'Amato (R-NY) and Helms. In their letter of protest to the NEA, signed by a number of other colleagues, including Democratic Senator John Kerry (D-MA), they argued, "This matter does not involve freedom of artistic expression—it does involve the question whether American taxpayers should be forced to support such trash." Meanwhile, in June 1989, officials at the Corcoran Gallery of Art in Washington, D.C., decided to cancel the Mapplethorpe exhibit rather than put in jeopardy its annual federal funding of $300,000. To protest what they regarded as an act of censorship, many artists withdrew their exhibits from the Corcoran and some benefactors withdrew monetary support. The Washington Project for the Arts, located down the street from the Corcoran, carried the Mapplethorpe exhibit, which in July was viewed by 50,000 visitors. The Religious Right, specifically Donald Wildmon's American Family Association and Pat Robertson's Christian Coalition, accused the NEA of supporting artwork that seeks to undermine Christian morality.

Congress responded to the Serrano-Mapplethorpe

Members of the congressional Conservative Action Team, including Majority Leader Dick Armey (R-TX, at podium), call for the abolition of the National Endowment for the Arts in 1997. House Republicans slashed the NEA budget, citing "decency" issues. *(Scott J. Ferrell/Congressional Quarterly/Getty Images)*

controversy in several ways. First, Representative Dana Rohrabacher (R-CA) mounted a legislative effort to eliminate the NEA altogether; his bill was ultimately rejected. On July 26, Senator Helms introduced an amendment to the NEA appropriations bill prohibiting any future funding of "obscene" artwork. In September, the House and Senate rejected the Helms amendment by votes of 264–53 and 62–35, respectively. Instead, Congress passed Public Law 101–122, which incorporated some of the language of the Helms amendment, stipulating that NEA funds may not be used "to promote, disseminate, or produce materials which . . . may be considered obscene," as defined by the U.S. Supreme Court decision in *Miller v. Sullivan* (1973).

Continuing Controversies

In 1990, Karen Finley, John Fleck, Holly Hughes, and Tim Miller, solo performing artists who would become known as the NEA Four, were rejected for NEA fellowships despite receiving recommendations from peer-review panels. The performances of these artists, three of them homosexual, focused on controversial themes, including the human body, abortion, AIDS, and sexual orientation. NEA chair John E. Frohnmayer (1989–1992) later admitted that his decision to decline funding for the four artists was based on decency standards. Later, the U.S. Supreme Court, in *National Endowment for the Arts v. Finley* (1998), affirmed the constitutionality of the NEA to consider "general standards of decency and respect for the diverse beliefs and values of the American people" in determining what art proposals to fund.

In 1992, conservative Patrick Buchanan challenged President Bush on the NEA issue during the Republican presidential primary, arguing that the Serrano-Mapplethorpe crisis was proof that the incumbent was out of touch with the public. The criticism prompted Bush to ask his NEA chair, Frohnmayer, to resign. Buchanan ultimately endorsed the Bush candidacy, but at the same time delivered his famous "culture wars" speech at the Republican National Convention. During the presidential campaign that fall, Democratic candidate Bill Clinton—much like Reagan before him—accused his opponent of having politicized the NEA.

President Clinton appointed actress Jane Alexander as chair of the NEA. During her tenure (1993–1997), Alexander reformed the process for issuing grants, shifting awards from nontraditional organizations to mainstream museums. In June 1994, a controversy erupted in response to a performance-artist show held in Minneapolis that featured Ron Athey, a homosexual who was HIV-positive, drawing blood from a fellow performer. In response to the Athey incident, Congress reduced the NEA budget by 2 percent. The following year, with Republicans in control of the House, the NEA budget was slashed from $162.3 million to $99.5 million, a 39 percent reduction. By 1997, moreover, Congress had become decidedly more active in its oversight of the NEA.

Although the NEA budget increased in subsequent years—reaching $144.7 million in fiscal year 2008—its budget was still nearly $40 million less than what it was prior to the Serrano-Mapplethorpe scandal. NEA chair Dana Gioia, appointed in 2003 by President George W. Bush, declared his mission "to bring the agency beyond the culture wars to create an institution which Americans trust and esteem." Under Gioia's watch, Shakespeare festivals and jazz concerts were major NEA-sponsored events.

Roger Chapman

See also: Alexander, Jane; Censorship; Christian Coalition; Great Society; Helms, Jesse; Johnson, Lyndon B.; Literature, Film, and Drama; Mapplethorpe, Robert; Serrano, Andres; Wildmon, Donald.

Further Reading

Binkiewicz, Donna M. *Federalizing the Muse: United States Arts Policy and the National Endowment for the Arts 1965–1980.* Chapel Hill: University of North Carolina Press, 2004.

Brenson, Michael. *Visionaries and Outcasts: The NEA, Congress, and the Place of Visual Arts in America.* New York: New Press, 2001.

Jensen, Richard. "The Culture Wars, 1965–1995: A Historian's Map." *Journal of Social History* 29 (1995): 17–37.

National Endowment for the Arts Web site. www.nea.gov.

Zeigler, Joseph Wesley. *Arts in Crisis: The National Endowment for the Arts Versus America.* Chicago: A Capella Books, 1994.

National Endowment for the Humanities

The National Endowment for the Humanities (NEH) is an independent agency of the U.S. federal government founded in 1965—under the National Foundation on the Arts and the Humanities Act, which also established the National Endowment for the Arts—to support research, education, and preservation programs in the humanities. The NEH pursues its mission chiefly by offering grants to cultural institutions such as museums, libraries, archives, colleges and universities, and public television and radio stations, as well as individual scholars and artists for research, writing projects, and media productions. According to the NEH, the humanities are vital to the nation in that they reveal "lessons of history" for gaining "wisdom" essential to a democratic republic. Beginning in the 1970s, political conservatives sharply criticized the NEH for sponsoring "leftist" programs and projects. During the 1980s and early 1990s, when Republican appointees were in control of the agency, liberals complained that the NEH was blocking innovative proposals for purely ideological reasons.

The NEH was established in the midst of the Cold War, when it was argued that the arts and humanities, in addition to the sciences, should be enlisted in the campaign against world communism. In the first thirty-five years of its existence, the NEH sponsored a total of 58,000 projects, issuing grants worth $3.72 billion while generating $1.63 billion in private donations. The NEH sponsored a wide range of projects, including a traveling exhibition of the treasures of King Tut's tomb, Ken Burns's PBS documentary series on the U.S. Civil War, the *Papers of George Washington* (projected to be ninety volumes when completed in 2016), and a number of research projects that led to award-winning books. The NEH has also appropriated $370 million to regional projects, including studies of the South and the Great Plains. Its American newspaper project had microfilmed 63.3 million pages of newsprint by the early 2000s, with a longer-term effort to convert the material into digital format and make it available online.

Of the appointed chairpersons since the body's inception—Barnaby C. Kenney (1966–1970), Ronald S. Berman (1971–1977), Joseph D. Duffey (1977–1981), William J. Bennett (1981–1985), Lynne V. Cheney (1986–1993), Sheldon Hackney (1993–1997), William R. Ferris (1997–2001), and Bruce Cole (2001–2009)—the two most controversial were those appointed by President Ronald Reagan, Bennett and Cheney, who saw it as their task to reel in the NEH and keep it from supporting liberal perspectives.

In his book *The De-Valuing of America* (1992), Bennett devotes the first chapter, titled "The Fight Begins: Identifying the Enemy," to the NEH. The "enemy," according to Bennett, is a liberal academic elite whose disdain for traditional morality, patriotism, and the American Dream has left it out of touch with the pulse of the nation—and who ought not be eligible for NEH funding. Bennett was thus dismayed to learn that his agency, through the Wisconsin Humanities Committee, had sponsored a documentary film by the International Women's Project, titled *From the Ashes . . . Nicaragua Today* (1982), that was sympathetic to the left-wing Sandinista rebels of Nicaragua. Bennett denounced the film, which later won an Emmy, as "unabashed socialist realist propaganda" and informed the heads of the state humanities councils that under his charge they were not to endorse "partisan" works.

Cheney's debut began with an attack on *The Africans* (1986), a nine-part NEH-supported film that linked the problems of modern Africa to the legacies of Western colonialism. Calling the documentary an "anti-Western diatribe," Cheney demanded that the agency be removed from the film's credits, despite the $600,000 in NEH funding. Scorning academic approaches to the humanities from the perspective of gender, race, and class, Cheney insisted that analysis should be based on "truths that pass beyond time and circumstance" and that the field not be reduced to texts about "politics" and "social power." Cheney thus was accused of stacking the cards against liberal scholars, especially multiculturalists and feminists, who applied for NEH funding. Defenders, emphasizing the stiff competition, accused losing applicants of sour grapes. Indeed, in 1991, only 1,776 projects were financed out of a total 8,132 applications. Even so, the *Chronicle of Higher Education* interviewed some NEH insiders who acknowledged that proposals were screened for political considerations. Cheney, like Bennett, deplored colleges and universities for deemphasizing the traditional Western canon and tended to back more traditional proposals. In her book *Telling the Truth* (1995), Cheney casts herself as a cultural warrior who as NEA chair suffered attacks from those who were politically biased, unfair, and irrational.

Cheney's successor, Hackney, led an initiative known as A National Conversation on American Pluralism and Identity (1994–1997), whose goal was to carry out President Bill Clinton's vision: "We must find in our diversity our common humanity." Hackney later wrote that some perceived the initiative as "a bugle call—for cultural war." Instead, he insisted, he wanted to create conditions for fostering a "civil society." Conservatives accused Hackney of attempting to impose a multicultural ideology, while liberals accused him of seeking to impose a melting pot ideology. Conservative columnist George Will pooh-poohed the idea of a national conversation, stating, "Subsidizing talk about diversity today is akin to subsidizing crabgrass: the problem is a surplus, not a shortage." The project moved forward at a cost of $7.3 million, involving citizen groups, state humanities councils, and college campuses, and was the subject of the PBS documentary *Talk to Me: Americans in Conversation* (1997).

In the meantime, both Cheney and Bennett recommended that the NEH be abolished, suggesting that the agency was beyond redemption. After Republicans gained control of Congress in 1994, the House Budget Committee voted to eliminate the NEH, and the Senate Budget Committee voted to reduce its budget by 50 percent. The agency survived, but funding fell from $152 million to $93 million in just one year (1995 to 1996). Ferris, the next NEH chair, deplored the cuts, stating, "Where is the peace dividend if we win the Cold War but lose the battle for our souls?"

After the attacks of September 11, 2001, the NEH under Cole initiated a program called We the People, which focused on American history and culture. "Our tolerance, our principles, our wealth, and our liberties have made us targets," Cole declared in a 2003 speech. "To understand this conflict, we need the humanities." Cole went on to assert that it was a matter of national security for Americans to overcome "amnesia" about their history and culture. In 2004, the NEH announced that the review process for grant proposals would no longer include assessments by independent specialists, a decision critics interpreted as ideology triumphing over quality. By 2006, the NEH budget stood at $141 million.

Roger Chapman

See also: Afrocentrism; Bennett, William J.; Cheney Family; Great Books; Multiculturalism and Ethnic Studies; National Endowment for the Arts; Reagan, Ronald; Revisionist History; September 11; Will, George.

Further Reading

Cheney, Lynne V. *Telling the Truth.* New York: Simon & Schuster, 1995.

Hackney, Sheldon. *One America Indivisible: A National Conversation on American Pluralism and Identity.* Washington, DC: National Endowment for the Humanities, 1997.

Miller, Stephen. *Excellence and Equity: The National Endowment for the Humanities.* Lexington: University Press of Kentucky, 1984.

National Endowment for the Humanities Web site. www.neh.gov.

Rediscovering America: Thirty-Five Years of the National Endowment for the Humanities. Washington, DC: National Endowment for the Humanities, 2000.

National Organization for Women

Inspired by the African-American civil rights movement, Betty Friedan's *The Feminine Mystique* (1963), and efforts by John F. Kennedy's Presidential Commission on the Status of Women (1963) to document the lives of women in postwar American society, a group of feminists attending a conference in June 1966 in Washington, D.C., founded the National Organization for Women (NOW). The organization, which included activists with backgrounds largely in the labor movement, focused initially on legal and political efforts to achieve gender equality in employment, education, and the media. The group's attack on sexual discrimination represented a controversial challenge to the notion of fixed, distinct, traditional gender roles that dominated American society at the height of the Cold War. Its success in such areas as lobbying the federal government to use the Civil Rights Act of 1964 to fight sexual discrimination in employment made NOW one of the most visible and enduring expressions of the rebirth of American feminism. As of 2007, the organization had more than half a million contributing members and 550 chapters across the United States.

In addition to criticism from social conservatives that NOW was irrelevant, or even dangerous, the liberal feminists who formed the organization also increasingly drew opposition from radical feminists in the women's liberation movement. While NOW relied on the efforts of middle-class, educated white women such as Friedan (its first president) to work for women's rights, radical feminism often centered on younger women more interested in consciousness raising and revolutionary challenges to patriarchy than liberal reform. While some conflicts were irreparable, the tension between NOW and radical feminism also resulted in NOW's eventual attention to issues such as the civil rights of lesbians, abortion rights, and the struggles of working-class women and women of color. By the late 1970s, NOW activists combined support for the Equal Rights Amendment (ERA) with recognition that the personal was indeed political for American women. The result was a polarizing critique of American society that addressed issues related to marriage, family, violence, and sexuality.

As NOW forged a modern American feminism, addressing gender equality in public and private life, political and social conservatives countered with their own organizations—such as Women Who Want to Be Women (WWWW), Happiness of Home Eternal (HOME), and Phyllis Schlafly's Eagle Forum. Conservatives from the New Right targeted NOW as a dangerous threat to American families and "traditional values," and, by the 1980s, antifeminism contributed to the ascendancy of the Republican Party. Conservative opponents associated NOW with the supposed cultural excesses of the 1960s, and, despite the fact that millions of American women created professional and personal lives that spoke to the ongoing struggle for gender equality, "feminism" increasingly became a pejorative term. Results of the backlash included the demise of the ERA in 1982, the increased erosion of support for

abortion rights and affirmative action, and a measurable gender gap among American voters in the last decades of the twentieth century. Rather than simply a battle between men and women, the continuing conflict over the role of NOW and feminism in American life became a protracted struggle over competing cultural ideals.

Richard L. Hughes

See also: Abortion; Affirmative Action; Civil Rights Movement; Equal Rights Amendment; Family Values; Feminism, Second-Wave; Friedan, Betty; Gay Rights Movement; Gender-Inclusive Language; Lesbians; Ms.; Schlafly, Phyllis.

Further Reading

Critchlow, Ronald. *Phyllis Schlafly and Grassroots Conservatism: A Woman's Crusade.* Princeton, NJ: Princeton University Press, 2005.

Evans, Sara. *Personal Politics: The Roots of Women's Liberation in the Civil Rights Movement and the New Left.* New York: Vintage, 1980.

National Organization for Women Web site. www.now.org.

Rosen, Ruth. *The World Split Open: How the Modern Women's Movement Changed America.* New York: Viking, 2000.

Rymph, Catherine. *Republican Women: Feminism and Conservatism from Suffrage Through the Rise of the New Right.* Chapel Hill: University of North Carolina Press, 2006.

National Public Radio

National Public Radio (NPR) is a nonprofit, publicly and privately funded media organization that produces and distributes radio programs to affiliate stations in the United States, providing an alternative to commercial broadcasting. While the organization does not broadcast a radio signal itself, NPR can be heard on more than 800 local radio stations in all fifty states. In the culture war controversy that surrounds NPR, the organization is variously described as either too liberal or not liberal enough in its reporting of the news. In the ongoing debate, economic and political actors take aim at NPR as a federally funded organization and create different political goals for it.

Established in 1970 and initiating broadcasts the following year on ninety charter public radio stations, NPR has grown significantly as a media distributor over the years. In NPR's first three decades of operation, its number of listeners climbed from tens of thousands to more than 26 million per week. Throughout its existence, NPR has struggled to reach diverse audiences and attain financial security. In 1983, however, it fell $7 million into debt after attempting to expand into other markets. Pacific Radio International and American Public Media, both rivals to NPR in public radio, gained from NPR's overstretch and found a stable niche in the market. Currently, NPR receives its funding from corporate gifts and grants from the Corporation for Public Broadcasting, the U.S. government, and other organizations. A third source of funding is the affiliate stations themselves, which pay their dues by holding on-air membership pledge drives. In 2004, NPR received a bequest of $236 million from the estate of Joan B. Kroc, the widow of McDonald's founder Ray Kroc. The main branches of NPR are located in Washington, D.C., and Culver City, California, with nineteen smaller bureaus around the country and sixteen international offices.

NPR has repeatedly found itself in the middle of the culture wars, at the nexus of liberal and conservative politics. Conservatives have consistently attacked NPR, referred to by some as National Precious Radio, for being overtly liberal, framing stories to favor liberals in general and Democrats in particular. Through the early and mid-1990s, especially, conservative politicians and talk show hosts charged that NPR's story selection and content were unequivocally liberal. At the helm of this attack was Speaker of the House Newt Gingrich (R-GA), Larry Pressler of the Senate Commerce Committee (R-SD), and popular conservative radio talk show host Rush Limbaugh. Among their accusations was that conservatives were routinely identified as "conservatives," but that liberals were never labeled as "liberals."

More broadly, conservatives took issue with NPR's program content, which they claimed was favorable to liberal social issues such as abortion and gay rights, and charged that liberal issues and candidates were cast in a favorable light and conservative issues and candidates in a negative light. In 1995, with the help of fellow Republicans, Gingrich and Pressler attempted to amend a bill so as to halt federal support for NPR. Citing free-market principles, Gingrich lamented government funding for public-media outlets and asserted the need for free competition in public radio. NPR countered by mobilizing local station managers to complain to their elected representatives. Gingrich finally lost support, and the amendment to end public funding of NPR was defeated on the floor of the House. Conservatives remained wary of NPR as a credible news source.

From the other end of the political spectrum, liberal critics have sometimes bemoaned NPR as an elitist institution that caters to the upper class. NPR's cultural programming, say these critics, inordinately represents the interests of the wealthy.

Statistically, NPR listeners are much more likely to be professionals, have advanced degrees, and earn higher incomes than the general American population. As a public media organization with government funding, however, it is said that NPR should be more representative of the nation as a whole and more interesting to more people. In addition, NPR accepts corporate funding in exchange for underwriting spots ("brought to you by" messages), yet some critics maintain that NPR fails to report on the misdeeds of its corporate sponsors. While underwriting messages are not strictly advertisements, they do tell listeners who funds NPR and may have the same effect as advertisements.

NPR remains one of the nation's most prominent media distributors. During the early twenty-first century, it had two of the three most popular radio programs in the country with *Morning Edition* and *All Things Considered*.

Ryan Gibb

See also: Abortion; Federal Communications Commission; Gay Rights Movement; Gingrich, Newt; Hill, Anita; Irvine, Reed; Limbaugh, Rush; Media Bias; Murrow, Edward R.; Public Broadcasting Service; Wildmon, Donald.

Further Reading
Engleman, Ralph. *Public Radio and Television in America: A Political History.* Thousand Oaks, CA: Sage, 1996.
McCauley, Michael. *NPR: The Trials and Triumphs of National Public Radio.* New York: Columbia University Press, 2005.
McCourt, Thomas. *Conflicting Communication Interests in America: The Case of National Public Radio.* Westport, CT: Praeger, 1999.
Mitchell, Jack W. *Listener Supported: The Culture and History of Public Radio.* Westport, CT: Praeger, 2005.
National Public Radio Web site. www.npr.org.

National Review

Launched in November 1955, the weekly (later biweekly) *National Review* has played a vital role in the emergence and definition of post–World War II American conservatism. Under the guidance of founder and longtime editor William F. Buckley, Jr., the magazine provided an important venue for the consolidation of diverse conservative perspectives.

Throughout the Cold War, the *National Review* remained staunchly anticommunist, often supporting an aggressive, confrontational approach to the Soviet Union. During the Vietnam War era, it rejected the message of the antiwar movement and criticized U.S. policymakers for failing to take a hard-line approach to winning the conflict. In domestic affairs, the magazine championed a free-market perspective and rejected the bureaucratic and ever-expanding administrative state as epitomized by Lyndon Johnson's Great Society. Its opposition to civil rights legislation during the same period also highlighted the magazine's opposition to extensive government intervention. While supporting integration in principle, its criticism of civil rights legislation rested on the perception of government's general incompetence to remedy social ills.

In another sign of its distrust of big government,

the *National Review* enthusiastically supported the 1964 presidential campaign of conservative Republican Barry Goldwater. After his landslide defeat at the hands of Johnson, the magazine turned its attention to Ronald Reagan, who gained national prominence during the campaign. The magazine proceeded to support Reagan in his successful bid for the California governorship and, in 1980, for president of the United States. Read widely in the Reagan White House, the *National Review* had a formative influence on young conservatives in that administration.

Buckley's Catholic sensibility was also evident in the magazine from the outset, although it was not unusual for editorials to be critical of church leadership, including American bishops for their pastoral letters on war and peace, and the economy. The magazine was openly critical of Pope Paul VI for his 1968 encyclical, *Humanae Vitae*, which reasserted the church's prohibition on artificial birth control.

After thirty-five years as editor in chief (1955–1990), Buckley stepped down and was replaced by John O'Sullivan (1990–1998). It was not until 2004, however, that Buckley officially relinquished control of the magazine by giving his majority share to a self-selected board of trustees. Rich Lowry (1998–) assumed the position of editor in chief with the departure of O'Sullivan.

Given its conservative perspective, the *National Review* has been a constant opponent of progressive intellectual and political movements and has taken criticism from them. At times, however, it has also been the object of disapproval by conservatives. Jeffrey Hart, a senior editor at the *National Review*, has subtly criticized the magazine for "downplaying conservative ideas and arguments of various conservative strands of thought" in favor of a reportorial and topical focus under the editorial leadership of Rich Lowry. A former trustee of the magazine, Austin Bramwell, criticized the magazine for abandoning its long-held conservative principles in support of President George W. Bush's war in Iraq.

Todd Scribner

See also: Birth Control; Buckley, William F., Jr.; Bush Family; Catholic Church; Civil Rights Movement; Cold War; Goldwater, Barry; Reagan, Ronald; Soviet Union and Russia; Vietnam War.

Further Reading

Bramwell, Austin. "Good-bye to All That." *American Conservative*, November 20, 2006.

Hart, Jeffrey. *The Making of the American Conservative Mind: National Review and Its Times.* Wilmington, DE: ISI Books, 2005.

National Review Web site. www.nationalreview.com.

National Rifle Association

On the 135th anniversary of the National Rifle Association (NRA) in 2006, President Sandra S. Froman detailed the mission of the organization: to defend the U.S. Constitution and Bill of Rights, support law and order and the national defense, train citizens in the safe handling and efficient use of small arms, promote shooting sports and competitions, and support hunter safety and hunting as a conservation activity. The primary focus of the NRA is protecting the Second Amendment to the U.S. Constitution (which guarantees "the right of the people to bear and keep arms"), characterized by Froman as "the cornerstone and guarantor of our Constitution and Bill of Rights."

Established following the Civil War, the NRA initially maintained close relationships with state and local governments, which provided assistance to the organization. With increasing urbanization, however, U.S. public officials began to place limitations on the ownership of firearms in order to limit their use in criminal activity. As the U.S. Congress passed gun control legislation (in 1934, 1938, 1968, and 1993), NRA officials intensified their opposition to government limitations on firearms ownership. A distinct cultural divide developed between those who support more extensive limitations on gun ownership and use, and those who regard firearms ownership as a crucial ingredient to a free society.

The NRA regards the U.S. Bureau of Alcohol, Tobacco, Firearms and Explosives (ATF)—the federal agency responsible for enforcing firearms legislation—with suspicion and at times with outright hostility. For example, Chris W. Cox, executive director of the NRA's Institute for Legislative Action, denounced the "heavy-handed" enforcement techniques that ATF agents reportedly used in 2005 at gun shows in Richmond, Virginia. One group the NRA considers a major opponent is the Brady Campaign to Prevent Gun Violence (formerly Handgun Control, Inc.), in which James and Sarah Brady have been active for many years—James Brady, the former White House press secretary, was shot in 1981 during an assassination attempt on President Reagan and has been wheelchair bound ever since. Another opposition group to the NRA is the Violence Policy Center, directed by Josh Sugarmann, who has called for an outright ban on handguns.

NRA leaders proudly declare that they campaigned successfully for the election of George W. Bush to the White House and a congressional majority (Republican) sympathetic to their cause (up until 2006). Following Senate ratification in 2005 and 2006 of President Bush's two Supreme Court nominees, John Roberts, Jr., and Samuel Alito, the NRA leadership announced that, with one additional Bush appointment, a five-justice majority could decide that the Second Amendment guarantees the right of *individual citizens* to keep and bear arms—this was

Actor Charlton Heston, president of the National Rifle Association, addresses the group's national convention in May 1999, following the Columbine (Colorado) High School shootings. Heston said gun owners were being unfairly blamed for the incident. *(Mark Leffingwell/AFP/Getty Images)*

realized in 2008 with the Supreme Court ruling *District of Columbia v. Heller*. Holding that self-protection is "the most basic human right of all," NRA officials have lobbied state legislatures to pass right-to-carry laws, which allow residents to carry a concealed weapon outside the home. The organization claims that in states with right-to-carry laws, the incidence of murder, rape, and robbery has declined significantly. As of 2007, forty states had passed such laws.

The NRA also worked for congressional passage of the Protection of Lawful Commerce in Arms Act (2005), a measure that prohibits lawsuits against firearm manufacturers and retailers for the criminal use of their products. Also, the NRA lobbied the Florida legislature to pass the "Castle Doctrine" law (2005), which establishes the right of citizens to defend themselves by using deadly force and eliminates the "duty to retreat" when faced with force outside the home and in a place they have a right to be. By May 2006, three other states had passed Castle Doctrine legislation In the international realm, Wayne LaPierre (executive vice president and CEO of the NRA) claimed that a well-funded group was attempting to persuade the United Nations to ratify an International Arms Trade Treaty that would restrict private ownership of firearms in the United States and establish gun control on a global basis. He urged gun rights supporters to oppose any UN action to regulate the firearms trade.

Gun control supporters, claiming that the NRA disregards the suffering caused by the easy availability

of firearms, seek regulation of the firearms industry, a crackdown on the illegal gun market, the establishment of product safety standards for firearms, and enhanced authority of the ATF to enforce regulations pertaining to firearms. Nonetheless, the NRA, a well-funded organization with more than 3 million members, has, with some exceptions, succeeded in preventing the adoption of additional firearms restrictions. Whether gun control supporters can compete effectively with the NRA may depend on their ability to raise funds, appeal to public opinion, and lobby effectively at various levels of government.

Glenn H. Utter

See also: Conspiracy Theories; Gun Control; Judicial Wars; United Nations.

Further Reading

Froman, Sandra S. "President's Column." *American Rifleman*, December 2005.
———. "President's Column." *American Rifleman*, June 2006.
LaPierre, Wayne. *The Global War on Your Guns: Inside the U.N. Plan to Destroy the Bill of Rights.* Nashville, TN: Nelson Current, 2006.
National Rifle Association Web site. www.nra.org.
Sugarmann, Josh. *Every Handgun Is Aimed at You: The Case for Banning Handguns.* New York: New Press, 2001.
———. *National Rifle Association: Money, Power and Fear.* Washington, DC: National Press, 1992.

Nelson, Willie

Willie Nelson is an iconic country music songwriter and performer from Texas whose unmistakable tremolo voice enlivens his recordings of such genre classics as "On the Road Again" (1980), "Mamas, Don't Let Your Babies Grow Up to Be Cowboys" (1978, with Waylon Jennings), and "Always on My Mind" (1982). One of the originators and leaders of the "outlaw" movement in country music, Nelson is also an outspoken figure outside the entertainment area, making his views known on such issues as drugs, factory farms, the environment, and the war in Iraq.

Born William Hugh Nelson on April 30, 1933, in Abbott, Texas, he later dropped out of high school, served eight months in the air force (1950), and briefly attended Baylor University. Nelson's early musical career took him far and wide before he finally settled in Nashville, Tennessee, in the late 1950s in search of stardom. Although he succeeded as a songwriter—penning "Crazy" (1961) for Patsy Cline, "Hello Walls" (1961) for Faron Young, and "Night Life" (1962) for Ray Price—the proprietors of the Nashville studios deemed Nelson's voice (and face) to be too offbeat for the upscale crossover audience they sought. In the 1970s, Nelson relocated to Austin, Texas, where he acted as a catalyst in a regional "hippie-redneck" subculture and style referred to alternately as "cosmic cowboy," "progressive country," "outlaw country," or "redneck rock." During this period, he cemented the crossover audience Nashville claimed he would never find, appealing to a younger, countercultural demographic with the concept albums *Yesterday's Wine* (1971), *Shotgun Willie* (1973), *Phases and Stages* (1974), *The Red-Headed Stranger* (1975), and *Wanted: The Outlaws* (1976). His "Blue Eyes Crying in the Rain" won the 1976 Grammy Award for best single. Nelson also went on to appear in a number of films, including *Honeysuckle Rose* (1980), which was based on his life.

Significantly, Nelson's deviation from the Nashville norm constituted a sartorial as well as an auditory rebellion. He grew his hair long, wearing it in braids, sported a beard, and presided over a group of like-minded artists—Waylon Jennings, Kris Kristofferson, and Jerry Jeff Walker, among others—who brought a 1960s sensibility to a musical genre that had often been critical of the counterculture movement. Curiously, Nelson succeeded in carrying his music to a new, younger, and politically progressive audience without alienating the core of his more traditional supporters.

Nelson also began to establish himself as a political populist in these years, appearing with the likes of both George Wallace and Jimmy Carter. In 1980, he sang the "Star Spangled Banner" at the Democratic National Convention, leaving out the words "And the rocket's red glare," prompting Republicans to accuse him of performing while under the influence. In 1985, Nelson organized the Farm Aid concert series to publicize the agricultural crisis threatening America's family-owned farms. From 1985 to 2006, the Farm Aid concerts raised $29 million for farmers. In 1990, the Internal Revenue Service indicted Nelson for failure to pay millions of dollars in taxes, further cementing his reputation as a rebel.

During the 2000 election, Nelson voiced support for Green Party candidate Ralph Nader, and in 2004, he was one of the higher-profile supporters of and fundraisers for the antiwar Democratic presidential candidate Dennis Kucinich. As an environmentalist, he has promoted Willie Nelson Biodiesel (or "BioWillie"), made from vegetable oils and animal fats produced on American farms. As a pot smoker—in *Willie* (1988), his autobiography, the singer boasts of once smoking a joint on the roof of the White House, unbeknownst to President Carter—he is a critic of the war on drugs and a backer of the National Organization for the Reform of Marijuana Laws (NORML). He came into conflict with the retail giant Wal-Mart over the marijuana leaf that graces the cover of his reggae album, *Countryman* (2005). In recent years, he has recorded a song critical of the war in Iraq

("Whatever Happened to Peace on Earth," 2004) and one documenting the phenomenon of gay cowboys ("Cowboys Are Frequently, Secretly Fond of Each Other," 2006).

Nelson remains a singular figure in the culture wars, as he maintains strong ties all along the cultural and political spectrum. The song "Highwayman" (1985), sung with Jennings, Kristofferson, and Johnny Cash, appealed to the New Agers with its allusion to reincarnation. With the conservative country singer Toby Keith, Nelson recorded "Beer for My Horses" (2002), a seeming lament on lawlessness and the anxiety of modern society but one that romanticizes lynching.

Nelson strikes a pose of creative freedom that can, at times, seem to place him above ideological wrangling, and he has been invoked on more than one occasion as a fitting symbol of the nation itself. Perhaps no moment better encapsulates this than his appearance on the celebrity telethon held in the wake of the September 11 terrorist attacks, concluding the program by leading all participants in singing "America the Beautiful." Thus, Willie Nelson's career as an artist and activist reveals much about the course of the culture wars in America, even as he confounds many of the assumptions regarding the much discussed red state–blue state divide.

Jason Mellard

See also: Counterculture; Country Music; Factory Farms; Lynching; Nader, Ralph; New Age Movement; Red and Blue States; Redneck; September 11; Wal-Mart; War on Drugs.

Further Reading

Malone, Bill. *Country Music U.S.A.* Austin: University of Texas Press, 2002.

Nelson, Willie, with Bud Shrake. *Willie: An Autobiography.* New York: Simon & Schuster, 1988.

Reid, Jan. *The Improbable Rise of Redneck Rock.* Austin: University of Texas Press, 2004.

Willie Nelson Official Web site. www.willienelson.com.

Willman, Chris. *Rednecks and Bluenecks: The Politics of Country Music.* New York: New Press, 2005.

Neoconservatism

Neoconservatism, which emerged in the United States during the second half of the twentieth century, emphasizes ideological constructs of freedom and democracy as the primary agent of historical change. This form of Americanism, neoconservatives believe, may be wielded like a weapon to destroy evil and injustice in the world. Conversely, neoconservatives promote constant vigilance at home, lest undesirable ideas corrupt American institutions and culture.

As a result of this philosophical foundation, neoconservatives tend to favor an activist and interventionist foreign policy and domestic policies that promote order, security, and the national interest. Unlike traditional conservatives, neoconservatives do not have an aversion to big government. However, they reject the liberal commitment to using big government to foster equality and social justice. From the neoconservative perspective, a large, powerful government is necessary for maintaining order and security at home and for promoting American interests abroad. Although they tend to be somewhat more liberal on many domestic issues than traditional conservatives—or "paleoconservatives," as the neoconservatives call them—they do not immerse themselves very deeply in domestic affairs. A sort of tacit agreement seems to have prevailed in which conservatives, mostly Republican in party affiliation, give social and religious conservatives sway over domestic questions, and the intellectual neoconservatives control foreign affairs.

European Origins

The origins of neoconservatism can be traced to Europe, in particular Weimar Germany (1919–1933). After the conclusion of World War I, many young Germans believed that liberal democracy had sapped the vitality of the German state and German culture. By the mid-1920s, a right-leaning nationalist reaction, which to some extent presaged the rise of National Socialism (Nazism), had emerged. Reactionary thinkers such as Martin Heidegger, Ernst Junger, and Carl Schmitt rejected both Bolshevism and Western-style liberal democracy as manifestations of historicism, scientism, and a licentious relativism that had, in their view, begun with the Enlightenment. As Europe drew closer to war in the 1930s, Heidegger's Jewish students Hannah Arendt, Leo Strauss, Herbert Marcuse, Karl Lowith, and Hans-Georg Gadamer fled Germany for America. There, over the course of the next two decades, the émigrés' philosophy entered American political thought, infusing older American traditions, on both sides of the political spectrum, with a new theoretical vitality. By the 1960s, for instance, Strauss had come to be identified with conservatism, while Marcuse was identified with the New Left.

The theoretical character of the émigrés' philosophy was highly attractive to many young intellectuals of the 1930s and 1940s. Almost the entire first generation of neoconservatives gravitated toward academia, the law, and various literary pursuits. Among them are Willmoore Kendall, Albert Wohlstetter, Gertrude Himmelfarb, Harry Jaffa, Allan Bloom, Irving Kristol, and Norman Podhoretz. Similarly, many of their students, protégés, and children, such as Francis Fukuyama, Paul Wolfowitz, William Kristol, and John Podhoretz, have gone on to careers in the same fields. In the aggregate, their work imparted a cohesiveness, sophistication, and intellectual authority to neoconservative thought that is unmatched by other strains of conservatism.

American Beginnings

Politically, the neoconservatives' trajectory has taken them from the far left to the far right. Many of the first-generation neoconservatives had been young anti-Stalinist socialists who abandoned socialism for the conservative wing of the Democratic Party during the Truman administration. Staunch anticommunists during the 1950s, the neoconservatives began to break with mainstream liberalism during the 1960s. The advent of the counterculture, the civil rights movement, and the war in Vietnam, as well as the social pressures engendered by these events, seemed to them to echo the sort of societal breakdown that had characterized Weimar Germany. Some, like Harry Jaffa, Norman Podhoretz, Midge Decter, Irving Kristol, and Gertrude Himmelfarb, became Republicans. It was Jaffa who in 1964 formulated Barry Goldwater's famous declaration: "Extremism in the defense of liberty is no vice . . . moderation in the pursuit of justice is no virtue." As the decade proceeded, Kristol, Podhoretz, and other neoconservatives held forth in the pages of *Commentary* and the *Wall Street Journal* on subjects as diverse as civil rights, women's rights, integration, the peace movement, the Great Society, and the generation gap.

Other neoconservatives, however, remained aligned with the Democratic Party, albeit opposed to the anti–Vietnam War stance that the party adopted in 1968. Most of these neoconservatives—a name bestowed on them by leftist commentator Michael Harrington when they refused to support the presidential candidacy of George McGovern in 1972—aligned themselves with Senator Henry M. Jackson (D-WA). One of the most senior and powerful figures in Washington, Jackson was an expert in defense matters, a staunch supporter of Israel's interests, and a man with presidential ambitions. During the 1970s, Jackson made it his business to ensure that the Nixon administration did not give away too much as it pursued arms control agreements with the Soviet Union. In order to assist Jackson in his jousting with the administration, his chief of staff, Dorothy Fosdick, brought in talented young neoconservatives such as Richard Perle, Charles Horner, Douglas Feith, Paul Wolfowitz, Elliot Abrams, and Richard Pipes to serve on or assist Jackson's staff.

The neoconservative assault on détente and arms control continued throughout the 1970s. Jackson shepherded the Jackson-Vanik Amendment (1974), which linked most favored nation trade status with increased Jewish emigration from the Soviet Union. Albert Wohlstetter attacked arms control and charged that the CIA had consistently underestimated Soviet nuclear missile deployments. Irving Kristol, Theodore Draper, and others inveighed against the Nixon, Ford, and Carter administrations' foreign policy and the effects on the American psyche of the "Vietnam syndrome."

Reagan Revolution

For neoconservatives, 1980 was a watershed year. The December 1979 Soviet invasion of Afghanistan had dealt the deathblow to détente and the Carter administration. However, Jackson learned that he had terminal cancer and retired from the Senate. Those neoconservatives who had remained Democrats now prepared to support, many for the first time in their lives, a Republican candidate for president. Ronald Reagan's call for a return to traditional values and his support for a muscular, confrontationist foreign policy resonated deeply with the neoconservatives.

Reagan's victory over Carter in 1980 allowed many neoconservatives to gain positions in the administration. Perle, Abrams, and Feith, for instance, secured jobs in the Defense Department as assistant secretaries. Jeane Kirkpatrick was appointed ambassador to the United Nations. Wolfowitz, named director of policy planning at the State Department, brought in several of his former students and associates, including I. Lewis Libby, Zalmay Khalilzad, Alan Keyes, and Francis Fukuyama. Pipes was given the post of director of East European and Soviet affairs on Reagan's National Security Council. On the domestic policy front, however, neoconservative representation was scant.

Despite Reagan's harsh, "evil empire" rhetoric, many neoconservatives were quickly disillusioned by the president's reticence to launch a global crusade against communism. Irving Kristol, writing in the *Wall Street Journal*, called Reagan's foreign policy a "muddle." Norman Podhoretz, editor of *Commentary*, detected an incipient "anguish" among neoconservatives. Many neoconservatives took their leave after Reagan's reelection and an improvement in Soviet-American relations. Held at arm's length by the less ideological administrations of George H.W. Bush and Bill Clinton, many neoconservatives and their allies spent their time outside government in think tanks such as the American Enterprise Institute and the Hudson Institute. They also formed several policy advocacy groups, the Jewish Institute for National Security Affairs and the Project for a New American Century being the most significant.

Returned to power with the presidency of George W. Bush, neoconservatives were the strongest promoters of a U.S. invasion of Iraq. Deputy Secretary of Defense Paul Wolfowitz is widely acknowledged as a chief architect of the Bush administration's decision to oust Saddam Hussein. The subsequent pressures generated by the outcome in Iraq caused divisions among neoconservatives, and some traditional conservatives, such as John McCain and Colin Powell, turned against the neoconservatives, who on past occasions had politically outmaneuvered them.

The conflict among neoconservatives, given the movement's cohesiveness over the years, surprised many observers. A notable example of the schism was a heated exchange between political scientist Francis Fukuyama and journalist Charles Krauthammer. In "The Neoconservative Moment," an article in the conservative *National Review*, Fukuyama described a 2004 speech given by Krauthammer on Iraq as "strangely disconnected from reality . . . without the slightest nod towards the new empirical facts that have emerged in the last year or so." Krauthammer, calling the criticism "bizarre," accused Fukuyama of "denying the obvious nature of the threat" represented by radical Islam.

Robert L. Richardson

See also: American Century; Cheney Family; Cold War; Communists and Communism; Israel; Keyes, Alan; Kristol, Irving, and Bill Kristol; Pipes, Richard, and Daniel Pipes; Podhoretz, Norman; Reagan, Ronald; Republican Party; September 11; Soviet Union and Russia; Strauss, Leo; Think Tanks.

Further Reading

Ehrman, John. *The Rise of Neoconservatism: Intellectuals and Foreign Affairs, 1945–1994*. New Haven, CT: Yale University Press, 1995.
Gerson, Mark. *The Neoconservative Vision: From the Cold War to the Culture Wars*. Lanham, MD: Madison Books, 1996.
Kristol, Irving. *Neoconservatism: The Autobiography of an Idea*. New York: Free Press, 1995.

New Age Movement

The New Age and neopagan (or contemporary pagan) movements are new religious movements (NRMs) that postdate World War II. They are particularly indebted to the 1960s' counterculture for their aesthetics, practices, and ideology, though they also have roots in earlier alternative religious movements such as theosophy, Western ceremonial magic, spiritualism, transcendentalism, and New Thought.

The practices and beliefs of New Agers and contemporary pagans are highly eclectic and diverse. Common threads include a disillusionment with mainstream religion as repressive, inauthentic, or spiritually barren; a conception of life as a journey of self-development; an optimistic view of human nature; a focus on holistic healing, both spiritual and physical; a belief in reincarnation and karma (the notion that actions in this life have effects on the next); the use of ritual to contact spiritual entities; religious syncretism; and a desire to connect with and protect the natural environment.

Most New Agers and many pagans adhere to a pantheistic worldview, believing that the divinity of the self and the interconnection of all things are the basis for an ethic of love, compassion, and social justice. The term "New Age" comes from the millennial belief that a new era of peace and prosperity will emerge from this evolutionary transformation of consciousness.

The differences between pagans and New Agers often come down to aesthetics. Although pagans occasionally gather for large festivals, they tend to work in small, personal groups without hierarchical authority. Unless they do healing work professionally, for example, as psychotherapists or acupuncturists, many are reluctant to charge money for healing. Contemporary pagan practices are often strongly nature oriented and draw on ancient and indigenous religions for their gods and myths, with the Celtic, Greek, and Egyptian pantheons as popular choices. Accordingly, the scholarly reconstruction of ancient religions is taken seriously by many pagans. Some are polytheists as they understand ancient cultures to have been, seeing deity as fundamentally multiple. It is more common, however, to understand all gods as part of one entity, often conceived of as a goddess. Many pagans also consider themselves witches, that is, practitioners of nature-based magic, with Wicca being the most widely known form of religious witchcraft.

New Agers, by contrast, tend to be more comfortable with professional–client relationships and with the exchange of money for healing work. They are less likely to call themselves witches, devote themselves to a particular pantheon, or practice a "tradition." Reading groups, learning centers, and workshops are more likely gathering places for New Age practitioners than covens or ritual groups. New Agers are also more likely to embrace practices and beliefs that blend religion and science, such as Kirlian photography (the capturing of auras on film) or the Gaia hypothesis (that the earth operates as a single organism), although pagans also participate in these. Channeling, whereby a spirit is allowed to speak through a human medium, is popular among New Agers, who look to these spirits for advice and guidance. Particularly famous among channeled books are the best-selling *A Course in Miracles* (1976) and *The Celestine Prophecy* (1993).

Evangelical Christians and rationalist skeptics are the most vocal critics of the New Age and contemporary pagan movements. Evangelicals have presented a host of biblical objections to New Age beliefs and practices, particularly targeting New Age assertions that Jesus is meant to be emulated, not worshipped; that human beings can attain their own wholeness or salvation; that acts that do no harm, such as consensual extramarital sex, cannot be considered wrong; that the divine can be experienced as feminine as well as masculine; and that evil is not an external force, but rather the product of an unnecessary disconnection from God.

More sophisticated evangelical critiques, such as journalist Russell Chandler's *Understanding the New Age* (1988), accuse the New Age movement of trivializing the problem of suffering as nothing more than an error in belief. Chandler also criticizes the moral relativism of some New Age writers, suggesting that the movement's intense individualism and lack of an external moral authority leave no basis for moral judgment. Elliot Miller's *A Crash Course on the New Age Movement* (1989) suggests that the New Age emphasis on mysticism encourages a retreat from the external world and undermines the work of social justice.

Skeptics such as Martin Gardner and Carl Sagan, in their books *The New Age: Notes of a Fringe Watcher* (1988) and *The Demon-Haunted World* (1995), respectively, assert that the emphasis on intuition and subjectivity in the New Age movement strips practitioners of the benefits of empirical fact checking. New Agers, they claim, are unable to distinguish science from pseudoscience and may subject themselves to useless or even dangerous practices.

Historian Ronald Hutton's largely sympathetic study *The Triumph of the Moon: A History of Modern Pagan Witchcraft* (1999) agrees that an overemphasis on intuition over rationalism can lead to dismissal of important scientific and historical data. Some critics, for example, are skeptical of the Goddess movement's theory of matriarchal prehistory. Some Native Americans have also been critical of New Agers and pagans, accusing them of irresponsible cultural borrowing. For Native Americans, the co-optation of their spiritual practices by such groups is part of an ongoing cultural imperialism by whites.

As some commentators note, the pagan belief that acts of love and pleasure are the rituals of the Goddess has sometimes led to a hedonism that is anything but spiritual. Pagans, however, are dedicated to celebrating sexuality, the natural world, and the body, and serious practitioners complain of "festival pagans," dabblers whose attendance at festivals is not based in regular religious practice or ethical commitments.

Christine Hoff Kraemer

See also: Anti-Intellectualism; Counterculture; Evangelicalism; Feminism, Second-Wave; Feminism, Third-Wave; Leary, Timothy; Men's Movement; Morgan, Robin; Postmodernism; Relativism, Moral.

Further Reading

Adler, Margot. *Drawing Down the Moon: Witches, Druids, Goddess-Worshippers, and Other Pagans in America Today*. Boston: Beacon, 1986.

Chandler, Russell. *Understanding the New Age*. Dallas, TX: Word, 1988.

Heelas, Paul. *The New Age Movement: The Celebration of the Self and the Sacralization of Modernity*. Oxford, UK: Blackwell, 1996.

Miller, Elliot. *A Crash Course on the New Age Movement*. Grand Rapids, MI: Baker Book House, 1989.

Pike, Sarah M. *New Age and Neopagan Religions in America*. New York: Columbia University Press, 2004.

Sagan, Carl. *The Demon-Haunted World: Science as a Candle in the Dark*. New York: Random House, 1995.

New Deal

The programs and policies for economic recovery and social reform advanced by the administration of President Franklin D. Roosevelt were collectively known as the New Deal. Most New Deal programs were intended as short-term solutions to facilitate economic growth during the Great Depression. Others, such as Social Security, had a lasting impact on American institutions. Ultimately, the New Deal created federal and state institutions that significantly expanded the role of government in American life, and its legacy has been frequently debated as part of the culture wars.

The New Deal originated in the Democratic Party, which was guided by its principles in the decades following the 1930s. Supporters of its programs and ideology were referred to as "New Deal Democrats" or members of the "New Deal coalition." The New Deal coalition consisted of politicians, special interest groups, including labor unions, and voting blocs that supported New Deal initiatives. Over time, the coalition became increasingly fragmented, finally beginning to disintegrate in the mid-1960s.

Critics opposed the New Deal on the grounds that it contained elements of socialism. Leading the opposition in the 1930s was Senator Robert Taft (R-OH), who believed that the New Deal placed too many restrictions on business. Taft argued that the New Deal would ultimately return the economy to a depression.

The New Deal remains controversial among American politicians, economists, and historians to the present day. Critics point to expanded federal control of the economy, reliance on deficit spending, creation of the "welfare state," and continued financial burdens of New Deal programs as negative legacies. Supporters point to New Deal programs as necessary and innovative responses to the Great Depression. They applaud programs such as the Federal Deposit Insurance Corporation and Social Security as beneficial to economic stability.

Support for the New Deal and its legacy has fallen primarily along party lines. Roosevelt's immediate successor was his vice president, Harry Truman, who sought ways to apply New Deal policies to postwar America. In his "Fair Deal" plan, he proposed universal health care. President Dwight D. Eisenhower, a Republican, resisted calls from his party to dismantle the social programs of the New Deal. John F. Kennedy began his political career as a New Deal Democrat and sought some form of its continuation in his plan for social reform, the "New Frontier." Kennedy's successor, Lyndon B. Johnson, also a Democrat, promoted the "Great Society," a program that called for expanded social reform.

Although the Environmental Protection Agency and the Occupational Safety and Health Administration were created on his watch, Richard M. Nixon, a staunch Republican, was committed to the ideal of limited government, especially rolling back the legacies of the New Deal. Thus, many New Deal programs had already been downsized by the time Republican Ronald Reagan assumed the presidency in 1980. Although Reagan greatly admired Roosevelt, his tenure as president is often viewed as the antithesis of New Deal leadership, with its emphasis on limited government interference in big business and on supply-side economics. For political conservatives Reagan represented the heroic counterpart to FDR and a realignment force. This is why Representative Mark Souder (R-IN) in 2003 proposed replacing the image of Roosevelt on the dime with that of Reagan. (The proposal was withdrawn after Reagan's widow, Nancy Reagan, voiced opposition.)

President Bill Clinton, a Democrat, referred to a "New Covenant" between government and the American people. Clinton, an ardent admirer of Roosevelt, proposed a wide range of initiatives aimed at social reform, including an unsuccessful attempt to introduce universal health care. Under Clinton, however, federal welfare programs were downsized.

Senator Hillary Rodham Clinton (D-NY) in 2003 accused President George W. Bush, a Republican, of trying to "undo the New Deal," and many other Democrats saw Bush's "compassionate conservatism" as an effort to roll back the New Deal in favor of a system of privatized social services. His extensive tax cuts seemed to follow Grover Norquist's plan to return to the days before the New Deal, including a widening of the wealth gap. Critics argue that Bush's Medicare prescription drug plan, which favored privatization, and his proposal to offer private investment options as part of the Social Security system showed his antipathy toward the New Deal. But supporters of the Bush administration argued that the president approved an expansion, not a reduction, of entitlement programs, most notably the Medicare prescription drug plan. Following the collapse of the credit market in 2008, the Bush administration launched a $700 billion financial bailout, which critical observers suggested was a return to the New Deal.

Melanie Kirkland

See also: Bush Family; Clinton, Bill; Clinton, Hillary; Compassionate Conservatism; Great Society; Health Care; Norquist, Grover; Social Security; Supply-Side Economics; Taft, Robert A.; Wealth Gap; Welfare Reform.

Further Reading

Brinkley, Alan. *The End of Reform: New Deal Liberalism in Recession and War*. New York: Alfred A. Knopf, 1995.

Chafe, William H., ed. *The Achievement of American Liberalism: The New Deal and Its Legacies*. New York: Columbia University Press, 2003.

Fraser, Steve, and Gary Gerstle, eds. *The Rise and Fall of the New Deal Order, 1930–1980*. Princeton, NJ: Princeton University Press, 1989.

Phillips-Fein, Kim. *Invisible Hands: The Making of the Conservative Movement from the New Deal to Reagan.* New York: W.W. Norton, 2009.

New Journalism

New Journalism emerged during the 1960s and 1970s as an innovative style of reporting in harmony with the counterculture movement. New Journalists saw themselves as taking over the role of the traditional novelist by addressing the broad social and cultural movements of their day, which they felt novelists had abandoned. While conventional journalists argued that a degree of objectivity could be achieved by maintaining a distance from their subjects, New Journalists contended that objective writing was not only untenable, but undesirable. By combining literary and journalistic devices, New Journalists hoped to create a more engaging and emotionally charged writing style that would go beyond answering the standard questions of who, what, where, when, why, and how.

In his introduction to *The New Journalism* (1973), Tom Wolfe defines the contours of New Journalism, explaining that it is a new literary form combining traditional reporting with novelistic devices such as telling stories using scenes rather than a chronological narrative; including conversational speech or full dialogue; adopting a personal point of view; and recording the details of everyday life. Wolfe's *The Electric Kool-Aid Acid Test* (1963), which documents the LSD activities and cross-country escapades of Ken Kesey and the Merry Pranksters, is written in this style. Hunter S. Thompson's *Hell's Angels: A Strange and Terrible Saga* (1967) uses a similar approach as he describes his travels with this counterculture motorcycle gang. Other books that have been identified as leading examples of New Journalism include Truman Capote's *In Cold Blood: A True Account of a Multiple Murder and Its Consequences* (1965); Joan Didion's *Slouching Towards Bethlehem* (1968), a series of articles about life in San Francisco; and Norman Mailer's *Armies of the Night: History as a Novel, the Novel as History* (1968), which documents his experience during a 1967 anti–Vietnam War march on Washington, D.C.

Critics of New Journalism quickly argued that by combining the literary devices of novels and journalism, New Journalists corrupt both forms. The insertion of the reporter's internal dialogue and worldview into a text labeled journalism, critics suggested, leads readers to assume that the reporter is an unreliable source. Such detractors dismissed New Journalism, with the reporter having a central role in the story, as symptomatic of the self-absorption of the 1960s counterculture. New Journalists countered that the goal of objectivity in reporting is patently unrealistic.

During the late 1960s, writers such as Hunter S. Thompson pushed the concept of New Journalism even further, arguing that reporters should not only be forthcoming about their perceptions, but they should experience the events they describe firsthand. As chroniclers of the counterculture, "Gonzo journalists"—practitioners of Thompson's style of subjective, first-person narrative—often consumed copious amounts of alcohol and drugs as part of their work. This served as additional fodder for those who argued that New Journalists were simply self-indulgent. The legacy of New Journalism, with its emphasis on the role of the reporter in the construction and telling of a story, remains evident in such magazines as *Rolling Stone.*

Jessie Swigger

See also: Counterculture; Literature, Film, and Drama; Mailer, Norman; Thompson, Hunter S.; Wolfe, Tom.

Further Reading

Weingarten, Marc. *The Gang That Wouldn't Write Straight: Wolfe, Thompson, Didion, and the New Journalism Revolution.* New York: Crown, 2006.

Wolfe, Tom, and E.W. Johnson, eds. *The New Journalism.* New York: Harper and Row, 1973.

New Left

The New Left movements that flourished during the 1960s and early 1970s challenged discrimination against blacks, ethnic minorities, and women; promoted freedom in dress, language, sexuality, and other aspects of personal expression; and opposed the nuclear arms race and the war in Vietnam. These movements exposed the fault lines in American society and politics by pressing for a radical extension of democracy to every person regardless of color, gender, sexual orientation, or origin. In foreign affairs, New Left activists challenged the consensus to contain communism at any cost by protesting a war that increasingly seemed without strategy, morality, or purpose.

The New Left germinated during the conservative 1950s, when communists, socialists, and anarchists of the Old Left appeared moribund. It found scattered models of resistance in African-American struggles for civil rights; Christian pacifist groups such as the War Resisters' League; and the Committee for a Sane Nuclear Policy, formed in 1957 to oppose nuclear testing. In the early 1960s, the New Left drew inspiration from black student sit-ins in the South and the Student Nonviolent Coordinating Committee (SNCC), which helped guide those campaigns. It drew, too, on the idealism of affluent Baby Boom youths eager to act on John F. Kennedy's inaugural exhortation to "ask what together we can do for the freedom of man."

White college students were prominent in the emerging New Left because they were relatively privileged, articulate, sheltered from the demands of the work world, and part of a fast-growing cohort marked by a strong generational identity. Students for a Democratic Society (SDS), originating as an offshoot of the socialist League for Industrial Democracy, in 1962 circulated an influential reform vision, the "Port Huron Statement," written chiefly by Tom Hayden, which urged "participatory democracy," to let individuals shape decisions that affected them in a bureaucratized society dominated by corporations and the military. In 1964, the Free Speech Movement at the University of California at Berkeley applied this philosophy by staging nonviolent student sit-ins that restored student rights to engage in political activity on campus.

Early New Left activists fit comfortably within the liberal Democratic coalition that enacted civil rights laws, advocated equal rights for women, expanded federal aid to education, and sought to empower the poor through community action programs. Beginning in March 1965, however, the sustained American bombing of North Vietnam and the deployment of ground troops to South Vietnam alienated New Left groups from the nation's liberal leaders and a "system," as Paul Potter of the SDS declared in April 1965, that "put material values before human values."

The New Left became larger, more diverse, and more radical during the late 1960s and early 1970s. In 1966, Stokely Carmichael of the SNCC advocated Black Power based on militant racial solidarity rather than integration, liberal coalition, and nonviolence. Chicanos (Mexican Americans), Puerto Ricans, Asian Americans, Native Americans, gays and lesbians, and other groups also asserted their identity, pride, and grievances toward mainstream institutions and values. Opponents of the Vietnam War engaged in civil disobedience at draft induction centers, held the March on the Pentagon in October 1967, and drew half a million demonstrators to Washington, D.C., in November 1969. During a student protest at Kent State University in Ohio on May 4, 1970, National Guard troops killed four students, precipitating student "strikes" that shut down hundreds of colleges and universities.

While Yippies (members of the Youth International Party) declared that "revolution is fun," and some members of other New Left groups flirted with the idea of violent revolution, their extreme actions led to a backlash in public opinion; electoral shifts toward conservative Republicans over liberal Democrats; and repression by local police, the National Guard, and the FBI. In his successful campaign to become governor of California in 1966, Ronald Reagan branded activists at the University of California at Berkeley a disruptive "minority of hippies, radicals, and filthy speech advocates" who

should be "thrown off campus—permanently." When protestors outside the Democratic National Convention in Chicago in August 1968 met with police brutality, however, the American public was shocked by the city's use of violence. But the backlash continued against the New Left, fed on resentment of all protests; hostility toward blacks, feminists, gays, and lesbians; tensions between blue-collar workers and more affluent antiwar demonstrators; and fears of violence stoked by ghetto riots and bombings by New Left splinter groups like the Weather Underground.

The SNCC, the SDS, Yippies, and similar groups faded after the early 1970s, but in its brief heyday the New Left transformed American society and politics. It helped topple the South's legalized racial caste system; established a new consensus that groups long on the margins of public life, including blacks and women, deserved rights, opportunities, and positions of authority; brought issues of gay and lesbian rights to the center of national politics; expanded the boundaries of acceptable cultural expression and relationships; and made dissent against U.S. foreign policy respectable even in wartime.

Robert Weisbrot

See also: Black Panther Party; Chicago Seven; Civil Rights Movement; Communists and Communism; Counterculture; Gay Rights Movement; Hayden, Tom; Hoffman, Abbie; Nuclear Age; Sexual Revolution; Students for a Democratic Society; Vietnam War; War Protesters.

Further Reading
Gitlin, Todd. *The Sixties: Years of Hope, Days of Rage*. New York: Bantam Books, 1987.
Gosse, Van. *Rethinking the New Left: An Interpretive History*. New York: Palgrave Macmillan, 2005.
Isserman, Maurice, and Michael Kazin. *America Divided: The Civil War of the 1960s*. New York: Oxford University Press, 2000.
Miller, James. *"Democracy Is in the Streets": From Port Huron to the Siege of Chicago*. New York: Simon and Schuster, 1987.

New York Times, The

Founded in 1851 and often referred to as "the Gray Lady" (for its plain appearance and traditional status), the *New York Times* has for years been the nation's most prominent newspaper. As such, it has unofficially functioned as the "newspaper of record," providing American society with the "first draft of history" and acting as a sort of "fourth estate" of the national sphere. In 2009, as the paper boasted the largest staff of any other newsroom in the country (some 1,200 staffers) and maintained a daily print circulation of 1 million (with Sunday circulation of 1.4 million), the New York

Times Company experienced severe financial strain ($1.1 billion in debt), which was exacerbated by a 7.7 percent decline in advertising revenue due to a faltering economy as well as the trend of more people relying on the Internet for their primary source of news.

From its beginnings as the *New York Daily Times*, the paper sought to be more substantive and less sensational than the rival newspapers of the day, as then explained by founder Henry J. Raymond: "[W]e do not mean to write as if we were in a passion." In 1896, the struggling paper was bought by Adolph S. Ochs. The new owner, wishing to set a course for higher journalism standards, added a motto to the paper's masthead: "All the News That's Fit to Print." Within four years, the newspaper attracted more advertising and increased its circulation from 25,000 to 100,000 by bolstering market reports and coverage of government news. During the paper's early years, the staff worked out of Times Tower on Broadway, a prominent location that came to be called Times Square. By the 1920s, circulation reached 330,000, with Sunday sales topping 500,000. Ochs remained publisher until his death in 1935, and all subsequent publishers have been his descendants: Arthur Hays Sulzberger (1935–1961), Orvil E. Dryfoos (1961–1963), Arthur Ochs "Punch" Sulzberger (1963–1992), and Arthur Ochs Sulzberger, Jr. (1992–). Although the company began issuing stock during the 1960s, the family has retained majority control. In 2007, the paper moved its operation into a new fifty-two-story neo-Gothic tower on Eighth Avenue between 40th and 41st streets in Midtown Manhattan.

Omissions and Biases

The *New York Times* has been praised for its coverage of such landmark twentieth-century events as the sinking of the *Titanic*, the Armenian genocide during the breakup of the Ottoman Empire, and the two world wars. However, it has been criticized for inaccuracies and/or omissions pertaining to the civil war following the 1917 Russian Revolution, the Holocaust, the Pinochet regime in Chile, and, most recently, the lead-up to the Iraq War. In 2003, Walter Duranty, a Stalin apologist who was a *Times* correspondent in Moscow during the 1920s and 1930s, was nearly posthumously stripped of his 1932 Pulitzer Prize for allegedly misleading his editors and readers about the Ukrainian famine.

In the culture wars, the *Times* has been criticized by both conservatives and liberals alike. For those who are politically to the right, the *Times* is a liberal newspaper that fails to reflect the values of the larger American culture. The conservative Media Research Center, founded in 1987, maintains a "Times Watch" Web page "dedicated to documenting and exposing the liberal political agenda of the *New York Times*."

It can also be argued, however, that the editorial positions of the paper are largely in harmony with the cosmopolitan mores of its immediate readership, the residents of New York City. Some have contended as well that the *Times* is often judged by the standards of advocacy journalism and narrowcasting rather than a dialectical "both sides" approach. In recent times, the *Times*'s op-ed page has included liberal columnists such as Maureen Dowd and the Nobel laureate economist Paul Krugman while also providing a rightward forum to former *Weekly Standard* editor David Brooks and globalization advocate Thomas Friedman. From 2007 to 2009, Bill Kristol, the leading figure of the neoconservative movement, was a regular columnist.

Although the *Times* supported the adoption of the Twenty-second Amendment, a conservative initiative to limit a president to two terms of office in negative response to Roosevelt winning four terms, its editorial page has not endorsed a Republican presidential candidate since Dwight D. Eisenhower. In fact, the *Times* was part of the small 16 percent of newspapers that endorsed John F. Kennedy for president in 1960. Writing in *Newsday* in 2000, Charles Krauthammer argued that the *Times*'s headline of September 7—"Gore Offers Vision of Better Times for Middle Class"—was what "*Pravda* used to run for Leonid Brezhnev's campaigns." That same year, Republican presidential candidate George W. Bush was inadvertently caught on an open mike complaining about *Times* reporter Adam Clymer, whom he referred to with an expletive.

In one of the most infamous attacks against the paper, the conservative pundit Ann Coulter wrote in the *New York Observer*, "My only regret with Timothy McVeigh [the bomber of the Oklahoma City federal building] is he did not go to the *New York Times* building" (August 26, 2002). As the late Reed Irvine of Accuracy in Media earlier accused the paper of projecting a liberal bias, MIT professor Noam Chomsky was advancing the argument that the *Times*, by acting as an "agenda setter" of the mainstream media, has narrowed the spectrum of public debate to the point that what is considered liberal is actually quite conservative.

Conservative radio talk show host Rush Limbaugh has often ridiculed the paper, despite the fact that he has for years drawn material from it. Ironically, the liberal watch group Media Matters was displeased by an "ego-stroking profile" of Limbaugh that appeared in the *New York Times Magazine* (July 6, 2008), calling Zev Chafets, the reporter who wrote the piece, "a toothless tiger." In February 1994, Limbaugh criticized the *Times* for not running a front-page article about Whitewater, a real estate scandal involving the Clintons, even though two years earlier the paper broke the story on page one. Liberals, in fact, accused the *Times* of having revived Whitewater, which had otherwise been a dead issue, and they point out that earlier the paper largely stood on the sidelines while the *Washington Post* investigated the Watergate scandal.

Since Whitewater involved a Democratic administration and Watergate a Republican one, some liberal critics suggest an inconsistency.

An "Establishment" Paper

For years the *Times* was regarded as an "establishment" newspaper. This is why it was chosen by the federal government in 1945 to write the history of the development of the atomic bomb. Science reporter William Laurence was assigned this exclusive task and even accompanied the August 9 bombing mission of Nagasaki, winning a Pulitzer Prize for his eyewitness account of the devastation. On many occasions, the *Times* cooperated with American officials by either not publishing stories or delaying their release. In 1954, as the Central Intelligence Agency (CIA) was about to launch a coup in Guatemala, the *Times* management ordered reporter Sydney Gruson out of that country—as later divulged, the decision was prompted by "security concerns" raised by CIA director Allen Dulles, who wanted the event left unreported. Later, as the CIA made preparations for the Bay of Pigs invasion of Cuba, the paper acquiesced to the Kennedy administration and held back on its coverage. Over the years, it was speculated that the paper was occasionally used as a cover for the CIA, a subject explored at length in *Without Fear or Favor: The* New York Times *and Its Times* (1980) by former *Times* reporter Harrison E. Salisbury. In 1956, the *Times* joined other American newspapers in declining China's invitation to send correspondents because it did not wish to embarrass the U.S. government.

Despite any perceived coziness with Washington officialdom, the *Times* had its conservative detractors who were displeased by the paper's support of New Deal programs and the civil rights movement. The paper's editorial stance, such as in 1951 when it sided with President Harry Truman in the firing of General Douglas MacArthur, would sometimes be out of sync with the prevailing public mood. In 1956, Senator James O. Eastland (D-MS) launched an inquiry of the *Times,* charging that 100 communists were on its staff. Ironically, this came after the Kremlin had publicly attacked the paper for distorting the policies of the Soviet government. Later, segregationists sued for libel after being inaccurately depicted in a political ad placed in the paper by a civil rights group. In the resulting U.S. Supreme Court decision, *New York Times Co. v. Sullivan* (1964), the Court ruled against the plaintiffs on the grounds that criticism of public officials does not warrant libel unless "actual malice" can be proven. Some believe that the paper's liberal bias drove it in October 1965 to unnecessarily reveal that Daniel Burros, the New York head of the Ku Klux Klan and a member of the American Nazi Party, had been born Jewish but was keeping it concealed; Burros, who some thought was mentally disturbed, committed suicide following the publication of a front-page article on his background.

During the Vietnam War, the paper became increasingly critical of American foreign policy. Beginning in 1962, *Times* reporter David Halberstam became the first war correspondent to offer a negative account of what was occurring in Vietnam; two years later he won the Pulitzer Prize. In 1966, Harrison E. Salisbury reported, in contradiction to official statements of the Lyndon Johnson administration, that American B-52s were bombing civilian targets in North Vietnam. Although an advisory board recommended Salisbury for the Pulitzer Prize, the decision was overruled by a 6–5 vote, apparently over disenchantment with the embarrassment caused for the government. In late 1969, frustrated by the growing antiwar sentiment of the news media, Vice President Spiro T. Agnew publicly denounced the biases of the "eastern establishment," clearly counting the *New York Times* as one of the "nattering nabobs of negativism." After the *Times* began publishing the Pentagon Papers, the government's top-secret history of the Vietnam War, the Nixon administration sought a court injunction to halt the serialization, but in *New York Times Co. v. United States* (1971), the Supreme Court sided against the government, 6–3.

Iraq War

In *Off with Their Heads* (2003), political consultant and Fox News analyst Dick Morris includes a chapter entitled "The New *New York Times,*" faulting the paper for failing to support President Bush after the terrorist attacks of September 11, 2001. Howell Raines, who became managing editor days prior to the terrorist attacks, is blamed by Morris for being a "partisan cheerleader, sending messages of dissent, and fanning the flames of disagreement on the left." Conservative critics have also questioned the newspaper for labeling the unrest in Iraq a "civil war" and for the persistent usage of the term "insurgents" instead of "terrorists." (Similarly, there was objection to articles that referred to Hurricane Katrina survivors as "refugees" instead of "evacuees.") In an opposite conclusion, liberals such as Arianna Huffington of the Huffington Post group blog fault the *Times* for its stenography-like reporting in the lead-up to the Iraq War. Huffington and others were especially condemning of *Times* reporter Judith Miller, believing that she quoted officials without doing real reporting. According to this critique, Miller in 2002 and 2003 played up the story on weapons of mass destruction in Iraq (which later proved to be nonexistent), sanctioning the efforts of the Bush administration.

In 2006, the *Wall Street Journal* editorialized that preventing the United States from winning the War on Terror was "a major goal" of the *New York Times.* This judgment followed the *Times* breaking a news story that the U.S. government was tracking international banking data in an attempt to uncover terrorist funding. Vice President Cheney criticized the paper for disclosing "vital national security programs" and said that doing so would make it "more difficult . . . to prevent future attacks against the American people." Defending itself in an editorial (June 28, 2006), the *Times* argued that terrorists obviously knew that transferring money by wire was subject to government monitoring. The real issue, the editorial continued, was "an extraordinarily powerful executive branch, exempt from the normal checks and balances of our system of government."

Roger Chapman

See also: Central Intelligence Agency; Clinton Impeachment; Coulter, Ann; Holocaust; Kristol, Irving, and Bill Kristol; Krugman, Paul; Limbaugh, Rush; Media Bias; September 11; Vietnam War; *Washington Times, The*; Watergate.

Further Reading

Friel, Howard, and Richard A. Falk. *The Record of the Paper: How the* New York Times *Misreports US Foreign Policy.* New York: Verso, 2004.

Hirschorn, Michael. "End Times." *Atlantic,* January–February 2009.

Morris, Dick. *Off with Their Heads: Traitors, Crooks & Obstructionists in American Politics, Media & Business.* New York: Regan Books, 2003.

New York Times Web site. www.nytimes.com.

Salisbury, Harrison E. *Without Fear or Favor: The* New York Times *and Its Times.* New York: Times Book, 1980.

Talese, Gay. *The Kingdom and the Power. Behind the Scenes at the* New York Times: *The Institution That Influences the World.* New York: Random House Trade Paperbacks, 2007.

Tifft, Susan E., and Alex S. Jones. *The Trust: The Private and Powerful Family Behind the* New York Times. Boston: Little, Brown, 1999.

TimesWatch Web site. www.timeswatch.org.

News Reporting

See Media Bias

Niebuhr, Reinhold

Identified by *Time* magazine in 1950 as "the number one theologian of United States Protestantism," Reinhold Niebuhr spent an academic career critiquing domestic and foreign affairs through the prism of what he called "Christian realism." Ever against any political idea, doctrine, policy, or movement that he regarded as excessively idealistic, naive, unjust, or showing signs of hubris, Niebuhr over the years criticized pacifism, the Christian social gospel, secular liberalism, fascism, the American atomic bombings of Japan, Stalinism, Soviet aggression, McCarthyism, nuclear brinkmanship, southern segregation, and the Vietnam War.

A neo-orthodox Protestant, Niebuhr in his writings, speeches, and sermons offered political analysis and social commentary that were infused with the doctrine of Original Sin and the belief that human beings are incapable of making an ideal society. Yet Niebuhr was not a conservative; he leaned to the left, affiliating for a time with the Socialist Party (1929–1941), embracing many of the tenets of Marxism, and eventually supporting New Deal liberalism. He believed that "children of light" should strive to make the world better even if it will always be less than perfect. As he once concluded, "Democracy is a method of finding proximate solutions for insoluble problems." Niebuhr's "Serenity Prayer" (early 1940s), which became engrained in American popular culture during World War II and the postwar years, expresses such views concerning human limitations. One version reads in part: "God, give us grace / to accept with serenity / the things that cannot be changed, / courage to change the things / that should be changed, / and wisdom to distinguish / the one from the other." The poem was adopted by Alcoholics Anonymous, but Niebuhr's authorship has been called into question— most recently in 2008 by a librarian at Yale University whose research uncovered examples of other individuals reciting similar prayers during the 1930s.

Karl Paul Reinhold "Reinie" Niebuhr, the son of a German immigrant and pastor of the Evangelical Synod (Lutheran), was born on June 21, 1892, in Wright City, Missouri, and grew up in Lincoln, Illinois. After graduating as valedictorian at both Elmhurst College (1910) and Eden Theological Seminary (BD, 1913), near Chicago and St. Louis, respectively, he completed his studies at Yale University (BD, 1914; MA, 1915). A pastorate stint at the Bethel Evangelical Church in Detroit (1915–1928), where Niebuhr supported the cause of the labor movement and denounced the policies of Henry Ford, was followed by a long teaching career at Union Theological Seminary in New York (1928–1960). A prolific essayist, Niebuhr was a regular contributor to the *Christian Century* (1922–1940), the *Nation* (1938–1950), and the *New Leader* (1954–1970). In 1935, he founded *Radical Religion* (later renamed *Christianity and Society*), a journal of current affairs he edited for three decades. In 1941, he founded a second journal, *Christianity and Crisis.*

Niebuhr also wrote nearly twenty books, including *Moral Man and Immoral Society* (1932), a criticism of both secular and religious liberalism; *The Nature and Destiny of Man* (1941, 1943), his central work, which in two volumes presents a theory of history and the human condition; *The Children of Light and the Children of Darkness* (1944), an endorsement of democracy with a warning of its human limitations; and *The Irony of American History*

(1952), a treatise that discusses the inherent weakness of national power. One of his later books, *The Structure of Nations and Empires* (1959), advocated U.S.-Soviet coexistence in the nuclear age.

As a Cold Warrior, Niebuhr quit writing for the *Nation* because he thought its editorials were supportive of Stalinism. He was the first national chairman of the Union for Democratic Action, which in 1947 was renamed the Americans for Democratic Action (ADA), a liberal organization staunchly committed to the Cold War policy of containment against the Soviet Union. He was consequently a booster of the Marshall Plan, believing it was prudent to help Western Europe rebuild after World War II in order to keep it safe for democracy. During the late 1940s, he was a chief adviser to the U.S. State Department's Policy Planning Staff, influencing Cold War strategists such as George Kennan, who called Niebuhr "the father of us all." During this time, Niebuhr also worked closely with the historian Arthur M. Schlesinger, Jr.

Although awarded the Presidential Medal of Freedom in 1964, Niebuhr was the subject of an FBI probe directed by President Richard Nixon after the theologian spoke out against the Vietnam War and expressed support for the civil rights movement. Niebuhr died on June 1, 1971. Today his ideas continue to influence activists on both the left and the right.

Roger Chapman

See also: Civil Rights Movement; Cold War; Graham, Billy; Hiroshima and Nagasaki; Labor Unions; Marxism; *Nation, The*; Nixon, Richard; Nuclear Age; Schlesinger, Arthur M., Jr.; Soviet Union and Russia; Vietnam War.

Further Reading
Brown, Charles C. *Niebuhr and His Age: Reinhold Niebuhr's Prophetic Role in the Twentieth Century.* Philadelphia: Trinity Press International, 1992.
Fox, Richard Wightman. *Reinhold Niebuhr: A Biography.* New York: Pantheon Books, 1985.
Link, Michael. *The Social Philosophy of Reinhold Niebuhr.* Chicago: Adams Press, 1975.
Scott, Nathan A., Jr., ed. *The Legacy of Reinhold Niebuhr.* Chicago: University of Chicago Press, 1975.
Sifton, Elisabeth. *The Serenity Prayer: Faith and Politics in Times of Peace and War.* New York: W.W. Norton, 2003.
Tinsley, E.J., ed. *Reinhold Niebuhr, 1892–1971.* London: Epworth Press, 1973.

Nixon, Richard

One of the most influential and controversial figures in postwar American politics, Republican Richard M. Nixon served as congressman, senator, vice president, and thirty-seventh president of the United States. In 1974, he resigned the presidency to avoid impeachment over his cover-up in the Watergate scandal. A politically polarizing figure and a culture warrior in his own right, Nixon remains a topic of the culture wars into the twenty-first century, as various factions debate the meaning of his presidency and his overall political legacy.

Richard Milhous Nixon was born on January 9, 1913, in Yorba Linda, California, and raised in a financially struggling Quaker household. After attending Whittier College (BA, 1934) and Duke University Law School (JD, 1937), Nixon served in World War II in the U.S. Navy. When the war was over, he returned to California and began his career in politics, winning election to the U.S. House of Representatives (1947–1950) and the U.S. Senate (1950–1953). After two terms as vice president under Dwight D. Eisenhower (1953–1961), Nixon lost the 1960 presidential race to Democrat John F. Kennedy by less than 113,000 votes out of 68 million ballots cast. Two years later, he lost the race for California governor to Democrat Edmund G. "Pat" Brown, only to make an amazing political comeback by twice wining the U.S. presidency (1968 and 1972). On August 9, 1974, Nixon resigned as president. For the remainder of his life he sought to rehabilitate his image and present himself as a statesman. He died on April 22, 1994.

"Red-Baiter" of Liberals

Nixon's various political campaigns shared the same elements: an emphasis on the dangers of America's Cold War enemies and "red-baiting" of liberal opponents. He was first elected to public office in 1946 when he defeated Congressman Jerry Voorhis, a five-term Democratic incumbent from California's Twelfth District. Nixon was catapulted into national celebrity in 1948 when, as a member of the House Committee on Un-American Activities (HUAC), he played an instrumental role in exposing Alger Hiss's connection with the Communist Party while working in the U.S. State Department. Nixon became a hero of the political right and used that momentum to gain a Senate seat. In that campaign he again used a red-baiting strategy, referring to opponent Helen Gahagan Douglas as "pink right down to her underwear." In response, Douglas branded Nixon with the "Tricky Dick" epitaph, which followed him for the rest of his life.

Nixon's popularity among Republicans led to his nomination as Eisenhower's vice-presidential running mate in 1952. However, he was almost removed from the ticket after the media reported his personal use of an $18,000 political "slush fund." He saved his reputation and place on the ticket with a paid televised response—his famous "Checkers Speech"—in which he detailed his household finances and explained that his wife did not

Future Republican president Richard Nixon (far left) achieved national prominence—and a leading role in the culture wars—as a "red-baiting" congressman during the Alger Hiss spy case in 1948. *(James Whitmore/Time & Life Pictures/Getty Images)*

own a fur coat but only a "a respectable Republican cloth coat"; the only political gift he ever accepted, he went on, was a cocker spaniel named Checkers, a dog he was not going to return because his children were attached to it. Perhaps Nixon's most well-known moments as vice president were the stoning of his motorcade during a visit to Venezuela (1958) and the "kitchen debate" he had with Soviet Premier Nikita Khrushchev over capitalism versus communism (1959).

Defeats and Political Comeback

Nixon's plan to move into the Oval Office after the end of Eisenhower's second term was dashed by Kennedy, who narrowly won the 1960 election. Critics charged that the Democrat victory was rooted in voter fraud, while others argued that Nixon's defeat was the result of his poor performance in the country's first televised presidential debate. Television audiences saw two very different politicians during that debate: JFK, who looked "presidential" and directly at the camera; and Nixon, who appeared ashen, unshaven, sweaty, and "shifty-eyed" as he could not decide whether to turn toward the camera or to the man he was addressing. Those who watched the debate on television said JFK had won; radio listeners felt Nixon outdid the young Democrat.

Many believed that Nixon's political career was over after his failed presidential run, which was followed by a losing race for the California governorship in 1962. At his farewell press conference, implying that liberal media bias was to blame for his two defeats, he bitterly told the reporters they would not have Nixon "to kick around anymore." Some commentators have argued that

the lasting effects of those setbacks made Nixon a paranoiac, later leading him to keep an "enemies list" and to resort to illegal campaign tactics in order to maintain an edge over opponents.

As the Vietnam War divided the country, Nixon returned to national politics in 1968 for a second try for the presidency. The Democratic Party was in a deep crisis—suffering infighting over the war and a serious backlash for its advocacy of civil rights legislation and other social programs. While President Lyndon B. Johnson announced that he would not seek reelection and the Democrats remained in disarray, Nixon promised to achieve "peace with honor" in Vietnam and to promote respect for law and order in American society. These two platforms appealed to many war-weary voters who were also unhappy with radical antiwar protests. With the support of "Middle America," Nixon easily defeated Hubert Humphrey in the November election.

Domestic and Foreign Policies

Historians critical of Nixon argue that when he assumed the presidency in 1969 he took advantage of the political and social divisions in the nation to advance his partisan ambitions. Referring to its supporters as the "great silent majority," the Nixon administration dismissed the youth counterculture and antiwar movement as a loud minority that did not represent the values of "real" Americans. At the same time, it was said, Nixon tapped into the resentments of whites by delaying enforcement of civil rights in the South and refusing to endorse school busing. Such policies were often referred to as the Republican Party's "southern strategy," which used issues such as race to appeal to white southern voters in order to gain the electoral edge.

On matters of race, however, Nixon's policies were far nobler than his negative rhetoric. His tenure did see gains in school integration—whereas 68 percent of African-American children in the South and 40 percent in the nation as a whole attended all-black schools in 1968, the figures fell to 8 percent and 12 percent, respectively, only two years later. Nixon also spent significantly on civil rights enforcement, bolstering the Equal Employment Opportunity Commission (EEOC) and the civil rights division of the Justice Department. Whereas civil rights outlays in President Johnson's final budget totaled $911 million, the 1973 budget drafted by Nixon called for $2.6 billion.

Many conservatives look back on Nixon's handling of domestic and economic issues and brand him a liberal. His administration oversaw the creation of the Environmental Protection Agency (EPA) and the National Oceanic and Atmospheric Administration (NOAA); the introduction of automatic cost-of-living adjustments (COLAs) for Social Security recipients; and the establishment of the Supplementary Security Income (SSI), guaranteeing an annual income for the elderly, blind, and disabled. Controversially, Nixon dealt with inflation by instituting wage and price controls, a policy critics regarded as a violation of free-market principles. Under Nixon's watch, for the first time since World War II, federal spending on social programs exceeded expenditures on defense.

As a matter of consensus, Nixon's greatest successes as president came in the area of foreign policy. He and Henry Kissinger, his national security adviser, set upon a policy that fundamentally changed the direction of the Cold War. This included establishing diplomatic relations with China (which some Democrats characterized as a strategy to overshadow the 1972 presidential campaign and strengthen Nixon's reelection chances) and negotiating the first Strategic Arms Limitation Treaty (SALT) with the Soviet Union in 1971. Thus, the Nixon era ushered in détente, a period of reduced tensions between the superpowers. In 1973, after engaging the United States in a secret bombing and invasion of Cambodia, Nixon and Kissinger negotiated the long-awaited end of U.S. involvement in Vietnam. Perhaps only because of Nixon's well-established anticommunist credentials was he able to pursue many of these foreign policies without being labeled an appeaser or simply soft on communism.

Watergate and Rehabilitation

In August 1974, Nixon became the first American president to resign from office, the culmination of the Watergate scandal—the break-in and bugging of the Democratic National Committee headquarters in 1972 and the subsequent cover-up and obstruction of justice by the Nixon White House. Had Nixon not resigned, he surely would have been impeached and most likely would have been removed from office. His subsequent pardon by President Gerald Ford caused an uproar and led to accusations that the two had made a secret deal. Adding to Nixon's disgrace was the decision of Duke University not to allow its campus to be the site of the Nixon Presidential Library. (It would eventually be built in San Clemente, California.)

Nixon did not fade away. In 1977 he collected $1 million for a series of taped interviews conducted by the British television personality David Frost. Although viewers heard Nixon argue that a course of action taken by the president is automatically legal, they also saw him express regret over Watergate. By the end of the decade, following the publication of *RN: The Memoirs of Richard Nixon* (1978), the former president was living in Saddle River, New Jersey, to be near the political elites and news media outlets of the Northeast. Popularly received during travels to Paris, Jidda, and Beijing, Nixon struck the pose of an elder statesman and informally advised presidents from Reagan to Clinton. He also wrote numerous works on foreign affairs, including *The Real War* (1980), *No More Vietnams* (1987), and *Beyond Peace* (1994). At the request of President Ronald Reagan, Nixon in 1981 joined Ford and Carter in representing the United States at the funeral of slain Egyptian leader Anwar Sadat. In 1984, after addressing the American Newspaper Publishers Association, Nixon to his surprise received a standing ovation. The cover of the May 1986 issue of *Newsweek* magazine featured the former president with the title "The Rehabilitation of Nixon."

Nixon's defenders, citing the foreign policy successes of his administration, argue that it is wrong to reduce his presidency to the Watergate scandal. Some conservatives have since blamed Nixon's downfall on "liberals," downplaying the enormity of the abuse of power. Conservative radio commentator Rush Limbaugh has dwelled on the media bias against Nixon. Arguably, the intensification of the culture wars is one of Nixon's major legacies. His White House staff included a number of people who would continue to wage the culture wars in other Republican administrations, including Dick Cheney and Donald Rumsfeld. In addition, Nixon appointed four justices to the U.S. Supreme Court, all of whom played a significant role in shaping the culture wars on issues such as abortion, affirmative action, school prayer, and states' rights. Most significantly, Nixon appointed perhaps the most conservative justice on the bench—William Rehnquist—who for fourteen years had been an associate justice before serving nineteen years as chief justice.

Maria T. Baldwin

See also: Agnew, Spiro T.; Busing, School; China; Cold War; Communists and Communism; Environmental Movement; Hiss, Alger; Judicial Wars; Presidential Pardons; Rehnquist, William H.; Republican Party; Silent Majority; Watergate.

Further Reading

Ambrose, Stephen E. *Nixon*. 3 vols. New York: Simon & Schuster, 1987–1991.

Greenberg, David. *Nixon's Shadow: The History of an Image*. New York: W.W. Norton, 2003.

MacMillan, Margaret. *The Week That Changed the World*. New York: Random House, 2007.

Mitchell, Greg. *Tricky Dick and the Pink Lady: Richard Nixon vs. Helen Gahagan Douglas—Sexual Politics and the Red Scare, 1950*. New York: Random House, 1998.

Nixon, Richard. *RN: The Memoirs of Richard Nixon*. New York: Grosset & Dunlap, 1978.

Reston, James, Jr. *The Conviction of Richard Nixon: The Untold Story of the Frost/Nixon Interviews*. New York: Harmony Books, 2007.

Norquist, Grover

As founder and executive director of the antitax lobbying group Americans for Tax Reform, established in 1985,

Grover Norquist has worked to prompt elected officials to cut taxes for the ultimate goal of decreasing the size of the federal government. The New Deal, he argues, has left a negative legacy of an oversized public sector that has put a drag on the economy and hampered individual freedom. As Norquist has said, "I don't want to abolish government. I simply want to reduce it to the size where I can drag it into the bathroom and drown it in the bathtub." Critics maintain that Norquist's antitax campaign has led to growing budget deficits, a reduction in the quality of life, and a widening of the wealth gap.

The son of a senior executive at Polaroid, Grover Glenn Norquist was born on October 19, 1956, and grew up in the Boston suburb of Weston. His interest in conservative politics took shape during the Cold War, when at age thirteen he read J. Edgar Hoover's book on communism, *Masters of Deceit* (1958), and Whittaker Chambers's autobiography, *Witness* (1952). His father also instilled in him an outrage over taxes. Norquist attended Harvard University, earning a bachelor's degree in economics (1978) and a master's degree in business administration (1981).

As a graduate student, Norquist volunteered in Ronald Reagan's presidential campaign, in the experience befriending Jack Abramoff, the future K Street lobbyist and convicted felon who was then a student at Brandeis University. He later helped Abramoff get elected chairman of the College Republicans. In 1985, Norquist established his niche at Americans for Tax Reform, an advocacy group in step with the philosophy of the Reagan administration.

Norquist claims credit for President George H.W. Bush's reelection defeat in 1992, declaring that it was retribution for breaking a promise not to raise taxes. Since then, his group has persuaded many candidates, including George W. Bush, to sign pledges not to increase taxes. Representative Newt Gingrich (R-GA) consulted with Norquist when crafting the Contract with America in 1994. Since then, Norquist has helped maintain a broad conservative coalition. Over the years his "Wednesday meetings" in Washington, D.C., attracted many prominent conservative activists and elected officials for strategizing policy and tactics. He has dubbed his political network the Leave Me Alone Coalition, explaining that the glue that bonds the disparate factions is the desire for less government intrusion.

Roger Chapman

See also: Bush Family; Chambers, Whittaker; Contract with America; Federal Budget Deficit; Hoover, J. Edgar; New Deal; Reagan, Ronald; Social Security; Tax Reform; Wealth Gap.

Further Reading

Americans for Tax Reform Web site. www.atr.org.

Cassidy, John. "The Ringleader." *The New Yorker*, August 1, 2005.

Easton, Nina J. *Gang of Five: Leaders at the Center of the Conservative Crusade*. New York: Simon & Schuster, 2000.

Norquist, Grover. *Leave Us Alone: Getting the Government's Hands Off of Our Money, Our Guns, Our Lives*. New York: W. Morrow, 2008.

North, Oliver

Marine lieutenant colonel Oliver North, Jr., achieved notoriety during the televised Iran-Contra hearings in the summer of 1987 and went on to a career as a conservative political commentator and aspirant to elective office. A little-known member of the National Security Council (NSC) during the Ronald Reagan administration, Lieutenant Colonel North was implicated as a key player in a scandal that was a direct defiance of a federal law not to fund the Contras, or counterrevolutionaries, fighting to overthrow the leftist Sandinista government in Nicaragua.

The son of middle-class parents, Oliver Laurence "Larry" North, Jr., was born in San Antonio, Texas, on October 7, 1943. After studying at the State University of New York at Brockport (1961–1963), he attended the U.S. Naval Academy (BS, 1968). North saw combat in Vietnam (1968–1969) and was awarded the Silver Star, Bronze Star, and two Purple Hearts for his service. In November 1986, "Ollie," as President Ronald Reagan called him, resigned his post along with the head of the NSC, Vice Admiral John Poindexter, when U.S. Attorney General Edwin Meese announced that sophisticated weapons systems had been sold to Iran and that money from the sales had been diverted to buy weapons for the Contras. Earlier, because the Contras had attacked Nicaraguan civilians and were charged with human rights abuses, Congress had cut off U.S. military aid.

Lieutenant Colonel Oliver North (left, with his attorney) testifies before congressional investigators in the Iran-Contra hearings of July 1987. Criminally convicted for his role in the affair, North was viewed by many as a scapegoat and by some as a hero. *(Chris Wilkins/AFP/Getty Images)*

When congressional hearings investigating the scandal were carried live on television, the media spotlight glowed favorably over North, who just as easily could have been cast as the villain. Portrayed as the heroic, battle-weary soldier—media professionals described him as "fascinating"—North was successful at deflecting criticism for his role in the scandal, and the public generally viewed him as a scapegoat. Although North admitted to supplying the Contras in defiance of the congressional ban—action that was not only illegal but unconstitutional—his three felony convictions were overturned on a technicality because he had been granted immunity for his testimony before Congress.

North later founded a company that manufactures bulletproof vests and promoted his folk-hero status by writing an account of his military career, *Under Fire: An American Story* (1991). During the 1994 election, he was an unsuccessful Republican candidate for a U.S. Senate seat in Virginia, challenging Democratic incumbent Chuck Robb. Filmmakers were given access to North's campaign, and the subsequent documentary, *A Perfect Candidate* (1996), features scenes of North expressing his born-again faith juxtaposed with footage of cynical political strategists plotting to use rumors of drugs and infidelity against Robb. During the campaign, North caused an uproar when he asserted that President Reagan all along "knew everything" about the diversion of funds to the Contras. Although North lost a close race, he reaffirmed his image as affable war hero and devoted family man. North went on to host *Common Sense*, a right-wing radio talk show on Radio America (1995–2003), and *War Stories with Oliver North* (2001–), a military history series on the Fox News Channel. In addition to appearing regularly on Fox as a political commentator, he has been a syndicated columnist, featured public speaker, and co-author of action novels.

Robin Andersen

See also: American Civil Liberties Union; Cold War; Human Rights; Iran-Contra Affair; Presidential Pardons; Reagan, Ronald.

Further Reading
Andersen, Robin. *A Century of Media, A Century of War.* New York: Peter Lang, 2006.
Fried, Amy. *Muffled Echoes: Oliver North and the Politics of Public Opinion.* New York: Columbia University Press, 1997.
Meyer, Peter. *Defiant Patriot: The Life and Exploits of Lt. Colonel Oliver L. North.* New York: St. Martin's Press, 1987.
Pasternak, Douglas. "Oliver North's New Crusade." *U.S. News & World Report,* June 6, 1994.

Not Dead Yet

The disability rights activist group Not Dead Yet was founded by Diane Coleman on April 27, 1996, after euthanasia advocate Jack Kevorkian was acquitted of murder charges in the deaths of two women with disabilities whom he had helped to commit suicide. Not Dead Yet believes that legalized euthanasia will lead to pressure to end the lives of people with disabilities. The group positioned itself against the Hemlock Society (since renamed Compassion and Choices), which has sought broadening assisted suicide laws to apply to people with nonterminal disabilities.

The controversy associated with Not Dead Yet intensified because of its alliance with conservative religious groups in opposing euthanasia. The Terri Schiavo controversy galvanized this alignment in 1998. Schiavo, who had collapsed in her home in 1990 and was diagnosed as being in an irreversible persistent vegetative state, became the center of a dispute involving her husband's decision to remove her feeding tube. He argued that it was what his wife would have wanted, despite the absence of a living will. Her parents argued that because she was Catholic, she would be opposed to euthanasia. Not Dead Yet filed *amicus* (friend of the court) briefs on behalf of the parents, advancing a disability rights position and denouncing the work of bioethicist Peter Singer, who has argued that the lives of cognitively impaired people are of lesser value than the lives of those who are unimpaired. After various appeals courts supported her husband's decision, Schiavo's feeding tube was removed in 2005, and she died almost two weeks later.

In response to depictions in the critically acclaimed films *Million Dollar Baby* (2004) and *The Sea Inside* (2004), Not Dead Yet challenged the notion that disability is worse than death. The group staged demonstrations at the Chicago Film Critics Association awards and the Oscar ceremonies, sparking public debate. As in the Schiavo controversy, however, much of the disability rights message was drowned out by broader arguments between social conservatives and liberals.

Not Yet Dead also took a stand against Oregon's Death with Dignity Act, in which state voters legalized physician-assisted suicide in 1994. The group supported federal legal attempts to overturn the law, but the U.S. Supreme Court upheld the measure in *Gonzales v. Oregon* (2006). Not Dead Yet criticized the Bush administration for failing to challenge the law from a disability rights perspective.

Laura Hague

See also: Abortion; Bush Family; Catholic Church; Kevorkian, Jack; Operation Rescue; Right to Die; Schiavo, Terri.

Further Reading
Fleischer, Doris Zames, and Freida Fleischer. *The Disability Rights Movement: From Charity to Confrontation.* Philadelphia: Temple University Press, 2001.

Nuclear Age

The $2.2 billion Manhattan Project, which developed the atomic bombs used against Japan on August 6 and 9, 1945, brought World War II to a close while ushering in the nuclear age. At the same time, it laid the groundwork for the Cold War and the mammoth U.S. military-industrial complex, including nuclear research and development, all of which shaped postwar domestic politics and contributed to the culture wars.

Big Science

The making of the atomic bomb represented the partnership of the scientific community and the federal government, involving some 120,000 individuals. Although considerably downsized after the war, work continued at national laboratories in Los Alamos, New Mexico; Oak Ridge, Tennessee; and other sites used during the Manhattan Project. The federal commitment in this field meant that 60 percent of college physics programs in 1949 were financed by the U.S. government. Merle Tuve, an American physicist who during the 1940s had quit working in nuclear research because it had become "a business," challenged the system with his 1959 *Saturday Review* essay "Is Science Too Big for the Scientist?" The year prior marked the establishment of the National Aeronautics and Space Administration (NASA), which headed rocket research and the manned space program. When President Dwight Eisenhower left office in 1961, he warned of a military-industrial complex, which included NASA and the nuclear industry. Alvin Weinberg, the director of the Oak Ridge lab from 1955 to 1973, coined the negative term "big science" in reference to expensive ongoing programs involving applied research for primarily warfare purposes. Weinberg's *Reflections on Big Science* (1967) warned that these colossal projects have the potential of bankrupting society. It has been estimated that from the time of the Manhattan Project to the end of the Cold War the United States spent $5.5 trillion on its nuclear arsenal.

Americans at first were proud of the atomic bomb, regarding the mushroom cloud as a symbol of progress and modernity. However, ambivalence and social tensions were apparent early on. As the country-and-western song "When the Atomic Bomb Fell" (1945) celebrated the defeat of the "cruel Jap," the U.S. Army was dismissing reports of radiation sickness at Hiroshima and Nagasaki as "Jap propaganda." The following year, the Hollywood docudrama *The Beginning or the End* portrayed the physicists of the Manhattan Project as heroes for saving lives by bringing the war to a speedy conclusion, while John Hersey's nonfiction work *Hiroshima* presented a sobering account of the human suffering caused by the first bomb dropped on Japan. Indignant about the way government officials were downplaying the dangers of atomic science,

a group of Manhattan Project researchers in 1945 formed the Federation of Atomic Scientists (FAS)—soon renamed the Federation of American Scientists—and resorted to fear tactics in an attempt to convince the public that nuclear weapons should be placed under international control. According to historian Paul Boyer, the "politicization of fear" the scientists introduced backfired and ultimately led to a nuclear arms race.

Doomsday Clock

In 1946, Bernard Baruch, the U.S. representative to the United Nations Atomic Energy Commission, submitted a plan (called the Baruch Plan) to create an international agency that would oversee all production facilities and research pertaining to atomic energy. This seemed exactly what the FAS wanted, but some observers saw the proposal as a ploy simply to make the Soviet Union look bad. Under the Baruch Plan, the United States would agree to turn over its atomic weaponry and open its pertinent research laboratories to international inspectors on the condition that other countries, including the Soviet Union, be subject to UN inspections as well. All nuclear activities would have to be licensed by the UN. In other words, the U.S. government wanted to prevent all other countries from breaking its nuclear monopoly.

Although the UN General Assembly passed the Baruch Plan, the Soviet Union vetoed it when the measure came before the Security Council. At the time, the Soviets were busy at work secretly developing an atomic bomb. With hopes for international control of atomic energy dashed, the FAS the following year began publishing the *Bulletin of the Atomic Scientists* in an effort to lift the veil of military secrecy and prompt public debate on the hazards of the nuclear age, something the scientists felt was not happening despite the creation of the U.S. Atomic Energy Commission (1946), which purportedly placed atomic energy under civilian control. The June 1947 issue of the *Bulletin* introduced the so-called Doomsday Clock, showing how many "minutes before midnight," or nuclear tragedy, the world stood. After the Soviet Union detonated its first atomic bomb on August 29, 1949, the clock was set at three minutes to midnight.

On April 5, 1951, Judge Irving Kaufman sentenced Julius and Ethel Rosenberg to death for passing atomic secrets to the Soviet Union, blaming them for "putting into the hands of the Russians the A-bomb years before our best scientists predicted Russia would" and emboldening the communists to start the Korean War. Earlier that year, the Federal Civil Defense Administration was established with the goal of establishing a nationwide fallout shelter program. In 1952, schoolchildren began watching the film *Duck and Cover* to learn how to dive under school desks during a sudden atomic attack. On November 1, 1952, the United States exploded a hydrogen bomb at Enewetak Atoll in the Pacific, pushing the Doomsday Clock up to two minutes to midnight. The Soviet Union responded with its own hydrogen bomb on August 12, 1953.

H-Bomb to Nuclear Treaties

The H-bomb introduced a new wave of nuclear protest, led by physicist Albert Einstein, philosopher Bertrand Russell, and Pope Pius XII. Following a U.S. test explosion on March 1, 1954, at Bikini Atoll in Micronesia, nuclear fallout spread across the Pacific in areas that had not been cleared of shipping due to a shift in the winds. Consequently, twenty-three crew members of the Japanese fishing trawler *Lucky Dragon* suffered from radiation poisoning that resulted in one fatality. "Our fate menaces all mankind," said one of the fishermen as he was being treated at the hospital. Fear and fascination about nuclear war and nuclear fallout were expressed in a number of popular novels—Dexter Masters's *The Accident* (1955), Nevil Shute's *On the Beach* (1957), and Walter M. Miller, Jr.'s *A Canticle for Leibowitz* (1959)—and movies—*The Incredible Shrinking Man* (1957), *Attack of the Crab Monsters* (1957), and *H-Man* (1958). Meanwhile, in June 1957, *Saturday Review* editor Norman Cousins and others established the National Committee for a Sane Nuclear Policy (SANE), urging a halt to nuclear testing. In 1958, others tried to disrupt nuclear tests by sailing ships into the Pacific proving grounds. Albert Bigelow, a former U.S. naval commander, was arrested as he headed *The Golden Rule* toward the forbidden waters, but Earle Reynolds managed to enter the area with his ship, *Phoenix of Hiroshima.*

In 1954, the United States focused its attention on a nuclear delivery system, developing the B-52 long-range bomber. By 1956, nearly 2,000 bombers with 7,000 nuclear bombs were at the American ready. The new trend, however, was missile technology with nuclear warheads. This is why the successful Soviet launching of *Sputnik* in October 1957 greatly alarmed Americans. John F. Kennedy campaigned for president on the perception that there was a "missile gap" between the Soviets and the Americans, even though in 1960 the United States introduced the nuclear-powered ballistic missile submarine, capable of launching a nuclear strike from the ocean depths. Later, in October 1962, the two superpowers had a tense standoff over medium-range missiles the Soviets had set up in Cuba to counter the U.S. long-range missile capability. After the Cuban Missile Crisis, there was a relaxing of tensions between Washington and Moscow, marked by the 1963 signing of a partial test-ban treaty that henceforth restricted nuclear testing to below ground.

With the specter of the mushroom cloud seeming to fade, anxiety about the nuclear age subsided somewhat. The inherent danger remained very much alive in public consciousness, however, as reflected in the dark, satirical humor of Stanley Kubrick's film *Dr. Strangelove, or: How I Learned to Stop Worrying and Love the Bomb* (1964). The politicization of fear in regard to atomic weaponry inspired the first television campaign attack ad. On September 7, 1964, the Lyndon B. Johnson presidential campaign ran the minute-long "daisy ad" on NBC's *Monday Night at the Movies.* The commercial showed a little girl standing in a meadow, plucking petals from a daisy while counting aloud. At a given point, her voice melds into that of a man counting down to a nuclear explosion. "These are the stakes," a message at the end warns. "To make a world in which all of God's children can live, or to go into the dark. We must either love each other, or die." Although the spot did not mention the name Barry Goldwater, the Republic presidential candidate, it was clear that he was being construed as an extremist who might unleash nuclear war. Republicans and others objected to the ad, which was run only once but played numerous times as a news story.

Meanwhile, efforts to halt nuclear proliferation led to the Nuclear Non-Proliferation Treaty of 1968, signed by the five nuclear powers at the time—the United States, the Soviet Union, Great Britain, France, and China—as well as 140 non-nuclear countries (excluding Israel, India, Pakistan, and North Korea, all of which later became nuclear powers). In 1972, the Nixon administration negotiated with the Soviets the first Strategic Arms Limitation Treaty (SALT), establishing limits on missiles and bombers that deliver nuclear weapons to their targets. Further limits on delivery systems were imposed by SALT II (1979), which the U.S. Senate refused to ratify but was nonetheless followed by both the Carter and Reagan administrations.

Reagan to Yucca

By the 1980s, the two superpowers possessed a total of 50,000 nuclear weapons, more than enough for mutual destruction. All the bombs dropped during World War II were the equivalent of 3 megatons (equal to 3 million tons of TNT), while in 1983 the combined U.S.-Soviet nuclear arsenal represented 15,000 megatons. Despite these figures, Ronald Reagan campaigned for the presidency in part to modernize America's nuclear arsenal. The nation's nuclear capability should not be based on deterrence, he contended, but on defeating the enemy. As president, Reagan authorized 100 MX missiles, called for the development of the Trident submarine (each capable of carrying 24 missiles with a total of 336 warheads), reactivated plans for the B-1 bomber (which President Jimmy Carter had canceled), and announced a long-term space-based ballistic missile defense system called the Strategic Defense Initiative. These developments alarmed many observers and emboldened a popular nuclear-freeze movement, which began in Europe and spread to New England town meetings. The dangers of the nuclear age were underscored by the radioactive fallout across Europe from the 1986 explosion of the Chernobyl nuclear power station in the Soviet Union. Eventually, Reagan and his Soviet counterpart, General Secretary Mikhail Gorbachev, negotiated the Intermediate-Range Nuclear Forces Agreement (1987).

In the years after Reagan, the two superpowers agreed to the first Strategic Arms Reduction Treaty (START) in 1991, followed by START II in 1993. The Comprehensive Test Ban Treaty of 1996, which was signed by 71 nations (including Russia), bans all forms of nuclear testing, but the U.S. Senate refused to ratify it. Ever since the demise of the Soviet Union, concerns have been raised that Russian "loose nukes" might fall into the hands of terrorists, prompting the U.S. government to allocate funds to help Russia decommission its old atomic supply. After the terrorist attacks of September 11, 2001, U.S. officials reiterated their concern that a "dirty bomb" could be constructed out of Cold War–era nuclear material and detonated in a highly populated area, spreading lethal levels of radiation. In addition, the United States recommitted itself to missile defense.

Meanwhile, environmentalists have been concerned about the problem of nuclear waste. As of 2008, nuclear waste was being stored at 121 temporary sites in nearly forty states. Plans were made for the Yucca Mountain underground storage facility in Nevada, located about 90 miles (145 kilometers) northwest of Las Vegas, to be opened by 1986 for the purpose of burying the spent nuclear fuel and radioactive waste from the nation's 104 nuclear reactors as well as material waste from the military nuclear weaponry. (Each year the reactors produce 2,000 metric tons of spent fuel.) More recently, the U.S. Department of Energy, which oversees the project, projected a 2020 operation date for the facility. As of 2008, the estimated cost of the facility was $96.2 billion—up from $57.5 billion seven years earlier. Residents of Nevada and a number of elected officials and politicians have opposed the opening of the Yucca site.

Roger Chapman

See also: Cold War; Communists and Communism; Cuba; *Enola Gay* Exhibit; Hiroshima and Nagasaki; Johnson, Lyndon B.; Kubrick, Stanley; Oppenheimer, J. Robert; Postmodernism; Science Wars; Soviet Union and Russia; Strategic Defense Initiative; Teller, Edward; Three Mile Island Accident; War Protesters.

Further Reading

Boyer, Paul. *Fallout: A Historian Reflects on America's Half-Century Encounter with Nuclear Weapons.* Columbus: Ohio State University Press, 1994.

Bulletin of Atomic Scientists Web site. www.thebulletin.org.

DeGroot, Gerard J. *The Bomb: A History.* Cambridge: Harvard University Press, 2005.

Hughes, Jeff. *The Manhattan Project: Big Science and the Atomic Bomb.* New York: Columbia University Press, 2002.

Newton, David E. *Nuclear Power.* New York: Facts On File, 2006.

Schwartz, Stephen. *Atomic Audit: The Costs and Consequences of U.S. Nuclear Weapons Since 1940.* Washington, DC: Brookings Institution Press, 1998.

Zeman, Scott C., and Michael A. Amundson. *Atomic Culture: How We Learned to Stop Worrying and Love the Bomb.* Boulder: University Press of Colorado, 2004.

Obama, Barack

The first African American to be elected president of the United States, Barack Obama achieved his 2008 victory running as a self-described post-partisan candidate with a left-of-center message emphasizing "change" and "hope." In that election, coinciding with two protracted wars and the worst economic crisis since the Great Depression, the Democrats not only won the White House but significantly expanded their majority in both houses of Congress. Some commentators immediately predicted that the election would go down in history as on par with the political realignments of 1932 and 1980. "Emphatically, comprehensively," the *New Yorker* editorialized, "the public has turned against conservatism at home and neoconservatism abroad."

Obama became the forty-fourth president by defeating Senator John McCain (R-AZ), garnering nearly 53 percent of the popular vote and carrying the swing states of Ohio and Florida as well as such traditional red states as Virginia, North Carolina, and Indiana. In the end, Obama and his running mate, Joe Biden (the long-time senator from Delaware), won the Electoral College by 365–173 votes. This had been preceded by Obama's surprising defeat of Senator Hillary Clinton (D-NY) in a hotly contested Democratic primary.

Early Life and Career

The son of a Kenyan father and white American mother, Barack Hussein Obama was born on August 4, 1961, in Honolulu, Hawaii. When Obama was two, his parents separated and the father eventually returned to Africa. Obama spent part of his childhood in Djakarta, Indonesia (1967–1971), where his mother remarried, this time to an Indonesian. Obama was later raised by his maternal grandparents in Hawaii, where, going by the name of Barry, he attended the Punahou Academy prep school. He went on to study at Occidental University in Los Angeles (1979–1981) and then transferred to Columbia University in New York (BA, political science, 1983). Following graduation, Obama briefly worked on Wall Street before moving to Chicago, where he was a community organizer.

After attending Harvard Law School (JD, 1991), where he served as the first black president of the *Harvard Law Review*, Obama returned to Illinois and directed PROJECT VOTE! (1992). He also joined a private law firm, published an autobiography, *Dreams from My Father: A Story of Race and Inheritance* (1995), lectured at the University of Chicago, and served in the Illinois Senate (1997–2005). As a state senator, he sponsored legislation

for tax credits to the working poor and a measure that mandated videotaping of all interrogations conducted by state and local police forces. In 2000, he lost a primary race for Congress against Democratic incumbent Bobby Rush, a prominent civil rights leader. In 2004, Obama won an open U.S. Senate seat, defeating the conservative Republican Alan Keyes.

Obama's unlikely trajectory to the White House began with a 2004 keynote address at the Democratic National Convention. In that speech he deplored the culture wars, asserting that there is only one United States of America, not "a liberal America and a conservative America" and not "a black America and white America and Latino America and Asian America." He called on Americans to turn from the "politics of cynicism" and to participate in the "the politics of hope." This post-partisan message was the theme of his presidential run, which was launched two years later with the publication of his second book, *The Audacity of Hope: Thoughts on Reclaiming the American Dream* (2006).

Contentious Democratic Primary

In the Democratic primary, Obama criticized Clinton, his main opponent, for her 2002 vote sanctioning the invasion of Iraq. Although not a U.S. senator at the time, he was publicly against that war from the onset. As a presidential candidate, he called for a phased withdrawal of U.S. troops from Iraq. Clinton, who refused to concede defeat until the very end, said the freshman senator did not have enough experience to be commander in chief. Obama's supporters argued that their candidate would be "more electable" in the general election than Clinton, whom they viewed as politically polarizing. After the election, Clinton was appointed secretary of state in the Obama administration.

Obama's early campaigning was given a boost by the active support of Oprah Winfrey, the black television talk show host, who rallied voters during the Iowa caucus and South Carolina primary. As Obama's campaign rallies drew throngs of people who were buoyed by his eloquent speeches calling for political "change," critics dismissed his "feel good" messages as lacking in substance.

Throughout the campaign, Obama faced attacks that suggested he was un-American. Certain detractors referred to him as "Osama" (alluding to Osama bin Laden, the al-Qaeda leader who masterminded the terrorist attacks of September 11, 2001) and emphasized his middle name (Hussein, like the name of the late Iraqi dictator). Some conservative conspiracy theorists on the Internet and talk radio communicated the notion that Obama was a secret Muslim, perhaps even an al-Qaeda "Trojan horse." *The New Yorker*, in its cover cartoon of July 21, 2008, offered a satirical depiction of such fear, presenting the candidate in a robe and turban giving a fist bump to his wife, Michelle, who was dressed as a rifle-toting black radical. Supporters of Obama cried foul over the magazine's sense of political humor, arguing that some readers would take the drawing literally.

In the primary as well as the general election, the issue of race was raised frequently. After Clinton had spoken of the courageous accomplishment of President Lyndon Johnson in signing the Civil Rights Act of 1964, claiming that she would be that kind of forward-thinking president, Obama accused her of dismissing the efforts of the civil rights activists. Geraldine Ferraro, the Democratic vice-presidential nominee in 1984 and a Hillary supporter, suggested that Obama was receiving preferential treatment because of his race: "If Obama was a white man, he would not be in this position. And if he was a woman of any color, he would not be in this position." When criticized for her comments, Ferraro retorted, "Every time that campaign is upset about something, they call it racist. I will not be discriminated against because I'm white." Rush Limbaugh, the king of conservative talk radio, satirized white supporters of Obama with the song "Barack the Magic Negro," belittling them for supposing the election of a black president would assuage their guilt over slavery and other past wrongs. Civil rights activists such as the Reverend Jesse Jackson thought Obama was catering too much to white voters, but the candidate saw himself as part of the "Joshua Generation" of the civil rights movement, meaning a new kind of black leader for a new period.

At one point the spotlight focused on some inflammatory statements of the Reverend Jeremiah Wright, the preacher at the Chicago church the Obamas had attended for many years. In one controversial sermon on racial injustice, Wright shouted, "God damn America!" Many began to ask how Obama could be a follower of such a spiritual leader. To diffuse the situation, on March 18, 2008, Obama gave a speech on race in America titled "A More Perfect Union" at the National Constitutional Center in Philadelphia, disagreeing with Wright (calling his remarks "distorted") but refusing to disown him (although Obama later withdrew his church membership). Obama was praised by many for daring to candidly address the complexities of race, especially by sharing how his white grandmother, who raised him during his teenage years and loved him deeply, sometimes feared blacks. In that speech, Obama compared his mixed-race background to the larger American experience "that out of many, we are truly one."

A New Era

The strategy Obama used in defeating McCain was to link him with the policies of President George W. Bush. Desperate for political traction, McCain picked Sarah Palin, the popular conservative governor of Alaska, as his running mate. Pro-life, pro-gun, and Pentecostal, Palin temporarily breathed new life into McCain's campaign as the Religious Right rallied around her. For a short while, the McCain-Palin ticket actually led in the polls, but the momentum stalled after the vice-presidential nominee became a national laughingstock following some bungled television interviews. Obama, in the meantime, benefited by endorsements from Colin Powell, a former secretary of state under Bush, and writer Christopher Buckley, son of the late conservative icon William F. Buckley, Jr.

As the campaign peaked, the economy tanked and a financial crisis unfolded, which Obama blamed on years of Republican deregulation. During the last presidential debate, McCain tried to reenergize his campaign by calling attention to "Joe the Plumber," a voter and small businessman in Ohio who had challenged Obama's plan to increase taxes on the wealthy. Meanwhile, Palin heated up the culture wars by referring to her small-town supporters as the "real America" and pointing out that Obama had earlier referred to rural Americans who cling to religious fundamentalism and guns as "bitter." Obama weathered these and other attacks by accusing his opponents of having no fresh ideas, but simply the old politics of fear.

On inauguration day, Obama declared a new era that would "set aside childish things." The inaugural address was viewed by many as a repudiation of eight years of Bush. "On this day, we gather because we have chosen hope over fear, unity of purpose over conflict and discord," said the new president. "On this day, we come to proclaim an end to the petty grievances and false promises, the recriminations and worn-out dogmas that for too long have strangled our politics." The speech, critics said afterward, was hardly post-partisan.

Roger Chapman

See also: Clinton, Hillary; Democratic Party; Election of 2008; Ferraro, Geraldine; Limbaugh, Rush; McCain, John; Neoconservatism; Palin, Sarah; Race; Red and Blue States.

Further Reading

Asim, Jabari. *What Obama Means—For Our Culture, Our Politics, Our Future.* New York: William Morrow, 2009.

Corsi, Jerome. *The Obama Nation: Leftist Politics and the Cult of Personality.* New York: Threshold Editions/Simon & Schuster, 2008.

Ifill, Gwen. *The Breakthrough: Politics and Race in the Age of Obama.* New York: Doubleday, 2009.

Lizza, Ryan. "Battle Plans." *The New Yorker,* November 17, 2008.

Obama, Barack. *The Audacity of Hope: Thoughts on Reclaiming the American Dream.* New York: Crown Publishers, 2006.

———. *Dreams from My Father: A Story of Race and Inheritance.* New York: Three Rivers Press, 1995.

Silverstein, Ken. "Useful Idiots." *Harper's Magazine,* November 2008.

Obesity Epidemic

Since the mid-1990s, alarm in scientific circles and popular discourse over what has been called "the obesity epidemic" and "the obesity crisis" have coincided with the concern of health officials over the increasing body weight of Americans. In 2003, U.S. Surgeon General Richard H. Carmona, concerned that fewer young people were meeting the physical fitness standards required of military recruits, declared obesity a threat to U.S. national security more dire than weapons of mass destruction. Although there is general agreement that Americans today are larger than those of previous generations, following a global trend, not everyone accepts "obesity" as a meaningful scientific categorization. Furthermore, regardless of any health risks posed by obesity, unanimity is lacking on what, if any, response is warranted on the part of individuals, the government, or the medical profession. Since a higher percentage of the poor, among them African Americans and Hispanics, tend to be overweight, some critics of anti-obesity campaigns view them as racial or class snobbery, especially since being overweight is often stereotypically linked with lack of discipline. Opinions about obesity often fall into two warring camps: one focuses on public health measures for the common good, and the other emphasizes freedom of choice and individual responsibility.

Obesity is generally defined in terms of the body mass index (BMI), calculated by dividing weight in kilograms by the square of height in meters (BMI = kg/m^2). For adults age twenty and older, a person with a BMI of less than 18.5 is classified as underweight, 18.5–24.9 as normal weight, 25.0–29.9 as overweight, 30–39.9 as obese, and 40 and over as morbidly obese. For an adult who is 5 feet and 6 inches (168 centimeters) tall, a normal body weight would be in the range of 118–160 pounds (54–73 kilos), while a weight of 216 pounds (98 kilos) or more would be considered obese. Of course, these categories are somewhat arbitrary—Why should 159 pounds (72 kilos) be considered normal and 161 pounds (73 kilos) overweight? BMI can also be misleading, as in the case of professional athletes who would be classified as overweight or obese because they are extremely muscular. For children and adolescents age nineteen and younger, growth charts are used to evaluate a child's weight-to-height ratio in relation to children of the same age and sex.

According to the U.S. Centers for Disease Control and Prevention (CDC), more than one-third of American adults were obese in 2006, double the percentage reported in 1980. Among U.S. children and adolescents (ages two to nineteen), obesity tripled between 1980 and 2002. In the view of most doctors, these statistics are cause for concern because obesity is generally associated with increased risk for many diseases as well as premature death. However, other researchers question whether obesity per se is a health risk, noting that it is prevalent in social groups (such as nonwhites and the poor) that have less access to health care, lead more stressful lives, and so on. Furthermore, while a 2004 study showed that obesity was second only to smoking as a cause of excess mortality, a study three years later suggested that overweight individuals were actually at lower risk of mortality than their normal-weight counterparts.

Some blame increased obesity on a "toxic environment" in which unhealthy and fattening foods are readily available. This view has led to a number of lawsuits, the first filed in New York in 2002, claiming that fast-food producers should bear some responsibility for the weight gain and ill health suffered by those who order from their menus, analogous to claims against tobacco companies for the health problems of smokers. Although none of these suits had been successful, the U.S. House of Representatives in 2004 and 2005 approved the Personal Responsibility in Food Consumption Act (known as the "Cheeseburger Act") to shield the food industry and restaurants from liability claims by obese customers. Although the Senate let the bill die on both occasions, more than a dozen states, beginning with Louisiana in 2003, passed their own "cheeseburger laws." Meanwhile, in 2006, the board of health in New York City unanimously passed an ordinance requiring restaurants to phase out artificial trans fats in the food they serve, arousing the ire of the National Restaurant Association. In 2008, California passed a law requiring restaurant chains to include food-calorie information on menus.

The concern about childhood obesity, heightened by the recommendation of the American Academy of Pediatrics to routinely screen individuals nineteen years and younger for weight problems, has led some school districts to begin reporting children's BMI to parents, as was mandated in Arkansas in 2003. Although motivated by a concern for children's health and welfare, BMI reports have been criticized for overemphasizing a single health measure at the risk of stigmatizing children who otherwise may outgrow being overweight, and providing insufficient contextual information for parents. Organizations such as Commercial Alert and the Kaiser Family Foundation have recommended a ban on "junk food" advertising to children and limitations on snack foods and soft drinks sold in schools. Although campaigns to prohibit television or print advertising have been unsuccessful, California, West Virginia, Colorado, Connecticut, and Texas have instituted restrictions on the sale of unhealthy food and drinks in school buildings.

The debate on diet and personal responsibility was intensified by the release of the documentary *Super Size Me* (2004), which portrayed filmmaker Morgan Spurlock gaining 24 pounds (11 kilos) and seriously impairing his health after only a month of eating three meals a day at McDonald's. Although McDonald's discontinued its "SuperSize" meals due to negative publicity surrounding *Super Size Me*, many viewers took issue with the film's claim that fast food is inherently unhealthy. Other documentaries—including *Bowling for Morgan* (2004), made by Scott Caswell, and *Me and Mickey D* (2005), made by Soso Waley, an adjunct of the Competitive Enterprise Institute—offered the counterargument that a person may eat fast food and stay healthy, emphasizing the personal responsibility of the consumer in making intelligent choices.

The Center for Science in the Public Interest and the World Health Organization have endorsed special taxes on fast food, analogous to the taxes on soft drinks and snack foods that already exist in eighteen states and the District of Columbia. Efforts to tax fast-food chains have not been successful, however, partly because of the difficulty of defining what constitutes fast food—for instance, taxing a salad at McDonald's but not a hamburger at a formal restaurant is inconsistent. In addition, a fast-food tax has been criticized as interfering with individual freedom of choice and of disproportionately penalizing the poor.

Sarah Boslaugh

See also: Health Care; McCarthyism; Tobacco Settlements.

Further Reading

Brownell, Kelly D., and Katherine Battle Horgan. *Food Fight: The Inside Story of the Food Industry, America's Obesity Crisis, and What We Can Do About It.* New York: McGraw-Hill, 2003.

Campos, Paul. *The Obesity Myth: Why America's Obsession with Weight Is Hazardous to Your Health.* New York: Penguin, 2004.

Critser, Greg. *Fat Land: How Americans Became the Fattest People in the World.* Boston: Houghton Mifflin, 2003.

Metcalf, Tom, and Gena Metcalf. *Obesity.* Detroit, MI: Thomson/Gale, 2008.

Oliver, J. Eric. "The Politics of Pathology: How Obesity Became an Epidemic Disease." *Perspectives in Biology and Medicine* 49:4 (August 2006): 611–27.

Occupational Safety

When President Richard Nixon signed the Occupational Safety and Health Act into law on December 29, 1970, he hailed the legislation as "the American system at its best." The act established the Occupational Safety and Health Administration (OSHA) "to assure so far as possible every working man and woman in the Nation safe and healthful working conditions." Over the years, OSHA has come to symbolize the rift between those who look to the government to protect individuals and those who advocate a more libertarian society. In 2008, with more than 2,100 personnel and an operating budget of over $490 million, OSHA conducted nearly 40,000 workplace inspections for the purpose of enforcing worker safety.

Occupational safety mandated by the government dates back to the 1870s, when Massachusetts passed laws for industrial safety. In 1913, the federal government became involved in improving working conditions with the establishment of the U.S. Department of Labor. Later, the passage of the Walsh-Healey Act (1936) gave government contract workers certain protections, including workplace safety and sanitation standards. The Fair Labor Standards Act (1938) implicitly promoted worker safety by limiting the work week to forty-four hours and restricting child labor. In response to a number of accidents at coal mines, Congress passed the Federal Coal Mine Safety Act (1952). After television journalist Edward R. Murrow aired the documentary *Harvest of Shame* (1960), detailing the harsh working conditions of migrant farm workers, Congress passed the Migrant Health Act (1962). All of this set the stage for OSHA, which was designed to build on existing laws and efforts at both the federal and state levels.

As an independent agency under the Department of Labor, OSHA works in concert with its research and education arm, the National Institute for Occupational Safety and Health (NIOSH), the latter an independent agency under the Department of Health and Human Services. The idea for federal regulatory bodies to improve occupational safety was proposed in 1968 by President Lyndon B. Johnson. At a time when the Vietnam War was raging, it was argued that the American workplace, averaging about 15,000 deaths, 7 million injuries, and 2 million disabilities annually, was exacting a heavier toll than the battlefields of Southeast Asia. Critics of OSHA later suggested that the decline in fatal on-the-job accidents was a trend well under way prior to federal involvement in occupational safety. In 1979, the U.S. Chamber of Commerce complained that fatal injuries on the job increased by 24 percent from 1976 to 1977, adding that businesses were forced to spend $25 billion between 1972 and 1979 to comply with "piles of more OSHA rules and paperwork." In actuality, the 1977 spike of 5,560 work-related deaths was considerably lower than the pre-OSHA figures.

After its first full year of operation, OSHA in 1973 was vilified by conservatives as an intolerable government intrusion on private enterprise. While the John Birch Society launched a flamboyant "Put OSHA Out of Business" campaign, arguing that the regulatory body was the first step toward the nationalization of the economy (in other words, communism), alarmist business leaders argued that "OSHAcrats" were violating the privacy of corporations by conducting workplace inspections. In reaction to the outrage of the business community, Congress introduced numerous bills to scale back OSHA. During the Reagan administration Thorne Auchter, a construction executive whose firm had been previously cited for safety violations, was put in charge of OSHA, prompting the consumer advocate Ralph Nader to declare the agency "shackled."

Over the years, critics have blamed OSHA for driving up the cost of doing business while reducing worker productivity. According to the findings of a 1987 study by Clark University economist Wayne B. Gray, about 30 percent of the overall drop in productivity experienced by the American manufacturing sector during the period 1958–1978 was the consequence of governmental regulation. However, proponents of federal oversight of occupational safety—in accord with the OSHA maxim "Safety is good business"—noted that in 2006 alone American employers paid $48.6 billion for job-related injuries, a business expense that could be reduced by improving worker safety. Conservatives, on the other hand, insist that they believe in safety just as strongly but think the matter should be left to voluntary compliance because businesses know more about their work environments than OSHA "desk jockeys" do. Business executives often complain that OSHA regulations fail to consider the unique situation of each workplace and instead issue "one size fits all" regulations. OSHA inspectors, critics charge, issue fines to companies that fail to meet some obscure regulation yet otherwise have an excellent safety record. In 2006, OSHA issued fines totaling about $85 million.

While OSHA and NIOSH have given serious attention to worker exposure to uranium, lead, cotton dust, coal dust, asbestos, and chemicals, the most common OSHA violation pertains to scaffolding safety—the cause of 9,000 citations issued in 2006. Meanwhile, reducing repetitive stress injuries has been an ongoing concern of OSHA and NIOSH. Such injuries are common to workers in jobs that require the same motion over and over—it has been estimated that nearly four out of ten workers suffer from this kind of injury. With the advent of computers and more jobs requiring keyboarding, repetitive stress injuries have risen in recent years. In response, OSHA has emphasized ergonomic solutions, involving the design and placement of machinery and equipment. In March 2001, arguing that implementation costs would be too financially burdensome for businesses, Congress and President George W. Bush rescinded OSHA regulations that would have introduced comprehensive ergonomics in the workplace.

Roger Chapman

See also: Bush Family; John Birch Society; Johnson, Lyndon B.; Labor Unions; Migrant Labor; Murrow, Edward R.; Nader, Ralph; Nixon, Richard; Reagan, Ronald; Smoking in Public.

Further Reading

Cullen, Lisa. *A Job to Die For: Why So Many Americans Are Killed, Injured or Made Ill at Work and What to Do About It.* Monroe, ME: Common Courage Press, 2002.
Gray, Wayne B. "The Cost of Regulation: OSHA, EPA, and the Productivity Slowdown." *American Economic Review* 77:5 (December 1987): 998–1006.
Mintz, Benjamin W. *OSHA: History, Law, and Policy.* Washington, DC: Bureau of National Affairs, 1984.
Occupational Safety and Health Administration Web site. www.osha.gov.

O'Connor, Sandra Day

The first woman to serve as a justice of the U.S. Supreme Court, Sandra Day O'Connor was born on March 26, 1930, in El Paso, Texas. She grew up on a cattle ranch in southeastern Arizona and graduated from Stanford University with a BA in economics in 1950. Two years later, she earned a law degree from Stanford Law School, where she served on the *Stanford Law Review* and graduated near the top of her class (which included future chief justice William Rehnquist).

When O'Connor embarked on a career, law was extremely male dominated, and California law firms were unwilling to hire her, offering her only a position as a secretary. Turning to public service, she became deputy county attorney of San Mateo County, California (1952–1953), and later a civilian attorney for Quartermaster Market Center in Frankfurt, Germany (1954–1957). She practiced law in the Phoenix area before serving as the state's assistant attorney general (1965–1969), a stint that ended when she was appointed to the Arizona State Senate. A Republican, she served as a senator until 1975, when she was elected judge of the Maricopa County Superior Court. Four years later, she was appointed to the Arizona Court of Appeals. On August 19, 1981, upholding a campaign promise to appoint the first woman to the U.S. Supreme Court, President Ronald Reagan nominated O'Connor. A month later, the Senate unanimously confirmed her appointment.

As an associate justice on the Supreme Court, O'Connor was the object of criticism from diverse interest groups. Her approach was simple: She considered each case narrowly. She tried to limit the generality of her decisions, which would allow more latitude in future, similar cases. It was difficult to extrapolate broad ideological interpretations from her decisions because they tended to be restricted to the narrow confines of the specific issue before the Court.

Women's organizations were disappointed that O'Connor would not advance the cause of women's rights more ardently. Many more were troubled because O'Connor's votes on abortion cases were clearly pro-life. Her abortion decisions—particularly *Planned Parenthood v. Casey* (1992), which narrowed the right to abortion by striking down provisions of a Pennsylvania state law—are regarded as her most controversial.

Conservatives and Republicans were dismayed by

some of O'Connor's decisions. Because she was appointed by Reagan and a registered Republican, they felt confident that she would regularly side with them. As the Court became more conservative, O'Connor emerged as a centrist. She was often the deciding vote and was in the majority more often than any of her cohorts. Conservatives were particularly disappointed by her decision in *Lawrence v. Texas* (2003), in which the Court deemed unconstitutional a Texas law that made homosexual sodomy a crime.

On July 1, 2005, O'Connor announced she would retire upon the confirmation of a successor to the bench. Originally, she was to be replaced by John Roberts, Jr., but the unexpected death of Rehnquist that September prompted President George W. Bush to renominate Roberts for the chief justice position. O'Connor delayed her retirement until the January 31, 2006, confirmation of Samuel Alito. Shortly after leaving the bench, in a speech at Georgetown University, she criticized Republican leaders who had been calling for judicial reform and warned that the lack of an independent judiciary is the hallmark of a dictatorship.

James W. Stoutenborough

See also: Abortion; Bush Family; Coulter, Ann; Gay Rights Movement; Judicial Wars; Planned Parenthood; Reagan, Ronald; Rehnquist, William H.; Sodomy Laws.

Further Reading

Biskupic, Joan. *Sandra Day O'Connor: How the First Woman on the Supreme Court Became Its Most Influential Justice.* New York: Ecco, 2005.

Chemerinsky, Erwin. "The O'Connor Legacy." *Trial* 41:9 (2005): 68–69.

Herda, D.J. *Sandra Day O'Connor: Independent Thinker.* Springfield, NJ: Enslow, 1995.

O'Connor, Sandra Day. *The Majesty of the Law: Reflections of a Supreme Court Justice.* New York: Random House, 2003.

O'Hair, Madalyn Murray

A key figure in the battle over the separation of church and state, who was branded by *Life* magazine in 1964 as the "most hated woman in America," Madalyn Murray O'Hair served as the public face of American atheism from the 1960s to her disappearance and death in 1995.

Born Madalyn Mays on April 13, 1919, in Beechview, Pennsylvania, she was a U.S. Army cryptographer during World War II, attended Ashland College in Ohio (BA, 1948) and South Texas College of Law (JD, 1952), and began a career as a social worker.

While living in Baltimore in the early 1960s, O'Hair filed a lawsuit protesting religious observances in her son

William's school. The case went all the way to the U.S. Supreme Court, which ruled in her favor in *Murray v. Curlett* (1963), holding that school-sponsored prayer and Bible study were to be prohibited in all public schools. In the late 1970s, however, her bid to have the words "In God We Trust" removed from the national currency failed. In the midst of these struggles, O'Hair founded American Atheists as a civil liberties organization for nonbelievers. As the lifetime leader of American Atheists, she produced a radio program to spread her views and became involved in a number of lawsuits policing the appearance of religion in the public sphere.

In 1980, William O'Hair became a born-again Christian, sparking a series of mutual renunciations between son and mother. Like the later religious conversion of Norma McCorvey ("Jane Roe" of the landmark 1973 *Roe v. Wade* ruling affirming a woman's right to an abortion), William's conversion was invoked by the Religious Right in their public relations strategy of reaching out to "victims" of liberal elitism and judicial activism. O'Hair was a contentious figure among secular progressives and within the community of atheist activists, many of whom regarded her as a fractious, ill-mannered militant.

After the August 1995 disappearance of O'Hair from her home in Austin, Texas, rumors circulated that she had left the country or that she had died and her children were involved in a cover-up so that William could not subject his mother to the indignity of a Christian funeral. Slowly, evidence surfaced that ex-convict David Roland Waters, who had been loosely involved with American Atheists, had kidnapped and killed O'Hair, her son Jon, and her granddaughter Robin in order to steal over $500,000 in gold coins. After her death, e-mail messages perpetuated a rumor, which first began in 1975, that O'Hair was petitioning the Federal Communications Commission to ban all religious references from television programming.

Jason Mellard

See also: American Civil Religion; Church and State; Cold War; Conspiracy Theories; Evangelicalism; Federal Communications Commission; Fundamentalism, Religious; Judicial Wars; *Roe v. Wade* (1973); School Prayer; Secular Humanism; Ten Commandments.

Further Reading

Dracos, Ted. *Ungodly: The Passions, Torrents, and Murder of Atheist Madalyn Murray O'Hair.* New York: Free Press, 2003.

Le Beau, Bryan. *The Atheist: Madalyn Murray O'Hair.* New York: New York University Press, 2003.

Seaman, Ann Rowe. *America's Most Hated Woman: The Life and Gruesome Death of Madalyn Murray O'Hair.* Harrisburg, PA: Continuum International, 2005.

O.J. Simpson Trial

The 1995 murder trial of former football star, actor, and television commentator O.J. Simpson revealed an abiding racial polarization in American society and brought fundamental issues of race and crime to the forefront of national discourse.

On June 12, 1994, Nicole Brown Simpson, the former wife of O.J. Simpson, and friend Ron Goldman were murdered in front of her condominium residence in the Brentwood section of Los Angeles. Police soon began to view O.J. Simpson as a suspect. After being formally charged on June 17, Simpson and friend Al Cowlings fled Los Angeles in his vehicle, a Ford Bronco. After being spotted in Orange County, he led a phalanx of police cars in a nationally televised low-speed chase that ended up back at Simpson's own house.

On July 22, Simpson pleaded "absolutely not guilty" to the murders, and on January 24, 1995, after months of jury selection and legal maneuvering, the trial got under way. The prosecution presented evidence that Simpson had physically abused Nicole during their marriage and contended that the abuse had escalated, culminating in the murders. Since there were no witnesses, confession, or fingerprints (a single bloody fingerprint was not detected in time to be included in the trial) and the murder weapon was never found, the prosecution's case was based purely on circumstantial evidence. In such instances, the prosecution must not only prove its case "beyond a reasonable doubt," but it must also disprove any plausible theory of innocence.

According to the defense team, a racist detective of the Los Angeles Police Department (LAPD), Mark Fuhrman, disapproved of Simpson's marriage to a white woman and moved incriminating evidence—a bloody glove—from the murder scene to Simpson's home. To establish this, the defense invoked past racial statements by Fuhrman and noted that he had been the one to discover many of the key pieces of evidence in the case. On cross-examination, defense attorney F. Lee Bailey got Fuhrman to deny that he had ever used the "N word" ("nigger") in the past ten years. Later in the trial, the defense presented tape recordings of recent conversations in which Fuhrman used the word frequently, expressed a general hostility toward blacks, and discussed planting evidence and framing men in interracial relationships. Fuhrman invoked the Fifth Amendment when asked if he had planted evidence in the Simpson case.

The prosecution was ill prepared to counter this strategy, having built its case on the volume of circumstantial evidence amassed against Simpson. This included a trail of blood extending from Nicole's house to Simpson's car to Simpson's property, and all the way inside his house up to his bedroom. Among the most incriminating evidence was a mixture of O.J. Simpson's blood and Goldman's blood found inside the defendant's car. Testing also revealed that

The highly publicized double-murder trial of former football star O.J. Simpson in 1995 divided the nation along racial lines: African Americans felt that justice was served by the "not guilty" verdict; whites were convinced that Simpson had committed the crimes. *(Vince Bucci/AFP/Getty Images)*

carpet fibers found on Goldman's body were identical to the carpet in Simpson's car, and that fewer than 100 carpets like that existed. Because of a procedural error by the prosecution, however, the jury never heard the carpet evidence.

Critics of the not-guilty verdict—rendered on October 2, 1995, after just three hours of jury deliberation—blamed the outcome on various missteps by Judge Lance Ito and prosecutors. One crucial decision by Ito was to exclude from the jury anyone who read a newspaper. Critics contended that this ensured a jury with a low intelligence level that would not be able to understand the complex scientific evidence about DNA that was central to the case.

By virtually all accounts, race was a central element in the trial, its coverage in the media, and Simpson's acquittal. Many observers believed that the lead prosecutor, Marcia Clark, was ill suited to try the case. Once it was established that the jury would be composed primarily of black women, research by the prosecution's own focus group found that black women in general did not like Clark, who was white, and did not subscribe to her domestic violence theory of the murders. Despite this, no effort was made to replace Clark or alter the prosecution's theory of the case. Meanwhile, realizing the racial implications of the jury composition and the police misconduct theory, the defense replaced lead counsel Robert Shapiro with Johnnie Cochran, a prominent black lawyer. Clark was also admonished by her critics for failing to establish rapport with the jury and, at one point, for going three months without examining a witness. Also in terms of the racial dynamic, Clark's informal banter with co-counsel Christopher Darden, who was black, was believed by some observers to have been alienating to the black women on the jury. The jury itself—sequestered in isolation for the duration of the trial—was paralyzed by infighting, some of which involved racial issues, even during the testimony phase.

The announcement of the final verdict polarized the country along clear racial lines. Blacks cheered for what they regarded as a repudiation of racially driven police misconduct; whites were stunned to silence over what they regarded as the exoneration of a brutal killer.

In a civil trial for wrongful death brought by the families of the two victims, Simpson was found liable in February 1997 and ordered to pay $33.5 million in damages. The reversal of outcome was widely explained by the lower standard of proof required to find against the defendant in a civil case ("a preponderance of the evidence") than in a criminal case ("beyond a reasonable doubt") and by differences in nuance, if not substance, in witness testimony.

A new controversy erupted in late 2006 after ReganBooks announced that it would publish a book by Simpson—prospectively titled *If I Did It*—in which he offered an account of how he "might" have carried out the murders. In response to public outrage, Rupert Murdoch, the owner of the publishing house, stopped the project. Simpson denied that the book was a confession to the crime, but he did concede that he was trying to capitalize on it—reigniting the outrage of those who believed he got away with murder. In August 2007, a Florida court awarded publication rights to the family of Ron Goldman as partial payment for Simpson's unpaid civil judgment. The book was finally published later that year under the title *If I Did It: Confessions of the Killer*, with comments by the Goldman family.

In September 2007, Simpson was arrested for leading a raid and armed robbery at a casino hotel in Las Vegas, Nevada. Simpson claimed that he was retrieving stolen sports memorabilia that belonged to him. Later, a jury found him guilty of twelve felony counts. In December 2008, a Clark County District Court judge sentenced Simpson, then age sixty-one, to a prison sentence of nine to thirty-three years. Jackie Glass, the presiding judge, publicly stated that neither the jury nor the court had been influenced by the 1995 murder trial.

Tony L. Hill and Roger Chapman

See also: Morrison, Toni; Murdoch, Rupert; Race.

Further Reading

Bosco, Joseph. *A Problem of Evidence: How the Prosecution Freed O.J. Simpson.* New York: William Morrow, 1996.

Bugliosi, Vincent. *Outrage: The Five Reasons Why O.J. Simpson Got Away with Murder.* New York: W.W. Norton, 1996.

Riccio, Thomas J. *Busted! The Inside Story of the World of Sports Memorabilia, O.J. Simpson, and the Vegas Arrests.* Beverly Hills, CA: Phoenix Books, 2008.

Spence, Gerry. *O.J.: The Last Word.* New York: St. Martin's Press, 1997.

Toobin, Jeffrey. *The Run of His Life: The People v. O.J. Simpson.* New York: Random House, 1996.

Operation Rescue

Operation Rescue, a Christian Fundamentalist direct-action organization, uses graphic imagery, civil disobedience, and intimidation tactics in a campaign to prevent abortion in America. Between 1986 and 1994, the group's "rescues" were some of the most high-profile examples of militant civil disobedience by the Religious Right. Operation Rescue argues that they are doing God-inspired work to prevent a "holocaust of unborn children." They regard abortion as a perversion of God's law that is indicative of a catastrophic diminution of biblical morality in society.

Randall Terry, a born-again charismatic Christian, founded the group in 1986 in Binghamton, New York, and led it through its most controversial early years. Operation Rescue protesters used confrontation, intimidation, and physical harassment to prevent women and doctors from entering abortion clinics. Terry was arrested several times, once for arranging to have an aborted fetus delivered to presidential candidate Bill Clinton at the 1992 Democratic National Convention. A *Washington Post* report estimated that over 40,000 people were arrested in Operation Rescue demonstrations between 1986 and 1990, one of the highest incarceration rates of any social movement organization in American history.

After the mid-1990s, deep internal dissent, mounting legal costs, prison sentences, and leadership strife led to organizational splintering. Some members began to employ increasingly violent tactics. Several were convicted in the slayings of abortion clinic doctors, nurses, employees, and volunteers. Finally, Congress passed the 1994 Freedom of Access to Clinic Entrances Act, which prohibits the use of intimidation or physical force to discourage people from gaining access to reproductive health care facilities.

Renamed Operation Save America (to distinguish it from various local Operation Rescue splinter groups, the organization carries on with a lower profile, maintaining an active Web site, producing exposés on abortion providers, and organizing prayer vigils outside clinics. In 1995, Norma McCorvey ("Jane Roe" in the 1973 Supreme Court case upholding a woman's right to have an abortion, *Roe v. Wade*) became a member of Operation Save America and was baptized by its leader, Reverend Phillip Benham.

Operation Rescue has had critics across the political

spectrum. Within the anti-abortion movement, some fear that the group's inflammatory statements and illegal tactics have drawn too much negative attention to the pro-life cause. Pro-choice critics argue that the group's ranks are filled with dangerous zealots whose tactics create a climate of fear that severely compromises women's legal right to obtain a safe, medically supervised abortion. Both sides agree that Operation Rescue's protests and tactics created a chilling effect on the available pool of medical personnel willing to perform abortions. Social and cultural analysts of abortion in American politics tend to focus on Operation Rescue's seminal role in pushing Christian Fundamentalism into national politics and contributing to a "culture of violence" and a highly polarized discourse between pro-life and pro-choice camps.

Steve G. Hoffman

See also: Abortion; Clinton, Bill; Evangelicalism; Family Values; Fundamentalism, Religious; Religious Right; *Roe v. Wade* (1973); Rudolph, Eric.

Further Reading

Blanchard, Dallas. *The Anti-Abortion Movement and the Rise of the Religious Right: From Polite to Fiery Protest.* New York: Twayne, 1994.
Ginsburg, F.D. "Rescuing the Nation: Operation Rescue and the Rise of Anti-Abortion Militance." In *Abortion Wars: A Half Century of Struggle, 1950–2000,* ed. Rickie Solinger, 227–250. Berkeley: University of California Press, 1998.
Maxwell, J.C. *Pro-Life Activists in America: Meaning, Motivation, and Direct Action.* Cambridge, MA: Cambridge University Press, 2002.
Risen, James, and Judy L. Thomas. *Wrath of Angels: The American Abortion War.* New York: Basic Books, 1998.

Oppenheimer, J. Robert

The American nuclear physicist J. Robert Oppenheimer directed the Los Alamos National Laboratory for the Manhattan Project during World War II and oversaw the production of the atomic bombs dropped on Japan in August 1945. During the Cold War in the early 1950s, in response to Oppenheimer's prior communist affiliation, his open opposition to development of the thermonuclear weapon (hydrogen bomb), and his support for international controls of atomic weapons, a federal "loyalty" board stripped him of his security clearance.

Julius Robert Oppenheimer, born on April 22, 1904, in New York City, graduated from Harvard University (1925), did postgraduate work at the Cavendish Laboratory in Cambridge, England, and received his PhD in physics from the University of Göttingen (1927) in Germany. There, he studied under the prominent physicist Max Born and met Werner Heisenberg, later the director

of the Nazis' short-lived nuclear weapons program at the Kaiser-Wilhelm Institute. Oppenheimer taught at the University of California, Berkeley, and the California Institute of Technology (1929–1947), taking leave to serve as director at Los Alamos in New Mexico (1943–1945). After the war, Oppenheimer served as director of the Institute for Advanced Study at Princeton University (1947–1966). For his role in developing the weapons that forced the Japanese surrender, Oppenheimer was given the Army-Navy Excellence Award (1945) and the Presidential Medal of Merit (1946).

As director of the Manhattan Project during the war, Oppenheimer was decisive in recruiting scientists and engineers, acquiring materials, and developing the neutron-splitting fission weapons that would dramatically escalate the destructive capacity of America's weapons. Despite his postwar antinuclear activism, while at Los Alamos he believed scientists should implement government directives and avoid influencing policy. He disallowed the circulation of physicist Leo Szilard's petition recommending vaguely defined conditional-surrender terms prior to using uranium- or plutonium-based weapons in the Pacific War. Within months of the end of the war, however, Oppenheimer acknowledged the "sin" of the physicists who had developed the atomic bomb. In a 1965 television broadcast, Oppenheimer repeated the lamentation from the Hindu *Bhagavad Gita* that he had uttered after the initial atomic-test explosion: "Now I am become death, the destroyer of worlds."

During the McCarthy era, Oppenheimer became a target of national security elites advocating modernization of America's nuclear arsenal and a confrontational containment policy. Oppenheimer was serving as chair of the General Advisory Committee of the Atomic Energy Commission (AEC) in October 1949 when he advised against development of the hydrogen bomb. That recommendation, as well as previous associations with the Popular Front and Communist Party (though he was never a member), led to speculation—stoked by FBI director J. Edgar Hoover—that he was a security risk. When President Dwight D. Eisenhower asked him to resign, Oppenheimer requested a formal hearing. Based in part on the testimony of physicist Edward Teller, a chief advocate of the hydrogen bomb, the AEC Personnel Security Board ruled in 1954 to revoke Oppenheimer's security clearance, despite finding him "a loyal citizen" who had violated no laws. A catalyst of the nuclear age, as well as one of its most controversial figures, Oppenheimer died of throat cancer on February 18, 1967.

Peter N. Kirstein

See also: Cold War; Communists and Communism; *Enola Gay* Exhibit; Hiroshima and Nagasaki; LeMay, Curtis; McCarthyism; Nuclear Age; Science Wars; Teller, Edward.

Further Reading

Bernstein, Jeremy. *Oppenheimer: Portrait of an Enigma*. Chicago: Ivan R. Dee, 2004.

Bird, Kai, and Martin J. Sherwin. *American Prometheus: The Triumph and Tragedy of J. Robert Oppenheimer*. New York: Alfred A. Knopf, 2005.

McMillan, Patricia J. *The Ruin of J. Robert Oppenheimer and the Birth of the Modern Arms Race*. New York: Viking, 2005.

Strout, Cushing, ed. *Conscience, Science, and Security: The Case of Dr. J. Robert Oppenheimer*. Chicago: Rand McNally, 1963.

O'Reilly, Bill

Television and radio personality, columnist, and author Bill O'Reilly has contributed to the culture wars by hosting the Fox News Channel program *The O'Reilly Factor* (1996–), which became the highest-rated news show on cable television. A self-described "culture warrior," O'Reilly places himself at the center of what he regards as a war between "traditionalists" and "secular-progressives." His frequent targets include the American Civil Liberties Union (ACLU), the *New York Times*, Hollywood, and the likes of philanthropist and political activist George Soros. O'Reilly defines his traditional principles as opposition to abortion, immigration rights, the death penalty, sex education, same-sex marriage, and the separation of church and state; and support for the War on Terror, limited government, greater privatization (in particular, of schools), and the use of coerced interrogation of suspected terrorists. Critics such as comedian and political commentator Al Franken, in his book *Lies and the Lying Liars Who Tell Them* (2003), accuse O'Reilly of misrepresenting and fabricating the truth. O'Reilly has likewise been condemned for his practice of shouting down guests and cutting off their microphones when they disagree with him.

The son of an accountant, William James "Bill" O'Reilly, Jr., was born into an Irish Catholic family on September 10, 1949, in Manhattan, New York, and was raised in nearby Long Island. He studied at Marist College (BA, history, 1971), Boston University (MA, broadcast journalism, 1975), and Harvard University's Kennedy School of Government (MA, public administration, 1995). After briefly teaching history and English at the Jesuit-run Monsignor Edward Pace High School in Opalocka, Florida (1971–1973), O'Reilly retooled himself and began a broadcasting career at WNEP-TV in Scranton, Pennsylvania. During the 1980s, after years of reporting local television news at some half-dozen locations across the country and winning two Emmys, he became a reporter at the network level at ABC and CBS. O'Reilly had his first popular success anchoring the syndicated entertainment program *Inside Edition* in 1989.

His show on the Fox News Channel, originally called *The O'Reilly Report*, coincided with Roger Ailes's launch of the station itself for Australian News Corp owner Rupert Murdoch in 1996. Ailes, a former Republican consultant who worked in the presidential campaigns of Richard Nixon, Ronald Reagan, and George H.W. Bush, made a concerted effort to offer a conservative news alternative to the three major networks (ABC, CBS, and NBC). O'Reilly's program harmonized with that overall mission. By the 2000 election, *The O'Reilly Factor* was at the top of cable news ratings. By 2007, in its eleventh year, the show was drawing an audience of several million viewers per night.

The O'Reilly Factor relies on the personality of its host for its appeal. O'Reilly presents himself as a righteously opinionated working-class hero taking on the intellectual elites, declaring his show a "no-spin zone." He frequently responds to negative e-mail and letters on the air, and uses his "unpopularity" to bolster his image as an underdog. Specifically geared to counter a perceived left-leaning bias in the media, *The O'Reilly Factor* provides a predominantly but not exclusively conservative editorial perspective. In 2002, O'Reilly began hosting *The Radio Factor*, a daily afternoon radio program that soon was heard on more than 400 stations. He has produced a weekly syndicated newspaper column and has written several books, including the best-seller *The O'Reilly Factor: The Good, the Bad, & the Completely Ridiculous in American Life* (2000), *Culture Warrior* (2006), and *A Bold Fresh Piece of Humanity* (2008).

Critics cry foul over O'Reilly's lack of concrete evidence at times, citing his presentation of blatantly untrue information. The media watch group FAIR (Fairness and Accuracy in Reporting) calls O'Reilly the "most biased name in news," and Media Matters named him its "Misinformer of the Year" in 2004. The Media Matters Web site also lists specious claims from *The O'Reilly Factor*, including a statement that a woman could "never" be "in danger" from pregnancy complications, incorrect statistics on the dropout rates for black students, and labeling the American Civil Liberties Union (ACLU) "a terrorist group."

A particularly notable example of O'Reilly's on-air style was seen on February 4, 2003. His guest was Jeremy Glick, whose father had been killed in the World Trade Center attacks on September 11, 2001. When Glick surprised O'Reilly by suggesting that some of the blame for 9/11 fell on the foreign policy of Republicans, Bill's characteristic shouting ("I've done more for the 9-11 families . . . than you will ever hope to do . . .") and baiting ("I hope your mom isn't watching this . . .") failed to rile Glick. After repeatedly screaming at the bereaved Glick to "shut up," O'Reilly cut off his microphone.

In 2004, a sex harassment suit filed against O'Reilly by one of his producers, Andrea Mackris, was settled for an undisclosed amount. Controversy surrounding the incident raised O'Reilly's audience ratings by as much as one-third during the week the settlement was announced.

Sue Salinger

See also: Abortion; American Civil Liberties Union; Capital Punishment; Christmas; Church and State; Media Bias; Privatization; Republican Party; Same-Sex Marriage; September 11; Sex Education; Sexual Harassment; Soros, George.

Further Reading
Hart, Peter, and Fairness and Accuracy in Reporting (FAIR). *The Oh Really? Factor: Unspinning Fox News Channel's Bill O'Reilly.* New York: Seven Stories Press, 2003.

Kitman, Marvin. *The Man Who Would Not Shut Up: The Rise of Bill O'Reilly.* New York: St. Martin's Press, 2007.

Lemann, Nicholas. "Fear Factor." *The New Yorker*, March 27, 2006.

O'Reilly, Bill. *Culture Warrior.* New York: Broadway Books, 2006.

Outing

Outing is the act of publicly exposing the sexual orientation of a gay person without his or her consent—it is short for taking someone "out of the closet." Outing might also include identifying individuals living with HIV or AIDS. Since publicly proclaiming one's homosexual identity is considered a very private and personal decision, members of the gay, lesbian, bisexual, transgender, and queer (GLBTQ) community, including the gay press and national gay political and social organizations, generally oppose outing in strong terms. Some argue, on the other hand, that outing may be necessary for advancing gay rights in certain circumstances.

Although outing began as a political tactic to garner national funding for AIDS education and awareness, opponents emphasize that it irresponsibly exposes individuals to potential antigay violence and stigma due to the fear of AIDS. Homosexuals, they argue, have the right to remain closeted in order to avoid personal harm or harassment. In the armed forces, outing can ruin the subject's military career because the Don't Ask, Don't Tell policy prohibits gays and lesbians from serving. More complicated is the issue of gay identity, which some view as self-ascribed and not solely a matter of same-sex activities. Proponents of outing, however, invoke the cause of gay liberation, arguing that homosexuals will never reach full political and personal freedom until their numbers are revealed and people no longer fear coming out of the closet.

In the late 1980s and early 1990s, journalist Michelangelo Signorile, in the weekly gay and lesbian magazine *OutWeek*, outed a number of public figures, including multimillionaire and publishing tycoon Malcolm Forbes, the son of conservative political activist Phyllis Schlafly, and news correspondent Pete Williams. Signorile provided one of the first intellectual arguments justifying outing as a way to diminish homophobia in American society. To respect the rights of the closeted celebrity, he contended, is to respect homophobia. Others, both conservatives and liberals, have used outing for political purposes, to topple gays from power, or to expose the hypocrisy of the closeted gay who publicly opposes gay rights. In the case of the latter, in 2004 gay rights activist Michael Rogers outed Congressman Edward Schrock (R-VA), who was on record against same-sex marriage and gays serving in the military.

Mary Cheney, the lesbian daughter of Vice President Dick Cheney, became the target of numerous gay activist groups who accused her of forsaking gay rights in order to run her father's reelection campaign in 2004. In particular, she was criticized for remaining silent after the Bush administration backed a constitutional amendment banning same-sex marriage—the Web site DearMary.com, spoofing a missing child notice, posted a photo of her on a milk carton under the title, "Have you seen me?" In 2004, Democratic presidential candidate John Kerry was criticized for outing Mary Cheney when he mentioned her sexual orientation during a televised debate, even though it was already public knowledge.

Beginning in 2006, the sexuality of popular celebrities became a hot topic within the Internet blogging community. In short succession, Mario Lavandeira of PerezHilton.com outed three Hollywood celebrities—Lance Bass, Neil Patrick Harris, and T.R. Knight. All three publicly admitted to being gay after the site attacked them for remaining closeted. While some argue that the visibility of homosexuals in popular culture helps others who are dealing with their own sexuality, others argue that there is a big difference between outing a celebrity who is just living his or her life and outing politicians who affect public policy.

Elizabeth M. Matelski

See also: AIDS; Cheney Family; Gay Rights Movement; Gays in the Military; Gays in Popular Culture; Kerry, John; Lesbians; Privacy Rights; Same-Sex Marriage; Transgender Movement.

Further Reading
Gross, Larry. *Contested Closets: The Politics and Ethics of Outing.* Minneapolis: University of Minnesota Press, 1993.

Johansson, Warren, and William A. Percy. *Outing: Shattering the Conspiracy of Silence.* New York: Haworth Press, 1994.

Mohr, Richard D. *Gay Ideas: Outing and Other Controversies.* Boston: Beacon Press, 1992.

Signorile, Michelangelo. *Queer in America: Sex, the Media, and the Closets of Power.* New York: Random House, 1993.

Packwood, Bob

Republican politician Bob Packwood served twenty-six years as a U.S. senator from Oregon (1969–1995) before resigning in the wake of a sexual harassment scandal. Known for being independent minded, Packwood was a leader of upholding woman's reproductive rights and environmental causes, voted against the confirmation of Clarence Thomas to the U.S. Supreme Court in 1991, and was the only senator in 1993 to vote against mandatory life sentences for people convicted of a third violent felony.

Born Robert William Packwood in Portland, Oregon, on September 11, 1932, he attended Willamette University in Salem, Oregon (1950–1954), and New York University School of Law (1954–1957). Packwood had a private law practice in Oregon from 1957 to 1963 and was a member of the Oregon state legislature from 1963 to 1968. During his tenure in the U.S. Senate, he served as chair of the Republican Senatorial Campaign Committee, the Republican Conference, and the Committee on Finance, and he was a member of the Committee on Commerce, Science, and Transportation.

Oregon voters, who largely viewed Packwood as a man of principle, became disenchanted with him following allegations of his unwanted sexual advances toward at least twenty-nine women. When the *Washington Post* first broke the story in November 1992, Packwood denied the allegations and went so far as to attempt to discredit his accusers. He postponed giving requested evidence (a personal diary) to the Senate Ethics Committee until after the 1992 election. Later, when hard evidence was presented, he claimed not to remember the incidents because of alcohol abuse. Women's groups that had once supported him, such as the National Organization for Women, lobbied for his resignation. The report of the Senate Ethics Committee confirmed the allegations as well as the fact that Packwood had altered evidence relevant to the committee's inquiry. Packwood resigned in disgrace effective October 1, 1995. He then founded Sunrise Research Corporation, a lobbying firm, and played a key role in the 2001 fight to repeal the estate tax.

Packwood's role in the culture wars centered on the contradiction between his professional actions and his personal behavior. By choosing not to confirm Clarence Thomas, who had been accused of sexual harassment, to the U.S. Supreme Court, Packwood enforced a standard of personal conduct he could not meet. He also profited from his misconduct by publishing *Senator Bob Packwood's Secret Diary* (1994).

Cyndi Boyce

See also: Abortion; Clinton Impeachment; Hill, Anita; Thomas, Clarence.

Further Reading
Kirchmeir, Mark. *Packwood: The Public and Private Life from Acclaim to Outrage.* New York: HarperCollins, 1994.

Paglia, Camille

Social critic, writer, professor, and self-described pro-sex feminist Camille Paglia entered the fray of the culture wars with the publication of *Sexual Personae: Art and Decadence from Nefertiti to Emily Dickinson* (1990), a controversial survey of Western literature and art. Her main thesis is twofold: (1) that sex differences between males and females are based on biological determinism; and (2) that the Western canon has served to subvert biology by culturally creating a variety of sexual personae. Criticized in publications of the right (such as *Commentary*) and the left (the *Nation*), Paglia has offended in equal measure the social sensibilities of liberals and conservatives with her eclectic ideas and assertions.

Camille Anna Paglia was born into a Catholic family in Endicott, New York, on April 2, 1947. After graduating from the State University of New York at Binghamton (BA, 1968) and Yale University (MPhil, 1971; PhD, 1974), she taught at several institutions, including Bennington College (1972–1980), Wesleyan University (1980), Yale University (1981–1984), and the University of the Arts in Philadelphia (1984–). After the debut of *Sexual Personae*, Paglia continued in the same vein with *Sex, Art, and American Culture* (1992) and *Vamps and Tramps* (1994), compilations of essays originally published in national and international publications on a wide range of topics, including the pop star Madonna, academia, politics, the Internet, film, and music. This was followed by *The Birds* (1998), an analysis of the Alfred Hitchcock film by the same name; and *Break, Blow, Burn* (2005), an anthology of poems with commentary. She was a columnist for the online magazine *Salon* (1996–2001) and then became a contributing editor for *Interview Magazine*.

Paglia's support of pornography, her dismissive views on rape (arguing, for example, that there is a "fun element in rape, especially the wild, infectious delirium of gang rape") and sexual harassment (which she categorizes as "sexual banter"), and her romanticizing of the prostitute over the "desexed professional woman" have consistently placed her at odds with the feminist establishment. Instigating feuds with major feminists, including Naomi Wolf (who described her as "full of howling intellectual dishonesty"), Paglia has called the women's movement the "Steinem politburo" while critiquing it as "infantilizing and anti-democratic" and embracing of victimhood. Although an advocate of homosexuality and transvestism,

Paglia has characterized the gay rights movement as "Stalinist."

As for the political left, Paglia denigrates it as "white upper-middle-class elitism" that is "paternalistic and condescending." She sees academic elites as engaging in class warfare, but argues that blue-collar men contribute more to society than male scholars. Paglia has also criticized humanities professors of the Ivy League for their inclusion of poststructuralist theory in the curriculum. She believes in educational reform that encompasses a balance between high art and popular culture. A libertarian, Paglia favors abortion, the legalization of prostitution, the reduction of the age of consent to fourteen, and the legalization of drugs.

Gehrett Ellis

See also: Abortion; Feminism, Second-Wave; Feminism, Third-Wave; Gay Rights Movement; Great Books; Pornography; Sexual Assault; Sexual Harassment; Sexual Revolution; Structuralism and Post-Structuralism; Transgender Movement; Victimhood; Wolf, Naomi.

Further Reading

James, Martin. "An Interview with Camille Paglia." *America*, November 12, 1994.
Menand, Louis. "Nietzsche in Furs." *Nation*, January 25, 1993.
Paglia, Camille. *Vamps and Tramps: New Essays.* New York: Vintage, 1994.
Wolf, Naomi. "Feminist Fatale." *New Republic*, March 16, 1992.

Palin, Sarah

As governor of Alaska and the Republican Party's first female vice-presidential candidate, Sarah Palin heated up the culture wars during the 2008 general election, campaigning as "an average hockey mom" who identified with "Joe Sixpack." Her conservative profile—mother of five, Pentecostal, anti-abortion (even in cases of rape and incest), lifetime member of the National Rifle Association, and nemesis of environmentalism (opposed to listing the polar bear on the federal endangered species list, skeptical of the view that global warming is linked to human activities, and supportive of oil drilling in the Arctic National Wildlife Refuge)—was to provide a boost to John McCain's bid for the White House, but polls on election day revealed that 60 percent of voters found Palin unqualified for the vice presidency.

She was born Sarah Louise Heath on February 11, 1964, in Sand Point, Idaho, and grew up in Alaska. She majored in journalism at the University of Idaho (BS, 1987), after having attended Hawaii Pacific University in Honolulu, North Idaho College in Coeur d'Alene,

and Matanuska-Susitna College in Palmer, Alaska. At age twenty, she was runner-up in the Miss Alaska beauty pageant. After college she married her high school sweetheart, Todd Palin, and briefly worked as a television sports reporter in Anchorage, Alaska. Her political career began in 1992 when she was elected to the town council of Wasilla, her hometown of about 6,000. Later, she served as Wasilla's mayor (1996–2002), lost a race for lieutenant governor (2002), and chaired the Alaska Oil and Gas Conservation Commission (2003–2004). In November 2006, campaigning for reform and ethics in state government, Palin was elected Alaska's eleventh governor, becoming the first woman to hold the post. In July 2009, she abruptly resigned as governor.

In a move that surprised political observers and even his own campaign advisers, McCain selected Palin to be his vice-presidential nominee in an attempt to appeal to his party's conservative base, in particular the Religious Right. Observers noted a similarity to the 1988 selection by George H.W. Bush, wishing to assuage conservatives, of Dan Quayle for his running mate. McCain also hoped to draw the "Wal-Mart moms" demographic as well as women voters who were disappointed by Hillary Clinton's failure to win the Democratic primary or be selected as Barack Obama's running mate. In addition, since Palin had a record in Alaska of opposing her own political party (having reported several officials, including the state Republican chairman, for ethics violations), McCain regarded her as a kindred maverick.

Immediately upon her insertion into the campaign, Palin ridiculed Obama's experience as a community organizer, suggesting that it did not match her executive credentials as a former mayor and current governor. Presenting herself as a fiscal conservative who cuts government spending, she boasted of taking a reduction in pay as governor, putting a state jet up for sale on eBay, and halting the federally funded boondoggle known as the "Bridge to Nowhere." (It was later reported that her salary cut had been followed by a raise, that the jet sold underpriced after finding no buyer on eBay, and that the money for the bridge was not returned to the federal government but spent elsewhere.) As the campaign progressed, Palin spoke of her red-state and small-town supporters as "the real America" and referred to the opposition as "elitists." Over and over she accused Obama of "palling around with terrorists" because he once sat on an antipoverty board with Bill Ayers, a university professor who years earlier had co-founded the radical Weather Underground.

The "mommy wars" broke out almost immediately after Palin became a candidate. It was asked why this woman desired to be a national leader at a time when she was caring for a newborn with Down syndrome, a question her supporters argued would never have been raised had she been the father. The question was repeated when it was learned that one of her unmarried teenage daughters was five months pregnant. As some pundits viewed the daughter as a case of conservative moral hypocrisy and an example of why schools need to teach about birth control, pro-lifers affirmed the daughter's decision not to terminate the pregnancy. In another family matter, Palin was under investigation for using her office as governor to try to arrange the firing of her ex-brother-in-law, an Alaskan state trooper. The candidate argued that her family's privacy had been violated, but her detractors answered that it was she who first used her family as a campaign prop.

The major setback for Palin, however, was her failure to appear knowledgeable on television. In an ABC interview conducted by Charles Gibson, she did not seem to know about the controversial Bush Doctrine, a policy of preemptive war for opposing potential terrorist attacks. Worse was the CBS interview by the news anchor Katie Couric, which showed a candidate critical of Supreme Court rulings yet unable to name specific cases she regarded as judicial activism. In addition, Palin continued to insist that living in Alaska provided her with foreign-policy experience because of its close proximity to Russia. In skits that often were word-for-word from actual interviews, Palin was ruthlessly lampooned by Tina Fey on the television comedy show *Saturday Night Live.* (The Associated Press went on to name Fey the Entertainer of the Year.)

Although Palin and her supporters dismissed the bad press—including reports that the campaign spent tens of thousands of dollars on Palin's wardrobe at stores such as Saks and Bloomingdales and for a fashion consultant, hair stylist, and makeup artist—as proof of liberal media bias and gender bias, many conservatives and women publicly expressed doubts over McCain's choice of a running mate. For example, in a *Wall Street Journal* column of October 17, 2008, Peggy Noonan, a former speechwriter for President Ronald Reagan, described Palin as "a person of great ambition" who has shown "little sign that she has the tools, the equipment, the knowledge or the philosophical grounding one hopes for, and expects, in a holder of high office." Palin, Noonan added, "does not speak seriously but attempts to excite sensation."

Roger Chapman

See also: Abortion; Clinton, Hillary; Election of 2008; Endangered Species Act; Global Warming; McCain, John; Media Bias; National Rifle Association; Obama, Barack; Religious Right; Republican Party; Stay-at-Home Mothers.

Further Reading

Gibbs, Nancy. "#4 Sarah Palin." *Time,* December 29, 2008.
Gourevitch, Philip. "The State of Sarah Palin." *The New Yorker,* September 22, 2008.
Hilley, Joseph H. *Sarah Palin: A New Kind of Leader.* Grand Rapids, MI: Zondervan, 2008.
Johnson, Kaylene. *Sarah: How a Hockey Mom Turned the Political Establishment Upside Down.* Kenmore, WA: Epicenter Press, 2008.

Parks, Rosa

A seamstress by trade, Rosa Parks was an activist with the National Association for the Advancement of Colored People (NAACP) whose refusal in 1955 to surrender her bus seat to a white passenger in Montgomery, Alabama, inaugurated a year-long bus boycott by black residents, propelled the Reverend Martin Luther King, Jr., to national prominence as a civil rights leader, supplied a blueprint for resisting segregation in the United States, and transformed the American civil rights campaign into a mass movement of national scope.

Born Rosa Louise McCauley on February 14, 1913, in Tuskegee, Alabama, Parks moved, after her parents' divorce, to Pine Level, Alabama, where she was homeschooled and joined the African Methodist Episcopal Church. At age eleven, she attended the Industrial School for Girls in Montgomery before entering an auxiliary institution of the Alabama State Teachers College for Negroes for secondary instruction. Family illnesses forced her to leave school, and she did not receive her high school diploma until 1933. The previous year she married Raymond Parks, a Montgomery barber and NAACP activist, joined the Montgomery NAACP in December 1943, and served as chapter secretary until 1957.

On December 1, 1955, Parks returned home from her job as a seamstress in a Montgomery department store on a municipal bus. A long-time municipal ordinance mandated segregation on public buses; white passengers enjoyed priority seating, while black passengers would sit, stand, or exit outright according to the placement of a "Colored" sign that limited seating for black passengers. Parks sat in the appropriate section until the number of white passengers exceeded the available seating. Driver James F. Blake then repositioned the "Colored" sign behind Parks and three other black passengers and demanded that they move; Parks alone refused. She was subsequently arrested for disorderly conduct and violating a local ordinance. On December 5, she was tried, convicted, and fined fourteen dollars—a verdict she later appealed.

Local NAACP president Edgar D. Dixon posted Parks's bond and conceived a community-wide boycott of the Montgomery bus system. A citizens' group called the Montgomery Improvement Association (MIA) was formed to coordinate the boycott, with local pastor Martin Luther King, Jr., chosen to lead that organization. The boycott began on December 5, 1955, and lasted 381 days, until the U.S. Supreme Court ruled in *Browder v. Gayle* (1956) that municipal bus segregation laws were unconstitutional.

Rosa and Raymond relocated in 1957 to Detroit, where Rosa worked as a seamstress until 1965, when African-American U.S. Representative John Conyers (D-MI) hired her as a secretary for his local office—a position she retained until her retirement in 1988. Parks spoke extensively, published memoirs in 1992 and 1995, and recaptured national attention in 1999 after the hip-hop music duo OutKast released a song titled "Rosa Parks" without her permission. Parks sued and, after multiple appeals, agreed in 2005 to an undisclosed settlement with the group and its affiliates. Rosa Parks died on October 24, 2005, after a year-long bout with progressive dementia. During the national funeral tribute, her body lay in state under the U.S. Capitol Rotunda in Washington, D.C.; it was the first time a woman was so honored.

Kevin C. Motl

See also: Civil Rights Movement; Homeschooling; National Association for the Advancement of Colored People; Race; Rap Music.

Further Reading

Branch, Taylor. *Parting the Waters: America in the King Years, 1954–1963.* New York: Touchstone, 1989.

Brinkley, Douglas. *Rosa Parks.* New York: Penguin, 2005.

Kohl, Herbert R. *She Would Not Be Moved: How We Tell the Story of Rosa Parks and the Montgomery Bus Boycott.* New York: New Press/W.W. Norton, 2005.

Parks, Rosa, with Jim Haskins. *Rosa Parks: My Story.* New York: Puffin Books, 1999.

Penn, Sean

Actor, film producer, and Tinseltown activist, Sean Penn has stirred controversy over the years for his public pronouncements critical of American foreign policy. He accused President George W. Bush of committing impeachable offenses with respect to the Iraq War. Critics have branded Penn as a disloyal American for traveling overseas to meet with authoritarian leaders who are hostile to U.S. interests. In October 2005, the conservative magazine *Human Events* listed Penn number three in its top ten "unhinged celebrities," explaining: "He's the actor who claimed that Fox News host Bill O'Reilly, shock jock Howard Stern and the U.S. government are greater threats to the American people than Osama bin Laden."

Penn was born into an acting family in Santa Monica, California, on August 17, 1960. His father, Leo Penn, a communist sympathizer or "fellow traveler," was blacklisted for supporting the Hollywood Ten and refusing to cooperate with the House Committee on Un-American Activities. At age fourteen, Penn made his acting debut on *Little House on the Prairie*, a television series directed by his father. After graduating from Santa Monica High School, Penn studied acting at the Repertory Theatre of Los Angeles and briefly attended Santa Monica Junior College. He emerged as Hollywood's "bad boy" during his tempestuous marriage to the pop singer Madonna (1985–1989), a period in his life highlighted by drunkenness and fights with paparazzi. In 1987, Penn spent over a month in the Los Angeles County jail after assaulting a fellow actor who sought to take his photograph. Since 1996 he has been married to the actress Robin Wright.

As an actor, Penn has often played loners, misfits, and desperate tough guys, starring in films that examine social problems or have political themes. He has played troubled youth, including a rebellious cadet at a military school (*Taps*, 1981); a surfer (*Fast Times at Ridgemont High*, 1982); a juvenile delinquent in reform school (*Bad Boys*, 1983); and a drug smuggler (*The Falcon and the Snowman*, 1984). He has portrayed men living on the edge, such as a street cop (*Colors*, 1988); an army sergeant in Vietnam who directs his men in a gang rape of a civilian (*Casualties of War*, 1989); a cocaine-snorting lawyer (*Carlito's Way*, 1993); a killer on death row (*Dead Man Walking*, 1995); a disturbed Hollywood film director (*Hurlyburly*, 1998); a cynical army first sergeant in World War II (*The Thin Red Line*, 1998); and a mathematics professor in need of a heart transplant (*21 Grams*, 2003). In narratives about raw justice, Penn has been a mentally disabled man who seeks custody of his child (*I Am Sam*, 2001); an ex-con who seeks revenge for the murder of his teenage daughter (*Mystic River*, 2003), a role that won him the Academy Award for Best Actor; and a disillusioned businessman who attempts to hijack a plane and ram it into the White House in order to kill President Richard Nixon (*The Assassination of Richard Nixon*, 2004). Penn's two political performances are his portrayals of Huey Long, the populist Louisiana governor (*All the King's Men*, 2006), and of Harvey Milk, the gay San Francisco elected official (*Milk*, 2008).

In addition, Penn has directed a number of films, namely *The Indian Runner* (1991), based on a Bruce Springsteen song about two brothers, one who loses a farm to foreclosure and the other a war veteran returning from Vietnam; *The Crossing Guard* (1995), about a man who seeks homicidal revenge on a drunk driver who killed his young daughter; *The Pledge* (2001), about a man who seeks revenge on a child molester; and *Into the Wild* (2007), based on the true story of a young traveler who dies alone in the Alaskan wilderness.

Over the years, Penn has been quoted in the media for his strong political views. He referred to President George H.W. Bush as a "murderer" for launching the invasion of Panama (1989) and the Gulf War (1991). He once called the pope a "monster" for rejecting the use of condoms to combat the AIDS epidemic. Critics have accused Penn of being a publicity hound, suggesting that this was why he ventured into Los Angeles during the riots sparked by the Rodney King police beating (1992) and why he visited New Orleans immediately following Hurricane Katrina (2005). By contrast, in Spike Lee's 2006 documentary film about Katrina, *When the Levee Broke*, Penn is highlighted as a genuine rescuer.

Sean Penn has been involved in several antiwar groups, including Not In Our Name, Artists United to Win Without War, and MoveOn.org. In the lead-up to the Iraq War, he placed a nearly full-page "open letter" to Bush in the *Washington Post* (October 19, 2002), asking the president to show restraint: "Defend us from fundamentalism abroad but don't turn a blind eye to the fundamentalism of a diminished citizenry through loss of civil liberties, of dangerously heightened presidential autonomy through acts of Congress, and of this country's mistaken and pervasive belief that its 'manifest destiny' is to police the world." That December he traveled to Iraq, where in its capital he held a press conference denouncing the imminent American invasion. Later, in a full-page ad in the *New York Times* (May 30, 2003), he accused the Bush administration of bringing misery to Iraq while benefiting American war contractors. In December 2006, Penn was presented the first annual Christopher Reeve First Amendment Award and used the occasion to call for the impeachment of Bush and Cheney over misrepresentations leading up to the Iraq War. Penn shocked his audience by arguing that if Bill Clinton could be impeached for lying about having oral sex with an intern, then to not impeach the Bush administration for lying about the war would be the equivalent of a semen stain on the American flag.

Penn has visited such politically forbidden places as Iran, Venezuela, and Cuba, meeting with rogue dictators and outspoken critics of American neoconservative foreign policy, and afterward writing about his experiences for the *San Francisco Chronicle* and the *Nation.* In October 2008, he visited Venezuela and Cuba with historian Douglas Brinkley and journalist Christopher Hitchens. Raul Castro, the president of Cuba, gave Penn an exclusive interview. Venezuela and Cuba, Penn argued, have the right to be autonomous and "imperfectly their own."

Roger Chapman

See also: Bush Family; Clinton Impeachment; Cuba; Hurricane Katrina; King, Rodney; Milk, Harvey; Neoconservatism; September 11; Stern, Howard; War Protesters; Watts and Los Angeles Riots, 1965 and 1992.

Further Reading

Hirschberg, Lynn. "What's Sean Penn Angry About Now?" *New York Times Magazine*, December 27, 1998.
Kelly, Richard T. *Sean Penn: His Life and Times.* New York: Canongate U.S., 2005.
Lahr, John. "Citizen Penn." *The New Yorker*, April 3, 2006.
Penn, Sean. "Conversations with Chávez and Castro." *Nation*, December 15, 2008.
Rabb, Scott. "Penn." *Esquire*, September 2007.

People for the Ethical Treatment of Animals

People for the Ethical Treatment of Animals (PETA), based in Norfolk, Virginia, was founded as a nonprofit organization in 1980 by Ingrid Newkirk and Alex Pacheco for waging a campaign for the total elimination of animal "exploitation" worldwide. By its twenty-fifth year PETA was boasting 1.6 million members and operating on an annual budget of $29 million. The group views any use of animals for consumer products, medical and scientific needs, and entertainment as a selfish manipulation of the animal kingdom by human beings. PETA's core philosophy calls for the elimination of human-centered thinking, and the group considers any measures to meet those ends valid. It also opposes the use of helper animals, such as Seeing Eye dogs and helper monkeys, as "speciesist" representations of a human-centric worldview. PETA promotes the health benefits of a vegan diet, offers free speakers and educational programming, funds other educational organizations, stages boycotts and protest campaigns, and accepts animals from those unable to care for them as an alternative to Humane Society shelters.

PETA spends 40 percent of its income on advertising and promotion, inspiring both critical acclaim and derision with its message. Its headline-grabbing multimedia campaigns are targeted at all ages and have been supported by celebrities such as Paul McCartney, Dick Gregory, Al Sharpton, and Cornel West. One effort compared the treatment of livestock on farms to the abuse of American slaves and concentration camp victims. The group also suggested that it is healthier for college students to drink beer than milk. With the slogan "I'd rather go naked than wear fur," accompanied by photos of nude women, PETA used a letter-writing campaign to scold television host Oprah Winfrey for featuring leather and fur clothing on her programs. A comic book suggested that children ask their mother "how many dead animals she killed to make her fur clothes," showing a cartoon image of a woman smiling as she raises a bloody knife over a terrified rabbit. Such campaigns have been variously praised for promoting a more "cruelty-free" lifestyle and criticized for inaccurate information, disturbing imagery, objectification of women, and preying on children's insecurities.

Over the years, PETA has been accused of supporting violent behavior and even terrorism in the pursuit of its cause. Incidents range from encouraging the defacement of school displays that promote meat and dairy products in the cafeteria, to supporting individuals and groups classified by the Department of Homeland Security as terrorist threats. PETA has made donations to organizations such as the Animal Liberation Front (ALF), the Earth Liberation Front (ELF), and Stop Huntingdon Animal Cruelty (SHAC). Both the ALF and the ELF engage in "animal liberation" activities, such as stealing animals from zoos, circuses, and research laboratories to release them from captivity; firebombing research clinics and other facilities; and running harassment campaigns against researchers and animal-control agents. Opponents of PETA have complained that it is unethical to accept money donated for animal welfare activities and use it to support terrorist activities, and hypocritical to engage in violence against those one accuses of violence.

Opposition to the group has increased with accusations that while PETA targets Humane Society employees and others involved in euthanizing stray animals, they have put to sleep many of the animals that they accept or rescue. In 2006, PETA employees were charged with administering lethal injections to animals that they had accepted with donations for their continued care, and of illegally dumping animal remains.

Solomon Davidoff

See also: Animal Rights; Ecoterrorism; Factory Farms; Fur; Sharpton, Al; West, Cornel; Winfrey, Oprah.

Further Reading

Best, Steven, and Anthony J. Nocella II, eds. *Terrorists or Freedom Fighters? Reflections on the Liberation of Animals.* New York: Lantern Books, 2004.

Guillermo, Kathy Snow. *Monkey Business: The Disturbing Case That Launched the Animal Rights Movement.* Washington, DC: National Press Books, 1993.

Guither, Harold D. *Animals Rights: History and Scope of a Radical Social Movement.* Carbondale: Southern Illinois University Press, 1997.

Newkirk, Ingrid. *Free the Animals: The Story of the Animal Liberation Front.* New York: Lantern Books, 2000.

People for the Ethical Treatment of Animals (PETA) Web site. www.peta.org.

Workman, Dave. *PETA Files: The Dark Side of the Animal Rights Movement.* Bellevue, WA: Merril, 2003.

Perot, H. Ross

A maverick Texas billionaire and political populist, H. Ross Perot was a third-party presidential candidate in the 1992 and 1996 elections. He left an indelible mark on the politics of that decade, shaping the 1992 election that sent Bill Clinton to the White House and inspiring the Republican Contract with America in 1994.

The son of a cotton broker, Henry Ross Perot was born on June 27, 1930, in Texarkana, Texas. After graduating from Texarkana Junior College (1949) and, as president of his class, the U.S. Naval Academy (1953),

he served in the U.S. Navy (1953–1957). He went on to work as a data-processing salesman for IBM (1957–1962), finally leaving the company to found Electronic Data Systems (EDS), headquartered in Dallas, Texas. The company's big break came when it won a contract to process Medicare claims. When EDS was listed on the New York Stock Exchange in 1968, Perot was suddenly worth $2 billion. In 1984, EDS was sold to General Motors for $2.5 billion, and two years later General Motors purchased Perot's remaining shares for $700 million. In 1988, Perot founded Perot Systems Corporation, based in Plano, Texas; he remained chairman of that company until his retirement in 2004.

In 1969, Perot leased two 707 jet airplanes to fly dinner, letters, and Christmas packages to American prisoners of war (POWs) in North Vietnam, but the communist regime blocked his plan. That same year he founded United We Stand, an organization that publicized the POW-MIA situation and gave support to President Richard Nixon's "Vietnamization" policy for a gradual U.S. troop withdrawal. In 1979, Perot was in the news again after successfully organizing a rescue of two EDS employees who had been taken captive in Tehran, Iran, by Islamic revolutionaries. In order to free them, Perot hired a retired Army Ranger and Green Beret to conduct a jail break, an exploit heralded in Ken Follett's *On Wings of Eagles* (1983). As head of a Texas task force on the war on drugs during the 1980s, Perot enlisted the help of First Lady Nancy Reagan, who was inspired to launch the "Just Say No" campaign. In 1984 and 1985, Perot headed a Texas task force to study education reform.

In the early 1990s, after speaking out with increasing frequency about the problems of the federal government, Perot was persuaded by the anti-incumbency activist Jack Gargan to run for president. On February 20, 1992, on the television interview program *Larry King Live*, Perot announced that he would run if volunteers gathered the necessary signatures for listing his name on the ballot in all fifty states. Viewers responded favorably, and Perot initiated an organization, called United We Stand America, to facilitate their efforts. Perot's campaign would continue the strategy of direct televised appeals to spur grassroots activism among disaffected voters. A hallmark of the campaign was the "infomercials" in which Perot sat behind a desk and talked in a folksy manner about the economy and other issues while using a pointer with charts and graphs. During an address before the National Association for the Advancement of Colored People (NAACP), he offended his audience by referring to African Americans as "you people." He also clashed with reporters who demanded more program specifics.

Perot outlined his political ideas in a book titled *United We Stand: How We Can Take Back Our Country* (1992). Outraged by what was then a $4 trillion federal debt, he called for an end to deficit spending. He proposed a 15 percent cutback in federal discretionary spending,

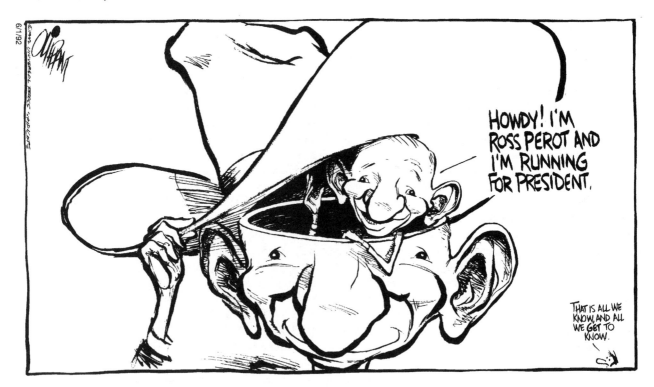

Texas entrepreneur and political maverick H. Ross Perot introduces himself to voters in this Oliphant cartoon during the 1992 presidential campaign. While some said he was short on specifics, the folksy third-party candidate emerged as a major contender. *(OLIPHANT ©1992 UNIVERSAL PRESS SYNDICATE. Reprinted with permission. All rights reserved.)*

a line-item veto, and a cut in the military budget. At the same time, he called for limiting tax deductions on interest to mortgages of $250,000 or higher, raising the marginal income tax on the wealthy from 31 to 33 percent, lifting the cap on income tax for entitlement programs such as Social Security and Medicare, increasing gas and cigarette taxes, and having Japan and Germany pay more for collective security. He encouraged political reform, including term limits, abolition of the Electoral College, the creation of an independent national health board to contain health costs, trade protectionism, and a libertarian social agenda (pro-choice and neutrality on gay marriage). The North American Free Trade Agreement (NAFTA) emerged as his key issue, about which Perot famously warned that there would be a "giant sucking sound" of American jobs leaving for Mexico if the treaty were enacted. In the end, Perot garnered 19 percent of the national vote, the best showing for a third-party candidate since Theodore Roosevelt's run on the Bull Moose ticket in 1912. Perot reportedly spent more than $72 million of his personal wealth on the campaign.

Remaining active in politics through the 1990s, Perot returned to *Larry King Live* in 1993 to debate Vice President Al Gore over NAFTA, a debate most viewers thought Gore won. Congressman Newt Gingrich (R-GA) conferred with Perot when crafting the conservative Contract with America legislative agenda in 1994. Perot ran for president again in 1996 as a candidate for the Reform Party and gained 9 percent of the vote. Thereafter, however, he opted out of the Reform Party he had founded, mocking former wrestler Jesse Ventura's bid for Minnesota governor under the party's banner in 1998 and steering clear of Pat Buchanan's bid for the party's presidential nomination in 2000. Pundits noted the irony when Perot Systems announced in 2006 that it was opening an office in Guadalajara, Mexico, in order to take advantage of the lower costs in hiring engineers. Although Perot was no longer in charge of the company, it was being operated by his son, H. Ross Perot, Jr.

Jason Mellard and Roger Chapman

See also: Clinton, Bill; Contract with America; Federal Budget Deficit; Globalization; Gore, Al; Nixon, Richard; Tax Reform; Third Parties; Vietnam Veterans Memorial; Vietnam War; War on Drugs.

Further Reading

Jelen, Ted, ed. *Ross for Boss: The Perot Phenomenon and Beyond.* Albany: State University of New York Press, 2001.

Mason, Todd. *Perot: An Unauthorized Biography.* Homewood, IL: Dow Jones–Irwin, 1990.

Perot, H. Ross. *My Life & the Principles of Success.* Fort Worth, TX: Summit Group, 1996.

Posner, Gerald. *Citizen Perot: His Life and Times.* New York: Random House, 1996.

Phelps, Fred

As founder and leader of the notorious Westboro Baptist Church in Topeka, Kansas, the Reverend Fred Phelps has led antigay protests across the nation, proclaiming that God has punished and will continue to punish the United States as long as it shows tolerance toward and acceptance of homosexuality. Phelps claims that from 1991 to 2008 the Westboro church conducted more than 34,000 antihomosexual demonstrations.

Fred Waldron Phelps was born on November 13, 1926, in Meridian, Mississippi. After attending John Muir College (AA, 1951), he moved to Topeka, Kansas, where he began a church while continuing his education at Washburn University (BA, 1962; JD, 1964). A primitive Baptist by his own definition, Phelps was originally ordained as a Southern Baptist. He practiced law for several years but reportedly was disbarred in 1979 for ethical misconduct.

Phelps, who views himself as a prophet, has declared that divine retribution for gay culture lay behind the September 11 terrorist attacks and natural disasters such as Hurricane Katrina. The placards he and his followers have used at demonstrations are viewed as hateful by almost all observers, including conservative Christians: "God hates fags" is a common refrain. Other slogans include "Thank God for AIDS," "No tears for queers," and the like. In 1998, Phelps shocked the nation by chanting "Matt is in hell" during the funeral of Matthew Shepard, a young gay man who had been brutally murdered in Wyoming. Later, Phelps and his followers protested at U.S. military funerals, attributing America's war deaths in Iraq and Afghanistan to God's displeasure over sodomy. Some Evangelicals have expressed concern that "leftists" have unfairly tried to equate Phelps's extremist message with mainstream Christian thought.

The Westboro church, which meets in the leader's home, is attended primarily by family members; Phelps is the father of some dozen adult children with children of their own. In cult-like gatherings, Phelps preaches a strict form of Calvinist theology, believing that all but a tiny elect are predestined to hell. At the church's main Web site, GodHatesFags.com, visitors are referred to as "depraved sons and daughters of Adam." To those who think his message against gays is harsh and unloving, Phelps argues that he is uncompromising about what the Scriptures teach concerning homosexuality. America's "kissy-pooh preachers," he maintains, have turned churches into "candy stores" and church members into "moral diabetics." Phelps refers to his antigay protests as "Love Crusades" in which warnings are offered out of brotherly concern.

Phelps's actions have led to lawsuits, legislation, and numerous counter-protests. In November 2007, a jury in Baltimore, Maryland, ruled against the Westboro church and awarded nearly $11 million in damages to a family whose funeral service for their son, a U.S. Marine who had been killed in Iraq, was disrupted by antigay protesters. In April of that same year, Kansas passed a law requiring a protest-free buffer around military funerals. About a dozen other states passed similar legislation. On Memorial Day 2007, President George W. Bush signed a similar federal law, the Respect for America's Fallen Heroes Act. In the meantime, American Legion groups across the country formed motorcycle honor guards to protect the sanctity of military burial against protesters. In addition, a group calling itself FreeRepublic.com was formed to stage demonstrations against the Westboro demonstrators.

Roger Chapman

See also: Evangelicalism; Fundamentalism, Religious; Gay Rights Movement; Hate Crimes; Hurricane Katrina; September 11; Shepard, Matthew.

Further Reading

GodHatesFags Web site. www.godhatesfags.com.
Van Biema, David. "The Harley Honor Guard." *Time*, May 8, 2006.
Veenker, Jody. "Called to Hate?" *Christianity Today*, October 25, 1999.

Philadelphia, Mississippi

Philadelphia, Mississippi, a town with about 7,300 residents, is remembered for the brutal slayings of three civil rights workers in 1964 as well as a controversial campaign stop by presidential candidate Ronald Reagan in 1980. Although rurally isolated, the town is a recognized symbol of the culture wars.

On June 21, 1964, members of the local Ku Klux Klan beat and shot to death James Chaney, Andrew Goodman, and Michael Schwerner, who had come to the area as volunteers in the "Freedom Summer" black voter registration drive. The three men—two white and one black, all in their early twenties—were stopped for a minor traffic violation, temporarily jailed, and upon their release, ambushed by Klansmen organized by Edgar Ray Killen, a part-time Baptist minister. Their bodies were found weeks later buried under an earthen dam outside of town. In 1967, eighteen suspects were indicted on federal conspiracy charges in connection with the case, but only seven were convicted. Killen was set free because of a hung jury.

Despite Philadelphia's lingering stigma, it was the setting for Reagan's first major campaign speech after gaining the Republican nomination for president. In his August 3, 1980, address at the Neshoba County Fair, Reagan proclaimed, "I believe in states' rights" and promised that as president he would work to "restore to states and local governments the power that properly belongs to them." Critics interpreted these remarks as signaling sympathy to white southerners for resisting federally imposed civil rights for African Americans. Defenders of Reagan say it is unfair to characterize the term "states' rights" as code language for white segregation; they also point out that Democratic presidential candidate Michael Dukakis spoke at the same fair in August 1988. Dukakis, however, did not defend states' rights but pledged to "bring down the barriers to opportunity for all our people."

The emergence of new evidence in the murder of Chaney, Goodman, and Schwerner led to a reopening of the case and a new trial in the town. On June 21, 2005, a jury found Killen, then eighty years old, guilty of three counts of manslaughter; he was promptly sentenced to sixty years in prison. That same month, the U.S. Senate issued a formal apology for having failed to enact antilynching legislation; Mississippi's two Republican senators, Trent Lott and Thad Cochran, were among the several who refused to co-sponsor the resolution. Although most Philadelphia residents welcomed the Killen trial, some saw it as reopening old wounds and believed that it was wrong to bring a man to trial four decades after the fact.

The events of June 1964 and the original legal proceedings were depicted in the 1988 motion picture *Mississippi Burning*. The evidence that finally led to Killen's conviction was turned up by investigative journalist Jerry Mitchell, with the help of an Illinois high school teacher and three students.

Roger Chapman

See also: Civil Rights Movement; Dukakis, Michael; Hate Crimes; Kennedy Family; Lott, Trent; Lynching; Reagan, Ronald; Republican Party; Rockwell, Norman; Till, Emmett; White Supremacists.

Further Reading

Ball, Howard. *Justice in Mississippi: The Murder Trial of Edgar Ray Killen.* Lawrence: University Press of Kansas, 2006.

Cannon, Lou. *Reagan.* New York: G.P. Putnam's Sons, 1982.

Huie, William Bradford. *Three Lives for Mississippi.* Introduction by Martin Luther King, Jr. New York: New American Library, 1968.

Mars, Florence. *Witness in Philadelphia.* Baton Rouge: Louisiana State University Press, 1977.

Younge, Gary. "Racism Rebooted: Philadelphia, Mississippi, Then and Now." *Nation,* July 11, 2005.

Pipes, Richard, and Daniel Pipes

Richard Pipes and Daniel Pipes, father and son, respectively, are neoconservatives known for their critiques on the American enemy of the day—for the former, the Soviet Union; for the latter, Islamic fundamentalism.

Richard Edgar Pipes was born on July 11, 1923, in Cieszyn, Poland, eventually immigrating to the United States with his parents. He was educated at Muskingum College in New Concord, Ohio (1940–1943), Cornell University (BA, 1945), and Harvard University (PhD, 1950). As a Harvard professor (1950–1996), he was an expert on Russian history and the Soviet Union, authoring or editing more than two dozen books, including *Formation of the Soviet Union* (1954); *The Russian Intelligentsia* (1961); *Soviet Strategy in Europe* (1976); *Russia Observed: Collected Essays on Russian and Soviet History* (1989); *Communism, the Vanished Specter* (1994); and *Three "Whys" of the Russian Revolution* (1997). The 1917 communist revolution in Russia, he maintained, was not representative of the people's will but simply the result of Lenin's tenacity and audacity.

Politically active during his academic career, Richard Pipes was an officer and member of the anticommunist Committee of the Present Danger (1977–1992) and served during the 1980s as an adviser to President Ronald Reagan on Eastern Europe and the Soviet Union. Critics accused him of being overly pessimistic toward the Soviet Union, including a lack of enthusiasm during arms limitation talks between Moscow and Washington. According to defenders, however, his influencing Reagan's hard stance against the Soviets helped paved the way for the United States to win the Cold War.

Born on September 9, 1949, in Boston, Massachusetts, Daniel Pipes studied at Harvard University (BA, 1971; PhD, 1978) and also attended schools in the Middle East, including the University of Tunis, University of Cairo, and Al-Azhar University in Cairo. From the 1970s through the 1990s, he held teaching and research positions at a number of prestigious universities and institutes, including Princeton University (1977–1978), the University of Chicago (1978–1982), Harvard University (1983–1984), the Naval War College (1984–1986), and the Foreign Policy Research Institute (1986–1993); he also served a stint on the policy planning staff at the U.S. Department of State (1982–1983).

Daniel's early writings, including *Slave Soldiers and Islam: The Genesis of a Military System* (1981) and *In the Path of God: Islam and Political Power* (1983), explained the history of Islam to those who were unfamiliar with its principles and teachings. In *The Rushdie Affair: The Ayatollah, the Novelist, and the West* (1990), he offered an explanation for the violent reaction of Islamic leaders to the publication of Salman Rushdie's 1989 novel *The Satanic Verses* and suggested that the novelist should have anticipated the negative reaction. During the 1990s, Pipes wrote essays warning against the dangers of Islamic fundamentalism to the United States. Critics accused him of racism and repeated the charge following the attacks of September 11, 2001, when he updated and anthologized many of the essays, publishing them under the title *Militant Islam Reaches America* (2002).

Shortly after the September 11 attacks, Daniel Pipes co-founded Campus Watch, a Web site dedicated to the study of Middle Eastern history and culture on college campuses. In 2002, Campus Watch published a list of academics whom Pipes judged to be overly critical of U.S. foreign policy. Many of the accused retaliated, calling Campus Watch and him anti-American. Several critics suggested that Pipes's activities bore similarities to the Red Scare tactics of McCarthyism.

Margaret Barrett and Roger Chapman

See also: Academic Freedom; American Century; Cold War; McCarthyism; Muslim Americans; Neoconservatism; Saudi Arabia; September 11; Soviet Union and Russia.

Further Reading

Pipes, Daniel. *Militant Islam Reaches America.* New York: W.W. Norton, 2002.
Pipes, Richard. *Vixi: Memoirs of a Non-Belonger.* New Haven, CT: Yale University Press, 2003.
Schrecker, Ellen. "The New McCarthyism in Academe." *Thought & Action* 21 (Fall 2005): 103–18.

Planned Parenthood

The organization Planned Parenthood Federation of America, with nearly 900 centers across the nation, provides birth-control materials, abortion and sterilization procedures, testing for sexually transmitted diseases, and screening for cervical and breast cancer. Twenty-five percent of American women reportedly use the services of Planned Parenthood at least once in their lives. According to its 2006–2007 annual report, Planned Parenthood performed 289,750 surgical abortions in 2006, representing 3 percent of the total services it provided.

From the perspective of its 4 million activists, donors, and supporters, Planned Parenthood champions reproductive rights by offering women confidential counseling and safe options in rational family planning. Its pro-life detractors, on the other hand, regard the organization as primarily a network of abortion clinics responsible for the murdering of the unborn. Even some pro-choice advocates have been critical of Planned Parenthood, calling it the "Wal-Mart of abortion clinics" because it typically drives small-size abortion clinics out of business by providing cheaper but inferior services.

Planned Parenthood was founded by the pioneering birth-control crusader Margaret Sanger, who coined the term "birth control." The roots of the organization date back to 1916 when Sanger established a birth-control clinic in Brooklyn, New York. As an obstetrical nurse she became interested in birth control from working among immigrants in the slums of Manhattan's Lower East Side. This experience radicalized her to begin disseminating printed materials on birth control. She was later indicted for violating the Comstock Laws of 1878, which banned the use of the mail service for disseminating sexually related material or anything that could be broadly construed as pornographic. In her work *Women and the New Race* (1920), Sanger promoted birth control as a way to ensure a woman's right to "voluntary motherhood."

In 1923, Sanger's clinic became the basis of the American Birth Control League, which in 1942 was renamed Planned Parenthood. Controversially, Sanger as well as others in the birth-control movement advocated eugenics, including sterilization for the "unfit" (poor). Many of those designated poor were Catholic and Jewish immigrants as well as blacks. By the late 1930s the general public came to associate eugenics with Nazi racism, giving birth control a negative connotation. On the advice of a public relations consultant, Sanger's organization adopted the name "planned parenthood" in lieu of "birth control."

In 1948, Planned Parenthood provided a research grant to the biologist Gregory Pincus, whose work ultimately led to the development of oral contraception, popularly known as "the pill." On May 9, 1960, the Food and Drug Administration approved the pill's availability to the public. This new form of birth control proved to be more effective than condoms, diaphragms, or chemicals, resulting in greater sexual freedom for women minus the consequences of unplanned pregnancy. By 1965 one-fourth of married women in the United States were using the pill. Oral contraception, most agree, was a major factor in precipitating the sexual revolution.

Following the introduction of oral contraception, Planned Parenthood turned its attention to abortion. That effort was indirectly facilitated by a challenge of the Connecticut ban on contraceptives. The Planned Parenthood League of Connecticut, headed by Estelle Griswold, took that issue to the Supreme Court, which in the ruling *Griswold v. Connecticut* (1965) overturned all such state laws on the grounds of privacy rights. Afterward, a number of states not only rescinded their laws banning contraceptives, but liberalized abortion laws as well. The *Griswold* decision was part of the cited case law that was used in *Roe v. Wade* (1973), the landmark Supreme Court decision that declared a woman's right to abortion to be part of her constitutional right to privacy.

After the legalization of abortion in 1973, Planned Parenthood became a target of derision by the pro-life movement. During the mid-1980s a number of Planned Parenthood clinics across the nation were bombed, set on fire, or vandalized. Later, Planned Parenthood lost ground in the judicial war over abortion. In *Planned Parenthood v. Casey* (1992), the Supreme Court ruled against the requirement for spousal notification prior to an abortion procedure; however, the same decision upheld state law requiring a mandatory cool-off period for all abortions and parental notification in cases involving minors. In *Gonzalez v. Planned Parenthood* (2007), the Supreme Court upheld the federal ban on D and X (dilation and extraction) abortion, which critics dub "partial-birth abortion."

Roger Chapman

See also: Abortion; Birth Control; Douglas, William O.; Food and Drug Administration; National Organization for Women; Operation Rescue; *Roe v. Wade* (1973); Sex Education; Sexual Revolution; Wal-Mart.

Further Reading

Coates, Patricia Walsh. *Margaret Sanger and the Origin of the Birth Control Movement, 1910–1930: The Concept of Women's Sexual Autonomy.* Lewiston, NY: Edwin Mellen, 2008.

Gordon, Linda. *The Moral Property of Women: A History of Birth Control Politics in America.* Urbana: University of Illinois Press, 2002.

Grant, George. *Immaculate Deception: The Shifting Agenda of Planned Parenthood.* Chicago: Northfield, 1996.

Johnson, John W. Griswold v. Connecticut: *Birth Control and the Constitutional Right of Privacy.* Lawrence: University Press of Kansas, 2005.

Planned Parenthood Federation of America Web site. www.plannedparenthood.org.

Podhoretz, Norman

As editor of the magazine *Commentary* from 1960 to 1995, Norman Podhoretz established the publication as an influential—if ideologically shifting—journal of opinion. At first, he published authors who shaped the emergence of the New Left in the early and mid-1960s. By the end of the decade, however, his magazine was opposing much of the radical agenda and shifting toward what would emerge as neoconservatism.

The son of Jewish immigrants, Podhoretz was born on January 16, 1930, and raised in Brooklyn, New York. His father, a milkman, wanted him to have a Jewish education, so in addition to attending a public high school during the day, he went to a night school where classes were taught in Hebrew. After completing high school in 1946, Podhoretz attended Columbia University (AB, 1950), where he studied with the distinguished critic and writer Lionel Trilling. At the same time, Podhoretz also studied Judaism and Jewish history at the College of Jewish Studies of the Jewish Theological Seminary (BHL, 1950). He completed his formal studies at Cambridge University in England (MA, 1957).

Upon completing service in the U.S. Army (1953–

As the editor-in-chief of *Commentary* magazine and author of several influential books, former leftist Norman Podhoretz emerged in the early 1970s as a leading voice of the fledgling neoconservative movement. *(James Keyser/Time & Life Pictures/Getty Images)*

1955), Podhoretz joined the staff of *Commentary*, the journal of the American Jewish Committee, rising to the position of editor-in-chief in 1960. He was already active in leftist politics, supporting a nuclear test ban and disarmament. Under his editorship, contributions were published by such authors as Paul Goodman, Staughton Lynd, Herbert Marcuse, and Norman O. Brown, thereby contributing to the intellectual foundations of the emerging New Left.

By the late 1960s, Podhoretz had become disenchanted with what he regarded as the New Left's anti-American, anti-Semitic, and totalitarian tendencies. Moving to the right politically, he described the New Left as "Stalinist," declared Lyndon Johnson's War on Poverty a failure, and opened the pages of his journal to critiques of the counterculture. By the early 1970s, nearly every issue of *Commentary* included an article by a disillusioned liberal. The magazine came to be regarded as a conservative rival to the *New York Review of Books*, whose editor, Jason Epstein, had had a falling out with Podhoretz.

Although *Commentary* addressed a wide range of issues, novelist Gore Vidal argued in a 1986 article that Podhoretz was interested primarily in Israel, wanting to use American influence to advance its cause, and had little genuine interest in other matters. Podhoretz, however, believed that he was challenging the "appeasement" culture of the left.

In addition to editing *Commentary* and writing articles, Podhoretz published several books, among them a trilogy of memoirs recounting his political passage and its consequences—*Making It* (1967), *Breaking Ranks* (1979), and *Ex-Friends* (2000)—and an autobiography, *My Love Affair with America* (2002). From 1981 to 1987, he worked for the United States Information Agency. After leaving *Commentary* in 1995, he joined the Hudson Institute, a conservative think tank, where he was a senior fellow until 2003. His son, John, was appointed editor of *Commentary* in 2007.

Gary Land

See also: Anti-Semitism; Ginsberg, Allen; Israel; Mailer, Norman; Neoconservatism; New Left; Vidal, Gore; War on Poverty.

Further Reading

Gerson, Mark. *The Neoconservative Vision: From the Cold War to the Culture Wars.* Lanham, MD: Madison Books, 1996.

Jeffers, Thomas L., ed. *The Norman Podhoretz Reader: A Selection of His Writings from the 1950s Through the 1990s.* New York: Free Press, 2004.

Vidal, Gore. "The Empire Lovers Strike Back." *Nation,* March 22, 1986.

Winchell, Mark Roydon. *Neoconservative Criticism: Norman Podhoretz, Kenneth S. Lynn, and Joseph Epstein.* Boston: Twayne, 1991.

Police Abuse

Police abuse has been a divisive topic of the culture wars, placing law and order in tension with individual rights. Prior to the 1960s, concern about police abuse generally centered on corruption, but later attention shifted to police brutality, coercive interrogation, the planting of false evidence, unlawful search and surveillance, and racial profiling.

In most debates on police abuse, conservatives generally defend law enforcement agencies, stressing the hazards of police work—from 1946 to early 2009, 4,565 police officers were shot and killed in the line of duty—and its importance in maintaining law and order. When questions arise over police conduct, conservatives tend to give the officers the benefit of the doubt. Accusations of police abuse, many conservatives feel, are grossly exaggerated. Liberals emphasize that law and order must be applied to all segments of society, including its 800,000 law enforcement personnel. The rights of the accused, which liberals believe are important safeguards against police abuse, are considered "criminal rights" by many conservatives who fear that an excessive focus on such matters hinders police from doing their job. Public perception of police abuse is polarized by race, with a higher percentage of blacks than whites viewing it as a major problem.

Organizations such as the American Civil Liberties Union have promoted the establishment of civilian review boards to provide external investigations when citizens file complaints of police abuse, such as racial profiling and police brutality. Opponents of the review boards argue that police should be judged by other police, not individuals who lack training in law enforcement and who have never dealt with the everyday realities of police work. Although most of the nation's largest cities now have these boards in place, critics argue that their limited power makes them ineffective. In conjunction with review boards is the trend for the videotaping of arrests and interrogations in order to provide a "record" should there later be accusations of excessive force.

Police corruption was a major concern during the 1960s and 1970s. It often involved police officers accepting bribes from criminal syndicates that were involved with gambling, prostitution, illegal alcohol, and the fencing of stolen goods. The bribed police would shield the syndicate, which would in turn pledge not to commit any robberies within the city limits. In 1961, there was a major investigation of such a corrupt bargain in Kansas City, Missouri. That same decade the Chicago police force underwent a major reform and established an internal investigation division to address corruption within its ranks. Frank Serpico made headlines during the late 1960s and early 1970s by reporting the corruption he witnessed while serving as an officer of the New York Police Department (NYPD). Occasional news items continue to report of police officers who are "on the take" and providing protection to drug dealers and their operations.

Police brutality emerged as a public issue during the 1960s and 1970s in connection with the civil rights movement and protests against the Vietnam War. On March 3, 1963, in Birmingham, Alabama, police repulsed young civil rights marchers with high-pressured fire hoses and attack dogs. Since this event was televised, many Americans saw it on the evening news. Birmingham's chief of police, Eugene "Bull" Connor, appeared on camera and vowed that his men would do it all over again if the "outside agitators" continued to stir trouble. Another iconic event in the annals of police brutality took place in Chicago during the August 1968 Democratic National Convention. Police descended upon the protesters with clubs and indiscriminately attacked all who stood in their path—a "police riot" was the official verdict and several police officers were indicted on charges of abuse of power.

Nearly forty years later, in 2004, police in New York City reacted to a smaller group of demonstrators outside the Republican National Convention protesting the Iraq War. Using little discretion, the NYPD arrested nearly 2,000 protesters and bystanders. Most were herded into holding pens in the city's jails and held without charge until the convention was over. Conservatives argued that such "preventive detention" was appropriate to protecting government officials and preserving law and order. Liberals complained that imprisonment without timely charges was an outrage.

Over the years much controversy has been stirred over police surveillance. In numerous cases, the police were found to have been monitoring political groups as opposed to criminal suspects. Most notorious was the FBI's "counter intelligence program," known as COINTELPRO, which was active between 1956 and 1971. This federal dragnet primarily targeted liberal and leftist groups, including organizations affiliated with the civil rights movement. After the terrorist attacks of September 11, 2001, there were a number of reports of police monitoring of antiwar groups.

Most controversies pertaining to police abuse, however, are not related to politics as much as they are to the manner in which law enforcement officials interact with the local citizenry. The Los Angeles Police Department (LAPD) became notorious for the rough treatment of minority suspects, especially African Americans and Latinos. Between 1963 and 1965, Los Angeles police officers shot and killed a total of 60 blacks; 25 were unarmed and 27 were shot in the back. This pattern of behavior was one of the triggers for the Watts Riots of 1965, which began when a white police officer stopped a black motorist and subjected him to an abusive interrogation in public. More than twenty-five years later, in 1991, a bystander videotaped members of the LAPD clubbing and kicking African American Rodney King after a high-speed chase. When the officers were acquitted of charges in the beating in 1992, the city erupted into the most destructive urban rioting in decades. From 1980 to 1991, nearly 280 LA officers or sheriffs had been accused of assaulting civilians.

The LAPD was involved in a scandal of a different kind in 1998. Some thirty police officers in the antigang unit of its Rampart Division were accused of beating citizens, planting guns and drugs on suspects, stealing drugs and guns, taking bribes, conducting illegal searches, and imprisoning people on false evidence. The scandal resulted in overturned convictions in more than 100 cases, and in 2000, the city signed an agreement with the U.S. Justice Department to carry out major reforms.

The effect of police conduct on criminal convictions was strongly emphasized in 2000, when Governor George Ryan of Illinois, a Republican, imposed a moratorium on the state's use of the death penalty. He went a step further in 2003, commuting the sentences of all 167 death row inmates in the state. Ryan said that these actions were the result of evidence of widespread police and prosecutorial abuse, which included the torturing of suspects to extract confessions.

Joseph A. Rodriguez

See also: King, Rodney; Racial Profiling; Watts and Los Angeles Riots, 1965 and 1992.

Further Reading

Blum, Lawrence N. *Stoning the Keepers at the Gate: Society's Relationship with Law Enforcement.* Brooklyn, NY: Lantern Books, 2002.

Cole, David. *No Equal Justice: Race and Class in the American Criminal Justice System.* New York: New Press, 1999.

Geller, William A., and Hans Toch. *Police Violence: Understanding and Controlling Police Abuse of Force.* New Haven, CT: Yale University Press, 2005.

Klinger, David. *Into the Kill Zone: A Cop's Eye View of Deadly Force.* San Francisco: Jossey-Bass, 2004.

McShane, Larry. *Cops Under Fire: The Reign of Terror Against Hero Cops.* Washington, DC: Regnery, 1999.

Weitzer, Ronald John, and Steven A. Tuch. *Race and Policing in America: Conflict and Reform.* New York: Cambridge University Press, 2006.

Political Correctness

Political correctness, otherwise known as PC, has been used in the culture wars as a pejorative epithet to characterize what critics deem a destructive political ethos in American society since the 1980s. While accusations of PC have often focused on university practices, they are by no means limited to this venue. Since the early 1980s, the PC debate has attracted a national audience, framing much of the discussion of, among other things, race relations, public education, and citizenship.

Most often, the ethos that is attacked as politically correct is understood to be "liberal," while those who do the attacking tend to be identified as "conservatives"—even though some PC developed as a critique of liberalism as much as an extension of it, and liberals frequently join with conservatives in making accusations of PC. While the types of practices decried as instances of PC are familiar enough, it is often difficult to discern their commonality. Thus, some have claimed that it is simply an all-purpose pejorative epithet used by conservatives to attack any and all liberal practices of which they disapprove. Still, it is possible to present a coherent account or narrative of what critics might call the "Ideology of Political Correctness" (IPC).

Ideology of Political Correctness

IPC arises from taking the liberal principle of *equal respect* to absurd lengths. Classical liberals saw equal respect as embodied in a series of individual rights—the right to own property, the right to compete in the marketplace, the right to participate in the political process. While equal rights entailed (a rough) equality of *opportunity*, it was never intended to ensure equality of *outcomes*; acceptance of equal *rights* was not intended to entail equality of *worthiness*. The IPC champions not only equality of outcome but construes equal respect as equal worthiness, and equal worthiness to require a kind of *positive affirmation*.

But the individual whose worth the IPC is concerned to affirm is not just any individual. In fact, the IPC represents a shift from classical liberalism's emphasis on the individual *qua* individual to the individual *qua* group member, as embodied in the movements of multiculturalism and identity politics. The groups the IPC is concerned to affirm are those that historically have been discriminated against and excluded primarily on the basis of ethnicity, gender, or sexual orientation. The flip side of the affirmation of those oppressed and excluded is the denigration of the "oppressors," namely white European males. This may take a variety of forms, notably revisionist history and a rejection of the unique accomplishments of "Western" civilization" (as embodied, for example, in the "Western canon"). This rejection is supported by the ethos of multiculturalism, which sometimes exaggerates the accomplishments of non-European cultures, as well as by moral relativism, which denies the existence of universal standards according to which diverse cultural achievements can be assessed.

Speech Codes and Western Canon

During the 1980s and early 1990s, a number of universities, responding to complaints of discrimination and harassment on campuses throughout the country, began formulating what came to be known as "campus speech codes." By 1995, more than 350 public colleges and universities regulated certain types of "hate speech" in one form or another. Such codes have been denounced as instances of PC largely because of the emphasis placed on protecting women and minorities from speech deemed to create a hostile campus environment. To supporters, such codes are necessary to stop speech that is the equivalent of an assault on personal dignity (not unlike a physical assault) and that creates a hostile learning environment. Such codes recognize that some individuals have been, and continue to be, the target of past and present discrimination on the basis of their ethnicity, gender, or sexual orientation. For example, to call a fellow student "nigger" would be a violation of a campus speech code. On the other hand, to casually call a woman a "girl" might also be regarded as a violation of the speech codes.

Detractors of speech codes see them as an attempt to forcibly impose the politically correct ethos of positive affirmation of groups historically discriminated against by suppressing legitimate speech. Accusations of PC have been fueled by the fact that some campus speech codes appeared to go beyond prohibiting offensive racial epithets directed at specific individuals, for example, to proscribing the expression of certain points of view (according to critics, those that are "politically incorrect"). Some liberal advocates of expansive free speech rights have joined conservative critics in attacking such codes, several of which have been challenged in court and held to be unconstitutional.

In 1984, Secretary of Education William Bennett published a report titled "To Reclaim a Legacy: A Report on the Humanities in Higher Education," in which he argued that Western civilization should be the core of the American college curriculum "because it is a source of incomparable intellectual complexity, diversity, and depth; [and] because it is under attack." The "attack" of which Bennett warned was the development of a more "multicultural-," gender-, and race-conscious curriculum at American colleges and universities and a move away from teaching the "traditional" canon of "great" Western books. To those who approve the shift in emphasis, the traditional curriculum reflects a "white European male political bias" that systematically dismisses the philosophy, literature, and art of non-European cultures as "inferior." To those who oppose the changes in curriculum as a manifestation of PC, such changes are an attempt to both denigrate the accomplishments of the writers who comprise the Western canon—"the oppressors"—and to exalt "the oppressed" by including works largely on the basis of the race or ethnicity or gender of the author (rather than on the merits of his or her works). On the other hand, some who argue to keep the canon proposed expanding it to include previously neglected writings.

Revisionist History and National Identity

The controversy over the canon has been replicated in the controversy surrounding accusations of "politically correct" (or "revisionist") history, as it concerns both academic history and the content of college and public school education. A notable example of the former is the firestorm surrounding the publication of Martin Bernal's *Black Athena: The Afroasiatic Roots of Classical Civilization* (1989), which expounds the hypothesis that ancient Greece, and hence Western civilization, derives much of its cultural roots from Afroasiatic (Egyptian and Phoenician) cultures. While Bernal's hypothesis remains controversial among scholars, it has been denounced as a work of politically correct, revisionist, "Afrocentric" history by many involved in the PC debate (who often appear ill equipped to pass judgment on the scholarly merits—or lack thereof—of the work). Debates over teaching history in the public schools have focused on the charge that PC has transformed the teaching of American history into a one-sided story of racist and sexist exploitation by white European males, or the charge that American history is sometimes not taught at all but replaced by "multicultural history" (including "Afrocentric" history), emphasizing the story and accomplishments of non-European peoples.

In *The Disuniting of America: Reflections on a Multicultural Society* (1998), historian Arthur M. Schlesinger, Jr., argues that multicultural education, both in colleges and universities and in the public schools, and multiculturalism in general, pose a threat to American culture by rejecting a unifying national identity based on citizenship and replacing it with a fragmenting plurality of identities based on racial and ethnic differences. What is particularly ironic, Schlesinger argues, is that ascribing such importance to racial and ethnic identity is representative of the racist legacy of American history that progressive liberal democrats have fought to overcome. Defenders of multiculturalism argue that American national identity, far from transcending cultural and ethnic particularity, in fact embodies the cultural particularity of Anglo-Saxon Protestant males. Attempts to "assimilate" indigenous and immigrant ethnic and cultural minorities through public education in an American national identity are viewed as attempts to force them to abandon their own particular cultural identity for another particular (Anglocentric) cultural identity.

Evan Charney

See also: Afrocentrism; Bennett, William J.; D'Souza, Dinesh; Great Books; Multiculturalism and Ethnic Studies; Revisionist History; Schlesinger, Arthur M., Jr.; Speech Codes.

Further Reading

Berlinerblau, Jacques. *Heresy in the University: The Black Athena Controversy and the Responsibilities of American Intellectuals.* Piscataway, NJ: Rutgers University Press, 1999.

Berman, Paul, ed. *Debating P.C.: The Controversy over Political Correctness on College Campuses.* New York: Dell, 1992.

D'Souza, Dinesh. *Illiberal Education: The Politics of Race and Sex on Campus.* New York: Macmillan, 1991.

Ravitch, Diane. *The Language Police: How Pressure Groups Restrict What Students Learn.* New York: Alfred A. Knopf, 2003.

Schlesinger, Arthur, Jr. *The Disuniting of America: Reflections on a Multicultural Society.* New York: W.W. Norton, 1998.

Wilson, John. *The Myth of Political Correctness: The Conservative Attack on High Education.* Durham, NC: Duke University Press, 1995.

Pornography

Pornography was perhaps most famously defined by U.S. Supreme Court justice Potter Stewart in his concurring opinion in the case of *Jacobellis v. Ohio* (1964), where he wrote, simply, "I know it when I see it." Even that rather vague definition of pornography is appropriate for the wide-ranging political debate over obscene images and sexuality that has been a cornerstone of the culture wars since the second half of the twentieth century. Making strange bedfellows of groups as disparate as Christian conservatives and radical feminists, the antipornography movement has led to a flurry of legal and political activity restricting sexual expression on behalf of women, children, and civilization. On the other side, pornographers, free-speech advocates,

and sex radicals have argued that the government is stifling free speech and regard the antipornography movement as part of a broader antisex agenda on the part of conservatives.

The contemporary pornography industry in American has been much influenced by the growth of a mass-media empire that includes conventional publishing, such as magazines, as well as a booming film and video industry and, since the 1990s, the Internet. Pornography became a major mainstream commercial enterprise in part via the Playboy enterprise, in which founder Hugh Hefner not only began selling the men's magazine *Playboy* in 1953, but opened a chain of Playboy lounges and popularized the "Playboy lifestyle." Other media entrepreneurs benefited from the more permissive sexual environment of the 1960s and 1970s with more hard-core magazines like *Penthouse* and *Hustler*. During that same period, the film industry produced "porn flicks" of huge commercial success, including *Deep Throat* (1972) and *The Devil in Miss Jones* (1973). The advent of VHS tape was a further boon to the industry, providing a cheap medium that could be delivered to private homes.

The commercial success of the pornography industry prompted a strong legal and political backlash at the local, state, and federal levels. The beginnings go back to *Chaplinsky v. New Hampshire* (1942), in which the Supreme Court declared that pornography was not an automatic protected category of speech. This was followed by *Roth v. United States* (1957), which ruled that "community standards" could be applied to determine if questionable material was "utterly without redeeming social importance." Finally, in *Miller v. California* (1973), the high court established clearer parameters for states to regulate obscenity in accordance with community standards. In addition, two federal studies on the pornography industry were launched—the 1970 Commission on Obscenity and Pornography and the 1986 Attorney General's Commission on Pornography. The first recommended bolstering sex education and further study of the effects of pornography, findings denounced by both Congress and the White House. The second study, headed by U.S. Attorney General Edwin Meese of the Reagan administration and produced by mostly antipornography crusaders, recommended more active enforcement of federal and state anti-obscenity laws.

The Religious Right, specifically the Moral Majority, took aim at the pornography industry, encouraging legislation and boycotts of prominent chain stores that sold pornographic magazines. One of the most high-profile conflicts occurred between televangelist Jerry Falwell and Larry Flynt, the editor of *Hustler* magazine. In response to Falwell's public campaign against his magazine, Flynt published a satirical liquor ad using Falwell's likeness and describing, in grotesque detail, Falwell losing his virginity to his mother in an outhouse. Falwell sued for

The issue of pornography—including a lack of consensus over its very definition—has been one of the central, defining battles in America's culture wars. Here, antipornography demonstrators organized by the Moral Majority take to the streets of Dallas, Texas, in 1985. *(Shelly Katz/Time & Life Pictures/Getty Images)*

libel and the case eventually reached the Supreme Court, where Flynt's political speech was protected under the First Amendment. During the course of the trial, an apparent supporter of Falwell shot Flynt, leaving him partially paralyzed for life.

In spite of Falwell's limited success in curbing pornography, many groups have been politically and culturally effective in organizing campaigns against obscenity. Beginning in the late 1970s, for example, Donald Wildmon's American Family Association voiced opposition to many facets of the pornography culture by organizing boycotts of convenience stores that sold pornographic materials, criticizing mainstream television shows with gratuitous sexuality, and challenging the National Endowment for the Arts for funding "obscene" artwork. Wildmon was joined in the fight by the Family Television Council and the Concerned Women for America.

Not all antipornography activists were on the political right, however. Prominent feminists such as Catherine MacKinnon and Andrea Dworkin argued that pornography has a disproportionate impact on women in both the production of pornographic materials and the effects of them on male behavior. Their assertions were bolstered by porn star Linda Lovelace, who claimed that her performance in *Deep Throat* was under duress—including physical, sexual, and emotional abuse by husband-director Chuck Traynor. MacKinnon and Dworkin argued that pornography is bad for all women because it sexualizes male domination. The antipornography feminists were successful in building a large feminist movement against pornography, including Women Against Pornography. In the 1980s, they successfully lobbied for new laws at the local level, with MacKinnon, an attorney, working with municipalities to draft strict antipornography measures. One such law, in Indianapolis, explicitly cited the protection of women as grounds for banning pornography, and even sanctioned lawsuits against pornography producers for damages done to women; the ordinance was struck down in federal court.

Not all feminists agreed with the antipornography position. So-called sex radicals or pro-sex feminists believed that the arguments against pornography victimize women by robbing them of agency in their sexuality. Some feminists have sought political alliances with sex workers and the gay and lesbian movements, arguing that feminists have common ground with persons society views as sexually deviant. Groups such as FACT (Feminist Anti-Censorship Task Force) worked to oppose legislation and litigation against pornography on the basis of free speech. In addition, pro-sex feminists have been critical of the political ties mainstream feminists established with right-wing activists, whom they regarded as part of a broader agenda to limit access to birth control and abortion.

The antipornography campaign in the 1990s shifted to the Internet, where pornography images were more easily and cheaply transmitted and, presumably, more likely to reach children. In addition, many recognized that the Internet allows for greater ease and anonymity in the exchange of child pornography. Congress made several attempts to regulate the Internet, including the Child Online Protection Act (1998), which was struck down by a lower federal court on the grounds of speech rights, a decision upheld by the Supreme Court in *Ashcroft v. American Civil Liberties Union* (2002).

Claire E. Rasmussen

See also: Dworkin, Andrea; Falwell, Jerry; Feminism, Second-Wave; Feminism, Third-Wave; Flynt, Larry; Hefner, Hugh; Internet; MacKinnon, Catharine; Moral Majority; National Endowment for the Arts; Sexual Revolution; Wildmon, Donald.

Further Reading

Attorney General's Commission on Pornography: Final Report. Vols. I and II. Washington, DC: U.S. Department of Justice, 1986.

Califia, Pat. *Public Sex: The Culture of Radical Sex.* Pittsburgh, PA: Cleis Press, 1994.

Commission on Obscenity and Pornography (1967) Report. Washington, DC: U.S. Government Printing Office, 1970.

De Grazia, Edward. *Girls Lean Back Everywhere: The Law of Obscenity and the Assault on Genius.* New York: Random House, 1992.

Kipnis, Laura. *Bound and Gagged: Pornography and the Politics of Fantasy in America.* New York: Grove Press, 1996.

Lynn, Barry W. *Polluting the Censorship Debate: A Summary and Critique of the Final Report of the Attorney General's Commission on Pornography*. Washington, DC: American Civil Liberties Union, 1986.

Postmodernism

Although not easily defined, the term "postmodernism" refers to the contemporary period in Western culture—"after" modernism—and the corresponding view among scholars, cultural critics, and philosophers that new modes of thought and expression in the post–World War II era have broken down or transcended established rules and categories. Trends and concepts associated with postmodernism include the dominance of mass media, globalization and cultural pluralism, the blurring of national boundaries, artistic eclecticism and the mixing of genres, skepticism toward science and progress, parody and self-reference, a rejection of traditional concepts of knowledge, and a world of many equal and competing ideologies and "isms."

Any serious approach to understanding postmodernism begins with two foundational works, Fredric Jameson's *Postmodernism, or The Cultural Logic of Late Capitalism* (1991) and Jean-François Lyotard's *The Postmodern Condition: A Report on Knowledge* (1979). According to Jameson, the essence of postmodernism is the commercialism of culture, characterized by a consumerist demand for increasingly novel productions of art and knowledge, and a proliferation of texts that blur high culture and low culture without regard to authority or the cultural canon. According to Lyotard, postindustrial societies, due to computerization, have created a postmodern condition by altering the status of knowledge and power, rendering the end of the "grand narrative" in which knowledge is seen as whole and giving way to multiple narratives in which knowledge is fragmented.

In the American culture wars, social conservatives have generally equated postmodernism with moral and cultural relativism, which they blame on liberals. Critics charge that postmodern thought contradicts itself by making arguments that rely on the same conventional hermeneutics and epistemology it claims to reject—a theory and methodology that rejects theory and methodology. Opponents of postmodernism typically vilify proponents for failing to affirm traditional values and narratives. Part of this response is a call for a return to the cultural canon, or "great books." Cultural literacy, it is said, is about shared values necessary for social cohesion among members of society. Thus, the resurgence of religious fundamentalism is linked to the desire for certainty in postmodern times. Even some leftists have expressed contempt for postmodernism, seeing it as a threat to political activism. Without agreed-upon norms,

they argue, it is difficult to organize mass movements for promoting social justice.

Critics of postmodernism generally take a dim view of revisionist history, multicultural studies, and in particular literary analysis involving deconstructionism, structuralism, and post-structuralism, all of which they regard as being connected with intellectual anarchy and confusion. Especially worrisome to critics are the postmodern assertions that (1) language is signification of reality, not reality itself; (2) texts are subjective facsimiles of reality; and (3) much of what we feel and experience in our mass-communication society is an illusion, a "hyperreality" based on simulation, including a type of simulation ("simulacra") that has no corresponding reality.

Proponents of the postmodern influence on higher learning argue that the "dead white men" celebrated in traditional accounts of history and represented in the literary canon comprise only one strand of the national narrative. They regard the trend to incorporate considerations of race, class, and gender into the classroom as emancipating and democratic because it gives voice to the previously marginalized and opens space for other narratives. Postmodernists also emphasize that every text, whether a book, speech, song, painting, film, or other creative expression, is essentially incomplete, a fragment, and that much can be learned by considering what was left out. Defenders of postmodernism emphasize that grappling with complexity enlarges human understanding while developing the critical thinking skills necessary for the information age.

The postmodern critique of science, including a rejection of Enlightenment principles and optimism about human progress, is a reaction to the development of atomic weapons and the use of them on Japan at the end of World War II. Postmodernism sees science as having limitations, and scientists as being guided by ideology and blinded by hubris. Whereas modernism is said to have emphasized rational thought—or the need for it—postmodernism stresses the importance of emotion and feelings. In reaction to the postmodern attack on science, physicist Alan Sokal in the 1990s debunked critics by succeeding in getting a postmodern journal to publish his hoax essay which nonsensically asserted that physical reality is simply a social construct. On the other hand, years earlier Thomas S. Kuhn in *The Structure of Scientific Revolutions* (1962) reasonably argued that the scientific community depends fundamentally on groupthink and ritual, and is characterized by a reluctance to think outside the prescribed paradigm.

In the American political arena, the postmodern trend is reflected in less party loyalty and the rise of independent voters—with a corresponding, and paradoxical, rise in partisanship. While there is more information available about government, opinion polls show that it has not increased knowledge about what government is doing. Information is largely communicated in sound bites, even as government and other institutional Web sites post PDF files containing thousands of documents and reports. There is a prevailing sense that issues are too complex, contributing to the popularity of pundits who simplify issues and events, narrowcasting media that construct narratives for a specialized ideological audience, and Internet bloggers who challenge the conventional media hierarchy. Politics lapses into entertainment, with actors and professional wrestlers getting elected to high office and presidential candidates obligated to appear on *The Oprah Winfrey Show.*

It has been argued that postmodernism is a condition of contemporary life; like the weather, it is not something an individual accepts or rejects. That attribute was described early on by Alvin Toffler in his best-seller *Future Shock* (1970), which details the short-lived nature of products, families, and relationships in the contemporary world. Even before that, media theorist Marshall McLuhan warned of postmodern developments then under way, pronouncing in the 1960s that "the medium is the message" and predicting a "global village" of instantaneous communication. In the twenty-first century, the Internet is said to epitomize postmodernism, offering a vast storehouse of knowledge at the global level—culture that is both high and low, entertainment and commercialism, a mishmash of visual images, competing narratives, and communication that is characteristically fragmentary and fleeting.

Roger Chapman

See also: Deconstructionism; Fundamentalism, Religious; Great Books; Internet; McLuhan, Marshall; Multiculturalism and Ethnic Studies; Nuclear Age; Relativism, Moral; Revisionist History; Science Wars; Sokal Affair; Structuralism and Post-Structuralism.

Further Reading

Jameson, Fredric. *Postmodernism, or The Cultural Logic of Late Capitalism.* Durham, NC: Duke University Press, 1991.

Lyon, David. *Postmodernity.* 2nd ed. Minneapolis: University of Minnesota Press, 1999.

Lyotard, Jean-François. *The Postmodern Condition: A Report on Knowledge.* Trans. Geoff Bennington and Brian Massumi. Minneapolis: University of Minnesota Press, 1984.

Powell, Jim. *Postmodernism for Beginners.* New York: Writers and Readers Publishing, 1998.

Premillennial Dispensationalism

The term "premillennial dispensationalism" refers to the eschatological ("last things" or end times) belief system embraced by millions of Christian fundamentalists, evangelicals, and Pentecostal Protestants. As pre-millennialists, they believe that the return of Christ will precede (*pre*) the establishment of a thousand-year (*millennial*) kingdom on Earth (based on a literal interpretation of Revelation 20:1–6). As dispensationalists, they divide history into a number (usually seven) of distinct periods (*dispensations*). Many contemporary premillennial dispensationalists are convinced that human history is nearing the end of the second-to-last dispensation (the "church age"); as the largest constituency of the Religious Right, they support political positions that line up with their view of eschatology. They are often criticized for accepting as literal the figurative and metaphorical language of the Bible, such as insisting that references to Israel pertain to the modern secular nation rather than God's spiritual followers.

In interpreting current events, premillennial dispensationalists seek "signs of the times" in an attempt to pinpoint the fulfillment of specific prophecy from various apocalyptic biblical texts, including Ezekiel, Daniel, and Revelation. They teach of the "rapture," in which Christians who are alive will be "caught up" to heaven (based on an interpretation of 1 Thessalonians 4:15–17) and spared having to experience the "great tribulation" (a term found in Matthew 24:21). The tribulation, a terrible cataclysmic upheaval but with a relatively short duration, is said to be followed by the millennium, characterized by Christ reigning with 144,000 Jews. The end of the world comes with a literal battle of Armageddon (referred to in Revelation 16:16), in which Christ and the Jews successfully defend Jerusalem against the armies of a reconstituted Roman Empire (world government). Then there is the Final Judgment, with Satan (also known as the Antichrist, who had misguided many by posing as a peacemaker) being eternally damned along with his followers while God's people are ushered into the kingdom of heaven.

American culture was introduced to dispensationalism by the Anglo-Irish evangelist John Nelson Darby, a leader of the Plymouth Brethren sect, who conducted seven preaching tours in the United States (1867–1882). Reeling in the aftermath of the Civil War and undergoing social upheaval by industrialization and urbanization, the United States proved a fertile ground for this new teaching. Unlike progressive postmillennial eschatology that foresaw human civilization improving generation after generation to the point where it would usher in a Christian golden age culminating with the Second Coming, premillennial dispensationalism offered a grim picture of the future: wars, famine, natural calamities, and escalating human wickedness. Darby's dispensational system was further disseminated by (1) the *Scofield Reference Bible* (1909, 1917, 1967), a highly popular annotated edition of the King James Version; (2) *The Fundamentals* (1910–1915), texts sanctioning premillennial dispensationalism as fundamentalist orthodoxy; and (3) fundamentalist Bible schools such as the Moody Bible Institute (1889), Dallas Theological Seminary (1924), and Bob Jones University (1927). Graduates of the latter two institutions were instrumental in making premillennial dispensationalism a part of popular culture: Hal Lindsey, the author of the best-seller *The Late, Great Planet Earth* (1970), is a graduate of Dallas Theological Seminary; and Tim LaHaye, the co-author (with Jerry Jenkins) of the best-selling *Left Behind* fiction series (beginning in 1995), is a graduate of Bob Jones University. Perhaps equal in effectiveness at introducing premillennial dispensationalist theology to the masses has been Jack T. Chick, who in 1970 began producing cartoon tracts infused with the doctrine—over half a million copies have been sold.

In the culture wars, the politics springing from premillennial dispensationalism tend to be antiprogressive, antiscientific, and infused with an otherworldly pessimism about human potential. As time draws near to the end, society is expected to become more depraved and immoral—precisely how premillennial dispensationalists have interpreted the counterculture, feminist, and gay rights movements. In addition, an apostasy is to occur within the mainline churches, which premillennial dispensationalists see as being possibly carried out by the Christian ecumenical movement and the World Council of Churches. Efforts toward world peace and the reduction of nuclear arms are regarded as swimming against the tide of biblical prophecy and perhaps causing an unwanted delay of the Second Coming. Since prophecy suggests that the Antichrist will establish a world dictatorship, premillennial dispensationalists opposed the Soviet Union and the international communist movement, just as they have been negative toward the Roman Catholic Church, the United Nations, the European Economic Community, multinational corporations, and any form of governmental centralization. Since premillennial dispensationalists anticipate the rebuilding of the Jewish temple on the old site in Jerusalem (which for them would be a sign that the rapture is near), they lobby for an American foreign policy that highly supports the security of Israel.

Roger Chapman

See also: Bob Jones University; Chick, Jack; Counterculture; Evangelicalism; Fundamentalism, Religious; Israel; LaHaye, Tim, and Beverly LaHaye; Nuclear Age; Religious Right; Soviet Union and Russia; World Council of Churches.

Further Reading

Boyer, Paul. *When Time Shall Be No More: Prophecy Belief in Modern American Culture.* Cambridge, MA: Belknap Press of Harvard University Press, 1992.

Clark, Victoria. *Allies for Armageddon: The Rise of Christian Zionism.* New Haven, CT: Yale University Press, 2007.

Frykholm, Amy Johnson. *Rapture Culture: "Left Behind" in Evangelical America.* New York: Oxford University Press, 2004.

Kieruff, Stephen. "Belief in 'Armageddon Theology' and Willingness to Risk Nuclear War." *Journal for the Scientific Study of Religion* 30:1 (March 1991): 81–93.

Presidential Pardons

A presidential pardon is a grant of release from the punishment or consequences of a federal offense prior to or after conviction. President George W. Bush issued 189 pardons and commuted eleven prison sentences, the lowest number of any two-term president since World War II. In comparison, Harry S. Truman, who served eighty-two days short of two full terms, issued the most pardons, commutations, and remissions of fines in the postwar era, totaling 2,044. Dwight D. Eisenhower issued 1,157 in two terms; John F. Kennedy 575 in less than one term; Lyndon B. Johnson 1,187 in less than two terms; Richard Nixon 926 in less than two terms; Gerald R. Ford 409 in less than one term; Jimmy Carter 566 in one term; Ronald Reagan 406 in two terms; George H.W. Bush 77 in one term; and Bill Clinton 459 in two terms. Although most presidential pardons are noncontroversial, in the culture wars certain pardons have been publicly perceived as a political abuse of power.

The president's authority to issue pardons is established by Article II, Section 2, of the U.S. Constitution: "The President . . . shall have Power to grant Reprieves and Pardons for Offenses against the United States, except in Cases of Impeachment." The U.S. Supreme Court in *Ex parte Grossman* (1925) affirmed that the president is authorized to grant pardons before, during, or after a trial. In *Schick v. Reed* (1974), the high court ruled that a president's power to pardon is provided exclusively by the Constitution and "cannot be modified, abridged or diminished by Congress." With few exceptions, pardons are processed by the Office of the Pardon Attorney in the U.S. Department of Justice. Despite the lack of constitutional restrictions on the conferring of pardons, specific federal guidelines are in place to ensure an orderly review of pardon requests, with recommendations forwarded to the White House. Shortly after Eisenhower became president in 1953, he announced a new policy of openness in the granting of pardons, using the occasion to indirectly criticize Truman for issuing a number of pardons without first consulting with the Justice Department.

The most controversial pardon was the one Ford granted to Nixon in the wake of the Watergate scandal. On September 8, 1974, in a national telecast announcing the decision, Ford explained that he was pardoning Nixon for "any offenses against the United States, which he . . . has committed or may have committed while in office" in order to help the nation heal. Since Nixon had personally chosen Ford to succeed Spiro T. Agnew (who resigned the vice presidency while under a legal cloud), many suspected a quid pro quo—that is, that Ford was chosen as vice president with the understanding that he would issue Nixon a pardon once becoming president. Ford denied the accusation, but he did divulge that the Nixon administration had discussed the possibility that Nixon had the power, while still president, to pardon himself. Ford also admitted that certain Nixon staffers had approached him on the matter of a possible pardon. But Ford maintained that there had been "no deal" and that his decision to pardon Nixon was "out of my concern to serve the best interests of my country." The pardon virtually ended the Watergate investigation, leading critics such as Senator Robert Byrd (D-WV) to declare Ford's action "the cover-up of the cover-up." The political fallout from that decision is probably the main reason Ford lost the 1976 election to Carter.

Less controversial was Ford's 1977 pardon of Iva Toguri D'Aquino, also known as Tokyo Rose. Her pardon came long after she completed more than six years in prison for treason, specifically for broadcasting Japanese propaganda to American servicemen during World War II. Without offering an explanation, Ford pardoned her on his last day in office, restoring her U.S. citizenship. Ford also began pardoning individuals who had been convicted of draft evasion during the Vietnam War—a policy dramatically expanded by Carter, who, on his first day in office, granted unconditional amnesty to an estimated 10,000 draft dodgers. Veterans' groups were angered by Carter's blanket pardon, and Senator Barry Goldwater (R-AZ) called it "the most disgraceful thing that a president has ever done." Although Truman had earlier pardoned a number of individuals who had violated the Selective Service Act or deserted during World War II, most had already completed prison time.

The pardon granted to Nixon was not the only political pardon. In 1953, Truman pardoned two former congressmen: J. Parnell Thomas (R-NJ), once head of the powerful House Committee on Un-American Activities, and Andrew J. May (D-KY), both of whom had been convicted of fraud. In 1971, Nixon commuted the prison sentence of James R. "Jimmy" Hoffa, the former president of the International Brotherhood of Teamsters, who had been convicted of jury tampering and fraud; this was a controversial decision because of Hoffa's earlier support of Nixon. Reagan was under pressure to pardon certain figures involved in the Iran-Contra scandal, including Oliver North, but declined to do so. In 1980, Reagan did pardon two FBI officials, W. Mark Felt and Edward S. Miller, both convicted of directing the 1972–1973 break-ins, without search warrants, of suspected hideouts of Weather Underground fugitives. Felt probably would not have been pardoned had his identity as Deep Throat, the Watergate informant, then been known. (He revealed that role in 2005.) On December 24, 1992, nearing the

end of his presidency, George H.W. Bush pardoned six individuals connected with the Iran-Contra scandal, including former secretary of defense Caspar Weinberger, who was scheduled to go on trial. The prosecutor of the Iran-Contra scandal, Lawrence Walsh, charged that Bush's action amounted to a cover-up and that the outgoing president was simply hiding his own involvement in the scandal.

President-elect Bill Clinton, commenting on Bush's Iran-Contra pardon, stated, "I am concerned by any action that sends a signal that if you work for the government, you are beyond the law." Eight years later, however, Clinton caused a brouhaha by issuing 140 pardons on his last day in the White House. Most controversial was the pardon of Marc Rich, a fugitive financier under federal indictment for evading $48 million in taxes. The press quickly learned that Rich's pardon was lobbied for by his ex-wife, Denise Rich, a generous financial contributor to the Democratic Party and the Clinton Presidential Library.

Not wishing to be accused of quid pro quo, President George W. Bush in December 2008 pardoned an individual who had been convicted of real estate fraud, but shortly afterwards rescinded the pardon after learning that the individual's family had provided donations to the Republican Party. Although Bush issued relatively few pardons, he set off his own controversy on July 2, 2007, when he granted clemency to I. Lewis "Scooter" Libby, his vice president's former chief of staff, sparing him from going to prison for perjury and obstructing justice. Libby had been implicated during an investigation of the 2003 leaking of the identity of a CIA operative after her husband had written an op-ed piece accusing the Bush administration of misleading the public about weapons of mass destruction in Iraq.

Roger Chapman

See also: Agnew, Spiro T.; Bush Family; Eisenhower, Dwight D.; Felt, W. Mark; Ford, Gerald; Iran-Contra Affair; Nixon, Richard; North, Oliver; Truman, Harry S.; War Protesters; Watergate.

Further Reading

Krent, Harold J. *Presidential Powers.* New York: New York University Press, 2005.

Moore, Kathleen Dean. *Pardons: Justice, Mercy, and the Public Interest.* New York: Oxford University Press, 1989.

Ruckman, P.S., Jr. "Executive Clemency in the United States: Origins, Development and Analysis (1900–1993)." *Presidential Studies Quarterly* 27 (1997): 251–71.

Prison Reform

For more than three decades, since the early 1970s, the United States has undergone an unprecedented wave of prison expansion, building and filling prisons faster than at any time in human history. In 1972, federal and state prisons held 196,000 inmates, with another 130,000 in local jails. Since then, the national inmate population has dramatically risen. By 2008, 2.3 million people were behind bars in America—far exceeding any other nation in the world—and costing taxpayers $60 billion annually. Many politicians, both Democrats and Republicans, designed and continue to support incarceration policies that mandate long prison terms even for victimless crimes. In many respects, the packed jails and prisons (holding 751 people for every 100,000 of the population) are symbolic of the culture wars.

Advocates of "tough on crime" policies assert that the decline in crime rates proves that incarceration is the best way to preserve law and order. Even so, a wide range of professionals in the criminal justice system, from police officers and judges to legal aid workers and prison wardens, are in favor of reforming the current prison system. They argue that there are less expensive, more humane, and more effective ways to solve crime at the community law-enforcement level. Those concerned with social and racial injustice, together with the expanding numbers of family and community members affected by what critics call the U.S. incarceration binge, are also vocal supporters of prison reform.

Much of the increase in the U.S. prison population can be attributed to mandatory minimum sentencing, such as the "Three Strikes and You're Out" law passed in California in 1994 (calling for twenty-five years to life for any felony conviction following two prior convictions). In 2003, lawyers challenged the constitutionality of that law in two cases heard before the U.S. Supreme Court—*Ewing v. California* and *Lokyer v. Andrade*. In one case, a man was found guilty of stealing videotapes worth $153 from a retail store on two separate occasions and sentenced to fifty years to life. The other man stole three golf clubs from a sporting goods store and was sentenced to twenty-five years to life. The justices ruled that the law did not represent cruel and unusual punishment and let the sentences stand. Marc Mauer of The Sentencing Project, one of the main groups advocating prison reform, noted that, as a consequence of those rulings, California taxpayers would spend well in excess of $1 million to keep the two men in jail.

The policies adopted in the mid-1980s that declared a "war on drugs" have also led to a spike in the incarceration rate. Increased criminalization for drug possession resulted in long prison terms for many low-level dealers and drug addicts. From 1985 to 2000, nonviolent drug offenses alone accounted for 65 percent of the rise in the federal prison population. During the same period, violent criminals accounted for only 6 percent of the overall increase. From 1980 to 2008, the number incarcerated for drug-related crimes increased from about 40,000 to nearly 500,000.

With 70 percent of funding for the war on drugs directed to law enforcement that results in high arrest rates, treatment options for addicts became less available. Doctors and others in public health argue that drug addiction should be considered a medical problem rather than a crime, and believe that lack of treatment for addicts exacerbates demand. Those in favor of continued criminalization argue that the lifting of harsh sanctions will result in more addicts.

Even though the vast majority of drug users and a majority of dealers are white and live in the suburbs, street-level law enforcement has been carried out primarily in urban minority neighborhoods characterized by severe underemployment. In his book *Breaking Rank* (2005), former Seattle police chief Norm Stamper exposed racial profiling and the targeting of young African Americans. Critics argue that this approach to selective law enforcement has led to the disproportionate arrest and imprisonment of minorities and explains why, by the 2000s, nearly half of all prison inmates were African Americans.

In the era of prison expansion, meanwhile, crime dramas and high-profile violent crimes involving homicides were commonplace in U.S. television programming. Between 1990 and 1998, the number of crime stories on the network evening news rose from 542 to 1,392. Media watch groups have likewise documented dramatic increases in stories about homicide, even while the actual murder rate dropped 20 percent. Being "tough on crime" was considered a winning electoral strategy for both political parties, so campaigns that emphasized the need for "law and order" became election-year standards. While public fear of violent criminals and unsafe streets generates political support for long prison terms, statistics about the real jail population belie that concern. During the 1990s, for example, more than half of new inmates incarcerated in state and federal prisons were convicted of nonviolent drug and property offenses.

After more than three decades, reformers believe that changes in U.S. prison policy could be on the horizon. In an era of falling crime rates, crime seems to have lost some of its potency as a political "hot-button" issue—a trend that may bode well for agents of change. Financial concerns have drawn attention to the escalating costs of prisons at the expense of education and other social services. And the failure of the war on drugs to substantially reduce substance abuse, along with the recognition that drug criminalization policies increase economic distress in poor minority communities, has led to an openness toward exploring alternative policies. Amid continuing budgetary shortfalls in California, for example, *Corrections Management Quarterly* (1997) published a study demonstrating that almost a quarter of incoming prisoners could be diverted to community-based programs, at a savings of up to 20 percent for new prison admissions. In 1999 and 2000, voters in Arizona and California, respectively, approved legislation designed to handle thousands of low-level drug offenders through treatment rather than imprisonment.

Robin Andersen

See also: Gilmore, Gary; Horton, Willie; War on Drugs; Zero Tolerance.

Further Reading

Bennett, W. Lance. *News: The Politics of Illusion.* 5th ed. New York: Longman, 2003.

Donziger, Steven R. *The Real War on Crime: The Report of the National Criminal Justice Commission.* New York: HarperPerennial, 1996.

Mauer, Marc. *Race to Incarcerate.* New York: New Press, 2006.

Stamper, Norm. *Breaking Rank: A Top Cop's Exposé of the Dark Side of American Policing.* New York: Nation Books, 2005.

Privacy Rights

Privacy rights protect individuals from government intrusion into their personal affairs. The right to privacy is controversial in the United States not least because there is no language in the Constitution or Bill of Rights that explicitly guarantees such a right, yet it has been invoked by the Supreme Court to justify contentious decisions on hot-button social issues. By declaring that reproductive rights, abortion rights, and gay rights are protected by a constitutional right to privacy, the high court has thrust itself into the middle of the culture wars.

The Bill of Rights, consisting of the first ten amendments to the Constitution, explicitly enumerates the individual freedoms and limits on government power referred to as civil liberties. While the right to privacy is not among them, Justice Louis Brandeis argued in his dissent in *Olmstead v. United States* (1928) that the document was intended to embody the principle of limited government and therefore conferred "the right to be let alone." Yet the right to privacy was not formally recognized in constitutional law until *Griswold v. Connecticut* (1965), involving a state ban on the distribution of information about and the use of contraceptives. The majority opinion, written by Justice William O. Douglas, declared the law unconstitutional, claiming that a married couple's reproductive rights are protected from government interference by implied "zones of privacy." These privacy rights, while not specifically enumerated, were said to be found in the "penumbras" of individual freedoms guaranteed by the First, Third, Fourth, Fifth, Ninth, and Fourteenth amendments.

The *Griswold* decision opened the door to subsequent rulings that extended privacy rights beyond the issue of marital reproduction. First, *Eisenstadt v. Baird* (1972) guaranteed the right of unmarried couples to contraception. This was immediately followed by the landmark decision in *Roe v. Wade* (1973), which relied on the Due Process Clause of the Fourteenth Amendment to strike down a Texas state law prohibiting abortions and extended implied privacy rights to a woman's right to choose. This ruling represents one of the most controversial Supreme Court decisions in American history and catalyzed the polarization of society.

The constitutional protection of privacy rights occupies a particularly contentious position in the culture wars because it has incited battles on two fronts. The first involves the political and moral implications of the Supreme Court's decisions, which set social conservatism's commitment to traditional and transcendent principles against progressive liberalism's dedication to the freedom of personal lifestyle choices. This struggle has primarily played out in the context of abortion debates. On one side are social conservatives self-defined as pro-life, who believe that abortion is morally wrong because all life is sacred and begins at conception. This position is represented by the Religious Right and groups such as the National Right to Life Committee and Operation Rescue. On the other side are liberals self-defined as pro-choice, who argue that women have a guaranteed right to complete control over their individual body, including reproduction. This position is represented by groups such as NARAL Pro-Choice America and Planned Parenthood.

The second front on which the culture war over privacy rights is fought involves the procedural, and ultimately political, issue of how the Supreme Court arrived at these controversial decisions. Specifically, social conservatives have called into question the legitimacy of the high court by branding justices who have supported the constitutional protection of privacy rights as "judicial activists." This pejorative term connotes the willingness of justices to "disregard" the language of the Constitution and intent of the framers, and to base decisions on their own political convictions. In the words of Robert H. Bork, a conservative denied Senate confirmation as a Supreme Court nominee in 1987, liberal justices "invent a general right of privacy."

This controversy was again inflamed when a Court majority returned to the issue of privacy rights in *Lawrence v. Texas* (2003). The majority opinion in this case, written by Justice Anthony Kennedy, upheld the constitutional protection of sexual privacy, declaring a state antisodomy law an "intrusion into the personal and private life of the individual." Advocates for gay rights celebrated the decision as a major victory. Conversely, social conservatives pointed to the decision as evidence of rampant judicial activism and rallied around Justice Antonin Scalia's dissent, which claimed "the Court has taken sides in the culture war" and "largely signed on to the so-called homosexual agenda."

During the 2004 presidential election campaign, Republican incumbent George W. Bush roused the overwhelming support of social conservatives by suggesting that judicial activism and the Supreme Court's constitutional protection of privacy rights threaten the two principles they held most dear—the sanctity of marriage and the sanctity of human life. This strategic use of the culture wars for political gain helped deliver Bush a second term in the White House.

Richard Gibbons Holtzman

See also: Abortion; Birth Control; Bush Family; Douglas, William O.; Gay Rights Movement; Judicial Wars; Operation Rescue; Planned Parenthood; Religious Right; *Roe v. Wade* (1973); Sodomy Laws.

Further Reading

Bork, Robert H. *The Tempting of America: The Political Seduction of the Law.* New York: Free Press, 1990.

Garrow, David J. *Liberty and Sexuality: The Right to Privacy and the Making of* Roe v. Wade. Berkeley: University of California Press, 1998.

O'Brien, David M. *Privacy, Law and Public Policy.* New York: Praeger, 1979.

Roosevelt, Kermit, III. *The Myth of Judicial Activism: Making Sense of Supreme Court Decisions.* New Haven, CT: Yale University Press, 2006.

Tribe, Laurence H. "*Lawrence v. Texas:* The 'Fundamental Right' That Dare Not Speak Its Name." *Harvard Law Review,* 117:6 (2004): 1894–955.

Warren, Samuel V., and Louis D. Brandeis. "The Right to Privacy." *Harvard Law Review* 4:5 (1890): 193–220.

Privatization

A topic of the culture wars since at least the 1980s, privatization in contemporary America refers primarily to government outsourcing (contracting out) of public services to private companies, or, more radically, the full transfer of business ownership from the public to the private sector (government divestiture.) A government-issued school voucher that can be used to pay for education at a private school is one form of privatization. Supporters of privatization typically assert that government is a public monopoly that raises money through taxation and consequently lacks the incentive to reduce cost and improve performance. With privatization, they argue, the entrepreneurial virtues of choice, competition, and efficiency can be injected into the delivery of public services. Critics of privatization argue that public services, which are generally intended to improve the quality of life, invariably suffer when the profitability of the provider is the primary aim. In addition, it is said, outsourcing has sometimes led to corruption, lax governmental oversight, and increased costs to taxpayers (including user fees).

Early proponents of American privatization included Milton Friedman, the Nobel Prize–winning economist and author of *Capitalism and Freedom* (1962); Gordon Tullock, the public-choice theorist and author of *Private Wants, Public Means* (1970); Anthony Downs, the Brookings Institution fellow and author of *Inside Bureaucracy* (1967); William Niskanen, chairman of the libertarian think tank the Cato Institute and author of *Bureaucracy and Representative Government* (1971); and Peter Drucker, the specialist on modern management and author of *The Age of Discontinuity* (1968). It was Drucker who coined the term "reprivatization."

In 1969, after New York City municipal workers were slow in clearing the streets of a major snowfall, recommendations were made for contracting out municipal services, including a proposal for privatized garbage collection. However, the initiative was nixed after labor unions and others raised objections. During the 1970s, Robert W. Poole, Jr., of the Reason Foundation, launched a promotion of privatization via the newsletter *Fiscal Watchdog* (later renamed *Privatization Watch*). By the 1980s, municipalities across the nation began outsourcing services—according to a survey of 596 American cities, privatization increased by 121 percent from 1982 to 1992, with 28 percent of municipal services being carried out by private firms. By 1992, about half of the nation's large cities were contracting out solid-waste collection, with privatized prisons on the rise as well, beginning in 1984 in Hamilton County, Tennessee. Long-term privatization of public water utilities increased from 400 in 1997 to 1,100 in 2003. Controversy has occasionally erupted over contracting out services to foreign companies—as in 2006, when Mitch Daniels, the Republican governor of Indiana, leased for seventy-five years the 157-mile Indiana Toll Road to an Australian-Spanish consortium for $3.8 billion.

In 1985, President Ronald Reagan announced a federal initiative for privatization. He had been following events in Great Britain, where privatization had been introduced by Prime Minister Margaret Thatcher, who was swayed by arguments of the Adam Smith Institute. During her tenure, many state-owned companies were privatized, from British Petroleum (1979) to Rolls Royce (1987). In addition, in 1988 the British government began requiring competitive bidding for all local government services. Although Reagan's efforts led to the sale of few government-owned entities (one exception was the 1987 divestiture of the freight railroad, Conrail), there was an increase in the outsourcing of many federal support services, including data processing, building maintenance, guard services, and food services.

President George W. Bush, who viewed himself as continuing the "Reagan revolution," tried to extend the privatization argument to Social Security. In championing what he called the "ownership society," Bush recommended that each American worker be allowed to opt out of the public Social Security system and have the amount that is normally deducted from his or her paycheck placed in a private account that is owned and controlled by the individual. In the face of public skepticism, the proposal floundered. Bush's presentation, observers noted, avoided mentioning that, in addition to providing old-age income, Social Security is an insurance program that provides death and disability benefits—something privatized accounts would fail to match. Concern over the dismantling of the safety net is directly related to the controversy over governmental outsourcing—the workers of private firms performing the tasks previously done by government employees in many cases receive lower salaries and fewer benefits, a common method for reducing operational costs. In 2000, the Economic Policy Institute reported that 10 percent of the 1.4 million federal-contractor workers in the United States were receiving wages below the poverty level.

Although Bush failed to reform Social Security, federal outsourcing increased during his presidency, from $207 billion in 2000 to $400 billion in 2006. According to the Federal Procurement Data System, private contracting in 2005 amounted to $268.43 billion for the Department of Defense, $5.49 billion for the Department of State, and $10.33 billion for the Department of Homeland Security. Of all federal contracts issued in 2005, only 48 percent were competitive. In 2007, a no-bid contract worth up to $52 million was awarded by the Justice Department to the consulting firm owned by John Ashcroft, who had resigned as attorney general in 2005—an award called into question by the Democratic-controlled House. There was also criticism aimed at Halliburton, the military contractor formerly headed by Vice President Dick Cheney, as its government contracts increased by 600 percent during the first five years of the Iraq War. In the viewpoint of many observers, privatization is especially prone to political corruption. From 2000 to 2007, according to one report, the top twenty federal contractors in America spent $300 million on lobbying and $23 million on contributions to political campaigns.

Opponents argue further that privatization tends to make government activities less transparent, sometimes making it seem that government is being reduced when in fact it is being increased by proxy. By the fifth year of the Iraq War (2007), the private security firm Blackwater Worldwide, with 850 operatives in the war zone, had garnered more than $1 billion in no-bid federal contracts. That same year, there were 163,000 nonmilitary personnel in Iraq (including 6,467 armed-security personnel), working as contractors for the Pentagon. Such reliance on the private sector, critics argued, was a way for the Bush administration to avoid implementing the draft by hiring "mercenaries"; at the time, contractors represented 10 percent of the American presence in Iraq. Moreover, it was argued, since the battle-zone fatalities of contractors—more than 1,000 by 2007—are not part of the official tally of war dead, privatization enabled the U.S. government to minimize the true scale of the war's human cost.

Roger Chapman

See also: Bush Family; Charter Schools; Cheney Family; Compassionate Conservatism; Friedman, Milton; Reagan, Ronald; School Vouchers; Social Security; Welfare Reform.

Further Reading

Kahn, Si. *Fox in the Henhouse: How Privatization Threatens Democracy.* San Francisco: Berrett-Koehler, 2005.

Rasor, Dina. *Betraying Our Troops: The Destructive Results of Privatizing War.* New York: Palgrave Macmillan, 2007.

Reason Foundation Web site. www.reason.org.

Roland, Gérard. *Privatization: Successes and Failures.* New York: Columbia University Press, 2008.

Savas, E.S. *Privatization and Public Private Partnerships.* New York: Chatham House, 2000.

Shichor, David. *Punishment for Profit: Private Prisons / Public Concerns.* Thousand Oaks, CA: Sage, 1995.

Progressive Christians Uniting

Progressive Christians Uniting (founded in 1996 as Mobilization for the Human Family) is an ecumenical organization launched by John Cobb, Jr., and George Regas in the Los Angeles area to provide resources for Christian clergy, laity, and congregations that promote progressive political activism.

Eager to debunk the presumption that Christian theology is the exclusive preserve of Christian conservatives like Pat Robertson and James Dobson, the group challenges the Religious Right's appropriation of the Bible and Jesus to promote goals such as organized prayer in schools, pro-life legislation, and the teaching of intelligent design. In *Progressive Christians Speak* (2003), the organization denounces the Christian Right for promoting a "politics of nostalgia and fear" and a mythical past when the United States was "harmonious, paternal and hierarchical." Progressive Christians Uniting denies that such a past ever existed while questioning its theological justification.

Several contributors to *Getting on Message* (2005) lament that religious progressives have allowed the Religious Right to "hijack Jesus" for causes utterly inconsistent with the spirit of Christ. The group seeks to reclaim the progressive Jesus of scripture and discern biblical mandates for diversity, egalitarianism, reconciliation, economic justice, and equity. Progressive Christians Uniting argues that progressives are more faithful to the import of scripture because the Bible is an intrinsically progressive text.

A core set of theological beliefs, articulated in the group's Confession of Faith, inform the organization's work: (1) While professing commitment to scripture, the sacraments, and Christian history, Christian progressives should also read scripture in light of the best modern research. (2) Embracing, rather than resisting, contemporary scholarship is the most responsible way to apply Christian faith to the questions and concerns of present-day society. By belief and temperament, the organization is largely optimistic with regard to human will and potential. The group envisions progressive Christians—sustained by the Holy Spirit and informed by the tolerant principles of the Enlightenment—challenging and replacing conservative religious, ethical, and social norms with an inclusive and justice-centered option for society's marginalized and disinherited.

Progressive Christians Uniting publications, conferences, and mobilization efforts have stressed the need for criminal justice reform implementing restorative models, antisweatshop campaigns, treatment rather than incarceration of nonviolent drug offenders, gender equity, more accommodating immigration policies, and environmental protection. The organization was highly critical of the foreign policy of President George W. Bush, in particular the U.S.-led invasion of Iraq.

Richard C. Goode

See also: American Civil Religion; Campolo, Anthony "Tony"; Creationism and Intelligent Design; Dobson, James; Evangelicalism; Fundamentalism, Religious; Religious Right; Robertson, Pat; School Prayer; Sider, Ron; Wallis, Jim.

Further Reading

Cobb, John B., Jr., ed. *Progressive Christians Speak: A Different Voice on Faith and Politics.* Louisville, KY: Westminster John Knox Press, 2003.

Laarman, Peter, ed. *Getting on Message: Challenging the Christian Right from the Heart of the Gospel.* Boston: Beacon, 2005.

Progressive Christians Uniting Web site. www.progressivechristiansuniting.org.

Promise Keepers

An evangelical men's movement based in Denver, Colorado, Promise Keepers was created to help men remain faithful to their Christian ideals and to influence the

Members of Promise Keepers, a men's evangelical Christian group that promotes traditional family values, moral integrity, and personal spiritual commitment, attend a gathering of 25,000 adherents in Fayetteville, Arkansas, in 2005. *(Charles Ommanney/Getty Images)*

surrounding culture. Although promoted as a ministry, Promise Keepers has a political aspect that has placed it squarely in the midst of the culture wars.

Bill McCartney, former coach of the University of Colorado men's football team, started Promise Keepers in 1990 after attending a banquet of the Fellowship of Christian Athletes that March. The organization's first national men's conference was held in 1992, attracting attendance of more than 22,000. The movement grew quickly after McCartney appeared on James Dobson's *Focus on the Family* radio show in June 1992. Two years later, Focus on the Family published the group's manifesto, "Seven Promises of a Promise Keeper." During the summer of 1996, twenty-two Promise Keepers conferences were conducted in outdoor stadiums, attended by over a million men. The height of the group's national prominence came on October 4, 1997, with a rally in Washington, D.C., called "Stand in the Gap," which attracted an estimated 600,000 men.

Rooted in the tradition of revivalism, Promise Keepers maintains the mission of "igniting and uniting men to be passionate followers of Jesus Christ" through seven promises. A Promise Keeper agrees to read the Bible regularly, bond with other males, practice sexual purity, build a strong marriage, serve his local church, break down racial barriers, and transform the world through moral and spiritual integrity. Although membership peaked in 1996, Promise Keepers continues to hold conferences and develop resources in North America and internationally.

In 2003, after years of the group struggling financially, board member Thomas S. Fortson, Jr., replaced McCartney as president. In a press conference in April 2004, Fortson announced that Promise Keepers was moving from a "movement" to a "mission." He encouraged evangelical men to "prepare for battle" and "fight the culture war" for America's soul. Fortson's overt politicization of the ministry reaffirmed its connections to the Christian Right. Promise Keepers maintains ties with such evangelical leaders as James Dobson, Bruce Wilkinson, Jack Hayford, and Charles Swindoll. Although the *Nation* magazine has referred to the Promise Keepers as a "third wave" of the Religious Right, taking over for the late Jerry Falwell's Moral Majority and Pat Robertson's Christian Coalition, the organization's leadership argues that its stand is not political but moral.

Groups such as the National Organization for Women have argued that the Promise Keepers' commitment to traditional patriarchal family roles, its opposition to abortion rights and gay marriage, and its "manly" ethos are a threat to women and democracy. Defenders point out that there is no uniform gender ideology among its adherents and that Promise Keepers calls on men to treat their wives as equal partners, contribute more actively to the care of children, and encourage spouses to pursue vocational goals. While Promise Keepers has committed itself to breaking down racial barriers, others argue that its evangelical reliance on individual relationships and moral legalism prevent it from addressing the systemic causes of institutionalized racism.

Kurt W. Peterson

See also: Dobson, James; Evangelicalism; Falwell, Jerry; Family Values; Focus on the Family; Men's Movement; Million Man March; Moral Majority; National Organization for Women; Religious Right.

Further Reading

Bartkowski, John P. *The Promise Keepers: Servants, Soldiers, and Godly Men.* Piscataway, NJ: Rutgers University Press, 2004.

Conason, Joe, Alfred Ross, and Lee Cokorinos. "The Promise Keepers Are Coming: The Third Wave of the Religious Right." *Nation,* October 7, 1996.

Hardisty, Jean V. *Mobilizing Resentment: Conservative Resurgence from the John Birch Society to the Promise Keepers.* Boston: Beacon, 1999.

Hayford, Jack, et al. *Seven Promises of a Promise Keeper.* Nashville, TN: W Publishing, 1999.

Promise Keepers Web site. www.promisekeepers.org.

Williams, Rhys H., ed. *Promise Keepers and the New Masculinity: Private Lives and Public Morality.* Lanham, MD: Lexington Books, 2001.

Public Broadcasting Service

A nonprofit public television broadcasting network, the Public Broadcasting Service (PBS) operates under the Corporation for Public Broadcasting (CPB). Founded on November 3, 1969, PBS is a legacy of President Lyndon B. Johnson's Great Society. In 2009, the PBS network consisted of 356 member stations across the nation and U.S. territories, reaching more than 65 million people. Political conservatives who are philosophically opposed to federal funding of television think PBS should be privatized, arguing that the advent of cable and satellite TV as well as the Internet has rendered public television obsolete. In addition, conservatives have for years complained that PBS has a liberal bias. PBS supporters, liberals and moderates alike, argue that public television enriches society by offering meaningful programming that profit-driven broadcasters would never be motivated to produce or air.

From its broadcast inception of October 5, 1970, PBS has grown into an extensive and sophisticated network. Broadcasts have included children's programs (*Sesame Street, Mister Rogers' Neighborhood, Barney and Friends,* and the like); cultural programs (such as *Masterpiece Theatre, American Playhouse,* and *Live from the Met*); British television series (such as *Upstairs, Downstairs*); science programs (*Nova* and *Cosmos*); news programs (namely *NewsHour with Jim Lehrer*); and a heavy schedule of documentary programs. For fiscal year 2009, CPB awarded PBS $196.7 million for station grants and $76.8 million for programming. About 20 percent of PBS funding comes from the federal government; the rest derives from state and local governments, corporate underwriting, individual viewers, and the marketing of PBS merchandise.

PBS was founded for the purpose of bringing varied programming to the airways at a time when there were only three commercial broadcasters (ABC, CBS, and NBC). In a speech on May 9, 1961, Federal Communications Commission chairman Newton Minnow denounced commercial television as "a vast wasteland" that offers a "steady diet" of "westerns and private eyes." Such programming, Minnow said, is "obviously not in the public interest" and fails to cater to the "special needs of children." Six years later, the report of the Carnegie Commission on Educational Television warned that educational television, then consisting of 182 stations nationwide, would cease to exist without federal funding. In that context, the CPB was founded.

Upon signing the Public Broadcasting Act of 1967, President Johnson spoke idealistically about the "revolutionary" power of television to "change our lives." He expressed the hope that the public broadcasters would "direct that power toward the great and not the trivial purposes" in order to "help make our Nation a replica of the old Greek marketplace, where public affairs took place in view of all the citizens." He also stressed the need for the CPB to be "representative" and "responsible." Ultimately, Johnson believed that public television and radio would "enrich man's spirit" by offering "more than just material wealth."

The CPB originally partnered with National Educational Television (NET), which was founded in 1952 with funding from the Ford Foundation. However, NET had produced some provocative documentaries about the Vietnam War and race relations, rankling conservatives. That is when the CPB decided to form PBS. Later, NET was absorbed by WNDT New York (and renamed WNET) and became an important PBS affiliate, along with KCET Los Angeles, WGBH Boston, and WQED Pittsburgh.

Although it was envisioned for PBS to be independent of government control, that seemed tenuous after Congress balked at providing an automatic earmark tax for public broadcasting. Consequently, the CPB would have to make a budget request every year. The CPB board, moreover, was made up of political appointees. Beginning with President Richard Nixon, who regarded PBS as part of the "liberal establishment," attempts were made to get the CPB to dictate programming. At the same time, Nixon pushed for PBS to decentralize (accede more power to local stations) so that "grassroots localism" would dilute the East Coast liberal bias. In 1973, PBS won a partnership agreement from the CPB to standardize funding distribution to guard against political interference. In 1975, Congress passed the Public Broadcasting Financing Act, providing a two-year advance appropriation to the CPB to further protect editorial independence. This was a compromise on President Gerald Ford's recommendation of a five-year advance authorization.

PBS came under repeated attack during the 1980s. The documentary series *Frontline* was often criticized by conservatives, who wanted every program to show "both" sides of an issue. PBS officials, however, thought in terms of an overall programming balance. Indeed, a 1975 District of Columbia Circuit Court ruling affirmed this position, stating that balance is to be judged by the overall program schedule and not a single production or even a series. Meanwhile, conservative activist David Horowitz formed the Committee on Media Integrity to document the "leftist slant" of PBS programs on foreign affairs. Similarly, Reed Irvine of Accuracy in Media criticized the "communist" perspective of the thirteen-part PBS documentary *Vietnam: A Television History* (1983). On the other side, liberals noted that PBS had aired a number of conservative programs, from *Firing Line,* hosted by William F. Buckley, Jr., to Milton and Rose Friedman's ten-part *Free to Choose* (1980).

Following the 1995 Republican takeover of the House of Representatives, Speaker Newt Gingrich (R-GA) called public broadcasting "an elitist enterprise" and announced his goal to "zero out" its public funding. Gingrich was joined in that pledge by Representative Larry Pressler (R-SD), who two years later lost reelection in a campaign in which detractors passed out bumper stickers that read, "Let's Keep PBS and 'Privatize' Pressler." In time, Gingrich admitted that Republicans had underestimated public support for PBS. During the presidency of George W. Bush there was renewed controversy when Kenneth Tomlinson, the appointed chairman of the CPB, called on PBS to reflect "the Republican mandate." Tomlinson later resigned under a cloud, but not until after he singled out the program *NOW with Bill Moyers* as being too liberal.

PBS has been in the spotlight of controversy with respect to televised presidential debates, ten of which have been moderated by PBS news anchor Jim Lehrer. During the 2000 campaign, Lehrer wrapped up the first debate (held at the University of Massachusetts in Boston on October 3) by asking Republican candidate George W. Bush, "Are there issues of character that distinguish you from Vice President Gore?" For some observers, that question lent support to Bush's partisan "values campaign." When Gore suggested redirecting the discussion to focus on the nation's problems, Lehrer asked, "Are you saying all this is irrelevant, Vice President Gore?" For some observers, that episode made Lehrer seem less than neutral. Later, during the 2008 presidential election, observers called into question the neutrality of Gwen Ifill, a senior correspondent for the *NewsHour,* in connection with her moderating the vice-presidential debate (held on October 2 at Washington University in St. Louis, Missouri). An African American, Ifill at the time was finishing a book on Barack Obama scheduled to be released on inauguration day—*The Breakthrough: Politics and Race in the Age of Obama* (2009)—which she had not disclosed upfront to the debate commission.

Roger Chapman

See also: Buckley, William F., Jr.; Federal Communications Commission; Friedman, Milton; Great Society; Horowitz, David; Irvine, Reed; Johnson, Lyndon B.; Media Bias; National Public Radio; Nixon, Richard; Privatization; Rusher, William A.

Further Reading

Auletta, Ken. "Big Bird Flies Right." *The New Yorker,* June 7, 2004.

Bullert, B.J. *Public Television: Politics and the Battle over Documentary Film.* New Brunswick, NJ: Rutgers University Press, 1997.

Carnegie Commission on the Future of Public Broadcasting. *A Public Trust.* New York: Bantam, 1979.

Day, James. *The Vanishing Vision: The Inside Story of Public Television.* Berkeley: University of California Press, 1995.

Engelman, Ralph. *Public Radio and Television in America: A Political History.* Thousand Oaks, CA: Sage, 1996.

PBS Web site. www.pbs.org.

Stewart, David. *The PBS Companion: A History of Public Television.* New York: TV Books, 1999.

Punk Rock

Outrageous, confrontational, and outside the mainstream of conventional rock-and-roll culture, punk rock conjures images of ripped T-shirts, Mohawk haircuts, and safety pins. This youth subculture, however, has involved more than music and fashion. Railing against corporate culture, suburbia, and conservative politics in the late 1970s and 1980s, punks were primarily young, white, middle-class males. Through "in your face" music and lifestyle, punks attempted to merge the shock of avant-garde rebellion and New Left protest traditions at a time when liberalism was on the wane. With a do-it-yourself (DIY) ethic of self-production, punks rejected the corporatization of music, the Reagan Revolution's conservative values, and the mainstream media's negative stereotypes of punk.

The roots of punk rock extend to the mid-1960s garage rock of Link Wray, and late 1960s fringe rock bands such as the Stooges and the MC5. Punk rock itself originated in the mid-1970s with a group of New York City musicians inspired by beatniks, the Velvet Underground, and its patron, Andy Warhol. Congregating at CBGB-OMFUG, a bar in New York's Bowery District, early punks such as Patti Smith and Richard Hell took a populist stance similar to that of their hippie forebears. Their minimalist fashion sense and avant-garde approach to music formed the foundation for the DIY ethic, while the New York Dolls brought glamour and intensity to the movement. At a 1975 CBGB showcase, punk received international press attention. Record companies were particularly interested in the Ramones, whose music was sparse and powerful, and who would push the punk movement beyond the artistic realm.

On a British tour in 1976, the Ramones brought American punk sensibilities to that country's youth. British punk took the New York framework and created an outlet for working-class rage. This often anarchic expression of generational discontent was epitomized by the Sex Pistols, who reveled in confrontation and shock value. In 1976, the Sex Pistols' anthem "Anarchy in the UK" helped create the impression that punk rock was to be feared. In a June 1977 NBC news report on punk in Britain, the movement was represented as violent and nihilistic, a threat to mainstream society. The report brought attention to American punks and inadvertently created a social phenomenon.

While the American artistic punk scene mellowed into the New Wave (epitomized by Blondie) by the early 1980s, a harder, more political punk filled the void. This angrier, more extreme punk (known as hardcore) came from punks who refused to fall prey to the cooptation that had begun to take place with media exposure, especially with the spread of cable television channels such as MTV. Hardcore punk emerged in Los Angeles, San Francisco, and Washington, D.C., with bands such as Black Flag, the Dead Kennedys (fronted by Jello Biafra), and Minor Threat. Mass media quickly picked up the hardcore stereotype of anarchy dressed in ripped jeans; punks were demonized on film (*Class of 1984*, 1982) and television (*Quincy*, 1982). To the mainstream, hardcore threatened the social order.

Punks fought this misrepresentation in their music and in "zines" (noncommercial fan magazines), the most well known being *Maximum RocknRoll*. Such DIY communication networks were outlets for punk political and social action in going against the Establishment. To punks, Reaganism merged with the evils of corporatization. This disdain was counter to Reagan-era optimism, as actualized by punk's use of "direct action" in which radical protest strategies of the 1960s, like guerrilla theater, were made more aggressive. For example, in one particular demonstration, punks staged "die-ins" (mass mock deaths), posed as fanatical Christians, and threw fake blood at fur stores. This culminated in a mass-action day called "No Business As Usual Day" (NBAU) on April 29, 1985. Aimed at the escalating arms race, NBAU concerts and die-ins were staged in cities across the country, including Atlanta, Chicago, and San Francisco.

Political activity grew between 1984 and 1986: Positive Force, a punk political organization with chapters across the United States, arranged concerts for community and international causes such as anti-apartheid; and a road show called Rock Against Reagan toured the country. Punks were keen to act but were not interested in sophisticated intellectual analysis and lacked long-term political vision. Anarchy may have formed the movement's core, but voluntary cooperation was the goal, not chaos. Because of the movement's ahistorical perspective, a coherent plan for political change could never be achieved. Punks used New Left protest tactics but did not see the legacy that informed these actions as something to be built upon to obtain their own goals.

As punk political action peaked, the subculture's limits crystallized. Commercialism and commodification were the source of punk ire and anxiety. Many youths were drawn not to the movement's activism but to its style. Punk rock could not hold back consumerism, and the subculture was opened to the masses. Bands such as Green Day made the "new" punk—grunge—a corporate success. Like the counterculture a generation before it, punk became exclusionary, going underground as conservatism rose and consumer culture embraced rebellion.

Anna Zuschlag

See also: Biafra, Jello; Counterculture; Family Values; Fur; Generations and Generational Conflict; Rap Music; Reagan, Ronald; Record Warning Labels; Rock and Roll; Warhol, Andy; Zappa, Frank.

Further Reading

Friedlander, Paul. *Rock & Roll: A Social History.* 2nd ed. Cambridge, MA: Westview Press, 2006.

MacLeod, Dewar. "'Social Distortion': The Rise of Suburban Punk Rock in Los Angeles." In *America Under Construction: Boundaries and Identities in Popular Culture*, ed. Kristi S. Long and Matthew Nadelhaft, 123–37. New York: Garland, 1997.

Mattson, Kevin. "Did Punk Matter? Analyzing the Practices of a Youth Subculture During the 1980s." *American Studies* 42:1 (Spring 2000): 69–97.

Szatmary, David P. *Rockin' in Time: A Social History of Rock-and-Roll.* Upper Saddle River, NJ: Prentice Hall, 2000.

Quayle, Dan

As the forty-fourth vice president of the United States (1989–1993), former U.S. representative and senator Dan Quayle (R-IN) personified the young conservatives of the New Right. Critics viewed him as a political lightweight; supporters argued that he was a victim of liberal media bias.

The son of a wealthy newspaper publisher, John Danforth "Dan" Quayle was born on February 4, 1947, in Indianapolis, Indiana. He studied at DePauw University (BS, political science, 1969) and Indiana University of Law (JD, 1974), serving along the way in the Indiana National Guard (1969–1975) and various positions in the state government (1970–1974). Entering politics during the Reagan ascendancy, Quayle served two full terms in the U.S. House of Representatives (1977–1981) and one and a half in the Senate (1981–1989). During his years on Capitol Hill, he sponsored only one major piece of legislation, a job-training bill co-sponsored by Senator Ted Kennedy (D-MA). In 1988, Republican presidential nominee George H.W. Bush selected Quayle as his running mate; many criticized this decision, saying the Hoosier was too inexperienced and lacked intellectual heft.

Quayle's 1988 vice-presidential campaign was marked by unusually intensive media scrutiny. His poor academic record at DePauw was uncovered (he was a C student and failed his first attempt at the final exam in political science); he was accused of using family connections to get into the National Guard in order to avoid the Vietnam War; and questions circulated about an overnight golfing event involving an attractive female lobbyist. One of Quayle's most embarrassing moments came during his vice-presidential debate with Democratic counterpart Lloyd Benson in Omaha, Nebraska. After Quayle stated that he had more experience than John Kennedy when he was nominated in 1960, Benson retorted, "I knew Jack Kennedy . . . Senator, you're no Jack Kennedy." Quayle was left speechless as the studio audience cheered. He became fodder for late-night talk shows and partisan magazines as his misstatements—many apocryphal—were chronicled. The most famous gaffe took place during his vice presidency when, at a grade-school appearance, he misspelled the word "potato" (as "potatoe") on the chalkboard. Quayle partially redeemed his reputation by performing well in the 1992 campaign debate with Al Gore and with the publication of his well-received autobiography, *Standing Firm* (1994).

Many conservatives remained loyal, saying the press unfairly pounced on his every minor mistake. Further,

Vice President Dan Quayle delivers an attack on the "liberal media" and the Democratic Party during an August 1992 God and Country rally organized by the Christian Coalition to promote family values. *(Chris Wilkins/AFP/Getty Images)*

they praised Quayle's consistent support for reduced government spending and lower taxes, a strong military and the Strategic Defense Initiative (missile defense), and traditional family values. It was this last issue that most engaged Quayle in the culture wars. In a now famous 1992 speech in which he criticized Murphy Brown, a popular television series character, for having a baby out of wedlock, he was lambasted by liberals for being intolerant. (He said the show represented a "poverty of values.") Conservatives countered that Quayle had spoken the truth about the importance of fathers and claimed that the negative trend of fatherless families in America was the root cause of poverty and crime in inner cities.

E. Michael Young

See also: Bush Family; Family Values; Gore, Al; Kennedy Family; Media Bias; Palin, Sarah; Republican Party; Strategic Defense Initiative; Tax Reform; Vietnam War; Woodward, Bob; Zappa, Frank.

Further Reading

Broder, David C., and Bob Woodward. *The Man Who Would Be President: Dan Quayle.* New York: Simon & Schuster, 1992.

Fenno, Richard F., Jr. *The Making of a Senator: Dan Quayle.* Washington, DC: CQ Press, 1998.

Quayle, Dan. *Standing Firm: A Vice Presidential Memoir.* New York: HarperCollins, 1994.

Quayle, Dan, and Diane Medved. *The American Family: Discovering the Values That Make Us Strong.* New York: HarperCollins, 1996.

Queenan, Joe. *Imperial Caddy: The Rise of Dan Quayle and the Decline and Fall of Practically Everything Else.* New York: Hyperion Books, 1992.

Race

With its founding years steeped in slavery, the United States built a legal and social system around the concept of "race," with legacies that continue to the present day. A set of practices known as de jure segregation, or the social separation of groups based on racial difference and backed by law, followed the abolition of slavery. Historically, use of the word *race* as a term to classify human groups is a relatively recent one. It first came into use in late eighteenth-century Europe and was understood as group identity based on common ancestry and shared physical traits. By the 2000s, de jure segregation had been abolished in the United States, but informal de facto segregation remained widespread even though the concept of race as a definitive biological marker was being questioned. Despite the improvement of "race relations," people of color by and large fall short of full political and economic equality.

Although physical anthropologists and biologists had attempted to categorize Homo sapiens by such racial types as "Caucasoid," "Negroid," "Mongoloid," and "Australoid," by the late 1900s anthropologists had reached a consensus that race is an arbitrary social construct and not a scientific designator. At one time, even Irish, Italians, and Jews considered nonwhite. Sociologists and anthropologists today prefer the term *ethnicity*, which refers to a group that shares cultural affinities, such as geographical and ancestral roots.

Despite the discrediting of the scientific category, American society has continued to grapple with issues of race and racism. Laws against interracial marriage were abolished; the "one-drop rule" method of determining blackness discontinued; and people of color were elected to public office at local, state, and federal levels, all while social integration and equal opportunity have remained out of reach for many minorities. A trend toward the de facto resegregation of cities has been evident, ironically exacerbated by the upward mobility of African Americans and the phenomenon of "black flight" (in the wake of "white flight") to the suburbs. In major metropolitan areas, neighborhoods and schools have redivided along racial lines, characterized by economic disparities between whites and people of color, while those who can afford to do so relocate for better school districts and areas with less crime. The highest indices of white-black segregation are concentrated in the Northeast and northern Midwest.

In developing scientific measurements of population, the U.S. Census Bureau played a role in nineteenth-century race categorization, carefully examining whites for traces of nonwhite ancestry. By the end of the twentieth century, racial classification became more complicated with greater diversity from new immigrant waves and the rise of interracial marriage. The 2000 Census allowed respondents to identify themselves by choosing more than one race from a list of fifteen choices, and to check "some other race" if none applied. Critics deplored the omission of "Arab" from the list, wondering why they were subsumed under "white" or "some other race." Perhaps most problematic from a statistical point of view was the recording of the Latino population: while some checked "some other race" (believing themselves "Indian," as they were known in their home countries), 48 percent identified themselves as "white" and 2 percent "black." Political advocacy groups objected to the census list, fearing it would artificially lower the number of people of color and ultimately affect affirmative action decisions and electoral districting.

The concept and meaning of "race" has entered prominently into the debates of the culture wars. As sociologists and scientists were reaching a consensus on the meaninglessness of racial identity (except as a social construction), Richard J. Herrnstein and Charles Murray caused controversy by asserting in *The Bell Curve* (1994) that differences in I.Q. test scores were evidence of biologically inherited racial differences in intelligence. A barrage of detractors responded, charging that the authors made assumptions about "essentialist" biological differences between groups, misinterpreted data, erred in reasoning, conflated social class with race, and ignored research that cast doubt on strong links between genetics and intelligence.

Meanwhile, the post-1960s rise of new scholarship to include voices of people of color, revise historical texts to correct bias, and create new theory resulted in a burgeoning interest in cross-disciplinary fields such as critical race studies, whiteness studies (examining the social invention of "whiteness"), postcolonial studies, and African-American, Latino/a, and Asian studies. "Culture studies" departments were established, providing curricula that critically attempted to "de-center" scholarly perspectives and examine the academy's disciplinary regimes of power, using the terminology of French philosopher Michel Foucault. At the forefront of the discussion was often the perspective of the "canon" or the so-called "great books." While multiculturalists argued for scrapping the study of inherited Western, "Eurocentric" works (or to at least augment it with contributions and critical perspectives of marginalized groups, the global south, and the colonized), traditionalists such as Allan Bloom (author of the 1987 book *The Closing of the American Mind*) charged that to abandon the canon was to abandon America's founding religious and moral principles and to devolve into moral relativism.

The question of race explosively reentered the American public sphere in the 2008 Democratic presidential election primary with the success of U.S. Senator and presidential hopeful Barack Obama, son of African immigrant and white parentage. Revealing the unsettled state of the definition of race in American public culture were the questions: "Is America ready for a black president?" and "Is he black enough?" Throughout his candidacy, Obama walked a fine line between an attempt to appeal to groups across the racial divides and his stated commitment to address the disparities that communities such as African Americans continued to endure. He offered the color-blind proclamation that "there is not a black America and a white America. . . . There's the United States of America," but became ensconced in a spring 2008 controversy over language in a sermon by his pastor, the Reverend Jeremiah Wright, that was critical of white America. Although Obama went on to win not only the Democratic primary, but the general election, becoming the first black man elected president of the United States, there was no consensus on how this historic milestone was to be interpreted with respect to the everyday lives of ordinary people of color.

Susan Pearce

See also: Afrocentrism; *Bell Curve, The*; Civil Rights Movement; Great Books; Hispanic Americans; Loving, Richard, and Mildred Loving; Lynching; Multiculturalism and Ethnic Studies; Obama, Barack; Watts and Los Angeles Riots, 1965 and 1992; White Supremacists.

Further Reading

Baum, Bruce. *The Rise and Fall of the Caucasian Race: A Political History of Racial Identity.* New York: New York University Press, 2006.
Hannaford, Ivan. *Race: The History of an Idea in the West.* Baltimore: Johns Hopkins University Press, 1996.
Livingstone, Frank B. "On the Non-Existence of Human Races." In *The Concept of Race*, ed. Ashley Montagu, 46–60. Westport, CT: Greenwood Press, 1980.
Spickard, Paul R. "The Illogic of American Racial Categories." In *Racially Mixed People in America*, ed. Maria P.P. Root, 12–23. Newbury Park, CA: Sage, 1992.

Racial Profiling

Racial profiling involves the action of law enforcement officials based on race, ethnicity, or national origins rather than individual behavior or specific information about alleged criminal activity. Incidents of racial profiling typically occur in the context of traffic stops, neighborhood patrolling, and airport screening. African Americans and Hispanics have often been subject to this practice, especially by officers concerned about drug or immigration enforcement. Being pulled over by the police for questioning is such a common experience for African Americans that they characterize it as being stopped for DWB—"driving while black." Following the September 11, 2001, terrorist attacks, people of Middle Eastern descent have experienced a greater amount of police searches and surveillance.

In the culture wars most people agree that racial profiling is wrong, but there is no consensus over what actually constitutes the practice. Law scholars maintain that the Fourth Amendment (protecting against unreasonable searches) and the Fourteenth Amendment (guaranteeing equal protection under the law) render racial profiling unconstitutional. In *United States v. Brignoni-Ponce* (1975), for example, the Supreme Court ruled that it is unconstitutional for border officers of the Immigration and Naturalization Service to single out people of Mexican descent for additional questioning. Conservatives argue that purely discriminatory racial profiling occurs much less frequently than liberals claim. What one side calls racial profiling, the other views as criminal profiling. Public figures generally reject "hard profiling" (using race as the sole criterion), but "soft profiling" (using race as *part* of a larger profile) remains a contentious issue because the line drawn between the two can be subjective.

Conservatives, emphasizing law and order, argue that common sense would allow police to use racial and ethnic characteristics to identify possible suspects. They note that federal officials, fearing they would be guilty of racial profiling, failed to adequately investigate the influx of Arab students enrolling at flight schools prior to September 11. Criticism of racial profiling is sometimes seen as avoidance to address the disproportionate rate of criminality in certain racial and ethnic communities. Liberals who are skeptical of soft profiling suggest that hidden prejudice looms larger than what law enforcement officials would care to admit. They also maintain that the rate of criminality should not be misconstrued with the rate of arrest, especially if certain segments of society are subjected to greater police scrutiny.

Critics of racial profiling argue that police in America have historically targeted minorities for more intensive policing because of blatant racism. As recently as 1999, a drug sting in Tulia, Texas, a town of 5,000 people with a small African-American community, resulted in the arrests of forty black males—about a third of the town's total. The arrests, based on the testimony of one undercover narcotics officer, proved to have been made with fraudulent evidence. Nearly all the suspects were released, but many served several years in prison. The case became the subject of several films, depicting an example of blatantly biased police work in the drug war.

Historically, most police officers in the United States have been white; some harboring strong biases against African Americans and other minorities. One solution has been to recruit more nonwhites as police officers, particularly in cities and towns with large nonwhite populations. While this has helped reduce animosity between police and minorities in many cases, studies show that even minority police officers may police nonwhites more intensely.

Beginning in the 1950s, civil rights groups such as the Urban League and the National Association for the Advancement of Colored People (NAACP) began campaigning against bias and profiling in police work. More radical groups, such as the Black Panthers and Brown Berets, joined the campaign the following decade, some seeking to incite anger and resistance to law enforcement. The 1965 Watts Riots in Los Angeles, California, was triggered by an incident that was regarded by the black community as police racial profiling.

Racial profiling emerged again as a national issue during the 1980s, as a rapid rise in the use of cocaine led to a sharp increase in violent crimes in major U.S. cities. The federal government intensified the war on drugs, and police throughout the country targeted illegal drug dealers and users. Arrest rates in poor, inner-city neighborhoods soared, and jails soon were filled with alleged drug offenders. More than 75 percent of them were black or Hispanic. In the mid-1980s, new anticrime legislation allowed police to confiscate the property of drug dealers and other criminals, including cars, houses, and other possessions. In the 1990s, states passed three-strikes laws and long mandatory sentences for repeat felony offenders. Civil rights groups and minority leaders complained that the laws prescribed longer sentences for the sale or possession of crack cocaine (most often used by minorities) than for possession or sale of powdered cocaine, which is much expensive and more often used by whites.

In the 1980s, criminologists argued that if police enforce "quality-of-life" laws against graffiti, panhandling, jaywalking, loitering, vandalism, littering, disorderly conduct, and minor motor vehicle violations, it would send a message that a neighborhood was under surveillance and thereby dissuade more serious criminality. In practice, police began detaining individuals for minor infractions and searching on computer databases for outstanding warrants. During the 1990s, crime rates in many large cities declined, most remarkably in New York City, where Mayor Rudolph Giuliani, a former federal prosecutor, encouraged the police to enforce quality-of-life laws. In 1994, Giuliani's first year in office, New York's crime rate fell by 12 percent. After an unexplained rise in 1995, it continued to decline during his eight years in office. Critics charged that quality-of-life policing encouraged the police to harass minority residents and go on "fishing expeditions" in search of illegal guns or drugs. Conservatives pointed to opinion polls indicating that most citizens living in high-crime areas supported the enforcement of quality-of-life laws.

In the early 2000s, people in many parts of the country began noticing increasing populations of Hispanic residents in their towns and cities. An undetermined number had entered the country illegally, and others had overstayed their visas. In response to the demographic shift or local complaints about it, police stepped up their inquiries of suspects who appeared to be Hispanic. In some regions they began asking for identity papers to check immigration status. Along the border with Mexico, border police stepped up efforts to stop the flow of illegal drugs and other contraband and to curtail the flow of illegal immigrants. Since it was not practical to search every person at border crossings, customs officials also checked minority travelers at an increased rate. Of all women searched by customs officers in 1999, for example, 46 percent were black and only 23 percent were white.

Controversy over racial profiling erupted again after the September 11 terrorist attacks. Travelers who appeared to be Middle Eastern or Muslim came under intense law enforcement scrutiny, particularly in and around U.S. airports, with Middle Eastern passengers being screened more frequently. The 2001 USA PATRIOT Act allowed the U.S. attorney general to detain alien suspects for a week without charge. The government proceeded to jail 762 aliens, most of them from Arab nations, on immigration violations. Proponents argued that fighting terrorism justifies close scrutiny of anyone of Middle Eastern origin. Opponents claimed that targeting Muslims or Middle Easterners for questioning was discriminatory and unconstitutional and increased the risk of other terrorists going undetected.

Joseph A. Rodriguez

See also: American Civil Liberties Union; Hispanic Americans; Illegal Immigrants; Muslim Americans; Race; USA PATRIOT Act; War on Drugs; Watts and Los Angeles Riots, 1965 and 1992.

Further Reading

Harris, David A. *Profiles in Injustice: Why Racial Profiling Cannot Work.* New York: New Press, 2002.

Heumann, Milton, and Lance Cassak. *Good Cop, Bad Cop: Racial Profiling and Competing Views of Justice.* New York: Peter Lang, 2003.

MacDonald, Heather. *Are Cops Racist?* Chicago: Ivan R. Dee, 2003.

Meeks, Kenneth. *Driving While Black: Highways, Shopping Malls, Taxicabs, Sidewalks: How to Fight Back if You Are a Victim of Racial Profiling.* New York: Broadway Books, 2000.

O'Reilly, James T. *Police Traffic Stops and Racial Profiling: Resolving Management, Labor and Civil Rights Conflicts.* Springfield, IL: Charles C. Thomas, 2002.

Rand, Ayn

A novelist-philosopher, Ayn Rand developed a brand of atheistic libertarianism known as Objectivism, emphasizing objective reality, rationalism, heroic individualism, self-interest, and laissez-faire capitalism, boldly declaring selfishness moral. Although Rand's writings have influenced millions, the academic community has remained ambivalent about Objectivism, with many scholars saying it lacks rigor. Early on, Rand's ideology was rejected by conservatives such as William F. Buckley, Jr., and Whittaker Chambers due to its atheistic basis. Rand's followers, often regarded as cultish, have been routinely denigrated as "Randoids."

Rand was born Alyssa Zinovievna Rosenbaum on February 2, 1905, in St. Petersburg, Russia, into a middle-class Jewish family. In her youth she developed a love of heroic, strong-willed individuals from reading French novels and studying the philosophy of Aristotle and Nietzsche. She graduated from the University of Petrograd with a degree in history (1924) and immigrated to America in 1926. Prior to working in Hollywood, she chose the name Ayn (after a Finnish novelist) Rand (after her Remington-Rand typewriter) to conceal her identity and protect her family in the Soviet Union.

After writing the dystopian, anti-Leninist novels *We the Living* (1936) and *Anthem* (1938), Rand reached her philosophical mark with *The Fountainhead* (1943) and *Atlas Shrugged* (1957). In *The Fountainhead*, which was made into a Warner Brothers film starring Gary Cooper (1949), the hero Howard Roark, an architect, exemplifies Objectivist individualism by refusing to design buildings that conform to societal aesthetic norms, going so far as to detonate a construction site rather than to see his plans altered. John Galt, the hero of *Atlas Shrugged*, is a similarly decisive figure. Respondents to a 1991 poll by the Library of Congress and the Book-of-the-Month Club rated *Atlas Shrugged*, only after the Bible, as the most influential book they had ever read.

Nathaniel Branden (born Blumenthal), a disciple who had an adulterous affair with Rand, in 1958 founded the Nathaniel Branden Institute to systematize and promote Objectivism. In 1968, however, Rand dismissed him from the movement. Her most famous disciple, a member of what she jokingly called "the Collective," was Alan Greenspan, who went on to chair the Federal Reserve Board (1987–2006). Many of Rand's essays published in the *Objectivist Newsletter* (1962–1966), the *Objectivist* (1966–1971), and the *Ayn Rand Letter* (1971–1976) were later developed into books—*For the New Intellectual* (1961), *The Virtue of Selfishness* (1964), *Capitalism: The Unknown Ideal* (1966), *Introduction to Objectivist Epistemology* (1967), *The New Left: The Anti-Industrial Revolution* (1971), *The Romantic Manifesto* (1971), and *Philosophy: Who Needs It?* (1982).

Rand died on March 6, 1982, in New York City. Although some credited her with helping pave the way for the conservative resurgence of the 1980s, Rand rejected Ronald Reagan because of his alignment with the Religious Right. Rand's literary heir, Leonard Peikoff, in 1985 founded the Ayn Rand Institute (ARI) in Marina del Rey, California. In April 1997, ARI activists demonstrated at the presidential summit on volunteerism in Philadelphia, protesting, "I Have No Duty to Sacrifice Myself."

Andrew J. Waskey

See also: Buckley, William F., Jr.; Chambers, Whittaker; Reagan, Ronald; Religious Right; Secular Humanism; Soviet Union and Russia.

Further Reading

Ayn Rand Institute Web site. www.aynrand.org.
McDonald, Marci. "Fighting over Ayn Rand." *U.S. News & World Report*, March 9, 1998.
Sciabarra, Chris Matthew. *Ayn Rand: The Russian Radical.* University Park: Pennsylvania State University Press, 1995.
Sharlet, Jeff. "Ayn Rand Has Finally Caught the Attention of Scholars." *Chronicle of Higher Education*, April 9, 1999.
Walker, Jeff. *The Ayn Rand Cult.* Chicago: Open Court, 1999.

Rap Music

With origins in the 1970s hip-hop culture of urban New York, rap music became part of the culture wars after gaining commercial success and reaching audiences beyond America's black ghetto and urban centers. The stereotypical rap song that has caught attention in the culture wars is storytelling delivered with fast rhyme, alliteration, and an accompanying beat, expressing concerns of the black underclass with lyrics that can be raw, boastful, aggressive, violent, sexist, homophobic, obscene, and mocking. Having emerged from hip-hop culture (along with break dancing, deejaying, and graffiti), contemporary rap music also reflects a cultural dichotomy. On one hand, rap songs are often political, focusing on drugs, gangs, street violence, rape, police brutality, and the like, offering a message of defiance rather than hope. On the other hand, some rap music offers a utopian message of racial unity—though this form is often obscured by the dialogue of the culture wars and by rap music institutions themselves.

Outside of hip-hop subculture, the deeper cultural influences on rap include Jamaican "dub" and reggae culture, African "griot" music, funk, soul, disco, and even German "krautrock." A key moment in the American scene occurred when MCs (emcees) in urban neighborhood block parties (especially in the Bronx) transitioned from entertaining *between* songs or acts to "rapping" into the next song. Commercial success for rap began with the Sugarhill Gang's "Rapper's Delight" (1979), which sold several million copies and spawned other rap singles in the early 1980s, including number one hits by artists outside the hip-hop culture, such as Blondie, Falco, and the Pet Shop Boys.

Rap music almost immediately became a political vehicle. As an art form, rap offered a musical outlet to those formally untrained or unable to sing, and it was fairly easy and simple to produce. Its violation of traditional tropes of popular music also gave a musical freedom rarely afforded in other music forms. As such, rap music emerged as a liberating experience for the artist, who had an amplified voice to speak his or her mind about current issues, not the least of which were race and class. One early master of rap, Afrika Bambaata, promoted a quasi-religious utopian message while organizing block parties in the Bronx. Other politically minded rappers emerged, including Lawrence Krisna Parker (known as KRS-One), The Coup, Success-N-Effect, and Public Enemy.

While rap was being appropriated by white culture for mainstream success, "gangsta rap" emerged on the West Coast. Most notably, LA rapper Ice T's debut gangsta rap album, *Rhyme Pays* (1987), was a top-30 hit record and the first rap album to be sold with a "parental advisory" warning label. The following year, the N.W.A. album *Straight Outta Compton* (1988) prompted a protest from the FBI in reaction to a song title featuring an obscene epithet against the police. Gangsta rap's lyrical themes focus on the urban realities avoided by pop music and earlier rap music, and it is often accused of glorifying gang violence.

In 1990, obscenity laws were enforced by the state of Florida with the arrest of a record retailer for selling copies of the 2 Live Crew's *As Nasty As They Wanna Be* (1989). Their music legally defined as "obscene," the members of the group that same year were arrested for performing at a Fort Lauderdale nightclub. The album's first single, "Me So Horny," became a top-30 hit with little radio play, and the album eventually went on to sell more than three million copies, largely due to notoriety from the controversy.

In the aftermath of the Los Angeles riots of 1992, social activist and minor hip-hop music personality Sister Souljah (Lisa Williamson) commented, "If black people kill black people every day, why not have a week and kill white people?" Presidential candidate Bill Clinton, in a speech before the Rainbow Coalition, publicly denounced Souljah's remark as reverse racism, comparing it to the hate speech of a white supremacist. Jesse Jackson dismissed Clinton's comments as political posturing, while Souljah countered that Clinton was acting as a racist. From this episode was coined the term "Sister Souljah moment," defined as the use of a "straw man" for political grandstanding against a perceived extremist view. In 1994, the minister of the Abyssinian Baptist Church in Harlem, Calvin Butts, began a crusade against "morally degraded" rap music, citing its negative influence on black youth. Princeton professor Cornel West, who

has recorded hip-hop CDs, has argued that rap music is an expression of marginalized blacks who are victims of capitalism and racism.

Christopher D. Rodkey

See also: Censorship; Clinton, Bill; Gangs; Heavy Metal; Jackson, Jesse; Parks, Rosa; Police Abuse; Punk Rock; Record Warning Labels; Watts and Los Angeles Riots, 1965 and 1992; West, Cornel.

Further Reading

Chang, Jeff. *Can't Stop Won't Stop: A History of the Hip-Hop Generation.* New York: Picador/St. Martin's Press, 2005.

George, Nelson. *Hip Hop America.* New York: Penguin, 2005.

Light, Alan, ed. *The Vibe History of Hip Hop.* New York: Random House, 1999.

Rose, Tricia. *Black Noise: Rap Music and Black Culture in Contemporary America.* Hanover, NH: Wesleyan University Press/University Press of New England, 1994.

Sieving, Christopher. "Cop Out? The Media, 'Cop Killer,' and the Deracialization of Black Rage." *Journal of Communication Inquiry* 22:4 (1998): 332–53.

Watkins, S. Craig. *Hip Hop Matters: Politics, Pop Culture, and the Struggle for the Soul of a Movement.* Boston: Beacon Press, 2006.

Rather, Dan

Longtime television journalist Dan Rather signed off from his final broadcast as anchorman and managing editor of the *CBS Evening News* on March 9, 2005, bringing to a close a career that spanned a half-century and included firsthand coverage of virtually every major event and issue in the postwar era—from the civil rights movement and the assassination of President John F. Kennedy to the Vietnam War, Watergate scandal, and post-9/11 world. He wrote several books, including *The Camera Never Blinks* (1977); its sequel, *The Camera Never Blinks Twice* (1994); and *Deadlines and Datelines* (1999). His influence enabled him to secure interviews with such controversial figures as Fidel Castro and Saddam Hussein. Through all of this, he also encountered at least his share of controversy. Indeed, his retirement in 2005 came amid charges of political bias and shoddy journalism in reporting on the politically charged issue of President George W. Bush's service in the Texas Air National Guard during the 1960s.

Daniel Irvin Rather was born in Wharton, Texas, on October 31, 1931, to Byrl and Irwin "Rags" Rather. He later credited his father with cultivating his interest in journalism and shaping his understanding. He once described Rags as an "impulse subscriber" and remembered his childhood home as always filled with local and national newspapers. As a teen, Rather reported on sports for the school newspaper. His interest continued to grow in the early 1950s, after enrolling at Sam Houston State Teachers College in Huntsville, Texas, with a major in journalism. While still in college, he worked as a reporter for local wire services and radio stations. After earning his degree in 1953, he worked for the *Houston Chronicle* and radio station KTRH in that city.

A major turning point in Rather's career came in 1961, when he was hired as director of news and public affairs by KHOU-TV, CBS's Houston affiliate. For the next four decades CBS would be Rather's professional home. Following the national recognition obtained from covering President Kennedy's assassination in November 1963, Rather was named the network's White House correspondent and went on to cover the Lyndon Johnson and Richard Nixon administrations. In 1974, Rather was named anchor and chief correspondent for the show *CBS News Special Reports* and, in 1975, a correspondent for the popular television news "magazine" *60 Minutes*. In 1981, upon the retirement of the legendary Walter Cronkite, Rather took over as the network's prime-time news anchor and managing editor.

Known as an aggressive investigative journalist and interviewer with a sometimes volatile personality, Rather was the center of national controversy on several occasions during his career. In 2002, *60 Minutes* colleague Andy Rooney stated in a television interview that Rather was "transparently liberal"—echoing a longtime and widely held view. In the context of the culture wars, Rather had come to epitomize a perceived bias in the media and was accused of harboring an agenda that was both anticonservative and antigovernment. Indeed, since his early days as a White House correspondent, Rather had struggled to overcome claims that personal politics influenced his reporting. The most famous example came in 1974, when, as White House correspondent, Rather traded words with President Richard Nixon at the peak of the Watergate scandal. The exchange took place at a press conference when, after Rather rose to ask a question, Nixon wryly asked if the reporter was "running for something." Put on the spot, Rather responded in kind: "No, sir, Mr. President, are you?" The exchange cast Rather in the spotlight and had an enduring effect on his reputation as a journalist. Despite Rather's claim that his "job is to inform, not persuade," this was not the last time he was caught in the political crossfire.

Rather's ability to endure and overcome criticism from public figures as well as fellow members of the media came to an end in 2005, in the aftermath of the so-called Bush Memogate scandal. The controversy began in September 2004, when Rather reported a story on *60 Minutes* that documents had been discovered in the files of President Bush's former commanding officer in the Texas Air Guard indicating that Bush had been

CBS television anchorman Dan Rather, a mainstay of the network from the early 1960s, resigned in March 2005 over a purported case of liberal media bias: a mistaken report on President George W. Bush's service record during the Vietnam War. *(John Chiasson/Getty Images)*

barred from flying after failing to report for physical examination. The authenticity of the papers was immediately called into question and, despite Rather's insistence on the highest journalistic standards, they were soon proven to be spurious. CBS was forced to retract the story and, after an internal investigation, fired several producers associated with the story. Rather, who had been planning to retire anyway, stepped down amid uncertainty over whether he was asked to leave as a direct consequence of the incident. In any event, the scandal was pegged as yet another example of a liberal bias in the mainstream media. In 2008, Rather filed a lawsuit against CBS, seeking millions of dollars.

Liam van Beek

See also: Bush Family; Iran-Contra Affair; Media Bias.

Further Reading

Goldberg, Bernard. *Arrogance: Rescuing America from the Media Elite.* New York: Warner Books, 2003.

Rather, Dan. *The Camera Never Blinks: Adventures of a TV Journalist.* New York: William Morrow, 1977.

———. *The Camera Never Blinks Twice: The Further Adventures of a Television Journalist.* New York: William Morrow, 1994.

———. *Deadlines and Datelines: Essays at the Turn of the Century.* New York: William Morrow, 1999.

Weisman, Alan. *Lone Star: The Extraordinary Life and Times of Dan Rather.* Hoboken, NJ: John Wiley & Sons, 2006.

Reagan, Ronald

The fortieth president of the United States (1981–1989) and leader of a conservative revolution in American politics, former film actor and governor of California (1967–1975) Ronald Reagan has played a central and enduring role in America's culture wars. Essential to understanding that role is acknowledging Reagan's life-long struggle against communism, his opposition to the expansion of the federal government, and his somewhat contradictory positions on issues of moral controversy. Far from being monolithically conservative on the issues most important to moral and religious traditionalists, the Reagan record is quite nuanced, with much of his rhetoric focusing on the war against communism rather than on abortion, homosexuality, or feminism.

Early Life and Emerging Ideology

Ronald Wilson Reagan was born on February 6, 1911, in Tampico, Illinois. In 1932, he graduated from Eureka College, where he majored in sociology and economics. After a short stint working as a radio sports broadcaster, he passed a screen test with the Warner Brothers film studio in Hollywood and was hired as an actor in 1937. He appeared in more than fifty motion pictures, with a hiatus during World War II, when he narrated training films for the armed forces. In 1947, he was elected president of the Screen Actors Guild (SAG), serving as head of that Hollywood union until 1952 and again from 1959 to 1960. Also in 1952, three years after a divorce from the actress Jane Wyman, he married the actress Nancy Davis. Moving into television during the 1950s, he became a host and regular performer on *General Electric Theater* and, later, the western series *Death Valley Days.*

A New Deal Democrat during the 1930s and early 1940s, Reagan spoke out on behalf of President Harry Truman's government-centered efforts to contain inflation and unemployment created by military demobilization after World War II. During the course of the 1950s, however, Reagan's views began to change. As president of SAG, he developed a reputation as a staunch anticommunist. In fact, he was later identified as a primary source of information for FBI files opened on hundreds of suspected Hollywood communists during the McCarthy era. Indeed, Reagan's activities during this period—including testimony before the House Committee on Un-American Activities—reflect his commitment to the Cold War struggle that would become a major theme of his presidency.

Reagan's work as SAG president dovetailed into his next series of ideological battles, this time over the size and scope of the federal government. As his film career began to wane, he found work as a national spokesman for the General Electric Company in the late 1950s. Regular duties included visits to local GE plants throughout the year, providing experiences that led to a major shift in political views and, later, party affiliation. Central to this was a growing concern that government was taxing American workers to excess.

A belief that the Republic Party was more vigilant against the spread of communism led Reagan to support the presidential candidacies of Dwight Eisenhower in 1952 and 1956, and of Richard Nixon in 1960. By the early 1960s, Reagan's experiences with GE and his perception that the Democratic Party was becoming ever more liberal on the issues of government regulation and taxation led him to take a more active role in the GOP. His initial foray into politics came in October 1964, when he delivered a nationally televised address—titled "A Time for Choosing"—in support of Barry Goldwater's presidential bid. Although he had established his reputation as a Hollywood anticommunist crusader, Reagan used the speech to express his concern on a different matter: the idea of government expansion as a necessary evil in postwar America. On the strength of that address, California Republican leaders courted Reagan to challenge the incumbent Democratic governor, Edmund G. "Pat" Brown, in 1966. Running on similar themes outlined in his 1964 Goldwater speech, Reagan defeated Brown by more than one million votes.

Political and Cultural Issues

His background as an anticommunist and his first foray into Republican politics are central to an understanding of Reagan's role in the culture wars of the 1970s and 1980s. His original and primary political concerns centered on the threats to individual freedom and responsibility posed by communism and big government. Contrary to the views of some culture wars adversaries, he did not establish his political identity as an anti-abortion crusader or national moralist. Indeed, in his eight years as California governor, Reagan supported at least three policies antithetical to conservatives in the culture wars to come. The first was a liberalization of state abortion laws, for which Reagan argued that women have the right to protect themselves from the health risks associated with pregnancy. The new legislation widened the accepted definition of pregnancy risk to include mental and psychological stresses, resulting in an increase in the number of legal abortions sought and preformed. The second policy permitted no-fault divorce in the Golden State. And the third barred discrimination against homosexual public school teachers.

Reagan is lionized in conservative circles to this day for his generally "pro-life" position as president, successfully appealing to the Religious Right in the 1976, 1980, and 1984 elections by opposing abortion rights (except in cases of rape and incest). It should not be overlooked, however, that in the late 1970s he was forced to apologize for the abortion law he signed as governor of California.

A moderate tone and hints of political conciliation came through at various times during Reagan's presidency. In July 1981, he appointed the first woman to the U.S. Supreme Court—Sandra Day O'Connor. Continuing his relatively supportive position on gay rights, Reagan, via daughter Maureen, maintained cordial relations with the Log Cabin Republicans (a national gay and lesbian GOP organization). At the same time, however, he came under fire in his second term for ignoring the growing AIDS crisis and giving little attention to the issue of unequal pay for women.

Legacy

President Ronald Reagan left office in January 1989 amid Democratic criticism—which has endured—that his conservative fiscal policies inflicted serious, long-term damage on the national economy by implementing major tax cuts (especially for the rich) at the same time that he was dramatically increasing military spending. During his presidency, the tax rate for the wealthiest Americans was reduced from 70 percent to 50 percent and finally to 28 percent. According to the rationale known as Reaganomics—referred to as "supply-side economics" by proponents and "trickle-down economics" by opponents—a reduced tax burden for the richest Americans would enable them to invest more and thus stimulate the economy. Critics came to refer to the Reagan years as the "Second Gilded Age" for the windfall it brought the economic upper class. While the federal debt tripled to $2.7 trillion during his presidency, the wealth gap between the richest and poorest widened: the share of total national wealth owned by the nation's richest 1 percent of families increased from 27 percent in 1981 to 39 percent in 1989.

Although the final demise of the Soviet Union did not come until after Reagan left office, conservatives and others credit him with winning the Cold War. According to the conventional wisdom, Soviet communism finally collapsed because the Kremlin could not keep up economically with the American arms buildup during the Reagan years. It is argued, for example, that Reagan's support for developing a missile shield known as the Strategic Defense Initiative (referred to as "Star Wars" by critics) forced Soviet leader Mikhail Gorbachev to give up the nuclear arms race. According to critics, however, Reagan's foreign policy was reckless, putting the world at risk of nuclear war, and *prolonged* the Cold War due to the negative impact of his actions on Soviet hardliners.

During his White House tenure, Reagan was mockingly called the "Teflon president" by his critics, who regarded him as like a nonstick cooking pan because he was never stuck with blame for failed adventures—such as putting U.S. Marines in harm's way in Lebanon (where 241 were killed in a 1983 terrorist attack) and the Iran-Contra affair (in which arms were secretly sold to Iran and the proceeds illegally diverted to anticommunist Contra forces in Nicaragua). So enduring was his political influence, however, that as recently as 2008—some two decades after he left office and four years after his death on June 5, 2005—Republican candidates vied for the claim of being in the conservative tradition of Ronald Reagan.

Brian Calfano

See also: Abortion; AIDS; Cold War; Communists and Communism; Gay Rights Movement; Goldwater, Barry; Iran-Contra Affair; Religious Right; Republican Party; Strategic Defense Initiative; Supply-Side Economics; Tax Reform.

Further Reading

Arquilla, John. *The Reagan Imprint: Ideas in American Foreign Policy from the Collapse of Communism to the War on Terror.* New York: Ivan R. Dee, 2006.

Collins, Robert M. *Transforming America: Politics and Culture During the Reagan Years.* New York: Columbia University Press, 2006.

Diggins, John Patrick. *Ronald Reagan: Fate, Freedom, and the Making of History.* New York: W.W. Norton, 2007.

Skinner, Kiron K., Annelise Anderson, and Martin Anderson, eds. *Reagan: A Life in Letters.* New York: Free Press, 2003.

Troy, Gil. *Morning in America: How Ronald Reagan Invented the 1980s.* Princeton, NJ: Princeton University Press, 2005.

Record Warning Labels

Warning labels on recorded music albums, cassettes, and compact discs (CDs) with the words "Explicit Lyrics—Parental Advisory" were adopted in 1990 by the Recording Industry Association of America (RIAA), the industry's leading trade group. The labeling system, instituted as a result of lobbying by the Parents Music Resource Center (PMRC), was intended to restrict child access to music with "offensive" lyrics.

The PMRC was founded in 1985 by the wives of several members of Congress and senior Reagan administration officials. Its spokespersons were Tipper Gore, the wife of then-Senator Al Gore (D-TN), and Susan Baker, the wife of then-Secretary of State James Baker. In December 1984, Tipper Gore had bought Prince's album *Purple Rain* (1984) for her daughter and listened to the song "Darling Nikki," which contained a description of masturbation. Finding such content inappropriate for children, Gore decided to mount a public campaign. The PMRC goal was to inform parents of offensive lyrics and to protect children from the dangers of "porn rock." Along with the National Parent-Teachers Association, the PMRC lobbied the RIAA to develop guidelines similar to those that govern the movie industry.

The RIAA was a fifty-five-member trade group whose constituent companies produced more than 90 percent of the records sold in the United States. Although warnings had appeared on many albums prior to 1985, the wording varied and the design was often indistinct from the album cover. The PMRC hoped to institute uniform and visible labels that warned of explicit violence, the glorification of alcohol and illegal drugs, occultism, and explicit sexuality. The organization also sought to have all song lyrics printed on the record jackets of all albums so that parents could screen the content of their children's records.

The PMRC's attempt to regulate the lyrical content of rock-and-roll albums was informed by a number of other discourses on youth sexuality, including the 1985–1986 Attorney General's Commission on Pornography (AGCP), which viewed pornography as corrupting children and contributing to sexual violence against children. Borrowing language from the AGCP report, the PMRC's media campaign asserted that "rock music has become pornographic" and harmful to minors. Following a publicity campaign about the dangers of "porn rock," the PMRC used its political connections to secure a hearing before the Senate Committee on Commerce, Science, and Transportation in September 1985. As Tipper Gore testified, one of the committee members at the hearing was her husband.

At the hearing, the PMRC was opposed by the American Civil Liberties Union (ACLU) and popular musicians John Denver, Dee Snider, and Frank Zappa. The musicians asserted that labeling was a form of censorship. Zappa declared that the efforts of the PMRC were "the equivalent of treating dandruff with decapitation."

Although the Senate committee claimed that the hearing was strictly informational, the proceeding raised the possibility of future legislation, which placed pressure on the RIAA to adopt the labels voluntarily. At the same time, the RIAA was lobbying for passage of the Home Audio Recording Act, which would impose a tax on blank audiotape and home recording equipment, generating hundreds of millions of dollars for the RIAA members' companies. Critics of record labeling believed that the RIAA strategically agreed to the PMRC's demands because the husbands of four PMRC members sat on the Senate committee that heard arguments on the proposed tax legislation.

On November 1, 1985, shortly after the first hearings on the Home Audio Recording Act, the RIAA and the PMRC announced that they had brokered a deal that would require labels with uniform wording, design, and placement to be affixed to all records with explicit lyrics. Regulation was to be conducted by the record companies. However, the labeling system was not implemented with regularity and uniformity by the companies until May 1990, when the RIAA publicly promised to enforce its own labeling system in order to stave off pending legislation in nineteen states that would have required even more stringent warning labels. Major retail outlets such as Wal-Mart refuse to carry music with warning labels, thus pressuring artists to produce music with unobjectionable lyrics or to distribute "clean" versions of some albums.

The PMRC's campaign to institute record labeling was linked to other social struggles over issues such as sex education and pornography. Protecting the young from explicit sex also had implications for sexual expression among adults.

Gill Frank

See also: American Civil Liberties Union; Biafra, Jello; Censorship; Counterculture; Gore, Al; Heavy Metal Music; Pornography; Rap Music; Reagan, Ronald; Rock and Roll; Sexual Revolution; Wal-Mart; Zappa, Frank.

Further Reading

Gore, Tipper. *Raising PG Kids in an X-Rated Society*. Nashville, TN: Abingdon, 1987.

Nuzum, Eric. *Parental Advisory: Music Censorship in America*. New York: HarperCollins, 2001.

Recording Industry Association of America (RIAA) Web site. www.riaa.com.

Red and Blue States

The tinting of states as either "red" or "blue" during a presidential election has been the media's way of indicating which of the two dominant parties won the corresponding Electoral College votes. Such color-coded map displays—designating red for Republican and blue for Democratic—distort the reality of how people voted because of the "winner take all" voting system. Used as shorthand in the culture wars, the two colors have come to symbolize binary opposites: red for conservative and blue for liberal, another oversimplification.

The red-blue demarcation calls attention to the Electoral College system and how it gives greater weight to historically constituted geographies than to the actual population. Each state, no matter how small its population, is allotted a minimum of three votes in the Electoral College—based on the constitutionally guaranteed two seats for the Senate and one for the House of Representatives. Since there are a total of 435 seats in the House and each state is allowed at least one, the remaining seats are divided among the states in accordance with population. Thus, rural states have an advantage in that they are guaranteed a minimum number of Electoral College votes in a given presidential election; states with large urban populations divide the remainder among themselves.

There has not previously been a consistent attribution of color to particular parties in the postwar era. Clearly, the use of red and blue are taken from the colors of the U.S. flag to signify the inherent nationalism in both of the parties. Television, print media, and the Internet have been the primary purveyors of reductive voting patterns that paint states in a broad swath of color rather than the micro-variation in the actual precinct results. In the highly contentious and legally contested election of 2000, the electoral map of red and blue states was consistent across major television networks, newspapers, and Internet sites for well over a month, a phenomenon that appears to have permanently pigmented the two major parties. Moreover, it contributed to a rancorous political divide within American society.

The polar color schemata have loaded ideological resonances. In most postwar iconography, red was always associated with communism, revolution, insurgency, and passion. Blue was often associated with the status quo, the Union Army, and rationality, but sometimes depression. Red is traditionally used to note the left in European politics. Blue is sometimes associated with parties that are proponents of capitalism and conservativism, such as the British Conservative Party. The dissolution of the Soviet Union in 1991 began to dissipate the traditional color associations, but the polarization of political opinion and ad hominem style of broadcasting and print punditry since that time have certainly reinforced the association of red for Republican and blue for Democratic.

The red and blue color coding has served as a proxy for generalizations about the beliefs, culture, and ideology of a state's population. Red states are said to favor conservative, moral-driven policies and to oppose government regulation, social spending, public ownership, stem-cell research, abortion, and gay marriage. Blue states, in contrast, are said to support personal liberties, government intervention in the economy, public broadcasting, Social Security, scientific research, access to abortion, and gay rights. The generalizations are even extended to people and their consumption habits: blues are said to live in the "Porn Belt" and "debauched dystopias," drive Volvos, and drink lattes; reds reside in the "Bible Belt" and the "sticks," drive pickup trucks, tote guns, watch NASCAR, and drink Coca-Cola.

Such characterizations are also seen in Web sites such as "Blue State of Mind" and "A Red Mind in a Blue State." While the broad abstractions have been thoroughly debunked by social scientists and political analysts, pundits still rely on these easy stereotypes, and they continue to have resonance in public discourse.

Tom Mertes

See also: Abortion; Democratic Party; Election of 2000; Gay Rights Movement; Privatization; Republican Party; Same-Sex Marriage; Science Wars; Stem-Cell Research; Transgender Movement.

Further Reading

Fiorina, Morris. *Culture War? The Myth of a Polarized America.* New York: Longman, 2005.
Frank, Thomas. *What's the Matter with Kansas? How Conservatives Won the Heart of America.* New York: Metropolitan Books, 2004.
Gelman, Andrew. *Red State, Blue State, Rich State, Poor State: Why Americans Vote the Way They Do.* Princeton, NJ: Princeton University Press, 2008.

Redford, Robert

The acclaimed film actor and director Robert Redford is renowned for his work in such popular hits as *Butch Cassidy and the Sundance Kid* (1969), *The Sting* (1973), *All the President's Men* (1976), *The Natural* (1984), and *Ordinary People* (1980, for which he won an Academy Award for Best Director), as well as for his role in championing independent filmmaking in America. Since the 1970s, Redford has also been prominent as an environmentalist and supporter of Native American rights.

The son of a milkman (later accountant), Charles Robert "Bob" Redford, Jr., was born on August 18, 1937, in Santa Monica, California. In 1955, he attended the University of Colorado to play on its baseball team, but he lost his athletic scholarship because of drinking problems. In 1958, after working in the oil fields of Southern California and roaming Europe (studying art in France and Italy), Redford moved to New York City to study at the Pratt Institute of Art and Design. But it was while taking classes in set design at the America Academy of Dramatic Arts in Manhattan that Redford discovered acting and began his professional career. After performing on Broadway—most notably in Neil Simon's *Barefoot in the Park* (1963)—and various television series, he turned to film in the mid-1960s, achieving superstar status for his starring role (with Paul Newman) in *Butch Cassidy.*

Not coincidentally, a number of Redford's films have resonated in the culture wars for their recurring theme of mistrust of the federal government, or American institutions in general. Such works include *The Candidate* (1972), which portrays the compromises and disillusionment of an idealistic young candidate for the U.S. Senate; *The Way We Were* (1973), about the 1950s Red Scare in Hollywood; *Three Days of the Condor* (1975), about a sinister CIA conspiracy; *All the President's Men* (1976), about the *Washington Post* investigative reporters who uncover the Watergate scandal (Redford plays Bob Woodward); and *Quiz Show* (1994, director), about the television quiz show scandals of the 1950s and 1960s. Redford has also played in or directed several pictures with a strong environmental theme, such as *Jeremiah Johnson* (1972), about a mountain man in the American West during the mid-1800s; *The Milagro Beanfield War* (1988), about a struggle between a poor farmer and rich developers; and *A River Runs Through It* (1992), about fly fishing and growing up in Montana.

In the 1970s, while making his home outside Hollywood, Redford began buying property near Provo, Utah, in a gorge of the Wasatch Mountains. Proceeds from a ski resort he bought in the area—renamed Sundance Ski Resort, after his character in the 1969 film—helped support the nonprofit Sundance Institute he opened in 1981. As an alternative to the commercialism of Hollywood production, the Sundance Institute was founded as a resource center for aspiring filmmakers, screenwriters, and theater artists, providing financial and technical assistance for creative artistic development. Beginning in 1985, the institute began promoting independent films through the Sundance Film Festival, held annually in Park City, Utah. The Sundance Festival quickly became the largest independent film festival in the United States, and today it remains the world's premier venue for showcasing new independent motion pictures.

Redford's interest in environmentalism began in 1970 when he successfully fought a proposal for an eight-lane highway near his home in Provo. In 1975, he opposed plans to construct a $3.5-billion coal-fired power plant in southern Utah—a position for which he was burned in effigy by 500 pro-growth state residents who referred to the actor as "the hypocritical obstructionist." Later, as part of a coalition of activists, he supported the permanent preservation of the area as the Grand Staircase-Escalante National Monument. Redford's interest in ecological issues also led to his involvement in Native American rights. In his documentary *Incident at Oglala* (1992), Redford condemns the federal justice system for prosecuting Leonard Peltier, a leader of the American Indian Movement (AIM) and activist, for the 1975 murders of two FBI agents.

Jacob W. Olmstead and Roger Chapman

See also: American Indian Movement; Environmental Movement; Hollywood Ten; McCarthyism; Watergate; Woodward, Bob.

Further Reading

Downing, David. *Robert Redford*. New York: St. Martin's Press, 1982.

Quirk, Lawrence J., and William Schoell. *The Sundance Kid: An Unauthorized Biography of Robert Redford*. Lanham, MD: Taylor Trade, 2006.

Spada, James. *The Films of Robert Redford*. Secaucus, NJ: Citadel Press, 1977.

Redneck

The term "redneck" as a description of rural, working-class whites may date back to British usage but is now most commonly associated with poor whites in the American South. It is derived from the sunburned skin acquired from outdoor manual labor.

Although "redneck" is often a pejorative, southern populists and coal miners' unions in the early twentieth century adopted the term as an emblem of class solidarity. Newspapers of the day used "redneck" interchangeably with "communist" and "Bolshevik" in describing violent or rebellious unionists in central Appalachia. The term took on more widespread popularity during the Depression, as southern poverty began to receive unprecedented national attention.

In the civil rights era, "redneck" retained a class-based undertone but was used, most notably by Malcolm X, specifically to describe white racists. The conflation of racial politics and white class identity was heightened in the late 1960s, when opponents of integration made racially charged appeals to working-class whites in both the South and the North, as George C. Wallace did during his presidential campaigns. Amid the subsequent emergence of identity politics, whites readopted the term for themselves to describe a conservative, anti-intellectual ideal. As self-application of the word increased in popularity, "redneck" took on a greater cultural significance at the expense of racial, political, and economic connotations. The word has been frequently used in country music lyrics since the 1970s to portray a masculine working-class counterculture.

Because of its discursive malleability, "redneck" has remained a commonly used word on both sides of the political spectrum. Conservatives have used the term positively to convey an impression of white populism and negatively to dissociate the Republican Party from right-wing fringe groups like the Ku Klux Klan. Liberals have used the term to disparage opponents, particularly those from "red states," regarding issues such as gun control, abortion rights, and public displays of the Confederate flag. And many people use the term "redneck" for whites who fail to conform to bourgeois standards of living.

Some commentators condemn the use of "redneck" because it promotes class stratification. They argue that the word's dual role as a cultural and economic signifier justifies depictions of poverty as a lifestyle choice. Jim Goad's polemic *The Redneck Manifesto* (1997) attempted to reestablish "redneck" within a context of radical class consciousness among poor whites, and to reprimand urban liberals for ignoring economic inequality among white Americans.

T.R.C. Hutton

See also: Anti-Intellectualism; Civil Rights Movement; Confederate Flag; Country Music; Gun Control; Labor Unions; Malcolm X; Race; Red and Blue States; Republican Party; Wallace, George.

Further Reading

Boney, F.N. "The Redneck." *Georgia Review* 25:3 (1971): 333–42.

Goad, Jim. *The Redneck Manifesto*. New York: Simon & Schuster, 1997.

Huber, Patrick J. "Redneck: A Short Note from American Labor History." *American Speech* 69:1 (1994): 106–10.

———. "A Short History of *Redneck:* The Fashioning of Southern White Masculine Identity." *Southern Cultures* 1:2 (1995): 145–66.

Jarosz, Lucy, and Victoria Lawson. "'Sophisticated People Versus Rednecks': Economic Restructuring and Class Difference in America's West." *Antipode* 34:1 (2002): 8–27.

Reed, Ralph

Ralph Reed, a conservative political activist and leader of the Religious Right during the 1990s, came to prominence when Pat Robertson named him as the first executive director of the Christian Coalition in 1989. Reed's work at that fundamental Christian advocacy group heralded a new era of political sophistication for evangelicals in America, translating their concerns into a political platform. Allegations of financial impropriety ultimately tarnished Reed's reputation among the evangelical faithful, however, and he left the Coalition in 1997 to start a political consulting firm and otherwise promote a right-wing fundamentalist agenda—only to become embroiled in another financial scandal.

The son of a U.S. Navy surgeon, Ralph Eugene Reed, Jr., was born on June 24, 1961, in Portsmouth, Virginia. Raised a Methodist, he became an evangelical Christian while attending the University of Georgia (BA, history, 1985). As an undergraduate, Reed devoted much of his time to GOP causes, serving as executive director of the College Republican National Committee (1982–1984) and as president of the National College Republicans (1983). Working to align Republican and evangelical concerns, he was mentored by several prominent GOP strategists, namely Grover Norquist and Jack Abramoff. Reed completed his education at Emory University (PhD, U.S. history, 1991).

During his tenure at the Christian Coalition, based in Chesapeake, Virginia, Reed focused on grassroots organizing by establishing local and state affiliates to help Christian activists develop a political capacity. He circulated voter guides at conservative churches to show where the candidates stood on abortion, gay rights, funding for the National Endowment of the Arts, school prayer, and school vouchers, with the goal of increasing votes for Republicans. He also encouraged Christians to run for local office and developed workshops to train Christians for advocacy work. At the 1996 Republican National Convention, Reed successfully thwarted an attempt by some delegates to remove from the party's platform a position supporting a constitutional amendment banning abortion. Reed resigned from the Christian Coalition in April 1997, after the group's chief financial officer, Judy Liebert, informed federal prosecutors that he had allowed a close friend and contractor to over-bill the coalition. At the same time, the coalition was under investigation by

Named executive director of the Christian Coalition at age twenty-eight, Ralph Reed played a key role in translating evangelical principles into a viable political agenda. He left the organization over allegations of financial impropriety in 1997 and launched a consulting firm. *(AP Images/Dennis Cook)*

the Federal Election Commission for alleged violations of federal campaign law in distributing voter guides and directly supporting Republican campaigns, including the reelection of Congressman Newt Gingrich (R-GA) and Oliver North's U.S. Senate bid in Virginia.

Upon leaving the Christian Coalition, Reed formed Century Strategies, an Atlanta-based lobbying firm with a Republican clientele. He also served as chairman of the Georgia Republican Party (2001–2003) and headed the Southeast regional reelection campaign for President George W. Bush (2003–2004). In 2005, Reed once again became ensnared in scandal, this time involving a former mentor, super lobbyist Jack Abramoff, who bilked Indian tribal clients of $80 million. Federal investigators found evidence that Abramoff paid Reed to organize evangelical opposition to a proposed Indian casino that a rival tribal casino (and client of Abramoff's) regarded as a threat. Reed claims to have been unaware that his work was helping an existing gambling facility.

Many evangelicals expressed disappointment in Reed. Marvin Olasky, editor of the evangelical *World* magazine, wrote that Reed's involvement in the Abramoff affair repudiated the moral principles Reed had fought for at the Christian Coalition. Political commentators believe that his involvement in the scandal led to his defeat in the 2006 Republican primary for lieutenant governor of Georgia.

Carolyn Gallaher

See also: Abortion; Campaign Finance Reform; Christian Coalition; Gingrich, Newt; Indian Casinos; National Endowment for the Arts; Norquist, Grover; North, Oliver; Religious Right; Republican Party; Robertson, Pat; School Prayer; School Vouchers.

Further Reading

Gerson, Michael J. "Christian Coalition in Unprecedented Crisis." *U.S. News & World Report*, February 16, 1998.

Reed, Ralph. *Active Faith: How Christians Are Changing the Soul of American Politics.* New York: Free Press, 1996.

———. *Politically Incorrect: The Emerging Faith Factor in American Politics.* Dallas, TX: World, 1994.

Rehnquist, William H.

As an associate justice of the U.S. Supreme Court (1972–1986) and as the sixteenth chief justice of the United States (1986–2003), William H. Rehnquist was associated with some of the most conservative rulings of that body and left the high court a more conservative judicial body than the one he had joined more than three decades before. Rehnquist presided over the Supreme Court in two of the most contentious proceedings in America's culture wars—the Senate impeachment trial of President Bill Clinton in 1999 and the case of *Bush v. Gore* (2000), which effectively decided a presidential election.

Born William Hubbs Rehnquist on October 1, 1924, in Milwaukee, Wisconsin, he attended Kenyon College (1942) before serving in the U.S. Army during World War II. Upon returning home, he attended Stanford University on the GI Bill, earning degrees in political science (BA, 1947; MA, 1948). After earning another master's degree, in government, at Harvard University (1949), Rehnquist returned to Stanford to complete his education in law (LLB, 1952). Graduating as class valedictorian, he was offered a prestigious clerkship for U.S. Supreme Court justice Robert Jackson (1952–1953), during which time the Court heard initial arguments in the landmark school desegregation case of *Brown v. Board of Education.* Rehnquist wrote a memorandum to Jackson in which he argued that the Court should defer to the precedent of *Plessy v. Ferguson* and allow states to exclude blacks from public schools under the "separate but equal" principle. Rehnquist later claimed that he had written the memo on behalf of Justice Jackson, but legal experts have suggested that the memo represented Rehnquist's own view.

After working in private practice in Arizona and becoming active in Republican politics, Rehnquist moved to Washington, D.C., in 1969 to service as assistant attorney general in the Richard Nixon administration. Upon the retirement of Associate Justice John Marshall Harlan in 1971, Nixon nominated Rehnquist to the high court. Senate Democrats, regarding him as too conservative, criticized the nominee for his *Brown* memo nearly twenty years earlier and noted other questionable incidents from Rehnquist's past. Among these was a deed to his summer home that prohibited the sale or lease of the house to any Jewish person, and a deed to his Phoenix home in the 1960s that barred nonwhites from the property. Although some Democrats resisted the nomination, many recognized that Rehnquist's intelligence and experience would make him a more than capable justice. Republicans saw him as a member who might shift the high court in a more conservative direction. The Senate confirmed Rehnquist's appointment by a vote of 68–26, and he took his seat in January 1972.

It soon became clear that Justice Rehnquist would be as conservative as Nixon had hoped. He was a staunch believer in the principle of federalism, trusting that local governments would be more likely than the federal government to reflect their constituents' views. Thus, whenever possible, Rehnquist stressed the importance of states' rights and interpreted the Equal Protection Clause of the Fourteenth Amendment more narrowly than the liberal justices who preceded him. In his early years on the bench, Rehnquist became the justice with the most sole dissents on the (Warren) Burger Court; he was also one of two justices to dissent in the historic case of *Roe v. Wade* (1973), which legalized abortion in America.

As chief justice—appointed by President Ronald Reagan to replace the retiring Warren Burger in 1986—Rehnquist, along with fellow Republican appointees, indeed shifted the Supreme Court rightward. The first notable conservative ruling came during Rehnquist's first term as chief justice in *McCleskey v. Kemp* (1987). In a 5–4 decision, the court refused to overturn the death sentence of Warren McCleskey, a black man, even though solid statistical evidence showed that the race of McCleskey's murder victim likely was an important factor in handing down the death penalty. Then in *Wards Cove Packing v. Antonio* (1989), the justices ruled that a company did not discriminate against minorities even though strong statistical discrepancies existed regarding the races of employees and the positions they held. And in *Shaw v. Reno* (1993), the high court declared that North Carolina could not create a district that would increase the state's percentage of minority representation, even though U.S. attorney general William Barr had ordered the state to adopt just such a measure. All of these rulings marked a departure from the Supreme Court's previous broad definition of racial discrimination.

Nearly a year after it was announced that he was suffering from thyroid cancer, William Rehnquist died on September 3, 2005, at age eighty. He was the first Supreme Court justice to die in office since Robert Jackson, for whom he had clerked, in 1954. In the interim, in large measure due to Rehnquist's influence, the Court little resembled the liberal (Earl) Warren Court of the 1950s and 1960s, nor even the more moderate Burger Court of the 1970s and 1980s.

Rehnquist's tenure was a boon to conservatives, who had grown tired of what they perceived as the Supreme Court's "judicial activism." They regarded Rehnquist as a chief justice who helped reduce the influence of what they considered unnecessary or unjust programs such as affirmative action. They also applauded his concurring opinion in *Bush v. Gore* (2000), which ensured that conservative Republican George W. Bush would win election to the White House over his Democratic opponent, Vice President Al Gore.

Liberals, on the other hand, criticized Rehnquist not only for his consistent positions on curbing defendant rights (in the name of law and order) and against civil rights and labor, but also for his failure to build a legislative consensus beyond his own conservative bloc. The Rehnquist Court was known for an unusual number of 5–4 and 6–3 verdicts, resulting in a high number of dissenting arguments that thereby weaken the strength of court precedents. Liberals further accused the Rehnquist Court of engaging in right-wing "judicial activism," as it declared more federal laws unconstitutional per year than any other judiciary in American history.

Aaron Safane

See also: *Brown v. Board of Education* (1954); Bush Family; Capital Punishment; Civil Rights Movement; Election of 2000; Gore, Al; Judicial Wars; Kennedy Family; Warren, Earl.

Further Reading

Davis, Sue. "Federalism and Property Rights: An Examination of Justice Rehnquist's Legal Positivism." *Western Political Quarterly* 39:2 (1986): 250–64.

Keck, Thomas M. *The Most Activist Supreme Court in History: The Road to Modern Judicial Conservatism.* Chicago: University of Chicago Press, 2004.

Kennedy, Randall L. "*McCleskey v. Kemp:* Race, Capital Punishment, and the Supreme Court." *Harvard Law Review* 110:7 (1988): 1622–61.

Lawson, Steven F. *Civil Rights Crossroads: Nation, Community, and the Black Freedom Struggle.* Lexington: University Press of Kentucky, 2003.

Relativism, Moral

Moral relativism encompasses the view that there is no single true morality and that, instead, ethical norms depend on the society to which a person happens to belong. Therefore, according to the relativist, there is no absolute morality that applies to all people everywhere. The term "moral relativism" is employed with a wide range of meanings in nonacademic contexts, where it is used as everything from a synonym for tolerance to a synonym for immorality. Despite this range of uses, the term has taken on considerable symbolic importance. Many regard America's culture wars as a battle between moral absolutists and moral relativists.

Conservative commentators occasionally accuse others of moral relativism or moral laxity if someone's wrongdoing seems to be punished too lightly. Television commentator Bill O'Reilly, for example, has argued that moral relativism is the world's greatest danger. Sometimes moral relativism is depicted as the inevitable result of the secularization of ethics, and colleges are frequently identified as intellectual sources of moral relativism, although many conservatives now see it as pervasive in American culture. According to Allan Bloom in *The Closing of the American Mind* (1987), virtually all college students believe that truth is relative. William J. Bennett in *Why We Fight: Moral Clarity and the War on Terrorism* (2002) argues that moral relativism has become today's conventional wisdom.

The term is often used to describe and criticize the 1960s counterculture and its effects. It was widely used in this way during the debates surrounding the impeachment of President Bill Clinton in 1998–1999. For some of his critics, Clinton was a symbol of moral relativism. Journalist Joe Klein, for example, observed that the first of the Baby Boom generation's "alleged sins" is "moral relativism." The term also received attention when, shortly before he was elected pope in 2005, Cardinal Joseph Ratzinger claimed that the world was moving toward "a dictatorship of relativism."

The term "cultural relativism" is sometimes used synonymously with "moral relativism," but it more specifically expresses the more modest descriptive claim that moral beliefs vary from culture to culture. The term "moral subjectivism" refers to the view that moral truth is relative to the individual. Moral relativism tends to be identified as a form of moral skepticism and is often mistakenly identified with moral pluralism.

Daniel Callcut

See also: Bennett, William J.; Catholic Church; Clinton, Bill; Clinton Impeachment; Counterculture; Fundamentalism, Religious; O'Reilly, Bill; Postmodernism; Secular Humanism; September 11.

Further Reading

Callcut, Daniel. "The Value of Teaching Moral Skepticism." *Teaching Philosophy* 29:3 (2006): 223–35.

Klein, Joe. *The Natural: The Misunderstood Presidency of Bill Clinton.* New York: Doubleday, 2002.

Moser, Paul K., and Thomas L. Carson. *Moral Relativism: A Reader.* New York: Oxford University Press, 2001.

Shafer-Landau, Russ. *Whatever Happened to Good and Evil?* New York: Oxford University Press, 2004.

Religious Fundamentalism

See Fundamentalism, Religious

Religious Right

By the late 1970s, three important conservative constituencies or pressure groups had emerged within the Republican Party: fiscal conservatives, national security conservatives, and religious conservatives—the last widely known as the Religious Right. A counter to the ecumenical Christian National Council of Churches and the liberal Protestant and Catholic clergy, the Religious Right represents a loose coalition of Protestants, Catholics, and Jews; the movement has been dominated, however, by conservative Protestants (chiefly "born-again Christians"). In the close presidential elections of both 2000 and 2004, the Religious Right has been credited with providing the margin of victory to Republican George W. Bush. Like Ronald Reagan before him, Bush had openly courted religious conservatives.

Leaders of the Religious Right present themselves as patriotic Americans who champion the traditional values that made the nation great. Critics warn that the Religious Right is a threat to individual liberty and cultural diversity as it seeks to tear down the wall of separation between church and state. Some opponents charge that the chief aim of the Religious Right is to establish a theocracy. Within Christian circles, there are those who criticize the Religious Right for fostering the view that there is only one divinely approved position on political and social issues. Religious critics of the Religious Right argue further that the work of churches is to win people through evangelism and charity, not divide them by engaging in political activities.

The Religious Right began to form in the context of the Cold War, which took on religious dimensions as American politicians emphasized the inherent atheism of communism. After the surprise Soviet launch of the satellite *Sputnik* in 1957, which marked the beginning of the U.S.-Soviet space race, the American government began emphasizing science in school curricula, which rankled Christian fundamentalists who disagreed with the theory of evolution, including the concept of an "old earth," and were philosophically opposed to federal interference in local classrooms. In the 1960s, religious conservatives were also alarmed by the burgeoning youth counterculture, with its loose sexual mores, indulgence in drugs, student protests, and disdain for authority. Likewise, religious conservatives were generally hostile toward the civil rights movement (and the mixing of races), the new wave of feminism (and the proposed Equal Rights Amendment), and the fledgling gay rights movement. U.S. Supreme Court rulings that banned school prayer (*Engel v. Vitale* in 1962 and *Abington School District v. Kemp* in 1963) and legalized abortion (*Roe v. Wade*, 1973), combined with the decision of the Internal Revenue Service to strip private schools of their tax-exempt status if they practiced racial discrimination (1970) and President Jimmy Carter's decision to withdraw tax exemptions from private schools that were set up to avoid court-ordered public school desegregation (1978), further contributed to the outrage of religious conservatives.

Notable figures in the Religious Right since the 1970s have included the following:

- Robert J. Billings, a graduate of Bob Jones University, founder of the National Christian Action Coalition (1978), a critic of government interference in religious schools, an administrator in the Department of Education under President Ronald Reagan, and a founding organizer of the Moral Majority;
- James C. Dobson, the founder of Focus on the Family (1977), a participant in the White House Conference on Families under President Jimmy Carter (1980), and a panel member of the Commission on Pornography under President Reagan (1986);
- Jerry Falwell, a Baptist minister and founder of the Moral Majority (1979);
- Robert Grant, a graduate of Wheaton College and Fuller Theological Seminary; a founder of the American Christian Cause (1975), Christian Voice (1978), and the American Freedom Coalition (1987); and the publisher and distributor of "moral-issues report cards" on elected officials;
- Bob Jones, Sr., founder of Bob Jones University (1926);
- Beverly LaHaye, wife of Tim LaHaye, a Baptist and founder of Concerned Women for America (1979), which rallied to defeat the Equal Rights Amendment;
- Tim LaHaye, a Baptist minister and author of the antisecularist work *The Battle for the Mind* (1980), a co-founder of Christian Heritage College in San Diego (1970), founder of Californians for Biblical Morality (1980) and the American Coalition for Traditional Values (1983), and a prominent Reagan supporter;
- Clarence E. Manion, a Roman Catholic, conservative radio commentator (*Manion Forum of the Air*, 1950s–1960s), dean of the college of law at Notre Dame University, a founding member of the John Birch Society, and the inspirer and publisher of Barry Goldwater's *Conscience of a Conservative* (1960);
- Edward A. McAteer, a Memphis-based marketing specialist and active Baptist, founder of the Religious Roundtable (1979) who influenced the conservative takeover of the Southern Baptist Convention (1979) and backed the election of Reagan;
- Ralph Reed, executive secretary of the Christian Coalition (1989–1997), publisher, distributor of "Christian" voter guides, and conservative political strategist;
- Pat Robertson, Baptist-turned-charismatic evangelical; founder of the Virginia-based Christian

Broadcasting Network (1960), Regent University (1977), and the Christian Coalition (1989);

- James Robison, a Baptist and founder of the Texas-based James Robison Evangelistic Association (1965); televangelist preacher; an organizer of the Religious Roundtable; and a vocal opponent of abortion, gay rights, the Equal Rights Amendment, and secular humanism;
- Francis A. Schaeffer, a Presbyterian recognized as the father of modern fundamentalism, author of the antisecular *A Christian Manifesto* (1981), and an advocate of Christian activism to stop abortion;
- Robert H.W. Welch, Jr., founding president of the John Birch Society (1958), a disseminator of communist conspiracy theory, and an advocate of limited government;
- Paul Weyrich, a Roman Catholic and chief organizer of the Religious Right, headed the Washington, D.C.–based Committee for the Survival of a Free Congress (1974), coined the term "moral majority," and conceived the organization that later bore that name;
- Donald Wildmon, a Methodist minister; monitor of television programming for moral content; founder of the National Federation for Decency (1977), later renamed the American Family Association; and close associate of Jerry Falwell.

Roger Chapman

See also: American Civil Religion; Church and State; Dobson, James; Falwell, Jerry; Focus on the Family; John Birch Society; LaHaye, Tim, and Beverly LaHaye; Moral Majority; Reed, Ralph; Republican Party; Robertson, Pat; Schaeffer, Francis; Wildmon, Donald.

Further Reading

Balmer, Randall. *Thy Kingdom Come: How the Religious Right Distorts the Faith and Threatens America.* New York: Basic Books, 2006.

Diamond, Sara. *Spiritual Warfare: The Politics of the Christian Right.* Boston: South End Press, 1989.

Martin, William. *With God on Our Side: The Rise of the Religious Right in America.* New York: Broadway Books, 1996.

Viguerie, Richard A. *The New Right: We're Ready to Lead.* Falls Church, VA: Viguerie, 1981.

Wallis, Jim. *Who Speaks for God? An Alternative to the Religious Right—A New Politics of Compassion, Community, and Civility.* New York: Delacorte Press, 1996.

Reparations, Japanese Internment

In early 1942, shortly after America entered World War II, the U.S. government undertook a massive pro-gram of relocation and internment of people of Japanese ancestry—including U.S. citizens (about 60 percent of the total) as well as resident aliens. This coincided with a smaller effort affecting German and Italian resident aliens. During the postwar period, with the success of the civil rights movement, the emergence of a new multicultural perspective, and the clarity of retrospection, the injustice of Japanese internment and the issue of reparations became a matter of national debate.

The relocation program banned people of Japanese ancestry from residence in 137 areas on the West Coast and the southwestern border of the United States. In accordance with Executive Order 9066, signed by President Franklin D. Roosevelt in February 1942, approximately 5,000 Japanese were relocated outside the prohibited areas, and another 120,000 men, women, and children were interned in one of ten relocation centers run by the War Relocation Authority; the centers were not closed until June 1946.

Although the ostensible purpose of the internment was to protect the United States from sabotage or other disloyal acts in support of Japan's war effort, no effort was made to determine whether any individual or organization in fact posed such a threat; people of Japanese heritage were targeted as a group. A presidential commission established by President Jimmy Carter in 1980 to study the matter reported to Congress that the internment was "motivated largely by racial prejudice, wartime hysteria, and a failure of political leadership."

Although some Americans at the time opposed internment, the vast majority accepted this usurpation of the civil liberties of Japanese Americans. And in *Korematsu v. United States* (1944), the U.S. Supreme Court found the internment constitutional—a judgment that has never been reversed. After the war, the U.S. government maintained a list of potential subversives (although not based on ethnicity) and a detention plan in case of a national emergency.

When forced to relocate, many Japanese Americans lost not only their liberty but also their homes, businesses, and other property. In the aftermath, some initial restitution was paid for actual property losses, but it was not until passage of the Civil Liberties Act of 1988 that reparations were made to all those who had been interned or relocated. Beginning in 1990, each surviving internee was given a $20,000 cash payment, along with a letter of apology from the government. The official apology, signed by President George H.W. Bush, read in part: "We can never fully right the wrongs of the past. But we can take a clear stand for justice and recognize that serious injustices were done to Japanese Americans during World War II."

Although many Americans have looked back on the internment with a sense of shame and regret, the 1988 reparations legislation met with some resistance on the part of World War II veterans and such organizations as the American Legion. And in a conservative backlash after the terrorist attacks of September 11, 2001, some suggested that the Japanese internment provided a model for detaining suspects in America's "war on terror."

Larry W. DeWitt

See also: Abu Ghraib and Gitmo; Civil Rights Movement; Multiculturalism and Ethnic Studies; Revisionist History; September 11; Victimhood.

Further Reading

Daniels, Roger. *Prisoners Without Trial: Japanese Americans in World War II*. New York: Hill and Wang, 1993.

Hayashi, Brian Masaru. *Democratizing the Enemy: The Japanese-American Internment*. Princeton, NJ: Princeton University Press, 2004.

Malkin, Michelle. *In Defense of Internment: The Case for "Racial Profiling" in World War II and the War on Terror*. Washington, DC: Regnery, 2004.

Personal Justice Denied: Report of the Commission on Wartime Relocation and Internment of Civilians. Seattle: University of Washington Press, 1997.

Republican Party

The Republican Party, founded in 1854 in reaction to the expansion of slavery, has maintained identifiable cultural positions throughout its history, and since the 1960s has increasingly been identified as the political home of conservatism. Soon after its inception, the party dominated the North, a region that was home to two-thirds of the nation's population. This enabled Republican Abraham Lincoln to capture the presidency in 1860 without any southern electoral votes. Lincoln's Civil War legacy maintained a Republican majority in the North, where the organization gained the nickname "Grand Old Party" (GOP). But the "party of Lincoln" was unable to make inroads into the culturally conservative white South until the civil rights movement of the 1950s and 1960s.

During the 1860s and 1870s, the GOP was identified with racial liberalism. But after the end of Reconstruction, the massive immigration of non-Protestants, and the rise of industrial capitalism, the party shifted to the right. Thereafter, Republicans received support mainly from conservative groups: native-born Protestants (especially evangelicals); people of British, German, and Scandinavian ancestry; business; and the upper socioeconomic classes. To please these constituencies, the GOP promoted policies prohibiting alcohol, restricting immigration, suppressing inflation, and protecting domestic industry through tariffs. Although the party was split between conservatives and progressives on some economic and foreign policies, it maintained a nationwide electoral majority until the Great Depression.

1930s to 1960s

From the 1930s through the 1960s the Depression's legacy caused most Americans to reject the GOP's conservative economic policies in favor of the Democrats' New Deal programs, as even President Dwight D. Eisenhower, a Republican, conceded in the 1950s. Consequently, the GOP increasingly focused on cultural conservatism to attract white southerners, Catholics, and other conservatives away from the Democratic Party. Early in the Cold War, Senator Joseph McCarthy (R-WI) and other Republicans achieved some success by attacking Democrats' loyalty. When Democrats professed staunch patriotism during this period, Republicans sought other wedge issues. By 1960, race had become a divisive issue between liberals and conservatives, but it was not yet a partisan concern. In 1964–1965, however, the national Democratic Party under President Lyndon B. Johnson supported the Civil Rights and Voting Rights Acts. This began a chain reaction causing many cultural conservatives to abandon the Democratic fold.

During the 1960s, many Republicans embraced cultural conservatism to win over conservative Democrats. In the 1964 presidential election, Barry Goldwater's (R-AZ) opposition to the Civil Rights Act helped him win five southern states. In addition, the tumultuous cultural events of the 1960s—the Black Power movement, urban rioting, rising crime, the counterculture, the sexual revolution, feminism, and the Vietnam War protests—combined with a strong economy to shift voters' concerns to cultural issues. In 1968, GOP candidate Richard M. Nixon successfully pursued a culturally conservative "southern strategy," denying the Democratic candidate, Vice President Hubert Humphrey, any southern electoral votes except in Texas.

Since the Nixon era, Republicans have increasingly identified their party as the political home of cultural conservatism. As president, Nixon eschewed openly racial statements to avoid offending moderates, but he won over culturally conservative Democrats by using code words that let them know he was on their side. For example, he promoted "traditional values" and "law and order," launched a "war on drugs," and denounced abortion rights, affirmative action, Vietnam antiwar protestors, "forced busing" to integrate public schools, and "activist judges" who ordered desegregation and protected abortion and defendants' rights.

Nixon's success in shifting the country rightward was mixed, mainly because Democrats controlled Congress. He did effect some culturally conservative changes: pushing through crime and drug laws, nominating conservatives to the courts, and expanding the Vietnam War into Cambodia. Still, many conservatives mistrusted Nixon because he was not a right-wing ideologue; he was a calculating politician. Consequently, much of his cultural conservatism was merely rhetorical, and he followed a generally moderate line in economic and foreign policy. Moreover, the Watergate scandal undermined Republicans' identification with "traditional morality."

Nevertheless, Nixon's legacy bolstered conservative influence in the GOP. On the one hand, he served as a rallying point for conservatives who admired him and hated the liberals who despised him. On the other hand, right-wing ideologues were pleased that the disgrace of Nixon, whom they viewed as a closet moderate, opened the way for them to dominate the GOP.

1970s to 1980s

Since the 1930s, conservative intellectuals, politicians, and strategists had been working to take over the GOP. By the late 1970s, the backlash to the Democrats' liberal cultural, economic, and foreign policies had boosted the conservative movement. For example, the populist New Right reinforced cultural conservatism at the grassroots level, especially among white southerners and evangelical Protestants. At the same time, Republican operatives disseminated right-wing ideas to the rank and file through targeted mailing, fundraising appeals, and television commercials. By 1980, conservatives had united behind Republican Ronald Reagan.

Reagan was the most culturally conservative president since Calvin Coolidge in the 1920s. He emphasized religion, supported organized prayer in public schools, and wooed conservative televangelists such as Pat Robertson and Jerry Falwell. Reagan imbued his hawkish nationalistic foreign policy with religious imagery, peppering his speeches with "God Bless America" and strongly denouncing the Soviet Union as the "evil empire." He also pleased cultural conservatives by professing "family values"; venerating the military; increasing the defense budget; and opposing abortion, affirmative action, busing, crime, drugs, the environmental movement, the Equal Rights Amendment, and pornography. Because of Democratic opposition and his own focus on economic issues, however, Reagan managed just a few culturally conservative results: appointing conservatives to the judiciary, escalating the "war on drugs," and cutting back affirmative action programs. Nevertheless, the Reagan era increased partisan polarization in the culture wars, and Republicans became increasingly identified with conservatism.

Reagan's successor, Republican George H.W. Bush, also espoused culturally conservative rhetoric. In his 1988 campaign, Bush denounced his Democratic opponent, Michael Dukakis, for supporting abortion rights, opposing the outlawing of flag desecration, and allowing prisoner furloughs as Massachusetts governor. Bush's campaign connected the latter issue with race through an ad showing Willie Horton, an African-American convict who had raped a white woman while on furlough. As president, however, Bush faced a Democratic majority in Congress and cultural moderates in his own party, and he achieved little of substance culturally besides appointing conservative judges. He also presided over the U.S. victory in the 1991 Persian Gulf War.

1990s to 2000s

Despite Republicans' inability to enact significant culturally conservative laws, social conservatives remained loyal. They considered Democrats irredeemably liberal, and the GOP aggressively courted them. The lack of tangible results energized cultural conservatives to fight harder within the GOP against moderates and libertarian conservatives, who argued that government should not intervene in cultural matters.

Despite their differences, Republicans and the conservative movement united against Democrats, a stance that hardened after Bill Clinton captured the presidency in 1992. Cultural conservatives disliked Clinton's support for abortion rights, feminism, affirmative action, and allowing homosexuals to serve openly in the military. The GOP focused its attacks on the president's "immoral character," using the federal government to investigate his finances, womanizing, lying, and "criminal behavior."

By the mid-1990s, the Republicans had achieved an electoral majority in the South, and nationwide, by applying conservative rhetoric and attacks on Clinton's character. GOP congressional candidates united behind Newt Gingrich's "Contract with America" (1994), which proposed a number of culturally conservative policies, although it avoided divisive issues such as abortion. In the 1994 elections, the Christian Coalition and other right-wing groups helped the GOP capture Congress. Once in power, however, Republicans failed to enact many culturally conservative laws. Moreover, Clinton undercut them by supporting popular conservative measures. Additionally, former wedge issues like affirmative action, busing, crime, and immigration lessened in political salience during the 1990s economic boom. Consequently, Republicans rallied cultural conservatives by maintaining their attacks on Clinton, even impeaching him in 1998. The bitterness of the Clinton era widened the gap between the major parties in the culture wars.

Partisan polarization increased during the presidency of George W. Bush. In the 2000 campaign, Republicans united behind Bush, a staunch conservative whose evangelical religious beliefs shaped his worldview. In order to win, however, Bush needed the support of moderate independents, so he presented himself as a "compassionate conservative" and "a uniter, not a divider." Nevertheless, polls showed that he owed his success to conservatives, who supported him by an 81–17 margin. Bush's victory in the disputed 2000 election intensified the culture wars because it was ultimately decided by a Supreme Court dominated by Republican appointees. As president, Bush gave rhetorical support to cultural issues but focused on economic ones, especially tax cuts. Following the attacks of September 11, 2001, however, Republicans inflamed nationalistic feelings to gain support for the Iraq War (beginning in 2003), but the ongoing difficulties there once again polarized the nation, as did the contentious 2004 election, which Bush won narrowly. By the end of the Bush era, the Republican Party was a conservative bastion in the culture wars.

George Rising

See also: Bush Family; Cheney Family; Christian Coalition; Civil Rights Movement; Compassionate Conservatism; Contract with America; Evangelicalism; Family Values; Goldwater, Barry; Moral Majority; Neoconservatism; Nixon, Richard; Reagan, Ronald; Religious Right; September 11; Vietnam War; Watergate.

Further Reading

Barone, Michael. *Our Country: The Shaping of America from Roosevelt to Reagan.* New York: Free Press, 1990.

Berman, William C. *America's Right Turn: From Nixon to Clinton.* Baltimore: Johns Hopkins University Press, 1998.

Edsall, Thomas Byrne, and Mary D. Edsall. *Chain Reaction: The Impact of Race, Rights, and Taxes on American Politics.* New York: W.W. Norton, 1992.

Foner, Eric. *Free Soil, Free Labor, Free Men: The Ideology of the Republican Party Before the Civil War.* New York: Oxford University Press, 1970.

Fraser, Steve, and Gary Gerstle, eds. *The Rise and Fall of the New Deal Order, 1930–1980.* Princeton, NJ: Princeton University Press, 1990.

Gerring, John. *Party Ideologies in America, 1828–1996.* New York: Cambridge University Press, 1998.

Mayer, George H. *The Republican Party, 1854–1966.* New York: Oxford University Press, 1967.

Schaller, Michael, and George Rising. *The Republican Ascendancy: American Politics, 1968–2001.* Wheeling, IL: Harlan Davidson, 2002.

Revisionist History

Broadly defined, revisionist history refers to efforts by scholars to revise the shared, conventional understanding of the past based on the examination or reexamination of historical evidence. In the context of the culture wars, revisionist history has taken on a pejorative connotation. Referred to in the negative sense, historical revisionism is any attempt to revise historical understanding through political and ideological dishonesty. Historians who do work labeled "revisionist" are accused of pursuing scholarship driven by ideological goals—that is, begin with a thesis and then manipulate or manufacture evidence to support it.

American historians such as Howard Zinn, Eric Foner, and Ronald Takaki, among others perceived as "liberal" or "leftist," have been derided by critics and praised by supporters as "revisionists." Yet how one applies the term, in either its negative or its positive sense, depends largely on one's political context. Typically, critics on the right disparage any type of history labeled revisionist. Their opposition is generally based on an ideological position according to which America's "traditional history"—a collection of heroic narratives—represents the true, objective, usable past. The concept of a single shared past is politically useful to the right when traditionalism comes under attack, in reality or in perception, by those who seek to dishonor its inherent values. Said to be at stake in this debate is a sense of national identity that depends on particular historical narratives instilled in citizens.

In 1994, for example, the conservative writer Lynn Cheney (wife of Dick Cheney, the future vice president) criticized the proposed National History Standards for public education in America for presenting a "grim and gloomy" portrayal of the nation's history. The proposed standards, which addressed certain areas of U.S. history that had been commonly neglected, became the subject of national debate, prompted in part by Cheney's preemptive editorial strike. In an article titled "The End of History," Cheney maintained that a war for America's heritage was being waged. Right-wing intellectuals and pundits such as Cheney, televangelist Pat Robertson, and others characterized their opponents as tenured radicals and liberals, entranced with moral relativism, postmodern philosophy, and a "politically correct" agenda—eliciting countercharges of intolerance and elitism.

In the culture wars, proponents of conservatism have repeatedly framed themselves as defenders of the past as it "truly happened." Among historians who have been criticized as revisionists, conversely, the view of history as a single, shared, agreed-upon past is dismissed as a ridiculous construct. Historians such as Howard Zinn, author of *A People's History of the United States* (1980), a text frequently assailed by critics on the right, argue that the work of any historian is necessarily interpretive. All historical evidence, according to Zinn and like-minded others, must be selected and interpreted in order to make sense of the past. This viewpoint emphasizes that history is always constructed.

Even according to revisionists, however, arguing that history is interpretive does not negate the historian's commitment to accuracy, rigorous documentation and verification, and a balanced reconstruction of events. Historical education and responsible citizenship, it is said, require open inquiry, healthy skepticism, and open-mindedness to new perspectives. Zinn, for example, approaches history from the perspective of minorities and the working class rather than solely the heroic and elite figures that have been typically portrayed in traditional accounts. Rather than an example of history being "rewritten," as his critics charge, Zinn maintains that his work offers a renewed clarity through the exploration of perspectives that have been routinely marginalized. Likewise, much of the work done in recent years that has been derided as "revisionist" involves feminist or ethnic histories. Even as critics of these perspectives charge that popular history is being "hijacked," revisionists contend that they are responding to oversights in the historical record. As Ronald Takaki has noted, history can be seen as a mirror, and, in the case of socially marginalized populations, it is necessary to hold up a different mirror to reflect these silenced stories.

Revisionist historians contend that some stories have been systematically left out of mainstream historical accounts, ironically arguing that traditionalists have essentially been engaging in revisionist history of their own. For example, traditional accounts of the lives of Thomas Jefferson, George Washington, and James Madison focus solely on their positive attributes and great accomplishments, whereas more complete accounts would examine their relationship to slavery, colloquial provincial interests, political ambitions, and personal rivalries. The nation's founders, in short, have been characterized as icons of democracy, while in reality they were individuals with human frailties, complex motivations, and even contradictory behavior.

Conservative advocates sometimes argue that the traditional and prevailing view of the founders as heroes helps engender civic pride and responsibility among the people. While proponents of traditionalism argue that the perpetuation of these virtues is vital to national identity and pride, revisionists argue that the interests of contemporary citizens themselves should be reflected in the study of history. Furthermore, they argue, if historians do not continue to reanalyze the past, the study of history will become stagnant, discouraging new scholarship and intellectual curiosity. Zinn and his contemporaries argue that history should constantly reexamine the past and thereby improve understanding of the present.

Despite such serious academic disagreements, "revisionism" in the context of the culture wars generally remains a dirty word. Arguments on the right tend to paint the controversy as one of dishonest, agenda-driven ideologues who manipulate the past to promote their own views. By way of example, one may point to Holocaust deniers, who seek legitimacy by referring to themselves as "revisionists" while shamelessly manipulating the facts in pursuit of an anti-Semitic agenda. Examples of extreme dishonesty aside, understanding the necessity of revisionism in the historical method is key to understanding the real stakes in the controversy.

Neil Shepard

See also: Academic Freedom; American Exceptionalism; Cheney Family; Columbus Day; Deconstructionism; *Enola Gay* Exhibit; Founding Fathers; Great Books; Holocaust; Multiculturalism and Ethnic Studies; Postmodernism; Williams, William Appleman; Zinn, Howard.

Further Reading

Nash, Gary B., Charlotte Crabtree, and Ross E. Dunn. *History on Trial: The Struggle for National Standards in American Classrooms.* New York: Alfred A. Knopf, 1997.
Takaki, Ronald. *A Different Mirror: A History of Multicultural America.* Boston: Little, Brown, 1993.
Zinn, Howard. *A People's History of the United States.* New York: Harper & Row, 1980.

Right to Counsel

In the American criminal justice system, the right to counsel means that a person suspected or formally accused of committing a crime must be offered the assistance of a licensed attorney. The right to counsel protects the accused from the complexities of the criminal justice process and the vast legal resources possessed by the state. Although in theory this right is universally supported, the question of how to practically apply it has led to contentious debate, highlighting the tension between the protection of civil liberties and the enforcement of law and order.

Right to counsel protections stem from language in the Fifth, Sixth, and Fourteenth Amendments to the U.S. Constitution. Recognized by the Supreme Court in *Powell v. Alabama* (1932) as one of the chief expressions of the principle of due process, the right to counsel protections apply to criminal suspects and defendants in federal and state jurisdictions. As the Supreme Court has repeatedly held, the constitutional right to counsel applies in any instance where a person is subject to questioning by police while under the physical control of law enforcement officials (*Escobedo v. Illinois*, 1964; *Miranda v. Arizona*, 1966), in a police line-up (*U.S. v. Wade*, 1967), at trial (*Johnson v. Zerbst*, 1938; *Gideon v. Wainwright*, 1963; *Argersinger v. Hamlin*, 1972), or in the appeals process (*Douglas v. California*, 1963). Current doctrine holds that the right to legal counsel begins at the time of arrest and police questioning and extends to all stages of the criminal justice process after prosecutors have made a formal accusation against the arrestee.

Although the right to counsel is considered one of the Constitution's most fundamental liberties, questions about its ultimate reach are controversial. Many court observers argue that right to counsel protections suffered noticeably at the hands of conservative justices during the Rehnquist Court (1986–2005). Liberals are especially critical of decisions that have made it more difficult for defendants to claim on appeal that their convictions resulted from the ineffectiveness of counsel at trial. Liberals argue that because the poorest defendants are typically represented by public defenders or court-appointed attorneys burdened with heavy or even overwhelming caseloads, the spirit of the right to counsel is violated at trial and again when avenues of appeal are blocked.

Several cases examining Sixth Amendment issues pertaining to the right to counsel—e.g., *Texas v. Cobb* (2001) and *Mickens v. Taylor* (2002)—produced narrowly divided decisions and revealed strong ideological tensions on the Court that have shaped the outcome in interpreting defendants' rights.

Some criminologists suggest that the debate on the right to counsel reflects the opposing "crime control theologies" held by liberals and conservatives. According to this argument, conservatives emphasize the importance of the fear of punitive measures in promoting individual lawfulness, while liberals emphasize environmental factors as the underlying cause of criminality and believe that rehabilitation is better than punishment. Critics of that analysis, however, remind everyone that the right to counsel is a right of the *accused* and that a presumption of innocence is a cornerstone of American law.

Bradley Best

See also: Judicial Wars; Miranda Rights; Rehnquist, William H.

Further Reading

Dudley, Mark. E. *Gideon v. Wainwright (1963): Right to Counsel.* New York: Twenty-First Century Books, 1995.

Smith, Christopher E. *The Rehnquist Court and Criminal Punishment.* New York: Garland, 1997.

Spaeth, Harold J., and Jeffrey A. Segal. *The Supreme Court and the Attitudinal Model.* New York: Cambridge University Press, 1993.

Taylor, John B. *The Right to Counsel and the Privilege Against Self-Incrimination: Rights and Liberties Under the Law.* Santa Barbara, CA: ABC-CLIO, 2004.

Walker, Samuel. *Sense and Nonsense about Crime and Drugs.* Belmont, CA: Wadsworth, 1998.

Right to Die

Whether people have a right to die is one of the most controversial issues in modern American society. The right-to-die movement is a political and legal campaign that seeks respect for the desires of terminal, suffering, or persistently vegetative individuals, and to empower them (or their surrogates) in ways that help them maintain a measure of control over the time and manner of their death.

Competing Worldviews and Categories of Physician Assistance

The right-to-die debate is often framed by two competing worldviews: the "sanctity of life" versus "quality of life." Advocates of the "sanctity of life" viewpoint generally oppose any termination of human life, through either active or passive means. This position is often premised on the religious belief that since humans are created in the image of God, they consequently possess intrinsic dignity. The "sanctity of life" argument can also be founded on a rational, secular concept of life as a basic good to which all human beings, regardless of disease or disability, have an inviolate right.

In contrast, the "quality of life" approach holds that the good of life is balanced by the realities of human suffering and bodily deterioration. Advocates of this position argue that, in some instances, an individual's quality of life has deteriorated so much that death becomes a benefit. They support the right of terminally ill patients who are enduring serious suffering but are still mentally competent to make a life-and-death decision to seek a physician's assistance in committing suicide.

One form of physician assistance is actual, direct administration of a voluntarily requested lethal dose; in such cases, the act is commonly referred to as "voluntary active euthanasia." Similarly, a physician may assist by merely supplying the patient with a requested lethal dose of medication. The latter act is typically classified as "physician-assisted suicide," for the patient is the one who actually commits the suicidal act. The distinction between these two types of assisted suicide can be seen in the actions of euthanasia advocate Jack Kevorkian, a physician who helped a number of people commit suicide. If a terminally ill patient requested his assistance, Kevorkian would typically attach the patient to a homemade suicide machine that injected a lethal dose of drugs when the patient activated the mechanism. Kevorkian evaded criminal conviction until he moved beyond merely facilitating a patient's suicide and instead actively administered a lethal injection to an individual who no longer had use of his arms or legs. This constituted voluntary active euthanasia and led to Kevorkian's conviction and imprisonment for second-degree murder.

A third category is "passive euthanasia," which includes the withdrawal of life-sustaining medical treatments, such as ventilators and feeding tubes. Each of these three categories raises highly contested moral, medical, and legal questions regarding concepts of patient autonomy, state paternalism, and "quality of life" versus "sanctity of life."

Legal Landmarks: Quinlan *to* Schiavo

The modern right-to-die movement was sparked by the landmark New Jersey Supreme Court decision *In re Quinlan* (1976), a case involving passive euthanasia. At the age of twenty-two, Karen Ann Quinlan collapsed and ceased breathing for two fifteen-minute periods, depriving her brain of oxygen that left her neurologically devastated. Quinlan was diagnosed as being in a persistent vegetative state (PVS), requiring twenty-four-hour intensive nursing care, a respirator, a catheter, and artificial nutrition and hydration (ANH) received through a feeding tube. Convinced that his daughter had no chance of cognitive recovery and that a slow, inevitable deterioration was not in her best interests, Quinlan's father initiated court action seeking to turn off his daughter's respirator. The attending physicians refused, at least in part out of fear that they could be criminally liable for participating in the death of their patient.

The court ruled in favor of Quinlan's father, holding that because his daughter did not have the mental capacity to exercise her independent right of choice, she was entitled to a surrogate decisionmaker who would act in her best interests. Moreover, of significant relevance to physicians, the court distinguished between "the unlawful taking of the life of another and the ending of artificial life-support systems as a matter of self-determination." This reassured doctors facing similar scenarios that they would not be held criminally liable. Following the court victory, Quinlan's father had the respirator removed but not the feeding tube, and she lived for another ten years.

An incompetent patient's right to die versus a state's interest in promoting life's sanctity was the subject of the U.S. Supreme Court decision in *Cruzan v. Director, Missouri Dept. of Health* (1990). The case was about Nancy Cruzan, who on January 11, 1983, at age thirty, was involved in a car accident that caused a deprivation of oxygen to her brain. The lack of oxygen left Cruzan neurologically impaired, with no chance of regaining her mental faculties, and she was diagnosed as being in a PVS. After rehabilitation efforts failed, Cruzan's parents asked the hospital to withdraw the feeding tube that had been keeping her alive. The hospital's refusal to honor their request was backed by Missouri governor John Ashcroft, setting in motion a legal battle that wound its way to the U.S. Supreme Court. The justices held that a state may assert an "unqualified interest in the preservation of human life," affirming Missouri's requirement that clear and convincing proof of the patient's desire to withdraw ANH must be demonstrated before such action can be taken.

Justice Sandra Day O'Connor, in her concurring opinion in *Cruzan*, noted: "Artificial feeding cannot readily be distinguished from other forms of medical treatment." Even so, thirty years after *Quinlan*, in the Terri Schiavo case, those opposing removal of her feeding tube equated such an act with a cruel and unusual death by starvation not fit for a convicted murderer on death row or a rabid pit bull. Provocative rhetoric notwithstanding, by 2005, however, the legal, medical, and ethical consensus was nearly unanimous that ANH is not the moral equivalent of ordinary care, but a life-prolonging medical treatment no different from a respirator or other mechanical device. Such was the rationale repeatedly articulated by the Florida judiciary as it sought to resolve the intractable dispute between Terri Schiavo's husband and her parents over the question of whether to cease provision of ANH. Schiavo spent over fifteen years in PVS before her feeding tube was removed in March 2005; she died about two weeks later. Her case was the focus of unprecedented international media coverage, prompting a surge in public attention to end-of-life decision making and debates regarding the appropriateness of legal, political, judicial, religious, and medical interventions.

State Interests and Individual Liberties

Controversies surrounding the right to die in the United States have not been limited to passive euthanasia and PVS patients. When it passed the Death with Dignity Act in 1994, Oregon became the first state to legalize physician-assisted suicide. Under this law, physicians are permitted to prescribe lethal drugs if a written request is made by an adult patient who desires to end his or her life in a humane and dignified manner and who has been determined by the attending physician and a consulting physician to be suffering from a terminal disease. The legislation went into effect in 1997, having survived a repeal attempt and a federal court challenge to its constitutionality. During its first three years of operation, sixty-nine Oregonians died from lethal medication obtained pursuant to the procedures set forth in the Death with Dignity Act.

In 1997, the U.S. Supreme Court declared in *Washington v. Glucksberg* and *Vacco v. Quill* that the use of a physician in committing suicide is not a fundamental liberty protected by the Constitution. The Court held that a state's interest in preserving and protecting human life—regardless of a terminally ill patient's desire—is a rational and legitimate state interest, and that state prohibitions against physician-assisted suicide appropriately reflect this commitment to life. These rulings were championed by many who believe in the "sanctity of life" and that protections are needed for vulnerable populations including the elderly, the poor, and people with disabilities. Organizations such as Not Dead Yet argue that euthanasia implicitly devalues those who are different, which may ultimately lead to abuse, neglect, and murder of vulnerable members of society.

In 2001, U.S. attorney general John Ashcroft ordered a revocation of the medical licenses of physicians in Oregon who prescribed lethal substances, arguing that to do so was neither a legitimate medical practice nor lawful under federal drug control legislation. However, in *Gonzalez v. Oregon* (2006), the U.S. Supreme Court affirmed the right of states to regulate medical practice, holding that the attorney general did not have authority to prohibit physicians from prescribing regulated drugs for use in physician-assisted suicide procedures permitted under state law.

Questions about the role of medicine in the process of death are related to the role of medicine in procreation, abortion, and research on fetal tissue. Consequently, questions about the meaning of life become politically charged. As an unprecedented percentage of the American population becomes elderly, and as technology increases the sustainability of physiological existence without "quality of life," questions related to living and dying well—particularly regarding alleviation of pain—are expected to increase in number and intensity.

Joshua E. Perry

See also: Abortion; Health Care; Kevorkian, Jack; Medical Marijuana; Not Dead Yet; O'Connor, Sandra Day; Rehnquist, William H.; Schiavo, Terri; Stem-Cell Research.

Further Reading

Brock, Dan W. "Voluntary Active Euthanasia." *Hastings Center Report* (March–April 1992): 10–22.

Dworkin, Ronald. *Life's Dominion: An Argument About Abortion, Euthanasia, and Individual Freedom.* New York: Vintage Books, 1994.

Gostin, Lawrence O. "Deciding Life and Death in the Courtroom: From *Quinlan* to *Cruzan, Glucksberg,* and *Vacco*—A Brief History and Analysis of Constitutional Protection of the 'Right to Die.'" *Journal of the American Medical Association* 278: 18 (1997): 1523–28.

Keown, John. *Euthanasia, Ethics, and Public Policy: An Argument Against Legalisation.* Cambridge, MA: Cambridge University Press, 2002.

Kilner, John F., Arlene B. Miller, and Edmund D. Pellegrino, eds. *Dignity and Dying: A Christian Appraisal.* Grand Rapids, MI: Eerdmans, 1996.

Quill, Timothy E. "Death and Dignity: A Case of Individualized Decision Making." *New England Journal of Medicine* 324:10 (1991): 691–94.

Velleman, J. David. "Against the Right to Die." *Journal of Medicine and Philosophy* 17:6 (1992): 665–81.

Robertson, Pat

Televangelist and former Baptist minister Pat Robertson, a prominent leader of the Christian Right, greatly influenced American politics in the 1980s and 1990s. He also founded the nation's first Christian television network, launched the country's most popular and longest-running Christian talk show, created the largest and most successful Christian Right lobbying organization, started a university, ran for president, and wrote more than a dozen books. But he attracted widespread criticism from people who thought he violated the separation of church and state.

Marion Gordon "Pat" Robertson was born on March 22, 1930, in Lexington, Virginia. His father, Absalom, had been a member of Congress. Robertson graduated from Washington and Lee University (BA, 1950), Yale Law School (JD, 1955), and New York Theological Seminary (MDiv, 1959), in between serving as a U.S. Marine lieutenant in Korea (1950–1952). Originally intending to pursue a career in law or business, Robertson changed plans after experiencing a religious conversion in 1956. Five years later, although connected with the charismatic movement, he was ordained as a minister by the Southern Baptist Convention.

The year of his ordination, Robertson purchased a television station in Portsmouth, Virginia, using it to start the Christian Broadcasting Network. This undertaking eventually included not only religious programs but also a range of family movies and news analyses, including *The 700 Club,* a news talk show that Robertson began in 1966 and hosted for over forty years. By the mid-1980s, his television network, charitable organizations, and other ministerial operations had become a $230 million operation.

The televangelist became a lightning rod for criticism after announcing his candidacy for the 1988 Republican presidential nomination. Although he portrayed himself as a responsible conservative slightly to the right of President Ronald Reagan, critics voiced concern that he would not respect the separation of church and state. He claimed in 1985 that his prayer changed the course of a hurricane, confirming his decision to run for president. That same year, he said that only Jews and Christians were qualified to hold office, and implied that as president he might ignore the U.S. Supreme Court's ruling on abortion. Many conservative evangelicals, especially members of charismatic churches, appreciated Robertson's support for organized school prayer and family values, and his opposition to secular humanism. Born-again Christians enabled him to raise more money than any of his Republican opponents. Robertson won a few state party caucuses and a handful of delegates but received only 9 percent of the national Republican presidential primary vote.

With the help of Ralph Reed, a young Republican activist, Robertson in 1989 launched the Christian Coalition. Earlier Christian Right organizations, such as the Moral Majority, had attracted a lot of press coverage but achieved only minimal legislative or electoral influence. In contrast, the Christian Coalition focused on winning control of party organizations at the local level. Consequently, the Christian Coalition obtained far more electoral influence than its predecessors and became a powerful Christian Right pressure group within the GOP, forcing Republicans to maintain their opposition to abortion and gay rights in exchange for the Coalition's continued assistance in mobilizing evangelical support for Republican candidates. The Christian Coalition, at its peak in the mid-1990s, claimed 4 million members and had an operating budget of $25 million, but it experienced a rapid decline after Reed left the organization in 1997.

Televangelist Pat Robertson, an ordained Baptist minister and charismatic evangelical, founded the Christian Broadcasting Network and the Christian Coalition. He has been a leading light and controversial spokesman of the Religious Right since the 1970s. *(Marty Katz/Time & Life Pictures/Getty Images)*

Robertson viewed the Christian Coalition as only one component in a broader strategy to oppose liberal interest groups that he felt threatened Christian religious liberty. Regent University, which he founded in Virginia Beach in 1977, opened a law school in 1986 in order to give evangelicals legal training from a Christian perspective. This was followed four years later by the founding of the American Center for Law and Justice (ACLJ), a counterpoint to the American Civil Liberties Union (ACLU), which Robertson regarded as hostile to public expression of religion.

With the turn of the twenty-first century, Robertson became an increasingly controversial figure, even among evangelicals. The National Association of Religious Broadcasters' board of directors voted in 2006 not to renew Robertson's board membership because of their objections to his polemical statements, which included a call for Venezuelan president Hugo Chavez's assassination and a pronouncement that Israeli prime minister Ariel Sharon's stroke was God's punishment for authorizing a withdrawal from the West Bank. Although Robertson remains a renowned figure because of his formative role in launching the Christian Right, his influence has waned.

Daniel K. Williams

See also: American Civil Liberties Union; Christian Coalition; Christian Radio; Church and State; Evangelicalism; Family Values; Fundamentalism, Religious; Moral Majority; Religious Right; Republican Party; Televangelism.

Further Reading

Boston, Rob. *The Most Dangerous Man in America? Pat Robertson and the Rise of the Christian Coalition.* Amherst, NY: Prometheus Books, 1996.

Donavan, John B. *Pat Robertson: The Authorized Biography.* New York: Macmillan, 1988.

Foege, Alec. *The Empire God Built: Inside Pat Robertson's Media Machine.* New York: John Wiley & Sons, 1996.

Harrell, David Edwin, Jr. *Pat Robertson: A Personal, Religious, and Political Portrait.* New York: HarperCollins, 1988.

Martin, William. *With God on Our Side: The Rise of the Religious Right in America.* New York: Broadway Books, 1996.

Watson, Justin. *The Christian Coalition: Dreams of Restoration, Demands for Recognition.* 2nd ed. New York: St. Martin's, 1999.

Rock and Roll

More than a musical movement, rock and roll follows generations through life, changing in beat, lyrics, and style to reflect the cultural and social needs of its listeners. At its core, rock symbolizes youthful struggles for a voice in popular culture and politics. Teenage disaffection with parental control in the 1950s imbued early rock music. When that rebellion turned hostile and radical, rock and roll became the vehicle for challenging authority in the decades that followed.

With roots in the South, rock and roll was a mix of rhythm and blues, and country music, sounds from the margins where black and white subcultures coexisted uneasily. Northern radio stations catered to new audience tastes, playing the music carried north by black migration in the forties. In 1951, Alan Freed, a Cleveland disc jockey, used the term "rock and roll" to describe the hybrid music his multiracial audience craved. Freed organized rock concerts where black artists such as Chuck Berry and Little Richard performed for integrated audiences. Young white listeners showed their appreciation by flocking to record stores. The trend did not go unnoticed. With an eye to the racial climate, Sam Phillips, owner of Sun Records in Memphis, believed that a white performer with "black style" could help rock and roll corner the white music market. With "That's All Right, Mama" in 1954, Elvis Presley proved Phillips's intuition correct. White rock and rollers like Presley and Jerry Lee Lewis, covering black artists, brought the music to ever wider audiences and commercial success.

Cold War America saw the birth of the teenager, a new social demographic that enjoyed levels of security and affluence unknown to previous generations. With more leisure time and disposable income, teens in the 1950s became a bastion of consumerism, courted by the entertainment industry. Rock and roll's brash beat and suggestive lyrics spoke of experiences beyond staid parental lifestyles. With Presley's breakthrough television appearances on the *Ed Sullivan Show* in 1956, rock and roll was entrenched in youth culture.

Cold War anxieties had created a rigid atmosphere of social and political homogeneity in the nation. Concomitant with this was a rise in racial tension as blacks pushed for equality. With its bold references to sex and rebellion, rock music faced the ire of authorities. Critics decried the erosion of teen morality through rock "leerics" and lewd performances. Interracial concert audiences concerned Christian fundamentalists and the Ku Klux Klan, who called for a ban on the "devil's music" to prevent the spread of juvenile delinquency and the "mongrelization" of white teens. Anti–rock-and-roll campaigns stretched across the country, culminating in the payola scandal of the late 1950s, in which the Federal Communications Commission targeted disc jockeys, like Freed, for accepting bribes to play specific rock songs.

Chastened by critics and controversy, rock and roll's brazen edges were smoothed over by the early 1960s when clean-cut teen idols (the likes of Frankie Avalon) were showcased on parentally approved television programs such as *American Bandstand*. Folk music provided the poignant social commentary missing from the new "wholesome" rock. As the civil rights movement turned violent and the Vietnam War accelerated, folk musicians such as Bob Dylan and Joan Baez injected politics into their lyrics. Folk music merged with rock in Dylan's "Like a Rolling Stone," released in 1965. Dylan's intense lyrics, and use of electric guitar, opened the door for rock and roll to be a vehicle for political views.

The enormous success of the Beatles in the mid-1960s solidified rock and roll's resurgence. It also reinvigorated claims that rock was damaging American teens. John Lennon's 1966 statement that the Beatles were more popular than Jesus caused a literal firestorm of protest, with record burnings held in states like South Carolina. To fundamentalists, rock music foreshadowed Christianity's destruction and was connected to communist plots to corrupt young America, as detailed in Christian polemics such as *Rock and Roll: The Devil's Diversion* (1967) by the televangelist Bob Larson. Performers such as Frank Zappa were deemed to be akin to the anti-Christ and faced calls for censorship. The Nixon administration carried on the crusade with a politically motivated campaign linking drug use to rock and roll.

The politicization of rock corresponded with the growth of the counterculture. Music was a common reference point for intersecting causes such as civil rights and the anti–Vietnam War movement. Psychedelic rock groups such as the Grateful Dead reflected the experimental attitude toward lifestyle and drugs emerging in San Francisco's Haight-Ashbury district, a gathering place for countercultural adherents. Eastern philosophy informed an intergenerational identity that, at its base, reflected a general "us" versus "them" mentality. In 1967, the "Summer of Love" displayed the hippie lifestyle and sounds in albums such as Jefferson Airplane's *Surrealistic Pillow* and the eponymous debut album, *The Grateful Dead*, as young Americans converged on San Francisco.

The gap between the mainstream and the counterculture widened as the 1960s radicalized. Rock and roll's mocking of authority transformed into a direct challenge to conservative America's way of life. Vietnam galvanized rockers against the dominant political establishment. Songs like "Eve of Destruction" (1965, Barry McGuire) and "Ohio" (1970, Crosby, Stills, Nash & Young) protested militarism and became antiwar anthems. Black artists such as Jimi Hendrix, steeped in the Black Power movement, called for revolution. The Woodstock Music and Art Fair, a massive three-day event in upstate New York in 1969, underscored the importance of rock festivals as countercultural political forums.

With defeat in Vietnam, rock and roll in the 1970s fell victim to the cultural and economic malaise that blanketed the nation. Activism gave way to hedonism. Glam rock and disco fed the decade's decadence. Rock was reborn with MTV's debut in 1981. Political and social commentary returned with Bruce Springsteen's *Born in the U.S.A.* (1984). Although embraced by the ultraconservative Reagan administration, the liberal album addressed the suffocating shadow of Vietnam. Springsteen, along with U2's Bono, has been instrumental in returning activism to rock music. Benefit concerts such as Live Aid in 1985, Live 8 in 2005, and Live Earth in 2007 pushed listeners to engage in social action. Rock and roll as a political medium continued with MTV's Rock the Vote. Springsteen coordinated the Vote for Change tour, a critical response to President George W. Bush's 2004 reelection campaign.

Though fragmented across many genres, rock and roll is still a strong musical and cultural force. Censorship campaigns continue, with record warning labels introduced to combat supposedly obscene lyrics. Cooptation of elements from the punk and rap subcultures kept rock and roll relevant through the 1990s, though a waning New Left may have blunted rock's political impact. Tastes change, but rock and roll's core is intact; it remains a communal experience and a beacon of freedom for all listeners.

Anna Zuschlag

See also: Baez, Joan; Bono; Censorship; Civil Rights Movement; Counterculture; Dylan, Bob; Federal Communications Commission; Generations and Generational Conflict; Record Warning Labels; Springsteen, Bruce; Vietnam War; War Protesters; Young, Neil; Zappa, Frank.

Further Reading
Altschuler, Glenn C. *All Shook Up: How Rock 'n' Roll Changed America.* New York: Oxford University Press, 2003.

Bennett, Andy. *Cultures of Popular Music.* Philadelphia: Open University, 2001.

Friedlander, Paul. *Rock & Roll: A Social History.* 2nd ed. Boulder, CO: Westview Press, 2006.

Halberstam, David. *The Fifties.* New York: Villard Books, 1993.

Martin, Linda, and Kerry Segrave. *Anti-Rock: The Opposition to Rock 'n' Roll.* New York: DaCapo Press, 1993.

Rockwell, George Lincoln

A striking figure as he strode the streets of Washington, D.C., in full Nazi-style regalia, George Lincoln Rockwell saw the battle for control of America as a continuation of the struggle of his hero, Adolf Hitler. Rockwell founded the American Nazi Party in 1959, gaining much publicity but negligible support.

At his northern Virginia headquarters in Arlington, Rockwell draped a large Nazi swastika flag and trained a unit of uniformed storm troopers that marched in demonstrations, which he led dressed in a suit and tie while puffing on a corncob pipe. Rockwell traveled nationwide to promote his views, often drawing counterdemonstrators and occasionally sparking violence.

The son of vaudeville performers, Rockwell was born in Bloomington, Illinois, on March 9, 1918. An extrovert as a teenager, Rockwell had a rebellious spirit that led to disciplinary problems at school and a mediocre academic record, but he entered Brown University in 1938 on the strength of exceptionally high aptitude test scores. Leaving college in 1941 to enlist as a U.S. Navy aviator, Rockwell served in the Pacific theater during World War II. He left active military service as a Naval Reserve lieutenant commander in 1945 and worked in Maine as a commercial artist while extending his skills at the Pratt Institute in Brooklyn, New York. Recalled to active duty for the Korean War, Rockwell became a supporter of the anticommunist crusade led by Senator Joseph McCarthy (R-WI). Becoming convinced that Marxism sought to organize inferior masses of people, Rockwell embraced Hitler's political tract *Mein Kampf* and his theories of white supremacy and anti-Semitism.

In 1962, Rockwell traveled to England and, with British neofascist Colin Jordan, formed the World Union of National Socialists. Returning to America, Rockwell helped establish nineteen chapters. He renamed his group the National Socialist White People's Party (NSWPP) in 1967. On August 25 of that year, Rockwell was assassinated in Arlington, Virginia, by a disgruntled former member of the organization.

Several NSWPP associates went on to form white supremacist groups that reached national prominence. Frank Collin led the National Socialist Party of America, gaining international attention in 1977 by threatening a march of neo-Nazis through Skokie, Illinois, a Chicago suburb that was home to many Jewish Holocaust survivors. William L. Pierce founded the National Alliance, which in the 1990s grew to prominence in part because of the success of an Internet-based, mail-order, white-power music business. Under the pseudonym Andrew Macdonald, Pierce wrote *The Turner Diaries* (1978), a work that partly inspired Timothy McVeigh's truck bombing of the Alfred P. Murrah Federal Building in Oklahoma City in April 1995.

Chip Berlet

See also: Anti-Semitism; Cold War; Conspiracy Theories; Holocaust; Marxism; McCarthy, Joseph; McCarthyism; McVeigh, Timothy; White Supremacists.

Further Reading
Schmaltz, William H. *Hate: George Lincoln Rockwell and the American Nazi Party.* Washington, DC: Brassey's, 1999.

Simonelli, Frederick J. *American Fuehrer: George Lincoln Rockwell and the American Nazi Party.* Urbana: University of Illinois Press, 1999.

Rockwell, Norman

Magazine illustrator and painter Norman Rockwell recorded the simplicity and nobility of American life through six decades of the twentieth century. Social conservatives esteemed Rockwell for his idealized renderings of old-fashioned, small-town family life, while progressives admired later works expressing support for the civil rights movement.

Norman Percevel Rockwell was born in New York City on February 3, 1894. He enrolled in the National Academy of Design in 1910 and soon thereafter in the Art Students League, both in New York. His first cover for the *Saturday Evening Post* was published in 1916, and over the next forty-seven years, he would produce more than 320 covers for that magazine, including the 1943 series of four paintings on the "Four Freedoms" espoused by President Franklin D. Roosevelt as a charter of universal human rights: freedom of speech, freedom of worship, freedom from want, and freedom from fear. His cover art also appeared on such popular periodicals as *Look, Life,* and *Literary Digest.*

Rockwell used his mastery of style and color, along with his sense of humor, to portray the themes and experiences of everyday life in small-town America. While some critics ridiculed his work for being overly optimistic, Rockwell explained, "I unconsciously decided that if it wasn't an ideal world, it should be, and so painted only the ideal aspects of it." Before 1963, most of his subjects were white people—of his hundreds of paintings on magazine covers, only three featured blacks. This changed during the civil rights era, however, when editors encouraged him to be more daring in addressing the starker realities of American culture.

On one 1964 cover of the *Saturday Evening Post,* Rockwell's painting *The Problem We All Live With* depicted four U.S. marshals escorting a young black girl to school. On a wall in the background are painted the words "nigger" and "KKK," along with red splotches from thrown tomatoes. The following year, the magazine published *Southern Justice* (which Rockwell called *Murder in Mississippi*), a reaction to the previous summer's murder of three civil rights activists in Philadelphia, Mississippi. The painting depicts two men, a white and a black, comforting each other with a fallen comrade at their feet.

During his long career, Rockwell was commissioned to paint portraits of several U.S. presidents: Dwight D. Eisenhower, John F. Kennedy, and Lyndon B. Johnson. In 1977, he was awarded the Presidential Medal of Freedom, the nation's highest civilian honor. He died on November 8, 1978, in Stockbridge, Massachusetts.

William T. Walker

See also: Civil Rights Movement; Eisenhower, Dwight D.; Family Values; Human Rights; Johnson, Lyndon B.; Kennedy Family; Philadelphia, Mississippi.

Further Reading

Claridge, Laura. *Norman Rockwell: A Life.* New York: Random House, 2001.

Gans, Herbert J. "Can Rockwell Survive Cultural Elevation?" *Chronicle of Higher Education*, April 21, 2000.

Marker, Sheery. *Norman Rockwell: Unabridged.* New York: World, 2004.

Rockwell, Norman, as told to Tom Rockwell. *Norman Rockwell: My Adventures as an Illustrator.* New York: Harry M. Abrams, 1994.

Rodman, Dennis

The antics and personality of Dennis Rodman, a talented but persistently controversial player in the National Basketball Association (1986–2000), generated much debate during the course of his career, raising broader issues about the public image of athletes and whether or not they have an obligation to be role models.

Born on May 13, 1961, in Trenton, New Jersey, Dennis Keith Rodman was raised in poverty. After playing basketball at Cooke County Junior College in Dallas (1982–1983) and Southeastern Oklahoma State University (1983–1986), he was drafted by the Detroit Pistons in 1986.

During his rookie year, Rodman became a key component in the Pistons' success. Nicknamed "the Worm," he was an "old school" player who played defense and rebounded with ferocity. He was one of the few players who could slow down such opposing stars as Michael Jordan, Magic Johnson, and Larry Bird while fitting into his team's "bad boy" style of play.

Late one night during the 1992–1993 NBA season, Rodman's tenure with the Pistons took a turn for the worse when team officials found him locked inside his pickup truck with a loaded shotgun. Rodman later described it as the moment the old Dennis died and the new Dennis emerged, when he stopped caring about the popular image of a black NBA star and decided to be himself—whether expressed by his tattoos, his ever changing hair colors, or his willingness to speak his mind. Shortly thereafter, the Pistons traded him to the San Antonio Spurs, where his play was marked less by his greatness as a rebounder and defender than by technical fouls, ejections, league fines, and suspensions. After the 1994–1995 season, the Spurs traded him to the Chicago Bulls.

Rodman's on-the-court prowess helped propel the Bulls to three straight championships, but with his behavior falling short of cultural expectations of the idealized sports figure, he was often criticized for his "selfish disrespect" for the game. He matched neither the image of the corporate, racially transcendent player, such as Michael Jordan, nor the image of the hip-hop street baller, such as Allen Iverson. Whereas in the media Jordan was "the good black," Rodman was "the bad black" because of his look and style. He regarded himself as "a real person," unwilling to conform to a contrived "normal" identity. Challenging homophobia, he sat for interviews at gay bars and sometimes cross-dressed, all the while flaunting his heterosexuality and interracial relationships with the singer Madonna and model-actress Carmen Electra.

On the court, he was no less controversial, racking up technical fouls and once kicking a cameraman in the groin, which led to an eleven-game suspension and a $1.1 million fine. He sometimes treated basketball as a burden that intervened with his party life, and he once described the NBA as 50 percent sex and 50 percent money. He made headlines for skipping practices and missing a playoff game.

Although often mentioned in tabloid magazines, Rodman is not remembered with the NBA greats. He and others believe this is due not to his basketball talents but to widespread disapproval of his image and behavior on and off the court. Rodman's autobiography *As Bad as I Wanna Be* (1997), widely viewed as a rationalization of irresponsibility and an attempt to shock readers, offers a testimony of individuality and a rejection of corporate basketball interests that seek to promote a contrived image of players.

David J. Leonard

See also: Counterculture; Madonna; Race; Transgender Movement.

Further Reading

Barett, Lindon. "Black Men in the Mix: Badboys, Heroes, Sequins, and Dennis Rodman." *Callalloo* 20:1 (1997): 102–26.

Lefrance, Melisse, and Genevieve Rail. "Excursions into Otherness: Understanding Dennis Rodman and the Limits of Subversive Agency." In *Sports Stars: The Cultural Politics of Sporting Celebrity*, ed. David L. Andrews and Steven J. Jackson. London: Routledge, 2001.

Remnick, David. *The Devil Problem and Other True Stores.* New York: Random House, 1996.

Roe v. Wade (1973)

Roe v. Wade, the landmark 1973 U.S. Supreme Court case establishing a woman's constitutional right to have an abortion during the first two trimesters of pregnancy, has been a persistent and highly contentious debate in the American culture wars from the moment it was handed down.

The case originated in March 1970 in Texas, where Norma McCorvey, an unmarried pregnant women using the alias "Jane Roe" to protect her privacy, filed suit against Dallas County district attorney Henry Wade to be allowed to have an abortion. McCorvey's lawyers, Linda Coffee and Sarah Weddington, argued that an 1856 Texas law forbidding abortion unless the pregnancy endangers the mother's life violated Roe's right of privacy. Their argument was based on the U.S. Supreme Court decision in *Griswold v. Connecticut* (1965), which ruled that a Connecticut statute prohibiting the use of birth control was unconstitutional because its enforcement violated "the zone of privacy" created by the Bill of Rights and the Fourth Amendment. These protections, the attorneys contended, gave Roe and other citizens the right to privacy in sexual and reproductive matters. District Attorney Wade argued that a fetus is a separate human being and has the right to live. Although the three-judge federal district court ruled for "Jane Roe," it refused to outlaw enforcement of the 1856 Texas law.

Both "Jane Roe" and Wade appealed to the U.S. Supreme Court, where the case was argued in October 1971 and reargued the following year. In 1973, after much debate, the Court ruled 7–2 in favor of "Jane Roe," thereby legalizing abortion in America. The majority opinion, written by Richard M. Nixon appointee Harry Blackmun, found that the privacy right to abortion, grounded in the Ninth and Fourteenth Amendments, was "broad enough to encompass a woman's decision whether or not to terminate her pregnancy" during the first trimester. In the second trimester, the state could regulate abortion if the pregnancy endangered the mother's life but could not otherwise prevent the procedure. Only during the third trimester could a state prohibit abortion altogether. Associate justices William H. Rehnquist and Byron White criticized the ruling, arguing that there was "no constitutional warrant for imposing such an order of priorities on the people and legislature of the States."

From the beginning, the *Roe* decision evoked support and opposition, further polarizing an electorate already divided over the issue of abortion. "Pro-choice" groups such as the National Organization for Women (NOW) insist that women have a "fundamental right" to decide whether to have an abortion. Arguing that life begins at conception, the Catholic National Right to Life Committee, Jerry Falwell's Moral Majority, and other "pro-life" organizations have rallied against the decision. McCorvey eventually revealed her identity and in 1995 converted to Christianity. She subsequently joined the pro-life movement, believing that abortion is harmful to women. In 2005, she unsuccessfully petitioned the U.S. Supreme Court to set aside the *Roe* decision on the basis that abortion procedures can cause harm to women.

Although unable to overturn the 1973 ruling, conservative politicians have succeeded in making it more difficult for women to have an abortion. Three years after the *Roe* decision, for example, Congress passed the Hyde Amendment, which barred federal funding for abortion. In 1989, Missouri legislators voted to deny the use of public facilities and employees to assist or perform abortions, a measure upheld by the Supreme Court in *Webster v. Reproductive Health Services* (1989). In 2003, Congress passed the Partial-Birth Abortion Act, outlawing late-term abortions carried out by a procedure known as "intact dilation and evacuation"; this law was upheld by the Supreme Court in *Gonzalez v. Carhart* and *Gonzalez v. Planned Parenthood* (2007). In 2006, the South Dakota state legislature and Mississippi's House Public Health Committee approved bills making it illegal for doctors to perform abortions. By the early 2000s, thirty-four states had passed legislation requiring minors to obtain parental consent or notify parents before having an abortion. These measures limited the scope of the *Roe* decision and suggested further erosion in the future.

Bruce E. Stewart

See also: Abortion; Birth Control; Catholic Church; Equal Rights Amendment; Feminism, Second-Wave; Feminism, Third-Wave; Judicial Wars; Moral Majority; National Organization for Women; Operation Rescue; Planned Parenthood; Rehnquist, William H.; Sexual Revolution.

Further Reading

Faux, Marian. Roe v. Wade: *The Untold Story of the Landmark Supreme Court Decision That Made Abortion Legal.* New York: Macmillan, 1988.

Garrow, David J. *Liberty and Sexuality: The Right to Privacy and the Making of* Roe v. Wade. Berkeley: University of California Press, 1998.

Hull, N.E.H., and Peter Charles Hoffer. Roe v. Wade: *The Abortion Rights Controversy in American History.* Lawrence: University Press of Kansas, 2001.

Rosenberg, Julius, and Ethel Rosenberg

The only American civilians executed for espionage, Julius and Ethel Rosenberg were an enduring cause célèbre of the Cold War era, memorialized by the left as martyrs to McCarthyite hysteria and reviled by the right as traitors who gave atomic secrets to the Soviet Union. Revelations by former KGB operatives and the U.S. government's release of decoded Soviet communications from the 1940s have led to a consensus among historians that Julius Rosenberg did engage in spying. Controversy lingers over several aspects of the case, however—notably the fairness of the trial and the extent of Ethel's involvement.

Julius Rosenberg and Ethel Greenglass Rosenberg, born on May 12, 1918, and September 28, 1915, respectively, grew up politically radical in New York City and met there in 1936 through the Young Communist League. Julius Rosenberg, a graduate of the City College of New York (1939) and an electrical engineer, worked as a civilian for the U.S. Army Signal Corps but was fired in 1945 for his past communist association. Ethel Greenglass, who worked as a secretary for a shipping company, became active in the labor movement. The couple married in 1939.

Their prosecution arose from the arrest in 1950 of David Greenglass, Ethel's brother and an army machinist who worked on the U.S. atom bomb project at Los Alamos, New Mexico. Charged with providing notes and sketches of bomb components to Soviet agents, Greenglass told the FBI that Julius had recruited him into a spy ring. Ethel was also arrested in the hope that her prosecution would pressure Julius into confessing. The Rosenbergs were convicted under the Espionage Act of 1917 in a March 1951 trial that launched the public career of anticommunist attorney Roy Cohn. Judge Irving Kaufman imposed the death penalty, asserting that the Rosenbergs had committed "worse than murder" and bore responsibility for the Korean War. After a series of failed appeals, and despite international calls for clemency, the Rosenbergs were electrocuted on June 19, 1953, at Sing Sing prison in New York.

For decades after their execution, the Rosenbergs were widely viewed as victims of a witch hunt. The fact that Cohn had helped steer the case to Kaufman, that the judge agreed with authorities beforehand to impose the death sentence, and that Ethel was directly linked to the case only by Greenglass's claim that she typed up meeting notes (which he recanted fifty years later), fueled feelings that the Rosenbergs had been railroaded. Political activ-ists, liberal celebrities, and the couple's orphaned sons, Robert and Michael Meeropol, campaigned to reopen the case. The Rosenbergs, particularly Ethel, were treated sympathetically in the best-selling novels *The Book of Daniel* by E.L. Doctorow (1971) and *The Public Burning* by Robert Coover (1977) and Tony Kushner's Pulitzer Prize–winning play *Angels in America* (1993).

In 1983, historians Ronald Radosh and Joyce Milton renewed debate on the case with their book *The Rosenberg File*, which concluded that Julius had been a Soviet agent. In the 1990s, U.S. government declassification of portions of the files of the Venona project, a U.S.-British decryption program of Soviet intelligence communications during and after World War II, and revelations by former KGB agents further implicated Julius in running a spy ring. His guilt—but not Ethel's—is now generally accepted by historians, as is the notion that others played a greater role in advancing the Soviet atomic program.

Andy Markowitz

See also: Capital Punishment; Cold War; Communists and Communism; Hiss, Alger; Kushner, Tony; McCarthy, Joseph; McCarthyism; Nuclear Age; Soviet Union and Russia.

Further Reading

Carmichael, Virginia. *Framing History: The Rosenberg Story and the Cold War.* Minneapolis: University of Minnesota Press, 1993.

Meeropol, Robert. *An Execution in the Family: One Son's Journey.* New York: St. Martin's Press, 2003.

Radosh, Ronald, and Joyce Milton. *The Rosenberg File: A Search for the Truth.* 2nd ed. New Haven, CT: Yale University Press, 1997.

Roberts, Sam. *The Brother: The Untold Story of Atomic Spy David Greenglass and How He Sent His Sister, Ethel Rosenberg, to the Electric Chair.* New York: Random House, 2001.

Rove, Karl

A controversial Republican campaign strategist, Karl Rove was credited as the "architect" of George W. Bush's election victories—for governor of Texas in 1994 and 1998, and for president of the United States in 2000 and 2004—and often identified as "Bush's brain" for his role in shaping White House policy to appeal to the Republican Party's conservative base.

During the first six years of the Bush administration, admirers called Rove a "political genius" for developing a winning electoral alliance out of a loose coalition of neoconservatives, libertarians, corporate leaders, and Religious Right groups, despite the many issues that otherwise divided them. In contrast, detractors labeled Rove "an evil genius," regarding him as an unprincipled operator who escalated the culture wars. In 2006, after

Democrats for the first time since 1994 gained control of the House of Representatives, effectively dashing Republican hopes for a GOP ruling majority lasting a generation or longer, Rove was cast as the scapegoat by members of his party who blamed his polarizing tactics for triggering a voter backlash. At that point, Rove was disparaged as the architect of Republican defeat.

Karl Christian Rove was born on February 25, 1950, in Denver, Colorado. He grew up in a dysfunctional family (learning as a young adult, for instance, that his biological father was not the man married to his mother), leading biographers to speculate that his attraction to politics was rooted in a search for belonging. This view has been supported in part by those who, observing him up close, suggest that Rove does not have passionate ideological conviction but thinks purely in terms of political strategy.

From 1969 to 1977, Rove attended the University of Utah, University of Maryland, George Mason University, and University of Texas but never completed the degree in political science he sought. His political education was obtained outside the classroom, serving as the executive director of the College Republicans (1971–1972), chair of the College Republicans (1973–1974), and special assistant to the chairman of the Republican National Committee, George H.W. Bush (1973). By the mid-1970s, Rove was working as a political consultant in Virginia while serving as finance director of the Virginia Republican Party. At Bush's request, Rove moved to Texas for the purpose of fundraising for a presidential exploratory committee.

Political strategist Karl Rove (right) engineered the ascendancy of George W. Bush from Texas to the White House. Rove sought to build a conservative Republican coalition that would last a generation; he resigned from the Bush administration amid scandal. *(Chip Somodevilla/Getty Images)*

In 1977, Rove did campaign work for both Bushes as well as Bill Clements, who was elected Texas governor. After serving as Clements's chief of staff (1977–1981), Rove ran an Austin-based marketing firm, Karl Rove & Co. (1981–1991), raising the funds that enabled Republicans to gain control of Texas. Essentially a party boss, Rove picked the Republican candidates to financially support. As the linchpin of George W. Bush's political career, Rove was his political adviser and chief strategist (1993–2001) and later senior White House adviser (2001–2007) and deputy chief of staff (2005–2006). Following the 2004 election, Bush was designated *Time* magazine's "Man of the Year," with Rove as runner-up.

Rove's political instincts enabled him to tap into issues that resonated with suburban swing voters. Accordingly, he directed his candidates to support tax cuts, welfare reduction, tort reform, improvement in education, and family values. His strategy was simple: build a large campaign war chest (for example, Bush outdid all other Republican challengers in 2000, raising $36 million) and repeat a simple message (during the 2004 presidential election, a central theme of the Bush reelection campaign was that Kerry, the Democratic rival, was a "waffler" on the War on Terror). Rove was considered a master of voter turnout strategy and is credited with developing issues that attracted evangelical voters to the polls in 2004. During that campaign, Rove arranged for the Republican National Convention to be held in New York City, not far from Ground Zero, in order to cast his candidate as the strong avenger of terrorism. Later, Rove organized Bush's push for Social Security privatization, but the issue failed to gain traction.

Rove's critics focus on his hardball campaign tactics, arguing that unethical practices date back to his College Republican days when he worked closely with Lee Atwater, the mastermind of the "whisper campaign" (an anonymous or "off the record" spreading of malicious gossip about a rival candidate) and "push polling" (telephone "polls" of prospective voters in which the questions provide negative and inaccurate information about the political opposition). In one early campaign trick, directed at a Democratic candidate running for Illinois state treasurer in 1970, Rove printed and distributed stolen campaign stationery advertising "free beer, free food, girls and a good time."

Critics have made numerous allegations against Rove for taking the political low road, but none has been substantially proven. Among other things, he is accused of involvement in a whisper campaign suggesting Texas governor Ann Richards was a lesbian (1994); the distribution of negative fliers against a Republican candidate running for the Alabama Supreme Court for the purpose of duping voters into believing the Democratic opponent was resorting to smear tactics (1996); a whisper campaign against John McCain during the South

Carolina Republican presidential primary in which questions were raised about the former POW's mental health (1999); and the Swift Boat Veterans for Truth campaign attack against the war record of Bush's Democratic rival John Kerry (2004).

Rove came under suspicion in the 2003 CIA leak case in which an agent's identity—Valerie Plame—was illegally divulged to the press after her husband, former diplomat Joseph C. Wilson IV, had publicly accused the Bush administration of fabricating evidence about Iraqi weapons of mass destruction. Rove was not charged with breaking federal law, but his chief of staff, I. Lewis "Scooter" Libby, was indicted, tried, and found guilty of perjury and obstruction of justice. (Libby's sentence was subsequently commuted by President Bush.) After leaving the White House, Rove came under a legal cloud over the improper firing of attorneys at the Justice Department (they had been removed for ideological reasons and replaced by Republican Party loyalists) and over his refusal to testify about it before Congress. In the meantime, the former political strategist was working as an analyst and commentator for Fox News and other media outlets.

Roger Chapman

See also: Atwater, Lee; Bush Family; Education Reform; Election of 2000; Neoconservatism; Privatization; Republican Party; September 11; Social Security; Tax Reform; Tort Reform; Welfare Reform.

Further Reading

Alexander, Paul. *Machiavelli's Shadow: The Rise and Fall of Karl Rove.* New York: Modern Times/Macmillan, 2008.

Barnes, Fred. "Karl Rove, White House Impresario." In The Weekly Standard: *A Reader: 1995–2005,* ed. William Kristol, 152–60. New York: HarperCollins, 2005.

Moore, James. *The Architect: Karl Rove and the Master Plan for Absolute Power.* New York: Crown, 2006.

Ruby Ridge Incident

Ruby Ridge is the name of a bluff in Boundary County, Idaho, where a deadly confrontation erupted in 1992 between federal agents and a forty-five-year-old survivalist and former Green Beret named Randy Weaver. Weaver had moved his family to Ruby Ridge in the mid-1980s and embraced Christian Identity, an anti-Semitic belief system. He also occasionally visited Richard Butler's then nearby Aryan Nation compound. Scholars believe that the incident at Ruby Ridge, and a similar standoff in Waco, Texas, the following year, sparked the rise of the modern-day militia movement.

The government's aggressive responses at Ruby Ridge and Waco were held up by nascent militia organizers as a testament to an out-of-control federal government. Militia leaders complained that federal agencies such as the FBI and the U.S. Marshals were illegally using military force against American citizens, and they encouraged potential recruits to arm themselves for a showdown with the government. Some militia recruiters also used racist language to encourage white men to "take back" their country from minorities, foreigners, and the United Nations.

The event that would become the militia movement's rallying cry began when an undercover federal agent approached Weaver for help purchasing sawed-off shotguns. Weaver delivered two guns in 1989 and was threatened with arrest. The agent offered to withhold charges if Weaver became an undercover informant on the Aryan Nations compound. Weaver refused and was formally arrested in January 1991. He failed to show up for his court date in February, although evidence suggests the wrong trial date was printed on the summons. The U.S. Marshal's office decided to arrest Weaver and to that end set up a surveillance operation on the perimeter of Weaver's property to monitor his movements.

On August 21, 1992, federal marshal William Degan was scouting terrain near the house when the family dog began barking. Randy Weaver, his son Samuel, and Kevin Harris, a friend living at the compound, went to investigate. A shootout ensued and Degan and Samuel were mortally wounded; Harris badly injured. Weaver claimed the government fired the first shot; the government asserted that it was returning fire. The next day, the rules of engagement were changed to permit agents to shoot to kill any armed male on the property, but somehow FBI sharpshooter Lon Horiuchi killed Vicky Weaver as she held the door open for her husband. Horiuchi claimed he was aiming at Randy Weaver, who surrendered nine days later.

Weaver's supporters argued that the government overstepped its constitutional authority by using military tactics to apprehend him and, in the process, murdered his son and wife, both unarmed. Some militia leaders regarded the government's refusal to accept blame as evidence of a Zionist plot to co-opt the executive branch of the U.S. government. For the nascent militia movement, the siege at Ruby Ridge represented federal tyranny, requiring a defense against it that was best provided by the citizens' militia.

Detractors argued that while the deaths of Vicky and Samuel Weaver were tragic, Weaver was responsible because he broke the law and refused to answer the charges against him in a court of law. Detractors noted that the Weavers espoused a violent ideology that defined African Americans and Jews as subhuman and called for their expulsion from the country.

In 1995, the Weaver family settled a lawsuit against the U.S. Department of Justice. The government did not acknowledge wrongdoing but paid the family $3 million to compensate for the shooting deaths of Vicky and Samuel Weaver.

Carolyn Gallaher

See also: Aryan Nations; McVeigh, Timothy; Militia Movement; Montana Freemen; Waco Siege; White Supremacists.

Further Reading

Dees, Morris. *Gathering Storm: America's Militia Threat.* New York: HarperCollins, 1996.

Gallaher, Carolyn. *On the Fault Line: Race, Class, and the American Patriot Movement.* Lanham, MD: Rowman & Littlefield, 2003.

Levitas, Daniel. *The Terrorist Next Door: The Militia Movement and the Radical Right.* New York: St. Martin's Press, 2002.

Walter, Jess. *Ruby Ridge: The Truth and Tragedy of the Randy Weaver Family.* New York: ReganBooks, 2002.

Rudolph, Eric

Widely identified in the media as a "Christian terrorist," Eric Rudolph was sentenced in 2005 to life imprisonment without parole for four bombings in the 1990s that killed two people and injured more than a hundred others. Among his targets were the 1996 Summer Olympics in Atlanta, Georgia, and abortion clinics in Georgia and Alabama.

Eric Robert Rudolph was born on September 19, 1966, in Merritt Island, Florida. Following his father's death in 1981, the family moved to North Carolina. Homeschooled during his teens, Rudolph passed the GED and briefly attended Western Carolina University in Sylva (1985–1986). He served in the U.S. Army with the 101st Airborne Division (1987–1989), but was discharged early because of insubordination and marijuana use. He then took up work as a carpenter. According to various sources, Rudolph was influenced by the ideology of the Christian Identity movement, which teaches that Jews are descendents of Satan, responsible for homosexuality, and part of an abortion conspiracy to end the white race.

Rudolph's bombing spree included the Centennial Olympic Park in Atlanta, killing a woman and injuring over a hundred others (July 27, 1996); the Sandy Springs Professional Building, a complex housing the Northside Planning Services abortion clinic in an Atlanta suburb, injuring six (January 16, 1997); the Otherside Lounge, a lesbian bar in Atlanta, injuring five (February 21, 1997); and the New Woman All Women Health Care, an abortion clinic in Birmingham, Alabama, killing an off-duty police officer and maiming a nurse (January 29, 1998). For more than five years, despite being on the FBI's 10 Most Wanted List with a $1 million bounty, he evaded arrest, living in the Appalachian wilderness of western North Carolina. In May 2003, he was finally captured

in Murphy, North Carolina. Rudolph, now incarcerated at the federal prison in Florence, Colorado, avoided the death penalty through a plea bargain in which he agreed to disclose his hidden stockpiles of explosives.

The bombing at the 1996 Summer Olympics in Atlanta, his most dramatic offense, was intended to embarrass the federal government for allowing abortion on demand. He hoped to defy the $303 million security operation and force the cancellation of the games, which he felt promoted the "despicable ideals" of "global socialism." He later apologized for that bombing but not the others.

After his arrest, Rudolph, claiming only Catholic affiliation, denied any formal link with the Christian Identity movement. In an eleven-page statement, he denounced the U.S. federal government as illegitimate for legalizing abortion. He characterized the Republican Party as "the Pharisaical sect," its pro-life supporters as duped, and President George W. Bush as a "coward" despite his talk about the "culture of life." Rudolph argued that the "plastic people" of America were hypocrites for supporting the war in Iraq while deploring violence against the U.S. government to stop the "murder" of unborn American citizens. As for homosexuality, he stated that violence should be used to keep it out of the public square.

Roger Chapman

See also: Abortion; Anti-Semitism; Aryan Nations; Capital Punishment; Catholic Church; Fundamentalism, Religious; Gay Rights Movement; Homeschooling; Lesbians; Vigilantism.

Further Reading

Schuster, Henry, with Charles Stone. *Hunting Eric Rudolph.* New York: Berkeley Books, 2005.

Vollers, Maryanne. *Eric Rudolph: Murder, Myth, and the Pursuit of an American Outlaw.* New York: HarperCollins, 2006.

Rusher, William A.

Convinced that the massive U.S. federal bureaucracy was a form of authoritarian collectivism sliding into socialism, William A. Rusher spent more than fifty years advocating a rollback of the policies and projects initiated by President Franklin D. Roosevelt in the 1930s. Rusher served from 1957 to 1988 as publisher of the magazine *National Review*, edited by William F. Buckley, Jr. His views were well circulated through a syndicated newspaper column, "The Conservative Advocate," begun in 1973, and regular appearances on television and radio as a commentator and political analyst. Rusher frequently wrote magazine articles and authored five major books.

Born in Chicago on July 19, 1923, Rusher mostly grew up in New York City. After graduating from

Princeton University (AB, 1943), where he was active in a campus Republican organization, he served in the U.S. Air Force in India during World War II, advancing from second lieutenant to captain. After earning a law degree at Harvard University (JD, 1948), he worked for seven years as an attorney for a Wall Street law firm and then as associate counsel to the Senate Internal Security Subcommittee (1956–1957), where he probed the alleged network of communists and subversives and others caught up in the Cold War and McCarthyism.

Rusher helped Buckley establish the conservative student group Young Americans for Freedom (1960), and then with a handful of other conservatives began the process of convincing Senator Barry Goldwater (R-AZ) to run for president in 1964. Although Goldwater was defeated by a wide margin, conservative campaign workers such as Phyllis Schlafly formed the nucleus of what would become the New Right, which came to power with the election of Ronald Reagan in 1980. From 1965 to 1970, Rusher was vice chair of the American Conservative Union, which had emerged from the Goldwater campaign. Rusher regularly appeared on the PBS debating series *The Advocates* (1969–1973), produced in response to the Nixon administration's criticism that television had a liberal bias.

When polling data in the mid-1970s indicated that more voters identified themselves as conservatives than liberals, Rusher set out to organize conservatives to create a third major political party to challenge the Republican Party, which he saw as having been hijacked by opportunistic politicians, including President Richard M. Nixon, whom Rusher felt had betrayed conservative principles. Rusher's *The Making of the New Majority Party* (1975) was one of a handful of books that sparked interest in and served as a blueprint for the conservative political resurgence. Rusher eventually (and reluctantly) joined forces with those conservatives who successfully took over the Republican Party.

From 1980 forward, Rusher continued his political activism as a senior statesman of the American conservative movement and as a distinguished fellow of the Claremont Institute in California. In *The Coming Battle for the Media* (1988), he accuses a "media elite" of infusing news coverage with a liberal bias.

Chip Berlet

See also: Buckley, William F., Jr.; Cold War; Communists and Communism; Goldwater, Barry; McCarthyism; Media Bias; *National Review*; Public Broadcasting Service; Republican Party; Schlafly, Phyllis; Schlesinger, Arthur M., Jr.; Student Conservatives.

Further Reading

Brennan, Mary C. *Turning Right in the Sixties: The Conservative Capture of the GOP.* Chapel Hill: University of North Carolina Press, 1995.

Schoenwald, Jonathan M. *A Time for Choosing: The Rise of Modern American Conservatism.* Oxford: Oxford University Press, 2001.

Ryan, George

Prior to his April 2006 conviction on eighteen federal counts of racketeering, mail fraud, tax evasion, and false statements, George Ryan, the one-term governor of Illinois (1999–2003), dramatically ended his political career by declaring a moratorium on state executions, emptying out the state's death row. While critics accused him of trying to bolster his legacy in the face of a political corruption scandal, foes of capital punishment praised him for focusing attention on the arbitrary and capricious nature of the death penalty. Although nominated for the Nobel Peace Prize and lauded in song by Illinois First, a Chicago rock band, Ryan in September 2006 was sentenced to six and a half years in prison for a bribery scandal involving the issuance of commercial driver's licenses when he was secretary of state.

A native of Kankakee, Illinois, a small town 60 miles (97 kilometers) south of Chicago, George Homer Ryan was born on February 24, 1934. After serving in the U.S. Army during the Korean War, he studied pharmacy at Ferris State College in Big Rapids, Michigan, graduating in 1961. For the next several years, he helped his father run the family's chain of drugstores but later opted for a career in Republican state politics. Advancing from the Kankakee county board (1968–1973) to the Illinois House of Representatives (1973–1983), he went on to hold statewide office as lieutenant governor under Governor James Thompson (1983–1991), secretary of state (1991–1999), and governor (1999–2003). For most of his political career, he took conservative to moderate positions on most issues.

On January 31, 2000, following new evidence that exonerated thirteen men on the state's death row, Ryan declared a halt to executions in Illinois. This led to the establishment of the Capital Punishment Commission, which studied 5,310 first-degree murder convictions in the state from 1988 to 1997. In its report of April 15, 2002, the commission offered eighty-five suggestions for reform, noting that the death penalty should be abolished if reform was not implemented. The commission found that those who murdered an African American were 60 percent less likely to receive the death penalty than those who murdered a white, and of the less than 2 percent of murder defendants who received the death penalty, the majority were poor, uneducated, and minorities. In addition, it was found, a number of death row inmates had been represented by attorneys who were later disbarred.

Clemency hearings in the wake of the report led Governor Ryan on December 19, 2002, to pardon three men who had been wrongfully convicted of murder. He pardoned four others on January 10, 2003, stating that they had confessed to murders they did not commit after being tortured by the Chicago police. Finally, on January 11, 2003, forty-eight hours before concluding his term, the governor commuted the death sentences of 167 inmates, relegating all but three to life in prison without the possibility of parole. In announcing the decision, Ryan stated, "Our capital system is haunted by the demon of error: error in determining guilt and error in determining who among the guilty deserves to die."

Roger Chapman

See also: Capital Punishment; Race.

Further Reading

Buchanan, Patrick J. "George Ryan's Pathetic Farewell." *Human Events*, January 20, 2003.

Sarat, Austin. *Mercy on Trial: What It Takes to Stop an Execution.* Princeton, NJ: Princeton University Press, 2005.

Shapiro, Bruce. "Ryan's Courage." *Nation*, February 3, 2003.

Warden, Rob. "Illinois Death Penalty Reform: How It Happened, What It Promises." *Journal of Criminal Law and Criminology* 95:2 (2005): 381–426.

Said, Edward

Edward Said was an influential and controversial Palestinian American literary theorist and critic whose life was as much an object of dispute as his scholarship and his pro-Palestinian politics. Of his twenty-three books, the best known is *Orientalism* (1978), a critical attack on the Eurocentric attitudes found in Western scholarship, art, education, and policymaking as well as the West's perspective of the Orient as the "Other"—the binary opposite of the West.

Edward Wadie Said was born on November 1, 1935, in Jerusalem to affluent Christian parents. He attended school in both Cairo and Jerusalem until the 1948 Arab-Israeli War made refugees of his extended family. He moved to the United States in 1951, earned degrees from Princeton University (BA, 1957) and Harvard University (MA, 1960; PhD, 1964), and became a professor of English and comparative literature at Columbia University (1963–2003).

Justus Reid Weiner, a scholar at the Jerusalem Center for Public Affairs, wrote a highly publicized article in 1999 that challenged the details of Said's biography. Weiner contended that Said's family never lived in Jerusalem, that he never studied there, and that the 1948 Arab-Israeli War therefore could not have rendered his family refugees. Said and a number of defenders vigorously refuted those accusations.

Despite this controversy, it is for *Orientalism* that Said is best known. Said defines the term "Orientalism" as the intellectual and editorial means by which scholars, writers, and political officials have defined, restructured, and dominated the East while obfuscating the inherent and universal humanity present in it. Orientalists define the Islamic World and Asia as static, backward, tyrannical, incapable of reform, and empirically inferior—racially and culturally—to the more advanced West. Said blames colonization and its associated modes of thought for encouraging this uneven comparison, explaining Orientalism in terms of binary opposition and a pervasive post-Napoleonic state of colonial inequality. Said proposes that the only honest portrayal of the non-European world is one that emphasizes humanity and individuality without relying on generalization and categorization to define one population in terms of the other.

Said did not confine his criticism to historical texts but also attacked contemporary scholarship. The public exchange between Said and Bernard Lewis, a professor of Near Eastern studies at Princeton, debated the merits of Orientalism in numerous academic journals. Critics continue to attack Said's thesis as a profoundly flawed account of Western scholarship, while Said's supporters contend that Western scholars remain so heavily influenced by Orientalist tradition that they are unable to present a fair and clear image of their subjects.

A passionate supporter of Palestinian statehood, Said served as an independent member of the Palestinian National Council until Yasir Arafat threw the Palestinian Authority's support behind Saddam Hussein in the 1991 Gulf War. At that point, Said became an increasingly vocal critic of Arafat's leadership. Shortly after Said's death from leukemia on September 25, 2003, Columbia University established the Edward Said Chair in Middle East Studies. In 2006, it was revealed that Said had been under FBI surveillance since 1971.

J.D. Jordan

See also: Israel; Lewis, Bernard; Multiculturalism and Ethnic Studies; Muslim Americans; Saudi Arabia; September 11.

Further Reading
Said, Edward. *Out of Place: A Memoir.* New York: Alfred A. Knopf, 1999.
Singh, Amritjit. *Interviews with Edward W. Said.* Jackson: University Press of Mississippi, 2004.
Weiner, Justus Reid. "'My Beautiful Old House' and Other Fabrications by Edward Said." *Commentary*, September 1999.
Williams, Patrick, ed. *Edward Said.* 4 vols. Thousand Oaks, CA: Sage, 2004.

Same-Sex Marriage

Same-sex marriage has been a significant issue in American law and politics since the early 1990s, when the Supreme Court of Hawaii in *Baehr v. Lewin* (1993) declared that the denial of marriage licenses to same-sex couples was a form of sex discrimination and in violation of the state's constitution. Hawaii and other states responded with a popular referendum that amended the state's constitution to define marriage as the legal union between a man and a woman.

The Hawaii court decision sparked a maelstrom of cultural controversy and led to concern that courts in other states would challenge the heterosexual basis of marriage. Politically, same-sex marriage emerged as an important issue at the federal level with the 1996 Defense of Marriage Act (DOMA), which was passed by an overwhelming majority in Congress and signed into law by President Bill Clinton. The law declared that the federal government may not recognize same-sex marriages for any purpose, and that no state can be compelled to recognize a same-sex marriage even if performed in another state. (The act also clarified that polygamous marriages would not be recognized.) As of 2007, forty-two states had passed a law or constitutional amendment restricting marriage to heterosexual unions. Several states also passed "SuperDOMAs," denying recognition not only of same-sex marriages but also of civil unions and domestic partnerships.

The debate was briefly rekindled in 1999 when Vermont's Supreme Court declared that denying marriage licenses to same-sex couples is a violation of equal protection under the law. The state legislature and the governor, Howard Dean, responded with a civil union bill that defined marriage as heterosexual but granted equal state benefits to same-sex couples. Most of the debate between 2000 and 2003 occurred at the state level, as individual states considered and usually passed DOMAs. Neither of the two major political parties made the approval of same-sex marriage a part of its platform, and few national politicians spoke out in favor of it. However, in 2002 the Alliance for Marriage, with the help of conservative legal scholar Robert Bork, drafted a federal marriage amendment that would define marriage in the U.S. Constitution as between a man and a woman.

After the U.S. Supreme Court overturned all state-level bans on sodomy in *Lawrence v. Texas* (2003), same-sex marriage once again became a high-profile issue at the national level. In his dissenting opinion, Justice Antonin Scalia warned that overturning the criminalization of sodomy would result in the overturning of marriage laws. The state of Massachusetts affirmed his fear in *Goodridge v. Massachusetts Department of Public Health* (2003), when its Supreme Judicial Court declared that the state's marriage laws violated equal protection guarantees and ordered the state to begin issuing marriage licenses to same-sex couples.

Following the Massachusetts decision, conservative leaders such as James Dobson and Pat Robertson pressured Republican politicians to pass the federal marriage amendment. The plan drew public support from President George W. Bush and many Republican members of Congress, although Bush and others did not push for immediate passage of the amendment. Bush's opponent in the 2004 election, John Kerry, opposed the amendment but supported civil unions rather than same-sex marriage. In the key state of Ohio, where a state amendment banning same-sex marriage was also on the ballot in the 2004 election, voter turnout was high, especially among conservatives. The Ohio amendment passed by a wide margin, and Bush narrowly won Ohio's electoral college votes.

While the general public's interest in same-sex marriage waned after the 2004 election, the issue remained an important one to the Religious Right, which continued to press for the federal amendment as well as further state provisions. Same-sex marriage was entangled with a number of other issues important to conservative Christians, such as the role of the courts, abortion, and sexuality. The issue is often cited in the right's indictment of "activist judges," meaning judges whose rulings are viewed as contrary to conservatives' understanding of settled law or the popular will.

Some opponents of same-sex marriage argue that recognizing nonheterosexual unions would imply state endorsement of same-sex relationships, in violation of the conscience of the majority of Americans and their religious views. Others, drawing on conventional wisdom about the family, argue that marriage between a man and a woman represents the most stable environment for rearing children. A two-parent household is more economically stable, it is argued, and the erosion of gender norms in nontraditional households is psychologically harmful to children.

While many social conservatives are united in their opposition to same-sex marriage, some conservatives and Republicans have voiced support for same-sex marriage or civil unions. Libertarian conservatives such as Andrew Sullivan argue that same-sex marriage would promote a stable family environment for gays and lesbians and discourage promiscuity. Monogamy and familial stability through marriage, it is argued, are more important goals than maintaining marriage as a heterosexual institution.

Gay and lesbian activists have generally lined up in support of same-sex marriage, and most major gay rights organizations, including the Lambda Defense League, have been involved in political and legal struggles in support of same-sex marriage. However, many others have expressed reservations about making same-sex marriage the central component of the gay rights movement. Some activists worry that working for same-sex marriage may interfere with the achievement of other important goals, such as antidiscrimination measures. Others, such as gender activist Michael Warner, argue that the marriage debate attempts to normalize gays and lesbians and demonize alternative sexual expression. Self-described queer activists worry that the gay rights movement has turned its back on the sexual liberation aspirations of the 1970s and has internalized heterosexist norms of the family.

Claire E. Rasmussen

See also: Bush Family; Clinton, Bill; Dean, Howard; Dobson, James; Family Values; Gay Rights Movement; Hay, Harry; Judicial Wars; Kerry, John; Religious Right; Robertson, Pat; Sexual Revolution; Sodomy Laws.

Further Reading

Eskridge, William N., Jr., and Darren R. Spedale. *Gay Marriage: For Better or for Worse? What We've Learned from the Evidence.* New York: Oxford University Press, 2006.

Goldberg-Hiller, Jonathan. *The Limits to Union: Same-Sex Marriage and the Politics of Civil Rights.* Ann Arbor: University of Michigan Press, 2002.

Mello, Michael. *Legalizing Gay Marriage*. Philadelphia: Temple University Press, 2004.

Wardle, Lynn, ed. *Marriage and Same-Sex Unions: A Debate*. New York: Praeger, 2003.

Wolfson, Evan. *Why Marriage Matters: America, Equality, and Gay People's Right to Marry*. New York: Simon & Schuster, 2004.

Sanders, Bernie

For many years the only independent in the U.S. House of Representatives, Bernard "Bernie" Sanders has been the rare radical political activist who has managed to carry his ideas into mainstream politics during an era of conservative dominance. A self-described democratic socialist, he was Vermont's only member of the House from 1991 to 2007. He was elected to the U.S. Senate in 2006.

The son of Polish immigrants, Sanders was born on September 8, 1941, and grew up in Brooklyn, New York. He graduated from the University of Chicago (BA, 1964), where he spent much of his time in political activism. He moved to Vermont in 1964 and entered politics in the 1970s as a member of the leftist Liberty Union Party. During that decade, he ran twice for senator under the party banner and twice for governor as an independent, in each case unsuccessfully. In 1981, running as an independent, he won the first of four consecutive terms as mayor of Burlington, the state's largest city, which some began calling "the People's Republic of Burlington." Mayor Sanders successfully pushed for a number of social, cultural, and economic programs, ranging from a public day care center to tax reform and the creation of an arts council.

Early in Sanders's mayoralty, a local political party, the Progressive Coalition, was formed to support his programs. The Vermont Progressive Party grew out of this effort. One of its candidates succeeded Sanders as mayor, and other party members won seats to the state legislature as well as local offices. Sanders's local political career helped galvanize the state's progressive elements.

Sanders was elected to the U.S. House of Representatives in 1990, defeating a first-term incumbent Republican. He increasingly worked with House Democrats, caucusing with them and being counted with them for such administrative purposes as committee assignments. He was a co-founder and first chairperson of the House Progressive Caucus; all other members were Democrats. He emphasized issues such as universal health care, veterans' issues, and the damaging effects of free trade, and he supported a variety of measures intended to address corporate influence in politics and the media. In 1999, to dramatize the problem of high-cost prescription drugs, he led a well-publicized bus trip in which a group of Vermonters went to Canada to buy the less expensive

Calling himself a "democratic socialist," Bernie Sanders of Vermont—posing before a portrait of socialist labor leader Eugene V. Debs—was elected to the U.S. Congress in 1990. After serving eight terms in the House, he was elected to the Senate in 2006. *(Steve Liss/Time & Life Pictures/Getty Images)*

medications available there. Other members of Congress soon followed suit.

Critics on the far left argue that Sanders has so compromised his principles that he is effectively a Democrat. His supporters contend that he has consistently emphasized his core values, representing the interests of working families, farmers, low-income families, veterans, students, and others underrepresented by a corporate-dominated political system. His populist policies have drawn support across the political spectrum, aided by his iconoclastic, outspoken style and no-nonsense practicality, and he has won a surprisingly enduring popularity in a traditionally Republican state.

Gary L. Bailey

See also: Democratic Party; Globalization; Health Care; Republican Party.

Further Reading

Conroy, W.J. *Challenging the Boundaries of Reform: Socialism in Burlington*. Philadelphia: Temple University Press, 1990.

Rosenfeld, Steven. *Making History in Vermont: The Election of a Socialist to Congress*. Wakefield, NH: Hollowbrook, 1992.

Sanders, Bernie, and Huck Gutman. *Outsider in the House*. New York: Verso, 1997.

Vermont Progressive Party Web site. www.answers.com.

Saudi Arabia

The largest country in the Middle East, comprising four-fifths of the Arabian Peninsula, Saudi Arabia possesses 20 percent of the world's known petroleum reserves and is perhaps the strictest fundamentalist Islamic society. Over the years, the United States has guaranteed the security of Saudi Arabia, providing military protection from first the Soviet Union and later Iraq and Iran, to safeguard the flow of oil. After the terrorist attacks of September 11, 2001, in which fifteen of the nineteen hijackers were Saudi nationals, Americans in greater numbers began questioning the wisdom of this strategic partnership. Critical observers charge that the Saudi monarchy sowed the seeds of al-Qaeda by fostering religious extremism.

King Ibn Saud, who founded the Kingdom of Saudi Arabia in 1932, based the laws of his society on Wahhabism, a puritanical Sunni Muslim doctrine that emphasizes jihad, or holy war. After Saud's death in 1953, his successors pursued the same course, infusing Wahhabi ideology in the nation's mosques, schools, and political system. Annually, Western monitors cite Saudi Arabia for human rights violations, but the U.S. government has avoided pressing the issue. Public worship other than Islam is outlawed, even for foreigners living inside the country. Non-Muslims are not allowed to be buried in the country because the ground, being the birthplace of Islam, is considered too sacred. Saudi Arabia is also known for imposing brutal punishment on lawbreakers, from amputation of limbs to decapitation. Between 1979 and 2008 there were over 1,800 executions in Saudi Arabia, of which more than half were foreign migrant workers. The British docudrama *Death of a Princess* (1980), based on the 1977 execution of a Saudi princess and her lover for adultery, aroused strong objection by Saudi Arabia when it was aired in the United States by PBS.

The American media have criticized Saudi Arabia for practicing "gender apartheid." Out in public a woman is required to wear a headscarf and a floor-length black garment called an *abaya*. Women are not allowed to drive and out in public must be escorted by male family members. Females may only attend all-girl schools. At restaurants women must eat in "family" sections, separated from single men. McDonald's Corp. and Starbucks Coffee Co. have been criticized for allowing their franchises in Saudi Arabia to operate with gender-segregated zones. American service women stationed in Saudi Arabia have also been subjected to some of these gender rules, prompting a 2001 lawsuit by Lieutenant Colonel Martha McSally, a U.S. Air Force fighter pilot, who objected to wearing a headscarf. (Congress rescinded the headscarf regulation, but the U.S. military still prohibits its female service members from driving while in Saudi Arabia.) A Saudi woman who in 2006 had been gang-raped was sentenced by a Saudi court to 200 lashes for being alone in an automobile with a non-relative male, but the negative foreign media attention led to her receiving a pardon. Some American women who married Saudis and were later divorced have been frustrated by Washington's lack

of intervention after their children were kidnapped in the United States and flown to Saudi Arabia, prompting books such as Patricia Roush's *At Any Price: How America Betrayed My Kidnapped Daughters for Saudi Oil* (2003).

As the custodian of Islam's two holiest sites (Mecca and Medina), Saudi Arabia has extended its religious influence to the larger Muslim world, even using oil proceeds to fund nations (primarily Egypt and Syria) and movements (such as the Palestinian Liberation Organization) that oppose Israel. During the 1980s Saudi males in large numbers, with the monarchy's blessings, traveled to Afghanistan to fight in a jihad against the Soviet Union. The United States through the CIA assisted some of those fighters, including Osama bin Laden, who in the late 1980s formed the al-Qaeda terrorist organization. Its members have since committed terrorist attacks inside Saudi Arabia, denouncing the monarchy for religious complacency that permitted U.S. forces to marshal in Saudi Arabia during the 1991 Gulf War. According to an October 2001 confidential poll of Saudi males (ages twenty-five to forty-one), 95 percent approved of bin Laden's jihad against the West.

Protecting the oil fields of the Middle East was the U.S. objective of the Gulf War, specifically to counterbalance Iraq, which had the largest military in the Middle East, and to force its withdrawal from Kuwait. American ties to Saudi Arabia date back to 1933 when Aramco (the Arabian American Oil Company) received a concession agreement giving it oil rights until 1999. In the early 1970s, however, Saudi authorities withdrew the concession. In 1973, oil was for the first time used as a political weapon, prompting Americans to coin the phrase "energy crisis." Members of the oil cartel OPEC (Organization of the Petroleum Exporting Countries), founded thirteen years earlier and dominated by the Saudi regime, imposed an oil embargo against the United States and other Western nations for supporting Israel during the 1973 Yom Kippur War. Despite such political twists and turns, between 1973 and 1980 the U.S. government allowed the Saudis to purchase $34 billion of American military hardware. During the early days of the Reagan administration, after acrimonious debate and a narrow 52–48 Senate vote, the United States agreed to sell Saudi Arabia AWACS—Airborne Warning and Control System—radar aircraft for monitoring the Saudi skies against surprise attack.

Since September 11 and the subsequent Iraq War, some liberal culture warriors have accused the Bush family of sinister ties with the Saudi monarchy—for example, Michael Moore's *Fahrenheit 911* (2004) and Craig Unger's *House of Bush, House of Saud* (2004). In the meantime, conservatives who have long advocated oil drilling in the Arctic National Wildlife Refuge in Alaska and offshore drilling along the Atlantic and Pacific coasts have argued that increasing domestic oil production would allow the

United States to end its energy dependency on authoritarian regimes such as Saudi Arabia.

Roger Chapman

See also: Bush Family; Cold War; Fundamentalism, Religious; Israel; Muslim Americans; Reagan, Ronald; September 11.

Further Reading

Baer, Robert. *Sleeping with the Devil: How Washington Sold Our Soul for Saudi Crude.* New York: Crown, 2003.

Bronson, Rachel. *Thicker Than Oil: America's Uneasy Partnership with Saudi Arabia.* New York: Oxford University Press, 2006.

Commins, David. *The Wahhabi Mission and Saudi Arabia.* New York: I.B. Tauris, 2006.

Posner, Gerald L. *Secrets of the Kingdom: The Inside Story of the Saudi-U.S. Connection.* New York: Random House, 2005.

U.S. Congress. *U.S. Relations with Saudi Arabia: Oil, Anxiety, and Ambivalence: Hearings before the Subcommittee on the Middle East and South Asia of the Committee on Foreign Affairs.* Washington, DC: US GPO, 2008.

Schaeffer, Francis

The evangelical philosopher and Presbyterian pastor Francis Schaeffer, once dubbed the guru of fundamentalism, fortified the Religious Right by linking secular humanism to pornography, the breakdown of the family, abortion, and the expansion of government. He blamed America's moral decline on the waves of immigrants that, after 1848, were lacking a Reformation background due to their largely Roman Catholic affiliation. He encouraged "true believers" to rise up in civil disobedience to cast aside immoral laws and reclaim the nation's Christian—that is, Protestant—heritage.

Francis August Schaeffer was born on January 30, 1912, in Germantown, Pennsylvania. He attended Hampden-Sydney College, graduating magna cum laude in 1935, and married Edith Seville, whose parents had served as missionaries with the Inland China Mission. He also attended Westminster Theological Seminary in Philadelphia (1935–1937), founded in the wake of a modernist-fundamentalist conflict at Princeton Theological Seminary and in opposition to the trend toward a liberal theological interpretation of the Bible. Orthodox Presbyterian leaders, among them Carl McIntire, organized Westminster, which eventually led to the formation of the Presbyterian Church in America. A new split established the Bible Presbyterian Church and its Faith Theological Seminary. Schaeffer graduated from the latter in 1938 and became the new denomination's first ordained pastor.

From 1938 to 1948 Schaeffer served in pastorates in several states. He then moved to Europe to start a youth ministry, which culminated in 1955 with the founding of L'Abri (The Shelter) in Switzerland. There Schaeffer taught Christian apologetics and helped establish the International Council of Christian Churches, a conservative counterpart to the World Council of Churches. (One of his students at L'Abri was Michael Ford, the son of President Gerald R. Ford.) Schaeffer wrote a number of books, including *Escape from Reason* (1968), *The God Who Is There* (1968), *True Spirituality* (1971), and *How Then Shall We Live?* (1976). His book *A Christian Manifesto* (1981) and the film series it inspired were criticized for offering a simplified rendering of Western history and philosophy. Some critics found him unscholarly; evangelical historian Mark Noll argued that Schaeffer's work presented a "simplified myth of America's Christian past."

Schaeffer died of leukemia on May 15, 1984, in Rochester, Minnesota. L'Abri centers still operate in Great Britain, Germany, the Netherlands, Sweden, Australia, South Korea, Canada, and the United States; and Schaeffer's teachings continue to influence many fundamentalists and other conservative Christians.

Andrew J. Waskey

See also: Abortion; American Exceptionalism; Catholic Church; Evangelicalism; Ford, Gerald; Fundamentalism, Religious; Immigration Policy; Koop, C. Everett; McIntire, Carl; Pornography; Religious Right; Secular Humanism; World Council of Churches.

Further Reading

Duriez, Colin. *Francis Schaeffer: An Authentic Life.* Wheaton, IL: Crossway Books, 2008.

Ruegsegger, Ronald W., ed. *Reflections on Francis Schaeffer.* Grand Rapids, MI: Academie Books, 1986.

Schaeffer, Francis A. *The Complete Works of Francis A. Schaeffer: A Christian Worldview.* 5 vols. Westchester, IL: Crossway Books, 1985.

Wellman, Sam. *Francis and Edith Schaeffer: Defenders of the Faith.* Uhrichsville, OH: Barbour, 2000.

Schiavo, Terri

Terri Schiavo garnered international attention as a symbol of what religious conservatives described as the "culture of death" and what end-of-life activists viewed as a person's right to die. For fifteen years, in a persistent vegetative state, she received nutrition and hydration through a feeding tube while a vitriolic legal battle was fought between her husband and her parents over whether to end that care. Her husband and legal guardian, Michael Schiavo, sought to remove the tube, claiming it was consistent with his wife's medical prognosis and her wishes. Mary and Robert Schindler, the woman's parents, took

The highly charged case of Terri Schiavo, a Florida woman in a vegetative state since 1990, pitted her husband, who asked that life support be discontinued, against her parents and anti-euthanasia groups. Schiavo died in 2005, thirteen days after the removal of her feeding tube. *(Matt May/Getty Images)*

legal action to block removal of the feeding tube because of their commitment to the sanctity of life and their belief that she might one day be restored to health.

Schiavo was twenty-six years old when, on February 25, 1990, she collapsed in the couple's apartment. Paramedics found her unconscious, not breathing, and without a pulse. A cause was never determined. Unable to swallow, Schiavo underwent surgical placement of a feeding tube for the delivery of nutrients. By the end of 1990, she was diagnosed as being in a persistent vegetative state, having never regained consciousness.

In 1998, after years of unsuccessful rehabilitation efforts and on the advice of his wife's physicians, Michael Schiavo petitioned the court to cease his wife's medical treatments, including the feeding tube. Removal of the feeding tube was opposed by the Schindlers, leading to a complex series of court battles and political interventions. The Schindlers were aided by an array of organizations and personalities—including Not Dead Yet, civil rights activist Jesse Jackson, Operation Rescue founder Randall Terry, and actor Mel Gibson—who joined in an attempt to "save Terri" through an Internet-based public relations campaign marked by disability rights rhetoric and anti-abortion slogans.

The scheduled removal of Schiavo's feeding tube in October 2003 and again in March 2005 created a media frenzy and ignited a political firestorm. Special laws designed to block the court-ordered removal and to provide federal judicial oversight of the Florida state court proceedings were passed by the Florida legislature and the U.S. Congress and signed, respectively, by Governor Jeb Bush and President George W. Bush. Despite these unprecedented legislative and executive interventions in an end-of-life court proceeding, the courts continued to uphold the decision of Schiavo's husband. Schiavo died on March 31, 2005, thirteen days after removal of the feeding tube.

In his *Focus on the Family* newsletter, James Dobson argued, "Terri's killing signifies conclusively that the judicial system in this country is far too powerful and . . . out of control." But a majority of legal, medical, and bioethical commentators found the Schiavo case a model of thorough legal proceedings, careful medical analysis, and appropriate protections of a patient's right to self-determination.

Joshua E. Perry

See also: Bush Family; Dobson, James; Evangelicalism; Focus on the Family; Gibson, Mel; Jackson, Jesse; Judicial Wars; Not Dead Yet; Operation Rescue; Right to Die.

Further Reading

Dobson, James. "Life, Death and Judicial Tyranny." *Focus on the Family Action Newsletter,* April 2005.

Perry, Joshua E., Larry R. Churchill, and Howard S. Kirshner. "The Terri Schiavo Case: Legal, Ethical, and Medical Perspectives." *Annals of Internal Medicine* 143:10 (2005): 744–48.

Schiavo, Michael. *Terri: The Truth.* New York: Dutton, 2006.

Schindler, Mary, and Robert Schindler. *A Life That Matters: The Legacy of Terri Schiavo—A Lesson for Us All.* New York: Warner Books, 2006.

Schlafly, Phyllis

Phyllis Schlafly, a prominent antifeminist leader best known for her relentless opposition to the Equal Rights Amendment (ERA), has actively participated in the conservative wing of the Republican Party since the 1950s. She has been called the "Gloria Steinem of the Right."

Phyllis McAlpin Stewart, born on August 15, 1924, in St. Louis, Missouri, was raised in a Catholic home and attended a female parochial school. She studied government and politics at Washington University in St. Louis (AB, 1944) and Radcliffe University (MA, 1945). Returning to Washington University decades later, she studied law (JD, 1978). On October 20, 1949, she married Fred Schlafly, Jr., of Alton, Illinois, a wealthy attorney and political conservative, and together they had six children.

Schlafly's marriage reinforced her growing conservatism, and during the 1950s and 1960s, she and her husband formed a dynamic couple in Illinois Republican Party politics. In 1952, she ran unsuccessfully for Congress and helped organize a GOP meeting in Alton on behalf of presidential hopeful Robert Taft, a U.S. senator from Ohio. The Schlaflys co-founded the Catholic anticommunist Cardinal Mindszenty Foundation in 1959. At some point Phyllis Schlafly was a member of the John Birch Society. During the 1964 presidential campaign, she wrote *A Choice Not an Echo* to promote the presidential drive of Barry Goldwater. In 1970, she once again failed at a bid for Congress.

Although she was exceptionally active in Republican Party politics at the state and local levels, it was her opposition to the ERA that propelled Schlafly into the national spotlight. Her initial opposition was based on the perception that the ERA was a threat to the family, which she defined in the February 1972 issue of the *Phyllis Schlafly Report* as "the basic unit of society, which is ingrained in the laws and customs of our Judeo-Christian civilization [and] is the great single achievement in the history of women's rights." With this basic philosophy, she and other conservative women in September 1972 founded Stop Taking Our Privileges (STOP ERA) to counter the ERA movement.

Through STOP ERA and later the Eagle Forum, founded in 1975, Schlafly articulated her opposition to the proposed amendment. If the ERA passed, she warned, courts would reinterpret legislation passed to protect women; abortion would continue unimpeded; women would be forced into combat situations through the draft; homosexual rights would be grafted into the Constitution; and laws governing child support, alimony, and divorce would be put in jeopardy. Any intended good of the ERA, Schlafly argued, was already provided by the Equal Pay Act of 1963, Title VII of the Civil Rights Act of 1964, and the Equal Employment Opportunity Act of 1972. Critics characterized her efforts as impeding the progress of women's rights.

Schlafly voiced her arguments against the ERA at protest rallies, congressional hearings, and lobbying sessions right up to the June 30, 1982, ratification deadline. In the decades after the amendment's defeat, she remained a strong voice in the conservative ranks of the Republican Party, publishing her monthly newsletter and writing a number of books on education, the courts, politics, and defense policy (she once described the atomic bomb as "a marvelous gift that was given to our country by a wise God"). In May 2008, students and faculty at Washington University protested against Schlafly being awarded an honorary doctorate degree.

Matthew C. Sherman

See also: Abortion; Equal Rights Amendment; Family Values; Feminism, Second-Wave; Gay Rights Movement; Goldwater, Barry; Judicial Wars; National Organization for Women; Same-Sex Marriage; Stay-at-Home Mothers; Taft, Robert, Jr.

Further Reading

Critchlow, Donald T. *Phyllis Schlafly and Grassroots Conservatism: A Woman's Crusade.* Princeton, NJ: Princeton University Press, 2005.

Felsenthal, Carol. *The Sweetheart of the Silent Majority: The Biography of Phyllis Schlafly.* New York: Doubleday, 1981.

Hoff-Wilson, Joan, ed. *Rights of Passage: The Past and Future of the ERA.* Bloomington: Indiana University Press, 1986.

Schlesinger, Arthur M., Jr.

Historian, author, adviser to presidents, and political activist Arthur M. Schlesinger, Jr., spent the second half of the twentieth century championing liberalism and defending the legacies of the New Deal. Schlesinger is perhaps best known for his cyclical theory of American political history, which suggests that the United States has a tradition of swinging back and forth between periods of reform and conservative resurgence. Similarly, he observed a tension between two views of the nation, the Puritan model (American exceptionalism and the belief of predestined national greatness) and the Founding Fathers model (a nation of bold experimentation, but nonetheless a nation among nations).

Himself the son of a prominent Harvard historian, Arthur Meier Schlesinger, Jr., was born on October 15, 1917, in Columbus, Ohio. A graduate of Harvard University (AB, 1938), he served during World War II with the Office of War Information (1942–1943) and the Office of Strategic Services (1943–1945). Despite not obtaining a doctoral degree, Schlesinger had a distinguished academic career at Harvard (1946–1961) and the City University of New York (1966–1995). In addition to teaching, Schlesinger served as a special assistant to President John F. Kennedy (1961–1963) and President Lyndon B. Johnson (1963–1964), and acted as a campaign adviser to Adlai Stevenson and Robert Kennedy. Schlesinger died in New York City on February 28, 2007.

A self-described "noncommunist leftist," Schlesinger helped found the liberal anticommunist organization Americans for Democratic Action (ADA, 1947), opposed McCarthyism and "Nixonism," warned against the "radical Right," and later declared the Vietnam War a "moral outrage." In defense of liberalism, Schlesinger argued that it serves as the "vital center" between the totalitarian extremes of communism and fascism. During a 1961 debate with conservative William F. Buckley, Jr., editor of the *National Review*, Schlesinger asserted that the welfare state is "deeply consistent with the American tradition" and is also "the best security against communism." That remark was scorned by Republicans and conservative Democrats, including Senator Everett Dirksen (R-IL), who characterized it as "a crisis in the mental history of Arthur Schlesinger."

Schlesinger is the author of many books, including *The Age of Jackson* (1945), a work placing Andrew Jackson in the liberal tradition, and which won a Pulitzer Prize; *The Vital Center: The Politics of Freedom* (1949), a defense of postwar liberalism; *The Age of Roosevelt* (1957, 1959, 1960), a three-volume work extolling the bold experimentation of the New Deal; *A Thousand Days: John F. Kennedy in the White House* (1965), a behind-the-scenes account of the Kennedy administration that won a Pulitzer Prize for Biography; *The Imperial Presidency* (1973), an analysis of the Johnson and Nixon presidencies and the abuse of executive power; and *The Disuniting of America: Reflections on a Multicultural Society* (1991), a repudiation of "politically correct" history, including black studies and Afrocentrism. Over the years, Schlesinger's harshest critics accused him of violating the objectivity of the historian by allowing partisanship to color his work, but he suggested that history is "the quest for an unattainable objectivity" and gained a wide following for his perceptive analyses.

Roger Chapman

See also: Afrocentrism; American Exceptionalism; Communists and Communism; Founding Fathers; Johnson, Lyndon B.; Kennedy Family; McCarthyism; Multiculturalism and Ethnic Studies; New Deal; Nixon, Richard; Political Correctness; Revisionist History.

Further Reading

Depoe, Stephen P. *Arthur M. Schlesinger, Jr., and the Ideological History of American Liberalism.* Tuscaloosa: University of Alabama Press, 1994.

Diggins, John Patrick, ed. *The Liberal Persuasion: Arthur Schlesinger, Jr., and the Challenge of the American Past.* Princeton, NJ: Princeton University Press, 1997.

Schlesinger, Arthur M., Jr. *A Life in the Twentieth Century: Innocent Beginnings, 1917–1950.* Boston: Houghton Mifflin, 2000.

School of the Americas

The School of the Americas (SOA)—renamed the Western Hemisphere Institute for Security Cooperation (WHISC or WHINSEC) in 2001—was founded in 1946 at the onset of the Cold War for the purpose of training Latin American military officers in tactics used for fighting communist insurgency. A U.S. Army facility operated in Spanish under Pentagon oversight, it was known as the Latin American Training Center until 1963. Originally located at Fort Gulick in Panama, the SOA was relocated to Fort Benning, Georgia, in 1984, after the signing of the Panama Canal Treaty. Since 1990 the school has been the scene of an annual protest led by Catholic activists.

From 1963 to 1996, the SOA trained 61,000 soldiers from eleven South and Central American countries. During the late 1980s and early 1990s, the facility became the object of public criticism because some of its graduates were linked to right-wing terror, death squads, and military takeovers. For example, SOA graduate General Romeo Lucas García was the dictator of Guatemala from 1978 to 1982, during which time that nation witnessed some 5,000 political murders and 25,000 civilian deaths; three Honduran generals, also SOA graduates, in the 1970s formed an army death squad called Battalion 3-16; and nearly all of the officers responsible for overthrowing the democratic government of Salvador Allende in Chile on September 11, 1973, were SOA graduates. It was the tarnished reputation of the SOA that compelled the Pentagon to rename it the Western Hemisphere Institute for Security Cooperation.

The existence of the SOA became more widely known after the shooting deaths of six Jesuit priests in El Salvador on November 16, 1989. Of the twenty-six soldiers implicated in the murders, nineteen were later found to have been trained by the SOA. On the first anniversary of the massacre, Maryknoll priest Roy Bourgeois, accompanied by protestors Charles Liteky and Patrick Liteky, entered SOA headquarters and poured blood over the photographs on display of the school's distinguished graduates. All three men were jailed, but their act of civil disobedience gave birth to the advocacy group School of the Americas Watch. Into the twenty-first century, that organization has continued protesting the operation of the training center, which it dubs the "School of the Assassins" and the "School of Coups." Each November, SOA Watch conducts a massive protest outside the gates of Fort Benning.

A 1992 internal Department of Defense investigative report, never intended for public dissemination, revealed that between 1982 and 1991 "torture manuals" had been a part of the SOA's curriculum. Newspapers across the country responded with editorials calling for the dismantling of the training center. In 1996, SOA Watch established an office in Washington, D.C., with the goal of lobbying Congress to do just that. In 1999, the U.S. House of Representatives voted 230–197 to reduce the school's funding from $4.5 million to $2 million, but the Senate opposed the reduction. In 2000, the House failed to pass a measure that would have shut down the school entirely. In the wake of the post–September 11 abuse of prisoners and detainees by American service personnel at Abu Ghraib prison in Iraq and the Guantánamo Bay detention camp in Cuba, critics have pointed to the SOA as proof of a long-standing and institutionalized darker side of the U.S. military system.

Roger Chapman

See also: Abu Ghraib and Gitmo; Catholic Church; Central Intelligence Agency; Cold War; Human Rights.

Further Reading

Gill, Leslie. *The School of the Americas: Military Training and Political Violence in the Americas.* Durham, NC: Duke University Press, 2004.
Nelson-Pallmeyer, Jack. *School of Assassins: Guns, Greed, and Globalization.* Maryknoll, NY: Orbis Books, 2001.
Quigley, Bill. "The Case for Closing the School of the Americas." *BYU Journal of Public Law* 20:1 (2006): 1–34.
School of the Americas Watch Web site. www.soaw.org.
Western Hemisphere Institute for Security Cooperation Web site. www.benning.army.mil/whinsec.

School Prayer

A test of the separation between church and state, the issue of mandatory prayer in public schools has been an ongoing and often controversial issue in the United States since the Cold War in the late 1940s and 1950s. The matter came to a head in the early 1960s, after a number of individuals filed federal lawsuits against public school districts for conducting prayer in the classroom and requiring students to take part. In several major rulings at that time, the U.S. Supreme Court declared such official rituals unconstitutional. While a bitter grievance of the Religious Right ever since, school prayer has not been an issue of utmost concern to most Americans. Nonetheless, a Gallup poll as recent as August 2005 showed that 76 percent of Americans support a constitutional amendment permitting voluntary school prayer.

Cold War Era

Before the Supreme Court ban on state-sponsored school prayer, only about one-third of the public schools in postwar America actually conducted classroom prayer. Some regions were more "prayer oriented" than others: 80 percent of elementary schools conducted prayer in the South and East; 38 percent did so in the Midwest; and only 14 percent in the West. State courts banned school prayer in Washington, California, South Dakota, Nebraska, Louisiana, Illinois, and Wisconsin.

The controversy surrounding school prayer emerged partly as a function of the Cold War, a time when many Americans equated atheism with communism. In this context, the phrase "In God We Trust" was inscribed on legal tender, and the words "under God" were inserted in the Pledge of Allegiance. In 1952, Congress directed the president to establish a National Day of Prayer. Although some school systems had a tradition of prayer and Bible reading dating back to the nineteenth century, others did not introduce devotional exercises until the Cold War era.

In *Everson v. Board of Education* (1947), the U.S. Supreme Court by a 5–4 majority interpreted the Establishment Clause of the First Amendment to the U.S. Constitution—"Congress shall make no law respecting an establishment of religion, or prohibiting the free exercise thereof"—as requiring a "wall of separation" between church and state. With the doctrine of separation in place, the high court in *McCollum v. Board of Education* (1948) then declared it unconstitutional for public schools to offer religious instruction. In *Engel v. Vitale* (1962), the high court declared mandatory prayer in public schools unconstitutional. This was followed by *Abington v. Schempp* (1963) and *Murray v. Curlett* (1963), which outlawed mandatory Bible reading and the recitation of the Lord's Prayer in public schools.

The Engel Case

In July 1958, the Herricks School Board in Nassau County on Long Island (New York) directed its teachers to recite the State Board of Regents' prayer each school day. Drafted in November 1951, the prayer read, "Almighty God, we acknowledge our dependence upon Thee, and we beg Thy blessings upon us, our parents, our teachers, and our country." New York governor Thomas Dewey endorsed the prayer, saying that it was useful for opposing "the slave world of godless communism." New York educational associations also endorsed the prayer, believing that it could serve as an antidote to "narcotics and alcohol." Protestant and Catholic leaders endorsed the recitation as well. Opposing the prayer directive were the liberal denominational magazine *Christian Century* (which warned that rote prayer can become an "empty formality"); the United Parents Association (which argued that students should not be forced to recite "what they do not even understand"); and several major Jewish organizations (which called it a violation of the separation of church and state).

After Herricks High School announced plans for implementing regular prayer, twenty-eight parents, representing thirty-nine students, requested that their children be excused from participating. In the legal case that ensued, *Engel v. Vitale*, the five plaintiffs, all Jewish parents, had one child each enrolled in the high school. Steven Engel opposed the Board of Regents' prayer after his son told him he should not have to attend synagogue since he was praying in school. Another plaintiff, Lawrence Roth, was an atheist who had painful memories of a brother being lynched in Pennsylvania for being a Jew, and did not want his son to be subjected to religious indoctrination. Roth, who had made the initial contact with the New York Civil Liberties Union over the matter, would receive hundreds of threatening phone calls and letters, many with anti-Semitic remarks; his driveway would later be the scene of a cross-burning. Another father, Monroe Lerner, regarded the prayer as a "mockery" and an "imposition," arguing that the provision allowing a student not to participate in the prayer only served to mark him or her as a "pariah." Daniel Lichtenstein op-posed the prayer because of his belief in the separation of church and state. The only female plaintiff, Lenore Lyons, was of Jewish descent but a member of the Unitarian Church.

The *Abington* and Murray *Cases*

As *Engel* wound its way through the lower courts, the *Abington* and *Murray* cases were also under way. In 1956, sixteen-year-old Ellery Frank Schempp, whose religious affiliation was Unitarian, objected to the daily ritual at Abington Senior High School (in a Philadelphia suburb) of reading ten verses out of the Protestant King James Version Bible and the recitation of the Lord's Prayer. Schempp did not agree with a literal reading of the Bible, thought the devotional was a violation of the Establishment Clause, and, with his parents' permission, filed a lawsuit with the aid of the American Civil Liberties Union. In 1960, Madalyn Murray, a social worker and an atheist, sued the Baltimore public school system for exposing her son, William, to daily Bible reading and the Lord's Prayer—morning devotionals she characterized as "brainwashing."

In all three cases, the U.S. Supreme Court ruled official school prayer a violation of the Establishment Clause. In *Engel*, the justices held, 6–1, that "daily classroom invocation of God's blessings as prescribed in the Regents' prayer . . . [is] a religious activity." The decisions in the *Abington* and *Murray* cases were consolidated, with the justices ruling, 8–1, that Bible reading and prayer in the present instances constituted "religious exercises, required by the States in violation of the command of the First Amendment that the Government maintain strict neutrality, neither aiding nor opposing religion."

Justice Potter Stewart dissented in both rulings, arguing that Thomas Jefferson's "sterile metaphor" about a "wall of separation" was "a fallacious oversimplification of the Establishment Clause." Americans, he went on, "are a religious people whose institutions presuppose a Supreme Being." Justice William O. Douglas, while siding with the majority, nevertheless admitted certain inconsistencies. In his *Engel* concurring opinion, the liberal Douglas wrote, "What New York does on the opening of its public schools is what we do when we open court. Our Crier has from the beginning announced the convening of the Court and then added 'God Save the United States and this Honorable Court.' That utterance is a supplication, a prayer in which we, the judges, are free to join, but which we need not recite any more than the students need to recite the New York prayer. What New York does on the opening of its public schools is what each House of Congress does at the opening of each day's business."

High school football players in Odessa, Texas, bow their heads in prayer before a game in September 2000. The prayer session was unsanctioned by the school because of a U.S. Supreme Court ruling in June that banned such activity as unconstitutional. *(Joe Raedle/Newsmakers/Getty Images)*

Aftermath

The general public voiced strong disagreement with the *Engel* decision. In the wake of *Brown v. Board of Education*

(1954), which banned school segregation, the outlawing of school prayer further convinced the right wing that Chief Justice Earl Warren should be impeached. The ultra-right John Birch Society, which responded to *Brown* by mounting a billboard campaign against Warren, used the issue of school prayer to bolster its argument. "Remove Warren, Restore God" was the slogan of a different group, the Committee to Restore God and Prayer in Our Schools. A cartoon in *The New Yorker* magazine depicted Whistler's Mother embroidering a pillowcase with the words, "Impeach Earl Warren."

In the wake of *Engel* and *Abington*, several attempts were made to pass a constitutional amendment that would allow school prayer. In spring 1964, at the urging of U.S. congressman Frank Becker (R-NY) of Long Island, the House Judiciary Committee conducted hearings on school prayer amendments. The "Amen Amendment," introduced by Senator Everett Dirksen (R-IL), failed a Senate vote on September 21, 1966. A second prayer amendment, offered by Congressman Chalmer Wylie (R-OH), was rejected by the House on November 8, 1971. And the Senate failed to approve President Ronald Reagan's prayer amendment on March 20, 1984.

Since the 1970s, state and local governments, emboldened by the influence of the Religious Right, have been testing the legal boundaries of the separation of church and state. In June 1978, Kentucky legislators mandated that public schools display the Ten Commandments, but the law was overturned by the U.S. Supreme Court in *Stone v. Graham* (1980). Alabama mandated a "moment of silence" each day in its school system, but the Supreme Court in *Wallace v. Jaffree* (1985) overturned that mandate on the grounds that its purpose was inherently religious. Clergy-led prayer at public high school commencement exercises was ruled unconstitutional in the high court ruling of *Lee v. Weisman* (1992). And in *Santa Fe Independent School District v. Doe* (2000), the Supreme Court ruled against student-led prayers before the start of school football games.

Roger Chapman

See also: American Civil Liberties Union; *Brown v. Board of Education* (1954); Church and State; Cold War; Communists and Communism; Douglas, William O.; John Birch Society; Judicial Wars; O'Hair, Madalyn Murray; Reagan, Ronald; Religious Right; Warren, Earl.

Further Reading

Dierenfield, Bruce J. *The Battle over School Prayer: How* Engel v. Vitale *Changed America.* Lawrence: University Press of Kansas, 2007.

"Pro and Con: Return Prayer to Public Schools?" *U.S. News & World Report*, September 15, 1980.

Solomon, Stephen D. *Ellery's Protest: How One Young Man Defied Tradition and Sparked the Battle over School Prayer.* Ann Arbor: University of Michigan Press, 2007.

School Shootings

Since the 1990s, deadly shootings on school grounds and college campuses across America have prompted much reaction from culture warriors who have linked the tragedies to various perceived social problems: lax gun control, media violence, declining family values, abandonment of religious instruction, rejection of personal responsibility, and victimization. On April 20, 1999, the worst school shooting to date took place at Columbine High School in Littleton, Colorado, where teenagers Eric Harris and Dylan Klebold utilized homemade bombs, shotguns, a carbine rifle, and a TEC-DC9 pistol to kill twelve fellow students and one teacher while wounding thirty-three others before taking their own lives. The deadliest college shooting occurred at Virginia Polytechnic Institute and State University (Virginia Tech) on April 16, 2007, when Seung-Hui Cho, a South Korean immigrant and senior at the school, used Glock and P22 pistols to shoot to death thirty-three (including himself) while wounding twenty-three others. Both of these attacks, as well as numerous others, involved assailants who were socially alienated, in some cases alleged victims of peer bullying, and struggling with mental health problems.

With each new incident, there is widespread debate over how society should best react to school shootings—specifically, the 333 fatalities between September 1992 and April 2008, as documented by the National School Safety Center. One side argues that media hype has ignored or downplayed statistics showing a decline in school-related shootings. Of the total youth homicides during that time period, less than 1 percent involved school shootings. In addition, of the nation's 30,000 annual shooting deaths, only a handful occur on college campuses. The media fixation on violent news events, they argue, inspires "copy cat" attacks (Cho of Virginia Tech, for example, referred to the Columbine assailants as "martyrs," while the Columbine attackers seemed to have been partially inspired by the Oklahoma City bomber Timothy McVeigh) and provides posthumous infamy (on the day of his attack, Cho mailed tapes and other materials to NBC News). In addition, they argue, too much attention on school shootings diverts limited financial resources from more serious social problems (such as violence that occurs off school grounds), leads to an oppressive school environment (involving metal detectors, surveillance cameras, lockdown drills, zero tolerance policies, and student snitching), and falsely suggests that adolescents are the main perpetrators of gun violence.

Those who think the focus on school shootings has been overblown point out that such violence is not new.

On January 29, 1979, for example, sixteen-year-old Brenda Spencer fired a .22-caliber rifle into a crowd at the Cleveland Elementary School in San Diego, California, across the street from her home, killing two and wounding seven. (Spencer's explanation for the crime—she said she did not like Mondays—inspired the 1979 single "I Don't Like Mondays" by the UK new wave band Boomtown Rats.) The first major college shooting occurred on August 1, 1966, when Charles Whitman, a former altar boy, Eagle Scout, and U.S. Marine, perched himself on the clock tower at the University of Texas at Austin and conducted sniper fire (he was equipped with Remington rifles, an M1 carbine, a shotgun, and other weapons), killing fourteen and wounding thirty-one before being gunned down by Austin police. Ten years later, on July 12, 1976, Edward Charles Allaway committed the so-called library massacre at California State University (Cal State), Fullerton, fatally shooting seven and wounding two with a .22-caliber rifle.

Regardless of these earlier incidents, many believe that the 1990s represented something new and concur with former CBS News anchorman Dan Rather who, following the tragedy at Columbine, pronounced school shootings a "national epidemic." This assessment was based on the increase of school rampage shootings in contradiction to the otherwise general trend of declining school violence. In the eighteen months preceding Columbine, school shootings killed three and wounded seven at Pearl High School in Pearl, Mississippi (October 1, 1997); killed three and wounded five at Heath High School in West Paducah, Kentucky (December 1, 1997); killed five and wounded ten at Westside Middle School in Jonesboro, Arkansas (March 24, 1998); killed one and wounded three at Parker Middle School in Edinboro, Pennsylvania (April 24, 1998); killed two and wounded one at Philadelphia Elementary School in Pomona, California (April 28, 1998); killed one at Lincoln County High School in Fayetteville, Tennessee (May 19, 1998); killed two and wounded twenty-two at Thurston High School in Springfield, Oregon (May 21, 1998); and wounded two at Armstrong High School in Richmond, Virginia (June 15, 1998).

Those advocating special action to curb rampage shootings have conceded that the saturation media coverage has been a factor in inspiring further violence, but they stress the importance of public awareness for foiling plots. Unlike typical school shootings of the past, rampage shootings are usually planned well in advance and even talked about ahead of time. In 2001, the *Journal of the American Medical Association* reported, "Although school-associated violent deaths remain rare events, they have occurred often enough to allow for the detection of patterns and the identification of potential risk factors."

Many of the proposed solutions for preventing school shootings betray a continuation of the culture wars, such as mandating moments of silence and displaying the Ten Commandments in schools; enforcing zero tolerance and requiring school uniforms; arming teachers and making guns more available; making guns less available; banning violent video games; and identifying alienated and disaffected individuals and victims of student bullying. *Bowling for Columbine* (2002), the polemical documentary film by Michael Moore, has linked school shootings to the National Rifle Association (which weeks after Columbine held an abbreviated annual meeting in Denver), the military-industrial complex (the defense contractor Lockheed Martin, it is noted, is the chief employer of Littleton), and class struggle. (Unlike others, Moore rejects the view that the music of Marilyn Manson and violent video games such as Doom were inspirational factors in the Columbine attack.)

In the wake of the Virginia Tech massacre—succeeded by the February 14, 2008, shooting at Northern Illinois University, in which Steven Kazmierczak used a shotgun and Glock pistol to kill seven (including himself) and injure fifteen others—many colleges across the country have bolstered campus security and implemented "alert messaging" systems that include panic buttons on computers.

Roger Chapman

See also: Family Values; Gun Control; Manson, Marilyn; McVeigh, Timothy; Moore, Michael; National Rifle Association; Rather, Dan; School Prayer; Ten Commandments; Victimhood.

Further Reading

Gabarino, James. *Lost Boys: Why Our Sons Turn Violent and How We Can Save Them.* New York: Free Press, 1999.

Lebrun, Marcel. *Books, Blackboards, and Bullets: School Shootings and Violence in America.* Lanham, MD: Rowman & Littlefield Education, 2009.

Moore, Mark Harrison. *Deadly Lessons: Understanding School Violence.* Washington, DC: National Academy Press, 2003.

Newman, Katharine S., Cybelle Fox, David Harding, Jal Mehta, and Wendy Roth. *Rampage: The Social Roots of School Shootings.* New York: Basic Books, 2004.

Zoba, Wendy Murray. *Day of Reckoning: Columbine and the Search for America's Soul.* Grand Rapids, MI: Brazos Press, 2000.

School Vouchers

Promoted as "school choice," school voucher programs give parents the option of sending their children to private or parochial schools instead of public schools by offering a voucher, tax credit, or scholarship to cover part or all of the tuition. The debate on school vouchers has raised fundamental questions regarding the purpose, control, and funding of public education in America.

Voucher proponents advocate market-based freedom of choice, arguing that it will increase educational opportunities for students attending failing public schools, as well as produce more effective schools and better educational outcomes for all children. Voucher programs, backers insist, promote equity by providing low-income families the option to leave underperforming schools—an option previously available only to families with greater financial means. Proponents also argue that school choice programs encourage increased parental involvement and more efficient educational organizations because the money allocated to parents and students flows directly from the parent to the school rather than through the local, state, or federal bureaucracy.

Opponents of school vouchers maintain that such programs lead to greater economic, racial, and religious stratification; weaken public schools; undermine the education profession; and threaten public school systems' ability to offer all children equal access to quality education. In general, opponents regard vouchers as part of the privatization movement that seeks to dismantle public services, including universal education. Critics of vouchers also point out that private schools are effectively out of reach to the poorest students because vouchers, tax credits, and other scholarship programs often do not cover the entire cost of tuition. Moreover, private schools, unlike public ones, have the right to reject students; thus, having a voucher does not necessarily mean having a choice.

The most controversial school choice programs allow parents to use vouchers to pay tuition at religious schools. One such program is the Cleveland (Ohio) Scholarship and Tutoring Program. Of all voucher students in Cleveland in the early 2000s, 99.4 percent attended religious schools. Opponents of government-subsidized faith-based programs view them as a violation of the separation of church and state. In the case of *Zelman v. Simmons-Harris* (2002), however, the U.S. Supreme Court upheld Cleveland's school voucher program, ruling that vouchers can be used to pay for tuition at sectarian schools without violating the Establishment Clause of the First Amendment.

Almost all existing school voucher programs have been the subject of legal challenge, with varying results. They have been upheld by state courts in Arizona, Illinois, Maine, Ohio, and Wisconsin but overturned in Vermont and Florida. Given the variations in the state programs, the divergent interpretations of state constitutional provisions, and the need to improve public schools, the debate over education and the efficacy of school voucher programs no doubt will continue.

Traci L. Nelson

See also: Academic Freedom; *Brown v. Board of Education* (1954); Busing, School; Charter Schools; Education Reform; Faith-Based Programs; Privatization.

Further Reading

Lupu, Ira C., and Robert W. Tuttle. "*Zelman*'s Future: Vouchers, Sectarian Providers, and the Next Round of Constitutional Battles." *Notre Dame Law Review* 78 (2003): 917–94.

Merrifield, John. *The School Choice Wars.* London: Scarecrow, 2001.

Omand, H. Lillian. "The Struggle for School Choice Policy After *Zelman*: Regulation v. Free Market." *Cato Institute Policy Analysis* no. 495, October 29, 2003.

Ravitch, Diane, and Maris A. Vinovskis, eds. *Learning from the Past: What History Teaches Us About School Reform.* Baltimore: Johns Hopkins University Press, 1995.

Smith, Colleen Carlton. "*Zelman*'s Evolving Legacy: Selective Funding of Secular Private Schools in State School Choice Programs." *Virginia Law Review* 89:8 (2003): 1953–2004.

Schwarzenegger, Arnold

The Austrian-born former world champion bodybuilder and Hollywood film star Arnold Schwarzenegger became governor of California in November 2003 after winning an election the previous month in which the incumbent, Democrat Gray Davis, was recalled. A Republican, fiscally conservative but socially liberal, Schwarzenegger went on to win reelection to a full term in 2006. His background has prompted comparison to both Ronald Reagan (an actor turned California governor, 1967–1975) and Jesse Ventura (a professional wrestler turned Minnesota governor, 1999–2003). In the culture wars, Schwarzenegger positioned himself as a political moderate, claiming to be "post-partisan."

The son of a Nazi army veteran, police chief, and champion curler, Arnold Alois Schwarzenegger was born in Graz, Austria, on July 30, 1947. He briefly served in the Austrian army (1965) and then went on to win thirteen world champion bodybuilding titles, including Mr. Olympia, Mr. World, and Mr. Universe (1965–1980). In the late 1960s, he moved to Los Angeles and by the 1970s was appearing in Hollywood movies. After studying at the University of Wisconsin at Superior (BA, business and international economics, 1980), Schwarzenegger became an American citizen in 1983. Three years later he married Maria Shriver, a television journalist and a member of the Kennedy clan. (Her mother was Eunice Kennedy Shriver, sister of the late president John F. Kennedy.) Beginning in the early 1980s, Schwarzenegger starred in a run of blockbuster action films, including *Conan the Barbarian* (1982), *The Terminator* (1984), *Predator* (1987), *Total Recall* (1990), *Terminator 2* (1991), and *Terminator 3* (2003). Before becoming governor, he served on national and state physical fitness councils.

Some believe that Schwarzenegger's attraction to public service was motivated in part to defuse criticism about the violent nature of his films. He cultivated a "family values" persona with his starring role in *Kinder-*

garten Cop (1990) and a $1 million donation to promote a California ballot initiative to increase after-school programs for children. Later, while a candidate for governor, his wholesome image was tarnished by reports of sexual misconduct against several young women. After the terrorist attacks of September 11, 2001, he served on a board to provide for the family victims of the World Trade Center disaster. Ironically, the release date of his film *Collateral Damage* (2001), about a terrorist plot in the United States, was delayed because of the real attacks in New York. As governor, Schwarzenegger came to be known as the "Governator," a play on his popular Terminator character.

In November 2005, Schwarzenegger flabbergasted Sacramento Republican circles when he announced that Susan P. Kennedy, a prominent local Democrat and lesbian, would be his chief of staff. Kennedy (no relation to Shriver) had been a deputy chief of staff for Governor Davis but agreed to work for Schwarzenegger because of his $222 billion plan to improve the state's infrastructure without raising taxes. The appointment of Kennedy followed a largely unsuccessful year for Schwarzenegger, in which he attempted to undermine the power of Democratic legislators (whom he called "girlie men") and steer the state in a more conservative direction by introducing four ballot measures—to extend probation for new public school teachers, restrict union political spending, alter legislative boundaries, and introduce a cap on the state budget—all of which the voters rejected. Despite that setback, Schwarzenegger overwhelmingly won reelection in November 2006. Since then, members of his own party have criticized him for moving to the left, as characterized by his endorsing an increase in the minimum wage, mandating a reduction in the state's greenhouse gas emissions, moving some nonviolent female criminals from jail to rehabilitation programs, and backing universal health care. Opponents of capital punishment were disappointed by his refusal to commute the death sentence of former Crips gang leader Stanley Tookie Williams in December 2005.

Roger Chapman

See also: Capital Punishment; Family Values; Gangs; Global Warming; Health Care; Prison Reform; Reagan, Ronald; Republican Party; September 11; Sexual Harassment; Ventura, Jesse.

Further Reading

Cooper, Marc. "Is the Terminator in Freefall?" *Nation*, October 31, 2005.

Leamer, Laurence. *Fantastic: The Life of Arnold Schwarzenegger.* New York: St. Martin's Press, 2005.

Wilentz, Amy. *I Feel Earthquakes More Often Than They Happen: Coming to California in an Age of Schwarzenegger.* New York: Simon & Schuster, 2006.

Science Wars

The wide-ranging political and religious conflicts over science in contemporary America—the "science wars"—reflect differences between the consensus view of a particular scientific community or discipline on the one hand, and the Religious Right, corporate economic interests, or advocates of a political ideology, usually conservative, on the other hand. The overarching context of the contemporary science wars is the growth of the federal government in the post–World War II era, leading to federal involvement in local education to bolster science curricula; a body of federal regulations regarding the environment, health, communication systems, transportation, and other areas of everyday life; and government spending on research and development for military-industrial endeavors.

The religious science wars, in particular, are fought over such issues as evolution versus creationism, stem-cell research, and the science of sexuality. Science wars driven by economic interests include the long struggle of the tobacco companies to deny the health risks of cigarettes and secondhand smoke, and the petroleum industry's support for skeptics of global warming. Conflicts between those espousing a conservative political agenda and the scientific community include those surrounding the Strategic Defense Initiative (SDI, or the "Star Wars" antimissile defense system) proposed during the Reagan administration in the 1980s but viewed by most scientists as impractical. Such is the prestige of science in modern society, however, that none of the opposition groups has declared itself directly in opposition to science. Instead, they typically claim to be the proponents of a more true and valid science than that of a corrupt or politicized scientific establishment.

Collaboration between business interests, political conservatives, and the Religious Right on various issues has strengthened the antiscience movement. In Congress, it has been strongest among Republicans. Various GOP presidential administrations, particularly those of Ronald Reagan and George W. Bush, have been known for supporting political positions that are in opposition to the mainstream scientific consensus.

Among the most prominent corporate science wars of the postwar era have been those waged in response to the environmental and public health movements. In both cases, scientific data and research findings have been ignored or attacked by corporate interests because of their negative commercial implications. The tactic was pioneered by the tobacco industry's decades-long campaign against scientific research linking smoking to cancer and other diseases. Another early example was the organized response of chemical and pesticide industries to Rachel Carson's environmentalist classic *Silent Spring* (1962), which highlighted the harmful effects of the insecticide DDT. Tactics used by commercial interests have included outright denial, character assassination, and the use of "fringe" scientists, often directly or indirectly compensated by the commercial interests themselves, to cast doubt on the mainstream position.

Several conservative think tanks have been especially associated with the science wars, among them the American Enterprise Institute, the Heritage Foundation, and the George C. Marshall Institute. These and other corporate-funded policy and research organizations issue scientific reports and technological assessments with the goal of making the mainstream view on certain issues seem inconclusive or in dispute. All three of the above-mentioned groups, for example, remain skeptical regarding the threat of global warming.

In media coverage, the conventions of journalistic "evenhandedness" and balance often cause reporters to present the scientific consensus and the claims of opponents on an equal footing. Corporate-backed science warriors have also developed a distinctive rhetoric, using terms such as "junk science" to condemn their opponents, while describing their own views as "sound science."

By no means are all environmental science wars driven by the political right. One issue that pits the scientific mainstream against forces on the environmentalist left is genetic modification of food crops. While organizations such as Greenpeace cast doubt on the safety of such foods, their relative lack of financial resources has made it harder for them to have an impact on this issue.

The religious science wars have centered primarily on the life sciences and spilled over into the social sciences. Among the oldest and most contentious issues, of course, is evolution, pitting the religious view, based on a literal account of creation in Genesis, against the overwhelming consensus of the scientific community that life has evolved in a natural process over billions of years. In *The Scandal of the Evangelical Mind* (1994), the evangelical academic Mark Noll titles one chapter "Thinking About Science," in which he laments "the damaging intellectual habits of fundamentalism" with its fixation on so-called creation science.

Other major and recurring concerns for conservative Christians are the ethical and religious issues raised by advances in medicine and the life sciences—or "bioethics." These range from the debate on abortion and the use of embryonic stem cells for scientific research to in vitro fertilization, euthanasia, genetic engineering, and the use of medical equipment to sustain brain-dead patients.

Religious science warriors often place their struggles in a cultural context, claiming that the real enemy is secularism and its "culture of death." They have sometimes forged alliances of convenience with postmodernists to attack established scientific truth in favor of intellectual pluralism, notably in the campaign to teach the "intelligent design" theory of the development of life alongside the scientific theory of evolution. Christian religious

activists have also opposed the scientific consensus in denying the effectiveness of condoms in preventing AIDS, asserting a link between abortion and breast cancer, and supporting "abstinence only" sex education.

Hostilities between the Republican Party and ideological conservatives on the one hand, and the nation's scientific community on the other hand intensified in the 1990s, particularly after the GOP won a majority in both houses of Congress in 1994. The new Republican Congress dismantled that body's respected scientific advisory body, the Office of Technology Assessment, in 1995. But the science wars reached new heights during the administration of George W. Bush, which was powerfully influenced by both religious conservatives and corporate interests. Bush's strongly conservative politics combined with his effort to subordinate nonpolitical executive branch appointees, including scientists, to political officials. The political appointees were often former industry lobbyists, Religious Right figures, or professional Republican operatives lacking scientific credentials and convinced that the scientific community was an enemy.

One major struggle in the Bush administration involved global warming. Climate researchers throughout the federal government complained that political pressure was put on them not to speak openly about climate change. References to global warming were often omitted from press releases, reports, and Web sites, while politically appointed supervisors controlled or blocked the scientists from speaking with the media. The issue was a politically sensitive one in the Bush administration, given that the president's rival in the 2000 election, Al Gore, had emerged as the world's most prominent advocate for changes in environmental policy.

In 2004, opposition to the Bush administration in the scientific community was voiced in a statement by the Union of Concerned Scientists, an environmental group located in Cambridge, Massachusetts. Eventually, forty-eight Noble laureates and many other distinguished American scientists would associate themselves with the statement. Many of the signatories and other scientists organized in support of John Kerry's 2004 campaign for president.

William E. Burns

See also: Anti-Intellectualism; Biotech Revolution; Carson, Rachel; Creationism and Intelligent Design; Food and Drug Administration; Fundamentalism, Religious; Genetically Modified Foods; Global Warming; Nuclear Age; Postmodernism; Religious Right; Smoking in Public; Sokal Affair; Strategic Defense Initiative; Think Tanks.

Further Reading

Forrest, Barbara, and Paul R. Gross. *Creationism's Trojan Horse: The Wedge of Intelligent Design.* New York: Oxford University Press, 2004.

Glantz, Stanton A., John Slade, Lisa A. Bero, Peter Hanauer, and Deborah E. Barnes, eds. *The Cigarette Papers.* Berkeley: University of California Press, 1998.

Mooney, Chris. *The Republican War on Science.* New York: Basic Books, 2005.

Noll, Mark A. *The Scandal of the Evangelical Mind.* Grand Rapids, MI: Eerdmans, 1994.

Secular Humanism

Secular humanism, a philosophy that looks to reason and science as the basis for moral decision making and cultural expression, has become a highly charged issue in America's culture wars. Those who espouse secular humanism generally regard organized religion, particularly traditional Christianity, as a threat to rationality and human progress. The Religious Right has attacked secular humanists for promoting a type of religion that eschews God, faith, moral rectitude, and traditional values.

The American Humanist Association, an organization founded to promote humanism, details its secular philosophy in Humanist Manifesto I (1933), Humanist Manifesto II (1973), and Humanist Manifesto III (2003). The first document, endorsed by the philosopher John Dewey and some thirty others, espoused "religious humanism" as a twentieth-century alternative to traditional religion. While not rejecting theism, the manifesto elevated "modern science" over "supernatural or cosmic guarantees." The second manifesto went on to denounce "traditional dogmatic or authoritarian religions that place revelation, God, ritual, or creed above human need or experience" and dismissed the notion of "divine purpose or providence for the human species." Firing a shot in the culture wars, the document validated birth control, abortion, and divorce, while largely blaming sexual repression on religion. Humanist Manifesto II was signed by a number of prominent individuals, including feminist Betty Friedan, behavioral psychologist B.F. Skinner, and science writer Isaac Asimov. Humanist Manifesto III defined humanism as "a progressive philosophy of life . . . without supernaturalism," emphasizing science and reason, and declared ethical values "derived from human need and interest as tested by experience."

Some of the signatories of the previous manifestos later endorsed "A Secular Humanist Declaration" (1980), which was drafted by philosopher Paul Kurtz and appeared in the debut issue of the *Free Inquiry*, the organ of the newly established Council for Democratic and Secular Humanism (later shortened to the Council for Secular Humanism). Kurtz was largely reacting to the Religious Right and its claim that secular humanism is a religion. His manifesto identified "democratic secular humanism" with "free inquiry" and maintained that people can lead wholesome lives without religion. Kurtz's critics regard his "free inquiry" as disingenuous, since it rejects theism outright.

Conservative Christians voiced their opposition to secular humanism in a variety of writings, among them Homer Duncan's *Secular Humanism: The Most Dangerous Religion in the World* (1979), Tim LaHaye's *The Battle for the Mind* (1980), Francis A. Schaeffer's *A Christian Manifesto* (1981), Josh McDowell and Don Stewart's *Understanding Secular Religions* (1982), and John W. Whitehead's *The Stealing of America* (1983). Opponents maintain that secular humanism is intolerant of Judeo-Christian beliefs and promotes moral relativism. Since secular humanism operates as a nontheistic religion, they argue, it should be subjected to the same constitutional constraints imposed on all other religions.

In the U.S. Supreme Court decision *Torcaso v. Watkins* (1961), secular humanism was classified as a religion in a footnote. This inspired the Religious Right to challenge the teaching of secular humanism in public schools, arguing that any promotion of its tenets in the classroom is a violation of the First Amendment's Establishment Clause. This argument was put to the test in Mobile, Alabama, in a legal showdown pitting Pat Robertson's National Legal Foundation against People for the American Way and the American Civil Liberties Union. In *Douglas T. Smith et al. v. Board of School Commissioners of Mobile County* (1987), U.S. District Court Judge W. Brevard Hand ruled that the Mobile school system had established "a religion of secularism" and ordered the removal of more than forty "secularism" books from the classroom. On appeal five months later, however, the ruling was overturned.

The Religious Right continues to argue that if public schools are allowed to advance the values of secular humanism while suppressing Judeo-Christianity, then the absence of a genuine marketplace of ideas renders by default a public religion of secular humanism. This viewpoint has resonated with many conservative Christian parents, propelling the homeschool movement. Fundamentalists have equated the teaching of evolution with secular humanism, arguing that the marketplace of ideas should require that the theory of intelligent design also be taught in the classroom. Some critics of the Religious Right argue that it labels anything not in accord with its perspective as secular humanism. Traditional religion and secular humanism, since they share some basic values, perspectives, and points of view, are not strictly binary opposites.

Roger Chapman

See also: American Civil Liberties Union; Book Banning; Church and State; Creationism and Intelligent Design; Evangelicalism; Friedan, Betty; Fundamentalism, Religious; Homeschooling; Relativism, Moral; Religious Right; Robertson, Pat; Schaeffer, Francis.

Further Reading

Deckman, Melissa M. *School Board Battles: The Christian Right in Local Politics*. Washington, DC: Georgetown University Press, 2004.

Ingber, Stanley. "Religion or Ideology: A Needed Clarification of the Religion Clauses." *Stanford Law Review* 41:2 (1989): 233–333.

Kurtz, Paul. *In Defense of Secular Humanism*. Buffalo, NY: Prometheus Books, 1983.

Tourney, Christopher P. "Evolution and Secular Humanism." *Journal of the American Academy of Religion* 61:2 (1993): 275–301.

Webber, Robert E. *Secular Humanism: Threat and Challenge*. Grand Rapids, MI: Zondervan, 1982.

Seeger, Pete

Renowned folk musician and social activist Pete Seeger has been a major figure in leftist causes, advocating the formation of labor unions, civil rights, the end of the Vietnam War, and environmental protection. He was also a driving force behind the socially conscious American folk music revival of the 1950s and 1960s, making the folk song an instrument of protest. In more recent times, he has influenced the music of Bruce Springsteen and others.

Born on May 3, 1919, Peter R. Seeger was the son of musicologist Charles Seeger and violinist Constance Seeger in New York City. Dropping out of Harvard at age nineteen, he traveled across the nation collecting songs for the musicologists John and Alan Lomax. A talented musician with an affinity for the working class, Seeger often sang at migrant camps and labor rallies during the Depression. In 1940, he met folk singer Woody Guthrie and that December formed a folk band, the Almanac Singers, with Guthrie, Lee Hays, and Millard Lampell. During this time, Seeger joined the Communist Party and was highly critical of President Franklin D. Roosevelt for not strongly supporting labor causes.

An avowed pacifist but also a hater of fascism, Seeger served in the U.S. Army during World War II. After his discharge, he founded People's Song, Inc. (1946), which published union songs and folk songs. He also formed the Weavers (1948), another folk singing group. By 1950, the group was under surveillance by the FBI and the McCarran Committee for alleged communist activities. Blacklisted in 1952, the Weavers disbanded. His detractors called Seeger "Khrushchev's songbird." In 1955, though five years earlier he had quit the Communist Party, he was summoned before the House Committee on Un-American Activities. Showing his disdain for the investigation but proclaiming that he had nothing to hide, he refused to answer questions, citing the First Amendment rather than the Fifth Amendment, which would have protected him from self-incrimination. Consequently, he was convicted of ten counts of contempt of Congress and sentenced to a year in prison. All was overturned on appeal.

Seeger continued his music and activism throughout the 1950s and 1960s, becoming involved in the civil rights movement and the folk music revival, and introducing Martin Luther King, Jr., to his version of "We Shall Overcome." His songs "Where Have All the Flowers Gone?" (1961) and "Turn, Turn, Turn" (1966) were a part of the Vietnam War protests. In his later years, Seeger also became involved in environmental causes, especially along the Hudson River in New York. In his mid-eighties, he actively opposed the U.S. invasion of Iraq. Bruce Springsteen's album *We Shall Overcome: The Seeger Sessions* (2006), which includes folk and protest songs that Seeger performed, was created in tribute to the artist. In 2009, Singer performed with Springsteen in an outdoor concert in front of the Lincoln Memorial in celebration of the election of Barack Obama as president.

Rachel Donaldson

See also: Civil Rights Movement; Communists and Communism; Environmental Movement; Guthrie, Woody, and Arlo Guthrie; Labor Unions; McCarthy, Joseph; McCarthyism; Springsteen, Bruce; Vietnam War; War Protesters.

Further Reading

Bromberg, Minna, and Gary Alan Fine. "Resurrecting the Red: Pete Seeger and the Purification of Difficult Reputations." *Social Forces* 80 (June 2002): 1135–55.

Dunaway, David King. *How Can I Keep from Singing: Pete Seeger*. New York: McGraw-Hill, 1981.

Seeger, Pete. *Where Have All the Flowers Gone: A Singer's Stories, Songs, Seeds, Robberies*. Bethlehem, PA: Sing Out, 1993.

Wilkinson, Alec. "The Protest Singer." *The New Yorker*, April 17, 2006.

Winkler, Alan M. *"To Everything There Is a Season": Pete Seeger and the Power of Song*. New York: Oxford University Press, 2009.

September 11

On the morning of September 11, 2001, nineteen terrorists hijacked four American commercial passenger aircraft and crashed three of them into high-profile targets in the United States. Two planes flew directly into the twin towers of the World Trade Center in New York, causing the buildings to collapse completely within a few hours. A third plane plowed into the Pentagon, the headquarters of the U.S. Department of Defense in Arlington, Virginia, just across the Potomac River from Washington, D.C., damaging one of its five sides. The fourth plane failed to reach its target in Washington, crashing in rural Somerset County, Pennsylvania. Passengers on that plane challenged the hijackers after learning about the earlier attacks, and the hijackers apparently responded by crashing the plane before being overpowered. Altogether, the attacks resulted in the deaths of nearly 3,000 people, including all onboard the four planes.

Initial Reaction

Americans responded to the attacks with a rush of patriotism, sympathy for the many victims, and anger at those who supported and carried out the attacks. In New York and Washington, the response of police and firefighters, many working around the clock at the indescribable disaster scenes, made them national heroes. President George W. Bush became a spokesman for the country's sorrow and rage, vowing that those responsible would be brought to justice. His approval rating soared to 86 percent, the highest ever attained by a U.S. president. New York City mayor Rudolph Giuliani became a national figure almost overnight as a spokesman for the city that sustained the most damage.

Within hours of the attacks, government investigators traced several of the hijackers to the terrorist organization al-Qaeda, whose leader, Osama bin Laden, directed international terror attacks from a headquarters in Afghanistan, under the protection of the ruling Taliban party, a fundamentalist Muslim group. Al-Qaeda had already been implicated in an earlier attack on the World Trade Center in 1993, in which a powerful bomb was detonated in the underground parking garage, causing six deaths and more than a thousand injuries as the smoke-filled towers were evacuated. In 1998, bin Laden publicly called for the killing of American civilians. His organization is believed to have planned and carried out a series of subsequent attacks. In 1998, terrorists carried out coordinated bombing attacks on the U.S. embassies in Kenya and Tanzania, both in eastern Africa; 12 Americans and more than 200 others were killed in the bombings. Two years later, terrorists rammed an improvised bomb against the side of the USS *Cole,* a U.S. Navy ship anchored in the harbor of Aden, the capital of Yemen at the southern tip of the Arabian Peninsula. Seventeen U.S. naval personnel were killed, and forty others were injured.

The Bush administration reported that al-Qaeda was motivated by a hatred of freedom and Western-style democracy. Bin Laden attributed the attacks to particular actions and policies of the U.S. government, including support of Israel against its Arab adversaries and the presence of U.S. military installations in Saudi Arabia, the home of Islam's most sacred places, since the end of the first Persian Gulf War in 1991. Bin Laden also accused the U.S. government of sowing discord among Muslim people; propping up cruel Middle Eastern regimes, including the Saudi monarchy; and exploiting Muslim countries to gain access to their huge oil reserves.

The Bush administration responded to the attacks by declaring a global "War on Terror" with the express goals of destroying al-Qaeda, bringing Osama bin Laden to justice, and preventing the further expansion of international terror networks. The primary tools of this campaign would be increased international intelligence and law enforcement, combined with economic sanctions and military action against states harboring terrorist groups. The first battle in this campaign began in early October 2001, when the U.S. led an international coalition on an invasion of Afghanistan to overthrow the Taliban, which had been harboring al-Qaeda, and to search for bin Laden and his lieutenants. The invasion succeeded in removing the Taliban from power, and the occupying authority set up a new Afghan government. Al-Qaeda and bin Laden slipped away, however, establishing new camps in the remote mountains of western Pakistan, near the Afghan border.

A year and a half later, the United States led a less inclusive coalition of countries in an invasion of Iraq that sought the removal of Saddam Hussein and the confiscation of the weapons of mass destruction (WMD) he was said to possess. The Bush administration claimed that there was a link between the Iraqi dictator and the September 11 attacks; although the president later backed down from that position, many Americans remain convinced of the initial allegations. Critics of the Bush administration and the Iraq War believe that the supposed tie was a fabrication to garner public support for the 2003 invasion.

Laying Blame

In struggling to understand the attacks, some Americans blamed the Islamic faith itself and its millions of adherents. Others blamed Muslims of Arab or Middle Eastern descent. In the weeks following the attack, a number of Arabs and natives of other Muslim countries were victims of hate crimes in several U.S. cities and towns. Others were subjected to verbal abuse and community suspicion. American Muslim organizations condemned the al-Qaeda attack and denied that their members were involved as participants or sympathizers. Saudi Arabia, where fifteen of the nineteen attackers were born, launched a public advertising campaign in the United States, condemning the attacks and pointing out that al-Qaeda had also committed terrorist acts on Saudi territory and against the Saudi government.

A few conservative American religious leaders attributed the September 11 attacks not only to Islam but to moral decay in the United States. The prominent televangelist Jerry Falwell blamed the attacks on pagans, abortionists, feminists, gays and lesbians, the American Civil Liberties Union, People for the American Way (a liberal lobbying group), and all "secularists." Whereas certain leaders of the Religious Right attributed the attacks to some form of divine punishment, the social conservative Dinesh D'Souza, in *The Enemy at Home: The Cultural Left and Its Responsibility for 9/11* (2007), asserts that Muslim anger against the United States is a "visceral rage" against American leftist cultural excesses.

Many found meaning in the works of the academics Bernard Lewis, Benjamin R. Barber, and Samuel P. Huntington. For years leading up to September 11, the Near Eastern scholar Lewis had maintained that Islamic fundamentalism is a reaction against secularism and modernism. Furthermore, as he explained in his seminal *Atlantic Monthly* essay "The Roots of Muslim Rage" (September 1990), Muslims feel aggrieved by their "lost superiority" as their societies lag further behind the West in power and wealth. It was Lewis who coined the phrase "clash of civilizations" to describe this conflict between Islamic fundamentalism and Western culture. After the September 11 attacks, Lewis elaborated on his thesis in *What Went Wrong? The Clash Between Islam and Modernity in the Middle East* (2002). The political theorist Barber, in *Jihad vs. McWorld* (1995), had earlier emphasized a conflict between "tribalism" and "globalism." The political scientist Huntington, borrowing a key phrase from Lewis, had written *The Clash of Civilizations and the Remaking of World Order* (1996), which predicted global instability in the wake of the Cold War due to cultural differences. These authors were frequently quoted by commentators who, in the aftermath of September 11, tried to make sense of "why they hate us."

Liberal critics found fault with U.S. military and foreign policy, charging that it had contributed to the rise of militant terrorist groups. In *9-11* (2001), the MIT professor Noam Chomsky, a longtime radical critic of U.S. policy, asserted that basic American foreign policy had contributed to the September 11 tragedy. He argued that the U.S. record of imperialism and abuse of other countries was sure to arouse violent and terrorist responses. In fact, he argued, the United States itself can be considered "a leading terrorist state." The former *New York Times* foreign correspondent Stephen Kinzer, in *All the Shah's Men: An American Coup and the Roots of Middle East Terror* (2003), likewise makes the argument that American foreign adventures laid the groundwork for September 11. These views of Chomsky and Kinzer harmonize with the thoughts of Ahmed Rashid, the Pakistani journalist, who in *Taliban: Militant Islam, Oil and Fundamentalism in Central Asia* (2000) suggests that the U.S. covert operations in Afghanistan during the Cold War acted as the "midwife" in giving birth to al-Qaeda.

One of the most controversial "laying blame" assessments was offered by Ward Churchill, an ethnic studies professor at the University of Colorado at Boulder. In his 2001 Internet essay "Some People Push Back: On the Justice of Roosting Chickens," Churchill argued that certain victims of the World Trade Center were not so innocent because they had been serving as "technocrats of empire." The September 11 attacks, he suggested, were a "befitting" way to harm "the little Eichmanns inhabiting the sterile sanctuary of the twin towers." These comments caught the attention of Fox News commentator Bill O'Reilly, who gave Churchill so much negative publicity that it led to the professor's firing in 2007. In another dramatic episode, again in outrage over the argument that the terrorist attacks were retribution for American foreign policy, O'Reilly in a February 4, 2003, broadcast angrily yelled at his on-air guest Jeremy Glick, whose father had been killed in the World Trade Center attacks.

Antiterrorist Measures and Their Critics

The U.S. government enacted several significant and controversial pieces of legislation in the wake of the September 11 attacks. One action involved a major reorganization of the executive branch to place nearly all domestic security agencies under a single cabinet-level organization, the new Department of Homeland Security. Although many commentators welcomed the reorganization, the department got off to a rocky start. One of its first acts was to create a Homeland Security Advisory System, a five-tier, color-coded threat scale to indicate the danger level of new terrorist attacks and trigger specific actions by federal and local authorities. The system was soon criticized because there were no publicly announced criteria for setting danger levels, and the nature of supposed threats was never disclosed. Critics complained that the threat scale could be used for political purposes—for example, to increase or decrease public apprehension about danger before an election or to pressure legislators to pass or vote down specific legislation. Other Homeland Security documents became targets for comedians and satirists. For example, a document recommending actions in case of a terror attack suggested that a house be sealed with plastic tape or duct tape to protect inhabitants from a chemical or biological attack.

Even prior to the establishment of the new security department, the government proposed and strongly pushed the USA PATRIOT Act, giving the president and executive departments sweeping powers to carry out the War on Terror. Critics charged that in providing for increased surveillance of terrorist suspects, the act allowed for the invasion of privacy of U.S. citizens and allowed illegal domestic intelligence gathering without court approval. Critics also complained that the provisions for detaining terrorist suspects recalled the Alien Registration Act of 1940, which was used after the United States entered World War II in 1941 to justify the internment of Japanese Americans and Japanese resident aliens. The USA PATRIOT Act was used to justify the fingerprinting and registration of approximately 80,000 Arab and Muslim immigrants to the United States and the detention of roughly 5,000 foreign nationals. A number of other countries also passed antiterror legislation, froze the accounts of suspected terrorists and their associates, and arrested thousands suspected of being members of terrorist cells.

Al-Qaeda and Taliban combatants, or suspects who were captured by allied forces in Afghanistan or by antiterror agents in other parts of the world, were designated "illegal enemy combatants." The U.S. government asserted that these individuals did not qualify for the protections extended to prisoners of war under international law and established a special detention center for them at the U.S. military base in Guantánamo Bay, Cuba. The government further maintained that the prison was not subject to international law since it was neither part of the United States nor under the control of the government of Cuba. Thus, interrogation methods, prisoner welfare, and criminal procedure would be decided solely by the executive branch of the U.S. government. Investigations later revealed that other "unofficial" prisons were being operated by U.S. intelligence agencies in other parts of the world. These prisons housed suspects who had been captured by "extraordinary rendition"—apprehension and removal by international intelligence officers with or without the cooperation of local law enforcement agencies. The treatment of prisoners in these undocumented prisons was not subject to review of any kind. In fact, the United States (and other governments suspected of cooperating) denied the existence of the prisons altogether.

Many of the government claims under the USA PATRIOT Act and related executive actions were later rejected by federal courts in cases brought by Guantánamo detainees, forcing changes in procedure in trying "enemy combatants." In 2008, the status of the Guantánamo Bay prison itself became an issue in the presidential campaign. Democratic candidate Barack Obama, who condemned the prison, was elected in November. Soon after his inauguration in January 2009, he issued an order that the prison be closed within one year.

Meanwhile, the events of 9/11 continued to bewilder many Americans. One conspiracy theory suggests that the U.S. government had prior information about the attack but failed to prevent it. Another suggests that agents of the United States actively planned and executed the attack, presumably to gain some benefit in international position or in dictating domestic policy. In 2004, Michael Moore's documentary film *Fahrenheit 9/11* suggested that the business relationship between the Bush family and the ruling Saud family of Saudi Arabia complicated the prevention of the attack and its later investigation.

J.D. Jordan and Roger Chapman

See also: Abu Ghraib and Gitmo; Bush Family; Central Intelligence Agency; Cheney Family; Chomsky, Noam; Conspiracy Theories; Falwell, Jerry; Moore, Michael; Muslim Americans; Saudi Arabia; September 11 Memorial; USA PATRIOT Act.

Further Reading
Chomsky, Noam. *9–11*. New York: Seven Stories Press, 2001.
Churchill, Ward. *On the Justice of Roosting Chickens: Reflections on the Consequences of U.S. Imperial Arrogance and Criminality.* Oakland, CA: AK Press, 2003.
Clarke, Richard. *Against All Enemies: Inside America's War on Terror.* New York: Free Press, 2004.
May, Ernest R. *The 9/11 Commission Report with Related Documents.* Boston: Bedford / St. Martin's, 2007.
Mayer, Jane. *The Dark Side: The Inside Story of How the War on Terror Turned into a War on American Ideals.* New York: Doubleday, 2008.
Meyssan, Thierry. *9/11: The Big Lie.* London: Carnot USA Books, 2002.

September 11 Memorial

In January 2004, a design titled *Reflecting Absence,* by architects Michael Arad and Peter Walker, was announced as the winner of an international competition to create a memorial plan for the World Trade Center site in New York City. The project was headed by the newly established Lower Manhattan Development Company (LMDC), whose aim was to rebuild ground zero and create a permanent memorial to the victims and heroes of the terrorist attacks of February 26, 1993, and September 11, 2001. At the heart of the project was a belief that the memorial should reflect both individual sacrifice and the shared values that had been threatened by the attacks. The LMDC also sought to shape a commemorative process that was unprecedented in its attention to public sentiment. Esteemed artists and architects, including the designer of the Vietnam Veterans Memorial, Maya Lin, made up the jury that chose the winning design, but the panel also included scholars, a widow of the September 11 attack, a resident, and a local business owner. Despite the attempts to accommodate a variety of interest groups, the project generated heated controversy.

The design criteria set out by the LMDC were motivated by several immutable factors, among them the limits of the space itself. In February 2003, Memory Foundations, the concept of Studio Daniel Libeskind, was selected as the principal element in the project to rebuild Lower Manhattan. Although the design preserved certain elements of the original site, including a remaining wall, it was also meant to inspire a sense of rebirth. The centerpiece was a 1,776-foot (541-meter) building known as the Freedom Tower. While Libeskind's plan was separate from the commemorative project, the structure would provide the physical context for the memorial. More important, the LMDC, with input from residents, survivors, and victims' families, developed a series of guiding principles for the design. The foremost goal was to create a place that underscored the compassion and honor of those who had sacrificed and to reaffirm American strength and commitment to freedom.

Despite criticism that the eight finalists had produced somewhat banal and similar concepts, Arad and Walker's proposal was said to best capture the central principles of the memorial project: enhance the physical landscape, preserve the "footprints" of the Twin Towers, incorporate the names of the dead, and include a below-ground cultural center and museum to tell the personal stories of the attacks. Still, problems quickly emerged that challenged the sought-after cohesion of the commemorative process. In particular, some New Yorkers began to question what the memorial would say about the event itself and its historical implications. *Reflecting Absence*, particularly in contrast to the overt patriotism of the Freedom Tower, seemed to focus too intently on grief and loss. Some detractors even argued that the design sanitized and de-historicized the memory of September 11 by avoiding comment on the horror of the attacks. Dissatisfaction with certain concept elements crystallized in a debate over the presentation of the names of the dead. Arad and Walker had chosen a random arrangement, believing that this would reflect the "haphazard brutality" of the terrorist strike. However, many of the city's firefighters believed that the attempt to universalize victimization failed to account for the distinctive sacrifice and courage of the first responders. This was not the first time that the city's most well-known heroes had challenged the process of commemoration.

One monument, to be erected outside the Fire Department Headquarters in Brooklyn, was proposed to commemorate the firefighters who had died on September 11. The bronze statue would be based on a photograph taken by Thomas E. Franklin of the *Record* (a Bergen County, New Jersey, newspaper) in the aftermath of the attacks. The now-famous image was of three firemen hoisting an American flag over the rubble at ground zero. Often compared to Joe Rosenthal's photograph of the flag raising at Iwo Jima, the image represented for many the patriotism and unity of all Americans. Nevertheless, in January 2002, debates raged about the decision to portray the group as racially diverse. Although the photograph was of three white men, professional models—one white, one black, and one Hispanic—were hired to pose for a more multicultural rendition. Incensed, local firefighters and residents protested the development of what they regarded as a politically correct "melting pot sculpture." Indeed, many saw the move as a political action that undermined the

historical authenticity of Franklin's original image. Ultimately, the design was abandoned in the hope of finding a more politically neutral monument.

The only group more vocal about the commemorative process was that of the families of the victims, particularly regarding the World Trade Center site. While their criticisms ranged from the placement of the names to the proposed symbolism of a below-ground memorial, their greatest battle came after the announcement of the International Freedom Center (IFC). Proposed as part of the site's cultural complex, the IFC would contain exhibits highlighting core American values and principles, as well as displays examining historical struggles for freedom in the United States and the world. Despite claims that the IFC would remain nonpartisan, fears quickly emerged that the museum would become a venue for leftists, academics, and protesters to denigrate the United States. The plan was finally stymied in 2005, after a successful "Take Back the Memorial" campaign was spearheaded by the families. While many concluded that the fight for freedom in America and abroad should be told, they believed that the World Trade Center site was not the place to do so.

Not unlike that of the ground zero memorial or the unsuccessful firefighter's statue, the IFC controversy revealed the tensions inherent in the commemorative process. In different ways, the debates facing each of these sites exposed the complicated relationship between memory and history. More important, they illustrated the larger difficulty in attempting to universalize and make palatable the still evolving experience of September 11. Perceptions of the overall design and its meaning no doubt will continue to change as interpretations of the terrorist attacks themselves also evolve.

Liam van Beek

See also: Multiculturalism and Ethnic Studies; Political Correctness; September 11; Vietnam Veterans Memorial.

Further Reading

Greenberg, Judith, ed. *Trauma at Home After 9/11.* Lincoln and London: University of Nebraska Press, 2003.
Lower Manhattan Development Corporation Web site. www.renewnyc.com.
Simpson, David. *9/11: The Culture of Commemoration.* Chicago and London: University of Chicago Press, 2006.

Serrano, Andres

The New York artist and photographer Andres Serrano became the center of a furious culture wars dispute over public exhibition of his notorious photograph, provocatively titled *Piss Christ* (1987), of a plastic crucifix in a transparent container of urine. Since Serrano had been awarded a fellowship from an art gallery sponsored by the National Endowment for the Arts (NEA), a debate soon erupted over the use of public funds to subsidize "offensive art."

Born in Brooklyn, New York, on August 15, 1950, Serrano grew up in a Catholic home of African-Haitian and Honduran heritage. Serrano had formal training in painting and sculpture at the Brooklyn Museum Art School (1967–1969), but he did not complete a degree program. His photography exhibits, which have shown at galleries and museums throughout the United States and Europe, include *The Unknown Christ* (1986), *Nomads* (1991), *KKK Portraits* (1991), *The Morgue* (1992), *Budapest* (1994), *The Church Series* (1994), *A History of Sex* (1998), and *Body and Soul* (2000). Serrano is known for works that use human bodily fluids for visual effect, including blood, milk, urine, and even sperm.

In 1986, Serrano was awarded a $15,000 fellowship from the Southeastern Center for Contemporary Art in Winston-Salem, North Carolina. The fact that the NEA did not directly dispense the grant to Serrano was immaterial to conservatives such as Senators Alphonse D'Amato (R-NY) and Jesse Helms (R-NC). In 1989, *Piss Christ* had been brought to the attention of Congress by the Tupelo, Mississippi–based American Family Association, a religious media watchdog, which declared the very title of the work blasphemous.

Senator D'Amato pronounced the Serrano work "a deplorable, despicable display of vulgarity" and insisted, "This is not a question of free speech. This is a question of abuse of taxpayers' money." In accordance with that view, Senator Helms in July 1989 introduced an amendment to the NEA appropriations bill for the purpose of prohibiting public funding of art deemed "obscene or indecent" or denigrating to religion or people. The amendment did not carry, but the final funding legislation included language calling on artists to meet "general standards of decency." The following year, the NEA began requiring grant recipients to sign an "obscenity pledge." NEA officials sought to provoke a legal challenge, believing that it would ultimately result in a judicial decision affirming artistic freedom. That strategy backfired when the U.S. Supreme Court in *National Endowment for the Arts v. Finley* (1998) ruled that the NEA may apply decency standards in determining what art projects to fund.

Meanwhile, debate continues over the meaning of Serrano's work. While some insist that a religious symbol immersed in urine is defiling, others believe the artist when he states that his intention was to provide a satire of religious kitsch. It has also been argued that, since the gospel itself is the story of Christ being degraded, the degradation of a symbol of Christ constitutes a retelling of the gospel. Another similar dispute over religious imagery occurred in 1999, when the Brooklyn Museum of Art exhibited Chris Ofili's *Holy Virgin Mary* (1996), a work featuring an African Virgin Mary partially painted with elephant dung.

Roger Chapman

See also: Censorship; Helms, Jesse; Mapplethorpe, Robert; National Endowment for the Arts; Religious Right; Warhol, Andy; Wildmon, Donald.

Further Reading

Baum, Joan. "On the Edge with Andres Serrano, Contemporary Photography's Artist Bad Boy." *Art Review*, December 20, 2000.

"Comments on Andres Serrano by Members of the United States Senate." *Congressional Record*, May 18, 1989.

Rambuss, Richard. "Sacred Subjects and Aversive Metaphysical Conceit: Crashaw, Serrano, and Ofili." *ELH* 71:2 (Summer 2004): 497–530.

Serrano, Andres. *Andres Serrano, Works 1983–1993.* Curated by Patrick T. Murphy. Essays by Robert Hobbs, Wendy Steiner, and Marcia Tucker. Philadelphia: Institute of Contemporary Art, University of Pennsylvania, 1994.

Sex Education

The sensitive association between children and sexuality has made sex education one of the most heated debates in the American culture wars. Questions of who should teach what about sex in public schools have been debated throughout the post–World War II era, perhaps most intensely since the 1980s. While America's relatively high rates of teenage pregnancy and the dangers of sexually transmitted diseases (STDs, also known as sexually transmitted infections, or STIs) have made sex education appear to be a practical necessity, the rise of the Christian Right has placed particular emphasis on the moral dimensions of sex education. As a consequence, sex education in America has become a political issue impacting debates at every level from local to national and, in part, facilitating the rise of the Christian Coalition's grassroots efforts to build a political coalition from school boards up to higher offices.

Historical Background

Sex has been a part of the public school curriculum and a subject of debate since at least the nineteenth century. At the turn of the twentieth century, moral crusaders such as Anthony Comstock sought a total ban on any "sexually explicit" material, including sex education materials. Reformers, primarily women's groups and Protestant organizations, sought to educate children about the moral dangers of sex. The primary advocates for sex education were sex hygienists, often led by medical professionals, who sought greater public knowledge about sexuality in order to prevent the spread of STDs. The limited curricula adopted at the time tended to focus primarily on sexual restraint, with an emphasis on the biology of sex and the dynamics of family life. In the 1950s, family life curricula were widely adopted and approved by professional associations.

In 1964, a small group of professionals concerned that information on sexuality and sexual activity was not readily available formed the Sexuality Information and Educational Council of the United States (SIECUS). The council adopted primarily a sexual hygiene curriculum, aimed at delivering scientifically factual information about pregnancy, STDs, and the science of sex. While eschewing moralizing language, SIECUS believed that promoting open dialogue about sex—including issues of birth control, pleasure, and desire—was the best way to ensure self-regulation. Prompted by SIECUS and other physicians and educators, the federal government began devoting significant resources to sex education. In 1965, the Elementary and Secondary Education Act (ESEA) made sex education a requirement in public schools. The legislation encouraged an approach known as comprehensive sex education, which attempted to inform students about the physical, moral, and psychological components of sex so as to enable them to make informed decisions. SIECUS was led by Dr. Mary Calderone, the former medical director of Planned Parenthood, an organization devoted to addressing issues of family planning and birth control.

The curriculum design for ESEA generally attempted to remain morally neutral in presenting the facts and scientific evidence about sexuality. It took the position that issues of sexual morality were best left to individuals and parents. Conservatives organized resistance to the new curriculum almost immediately despite its relatively conservative approach. At the time, social conservatives were also sensitive to the signs of a growing sexual revolution. The first birth-control pill had been made commercially available in 1961, raising widespread apprehension that it would lead to a decline in moral behavior and family values. In public education, social conservatives were also concerned about the teaching of evolution and court decisions limiting or ending prayer and religious instruction in public schools.

In the 1970s, conservative opponents of sex education produced counter-educational materials focusing on moral issues and sexual abstinence. Led by members of conservative Christian churches, the movement put up candidates for local school boards and local governments, emphasizing their stance against value-neutral sex education. The movement warned that sex education was encouraging teenage sexuality, often spreading stories of teachers encouraging sexual experimentation in the classroom and, later, that teachers were promoting homosexuality. Proponents of comprehensive sex education were generally less organized and less politicized. In 1979, Planned Parenthood created an education ser-vices department that provided information about sex education and birth control, but these efforts were less organized than the political and cultural pressures of the Christian Right.

By the 1980s, with the election of President Ronald Reagan and more conservative legislators across the country, the opposition to comprehensive sex education had well-placed allies in political positions, resulting in new legislation and greater funding for sex education programs that promoted abstinence. Abstinence education focused on teaching sexual restraint until marriage, often using fear tactics about the moral and health consequences of adolescent sexuality. In 1981, conservative senators Jeremiah Denton (R-AL) and Orrin Hatch (R-UT) sponsored the Adolescent and Family Life Act, popularly known as the Chastity Act, which provided funds to create and support abstinence-only sex education. The reach of these programs was extended in 1996, when as a part of the Personal Responsibility and Work Opportunity Reconciliation Act, also known as welfare reform, states were given block grants to implement abstinence-only or abstinence-plus programs that encouraged abstinence and offered minimal introductions to birth control and STD prevention. These programs were allowed to present information about contraception usage, but only in terms of failure rates, not in terms of obtaining contraception or its proper use. Educators were encouraged to discuss the damaging psychological consequences of sexual activity. In 2005, President George W. Bush increased funding for abstinence-only sex education by 25 percent.

In 2005 and 2007, Representative Barbara Lee (D-CA), a proponent of a more comprehensive approach, introduced the Responsible Education About Life Act to provide funds for broadening sex education beyond abstinence-only programs, and especially to inform young people that condoms can prevent STDs, including HIV-AIDS. Conservative opposition succeeded in blocking passage of the bill in the 110th Congress.

The pro-abstinence position also become a part of conservative foreign policy, which required, for example, that part of the money earmarked in the President's Emergency Plan for AIDS Relief be used to promote sexual abstinence. In 2009, however, during his early days in office, President Barack Obama withdrew some restrictions on the distribution of foreign aid for health and family planning. "For too long," he said, "international family planning assistance has been used as a political wedge issue, the subject of a back and forth debate that has served only to divide us. I have no desire to continue this stale and fruitless debate. It is time that we end the politicization of this issue."

Current Trends and Viewpoints

Today, sex education curricula vary significantly, but abstinence-plus programs like Sex Respect remain widely popular. These programs encourage abstinence until marriage and often use fear as a means of encouraging students to refrain from sexual activity. Many curricula emphasize the failure rate of contraception, resisting peer pressure, and the psychological and physical risks of sexual activity. For example, in a video entitled "No Second Chance" used in Sex Respect, an educator compares sex outside of marriage to Russian roulette, but with a greater chance of getting killed. A survey by the Kaiser Foundation in 2002 showed that as many as one-third of schools in America were taking an abstinence-only approach—the only one that allows a state school system to qualify for federal assistance. Since that time, several states have declined federal funds in order to teach comprehensive sex education.

Advocates for comprehensive sex education point out that the United States has a relatively high rate of teenage pregnancy. Pregnancy rates among teenagers have generally declined since 1991, but the United States compares poorly to industrialized countries that offer more comprehensive sex education. The abstinence-plus approach was also challenged by the AIDS epidemic. The use of condoms during sexual intercourse can prevent this most feared STD, but the noncomprehensive programs teach only about their failure rate (which is very small), subjecting teenagers who may be sexually active in spite of the program to the danger of contracting AIDS from unprotected sex.

Data on the effectiveness of differing programs are not conclusive. According to a 2007 study commissioned by Congress comparing groups that had received abstinence-only education to groups that had not, on average both groups had the same proportion of students who remained abstinent (about 50 percent) and who engaged in sex during the study period. Those who did have sex in the two groups were equally likely to use condoms or other contraceptives. The study called into question the effectiveness of the abstinence programs used by the groups in the study but shed no light on the effectiveness of comprehensive sex education.

Proponents of comprehensive sex education also point out that a large majority of parents favor comprehensive sex education over abstinence-only programs. The Guttmacher Institute reports that as many as 80 percent of parents wished their children had exposure to more information in the classroom. Even so, sex education in the schools remains a sensitive issue, and little has been done to shift from the abstinence-only approach.

Advocates of comprehensive sex education may gain support from the results of the 2008 election, in which Democrat Barack Obama was elected president and Democrats elected majorities in both houses of Congress. SIECUS has continued to promote and produce comprehensive sex education materials, and Planned Parenthood has also continued promoting the approach, but its role in the abortion debates has limited its ability to act as an advocate for sex education reform. Christian conservatives, on the other hand, continue to apply pressure to maintain sex education that concentrates on morals and values.

Claire E. Rasmussen

See also: Abortion; AIDS; Birth Control; Bush Family; Christian Coalition; Family Values; Gay Rights Movement; Kinsey, Alfred; Koop, C. Everett; Planned Parenthood; Religious Right; Sexual Revolution; Welfare Reform.

Further Reading

Campos, David. *Sex, Youth, and Sex Education: A Reference Handbook.* Santa Barbara, CA: ABC-CLIO, 2002.

Deckman, Melissa M. *School Board Battles: The Christian Right in Local Politics.* Washington, DC: Georgetown University Press, 2004.

Irvine, Janice. *Talk About Sex: The Battles over Sex Education in the United States.* Berkeley: University of California Press, 2003.

Levine, Judith. *Harmful to Minors: The Perils of Protecting Children from Sex.* Minneapolis: University of Minnesota Press, 2003.

Luker, Kristin. *When Sex Goes to School: Warring Views on Sex—and Sex Education—Since the Sixties.* New York: W.W. Norton, 2006.

Moran, Jeffery P. *Teaching Sex: The Shaping of Adolescence in the 20th Century.* Cambridge, MA: Harvard University Press, 2000.

Sex Offenders

A sex offender is an individual who has confessed to, or been convicted of, committing a sex crime, including rape, child molestation, and/or downloading from the Internet or distributing child pornography. Beginning in the 1990s, many states have passed strict tracking and residency laws in an attempt to protect society, especially children, from convicted sex offenders. Opinion polls show that most Americans support these measures, but a number of constitutional experts and public-policy consultants believe that such laws violate privacy rights, impose double jeopardy, waste funds, and fail to address the problem of sex offenders in the most constructive manner.

Although sex offenses in the United States have been on the decline since 1992, fear of sex offenders on the part of the general public has increased during the 2000s. As part of Operation Falcon (2005–2006), the U.S. Justice Department in a single day arrested some 1,600 unregistered or wanted sex offenders across twenty-seven states. Of the 190,000 federal prisoners in 2006, 11,000 were sex offenders. In 90 percent of cases, according to experts, child molestation is committed by family members, not strangers. Even so, most laws aimed at curbing pedophilia target the stranger.

In 1990, Washington became the first state to require sex offenders to register with police. Other states followed suit, and it became a federal requirement with passage of the Jacob Wetterling Act (1994), named after a missing child. Also in 1994, New Jersey passed Megan's Law, requiring community notification of any sex offender who takes up residency. Megan's Law was named after seven-year-old Megan Kanka, a kidnap-rape-murder victim of a neighbor with prior convictions for sex offenses. Other states and localities adopted variations of Megan's Law, leading to legal inconsistencies in the definition of sex offender and how information is to be collected and released to the public. Such confusion prompted passage in 2006 of the federal Adam Walsh Child Protection and Safety Act, named after the murdered son of John Walsh (the host of Fox Television's *America's Most Wanted*), which established national standards for registering, reporting, and public notification. By 2006, there were more than 560,000 registered sex offenders nationwide.

Laws against convicted sex offenders include the registration of all names in publicly accessed databases, the collection of DNA samples, state laws restricting where sex offenders can live and work, and the indefinite confinement of certain sex offenders to psychiatric centers after the completion of prison terms. As of 2006, eighteen states had laws allowing for the continued detention of sex offenders following the completion of their prison sentences. A few states have classified sex crimes as a capital offense. In addition, efforts have been made to regulate the Internet to thwart sexual predators.

Civil libertarians and other critics of sex-offender registries raise the issue of individual liberties, arguing that convicts who have served time for their offenses should be able to resume life as a citizen free from harassment. Some sex offenders have been rendered homeless because residency laws, like the one enacted in Georgia in 2006, have made it illegal for them to live near schools, parks, playgrounds, bus stops, churches, or any other place where children might gather. In certain cases, sex offenders have listed Wal-Mart parking lots as their official residence. When sex offenders are uprooted, health professionals warn, their treatment typically gets interrupted. Not only does this raise the risk of a repeat offense, but it also makes it more difficult for law enforcement officials to keep track of them. Since, in some states, persons convicted of having underaged consensual sex while in high school are officially listed as sex offenders, individuals who may pose no real danger to society can be adversely impacted by these measures.

As widespread access to the Internet has increased, some sex offenders have used it as a medium for illegally sharing and viewing child pornography. Social networking sites, where users create profiles and/or join chat groups, have also created a medium for finding and stalking potential victims. The problem came to light in 2004, largely due to exposure on the NBC television series *To Catch a Predator*. Working in collaboration with law-enforcement officials and the online watchdog group Perverted Justice, the show identifies predators online and, when they solicit sex from minors and arrange encounters with them, a camera crew shows up to wait for the predator to arrive. Critics of the show believe the exposé technique enables offenders to claim forced entrapment in a court of law, not to mention that it pushes the margins of ethical journalism. In its first three years, however, the program led to the arrest of more than 200 sex offenders.

Another important set of events surrounding sex offenders are the child molestation scandals that have plagued the Catholic Church in recent years. John Geoghan, a priest for thirty years and a significant figure in the Catholic Church sex scandals, was accused of sexual abuse by more than 130 individuals, defrocked in 1998, and sentenced to prison in 2002. He was later murdered in his prison cell by another inmate. Geoghan's case became the catalyst for a public interrogation of clergy sex abuse and concealment of information by church officials. It later inspired a string of similar court cases and a shift in church policy. Today, the archdiocese of Boston and the Vatican require members of the clergy and volunteers to report any accusations of child abuse to the proper authorities; however, the Vatican maintains the privacy of accused child abusers. The Catholic Church has acknowledged that from 1950 to 2007 there were 13,000 credible accusations of sex abuse by its priests in the United States.

Jennifer Lyn Simpson,
Merrit Dukehart, and Roger Chapman

See also: Bradley, Bill; Catholic Church; Pornography; Sexual Assault; Sexual Harassment.

Further Reading

Greenblatt, Alan. "Sex Offenders." *CQ Researcher*, September 8, 2006.

Jenkins, Philip. *Moral Panic: Changing Concepts of the Child Molester in America.* New Haven, CT: Yale University Press, 1998.

Perverted Justice Web site. www.Perverted-Justice.com.

Terry, Karen J. *Sexual Offenses and Offenders: Theory, Practice, and Policy.* Belmont, CA: Wadsworth, 2006.

Sexual Assault

Sexual assault is a category of criminal behavior that includes any sexual contact in the absence of uncoerced consent. While the legal definition of sexual assault is now widely accepted, the causes and consequences, appropriate prevention methods, and what constitutes a fitting social response remain contested.

According to the U.S. Department of Health and Human Services, sexual assault may include inappropriate touching; vaginal, anal, or oral penetration; rape; attempted rape; incest; or child molestation. Sexual assault does not require physical contact and may be perpetrated verbally, visually, or in any other way that forces someone to engage in unwanted sexual contact or attention. Specific laws governing what constitutes consent and at what age an individual is able to give it freely vary by state.

According to the Violence Against Women Grants Office, an estimated one in six women and one in thirty-three men have experienced an attempted or completed rape as either an adult or child. The rape/sexual assault rate for people ages sixteen to nineteen is nearly twice as high as for all other age groups. Rape and sexual assault are also among the most underreported of crimes due to the significant emotional trauma and enduring social stigma they produce. Rates of reported rape may be even lower for men than for women because of this stigma.

Since the 1970s, a large number of groups and organizations have formed to reduce and ultimately end sexual assault, though they have pursued a wide variety of approaches. Some, including AWARE (Arming Women Against Rape and Endangerment) and the Women's Self Defense Institute, have focused on promoting self-defense and increasing awareness for potential victims. These groups seek to prevent assaults by strangers (24 percent of assaults fall into this category, according to the 2002 National Crime Victimization Survey) and advocate "safe" behavior such as avoiding poorly lit areas, traveling with friends or companions (using the "buddy system"), and avoiding "provocative" behavior. The prevention efforts of other groups—such as the YWCA, National Sexual Violence Resource Center, RAINN (Rape, Abuse & Incest National Network), and MASV (Men Against Sexual Violence)—emphasize the prevention of acquaintance or "date" rape (76 percent of cases), changing cultural systems, the importance of educating men (who remain the most frequent perpetrators of sexual assault), and responsible bystander behavior to intervene in inappropriate or unwanted behavior among peers before an assault occurs. These groups also often challenge "victim blaming," arguing that because sexual assault is an act of violence and domination, not lust, it cannot be "provoked."

"Take Back the Night" rallies marked the first significant organized public protests of violence against women, first in England and then the United States in the late 1970s. These events are characterized by groups of women walking in solidarity through the streets to "reclaim" the night as safe for women and raise awareness about sexual violence. In the 1990s, the entire month of April was designated Sexual Assault Awareness Month; events are now held on college campuses and in communities across the country to raise awareness about sexual assault prevention. In 1998, *The Vagina Monologues* playwright Eve Ensler founded V-Day as "an organized response against violence toward women," arising from a demand that "rape, incest, battery, genital mutilation and sexual slavery must end now." Issues of sexual assault have influenced the debate over other politically charged issues as well. In the abortion debate, for example, some states that otherwise prohibit or restrict abortions make exceptions in the case of rape or incest; others do not.

Jennifer Lyn Simpson

See also: Abortion; Sexual Harassment; Sexual Revolution.

Further Reading

Buchwald, Emilie, Pamela Fletcher, and Martha Roth. *Transforming a Rape Culture.* Rev. ed. Minneapolis, MN: Milkweed Editions, 2005.

Foubert, John D. *The Men's Program: A Peer Education Guide to Rape Prevention.* 3rd ed. New York: Routledge, 2005.

Thornhill, Randy, and Craig T. Palmer. *A Natural History of Rape: Biological Bases of Sexual Coercion.* 3rd ed. Cambridge, MA: MIT Press, 2000.

Sexual Harassment

Sexual harassment includes a range of behaviors that subject persons to unwanted sexual attention. According to the U.S. Equal Employment Opportunity Commission (EEOC), sexual harassment is a form of sex discrimination that constitutes a violation of Title VII of the Civil Rights Act of 1964. In educational institutions, sexual harassment is also a violation of Title IX of the Education Amendments of 1972. While it may take many forms, two broad categories of behavior can be identified as constituting sexual harassment: quid pro quo demands for sexual attention, or behavior in exchange for rewards or protection from punishment; and behavior that is disturbing to the point of inhibiting work performance or creating undue stress in the workplace by creating a *hostile environment*. The sexual harassment debate today centers largely on free speech issues and the question of whether restricting speech can or will fundamentally alter the culture of sexism that gives rise to sexual harassment.

From 1997 to 2006, the number of cases reported annually to the EEOC declined by just under 25 percent, from almost 16,000 to just over 12,000. During the same time period, cases filed by men increased from 11.6 percent of total cases to 15.4 percent. Since sexual harassment is widely believed to be underreported because of fear of retaliation, reliable figures are hard to obtain.

According to a 2006 report by the American Association of University Women (AAUW), "Nearly two-thirds of college students experience sexual harassment at some point during college, including nearly one-third of first-year students."

The origins of the term "sexual harassment" can be traced to a 1974 Cornell University case in which a female laboratory employee quit her job after a scientist made regular unwanted sexual advances, and was denied unemployment insurance on the grounds that she did not have "good cause" to leave her job. The term was first used in a legal ruling in the federal district court case of *Williams v. Saxbe* (1976), which recognized sexual harassment as a form of discrimination under Title VII. Since then there have been numerous court decisions clarifying its definition and scope.

Several episodes in the early 1990s brought the issue of sexual harassment prominently into public discourse: the 1991 Supreme Court confirmation hearings of Clarence Thomas, in which University of Oklahoma law school professor Anita Hill gave testimony that Thomas had sexually harassed her when they worked together at the EEOC; the 1991 Tailhook convention of navy and marine corps aviators, and subsequent claims that seven men and eighty-three women had been sexually assaulted or harassed at the two-day event in Las Vegas, Nevada; and the 1994 sexual harassment lawsuit by Paula Jones against President Bill Clinton, alleging that he had sexually propositioned her when he was governor of Arkansas and she was a state employee. Media coverage of these widely reported events galvanized and sometimes polarized public conversation on the issue of sexual harassment in America.

While the term "sexual harassment" is broadly understood to include injurious and appalling behaviors, the definition of "offensive" behavior can vary by individual and context. The amorphous and ambiguous edges of sexual harassment policy have been widely criticized by defenders of free speech, by libertarian "small government" groups, and by feminist groups such as Feminists for Free Expression, who reject the notion that curtailment of speech will fundamentally change the culture of gender discrimination that gives rise to sexual harassment.

Jennifer Lyn Simpson

See also: Civil Rights Movement; Clinton Impeachment; Feminism, Second-Wave; Feminism, Third-Wave; Hill, Anita; MacKinnon, Catharine; Sexual Assault; Thomas, Clarence; Women in the Military.

Further Reading

Brant, Clare, and Yun Lee Too, eds. *Rethinking Sexual Harassment.* Boulder, CO: Pluto Press, 1994.

Langalan, Martha. *Back Off: How to Stop and Confront Sexual Harassers.* New York: Simon & Schuster/Fireside, 1993.

MacKinnon, Catharine A., and Reva B. Spiegel, eds. *Directions in Sexual Harassment Law.* New Haven, CT: Yale University Press, 2004.

Mink, Gwendolyn. *Hostile Environment: The Political Betrayal of Sexually Harassed Women.* Ithaca, NY: Cornell University Press, 2000.

Zimmerman, Jean. *Tailspin: Women at War in the Wake of Tailhook.* New York: Doubleday, 1995.

Sexual Revolution

The sexual revolution was an outburst of experimentation with sexual norms and practices that took place mainly during the 1960s. Participants in this liberalization viewed pleasure as the guiding criterion of sexual life. Opponents defended more conservative values of sexual modesty, premarital chastity, and self-control.

Origin in the 1950s

While the sexual revolution is often perceived as a generational struggle pitting 1960s nonconformists against the puritanical morality and middle-class "family values" of the previous decade, in fact the climate for sexual expression had been significantly liberalized during the 1950s. From Alfred Kinsey's pioneering studies of human sexual behavior to Elvis Presley's pelvic gyrations, from risqué films such as *Baby Doll* (1956) to tabloid coverage of transsexual celebrity Christine Jorgensen, from Hugh Hefner's *Playboy* magazine (founded in 1953) to scandalous works of literature such as Vladimir Nabokov's *Lolita* (1955) and Allen Ginsberg's "Howl" (1956), American culture of the period was marked by the highly visible, if controversial, presence of sexuality. The nostalgia for the 1950s evident in many attacks on the sexual revolution launched by social and religious conservatives is thus ironic, since the 1960s capitalized on the already growing openness of the postwar environment, admittedly pushing it to extremes of expression and conduct that could hardly avoid provoking a backlash.

Sexual explicitness in art increased markedly during the 1960s, prompted by a series of U.S. Supreme Court decisions striking down censorship efforts aimed at banning literary works by the likes of D.H. Lawrence and Henry Miller. The trickle-down effect of these decisions was to legitimate a wide range of sexual expression in cinema and print, including the surfacing of the porn industry from a shadowy underground. More daring competitors to *Playboy* magazine appeared, such as Al Goldstein's *Screw* and Larry Flynt's *Hustler*, and by the early 1970s, hard-core films such as *Deep Throat* (1972) and *The Devil in Miss Jones* (1973) were enjoying unprecedented critical and commercial success. Meanwhile, rock-and-roll music was promoting anti-establishment attitudes among contemporary youth, including an embrace of drugs and premarital sex.

By the mid-1960s, a counterculture of "hippies" had emerged on college campuses and in major cities, advocating "free love," among other things. In 1967, they launched the "Summer of Love" in San Francisco, inaugurated by a massive "Human Be-In" that featured public nudity and casual sex.

Advent of the Pill

Popular views of sexual morality were also relaxed by the advent of accessible birth control through the invention of oral contraceptives, approved for use by the FDA in 1960 and popularly known as "the Pill." Unlinking sex from reproduction meant that casual sex bore fewer obvious penalties, especially for women. As popular best-sellers such as Helen Gurley Brown's *Sex and the Single Girl* (1962) offered advice on how best to capitalize on the newly permissive environment, personal pleasure became the guiding standard for sexual ethics. Consequently, the institution of marriage suffered while divorce rates climbed, cohabitation became more widespread, and nonmonogamous behaviors grew. Some couples experimented with "swinging" practices such as spouse-swapping and "open" relationships. Bastions of traditional morality such as the Catholic Church inveighed against this sudden eruption of licentiousness: Pope Paul VI's encyclical *Humanae Vitae* (1968), for example, denounced all forms of "artificial" birth control as tending to undermine marital commitment. Even so, the sexual revolution continued undaunted.

One of its most controversial elements was the increasing visibility of a self-confident and unapologetic homosexual minority. During the 1950s, gay and lesbian subcultures had thrived in urban areas, and nascent "homophile" groups, such as the Mattachine Society and the Daughters of Bilitis, had begun to advocate for mainstream acceptance. The youth counterculture and the antiwar movement of the 1960s, however, tended to promote more militant attitudes among those who sought conformity to conservative social norms. Tensions exploded in the Stonewall Riots of June 1969, when homosexuals in New York City's Greenwich Village struck back against police harassment. The riots spawned a vocal coalition for "gay liberation." Gay and lesbian rights activists released incendiary manifestos, mounted freedom marches in major cities, and decried homophobic stereotypes in the mass media. At the same time, mainstream culture was pioneering more positive depictions of gays and lesbians in films such as *The Boys in the Band* (1970). In another battle with sexual orthodoxy, some more openly explored their bisexuality.

Feminist Reactions

An ambivalent response to the sexual revolution was displayed by second-wave feminism, which embraced women's newfound freedoms while condemning their exploitation as sexual objects. Anne Koedt's landmark essay "The Myth of the Vaginal Orgasm" (1970) discussed an autonomous female sexuality centered on clitoral pleasure, and lesbian feminists defended homosexuality as a political option for all women tired of "sleeping with the enemy." At the same time, feminist activists mounted powerful critiques of sexual objectification and violence, attacking the growing sex industry, picketing beauty pageants for commercializing women's bodies, and mounting consciousness-raising efforts to combat sexually degrading images of women throughout mainstream popular culture. Radical feminists converged with the Religious Right in their denunciations of pornography.

Reactions against the sexual revolution have been largely conservative in nature. Advocates of "family values" have opposed the sexual license of 1960s culture, defending the importance of traditional marriage. Religious conservatives have decried the "moral relativism" that allows sex to be viewed as a purely naturalistic act centered on personal gratification. Renewed efforts at censorship have taken aim at popular pornography and graphic works by artists such as Robert Mapplethorpe, while an antigay backlash has denounced the mainstreaming of homosexuality, sometimes pointing to AIDS as proof of the penalties for pursuing unfettered sexual pleasure.

Still, there can be little doubt that popular attitudes toward sexuality underwent a massive transformation during the 1960s. The legacy of the sexual revolution is unlikely to abate anytime soon.

Rob Latham

See also: Birth Control; Book Banning; Brown, Helen Gurley; Counterculture; Family Values; Feminism, Second-Wave; Gay Rights Movement; Generations and Generational Conflict; Hefner, Hugh; Kinsey, Alfred; Planned Parenthood; Pornography; Relativism, Moral; Religious Right; Rock and Roll; Sex Education.

Further Reading

Allyn, David. *Make Love, Not War: The Sexual Revolution—An Unfettered History.* New York: Little, Brown, 2000.

Escoffier, Jeffrey, ed. *Sexual Revolution.* New York: Thunder's Mouth, 2003.

Heidenry, John. *What Wild Ecstasy: The Rise and Fall of the Sexual Revolution.* New York: Simon & Schuster, 1997.

Jeffreys, Sheila. *Anticlimax: A Feminist Perspective on the Sexual Revolution.* New York: New York University Press, 1990.

Sharpton, Al

An outspoken African-American Baptist minister and political activist, the Reverend Al Sharpton emerged as a national figure during the 1980s and 1990s for orchestrating militant street protests in New York City in response to hate crimes, police brutality, and other perceived social injustices. Called "the Riot King," "Al Charlatan," and "the Reverend Soundbite" by those who believe he lacks substance and sincerity, Sharpton portrays himself as a political outsider who represents disenfranchised blacks. He has publicly criticized the Reverend Jesse Jackson, a former mentor, as a political insider who has abandoned his ideals for expanding civil rights. After surviving a stabbing by a white man during a street protest in 1991, Sharpton spoke of undergoing a spiritual transformation that has made him conciliatory and mainstream. Since then, he has used political campaigns to air his views, running as a losing candidate in several Democratic primaries—U.S. Senate (1992, 1994), mayor of New York (1997), and the U.S. presidency (2004).

Alfred Charles "Al" Sharpton, Jr., was born on October 3, 1954, in Brooklyn, New York. A "wonder boy preacher" beginning at age four, he was ordained as a minister of the Pentecostal Church in 1964. Sharpton's social consciousness developed during childhood after his divorced mother was forced to move the family from a middle-class neighborhood of Queens to the projects in Brooklyn. The poverty of ghetto life shocked Sharpton, who found the political complacency of its occupants confounding. He graduated from Tilden High School in Brooklyn (1972) and then attended Brooklyn College (1973–1975). After serving as youth coordinator of the Southern Christian Leadership Conference's (SCLC's) Operation Breadbasket in New York (1969–1971), Sharpton founded and directed the National Youth Movement (later renamed the United African Movement) (1971–1986). In 1991, he founded the National Action Network, Inc., also located in New York. In 1993, he was appointed coordinator of the minister division of Jackson's National Rainbow Coalition. In 1994, he left the Pentecostal Church and became the associate minister of Bethany Baptist Church in Brooklyn.

Sharpton has been criticized for focusing on violent crime committed by whites against blacks, while virtually ignoring what the conservative radio talk show host Rush Limbaugh and others call a more extensive problem: "black-on-black crime." Sharpton is further blamed for inflaming racial tensions and in some cases sparking riots, while others agree with him that New York is "perhaps the most racist city in the country," presenting situations that require extremist activism. Sharpton conducted protests in reaction to the incident involving so-called subway vigilante Bernhard Goetz, who in December 1984 shot four blacks who approached him for money in a New York subway car. Following the December 1986 murder of Michael Griffith, a black youth who had entered the white section of Howard Beach in Queens, Sharpton organized street protests to pressure the city to appoint a special prosecutor, which led to the eventual prosecution

The Reverend Al Sharpton, a high-profile activist for African-American justice, speaks to the media about the case of Amadou Diallo in 2000. Diallo, who had been unarmed, was shot forty-one times by four New York City police officers. *(Manny Ceneta/AFP/Getty Images)*

of the white assailants. Sharpton stood behind the allegations of Tawana Brawley, a black teenager who claimed that several white men had kidnapped and raped her in November 1987, although a subsequent investigation revealed that her story was a hoax to avoid punishment by her stepfather for staying out too late; Sharpton later had to pay $65,000 in damages for having accused a white attorney of being one of Brawley's assailants. Sharpton has led demonstrations against police brutality on several occasions, including the February 1999 shooting of Amadou Diallo—an unarmed African man who was shot by four white NYPD officers forty-one times after reaching into a pocket for his wallet.

During the 1980s, unknown to the people he was leading in street demonstrations, Sharpton was working as an informant for the Federal Bureau of Investigation (FBI). This came about because of his association with boxing promoter Don King, who had alleged ties to organized crime involving the laundering of drug money; the FBI threatened Sharpton with criminal prosecution if he did not cooperate with their investigation. Later, Sharpton was accused of spying on black radicals. He maintained that he forwarded information to the FBI only on suspected drug dealers, but the New York newspaper *Newsday* reported in 1998 that he provided the FBI with information that led to the arrest of a black man suspected in the shooting of a New Jersey state trooper.

Roger Chapman

See also: Goetz, Bernhard; Hate Crimes; Jackson, Jesse; Limbaugh, Rush; Police Abuse; Thurmond, Strom.

Further Reading

Biondi, Martha. *To Stand and Fight: The Struggle for Civil Rights in Postwar New York City.* Cambridge, MA: Harvard University Press, 2003.

Klein, Michael. *Man Behind the Sound Bite: The Real Story of the Rev. Al Sharpton.* New York: Castillo International, 1991.

Sharpton, Al. "What I've Learned." *Esquire,* January 2005.

Sharpton, Al, and Karen Hunter. *Al on America.* New York: Dafina Books, 2002.

Sharpton, Al, and Anthony Walton. *Go and Tell Pharaoh: The Autobiography of the Reverend Al Sharpton.* New York: Doubleday, 1996.

Sheen, Fulton J.

One of the most popular clerics in U.S. history, Archbishop Fulton J. Sheen helped fashion Roman Catholicism as part of the American mainstream with his highly rated prime-time television broadcasts during the 1950s. He condemned communism for its atheistic ideology, and he framed the Cold War as a cosmic struggle that would end with Russia returning to its Christian roots. Sheen converted thousands, including public personalities such as Heywood Broun, Clare Booth Luce, and Henry Ford II, as well as the former communists Louis F. Budenz and Elizabeth Bentley.

Born in El Paso, Illinois, on May 8, 1895, Fulton John Sheen grew up in nearby Peoria. After earning degrees at St. Viator College in Bourbonnais, Illinois (AB, 1917; MA, 1919), he received ordination in September 1919. He then continued his education in theology and philosophy at Catholic University of America in Washington, D.C. (STL and JCB, 1920), and the University of Louvain in Belgium (PhD, 1923). From 1926 to 1950, he taught at Catholic University of America, but it was his broadcast ministries—beginning with the national radio program *The Catholic Hour* in 1930 and the prime-time television show *Life Is Worth Living,* which ran from 1952 to 1957—that made him a household name.

The hosting of *Life Is Worth Living,* which won Sheen an Emmy in 1952, enabled him to promote religion and American values by speaking—sometimes humorously— on such diverse topics as modernity, fatigue, science, handling teenagers, psychiatry, and God. As he had done since the 1930s, Sheen continued to denounce Marxism as a counterfeit religion. In 1953, coincidentally nine days before the death of Soviet leader Joseph Stalin, Sheen presented a televised eulogy that parodied Marc Antony's funeral oration in Shakespeare's *Julius Caesar:* "Friends, Soviets, countrymen, lend me your ears; I come to bury Stalin, not to praise him." In the tract *Smokescreens* (1983), Christian fundamentalist producer Jack Chick argues that Sheen's anticommunism was part of a postwar Vatican conspiracy to shift attention away from the Catholic Church's support of the Nazis and to create a common enemy for forging a sense of unity between Catholics and Protestants.

From 1950 to 1966, Sheen served as national director of the Society for the Propagation of the Faith. As head of missionary activities for U.S. Catholics, he gained a strong sense of the needs of the disadvantaged poor, at home and abroad. This made him an advocate of social and racial justice in the American South. In the late 1950s, he began advocating governmental foreign aid, saying that "missionaries will not sell America, nor will they win military pacts. But America will gain by it in the end." In 1958, he spoke on the subject during a White House visit with President Dwight D. Eisenhower. He also brought concerns for social justice to Vatican Council II (1962–1965) as a member of the commission on missions. Sheen died on December 9, 1979.

Tim Lacy and Roger Chapman

See also: Budenz, Louis F.; Catholic Church; Chick, Jack; Civil Rights Movement; Cold War; Communists and Communism; Eisenhower, Dwight D.; Marxism; McCarthy, Joseph; McCarthyism; Televangelism.

Further Reading

Reeves, Thomas C. *America's Bishop: The Life and Times of Fulton J. Sheen.* San Francisco: Encounter Books, 2001.

Riley, Kathleen L. *Fulton J. Sheen: An American Catholic Response to the Twentieth Century.* Staten Island, NY: St. Paul's / Alba House, 2004.

Shelley, Martha

A radical feminist gay rights activist and controversial writer, Martha Shelley spearheaded the separatist radical lesbian-feminist movement in postwar America. Inspired by the Stonewall Riots of 1968, Shelley's influential articles "Notes of a Radical Lesbian" (1969), "Gay Is Good" (1970), and "Lesbianism and the Women's Liberation Movement" (1970) offered a radical link between the women's liberation and gay liberation movements. In her characteristically angry tone, she asserted that lesbians must strive for understanding, rather than toleration and superficial acceptance. For Shelley, true women's liberation is connected with the practice of lesbian sexuality because only in the complete rejection of patriarchy can women find their freedom.

Martha Shelley (née Altman) was born into a Jewish family on December 27, 1943, in Brooklyn, New York. A self-described "loner" in high school, she felt like an outsider until she joined the New York chapter of the lesbian organization Daughters of Bilitis (DOB) and became part of the fledgling gay rights movement. By the late 1960s, the young radical had found her voice. She legally changed her name to Martha Shelley in honor of her favorite poet, Percy Shelley, became the president of the DOB, participated in numerous antiwar protests, and joined the more radical Student Homophile League on the Barnard College campus. When the league failed to adequately address lesbians' concerns, Shelley and other young militants formed the anarchical and short-lived Gay Liberation Front in 1969. She later moved to Oakland, California, where she worked briefly with the ill-fated California Women's Press Collective. She has continued to publish articles, essays, and poems, including the verse collections *Crossing the DMZ* (1981) and *Lovers and Mothers* (1982).

Shelley defied the conservatism creeping into some of the nation's most high-profile consciousness-raising organizations. By appropriating the language of other civil rights activists, she likened the situation of lesbians in the women's and gay rights movements to the state of African Americans in larger society. In the late 1960s, radical lesbians found themselves at a crossroads. Believing that it could undermine the credibility of the entire women's movement itself, Betty Friedan's National Organization of Women (NOW) took a decidedly hostile approach to lesbianism. Gay rights organizations had similarly considered lesbianism something of a distraction. In response, Shelley co-founded the Lavender Menace, later renamed Radicalesbians, with NOW defector Rita Mae Brown in 1970. The organization's founding manifesto, titled "The Woman-Identified Woman," called for the inclusion of lesbians in the larger women's liberation movement. Although Radicalesbians folded the following year, NOW incorporated lesbian rights into its charter.

Kelly L. Mitchell

See also: Counterculture; Feminism, Second-Wave; Feminism, Third-Wave; Friedan, Betty; Gay Rights Movement; Lesbians; National Organization for Women; Sexual Revolution; Stonewall Rebellion.

Further Reading

Clendinen, Dudley, and Adam Nagourney. *Out for Good: The Struggle to Build a Gay Rights Movement in America.* New York: Simon & Schuster, 1999.

Marcus, Eric. *Making History: The Struggle for Gay and Lesbian Equal Rights, 1945–1990.* New York: HarperCollins, 1992.

Shelley, Martha. "Gay Is Good." In *Out of the Closets: Voices of Gay Liberation*, ed. Karla Jay and Allen Young, 31–34. New York: New York University Press, 1992.

———. "Notes of a Radical Lesbian." In *Women's Rights in the United States: A Documentary History*, ed. Winston E. Langley and Vivian C. Fox, 283–84. Westport, CT: Greenwood Press, 1994.

Shepard, Matthew

Matthew Shepard, a twenty-one-year-old college student in Wyoming, was brutally murdered in October 1998, the victim of an antigay hate crime, a robbery, or both, depending on who tells the story. Publicity surrounding the murder brought national attention to the issue of hate crimes.

Born on December 1, 1976, in Casper, Wyoming, Matthew Wayne Shepard grew up in a middle-class home and attended the American School in Switzerland. In 1995, after studying at Catawba College in Salisbury, North Carolina, and Casper College, he enrolled as a political science major at the University of Wyoming. Sometime after midnight on October 7, 1998, Shepard got a ride with two men he had met at a bar and who may have lured him away by pretending to be gay. He was driven to a rural area of Laramie and subsequently robbed, severely beaten and pistol-whipped, and left to die tied to a fence in freezing weather. Eighteen hours later, he was found barely alive by a passerby. Shepard, who suffered extensive lacerations and a fractured skull, died at Poudre Valley Hospital, in Ft. Collins, Colorado, on October 12.

At Shepard's funeral, the notorious "Reverend" Fred Phelps shocked the nation by staging an antigay protest, carrying inflammatory placards with slogans such as "GOD HATES FAGS." Shepard's attackers were Russell Henderson, who pleaded guilty to felony murder and kidnapping, and Aaron McKinney, who was found guilty at trial. The two gave conflicting statements about their motives for the crime. During the trial, they used the "gay panic defense," arguing temporary insanity caused by homophobia after Shepard had

Matthew Shepard, a gay University of Wyoming student viciously murdered in 1998, is memorialized in a candlelight vigil. The incident became a cause célèbre in the gay rights movement and spurred demands for stronger federal hate-crime legislation. *(Evan Agostini/Getty Images)*

propositioned them. At one point, they stated that the motive behind the crime was strictly robbery, a detail some later emphasized in arguing that the incident did not rate as a hate crime. Both men were sentenced to two consecutive life sentences, McKinney without the possibility of parole.

Shepard's parents later founded the Matthew Shepard Society, dedicated to promoting tolerance. In 2002, the murder and its aftermath were the subject of two television films, *The Matthew Shepard Story* by NBC and *The Laramie Project* by HBO, the latter based on an off-Broadway play. In 2007, Congress passed the Matthew Shepard Act (officially the Local Law Enforcement Hate Crimes Prevention Act), but it was vetoed by President George W. Bush (as an amendment to the Defense Authorization Bill). The measure would have expanded federal hate-crime law to include incidents motivated by bias against gender, sexual orientation, or disability.

Michael Johnson, Jr.

See also: Gay Rights Movement; Hate Crimes; Phelps, Fred.

Further Reading

Loffreda, Beth. *Losing Matt Shepard: Life and Politics in the Aftermath of Anti-Gay Murder.* New York: Columbia University Press, 2000.

Lynch, John. "Memory and Matthew Shepard: Opposing Expressions of Public Memory in Television Movies." *Journal of Communication Inquiry* 31:3 (July 2007): 222–38.

Matthew Shepard Society Web site. www.matthewshepard.org.

Ott, Brian L., and Eric Aoki. "The Politics of Negotiating Public Tragedy: Media Framing of the Matthew Shepard Murder." *Rhetoric & Public Affairs* 5:3 (Fall 2002): 483–505.

Patterson, Romaine, and Patrick Hinds. *The Whole World Was Watching: Living in the Light of Matthew Shepard.* New York: Advocate Books, 2005.

Shock Jocks

"Shock jocks," provocative radio talk show hosts or disc jockeys, are known for speaking in a deliberately offensive manner and treating their callers rudely. Most commonly associated with controversial radio personality Howard Stern, the term has become a pejorative label for irreverent broadcasters whose on-air behavior is meant to shock and offend the general listener. Although such radio shows remain popular, they have been increasingly subjected to fines and sanctions by the Federal Communications Commission (FCC), a trend that caused Stern to move his show to an unregulated satellite radio station.

Typically, shock jocks engage their audience in conversations about the more prurient aspects of sex as well as topics that promote racism, homophobia, exploitation of women, and the ridicule of disabled people. While many angry listeners simply file complaints with the FCC, others have taken more dramatic action. The number of suspects in the 1984 murder of Denver-based shock jock Alan Berg was so great that sixty police officers had to be assigned to the case. Berg's violent death brought national attention to the shock jock phenomenon and was the basis for Eric Bogosian's award-winning play *Talk Radio* (1987; film version, 1988).

Shock jocks are especially popular among young adult males. In addition to Stern, the most audacious radio personalities include Steve Dahl, a Chicago DJ who proposed making a "cocktail" of the corpses left floating after Hurricane Katrina; Mike Church, a regular target of the Southern Anti-Defamation League for his distasteful comments against the South; Todd Clem, also known as Bubba the Love Sponge, arrested in 2001 after slaughtering a live pig on the air; Opie and Anthony, fired after joking that Boston mayor Thomas Menino had been killed in an automobile accident; Tom Leykis, who revealed the name of the woman who accused basketball star Kobe Bryant of rape in July 2003; and Mancow Muller, who sent rival talk show host Howard Stern a box of excrement. A handful of women have managed to succeed in the field. One is Liz Wilde, a Floridian who promotes "Blow It Out Yer Ass" Fridays. Another is "The Radio Chick," Leslie Gold, whose New York show features titillating skits like "20 Questions with a Hooker."

Some critics blame shock jocks for a "renaissance of vulgarity" in American society. Others see shock jocks as a by-product of a society that has lost its moral compass. Radio and television pioneer Steve Allen speculated in his *Vulgarians at the Gate* (2001) that Stern and his "toilet talk fraternity" were being used by media conglomerates to grab ratings. Civil discourse may not sell, but controversy certainly does. Most shock jocks started out as Top 40 DJs and continue to serve the same commercial interests.

While Congress continues to boost FCC fines to more than $300,000 per violation, free speech advocates equate the tighter restrictions with a new brand of McCarthyism. Survey research suggests that a majority of listeners prefer radio personalities who "push the limits." Many argue that radio is no more explicit than network television or cable programs. In fact, some First Amendment experts have complained that shock jocks are being punished for broadcasting sexually explicit bits that are perfectly acceptable on daytime TV.

Cindy Mediavilla

See also: Censorship; Federal Communications Commission; Hurricane Katrina; McCarthyism; Political Correctness; Speech Codes; Stern, Howard; Talk Radio.

Further Reading

Allen, Steve. *Vulgarians at the Gate: Trash TV and Raunch Radio—Raising the Standards of Popular Culture.* Amherst, NY: Prometheus Books, 2001.

Hilliard, Robert, and Michael C. Keith. *Dirty Discourse: Sex and Indecency in American Radio.* Ames: Iowa State Press, 2003.

O'Connor, Roy. *Shock Jocks: Hate Speech and Talk Radio.* San Francisco: AlterNet Books, 2008.

Sider, Ron

The Canadian-born theologian and author Ron Sider became prominent among Christian evangelicals during the 1970s for his attacks on the wealthy, on indifference toward poverty, and on the perceived complacency of many North American Christians. As a professor at Philadephia's Messiah College, he wrote *Rich Christians in an Age of Hunger* (1977), a polemical work that sold more than 350,000 copies and generated intense debate over the relationship between Christianity and economics, and over the relative impact of structural factors and personal choices in determining individual success or failure. Like Tony Campolo and Jim Wallis, Sider combined evangelicalism and leftist politics in a way that earned great popularity on college and seminary campuses, as well as rebukes from all points on the political spectrum.

Ronald James Sider was born on September 17, 1939, in Stevensville, Ontario, and raised in a Brethren in Christ household. An offshoot of the Mennonites, the Brethren in Christ sect emphasizes pacifism, simple living, and the importance of community, ideas that inform all of Sider's later work. He received his BA from Waterloo Lutheran University, Ontario, and his Master's of Divinity and PhD in history from Yale University. In 1968, he took up his teaching position in Philadelphia, choosing to live in an impoverished neighborhood of that city. In 1972, Sider served as secretary of Evangelicals for McGovern and the following year helped found Evangelicals for Social Action, an organization that called for a biblical response to combating racism and poverty. His appeal at the 1984 Mennonite World Conference to send nonviolent Christian peacekeeping forces into zones of conflict led to the creation of Christian Peacemaker Teams, an organization that has participated in sometimes controversial interventions in the Middle East, Chechnya, Haiti, and Chiapas, Mexico.

Sider has published more than twenty books, including three updated versions of *Rich Christians*, as well as numerous articles for *Christianity Today*, *Sojourners*, *PRISM*, and other moderate and progressive religious serials. His work is unified by its attention to the systemic forces that underlie individual and regional poverty, the hypocrisy he sees in evangelicals who ignore issues of social justice, and the need for enhanced government programs—in conjunction with charitable giving—in order to redress economic inequalities. These views, along with his sometimes strident criticisms of American society, have led detractors to accuse him of anti-Americanism, simplistic and utopian economic theorizing, and/or outright Marxism. Religious conservatives have mounted a sustained attack against Sider since the mid-1970s, most notably through Christian reconstructionist David Chilton's *Productive Christians in an Age of Guilt Manipulators* (1981).

Sider has modified aspects of his views in response to these criticisms. Later writings reflect a growing appreciation for market economies and an increasing emphasis on the impact of personal choice on individual success. The link between individual morality and poverty, along with his belief in the ability of Christianity to transform economically detrimental personal behavior, has led Sider to support faith-based social programs. This endorsement, along with his opposition to abortion and same-sex marriage, has drawn condemnation from liberals within and beyond the Christian community.

Robert Teigrob

See also: Abortion; Campolo, Anthony "Tony"; Canada; Christian Reconstructionism; Compassionate Conservatism; Evangelicalism; Faith-Based Programs; Marxism; Religious Right; Same-Sex Marriage; Wallis, Jim; Wealth Gap.

Further Reading

Chilton, David. *Productive Christians in an Age of Guilt Manipulators: A Biblical Response to Ron Sider.* Tyler, TX: Institute for Christian Economics, 1981.

Martin, Paul. "Prophet or Siren? Ron Sider's Continued Influence." *Religion & Liberty* 10:1 (January and February 2000): 11–13.

Robbins, John. "Ron Sider Contra Deum." *Trinity Review* (March–April 1981): 1–6.

Sider, Ron. *Just Generosity: A New Vision for Overcoming Poverty in America.* Grand Rapids, MI: Baker, 1999.

———. *Rich Christians in an Age of Hunger: A Biblical Study.* Downers Grove, IL: InterVarsity Press, 1977.

Silent Majority

The term "Silent Majority" was a rhetorical device first used by President Richard Nixon in a televised speech on November 3, 1969, to cast the protesters of the Vietnam War as not representative of average Americans. The context was his attempt to restore public support for his policy to seek "peace with honor" rather than immediately withdraw U.S. forces. In that address, Nixon appealed to "the great silent majority of my fellow Americans" and asked them to help him "end the war in a way that we could win the peace." His strategy was to make the antiwar demonstrators seem like a small but loud minority out of step with the rest of American society, which believed in the fight to stop the spread of communism in Vietnam and Southeast Asia.

During his first months in office in 1969, the president established the Nixon Doctrine for implementing "Vietnamization," a plan to shift the war burden from the U.S. military to Vietnamese armed forces. Later, Nixon traveled to the region and met with American troops and the president of South Vietnam. Despite his efforts to decrease American involvement in the increasingly unpopular conflict, antiwar protests continued at home. Moreover, newspaper revelations of the My Lai massacre (in which hundreds of unarmed Vietnamese villagers had been killed by U.S. soldiers) inflamed protesters, further complicating efforts to secure public support for his war agenda.

It did not go unnoticed by Nixon that the protest movements included some of the same youthful, counterculture elements that were part of the earlier civil rights movement. He and many conservative politicians believed that media coverage of these "agitators" had skewed the public perception of their breadth and popularity. Most Americans, Nixon argued, were not only loyal supporters of the Cold War policy of containment but also opponents of the domestic riots and marches that threatened the social status quo of race relations and gender roles. Nixon's speech also appealed to veterans of past wars, many of whom viewed war protesters as unpatriotic.

In general, Nixon's argument resonated with blue-collar workers. On May 8, 1970, in a show of support for Nixon's war policies, helmeted construction workers, in a demonstration organized by the president of the Building and Construction Trades Council, wielded wrenches against antiwar students in New York City. After beating up students, the workers then marched to city hall and raised the American flag that had been lowered to half-mast to mourn the victims of the Kent State shootings four days earlier.

The "Silent Majority" claim was an integral part of the Republican strategy to win support of the white working class, especially in the Midwest and the South. Strategists also argued that media coverage of the war was unbalanced, offering excessive coverage to dissenting groups and thus displaying a liberal media bias. Similarly, when Jerry Falwell established the Moral Majority, the idea being communicated was that anything not in accord with the conservative viewpoint was outside the mainstream.

Angie Maxwell

See also: Civil Rights Movement; Cold War; Communists and Communism; Counterculture; Falwell, Jerry; Media Bias; Moral Majority; My Lai Massacre; Nixon, Richard; Republican Party; Vietnam Veterans Against the War; Vietnam War; War Protesters.

Further Reading
Black, Conrad. *Richard M. Nixon: A Life in Full.* New York: PublicAffairs, 2007.

Genovese, Michael A. *The Nixon Presidency: Power and Politics in Turbulent Times.* Westport, CT: Greenwood, 1990.

McNamara, Robert S. *In Retrospect: The Tragedy and Lessons of Vietnam.* New York: Times Books, 1995.

Simpsons, The

The Simpsons, an animated television series created by cartoonist Matt Groening, has been highly popular and controversial since its premiere in 1989. In following the lives of Homer, Marge, and their children, Bart, Lisa, and Maggie, *The Simpsons* pokes fun at a variety of social, political, and economic issues, including juvenile delinquency, alcoholism, race relations, gender roles, consumerism, and class divisions. The show's social commentary generally draws criticism from conservatives and praise from liberals, but its depiction of a modern family has found allies on the political right as well. In 2007, the cartoon series was the basis for the movie, *The Simpsons*, which was widely received.

Groening's series first appeared as a recurrent segment on *The Tracey Ullman Show* (1987–1990) and then became a weekly series on the Fox television network in 1989. Each member of the Simpson family provides fodder for satirical humor. Homer is more interested in drinking Duff Beer and eating donuts than in interacting with his family. Marge is an understanding, patient housewife but has a darker side and is secretly ambitious. Bart is an irreverent, self-described underachiever and is continuously in trouble for bucking authority. Lisa is a budding feminist, saxophone player, and vegetarian.

The other residents of the Simpsons' fictional hometown—Springfield, USA—also play a significant role in many of the storylines. Homer works at a nuclear power plant under the management of the greedy Mr. Burns and his assistant Mr. Smithers, allowing for plot lines exposing the sinister side of capitalism. Krusty the Klown, the children's favorite entertainer, is an off-stage alcoholic and compulsive gambler, which the show often uses to comment on the hypocrisy of entertainment and the media. Ned Flanders, the Simpsons' neighbor, is an evangelical Christian who is constantly trying to save Homer and his family. In a 2005 episode, Marge's sister Patty falls in love, comes out as a lesbian, and decides to marry.

Although *Simpsons* satire often comes at the expense of the political right, some conservatives have commended the show's portrayal of a stable nuclear family and of religion. Homer and Marge's marriage is often depicted as dysfunctional, but the couple continues to stay together. The character of Ned Flanders also finds support among conservatives. Although he is an evangelical Christian and is often ridiculed for his perpetual positive attitude, he is also portrayed as empathetic and kind. With its commitment to satirizing everyone, *The Simpsons* has found audiences on both sides of the political fence, and the series has drawn the attention of scholars as well.

Jessie Swigger

See also: Campolo, Anthony "Tony"; Comic Books; Comic Strips; Evangelicalism; Family Values; Lesbians; Nuclear Age; Race; Stay-at-Home Mothers.

Further Reading

Groening, Matt. *The Simpsons: A Complete Guide to Our Favorite Family*. New York: HarperPerennial, 1997.

Irwin, William, Mark T. Conrad, and Aeon J. Skoble, eds. *The Simpsons and Philosophy: The D'Oh of Homer*. Chicago: Open Court, 2001.

Pinsky, Mark, and Tony Campolo. *The Gospel According to the Simpsons: The Spiritual Life of the World's Most Animated Family*. Louisville, KY: Westminster John Knox Press, 2001.

Smoking in Public

Beginning in the 1970s, the issue of smoking tobacco in indoor public facilities has pitted libertarians against health advocates across the United States. For many opponents of government-imposed restrictions on smoking, lighting up a cigarette symbolizes individualism and freedom of choice. Smoking bans thus are seen as an attack on civil liberties and an example of "Big Brother" policing. On the other hand, for those concerned about the health risks of involuntary (secondhand) smoking— otherwise known as environmental tobacco smoke (ETS)—the public good warrants smoking bans in public transportation facilities, workplaces, and even restaurants and bars. By 2007, half of all Americans lived in states or local communities that had implemented smoking ordinances.

U.S. Surgeon General Leroy E. Burney in 1957 became the first U.S. federal official to declare a causal link between smoking and lung cancer, but it was not until seven years later that smoking was officially declared a health hazard. A report issued in January 1964 by Surgeon General Luther L. Terry's Advisory Committee on Smoking and Health compelled Congress the following year to require health warning labels on all cigarette packages. By 1972, the Surgeon General's office began warning about ETS.

In 1986, Surgeon General C. Everett Koop, as well as the National Research Council of the National Academy of Sciences, produced the results of a number of studies that linked ETS with lung cancer in nonsmokers. Reiterating the health risks of ETS, the U.S. Environmental Protection Agency in 1993 classified secondhand smoke

as a "Group A" carcinogen. In 2006, Surgeon General Richard Carmona warned that ETS is "more pervasive than we previously thought" and "a serious health hazard that can lead to disease and premature death in children and nonsmoking adults." Carmona argued that ventilation systems like the ones used in restaurants do not eliminate secondhand smoke.

In the wake of the first warnings against smoking by the Surgeon General's office, the tobacco industry in 1958 founded the Tobacco Institute, a think tank that would devote itself to disputing the scientific data on smoking. Its efforts would be offset, however, by those of various antismoking groups in the late 1960s and 1970s, including Action on Smoking and Health (ASH), founded in 1968; Group Against Smokers' Pollution (GASP), founded in 1971; and Fresh Air for Non-Smokers (FANS), founded in 1979.

The antismoking lobby scored an early victory in 1972, when Minneapolis and St. Paul, Minnesota, became the first municipalities in the nation to restrict smoking in public buildings. The anti-ETS movement was bolstered four years later by a ruling of the New Jersey Superior Court that affirmed the right of Donna Shimp, an employee of Bell Telephone and the plaintiff in the case, to work in a smoke-free office environment. In 1986, the U.S. General Services Administration banned smoking in federal buildings. In 1988, Congress banned smoking on domestic airline flights of two hours or less, extending the ban two years later to longer flights.

By the mid-1980s, the R.J. Reynolds Tobacco Company was publishing editorial advertisements in national publications in an attempt to block pending smoking ordinances across the country. Titles included "Smoking in Public: Let's Separate Fact from Friction," "Second-Hand Smoke: The Myth and the Reality," "Workplace Smoking Restrictions: A Trend That Never Was," "The Second-Hand Smokescreen," and the like. In a two-pronged approach, the campaign cast doubt on scientific claims about the health risks associated with ETS by suggesting that the data are inconclusive, and framed the issue of smoking in public as one that can be resolved by individuals applying "common sense" and "politeness." One ad characterized smoking bans as a form of "segregation," implying that smokers were being stripped of their civil rights.

Perhaps most controversial has been the debate over smoking in restaurants and bars. In 1995, tobacco giant Philip Morris provided the seed money for the establishment of the Guest Choice Network (later the Center for Consumer Freedom), a lobbying organization to oppose, among other things, government-imposed smoking bans in restaurants. Generally, the hospitality industry has emphasized market principles, arguing that proprietors should have the authority to decide whether or not to allow smoking in their establishments and that customers can decide for themselves whether or not to patronize them. In 1994, controversially, California became the first state to pass legislation that banned smoking in all buildings open to the public, including bars and restaurants (though the measure did not fully go into effect until 1998). New York City's 2003 smoking ordinance also banned smoking in bars and restaurants. One of the strictest smoking bans went into effect in Hawaii in 2006, forbidding outdoor smoking less than 20 feet (6.1 meters) from any door, window, or ventilation system of a hotel, restaurant, or bar.

Roger Chapman

See also: Koop, C. Everett; Science Wars; Tobacco Settlements.

Further Reading

Hilts, Philip J. *Smokescreen: The Truth Behind the Tobacco Industry Cover-up.* Reading, MA: Addison-Wesley, 1996.

Schaler, Jeffrey A., and Magda E. Schaler, eds. *Smoking: Who Has the Right?* Amherst, NY: Prometheus Books, 1998.

Sullum, Jacob. *For Your Own Good: The Anti-Smoking Crusade and the Tyranny of Public Health.* New York: Free Press, 1998.

U.S. Environmental Protection Agency. *Respiratory Health Effects of Passive Smoking: Lung Cancer and Other Disorders.* Bethesda, MD: National Institutes of Health, 1993.

U.S. Surgeon General. *The Health Consequences of Involuntary Smoking.* Rockville, MD: U.S. Department of Health and Human Services, 1986.

Socarides, Charles

Psychiatrist and author Charles Socarides argued in 1973 that the American Psychiatric Association (APA) "sacrificed our scientific knowledge" when it stopped listing homosexuality as a mental illness. Regarding same-sex desire as a "neurotic adaptation," Socarides devoted his career to the "treatment and prevention" of homosexuality.

A native of Brockton, Massachusetts, Charles William Socarides was born on January 24, 1922. At age thirteen, inspired by the writings of Sigmund Freud, he decided to become a psychiatrist. A graduate of Harvard College (1945), New York Medical College (1947), and the psychoanalytical clinic and research center at Columbia University's College of Physicians and Surgeons (1952), he served as a lieutenant in the U.S. Navy during the Korean War. While maintaining a private practice in New York City, he taught psychiatry at the Albert Einstein College of Medicine in the Bronx (1960–1996). Near the end of his career, in 1992, Socarides co-founded the National Association for Research and Therapy of Homosexuality, based in Encino, California, a nonprofit group "dedicated to affirming a complementary, male-female model of gender and sexuality."

After APA members in April 1974 voted 5,845 to 3,810 (out of 17,910 eligible voters) to uphold the 1973

board decision to declassify homosexuality as a psychological malady, Socarides and seven other psychiatrists demanded a second vote. APA members, they argued, had been misled because a letter about the referendum mailed to them by the board and signed by APA leaders was conceived and paid for by the National Gay Task Force. Indeed, the task force, which had been formed in October 1973 to "work for liberation of gay people and a change in public attitudes," spent $3,000 on printing and mailing the letter, a detail that was not at the time disclosed to the APA rank and file. In May 1975, an ad hoc committee of the APA rejected the request for a new vote, ruling that it was "opposed to the use of referenda to decide on scientific issues." But Socarides's faction saw the first vote as a case in which a scientific issue had been decided by a referendum—and one manipulated by political activism.

His detractors (much of the mental health profession as well as gay rights activists) believed that Socarides perpetuated the suffering of his patients by convincing them that homosexuality was something that had to be "fixed." His supporters (social conservatives and certain religious groups) regarded him as a brave scientist who followed where his research findings led and offered "reparative therapy" to help people overcome a pathological illness. Critics dismissed his claim to have "cured" 35 percent of his gay patients.

Socarides wrote numerous books, including *The Overt Homosexual* (1968) and *Homosexuality: A Freedom Too Far* (1995). His gay son, Richard, was a White House adviser on lesbian and gay issues to President Bill Clinton. Socarides, who died on December 25, 2005, was convinced that he had failed his son by not providing the kind of family atmosphere necessary for heterosexual development.

Roger Chapman

See also: Clinton, Bill; Gay Rights Movement; Gays in the Military; Hay, Harry; Milk, Harvey; Lesbians; Same-Sex Marriage; Science Wars; Sodomy Laws; Stonewall Rebellion; White, Reggie.

Further Reading

Bayer, Ronald. *Homosexuality and American Psychiatry: The Politics of Diagnosis.* New York: Basic Books, 1981.

Erzen, Tanya. *Straight to Jesus: Sexual and Christian Conversion in the Ex-Gay Movement.* Berkeley: University of California Press, 2006.

Socarides, Charles W. "How America Went Gay." *America*, November 18, 1995.

Social Security

The Social Security program—signed into law by President Franklin D. Roosevelt in 1935—was created to provide retired workers with a stable income. It has grown into one of the largest economic responsibilities of the U.S. federal government, accounting for nearly one-quarter of the government's annual spending. From the program's inception to 2008, over $10 trillion was paid out in benefits.

Social Security is a form of social insurance to which workers and their employers contribute a percentage of the workers' wages. Upon the retirement, disability, or death of a worker, the federal government pays a regular cash benefit to the worker or his or her surviving dependents. Benefits are not computed strictly on an actuarial basis (returns are not based strictly on considerations of individual equity), but elements of social policy are factored in as well (what policymakers call concern for *social adequacy*). For example, Social Security benefits are weighted so that the retirement benefit is proportionately higher for low-wage workers than for high-wage workers.

History

The Social Security Act of 1935 created only a retirement benefit and only for the individual worker. Only about half the jobs in the economy were covered under the original 1935 legislation. Major amendments adopted in 1939 changed the nature of the system from an individual retirement program to a family-based benefit, by the addition of dependent and survivor benefits. The provision of spouses' benefits, in particular, was premised on the model of the typical 1930s-era family, which featured a working father and a stay-at-home mother.

Between 1950 and 1972, the program expanded dramatically, providing coverage to new classes of occupations, significantly increasing the value of benefits, and adding new types of benefits. Cash disability benefits were made available in 1956, and health insurance for the elderly was provided under Medicare in 1965. In 1972, the program allowed for regular annual increases in benefits to keep pace with the cost of living. Since then, financing concerns have slowed policy expansion.

The impact of Social Security on the economic status of the elderly has been dramatic. Prior to the program, the majority of the elderly in America lived in some form of economic dependency—they were too poor to be self-supporting. In 2006, only 10 percent of the nation's elderly were living in poverty, a much lower rate due in large part to Social Security. It is also the nation's principal disability program, with 8 million people receiving disability benefits in 2006 and another 7 million receiving survivors' benefits. Of Social Security's 48 million beneficiaries in 2006, more than 3 million were children receiving benefits as dependents of insured workers. In 2008, some 50 million people received $600 billion in annual benefits under the program.

Ideological Viewpoints

As America's largest and most expensive social welfare program, Social Security has been a source of almost constant contention in the culture wars. In the 1980s, President Ronald Reagan's budget director, David Stockman, referred to the Social Security program as "the inner fortress of the welfare state" that the conservative movement would seek to dismantle. Social conservatives believe that the family rather than the government ought to provide such economic support. However, because the program is designed around the family as the economic unit, some social conservatives have been won over. Gary Bauer, the founder of the socially conservative Family Research Council and a Republican candidate for president in 2000, defended Social Security on the grounds that its benefit structure (especially the spousal benefit) encourages traditional families.

Fiscal conservatives complain that Social Security taxes are onerous, and that government is an inefficient provider of economic security compared to private markets. They argue that America would be better served by a privatized system of economic security rather than one sponsored by the government. Advocates of small government, such as libertarians, opposed on principle to government involving itself in issues of economic security, characterize Social Security and similar programs as part of a patronizing "nanny state."

Liberals, on the other hand, argue that government has an obligation to ensure a basic foundation of economic security for its citizens. Social Security has long been viewed as a principal achievement of the liberal welfare state and is fiercely defended by the Democratic Party as one of its signal political achievements. Some on the political left complain that the program is not generous enough, and that it should be structured more like traditional European social welfare programs. Linking benefits to work means that existing inequities in the workplace—such as lower wages and participation rates for African Americans and women—will be mirrored in the retirement benefits under the system. Accordingly, some liberals complain that the program does not provide compensatory features for women and minorities to offset prior discrimination in the workplace. Feminists argue that the spousal benefit implicitly supports patriarchal families. Some critics argue that the system is unfair to African Americans because their shorter life expectancies mean less in retirement benefits.

The division between private versus government-sponsored social support is one of the main political fault lines in the culture wars. It pits the conservative ideals of individual responsibility and the pursuit of individual equity against the liberal ideals of collective responsibility and concern for the less fortunate. The designers of the Social Security program tried to strike a balance between these two sets of ideals, with elements of both built into the system. But attacks from both ends of the political spectrum have been commonplace throughout Social Security's history. Since about the late 1980s, the critiques from the left have tended to fade, and the critiques from fiscal conservatives and libertarians have tended to be more prominent than critiques from social conservatives.

Long-Term Solvency and the Push for Privatization

The most active criticism of the Social Security system revolves around fiscal issues. The fiscal critique has gained traction in the early twenty-first century given the uncertain future solvency of the system. Because the financing of Social Security is highly sensitive to demographic changes, as the Baby Boom generation enters its prime retirement years, the financial demands on the system will be severe. In its 2007 report, the board of trustees for the system projected that the program will fall short of full funding by the year 2041.

Social Security thus faces a long-range solvency challenge that may require a tax increase or benefit reductions in the future. Debates about the future of Social Security are likely to involve issues of cost and intergenerational fairness, as future taxpayers may be asked to bear greater burdens or future beneficiaries to accept lesser benefits than prior cohorts.

Such uncertainty has provided a renewed opportunity for conservative critics to argue for privatization of the system. Privatization means that some or all of the tax revenues financing the program would be diverted from the government's accounts and invested in the stock market. Thus, a private equity account of some type would replace some or all of the benefits offered by the Social Security program.

In 2001, newly installed President George W. Bush signaled his intention to transform the system by shifting large segments of its financing to the private equity market. Bush appointed a special commission of experts to recommend ways to introduce private accounts into the system and campaigned hard for this idea at the start of his second term in 2005, but he was unable to generate a political consensus in support of his proposals.

Although there have been critics of the program throughout its history, Social Security has enjoyed a remarkable degree of public support. Its design has seemed to accord well with the values of the majority of American workers and taxpayers. Whether this consensus will endure as the solvency problem deepens remains to be seen.

Larry W. DeWitt

See also: Bush Family; Federal Budget Deficit; Generations and Generational Conflict; New Deal; Reagan, Ronald; Tax Reform; Welfare Reform.

Further Reading

Altman, Nancy J. *The Battle for Social Security: From FDR's Vision to Bush's Gamble.* Hoboken, NJ: John Wiley & Sons, 2005.

Berkowitz, Edward D. *America's Welfare State: From Roosevelt to Reagan.* Baltimore: Johns Hopkins University Press, 1991.

Diamond, Peter A., and Peter R. Orszag. *Saving Social Security: A Balanced Approach.* Washington, DC: Brookings Institution, 2004.

Ferrara, Peter J., and Michael Tanner. *A New Deal for Social Security.* Washington, DC: Cato Institute, 1998.

Social Security Administration Web site. www.socialsecurity.gov.

Sodomy Laws

Sodomy laws prohibiting various forms of nonreproductive sexual activity once existed in the penal codes of every U.S. state, but only fourteen maintained them by 2003, the year in which the U.S. Supreme Court in *Lawrence v. Texas* declared all such laws unconstitutional on the grounds that they violated a person's right to privacy. Because of the sexual practices they targeted, sodomy laws effectively criminalized gays and lesbians and thereby hindered their inclusion in mainstream society as respectable, law-abiding citizens.

Sodomy laws have both religious and historical roots. Prohibitions against same-sex intercourse, for example, are found in the Jewish and Christian scriptures. English law criminalized such behavior, establishing a precedent for colonial American jurisprudence to do the same. The mid-twentieth century, however, saw increasing divergence among the states regarding sodomy laws. Led by Illinois in 1961, certain states rescinded their sodomy laws for consenting adults. Others expanded the scope of these laws to include some heterosexual behaviors as well as same-sex acts between women. One notable battle over such laws occurred in California in 1975, when sodomy was decriminalized by a one-vote margin in the state senate. The conservative backlash led to the Briggs Amendment ballot initiative in 1978, which sought (but failed) to deny employment to gay and lesbian schoolteachers in California.

Sodomy laws continued to be a flashpoint for social conservatives and gay rights groups. During the peak of the AIDS crisis in the 1980s, when male-male sex acts were under attack as a health risk, the Supreme Court in *Bowers v. Hardwick* (1986) upheld the states' prerogative to criminalize sodomy. The Court thereby resisted recognizing a right to privacy for gays and lesbians expansive enough to protect consensual sexual activity, as it had done previously for heterosexuals. Social conservatives, already wary of the Court's expansive interpretation of privacy so key to the *Roe v. Wade* (1973) decision on abortion, embraced the *Bowers* ruling.

Although sodomy laws were rarely enforced by the 1980s, in some areas openly gay citizens were automatically presumed to be guilty of sodomy, and thus were regarded by some as criminals. Such stigmatization led to a number of court decisions depriving gays and lesbians of child custody rights or adoption privileges. Others lost their jobs for allegedly practicing sodomy. *Lawrence v. Texas* (2003), which overturned *Bowers* after just seventeen years, was therefore monumental in ending the association of homosexuality with criminality. In his dissent, Justice Antonin Scalia criticized the majority decision, complaining that the Court "has taken sides in the culture war" in favor of the "so-called homosexual agenda." Scalia went on to argue that the *Lawrence* decision means state laws against same-sex marriage, bigamy, adult incest, and prostitution are now subject to being challenged.

Phil Tiemeyer

See also: AIDS; Bryant, Anita; Douglas, William O.; Family Values; Gay Rights Movement; Judicial Wars; Milk, Harvey; *Roe v. Wade* (1973); Same-Sex Marriage.

Further Reading

Eskridge, William N., Jr. *Dishonorable Passions: Sodomy Laws in America, 1861–2003*. New York: Viking, 2008.

Franke, Katherine M. "The Domesticated Liberty of *Lawrence v. Texas*." *Columbia Law Review* 104:5 (June 2004): 1399–1426.

Ireland, Doug. "Republicans Relaunch the Antigay Culture Wars." *Nation*, October 20, 2003.

Sokal Affair

The "Sokal Affair" of the late 1990s was a literary conflagration that followed the publication of New York University physicist Alan Sokal's paper "Transgressing the Boundaries: Toward a Transformative Hermeneutics of Quantum Gravity" in the postmodern cultural studies journal *Social Text*. Sokal revealed that the piece was a hoax, designed to determine if a leading journal would "publish . . . nonsense if (a) it sounded good and (b) it flattered the editors' ideological preconceptions." A front-page article in the *New York Times* announced that the answer was "yes," setting off a heated debate over the intellectual substance of postmodernism.

A dedicated physicist and unabashed old leftist (he frequently quotes Noam Chomsky and taught math for the Sandinistas), Sokal had been disturbed by claims that the "academic left" no longer believed in the ability of science to obtain objective truth. (If one concedes that truth is simply an artifact of power, Sokal argued, it would be impossible to criticize power as being untruthful.) After considering the best way to respond, he finally settled on parody. Sokal spent several months writing

a comic pastiche that combined "vague rhetoric about 'nonlinearity,' 'flux' and 'interconnectedness'" while insisting "physical 'reality,' no less than social 'reality,' is at bottom a social and linguistic construct." In footnotes, he claimed that the mathematical axioms of choice and equality stemmed from pro-choice, pro-equality "liberal feminists" and that New Age theories of the collective unconscious were the basis of cutting-edge research into quantum gravity, citing Rebecca Goldstein's novel *The Mind-Body Problem* (1983) as a definitive text on the subject. More important, perhaps, the submission lavished praise on the editors of *Social Text* and called for scientists and mathematicians to subordinate their work to the left-wing political program.

After *Social Text* published the paper in its spring/summer 1996 issue on "The Science Wars," *Lingua Franca* published Sokal's essay revealing the hoax in its May/June issue. The editors of *Social Text* responded by calling Sokal a "deceptive" and "difficult, uncooperative author," and his article as "a little hokey," "somewhat outdated," and "not really our cup of tea." (At the same time, one editor refused to believe it was a hoax, instead maintaining that Sokal simply had "a folding of his intellectual resolve.") They refused to publish Sokal's afterword defending and explaining his paper.

Meanwhile, the Sokal hoax was invoked by countless popular and academic critics of postmodernism as definitive proof of the field's vacuousness. Still, Sokal was at pains to point out that "at most it reveals something about the intellectual standards of *one* trendy journal" and to insist there should not be a "science war" but an "exchange of ideas . . . to promote a collective search for the truth."

The following year, Sokal and French physicist Jean Bricmont together published *Fashionable Nonsense*, a book-length critique of the misuse of science by prominent postmodernists and a philosophical defense of scientific realism. The book led to more critiques of postmodernism in the popular press, but little response from the cultural studies community, which had largely written off Sokal as a mocking critic.

Aaron Swartz

See also: Anti-Intellectualism; Foucault, Michel; Postmodernism; Science Wars.

Further Reading

Bérubé, Michael. *Rhetorical Occasions: Essays on Humans and the Humanities*. Chapel Hill: University of North Carolina Press, 2006.

Editors of *Lingua Franca*. *The Sokal Hoax: The Sham That Shook the Academy*. Lincoln, NE: Bison Books, 2000.

Sokal, Alan, and Jean Bricmont. *Fashionable Nonsense: Postmodern Intellectuals' Abuse of Science*. New York: Picador, 1998.

Soros, George

A billionaire financier, entrepreneur, and philanthropist, George Soros is known not only for several high-profile financial deals but also for his writings on politics and economics. In the late 1970s, he began his long campaign of promoting social and political reform in Eastern Europe, but at the beginning of the twenty-first century, his outspoken opposition to the policies of President George W. Bush made him a prominent figure in the American culture wars.

Born György Schwartz on August 12, 1930, in Budapest, Hungary, Soros experienced the Nazi occupation and escaped the Holocaust by concealing his Jewish ethnicity. At age seventeen, he moved to England, where he earned a degree from the London School of Economics (1952) and came under the influence of the philosopher Karl Popper. After immigrating to the United States in 1956, he worked for a number of years as an arbitrage trader and then co-founded Quantum Fund (1969), which emerged as one of the world's most lucrative hedge funds. This was followed by the establishment of Soros Fund Management (1973), a highly successful international investment fund he continues to chair. Two of its controversial deals were a currency speculation in the British pound and the Malaysian ringgit during the 1990s that resulted in the devaluation of both currencies. In the former case, he was said to have earned $1 billion in one day by speculating that the pound would decline in value. His best-selling book *The Alchemy of Finance: Reading the Mind of the Market* (1988) is a treatise on investing.

Profoundly influenced by Popper's *The Open Society and Its Enemies* (1945), Soros applied his wealth to fostering reform in "closed societies" such as South Africa, China, and the Soviet Union and its Eastern Bloc. His Open Society Institute (OSI) was founded in 1979 to champion the creation of civil societies in countries shedding totalitarian systems. Operating in more than fifty countries, OSI continues to support education, human rights, economic development, women's concerns, and public health. His founding of Central European University in his native city of Budapest in 1991 was with the intention of training new public and academic leaders in the rapidly transforming countries of Central and Eastern Europe and the former Soviet Union. In *Opening the Soviet Union* (1990), Soros claimed some credit for the downfall of communism; he had supported the Solidarity trade union movement in Poland and the Charter 77 human rights organization in Czechoslovakia, both of which helped foster the demise of the Soviet bloc.

In the United States, OSI has initiated programs to promote reform in criminal justice, immigration, and youth empowerment. Some of Soros's positions have run counter to the viewpoints of political conservatives, such as his advocacy of needle exchange programs, medical marijuana, and medical-assisted suicide. The American public became more familiar with him during the 2004 presidential election, when he donated millions of dollars to organizations such as MoveOn.org to oppose the reelection of George W. Bush. In *The Bubble of American Supremacy: Correcting the Misuse of American Power* (2003) and *The Age of Fallibility: The Consequences of the War on Terror* (2006), Soros has characterized the Bush administration's foreign policy as delusional, arguing that it has undermined America's greatness through violations of human rights and actions representative of closed societies.

Susan Pearce

See also: Abu Ghraib and Gitmo; Bush Family; Cold War; Communists and Communism; Globalization; Holocaust; Human Rights; Medical Marijuana; Prison Reform; September 11; Soviet Union and Russia; War on Drugs.

Further Reading

Carter, Terry. "Mr. Democracy." *ABA Journal*, January 2000.
Kaufman, Michael T. *Soros: The Life and Times of a Messianic Billionaire*. New York: Alfred A. Knopf, 2002.
Open Society Institute Web site. www.soros.org.

Southern Baptist Convention

Organized in 1845 in Augusta, Georgia, the Southern Baptist Convention (SBC) is the largest Protestant denomination in the United States, the second-largest religious group in the United States (after the Roman Catholic Church), and the largest Baptist group in the world. In 2008, the SBC claimed more than 16 million members, worshipping in over 42,000 churches in the United States. Although SBC churches are highly concentrated in the American South, the denomination has expanded to include congregations in every U.S. state and throughout the world.

The SBC has figured prominently in the rise of the Christian Right since the 1980s, but historically it has been minimally involved in American politics. Southern Baptists faced controversy in their early history (over slavery, denominational structure, and missionary activity that split Northern and Southern Baptists, for example), but had little capacity or inclination for political-cultural engagement before the mid-twentieth century. The traditional marginalization of the South weakened SBC capability for national influence before post–World War II economic renewal. Moreover, Southern Baptists encountered difficulties in national mobilization due to their decentralized church polity (congregational, associational, confessional) and some internal tendencies toward separatism.

Southern Baptists first strongly embraced political-cultural engagement after evangelical leaders like Billy Graham, Carl F.H. Henry, and Charles Fuller spearheaded efforts to bring national revival and cultural renewal in the 1940s. Enthusiasm for confronting secularism was later bolstered by supporting Christian intellectual rationale, such as Richard John Neuhaus's book on church-state relations, *The Naked Public Square: Religion and Democracy in America* (1984).

As SBC willingness to engage with society grew, denominational transformation brought the organization into the political and cultural spotlight. Beginning in 1961, the denomination split between theologically liberal/moderate and conservative/fundamentalist camps, with the former holding ascendance until 1979 and the latter maintaining preeminence in the years since. In the so-called Conservative Resurgence or Fundamentalist Takeover, conservatives from 1979 on engineered successive SBC presidential victories and installed supporters in key positions on boards and seminaries. In addition, conservatives reformed denominational institutions to enable greater unity on doctrinal orthodoxy, especially biblical inerrancy and infallibility. The SBC today remains largely conservative, albeit with internal tension between liberals/moderates and old-line conservatives (who object to perceived SBC creedalism and centralization) that operate through local and national splinter entities.

The internal SBC theological struggle has had political implications as well, explaining such seeming paradoxes as the SBC's initial support and later criticism of *Roe v. Wade* (1973) and the competing ranks of politically liberal members (Jimmy Carter, Bill Clinton, Richard Gephardt, Al Gore) versus conservative ones (Newt Gingrich, Jesse Helms, Strom Thurmond, and Trent Lott). Since 1979, the SBC has become more politically active, typically supporting conservative causes through agencies like the Ethics and Religious Liberty Commission. Although the SBC includes members with diverse political leanings and endorses political activism according to biblical values over party lines, it has also proven to be an important Republican Party constituency.

The SBC opposes abortion, euthanasia, human cloning, electively aborted embryonic stem-cell research, pornography, premarital sex, homosexuality, same-sex marriage, sexuality and violence in the media, gambling, and alcohol/tobacco/drug use. It supports homeschooling, school choice, voluntary prayer and religious expression in public schools, capital punishment, and the appointment of conservative federal judges. Some SBC resolutions have been relatively uncontroversial, supporting environmental care, human rights, hunger relief, voluntary organ donation, disaster assistance, and benevolence (prison, homeless, and AIDS victim ministries); while renouncing sex trafficking, genocide,

religious persecution, terrorism, anti-Semitism, and racism. Other resolutions, however, proved to be polarizing, including affirmations of Ronald Reagan, Operation Desert Storm, Operation Iraqi Freedom, the Boy Scouts of America's leadership policies, the ban on homosexuality in the military, border control (though with social and economic justice for legal and illegal immigrants), and Israeli sovereignty (though calling for internationally just treatment of Israelis as well as Palestinians). The SBC has also stirred controversy for boycotting the Walt Disney Company and subsidiaries for pro-gay policies and programs (1997–2005), confining pastoral leadership to men, and stating that wives should submit graciously to their husbands (just as husbands must love their wives as Christ loved the church).

Although the SBC is politically conservative overall, its size, structure, and diffuseness has over the years allowed for variation in political approaches among leaders, members, and affiliated organizations. Thus, SBC resolutions are suggestive but nonbinding. The large tent of the SBC has accommodated those with nontraditional theological positions (i.e., Pat Robertson's Charismaticism) and those with vastly differing political positions (from Jerry Falwell to Rick Warren).

Erika Seeler

See also: Boy Scouts of America; Falwell Jerry; Gays in the Military; Graham, Billy; Immigration Policy; Israel; Pornography; Reagan, Ronald; Religious Right; Right to Die; Robertson, Pat; *Roe v. Wade* (1973); Same-Sex Marriage; Stem-Cell Research; Walt Disney Company; Warren, Rick; Women in the Military.

Further Reading

Ammerman, Nancy. *Baptist Battles: Social Change and Religious Conflict in the Southern Baptist Convention.* New Brunswick, NJ: Rutgers University Press, 1990.

Dockery, David S., ed. *Southern Baptists and American Evangelicals: The Conversation Continues.* Nashville, TN: Broadman & Holman, 1993.

Southern Baptist Convention official Web site. www.sbc.net.

Yarbrough, Slayden A. *Southern Baptists: A Historical, Ecclesiological, and Theological Heritage of a Confessional People.* Brentwood, TN: Southern Baptist Historical Society, 2000.

Soviet Union and Russia

After centuries of autocratic czarist rule, the 1917 Bolshevik Revolution brought Russia under communist control, leading to the establishment of the Union of Soviet Socialist Republics (USSR). Following the Soviet regime's implosion, triggered by reforms initiated by Kremlin leader Mikhail Gorbachev, the USSR in 1991 fragmented into a dozen independent republics with Russia as the dominant country. Whether Czarist Russia, Red Russia, or New Russia, this nation has traditionally been mistrusted by Americans and often characterized as the polar opposite of the United States.

Long before it became a communist dictatorship, Russia was widely viewed by Americans as a land of tyranny—Abraham Lincoln in the Lincoln-Douglas debates (1858), for instance, referred to Russia in this fashion. Earlier, the Monroe Doctrine (1823) and its assertion of American dominance of the Western Hemisphere was formulated in part as a warning to Russia, which at the time was colonizing Alaska and maintaining a fort as far south as what is today Sonoma County, California. And in his much-quoted study *Democracy in America* (1820–1840), Alexis de Tocqueville refers to the United States and Russia as "two great nations in the world, which started from two points," the former by "the plowshare" and the latter by "the sword."

World War I to Early Cold War

Although the American journalist and socialist John Reed wrote a celebratory account of the Bolshevik Revolution—*Ten Days That Shook the World* (1919)—most of his countrymen regarded the communist takeover of Russia as a tragedy. Moreover, Russia's unilateral withdrawal from World War I and its signing of a separate peace with Germany (the Treaty of Brest-Litovsk in 1918) were viewed as an act of treachery to the Western alliance, in particular Great Britain and the United States. With a civil war raging in Russia, the United States kept a military intervention force inside the country from 1918 to 1920. Meanwhile, the first Red Scare in the United States led to the roundup of "radicals" of Eastern European descent and their deportation to Russia on a ship nicknamed the "Soviet Ark."

Not until 1933, under President Franklin Roosevelt, did the United States formally recognize the Soviet government. During the decade of the Great Depression, many progressives were negatively labeled "fellow travelers" and "pinks" for making investigatory trips to the Soviet Union and then writing favorable assessments of planned economy. Violent labor disputes, such as the 1934 Electric Auto-Lite strike in Toledo, Ohio, were denigrated by conservative businessmen as "Bolshevik." In 1939, the Soviet government signed a nonaggression pact with the Nazi regime in Germany, inspiring the term "red fascism." Following Hitler's 1941 invasion of Russia, however, the Soviet Union became an ally, as heralded in the U.S. government's "Why We Fight" film, *The Battle of Russia* (1943). At the same time, Hollywood produced a number of positive films about Russia, including *Mission to Moscow* (1943), *The North Star* (1943), and *Song of Russia* (1944).

Nonetheless, the U.S.-Soviet wartime alliance was characterized by mutual mistrust. On July 25, 1945, after the United States' first successful atomic bomb test, President Harry Truman wrote in his diary, "It is certainly a good thing for the world that Hitler's crowd or Stalin's did not discover this atomic bomb." As it turned out, Soviet espionage penetrated the Manhattan Project, which would enable Russia to accelerate its own development of atomic weaponry. Once Russia acquired the bomb—which it tested successfully for the first time on August 29, 1949—the two superpowers embarked on a nuclear arms race. Already the Cold War had begun, largely due to the Soviet domination of Eastern Europe.

Culture Wars

As the Cold War played out and became a part of the culture wars, Americans largely regarded Russia as the opposite of what the United States stood for. The term "un-American" was a synonym for communist, meaning like the Soviet Union. Conservative culture warriors often branded their liberal opponents as being un-American or "far left." As the Soviet Union's official atheist stance was emphasized, the phrase "one nation under God" was inserted in the American flag pledge in 1954, and "In God We Trust" inscribed on U.S. currency in 1957, precipitating debates on the separation of church and state. The first stirrings of the Religious Right were related to the Christian opposition to Soviet curtailment of religious freedom, as evangelists such as Billy Hargis preached against communism (in 1964 he published *The Far Left, and Why I Fight for a Christian America*) and conducted ministry activities such as releasing hot air balloons with attached Bible verses over Soviet bloc nations.

For many cold warriors, the authoritarian Soviet system with its restrictions on individual freedom was what America was opposing. That was the message of the Freedom Train, which from 1947 to 1949 traversed the United States, stopping at major cities so that Americans could view original copies of the Bill of Rights and other "documents of liberty." In 1950, *Life* magazine reported the forty-eight-hour "communist takeover" of Mosinee, Wisconsin, a drama staged by the American Legion to underscore the freedom that would be lost under a Soviet-like system of government. The lesson was even less subtle in *Red Nightmare* (1957), a U.S. government propaganda film. Meanwhile, Isaiah Berlin's essay "Two Concepts of Liberty" (1958) prompted an intellectual debate over the distinction between negative liberty (freedom from restraint of the state, which the United States emphasized) and positive liberty (freedom to have what is necessary to reach one's full potential, which communists claimed to advance).

Americans largely viewed Russia as totalitarian and barbaric, based on news reports about its secret police (the Committee for State Security, known as the KGB), Stalinist purges, system of concentration camps (the Gulag), harassment and imprisonment of dissidents (such as writers, scientists, and intellectuals), and tight control over Eastern Europe (including the brutal crackdowns on Hungary in 1957 and Czechoslovakia in 1968). Nikita Khrushchev, who became the Soviet leader after Stalin's death in 1953, reinforced this negative image when he banged his shoe on a table during a debate at the General Assembly of the United Nations on October 12, 1960, and at various times said of the capitalist Western world, "We will bury you." The *Rocky and Bullwinkle Show*, an American television cartoon show that aired from 1959 to 1964, satirically portrayed the stereotype of sinister Russian behavior with the characters Boris Badenov and Natasha Fatale, an unsavory espionage duo that was hopelessly evil as well as incompetent. Some Americans thought President Ronald Reagan was too provocative when on March 8, 1983, he publicly declared the Soviet Union an "evil empire," but many agreed with him when he denounced as "savagery" the 269 deaths caused by the Soviet downing of a South Korean commercial airliner on September 1, 1983, after it had veered into Russian air space.

Americans long regarded Russians as backward and technologically inferior. This was despite the Soviet achievements of detonating a hydrogen bomb on August 12, 1953; launching the first artificial satellite on October 4, 1957; and conducting the first manned orbit of the earth on April 12, 1961. During the July 1959 "kitchen debate" at a trade exhibition in Moscow, U.S. vice president Richard Nixon boasted of the superiority of American consumer goods while hinting that the Soviet Union was below Western standards. The film comedy *The Russians Are Coming! The Russians Are Coming!* (1966), about a Russian submarine accidentally running aground off of Nantucket Island in Massachusetts, conveyed the view that the Soviets posed a danger that was canceled out by their own incompetence. For observant Americans, the Cuban Missile Crisis in October 1962 underscored Soviet vulnerability as the Kremlin sought some tactical way to offset the disadvantage of its lagging weapons delivery systems. When the two superpowers conducted the Apollo-Soyuz Test Project in 1975, some Americans grumbled that NASA had to give away trade secrets in order for the joint space venture to work. The Soviet space station *Mir* (1986–2001) was the butt of American jokes, even the subject of slapstick humor in the Hollywood film *Armageddon* (1998), because of its patchwork repairs and various mishaps, including a fire. The explosion of the Chernobyl nuclear reactor on April 26, 1986, which spewed radiation across Europe, was later attributed to Soviet design flaws as well as mismanagement. Many conservatives remain convinced that a main reason the Soviet Union came to a sudden end is that it was unable to keep up with American technological advances, especially after Reagan's March 1983 announcement of the Strategic Defense Initiative, a space-based antiballistic missile system.

Hope and Disappointment

In a commencement address at American University on June 10, 1963, President John F. Kennedy called on Americans to reexamine their attitudes about the Soviet people. "No government or social system is so evil that its people must be considered as lacking in virtue," Kennedy said. Although communism is "repugnant," he went on, Americans may nevertheless "hail the Russian people for their many achievements—in science and space, in economic and industrial growth, in culture and in acts of courage." Both sides, he insisted, have a "mutual abhorrence of war." Later, during the Moscow summit of May 1972, President Nixon offered similar sentiments, stating, "In many ways, the people of our two countries are very much alike . . . large and diverse . . . hard-working . . . a strong spirit of competition . . . a great love of music and poetry, of sports, and of humor . . . open, natural, and friendly. . . ." Both sides, explained Nixon, want "peace and abundance" for their children. Such hope was the theme of "Leningrad" (1989), a song by Billy Joel about two Cold War kids who grow up on different sides of the Atlantic but later meet in Russia, share a laugh, and embrace.

Perhaps one of the greatest American disappointments during the Cold War was the 1978 Harvard commencement address by the Russian dissident Alexander Solzhenitsyn. The author of *A Day in the Life of Ivan Denisovich* (1962) and *The Gulag Archipelago* (1973), among other works, Solzhenitsyn used the occasion to criticize Soviet tyranny but also to argue that Western society, due to its "spiritual exhaustion," was no model to follow. Since Solzhenitsyn had for two years been living in exile in the United States, his words were taken as a condemnation of American culture in particular. Later, during the 1980s, as Gorbachev introduced the reforms of *glasnost* (openness about social problems) and *perestroika* (restructuring of the economy), Americans gradually hoped that their former rival might become Westernized. After the demise of the Soviet Union on December 25, 1991, President George H.W. Bush suggested that the United States and the new Russia could begin a long era of friendly cooperation.

By Western democratic standards, the first leaders of post-USSR Russia—Boris Yeltsin (1991–1999), Vladimir Putin (2000–2008), and Dmitri Medvedev (2008–) —have proven to be autocratic. The Yeltsin years were characterized by "economic shock therapy" and "bandit capitalism" in which oligarchs and mafia ruled over a chaotic shift toward privatization. In October 1993, Yeltsin dissolved the Duma (Russian parliament) and then ordered tanks to shell the building when some of the legislators refused to leave. Stephen Cohen, a professor of Russian studies, at the time deplored the Bill Clinton administration for "supporting" Yeltsin's behavior. Cohen and others also criticized the "missionary economists" from the West who pushed for market reforms in Russia with apparently little concern for the consequent social upheaval. In September 2000, the Republican-dominated U.S. Congress issued a 209-page report titled *Russia's Road to Corruption: How the Clinton Administration Exported Government Instead of Free Enterprise and Failed the Russian People*, which concluded: "Russia today is more corrupt, more lawless, less democratic, poorer, and more unstable than it was in 1992." Eight years later, after two terms of the George W. Bush administration, an equally negative report could have been issued about "Putinism."

After the terrorist attacks of September 11, 2001, Russia gave tacit approval to the United States to use air bases in the former Soviet republics of Central Asia in the military campaign to oust the Taliban regime in Afghanistan and to search for Osama bin Laden. However, Russia did not approve of the United States going to war against Iraq in 2003. Relations between the two countries have suffered primarily due to the eastward expansion of the North Atlantic Treaty Organization (NATO) and Washington's unilateral withdrawal from the Anti-Ballistic Missile (ABM) Treaty in 2001, in conjunction with its intention of setting up a missile-defense system in Eastern Europe. In May 2007, Putin referred to the foreign policy of the United States and its NATO allies as kin to that of the Third Reich. U.S. defense secretary Robert Gates responded that "one Cold War was quite enough." Looking back in July 2007, Gorbachev observed, "We all lost the Cold War," explaining that the subsequent American "winner complex" has led Washington to adopt an aggressive and misguided foreign policy. Some Russian intellectuals have dubbed the United States "the new Soviet Union."

Roger Chapman

See also: American Exceptionalism; Central Intelligence Agency; Cold War; Communists and Communism; Cuba; Hiroshima and Nagasaki; Hiss, Alger; Marxism; McCarthyism; Rosenberg, Julius, and Ethel Rosenberg; Strategic Defense Initiative.

Further Reading

Cohen, Stephen. *Failed Crusade: America and the Tragedy of Post-Communist Russia.* New York: W.W. Norton, 2001.

Fried, Richard M. *The Russians Are Coming! The Russians Are Coming! Pageantry and Patriotism in Cold War America.* New York: Oxford University Press, 1998.

Goldgeier, James M., and Michael McFaul. *Power and Purpose: U.S. Policy Toward Russia After the Cold War.* Washington, DC: Brookings Institution Press, 2003.

LaFeber, Walter. *America, Russia, and the Cold War, 1945–2006.* Boston: McGraw-Hill, 2008.

Ostrovsky, Arkady. "Enigmas and Variations: A Special Report on Russia." *Economist,* November 29, 2008.

Sowell, Thomas

An African-American economist who favors laissez-faire policies, Thomas Sowell has studied race, politics, and economics from an international perspective while castigating liberals (whom he dubs "the anointed") for striving to build a society that offers economic justice (which he denigrates as "cosmic justice"). A multicultural conservative, Sowell has been at odds with black activists who resent his strong attacks on affirmative action programs. Often called a polemicist by critics, he has been accused of overstating his arguments and for showing little empathy for the plight of the economically disadvantaged. Others view him as a brave iconoclast who has attacked political correctness with candor and logic.

The culture wars, according to Sowell, represent a continuation of a battle that has been waged for the past two hundred years between two opposing ideological conceptions of human nature: the "constrained" versus the "unconstrained." As explained in his writings, the constrained view (adopted by conservatives) regards human nature as tragically flawed and social problems as a fact of life; the unconstrained view (adopted by liberals) regards human nature as perfectible and social problems as challenges that can be solved.

Sowell was born on June 30, 1930, in Gastonia, North Carolina, and grew up in New York. After serving in the U.S. Marines (1951–1953), he attended Howard University (1954–1955), Harvard University (AB, 1958), Columbia University (AM, 1959), and the University of Chicago (PhD, 1968). At the last institution, Sowell came under the sway of Milton Friedman, the leading exponent of laissez-faire economics. Although Sowell worked as an economist for the U.S. Department of Labor (1961–1962) and the American Telephone & Telegraph Company (1964–1965), he spent most of his career in academia, teaching at Rutgers University (1962–1963), Howard University (1963–1964), Cornell University (1965–1969), Brandeis University (1969–1970), and the University of California at Los Angeles (1970–1980). He has also been long affiliated with the Hoover Institution on War, Revolution, and Peace at Stanford University. Since the 1980s, he has been a widely syndicated newspaper columnist and has written articles for major magazines and journals.

His books include *Affirmative Action: Was It Necessary in Academia?* (1975), *The Economics and Politics of Race: An International Perspective* (1983), *Preferential Politics: An International Perspective* (1990), *The Vision of the Anointed: Self-Congratulation as a Basis for Social Policy* (1995), *The Quest for Cosmic Justice* (1999), *Affirmative Action Around the World: An Empirical Study* (2004), *Black Rednecks and White Liberals: And Other Cultural and Ethnic Issues* (2005), and *A Conflict of Visions: Ideological Origins of Political Struggles* (2007). He has also published an autobiography, *A Personal Odyssey* (2000).

In his writings and lectures, Sowell has denounced as fallacious the assumption that economic disparities constitute discrimination per se. Inequality, he insists, is largely due to negative "cultural patterns" that undermine self-development. He has been especially critical of affirmative action, labeling it reverse discrimination. Such policies, he asserts, contribute to racial tensions, nurture political grievances, confer victimhood status on their recipients, and in the end make minorities economically worse off. Sowell has also been critical of the American education system, believing that standards have been lowered in order to accommodate political correctness. He has been critical of Harvard's affirmative action program, stating that it has been harmful to many blacks by putting them in a situation for which they were not academically prepared. Sowell insists that since other minority groups have been mainstreamed in American society, including the Irish and Italians, the same opportunity exists for blacks.

Roger Chapman

See also: Affirmative Action; *Bell Curve, The*; Friedman, Milton; Multicultural Conservatism; Political Correctness; Race; Victimhood.

Further Reading

Kilson, Martin. "Anatomy of Black Conservatism." *Transition* 59 (1993): 4–19.

Magalli, Mark. "The High Priests of the Black Academic Right." *Journal of Blacks in Higher Education* 9 (Autumn 1995): 71–77.

Sowell, Thomas. *A Personal Odyssey.* New York: Free Press, 2000.

———. "A Personal Odyssey from Howard to Harvard and Beyond." *Journal of Blacks in Higher Education* 30 (Winter 2000/2001): 122–28.

Stewart, James B. "Thomas Sowell's Quixotic Quest to Denigrate African American Culture: A Critique." *Journal of African American History* 91:4 (Fall 2006): 459–66.

Speech Codes

Speech codes, as adopted by many American colleges and universities, prohibit "hate speech" by faculty, staff, or students, with the purpose of promoting a positive education environment free of expressions that could be regarded as "marginalizing" racial and ethnic minorities, women, homosexuals, and others. The Foundation for Individual Rights in Education (FIRE), founded in 1998, has over the years joined the American Civil Liberties Union in opposing campus speech codes, arguing that they violate the First Amendment.

Speech codes were introduced by university administrators beginning in the late 1980s and early 1990s in response to incidents of bigotry on college campuses.

The intention was to curb the "soft racism" that creates a "hostile environment" for learning. According to arguments rooted in critical race and legal theories, overt hostility toward minorities by the dominant culture tends to suppress the speech rights of those belonging to socially marginalized groups. Generally, speech codes were part of the larger goal of promoting multiculturalism.

By 1997 half of college campuses had promulgated some form of speech codes, which were largely patterned on restrictions against sexual harassment. The catalyst for speech codes was the news media's sensational coverage of campus episodes, including the 1990 expulsion of a student at Brown University who was found to have used slurs against blacks, homosexuals, and Jews. Earlier, in 1986, a Yale University student made the news for spoofing the school's annual Gay and Lesbian Awareness Days (GLAD) by passing out satirical fliers advertising BAD (for Bestiality Awareness Days).

While speech codes generally do not bar all offensive speech, they have sought to prevent and punish speech directed at and found offensive by the listener due to his or her respective race, religion, ethnicity, gender, and/or sexual orientation. The issue is often about etiquette and to what extent it should be codified. The controversy surrounding campus speech codes centers on the restriction of speech and expression that critics believe undermines academic freedom during discussions on social issues that pertain to minority populations. Many conservatives argue that speech codes typically favor liberal discourse at the expense of conservative and libertarian viewpoints. Some of the same critics, however, called for the dismissal of Ward Churchill, the University of Colorado professor who provoked controversy after characterizing the victims of the September 11 terrorist attacks as "little Eichmanns."

Proponents of speech codes equate offensive expression with "fighting words," or speech not protected by the U.S. Constitution. In 1942, for instance, the Supreme Court in *Chaplinsky v. New Hampshire* ruled against fighting words that "tend to incite an immediate breach of the peace." Opponents dismiss speech codes as "political correctness" thats restrict offensive opinions, which they regard as a violation of individual freedom and the central tenet of American political and social life that allows the airing of unpopular viewpoints. College Republicans, in a bold challenge to the restrictions imposed by speech codes, have held "affirmative action bake sales" in which cookies are sold to whites at a higher price than to minorities. Such demonstrations offer a purposefully hostile message to not only teach against affirmative action, but to flaunt free speech.

U.S. courts have invalidated speech codes when they have been found to be too vague, too broad, or discriminatory toward a particular viewpoint. Speech codes are deemed too vague when an individual must guess as to what conduct is or is not prohibited. In an effort to prohibit nonprotected speech (such as fighting words), they penalize individuals for protected speech such as political advocacy or expressions of opinion; and they are discriminatory if otherwise constitutionally protected speech or expression of opinion is punishable because the governing body considers the message politically offensive or distasteful.

Earlier versions of speech codes were struck down at both the state and federal levels. In *Doe v. University of Michigan* (1981), a federal district court ruled against the university's speech codes, which were used against someone who had argued that women are biologically programmed to be caregivers. The same court in *UWM Post Inc. v. Board of Regents of University of Wisconsin* (1991) rejected the Board of Regents' argument that speech codes were necessary to stop harassment of minorities, stating that the "commitment to free expression must be unwavering" despite the "many situations where, in the short run, it appears advantageous to limit speech to solve pressing social problems, such as discriminatory harassment." The ruling went on to declare "the suppression of speech" as "governmental thought control."

In *R.A.V. v. City of St. Paul* (1992), the U.S. Supreme Court indirectly weighed in on the controversy of campus speech codes when it overturned a municipal ordinance that criminalized the display of any symbol likely to provoke "anger, alarm or resentment in others on the basis of race, creed, religion or gender." This case focused on the actions of a juvenile who had allegedly burned a cross on the lawn of an African-American neighbor. The Court ruled that prohibiting symbols such as a burning cross or swastika constituted viewpoint discrimination, a violation of the First Amendment. In the wake of that ruling, many campuses had to modify or discard their speech codes. The same year of that decision Senator Larry Craig (R-ID) introduced legislation that would have cut off federal funding to any college that imposes speech rules.

In 2003, the U.S. Department of Education's Office of Civil Rights entered the debate on speech codes when it stipulated that speech codes focusing on harassment "must include something beyond the mere expression of views, words, symbols or thoughts that some person finds offensive." During the mid-2000s an estimated 700 American colleges and universities maintained some form of speech codes. A great many lower-level schools have also enforced speech codes as part of bans on offensive conduct and harassment. Some schools have begun experimenting with "free speech zones," select areas of campus where student protests and demonstrations can be carried out with minimal disrupting potential.

Traci L. Nelson

See also: Academic Freedom; American Civil Liberties Union; Censorship; Churchill, Ward; Diversity Training; Gender-Inclusive Language; Hate Crimes; Multiculturalism and Ethnic Studies; Political Correctness; Race; Sexual Harassment; Victimhood; Zero Tolerance.

Further Reading

Cleary, Edward J. *Beyond Burning the Cross: The First Amendment and the Landmark* R.A.V. *Case.* New York: Random House, 1994.

Delgado, Richard, and Jean Stefancic. *Understanding Words That Wound.* Boulder, CO: Westview Press, 2004.

FIRE—Foundation for Individual Rights in Education Web site. www.thefire.org.

Gould, Jon B. *Speak No Evil: The Triumph of Hate Speech Regulation.* Chicago: University of Chicago Press, 2005.

Shiell, Timothy C. *Campus Hate Speech on Trial.* Lawrence: University Press of Kansas, 1998.

Spock, Benjamin

Referred to as "Dr. Spock, the baby doc," pediatrician and psychiatrist Benjamin Spock became a leading authority on childrearing with his best-selling book *The Common Sense Book of Baby and Child Care* (1946), which has sold tens of millions of copies in nearly forty foreign languages. Many social conservatives blame Spock's permissive childrearing principles for the excesses of the counterculture generation. Spock further alienated conservatives by demonstrating against the Vietnam War and the nuclear arms race in the 1960s and 1970s.

Benjamin McLane "Benny" Spock was born on May 2, 1903, in New Haven, Connecticut. During his undergraduate years at Yale University (BA, 1925), he won a gold medal in rowing at the 1924 Olympic Games in Paris. After attending the Yale University School of Medicine (1925–1927), and Columbia University's College of Physicians and Surgeons (MD, 1929), he completed residencies in pediatrics and psychiatry at two New York hospitals. He served as a psychiatrist in the U.S. Navy during World War II and, after publishing his landmark work on childrearing, went on to hold positions at the Mayo Clinic in Rochester, Minnesota (1947–1951), University of Pittsburgh (1951–1955), and Western Reserve University in Cleveland (1955–1967). By the mid-1950s, Dr. Spock was an influential public figure with several magazine columns and his own television show. He died on March 15, 1988, in San Diego, California.

Spock was influenced by Sigmund Freud's theories of child development and brought these concepts to a broad audience, using everyday language and a friendly tone. He questioned the widely accepted view that parents should limit the amount of praise or affection they show children, and argued against the rigid feeding schedules advocated by most pediatricians. Although opponents charged that his "child-centered" model spoils children and exhausts parents, Spock's ideas were widely adopted.

Spock entered the political arena in 1960 by announcing his support for John F. Kennedy's presidential bid. Two years later, amid mounting concern over nuclear testing, he joined the National Committee for a Sane Nuclear Policy (SANE, or Scientists Against Nuclear Energy). In 1967, he marched with the Reverend Martin Luther King, Jr., against the Vietnam War. That year Spock resigned from SANE, as his increasingly radical stance alienated its leadership circle. The following year, Spock was convicted in federal court of aiding and abetting the draft-resistance movement and sentenced to two years in prison; the verdict was later overturned. In 1972, Spock ran for president of the United States as the nominee of the People's Party, getting on the ballot in ten states and winning nearly 80,000 votes on a platform of disarmament, free university education and health care, and the legalization of abortion and marijuana.

Spock's critics argued that his "permissiveness" was to blame for the social upheaval of the 1960s. In a widely publicized sermon, for example, conservative Christian preacher Norman Vincent Peale charged that Spock's childrearing advice had resulted in a lack of respect for authority on the part of Baby Boomers. Concurring, James Dobson, an evangelical who would later establish Focus on the Family, wrote *Dare to Discipline* (1970) to counter Spock.

In the 1970s, Spock faced criticism by such feminists as Gloria Steinem, for proposing that girls and boys should be raised differently and for assigning the majority of parenting responsibilities to women. Although he apologized for his sexism, Spock never accepted the charge of permissiveness and argued that critics misunderstood the balance between freedom and boundaries that he endorsed.

Manon Parry

See also: Abortion; Counterculture; Dobson, James; Family Values; Generations and Generational Conflict; Health Care; Kennedy Family; King, Martin Luther, Jr.; Nuclear Age; Steinem, Gloria; Third Parties; War Protesters.

Further Reading

Bloom, Lynn Z. *Doctor Spock: Biography of a Conservative Radical.* Indianapolis, IN: Bobbs-Merrill, 1972.

Maier, Thomas. *Dr. Spock: An American Life.* New York: Harcourt Brace, 1998.

Spock, Benjamin, and Mary Morgan. *Spock on Spock: A Memoir of Growing Up with the Century.* New York: Pantheon Books, 1985.

Springsteen, Bruce

Musician, songwriter, and sometime social commentator Bruce Springsteen was born on September 23, 1949, in Freehold, New Jersey. After growing up in an unhappy, uncommunicative, blue-collar family and being deemed ineligible for the military draft, he signed with Columbia Records in 1972 and assembled his legendary E Street Band. Two albums with relatively poor sales were followed by *Born to Run* (1975), which captured a huge audience. As the band's concert performances reached unprecedented success, fanfare increased to near-manic heights with its seventh album, *Born in the USA* (1984). Although he began as an apolitical chronicler of a New Jersey adolescent culture of cars, boardwalks, and ennui, Springsteen eventually was drawn closer to social issues and politics.

In 1981 Springsteen began his long sponsorship of Vietnam Veterans of America, using his concerts to champion local food banks, condemn plant closings, and alert audiences to the poverty and despair that lay beneath the American dream. "Born in the USA," Springsteen's 1984 anthem, was a lament for the shoddy treatment of Vietnam veterans. Yet both Democratic and Republican politicians, and even intellectual pundits such as George Will, misinterpreted the song to be a jingoistic celebration of America. After Ronald Reagan tried to enlist him in his "Morning in America" reelection campaign, Springsteen became more outspoken in his opposition to Reaganomics, plant closings, and hypocritical expressions of patriotism.

Tiring of the pressures of rock superstardom, Springsteen explored less popular musical avenues after 1986. In doing so, he deepened his connections to both contemporary and earlier leftist causes. In 1985, he supported the Live Aid performances to bring attention to Third World poverty and lent his voice to the Sun City protest against apartheid. He was also a leader of an unsuccessful attempt to prevent the closure of a 3M factory in his old hometown. Some of his later albums, such as *The Ghost of Tom Joad* (1995) and *We Shall Overcome: The Seeger Sessions* (2006), paid tribute to the idealistic radicalism of novelist John Steinbeck and folksinger Pete Seeger. In the aftermath of the September 11, 2001, terrorist attacks, Springsteen revived his connection to heartland sensibilities in *The Rising* (2002).

In 2004, publicly endorsing a candidate for the first time, Springsteen gave an eleven-state "Vote for Change" concert tour on behalf of Democratic presidential candidate John Kerry. The following year, Republican leaders in the U.S. Senate blocked a resolution commemorating the twentieth anniversary of the album *Born to Run*. Later, Springsteen condemned President George W. Bush's response to Hurricane Katrina, calling him "President Bystander." During the 2008 presidential election he performed at campaign rallies in support of Barack Obama's candidacy, in between songs imploring crowds, "I want my country back, I want my dream back."

Perhaps Springsteen's most important contribution in the culture wars has been to popularize a class analysis of American life and opportunity. Most notably, he has portrayed the blue-collar characters of his songs as clinging desperately to their version of the American dream in the face of depredation from powerful interests and an uncaring government.

Douglas Craig

See also: Bush Family; Globalization; Hurricane Katrina; Kerry, John; Obama, Barack; Reagan, Ronald; Seeger, Pete; September 11; Steinbeck, John; Supply-Side Economics; Vietnam War; Will, George.

Further Reading
Corn, David. "Springsteen for Change." *Nation*, October 25, 2004.

Cowie, Jefferson, and Lauren Boehm. "Dead Man's Town, 'Born in the U.S.A.,' Social History, and Working-Class Identity." *American Quarterly* 58:2 (June 2006): 353–78.

Levy, Joe. "Bruce Springsteen: The Rolling Stone Interview." *Rolling Stone*, November 1, 2007.

Marsh, Dave. *Bruce Springsteen: Two Hearts*. New York: Routledge, 2004.

Star Wars

See Strategic Defense Initiative

Starr, Kenneth

As an independent counsel beginning in August 1994, Kenneth Starr directed the federal investigation into an Arkansas land deal known as Whitewater that had involved Bill Clinton before he became president. The $52 million probe revealed a sex scandal that led to Clinton's impeachment. The 445-page *Starr Report* (1998), issued by Starr's office and later released over the Internet by the Republican-controlled Congress, recounted in salacious detail Clinton's affair with White House intern Monica Lewinsky.

Kenneth Winston Starr, the son of a Church of Christ minister, was born on July 21, 1946, in Vernon, Texas. He grew up in San Antonio and later attended George Washington University (AB, 1968), Brown University (MA, 1969), and Duke University School of Law (JD, 1973). After serving as a law clerk for Chief Justice Warren E. Burger (1975–1977), he practiced with a private firm in Washington, D.C., before taking a position in the U.S. Justice Department (1981–1983) during the Ronald Reagan administration. Reagan appointed him as a judge on the U.S. Court of Appeals for the District of Columbia Circuit (1983–1989), a position he resigned to

Special prosecutor Kenneth Starr testifies to the House Judiciary Committee in November 1998 that President Bill Clinton had engaged in obstruction of justice during the investigation into his relationship with White House intern Monica Lewinsky. *(Luke Frazza/AFP/Getty Images)*

serve as President George H.W. Bush's solicitor general of the United States (1989–1993).

On August 5, 1994, a three-judge panel called on Starr to replace Robert B. Fiske in the Whitewater investigation, a federal probe into a failed real estate development in Arkansas during the 1970s that involved Bill and Hillary Clinton. It was no secret that Republicans were displeased with Fiske's initial findings, and political pressure was brought to bear in finding a more aggressive figure to serve as independent counsel.

Other matters came up during the course of the investigation, including the allegedly improper termination of staff at the White House travel office (referred to as Travelgate) and purported White House mishandling of FBI files (Filegate).

In 1994, an Arkansas resident named Paula Jones filed a lawsuit against President Clinton, claiming that he had sexually harassed her when he was the governor. Jones's lawyers, financed by conservative operatives, questioned Clinton about his relationship with various women, including Lewinsky, in an effort to establish a pattern about his behavior that would give credence to their client's charge. Under oath, Clinton denied having illicit relationships with the women.

Starr then shifted his investigation to prove that Clinton had committed perjury in the Jones case. Although Starr did in the end prosecute some figures involved with Whitewater, Clinton's impeachment had nothing to do with the real estate scandal but centered on perjury and obstruction of justice about a consensual sexual relationship with Lewinsky.

In a 1998 nationally televised interview, First Lady Hillary Clinton referred to Starr and his investigation as part of a "vast right-wing conspiracy." Defenders of the president, such as political adviser James Carville, regarded Starr as "sex-obsessed." Critics in general characterized the Starr investigation as a "sexual inquisition." Joe Conason in *Big Lies* (2003) dismissed *The Starr Report* as "conservative public pornography." Indeed, wire reports quoting the document warned that the contents "may be OFFENSIVE to some readers," as every sexual episode between the president and the intern was recorded at least twice, in some cases three and four times.

Critics viewed Starr's investigation as "slash and burn" politics, a witch hunt that, in pornographic detail and at great expense to taxpayers, crossed lines of decency in delving too far into the private life of an individual. Defenders of Starr argue that the person to blame is Clinton, who perjured himself to hide his moral shortcomings. In *The Death of Outrage* (1998), the conservative commentator William J. Bennett hailed Starr as a man of great integrity and suggested that outrage should be directed at Clinton's impropriety.

While Starr's critics emphasize a need in politics to separate the public figure from the private person, noting that a president's job performance is what is important, Starr's supporters emphasize that the private person is inseparable from the public figure and that a president's character is vitally linked to job performance.

Starr, who in 2004 became the dean of Pepperdine University School of Law, has characterized himself a victim of undeserved notoriety, lamenting that the political fallout from his investigation has harmed his chances of ever being appointed to the Supreme Court. In a 2005 interview he said that, throughout the investigation, he compared his plight with that of Apostle Paul but made it his aim to be "upbeat" like Teddy Roosevelt. Starr is the author of *First Among Equals: The Supreme Court in American Life* (2002).

Roger Chapman

See also: Bennett, William J.; Clinton, Bill; Clinton, Hillary; Clinton Impeachment; Helms, Jesse; Pornography; Sexual Harassment; Thomas, Clarence; Victimhood.

Further Reading

Bennett, William J. *The Death of Outrage: Bill Clinton and the Assault on American Ideals.* New York: Free Press, 1998.

Schmidt, Susan, and Michael Weisskopf. *Truth at Any Cost: Ken Starr and the Unmaking of Bill Clinton.* New York: HarperCollins, 2000.

Toobin, Jeffrey. *A Vast Conspiracy: The Real Story of the Sex Scandal That Brought Down a President.* New York: Random House, 1999.

Stay-at-Home Mothers

"A woman's place is in the home," goes the old adage, but for years American women of all income levels have worked inside and outside the home, providing for their families in myriad ways. In the 1960s and 1970s, however, debates about stay-at-home mothers and working mothers became a central cultural issue. While many women worked outside the home during World War II, they were expected to become housewives and consumers once the fighting stopped. Some rebelled against this cultural expectation, and the women's movement of the 1960s and 1970s placed working women in the center of a political debate. Outspoken feminists such as Betty Friedan advocated for women's right to be employed outside the home and to receive equal pay and status with men in the workplace.

A popular cultural image of the 1980s and 1990s was working mothers as "supermoms" who balanced full-time work, home life, and child care. The number of working mothers continued to rise through the 1980s and peaked in the mid-1990s. Still, First Lady Hillary Clinton's remark in 1992 that "I could have stayed home and baked cookies and had teas, but what I decided to do was fulfill my profession" caused outrage among many social conservatives. By the early 2000s, media articles were highlighting reports about women who left high-powered careers to become stay-at-home moms.

The stay-at-home mom movement drew women who never worked outside the home as well as those who chose to temporarily or permanently leave careers in order to care for young children. This movement sought to gain recognition for the work women perform inside the home, and for the role they play in facilitating the lives of all family members. According to some analysts, the market value of a stay-at-home mom is roughly equivalent to a professional salary. Thus, for some families, a stay-at-home parent may be more economically and socially feasible than having two working parents.

Some observers argue that professional women who leave their careers to become stay-at-home moms do so because American society has not provided adequate support for dual-income families, such as affordable child care. Unlike European societies that are structured around family needs, the American system is based on the outdated model that full-time employees have a partner at home responsible for childrearing, social obligations, and the household. Also, since working mothers are still disproportionately in charge of the majority of home and child care duties, an extra burden falls on them. Expensive child care options, lack of family-friendly policies in the workplace, long commutes, schools that dismiss before the end of the work day, lack of flexibility from a spouse's employer, poor maternity/paternity leave options, and lack of support from spouses all may contribute to a woman's decision to be a stay-at-home mom, or a man's decision to be a stay-at-home dad.

Tanya Hedges Duroy

See also: Christian Coalition; Clinton, Hillary; Equal Rights Amendment; Family Values; Feminism, Second-Wave; Feminism, Third-Wave; Focus on the Family; Friedan, Betty; Palin, Sarah; Religious Right.

Further Reading

Bolton, Michelle K. *The Third Shift: Managing Hard Choices in Our Careers, Homes, and Lives as Women.* San Francisco: Jossey-Bass, 2000.

McKenna, Elizabeth Perle. *When Work Doesn't Work Anymore: Women, Work, and Identity.* New York: Dell, 1998.

Morgan Steiner, Leslie. *Mommy Wars: Stay-at-Home and Career-Moms Face Off on Their Choices, Their Lives, Their Families.* New York: Random House, 2006.

Peskowitz, Miriam. *The Truth Behind the Mommy Wars: Who Decides What Makes a Good Mother?* Emeryville, CA: Seal, 2005.

Steinbeck, John

The novelist and social commentator John Steinbeck, winner of the 1962 Nobel Prize in Literature, was born on February 27, 1902, in Salinas, California. He attended Stanford University (1919–1925) but never graduated. A New Deal Democrat, Steinbeck used his writing to explore economic and moral problems. Although his writings were generally praised for how they portrayed the poor and downtrodden with dignity and compassion, critics on the right accused him of being overly critical and unpatriotic. Critics on the left found him either too sentimental or not radical enough.

Steinbeck's first literary success was *Tortilla Flat* (1937), a collection of stories about a band of Mexican Americans in Monterey coping with the Great Depression. The economic downturn of the 1930s greatly shaped the author's art and politics. So, too, did his first wife, a Marxist and Communist Party member. During this period, Steinbeck attended radical meetings and labor rallies and even visited the Soviet Union. His novels of the Depression, *In Dubious Battle* (1936), *Of Mice and Men* (1937), and *The Grapes of Wrath* (1939), focus on the struggles of common people in an unjust economic system. His stories were based on labor unrest he actually witnessed, but the mostly Mexican migrants he encountered were changed to white characters.

Steinbeck is known most of all for *The Grapes of Wrath*, which depicts Depression-era Americans struggling for a better life. The work was condemned in Congress and today remains one of the nation's top fifty banned books. The Pulitzer Prize–winning novel was released as a major motion picture starring Henry Fonda in 1940. The main character of the novel lives on in Woody Guthrie's song "Tom Joad" (1940) and Bruce Springsteen's album *The Ghost of Tom Joad* (1995).

After a stint as a war correspondent, Steinbeck published the novel *Cannery Row* (1945), a subtle condemnation of Monterey's middle-class hypocrisy and materialism. Progressives condemned the book for failing to expose the system as he did in *The Grapes of Wrath*. Conservatives complained that he was criticizing American society at a time when soldiers were sacrificing their lives in World War II. Feminists criticized the misogynistic portrayal of the character Kate Ames in *East of Eden* (1952), a Cain and Abel morality tale set in California's Salinas Valley. The work reached a wide audience as a 1955 film starring James Dean. *The Winter of Our Discontent* (1961), Steinbeck's last fiction work, was a reaction to the television quiz show scandals of the 1950s and explores the theme of moral relativism.

The nonfiction works *Sea of Cortez* (1941) and *The Log from the Sea of Cortez* (1951), which record his adventures collecting marine samples, established Steinbeck's place as an early advocate of the environmental movement, emphasizing the interconnectivity of all living things. His travelogues *Travels with Charley* (1962) and *America and Americans* (1966) explore physical and cultural aspects of the United States. In the former, he bristles at a racist incident he witnessed in New Orleans involving white women intimidating a black child as she enters a previously segregated school. In one of his last controversies Steinbeck was criticized by war protesters for wearing army fatigues during a 1966 visit to Vietnam. Shortly before Steinbeck's death in New York City on December 20, 1968, President Lyndon B. Johnson awarded him the Medal of Freedom.

Roger Chapman

See also: Brown v. Board of Education (1954); Civil Rights Movement; Communists and Communism; Environmental Movement; Feminism, Second-Wave; Guthrie, Woody, and Arlo Guthrie; Labor Unions; Marxism; Migrant Labor; New Deal; Relativism, Moral; Vietnam War.

Further Reading

Benson, Jackson J. *The True Adventures of John Steinbeck, Writer: A Biography.* New York: Penguin, 1990.

Wartzman, Rick. *Obscene in the Extreme: The Burning and Banning of John Steinbeck's* The Grapes of Wrath. New York: PublicAffairs, 2008.

Steinem, Gloria

Feminist, activist, writer, and longtime editor of *Ms. Magazine*, Gloria Steinem first earned notoriety for a 1963 article detailing her undercover experience as a "bunny" at the New York Playboy Club. She went on to become the public face of American feminism.

Gloria Steinem was born on March 25, 1934, in Toledo, Ohio, where she had a middle-class upbringing. A Phi Beta Kappa graduate of Smith College (1956) and a postgraduate fellow in India (1957–1958), she devoted her career to writing and editing, first for the Independent Service for Information (1959–1960), which turned out to be funded by the Central Intelligence Agency (CIA), and then for the magazines *Glamour* (1962–1969), *New York* (1968–1972), and *Ms.* (1972–1987). Her books include the essay collections *Outrageous Acts and Everyday Rebellions* (1983), *Revolution from Within* (1992), and *Moving Beyond Words* (1993), as well as a biography of Marilyn Monroe entitled *Marilyn* (1986).

Steinem first encountered the feminist movement in 1969 during an assignment for *New York* magazine, covering an abortion speak-out and rally sponsored by the Redstockings, a radical feminist group. The event resonated with Steinem, who secretly had had an abortion while in college. The rally also illuminated and connected issues of sexism and patriarchy for her, fundamentally changing the direction of her life. In December 1971, a committed feminist, Steinem helped launch the first issue of *Ms.*, as a supplement to *New York* magazine.

Ms. was established in its own right the following year, with Steinem as editor. The publication proved highly successful at first, but its popularity dwindled by the 1980s. While receiving praise and attracting previously uninterested women into the second-wave feminist movement, *Ms.* was also under constant criticism from both feminists and antifeminists. Radical feminists disapproved of the magazine's carrying advertisements, arguing that it was too conservative, mainstream, and slanted toward white women. Others complained that it focused excessively on lesbianism.

Whatever the controversies, the popularity of the magazine brought public attention to Steinem, whose intelligence, composure, sense of humor, and charm helped make her a media darling. Through her public appearances and writings, she argued for legalized abortion and crusaded against sexism, while making women's liberation seem logical and beneficial for both sexes. Many of Steinem's feminist peers accused her of hijacking the movement, however, denigrating her as a late arrival to the cause, criticizing her less-than-aggressive style, and attempting to discredit her achievements and activism by criticizing her femininity and physical attractiveness. The Redstockings and Betty Friedan, the well-known feminist activist and co-founder of the National Organization for Women (NOW), falsely accused Steinem of having worked for the CIA (a distortion based on the secret subsidy of the media organization she earlier worked for) and using *Ms.* to collect personal information about feminists. Steinem also stirred controversy in 2000, when, at age sixty-six, after stating for years that a woman did not need a man, she married.

Alexandra DeMonte

See also: Abortion; Central Intelligence Agency; Feminism, Second-Wave; Feminism, Third-Wave; Friedan, Betty; Hefner, Hugh; Lesbians; Morgan, Robin; Ms.; National Organization for Women; Pornography.

Further Reading

Daffron, Carolyn. *Gloria Steinem.* New York: Chelsea House, 1988.

Farrell, Amy Erdman. *Yours in Sisterhood:* Ms. Magazine *and the Promise of Popular Feminism.* Chapel Hill: University of North Carolina Press, 1998.

Rosen, Ruth. *The World Split Open: How the Modern Women's Movement Changed America.* New York: Penguin Books, 2000.

Stern, Sydney Landensohn. *Gloria Steinem: Her Passions, Politics and Mystique.* Secaucus, NJ: Carol, 1997.

Stem-Cell Research

Stem cells are present in all animal life forms. In humans, they possess two important properties that differentiate them from most other cells in the human body: (1) they are unspecialized but under the right conditions can develop into many of the almost 200 different types of specialized cells in the body (such as brain cells or red blood cells); and (2) they are able to divide and renew themselves for long periods of time. Because of these properties, stem cells have the potential to grow replacements for cells that have been damaged or that a person's body no longer creates on its own. This, according to scientists, could lead to revolutionary treatments or cures for many diseases and conditions that have long stymied medical science, including Parkinson's disease, Alzheimer's disease, stroke, heart disease, burns, spinal cord injury, diabetes, and arthritis. However, the therapeutic promise of stem cells is tempered by the moral objections many people have to one of the most promising areas of stem-cell research, that involving human embryonic stem cells (hESC).

Science

There are two types of stem cells in the human body: adult stem cells and embryonic stem cells. Adult stem cells, also called somatic cells, are found in small numbers among differentiated cells and are used by the body to repair and replace the cells needed in the tissue in which they are found: for instance, hematopoietic stem cells are found in the bone marrow and can differentiate into all the types of blood cells found in the body. Research and treatments involving adult stem cells are much less controversial than those involving hESC, and therapies such as bone marrow transplantation (hematopoietic stem-cell transplantation, practiced since the 1960s) have become commonplace in modern medicine. Scientific use of adult stem cells is relatively uncontroversial because the cells come from consenting adult donors or from umbilical cord blood and do not require destruction of an embryo. However, their therapeutic potential is limited because each type of adult stem cell can develop only into limited types of cells, and because adult stem cells are relatively rare in the body and are not easily cultured (duplicated) in the laboratory.

Embryonic stem cells are believed to hold much greater therapeutic promise because of their ability to differentiate into any type of cell and because they are easy to culture in the lab. Mouse embryonic stem cells (mESC) were first isolated and cultured in 1981 by the British scientist Sir Martin John Evans, and independently that same year by Gail R. Martin, a professor of anatomy at the University of California in San Francisco. Human embryonic stem cells were first successfully cultivated in 1998, when James Thomson, a cell biologist at the University of Wisconsin, successfully generated hESC from blastocysts (pre-embryonic balls of cells).

Controversy

It is the source of human embryonic stem cells, rather than their therapeutic potential, that makes them controversial. As the name implies, hESC are created from human embryos, and the process of creating hESC destroys the embryo. For persons who believe that life begins at conception (the official position of the Catholic Church and many fundamentalist denominations), destroying an embryo is as repugnant as killing an adult human being. Advocates of hESC argue that this is selective morality (or political grandstanding) because opponents of stem-cell research seem not to be bothered by the fact that thousands of embryos are destroyed annually by fertility clinics, simply because they are no longer wanted or needed. Such embryos are created through in vitro fertilization (fertilization of an egg by a sperm outside a woman's body, in a test tube or the equivalent) in order to help infertile couples conceive, and many more embryos are created than will be needed for each individual couple. Advocates of hESC argue that couples should be allowed to donate the excess embryos to scientific research rather than have them destroyed.

Stem-cell research is not prohibited in the United States, but for a period of time was severely limited by restrictions on federal funding. In August 2001, President George W. Bush announced that federal funding for hESC research would be limited to the stem-cell lines (populations of cells grown from a single embryo) already in existence, a decision he justified as a compromise: it would not encourage further destruction of embryos, but

it allowed research to continue (since the original embryos used to create existing stem-cell lines were already dead). Nevertheless, the restrictions were viewed as serious impediments to the development of stem-cell research in the United States, because many of the existing stem-cell lines proved unsuitable for research and because the federal government is a major source of funding for most medical research. Many prominent scientists spoke out in favor of removing these restrictions, as did celebrities affected by diseases targeted by stem-cell researchers, including actor Michael J. Fox (Parkinson's disease), the late actor Christopher Reeve (spinal cord injury), and former First Lady Nancy Reagan (whose husband suffered from Alzheimer's disease). Two arguments often put forward for raising the restrictions in federal funding are that allowing individual religious beliefs to restrict scientific research is a violation of the separation of church and state, and that it is immoral to restrict potentially life-saving research due to the objections of a few individuals (who, after all, would themselves be allowed to benefit from any cures thus discovered).

President Bush remained firm in his refusal to expand federal funding for stem-cell research, and in July 2006 and June 2007 vetoed bills that would have permitted federal funding for research using new stem-cell lines. Given the vacuum created by the restrictions on federal funding, some U.S. states devoted substantial funding to promote stem-cell research, hoping to become scientific leaders in the field and to cash in on the profits available from successful therapies, as well as being poised to capitalize on federal funding when it becomes available. California was the first state to do so, passing Proposition 71 (the California Stem Cell Research and Cures Initiative) in November 2004. The measure provided $3 billion in funding for stem-cell research, to be allocated to California universities and research institutes. New York State followed suit by earmarking $600 million in the state budget over ten years to support stem-cell research. In New Jersey, however, a bill that would have provided $450 million for stem-cell research was defeated by voters in November 2007, partly due to a well-organized opposition campaign supported by, among others, New Jersey Right to Life (an anti-abortion organization) and the Catholic Church.

In November 2007 two scientists, Junying Yu in Wisconsin and Shinya Yamanaka in Tokyo, announced that they had independently developed a technique, called "direct reprogramming," that processes human skin cells so that they take on many of the qualities of stem cells, most important being capable of differentiating into any type of cell in the body. While this discovery may provide a means to develop hESC therapies without requiring the destruction of embryos (and was hailed as such by spokespersons for the Bush administration and the Catholic Church), much more research will be required before it is known if the direct reprogramming technique will result in the development of useful therapies. Shortly after becoming president, Barack Obama rescinded Bush's restrictions on stem-cell research.

Sarah Boslaugh

See also: Abortion; Bush Family; Catholic Church; Science Wars.

Further Reading

Herold, Eve. *Stem Cell Wars: Inside Stories from the Frontlines.* New York: Palgrave Macmillan, 2006.
Humber, James M., and Robert F. Almeder, eds. *Stem Cell Research.* Totawa, NJ: Humana Press, 2004.
Parson, Ann B. *The Proteus Effect: Stem Cells and Their Promise for Medicine.* Washington, DC: Joseph Henry Press, 2004.

Stern, Howard

America's most prominent shock jock, talk show host Howard Stern has pushed the limits of social discourse on the radio while claiming to champion liberty and freedom. Popular especially among young white males, Stern's raunchy and provocative syndicated morning show has consistently ranked number one in audience ratings.

Howard Allen Stern was born on January 12, 1954, on Long Island, New York. After studying communications at Boston University (BS, 1976), where he was fired from the campus radio station for broadcasting a racially inappropriate skit called "Godzilla Goes to Harlem," Stern began a career as a professional disc jockey. For about a decade, he perfected his irreverent radio persona at several stations on the East Coast. In 1985, he moved to New York City's WXRK-FM, where his outrageous style was allowed to flourish. In 2005, his show was syndicated in forty-five media markets. His employer, Infinity Broadcasting, paid a steep price for Stern's unbridled creativity, however. In the twenty years he worked there, the Federal Communications Commission (FCC) fined Infinity over $2 million for indecency.

To his fans, Stern is a master of his craft, has helped to liberate American culture from puritanical oppression, and is one of radio's most skilled interviewers. His critics argue that his crude, "in your face" style has debased society.

The self-proclaimed "King of All Media" abandoned traditional radio in early 2006, opting instead to join Sirius satellite radio, where he could broadcast unfettered by federal regulations. It remains to be seen whether his show will thrive in an uncensored environment. As veteran comic Tom Dreeson commented before Stern's first satellite broadcast, Howard's "kind of humor might only be funny because it was forbidden."

Cindy Mediavilla

See also: Censorship; Federal Communications Commission; Political Correctness; Shock Jocks.

Further Reading

Cegielski, Jim. *The Howard Stern Book: An Unauthorized, Unabashed, Uncensored Fan's Guide.* Secaucus, NJ: Carol, 1994.
Colford, Paul D. *Howard Stern: King of All Media—The Unauthorized Biography.* New York: St. Martin's, 1996.
Lucaire, Luigi. *Howard Stern, A to Z: The Stern Fanatic's Guide to the King of All Media.* New York: St. Martin's, 1997.
Menell, Jeff. *Howard Stern: Big Mouth.* New York: Windsor, 1993.
Stern, Howard. *Miss America.* New York: Regan Books, 1995.
———. *Private Parts.* New York: Simon & Schuster, 1993.

Stewart, Jon

The American actor, writer, and comedian Jon Stewart is best known for his work as the host of a "fake news" program on the cable television channel Comedy Central. Born Jonathan Stewart Leibowitz on November 28, 1962, in New York City and raised in New Jersey, he attended the College of William and Mary (BS, psychology, 1984) and then held a series of odd jobs before launching a career in New York as a stand-up comedian in 1986. He went on to work on various television and film projects and published a volume of comic essays, *Naked Pictures of Famous People* (1998), before becoming host of *The Daily Show* in 1999.

On the nightly program, Stewart satirizes current events and popular culture; his usual targets are politi-

Jon Stewart hosts a half-hour satirical news program called *The Daily Show* on cable television's Comedy Central channel. Viewer polls suggest that the show is an important source of news among young people. *(Frank Micelotta/Getty Images for Comedy Central)*

cians and the media. The show's popularity skyrocketed as a result of its special "Indecision 2000" coverage of the 2000 presidential election and since then has won several Peabody and Emmy awards. George W. Bush's reelection inspired the sequel, "Indecision 2004." Although *The Daily Show* has poked fun at people of many political persuasions, conservatives have charged that most of its humor comes at the expense of Republicans. When television and radio host Bill O'Reilly interviewed Stewart on his Fox News show in September 2004, he accused Stewart of playing to a left-leaning audience, despite Stewart's declaration that his program does not have "an agenda of influence."

Although media watchers note that *The Daily Show* has cultural and political significance—primarily for getting young people to think about politics and current events—Stewart insists that his program is strictly intended as comedy. Nevertheless, *The Daily Show* has become an increasingly popular venue for important figures in politics and the press. Democratic politicians have found it an especially congenial environment; both John Edwards and John Kerry made appearances on the show prior to their 2004 bids for the White House, for example.

Stewart further circulated his brand of political satire with his best-selling *America (The Book): A Citizen's Guide to Democracy Inaction* (2004), a work he co-authored with Ben Karlin and David Javerbaum. *Publisher's Weekly* named *America* book of the year, commending it for offering "a serious critique of the two-party system, the corporations that finance it and the 'spineless cowards in the press' who 'aggressively print allegation and rumor independent of accuracy and fairness.'" But Wal-Mart refused to carry the book in its stores because it features a doctored photograph with the heads of the Supreme Court justices attached to naked bodies. The opposite page has paper-doll cutouts of robes, and the reader is asked to "Restore their dignity by matching each justice with his or her respective robe."

Charlotte Cahill

See also: Bush Family; Campaign Finance Reform; Censorship; Election of 2000; Kerry, John; Media Bias; O'Reilly, Bill; Republican Party; Talk Radio; Wal-Mart.

Further Reading

Peyser, Mark, and Sarah Childress. "Red, White, and Funny." *Newsweek*, December 29, 2003.
"10 Questions for Jon Stewart." *Time*, September 27, 2004.

Stone, Oliver

Controversial filmmaker Oliver Stone has raised important social questions and explored many topics that have been part of the culture wars. His film on John F. Kennedy's assassination was criticized for its loose portrayal of real events and for presenting the assassination as a vast conspiracy. Eminent historian Arthur M. Schlesinger, Jr., argued that some of Stone's productions amount to "dramatic license . . . corrupted by ideology."

Stone, whose father was a Jewish-American stockbroker and his mother a French Catholic, was born in New York City on September 15, 1946. After a year attending Yale University (1964–1965), Stone wrote the semiautobiographical novel *A Child's Night Dream*, which did not get published until 1997. He taught English in Saigon, Vietnam, then served a year in the merchant marine and traveled to Mexico. In 1967, Stone joined the U.S. Army and was soon deployed to Vietnam, where he was twice wounded in battle. Afterward, he studied film under director Martin Scorsese at New York University, graduating in 1971. With *Midnight Express* (1978), a film about an American drug smuggler's ordeal in a Turkish prison, Stone won the Academy Award for Best Screenplay. Stone wrote and directed the horror film *The Hand* (1981) and wrote the screenplays for *Conan the Barbarian* (1982), *Scarface* (1983), *Year of the Dragon* (1985), and *8 Million Ways to Die* (1986).

In 1986, drawing on his experiences in Vietnam, Stone wrote and directed *Platoon*, which won Academy Awards for Best Picture and Best Director. In that production, Stone aimed to debunk the "sacred mission" concept of war and instead show the "true and gritty, from the inside out." In a surreal scene that reflects the My Lai massacre, a Vietnamese village is gratuitously razed and its inhabitants murdered. Stone also won an Academy Award (Best Director) for *Born on the Fourth of July* (1989), a film that features the struggles of a paraplegic Vietnam veteran who becomes an antiwar activist. Stone's *Heaven and Earth* (1993), which explores the war from the perspective of a Vietnamese woman, was not as successful as his other films about the Vietnam War.

Stone's films also criticize American culture and challenge historical interpretations of events. In *Wall Street* (1987), he sharply criticizes the greed that infests the American marketplace. In *Talk Radio* (1988), he explores the anger and rage of shock jocks and many Americans. *The Doors* (1991) romanticizes rock singer Jim Morrison while highlighting the excesses of the counterculture. *Natural Born Killers* (1994) is a satirical commentary on American violence and its connection with mass media.

Stone's *JFK* (1991), based on the book *Crossfire: The Plot That Killed Kennedy* by Jim Marrs (1989), created a firestorm of controversy. The film implies that the government was culpable in a vast conspiracy to kill President John F. Kennedy in order to prevent the withdrawal of troops from Vietnam. *Nixon* (1995), a surprisingly sympathetic portrayal of the Watergate president, was criticized for its nebulous implication that Nixon was involved in the CIA assassination plot against Castro that was somehow connected with the Kennedy assassination.

Stone's *World Trade Center* (2006) is based on the experience of two Port Authority officers trapped under the debris of one of the collapsed towers following the September 11, 2001, terrorist attacks in New York City. It received praise for its poignant and patriotic undertones and has been criticized by those who believe the film's release was the exploitation of a tragedy. As President George W. Bush's two terms in the White House drew to a close, Stone came out with *W* (2008), a biopic work of the forty-third president that a reviewer in *The New Yorker* declared "soulless."

Matthew C. Sherman and Roger Chapman

See also: Bush Family; Conspiracy Theories; Counterculture; Kennedy Family; My Lai Massacre; Nixon, Richard; Revisionist History; Schlesinger, Arthur M., Jr.; September 11; Shock Jocks; Vietnam Veterans Against the War; Vietnam War; War on Drugs.

Further Reading

Riordan, James. *Stone: The Controversies, Excesses, and Exploits of a Radical Filmmaker*. New York: Hyperion, 1995.

Silet, Charles P., ed. *Oliver Stone: Interviews*. Jackson: University Press of Mississippi, 2001.

Toplin, Robert Brent. *Oliver Stone's USA: Film, History, and Controversy*. Lawrence: University Press of Kansas, 2000.

Stonewall Rebellion

The Stonewall riots, also known as the Stonewall rebellion, took on mythic importance for the gay rights movement. In the early morning hours of June 28, 1969, police raided the Stonewall Inn, a gay bar located in Greenwich Village, New York City. Raids of nightclubs and other venues frequented by gays were common in large American cities during the middle decades of the twentieth century, when repression of homosexuality and gender-bending were at their height. Bar patrons ordinarily complied with orders to leave the premises and passively accepted arrest if they were unable to produce identification. On this particular night, however, the patrons, many of whom were transvestites, resisted the police action, and a raucous crowd joined them outside the bar. Part of the legend of Stonewall is that the mood of some of the gay patrons was especially sour because of the recent death of Judy Garland, a gay icon whose funeral had been held in New York earlier that day. The riots lasted for six days, with police and gays locked in violent clashes that included throwing bricks and other objects, setting fires, and damaging police vehicles and other property.

Much like Rosa Parks's refusal to give up her seat on a bus, the Stonewall rebellion came to symbolize the active resistance of an oppressed group. But Stonewall had more than symbolic importance for the gay rights movement. It also signified the movement's embrace of "gay liberation," which was characterized by more radical goals and militant tactics than the assimilationist aspirations and peaceful political strategies of other gay rights activists. The movement made several major breakthroughs on the heels of Stonewall and the activism that it inspired, including the 1973 decision of the American Psychiatric Association to remove homosexuality from its list of mental disorders.

Gary Mucciaroni

See also: Civil Rights Movement; Feminism, Second-Wave; Feminism, Third-Wave; Gay Rights Movement; Parks, Rosa; Police Abuse; Socarides, Charles; Transgender Movement; Vietnam War.

Further Reading

Duberman, Martin. *Stonewall*. New York: Plume, 1994.

Marotta, Toby. *The Politics of Homosexuality*. New York: Twayne, 1995.

Teal, Donn. *The Gay Militants*. New York: Stein and Day, 1971.

Strategic Defense Initiative

A Cold War defense program initiated in the early 1980s by President Ronald Reagan, the Strategic Defense Initiative (SDI)—popularly referred to as "Star Wars"—was based on a plan to use space-based weapons to shoot down potential incoming missiles from the Soviet Union. While some blamed the program for heightening Cold War tensions and intensifying the nuclear arms race, others credited it for hastening the decline of the Soviet Union.

The primary focus of SDI was to be large lasers orbiting Earth that could shoot down airborne Soviet missiles before they could enter American territory. Reagan inaugurated the program in a speech on March 8, 1983, stating, "I call upon the scientific community who gave us nuclear weapons to turn their great talents to the cause of mankind and world peace; to give us the means of rendering these nuclear weapons impotent and obsolete." About two weeks later, Reagan delivered another speech in which he called the Soviet Union an "evil empire." These two speeches launched a period of new intensity in the nuclear arms race.

The nickname "Star Wars," which was given to the program by its critics, brought complaints from filmmaker George Lucas, creator of the hugely popular movie series of the same name, which features intergalactic battle but with an ultimate message of compromise and cooperation. Although opponents of SDI used the name Star Wars to deride the program as science fiction, some proponents also used the term, in the belief that science fiction has inspired many real-life technologies.

SDI originated with the development of a laser that made use of nuclear and x-ray technologies. The laser was brought to fruition in the late 1970s at Lawrence Livermore National Laboratory in California, by scientist Peter Hagelstein. The development team, called the O Group, was descended from the efforts of Edward Teller, who had co-founded the laboratory in 1949 for research on advanced weapons systems. SDI was to use laser technology against Soviet intercontinental ballistic missiles (ICBMs) that could deliver nuclear warheads.

The Strategic Defense Initiative Organization (SDIO) was established in 1984 to foster further research. The organization was headed by U.S. Air Force Lieutenant General James Adam Abrahamson, a former director of the NASA Space Shuttle program. No SDI system was ever fully implemented, but research by SDIO led to technological advances in computer technology, sensors, and miniaturized components that have found other applications in military development and communications.

The doctrine underlying SDI was "strategic defense," as opposed to the Cold War offensive strategy of "mutually assured destruction." Among the critics of SDI was physicist Hans Bethe, who had worked on development teams for the atomic bomb and the hydrogen bomb in the early years of the Cold War. Bethe and others claimed that a space-based laser system would be scientifically impractical and prohibitively expensive, and the Soviets could easily destroy it or eliminate its usefulness by deploying decoy missiles. Based on his experience with weapons of mass destruction, Bethe believed that the Cold War could be resolved through diplomacy rather than new technologies.

Soviet premier Mikhail Gorbachev strongly opposed SDI, and the program became a major agenda item at his October 1986 summit with Reagan in Reykjavik, Iceland. In December 1987, the two leaders signed the Intermediate-Range Nuclear Forces Treaty, which proponents of SDI regarded as a sign of success. Supporters of the program later suggested that it helped bring about the demise of the Soviet Union in 1991, as the very threat of a space-based system shed light on the deficiencies of Soviet defenses. Opponents of SDI instead argue that Gorbachev's reforms and larger sociopolitical trends are responsible for the Soviet Union's dissolution. Some even suggest that SDI prolonged the Cold War because it galvanized the Kremlin hardliners, hindering Gorbachev's reforms and overtures for peace.

President George H.W. Bush kept the SDI project alive, but President Bill Clinton in 1993 shifted the focus from missile-based global to ground-based regional defense systems and redesignated SDIO as the Ballistic Missile Defense Organization (BMDO). Also in 1993, it was revealed that a breakthrough SDI test in 1984 had been faked—the targeted missile carried a homing beacon that enabled the interceptor to shoot it down easily. The Star Wars concept was revived by President George W. Bush in the wake of the September 11, 2001, terrorist attacks, this time under the title National Missile Defense; the name was changed to Ground-Based Midcourse Defense in 2002. New technologies developed under this program remain in the testing stage.

Benjamin W. Cramer

See also: Bush Family; Clinton, Bill; Cold War; Communists and Communism; Hiroshima and Nagasaki; Nuclear Age; Oppenheimer, J. Robert; Reagan, Ronald; Science Wars; September 11; Soviet Union and Russia; Teller, Edward.

Further Reading

Broad, William J. *Star Warriors: A Penetrating Look into the Lives of the Young Scientists Behind Our Space Age Weaponry.* New York: Simon & Schuster, 1985.

FitzGerald, Frances. *Way Out There in the Blue: Reagan, Star Wars, and the End of the Cold War.* New York: Simon & Schuster, 2000.

Lakoff, Sanford, and Herbert F. York. *A Shield in Space? Technology, Politics, and the Strategic Defense Initiative.* Berkeley: University of California Press, 1989.

Linenthal, Edward T. *Symbolic Defense: The Cultural Significance of the Strategic Defense Initiative.* Urbana: University of Illinois Press, 1989.

Strauss, Leo

A political philosopher cited as one of the intellectual leaders of American neoconservatism, Leo Strauss was born September 20, 1899, near Marburg, Germany. He studied classical and political philosophy under such prominent figures in the field as Ernst Cassirer, Edmund Husserl, and Martin Heidegger. His study of Thomas Hobbes led him to England, where he remained after the rise of Nazism, taking a teaching position at Cambridge University. In 1937, he emigrated to the United States, where he taught at the New School for Social Research in New York City (1938–1948) and the University of Chicago (1949–1968).

By the time of his death on October 18, 1973, Strauss had come to influence a number of conservative-oriented American intellectuals and political activists, including Allan Bloom, William J. Bennett, Irving and William Kristol, Alan Keyes, Carnes Lord, and Norman Podhoretz, all founding members of neoconservatism. Many of Strauss's followers were strong promoters of President George W. Bush's plan to invade Iraq.

Critics of the neoconservative movement claim that it represents a Straussian "conspiracy" to control American foreign policy, and some liberals claim that Strauss's theories are antidemocratic and encourage a "fascist" tyranny of the "wise." Supporters of Strauss have suggested that his critics are guided by anti-Semitism.

Strauss himself engaged in no political activity, preferring the life of a scholar-philosopher. He was critical of modern philosophy and social science. Instead, he sought a return to the earlier perspectives of classical Greek philosophers Plato and Aristotle and Jewish tradition as reflected in the Bible. His studies of the seventeenth-century philosophers Baruch Spinoza and Thomas Hobbes led him to conclude that modern philosophy and science did not refute the claims of religion, and that the conflict between religion and science is fated to remain perpetual.

Strauss distrusted liberalism, modernity, and multiculturalism. He argued that uncritical praise of democratic culture leaves unchallenged the weaknesses of "mass culture," which diminishes the value of the pursuit of excellence as a human ideal. To learn about humanity's highest values, Strauss and many of his followers encourage a return to the "great books" of the ancient and medieval tradition.

Martin J. Plax

See also: American Century; Anti-Semitism; Bennett, William J.; Bush Family; Great Books; Keyes, Alan; Kristol, Irving, and Bill Kristol; Neoconservatism; Podhoretz, Norman.

Further Reading

Drury, Shadia B. *Leo Strauss and the American Right*. New York: St. Martin's, 1997.

Lenzner, Steven, and William Kistol. "What Was Leo Strauss Up To?" *Public Interest*, Fall 2003.

Norton, Anne. *Leo Strauss and the Politics of American Empire*. New Haven, CT: Yale University Press, 2004.

West, Thomas. "Leo Strauss and American Foreign Policy." *Claremont Review of Books*, April 25, 2005.

Structuralism and Post-Structuralism

Structuralism is a method of analysis and philosophical approach to the understanding of human endeavors from language to literature and politics. According to this perspective, all of human-created reality, despite any apparent complexity, can be reduced to more simple basic facts or principles that remain the same regardless of a person's race, culture, gender, or ethnicity. This stands in direct opposition to poststructuralist methodologies, especially deconstructionism, which harshly criticize structuralism and insist that humanity is far less unified than the structuralist would suppose.

The Swiss linguist Ferdinand de Saussure is the originator of structuralism. Saussure's most important work, *Cours de linguistique générale* (Course in General Linguistics, 1916), begins by distinguishing between *langue* and *parole* (roughly "language" and "speech"). *Parole* (the spoken or written word) is public, and *langue* is

its underlying system. Whereas *parole* is arbitrary, *langue* is structured. For example, although two persons may use different *parole* (such as a case in which one speaks English and the other Chinese), they nonetheless share the same *langue*. The same thought process gives rise to different forms of speech. Thus, the work of the linguist committed to the tenets of structuralism is to cut through the surface *parole* and discover the underlying *langue*.

The impact of Saussure's methodology for understanding human language cannot easily be overstated. Almost immediately upon its publication, Saussure's *Cours* swept through higher education on both sides of the Atlantic, and into other fields such as anthropology, literature, and psychology. Saussurian linguistics bred a sense of optimism into the humanities and human sciences, as it was seen as offering a new form of progress for studies in these fields.

By way of example, if language is rule-governed, and if works of literature are but extended acts of language, then works of literature are also rule-governed. So, despite the fact that in literature there are a myriad of different characters, events, and narrative styles, the structuralist would maintain that they all contain the same, or very similar, structures. The Marxist structuralist might claim that works of literature create their plot and corresponding tension by combining or juxtaposing different social classes. All stories that address romantic love between two people of different social classes, for example, share the same structuralist core. A Freudian structuralist might hypothesize that the structure beneath such stories is a psychological one playing off our pre-linguistic egos, especially the desire to preserve one's life. This approach contrasts sharply with multicultural interpretations of texts, in which it is presupposed that autobiographical details of both the author and reader of a text make any single, universal meaning impossible. It contrasts even more sharply with deconstructionist methodologies that remove the author completely from the realm of meaning. According to such methodologies, meaning is created by the reader alone, and in no case does a reader uncover a preexisting meaningful structure created by the author.

Structuralism became especially influential in the field of anthropology. In such works as *The Elementary Structures of Kinship* (1949) and *La Pensée Sauvage* (The Savage Mind, 1962), French anthropologist Claude Lévi-Strauss utilized structuralist methodology to address core issues in anthropology. He argued, for example, that both the scientific engineer and the pre-scientific "savage" share the same theoretical core. The concept of kinship, he argued further, is reducible to the exchange of women consistent with the prohibition against incest; bound by that prohibition, the exchange encourages social cooperation and peaceful communication across clans. Thus, Lévi-Strauss concludes, kinship can be used to explain the origins of much larger phenomena such as politics and even religion.

In another realm, Joseph Campbell applied structuralistic methodology to the study of myth, arguing in *The Hero with a Thousand Faces* (1949) that all hero myths, regardless of culture, have the same structure. Specifically, they involve a hero born in an ordinary world who is called to an extraordinary one. Upon entering the extraordinary world, the hero wins a battle and returns to the ordinary world with newly acquired gifts and skills that he bestows on friends or clansmen.

A major blow to structuralism came at the height of its European popularity when, in 1966, the French philosopher Jacques Derrida delivered a paper that was highly critical of the movement. Derrida's paper prompted persistent questioning regarding the theoretical core of structuralism. Chief among the concerns of objectors is the strong disavowal of history and historical circumstance that pervades structuralist studies. Structuralists, it is said, view the facts of particular cultures as the unnecessary, arbitrary *parole* and that the essence lies in the *langue* that lies beneath—though it is not clear why historical or cultural facts are to be minimized or labeled "arbitrary." Others criticize the structuralist approach for its unwarranted insistence upon "essential" properties of human phenomena. For example, some structuralist critiques seem to assume that there is a genuine property of "maleness" and "femaleness" such that all persons have just one or the other, and that the two are complete, clearly defined categories. Postmodern feminists, among others, object to this view, regarding it as a veiled attempt to buttress arbitrary, culturally defined values.

The methodologies that replaced structuralism tend to capitalize on these objections. Post-structuralism and postmodern methodologies emphasize, contrary to structuralist tenets, the importance of contingent cultural and historical artifacts upon meaning. Deconstructionists directly challenge the alleged immutability of the so-called structure that underlies an observed system, and attempt to show how anything "beneath" the surface text can itself be deconstructed.

Craig Hanson

See also: Deconstructionism; Multiculturalism and Ethnic Studies; Paglia, Camille; Postmodernism; Relativism, Moral.

Further Reading

Campbell, Joseph. *The Hero with a Thousand Faces.* Novato, CA: New World Library, 2008.

Eagleton, Terry. *Literary Theory: An Introduction.* Minneapolis: University of Minnesota Press, 1996.

Lévi-Strauss, Claude. *The Elementary Structure of Kinship.* Boston: Beacon Press, 1971.

Saussure, Ferdinand de. *Course in General Linguistics.* LaSalle, IL: Open Court, 1998.

Student Conservatives

If at times less vocal than their liberal and radical counterparts, student conservatives have stood at the social, political, and intellectual vanguard of the American culture wars since at least the 1960s. During that tumultuous decade, they clashed with the New Left and the hippie counterculture, which they viewed as a radical, permissive, and secular movement corrosive to the traditions and values of American society. Between the 1970s and the 2000s, student conservatives broadened their efforts to combat issues such as abortion, feminism, and gay rights. In these disputes, they enjoyed the increasingly lavish support of conservative benefactors and institutions. This support, and the centrality of universities to the culture wars, nurtured a growth in the number, organization, and influence of student conservatives during this period.

Young Americans for Freedom (YAF), the first significant conservative student organization, played a vital role in the 1960s. Guided by adult conservatives like William F. Buckley, Jr., and William Rusher, YAF brought together a diverse group of conservative students from hundreds of college campuses. Its founding document, the Sharon Statement (1960), stressed the importance of a limited government to the preservation of liberty, moral order, and tradition. The 1964 presidential campaign of Republican Barry Goldwater energized conservative students, and YAF members such as Robert Croll and John Kolbe worked aggressively to spread Goldwater's conservative message. YAF's student journal, the *New Guard*, publicized the group's political activities and provided a forum for the discussion of conservative ideas on campus.

Young conservatives responded aggressively to the emergence of a new cadre of student radicals in the 1960s. The New Left and the hippie counterculture capitalized on a growing opposition to the Vietnam War in the mid-1960s to advance their political and cultural agenda on many college campuses. Student conservatives, many themselves opposed to the draft, answered by staging counterdemonstrations in support of the war and in opposition to the student radicals. "Bleed-ins" encouraged students to donate blood for the troops, and "bake-ins" raised money to send them cookies. College conservatives challenged the protests of student leftists at places such as Columbia University in 1968, when they blocked student radicals from taking over the university library. They led a campaign against the National Student Association, which they believed had become a political front for the New Left. Other organizations such as the Free Campus Movement, founded at the University of Southern California in 1968, and the Community of the Right, organized at Stanford University in 1969, provided opportunities for student conservatives to counter the collegiate left.

R. Emmett Tyrrell, a graduate student in history at Indiana University, founded in 1967 a conservative journal, *The Alternative*, which used satire and mockery in its attack on the New Left's influence at IU. He later helped orchestrate an electoral victory for conservatives and the removal of the leftists from key student government positions at the school. The journal proved even more successful. Later renamed the *American Spectator*, the journal continued to target the New Left and youth counterculture while playing an ecumenical role of sorts for conservatism. Anticipating larger trends in the American right, its pages brought traditionalist and libertarian conservatives together with a new group of disenchanted liberals called neoconservatives, united behind a growing disgust over the cultural and political direction of American liberalism.

Hostility to abortion rights, the feminist movement, gay rights, affirmative action, busing, and the drug culture nurtured a growth in the number of conservative students in the 1970s and 1980s. Christian student conservatives found abortion, legalized by the U.S. Supreme Court in *Roe v. Wade* (1973), a particularly galvanizing issue. Many students on the right, especially young women, participated in annual Right to Life marches and rallies on campuses and in capital cities. In the 1970s, young conservative women also fought against the feminist movement and the Equal Rights Amendment, which they believed would undermine the biological roles of the sexes and threaten the traditional family structure. Some female students, such as Mary Eberstadt at Cornell University and Heather MacDonald at Yale University, in the early 1980s shifted rightward in reaction to liberal ideas they encountered during their undergraduate and graduate years.

Many future conservative leaders worked for right-wing campus periodicals. At Dartmouth College, for example, Dinesh D'Souza developed his writing skills as editor of the *Dartmouth Review*, an independent conservative student publication that relentlessly assailed liberal stances, particularly the women's and gay rights movements. D'Souza would become a leading culture warrior and conservative commentator in the 1990s and 2000s. While attending the University of Virginia during the late 1980s, Rich Lowry, a future editor of the *National Review*, wrote for the conservative *Virginia Advocate* (founded in 1986). Overall, there was a dramatic expansion in the number of conservative student publications at the campuses of Harvard, Yale, and Duke, among others. These student periodicals proved effective training grounds for future conservative leaders of the culture wars.

Since the 1980s, student conservatives have continued to fight on the front lines of the culture wars, particularly over the issues of abortion, homosexuality, and affirmative action. For the cause of battling liberalism, they have been provided grants, fellowships, and internships by a growing body of conservative think tanks and foundations, including the Intercollegiate Studies Institute (1953), the Heritage Foundation (1973), and American Collegians for Life (1988). In addition, Morton Blackwell's Leadership Institute (1979) has provided leadership training, while James Dobson's Focus on the Family Institute (1995) has assisted evangelical conservative students.

Conservative colleges such as Hillsdale College in Michigan and Grove City College in Pennsylvania, and Catholic conservative colleges like the University of Dallas and Franciscan University of Steubenville, Ohio, have provided safe havens for the training of student conservatives and future culture warriors. Conservative Christian colleges, such as Indiana Wesleyan University and Taylor University in Indiana, have also contributed to training articulate young conservatives. The founding in 2000 of Patrick Henry College, a conservative Christian college in Purcellville, Virginia, dedicated to changing American culture, testifies to the continued salience of student conservatives to the culture wars.

Daniel Spillman

See also: Affirmative Action; Buckley, William F., Jr.; Counterculture; Equal Rights Amendment; Feminism, Third-Wave; Gay Rights Movement; Heritage Foundation; Hillsdale College; Neoconservatism; New Left; *Roe v. Wade* (1973); Rusher, William A.; Vietnam War.

Further Reading

Andrew, John A., III. *The Other Side of the Sixties: Young Americans for Freedom and the Rise of Conservative Politics.* New Brunswick, NJ: Rutgers University Press, 1997.

Eberstadt, Mary, ed. *Why I Turned Right: Leading Baby Boom Conservatives Chronicle Their Political Journeys.* New York: Threshold Editions, 2007.

Lantzer, Jason S. "The Other Side of Campus: Indiana University's Student Right and the Rise of National Conservatism." *Indiana Magazine of History*, June 2005.

Micklethwait, John, and Adrian Wooldridge. *The Right Nation: Conservative Power in America.* New York: Penguin Books, 2004.

Schneider, Gregory. *Cadres for Conservatism: Young Americans for Freedom and the Rise of the Contemporary Right.* New York: New York University Press, 1999.

Students for a Democratic Society

Founded in Ann Arbor, Michigan, in 1960, Students for a Democratic Society (SDS) was a radical student organization that flourished in the last half of the 1960s. It was the largest and most influential organization of the New Left movement, which called for radical social and political change in the 1960s and early 1970s.

The SDS grew out of the student branch of the League for Industrial Democracy, a socialist educational organization. The group's founding members drew inspiration from both the civil rights movement and organized labor. At the initial meeting in Ann Arbor, they elected Robert Alan Haber as president (officially field secretary). At the group's first convention in June 1962, it approved the Port Huron Statement, a manifesto (named for the town in which the gathering was held) drafted chiefly by co-founder, staff member, and Haber's successor as president, Tom Hayden. Beginning with the often-quoted words, "We are people of this generation, bred in at least modest comfort, housed now in universities, looking uncomfortably to the world we inherit," the document declared an "agenda for a generation": working for full civil rights for African Americans, an end to poverty, more political involvement on the part of college students, and the pursuit of true democracy and freedom in the world.

In its early years, the SDS focused its efforts largely on economic inequality. One of its better-known efforts was the Economic Research and Action Project (ERAP), a campaign for community organizing among unemployed whites in major northern cities. At the group's 1964 annual meeting, a split developed between supporters of ERAP and those who wanted to emphasize campus organizing. The majority sided with the ERAP supporters, but the drive toward campus activism would become increasingly important for SDS members.

The group did not focus heavily on the Vietnam War until 1965, after President Lyndon Johnson escalated the conflict under the Gulf of Tonkin Resolution. The group's membership grew slowly between 1960 and 1965, but the spike in U.S. troop deployment to Vietnam resulted in a massive increase in SDS membership. Local SDS chapters sprang up all over the country, mostly as a result of student opposition to the war. Members organized demonstrations on college campuses to protest U.S. involvement and the draft, and teach-ins to educate fellow students. The SDS staged one of the first national demonstrations against the war in April 1965, a protest that drew around 20,000 people to Washington, D.C. Meanwhile, the organization itself was changing in dramatic ways. Members voted to remove the anticommunist planks from the SDS charter, and the organization moved its headquarters from New York to Chicago, reflecting the desire of many members to make the group more national.

The year 1968 was also important for the SDS. In the spring of that year, members waged a series of rallies, teach-ins, and marches to protest continuing U.S. involvement in Southeast Asia. On April 26, the organization sponsored a one-day strike in which approximately one million students participated. At Columbia University in New York City, the local SDS chapter joined with other groups to protest the school's involvement with the Institute for Defense Analyses (IDA), a weapons research outlet affiliated with the U.S. Department of Defense. The conflict escalated when Columbia officials announced plans to build a new gymnasium on land originally intended for low-cost housing in Harlem. The protests, including the takeover of several university buildings, finally prompted the administration to scrap plans for the gymnasium and end its affiliation with the IDA. The widely publicized events at Columbia also put the SDS in the public spotlight and attracted new members to the organization.

The growing influence of the SDS on American college campuses convinced many of its supporters that a social revolution was possible. As expectations rose, however, the group became increasingly divided. As early as 1966, the Progressive Labor Party (PL), a Maoist group committed to communist principles, had begun using SDS as a recruitment vehicle and organized the Worker Student Alliance (WSA) to push its agenda. Although the vast majority of SDS members were anticommunist, they were also reluctant to expel communists from the group. The Revolutionary Youth Movement (RYM), led by Bernardine Dohrn, Mark Rudd, and others, organized in opposition to the WSA and tried to prevent what its leaders viewed as a hostile takeover of the organization by the WSA. They were particularly troubled by the hostility of many WSA members toward the Black Panthers.

The conflict came to a head at the 1969 SDS national convention in Chicago, where the WSA moved to take control of the national SDS. Led by Dohrn, the RYM faction voted to expel the PL from the convention and subsequently walked out of the building, leaving the SDS with two sets of leaders. The split at the 1969 convention was the death knell for SDS, which would hold no further annual conventions. The RYM faction formed the radical Weather Underground Organization, known popularly as the Weathermen, organized around the goal of a revolution that would overthrow the U.S. government. Believing that a revolutionary political party per se would be ineffective, the group's leaders called for militant direct action to bring about the demise of the federal government. The Weathermen remained active until 1975, at which time the New Left effectively collapsed.

Decades after its demise, however, the SDS continued to influence the social and cultural changes that transformed America. By organizing students around an agenda of radical social and political change, the group helped lay the groundwork for the cultural battles that would be a legacy of the 1960s. Indeed, in 2006, a group of former SDS members teamed with college students to advocate a revival of the group. They envisioned a multi-issue organization that would unite students across the country to support an agenda of leftist causes, including opposition to various forms of military action, support for protective environmental legislation, and a critique of global current trade agreements. By the end of 2006, the new SDS boasted hundreds of chapters on college campuses and thousands of members.

Blake Ellis

See also: Black Panther Party; Chicago Seven; Civil Rights Movement; Cold War; Communists and Communism; Counterculture; Hayden, Tom; Hoffman, Abbie; Marxism; New Left; Vietnam War; War Protesters.

Further Reading

Gitlin, Todd. *The Sixties: Years of Hope, Days of Rage.* New York: Bantam, 1987.

Isserman, Maurice. *If I Had a Hammer: The Death of the Old Left and the Birth of the New Left.* New York: Basic Books, 1997.

Miller, James. *Democracy in the Streets: From Port Huron to the Siege of Chicago.* Cambridge, MA: Harvard University Press, 1994.

Sale, Kirkpatrick. *SDS.* New York: Random House, 1973.

Summers, Lawrence

An economist, academic, and former government official, Lawrence "Larry" Summers served five years as president of Harvard University before resigning in February 2006 after a series of disputes with school faculty over sensitive political and social issues. Born Lawrence Henry Summers on November 30, 1954, in New Haven, Connecticut, he studied at the Massachusetts Institute of Technology (BS, 1975) and Harvard (PhD, 1982), where in 1983 he became the youngest tenured professor. After serving as chief economist of the World Bank (1991–1993) and secretary of the treasury (1999–2001) in the administration of President Bill Clinton, he was appointed president of Harvard. Although some attributed his demise as president to failing to apply a corporate approach in campus governance, and others blamed his shielding of a fellow Harvard economist accused of defrauding the federal government while serving as a consultant for Russian market reform, many portrayed him as a victim of the culture wars.

Summers's tenure as university president was characterized by a series of public gaffes. Most incendiary was his January 2005 statement that women are underrepresented in the fields of mathematics and science for reasons of "intrinsic aptitude." In 2001, he had challenged the prominent African-American professor Cornel West to apply more scholarly rigor in his work. An insulted West left Harvard for what he regarded as a more respectful environment at Princeton University. The following year, Summers offended Muslim students by characterizing them as anti-Semitic for lobbying Harvard to divest stock in companies that do business in Israel.

Although the student body, by a margin of three to one, sided with the president in the 2005 public dispute, the faculty of the arts and sciences, by a vote of 218 to 185 (with 18 abstentions), formally expressed its lack of confidence in Summers's leadership. When a second vote of no confidence was scheduled the following year, he announced that he would step down at the end of the 2006 school year.

Supporters of Summers regard him as a reformer who made enemies on campus because he violated "political correctness" and speech codes while demanding higher academic standards and denouncing grade inflation. His opponents argue that he was primarily undone by his arrogant and insensitive behavior and top-down management style.

Roger Chapman

See also: Academic Freedom; Anti-Semitism; Israel; Multiculturalism and Ethnic Studies; Muslim Americans; Political Correctness; Soviet Union and Russia; Speech Codes; Victimhood; West, Cornel.

Further Reading

Bradley, Richard. *Harvard Rues: Lawrence Summers and the Battle for the World's Most Powerful University.* New York: HarperCollins, 2005.

Lewis, Harry. *Excellence Without a Soul: How a Great University Forgot Education.* New York: Public Affairs, 2006.

Wilson, Robin. "The Power of Professors." *Chronicle of Higher Education*, March 3, 2006.

Supply-Side Economics

Supply-side economics is an approach pioneered in the 1970s that stresses the role of tax cuts in creating economic incentives and in fostering economic growth. Supply-side economics is commonly set in opposition to the demand-side perspective of Keynesian and monetarist economics.

The intellectual foundations of supply-side economics are attributed to economist Arthur Laffer's work, and especially to a drawing executed on a cocktail napkin that Jude Wanniski later called the "Laffer Curve" in his book *The Way the World Works* (1978). The curve depicts a relationship between tax rates and tax revenue, showing that each level of tax revenue corresponds to two levels of tax rates, one high and one low. Supply-siders argue that the tax rates prevailing in the United States are in the top section of the curve. They argued at the time that a decrease in those rates would not only increase people's income and incentives to work but also increase the amount of tax revenue collected by the government. Thus, a tax cut would pay for itself without requiring any adjustment in government spending.

Supply-side economics is often referred to as "trickle-down" economics because it is hypothesized that a decrease in the marginal tax rate will provide incentives for entrepreneurs to hire more workers, as they receive higher revenues and profits. Thus, the increase in income created by the decrease in tax rates would be passed on to the rest of society from the top down. Supply-side assumptions formed the economic foundation of Ronald Reagan's campaign platform in 1980 and were heavily implemented throughout his presidency.

Despite its endorsement by Nobel Prize laureate Robert Mundell, supply-side economics found relatively little support in the academic community. The Nobel Prize–winning economist and liberal commentator Paul Krugman has been one of the most vocal opponents of supply-side economics. In his book *Peddling Prosperity* (1994), Krugman observes that no economics department at any major American university has a specifically supply-side orientation. Through his books and op-ed pieces in the *New York Times*, Krugman has sought to convince the American public that supply-side economics is an ideology disguised as scientific theory. This sentiment echoed George H.W. Bush's characterization of supply-side economics in 1980 as "voodoo economics" and the confession of Reagan budget director David Stockman in *The Triumph of Politics* (1986) that supply-side economics was a ploy to justify tax cuts for the wealthy. In the realm of popular culture, Al Franken introduced "Supply-Side Jesus," a cartoon figure portraying Jesus Christ as a wealthy individual providing employment to poorer people through his thirst for luxury items.

The emphasis on tax cuts in the economic policies of President George W. Bush, in particular the elimination of the estate tax and the reduction of the tax on capital gains, has been interpreted by some as a revival of supply-side economics. In each year of the Bush administration following the first tax cuts in 2002, the Congressional Budget Office (CBO) forecast long-term budget deficits and increased national debt. The Democratic Leadership Committee, interpreting the CBO reports to mean that the tax cuts had failed to generate new wealth, declared the death of supply-side economics in 2003.

Quentin Hedges Duroy

See also: Bush Family; Democratic Party; Federal Budget Deficit; Franken, Al; Krugman, Paul; Norquist, Grover; Reagan, Ronald; Republican Party; Tax Reform; *Wall Street Journal, The*.

Further Reading
Bartlett, Bruce, and Timothy P. Roth, eds. *The Supply-Side Solution*. Chatham, NJ: Chatham House, 1983.
Krugman, Paul. *Peddling Prosperity: Economic Sense and Nonsense in the Age of Diminished Expectations*. New York: W.W. Norton, 1994.
Stockman, David. *The Triumph of Politics: Why the Reagan Revolution Failed*. New York: Harper and Row, 1986.
Wanniski, Jude. *The Way the World Works: How Economies Fail and Succeed*. New York: Basic Books, 1978.

Symbionese Liberation Army

The Symbionese Liberation Army (SLA) was a militant political group that carried out a series of violent crimes, including murder, kidnapping, armed robbery, and the planting of bombs, in the San Francisco Bay area during the first half of the 1970s. "Death to the fascist insect that preys upon the life of the people" was the group's slogan. Although the SLA was denounced by the Berkeley student newspaper and most leftist radicals, conservatives regarded it as symptomatic of counterculture excesses. At the time, some radicals hypothesized that the SLA was a creation of the FBI to discredit the left.

Made up of about a dozen members, predominantly white and middle class, the SLA proclaimed the goal of unifying "oppressed people" to fight against "the capitalist state and all its value systems." The group's logo was a seven-headed cobra, symbolizing the seven principles of Kwanzaa. Their leader, known as Field Marshal Cinque, was Donald DeFreeze, a black escaped convict and purported schizophrenic.

The notoriety of the SLA was based on two dramatic crimes. One was the assassination on November 6, 1973, of Marcus Foster, the black superintendent of the Oakland school system, because he favored student identification cards. The second was the February 4, 1974, kidnapping of Patricia "Patty" Hearst, the nineteen-year-old heiress of the Hearst newspaper chain.

In compliance with her captors' ransom demand, Hearst's parents established a $2 million charity fund and distributed food to over 30,000 people. In April, however, the SLA released a tape in which Hearst declared that she had taken the name Tania and enlisted in the terrorist army. She was photographed participating in a bank robbery that left one bystander dead, and a warrant for her arrest was issued immediately. She was captured in September 1975 and convicted of bank robbery six month later despite her claims of being brainwashed. Her seven-year prison sentence was commuted by President Jimmy Carter after she had served twenty-one months. She was granted a full pardon by President Bill Clinton in January 2001.

Six SLA members were killed in a shootout with Los Angeles police on May 17, 1974. After two more bank holdups, the group disbanded, its remaining members either arrested or gone underground. In 1999, former SLA member Kathleen Soliah, alias Sarah Jane Olson, was arrested. In October 2001, fearing that a fair trial would be impossible in the post-9/11 climate, she reluctantly pleaded guilty to having placed bombs under police cars in 1977 with the intention to kill. In November 2002, the last known SLA fugitive, James Kilgore, was captured in South Africa. And in February 2003, four former SLA members were given prison sentences for the 1975 robbery murder in which Hearst had participated; some of them had earlier served time for the Hearst kidnapping.

Roger Chapman

See also: Clinton, Bill; Conspiracy Theories; Counterculture; Kwanzaa; Marxism; Presidential Pardons; September 11; Stone, Oliver; Victimhood.

Further Reading

Graebner, William. *Patty's Got a Gun: Patricia Hearst in 1970s America.* Chicago: University of Chicago Press, 2008.

Hearst, Patricia, with Alvin Moscow. *Every Secret Thing.* Garden City, NY: Doubleday, 1982.

Pearsall, Robert Brainard, ed. *The Symbionese Liberation Army: Documents and Communications.* Amsterdam: Rodopi N.V., 1974.

Taft, Robert A.

Nicknamed "Mr. Republican," Robert A. Taft was a conservative U.S. senator from Ohio who opposed the New Deal, advocated a noninterventionist foreign policy, and supported McCarthyism

Robert Alphonso Taft was born on September 8, 1889, in Cincinnati, the eldest son of William Howard Taft (the only person to have served as both president of the United States and chief justice of the Supreme Court). Educated at Yale University (BA, 1910; MA, 1936) and Harvard Law School (LLB, 1913), Taft practiced law and set his sights on the White House but failed to secure the Republican nomination for president in 1940, 1948, and 1952.

Taft had a full public career: assistant counsel for Herbert Hoover's U.S. Food Administration (1917–1919); Ohio House of Representatives (1921–1926); Ohio Senate (1931–1932); and U.S. Senate (1939–1953).

He began his tenure in the Senate opposed to President Franklin D. Roosevelt's New Deal programs, which he regarded as socialistic, and in the postwar period he worked to reduce Roosevelt's legacy. Thus, with Representative Fred A. Hartley, Jr. (R-NJ) as co-author, he introduced the Taft-Hartley Act, a measure to curb labor activity by scaling back the Wagner Act (1935). Passed on July 23, 1947, over President Harry Truman's veto, Taft-Hartley included a provision requiring unions to adhere to an eighty-day "cooling off" period prior to going on strike during times of national emergencies. That same year, Taft campaigned against a plan for compulsory health insurance, denouncing it as "the federalization of medicine."

Taft urged the United States to maintain a strong military without diplomatic alliances and foreign entanglements. He put forth his views in *A Foreign Policy for Americans* (1951). One of his concerns was that that the Cold War might turn the United States into a "garrison state" with the undermining of national liberty. Taft was staunchly against communism, but he supported the Marshall Plan with misgivings and opposed Senate ratification of the North Atlantic Treaty Organization.

The postwar Red Scare brought out Taft's strongest partisan instincts. After Senator Joseph McCarthy (R-WI) alleged that the State Department had been infiltrated by communists, Taft encouraged him to "keep talking." It is believed that Taft counseled Eisenhower not to stifle McCarthy because McCarthy's claims were damaging to Democrats. Taft died of cancer in New York City on July 31, 1953. At least one biographer is convinced that had Taft still been a member of the Senate, he would not have voted to censure McCarthy in 1954.

Roger Chapman

See also: American Century; Cold War; Communists and Communism; Eisenhower, Dwight D.; Health Care; Kerouac, Jack; Labor Unions; McCarthy, Joseph; McCarthyism; Neoconservatism; New Deal; Republican Party; Schlafly, Phyllis.

Further Reading

Hayes, Michael T. "The Republican Road Not Taken: The Foreign-Policy Vision of Robert A. Taft." *Independent Review* 8:4 (2004): 509–25.

Kirk, Russell, and James McClellan. *The Political Principles of Robert A. Taft.* New York: Fleet, 1967.

Patterson, James T. *Mr. Republican: A Biography of Robert A. Taft.* Boston: Houghton Mifflin, 1972.

Robinson, Phyllis. *Robert A. Taft: Boy and Man.* Cambridge, MA: Dresser, Chapman and Grimes, 1963.

Talk Radio

A daily staple of millions of Americans, talk radio since the late 1980s has emerged as one of the most influential media in the United States. Indeed, by 2007, more than 80 percent of all AM radio stations included at least one talk show in their broadcast lineup. In fact, talk radio during the first decade of the twenty-first century was so popular that it supported more than 1,200 "all-talk" shows. These programs are often political in nature, usually polemical, and make little effort at being objective.

Although some historians credit regional call-in shows and early game shows as the inspiration behind talk radio, the format was not widely adopted until the 1960s, when stations such as KABC in Los Angeles and KMOX in St. Louis switched to all talk. Pioneering talk radio personalities included Long John Nebel, whose offbeat broadcasts featured discourses on UFOs and voodoo; Joe Pyne, a political conservative who supported the Vietnam War and abhorred hippies; Mort Sahl, a liberal political satirist who enjoyed poking fun at Richard Nixon; and Bill Ballance, host of the "Feminine Forum," the first so-called topless or sex talk program.

In talk radio, show hosts typically begin their broadcasts by introducing a provocative topic, often taken from that day's headlines or instigated as part of a conversation with an on-air guest. Listeners are then encouraged to call in with their comments and questions. Depending on the host, content may focus on one or more of the following topics: general issues, politics, sports, "hot talk" (also known as "shock jock"), popular culture, finance, home improvement, psychology and relationships, and "specialty" topics such as computers, cars, and travel. Fans generally tune in to hear how their favorite host will react to caller comments.

The most popular topic of on-air conversation by far has been politics. Of *Talkers Magazine*'s top 100 talk radio hosts in 2007, 40 percent identified their programs as politically conservative, moderate, or progressive. Until 1987, all radio content in the United States was regulated by the Fairness Doctrine, a federal law requiring broadcasters to provide balanced coverage of important controversial issues. Once the law was repealed, however, many hosts felt free to begin promoting specific political and social agendas, resulting in some decidedly one-sided programming. As Mary Beal, on-air personality and former board member of the National Association of Radio Talk Show Hosts, once said, "I don't care if I have a balanced viewpoint, because any opinion can be challenged by the people who call in."

The true power of unregulated talk radio became apparent in 1992, when presidential candidates Bill Clinton and Ross Perot both made optimum use of the medium in their campaigns. According to a *Congressional Quarterly* study, listeners learned more about the nominees through talk radio than any other medium. Many voters who had felt disenfranchised by the electoral process suddenly felt empowered because the candidates had come to them.

Rush Limbaugh, a leading figure in American talk radio since the 1980s, is an outspoken conservative who vociferously expounds on the "evils" of homosexuality, feminism, environmentalism, and liberalism in general. In 1992, his syndicated program the *Rush Limbaugh Show* was heard on 529 stations across the country. Within three years, he not only had expanded his reach to 660 stations, but he was credited with single-handedly helping the Republicans regain control of Congress. "I believe that the most effective way to persuade people is to speak to them in a way that makes them think that they reached certain conclusions on their own," he has said. By 2007, Limbaugh was the most popular radio broadcaster in the nation, with more than 13 million people tuning in to his show at least once a week.

Despite his popularity, Limbaugh is by no means the only conservative voice on the radio dial. During the first decade of the 2000s, right-wing commentator Sean Hannity had a weekly audience of 12 million, while the self-proclaimed "firebrand conservative" Michael Savage spoke regularly to more than 8 million listeners. On the more liberal side has been Ed Schultz, a "progressive" broadcasting from Fargo, North Dakota; as well as Randi Rhodes, a mainstay of the left-leaning radio network Air America. Other well-known radio talk show personalities include "Dr. Laura" Schlessinger, who dispenses family advice as well as political opinions; Christian broadcaster Mike Gallagher; and "shock jocks" Howard Stern, Mancow, and Opie & Anthony.

Talk radio has been called "the working people's medium." According to a 2004 Pew Research Center study, 17 percent of the American public regularly tune in to call-in radio shows. Of these, most are middle-aged men who are well educated and consider themselves conservative. *Talkers Magazine*'s 2007 talk radio survey revealed that nearly 75 percent of listeners voted in the 2006 election and that 58 percent were registered as independents.

National Public Radio personality Diane Rehm has described talk radio as America's "electronic backyard fence," where listeners can discuss issues anonymously over the air. On the other hand, she warned, talk radio can be "a provocative and even dangerous medium, capable of representing an extreme form of democracy," particularly in the hands of radio hosts "who attempt to use talk shows to spread their own political or social dogma." Especially worrisome are the "radio activists" who agitate their audiences by emphasizing only one side of whatever issue they are discussing. *Newsday* media critic Paul Colford has asserted that these types of on-air hosts are nothing more than "ambassadors in the culture of resentment." Likewise, Tim Rutten of the *Los Angeles Times* has called Limbaugh and his imitators the "tough guys and mean girls of AM talk," who use bullying tactics, instead of solid reasoning, to get their point across.

Cindy Mediavilla

See also: Bennett, William J.; Clinton, Bill; Donahue, Phil; Federal Communications Commission; Limbaugh, Rush; Media Bias; National Public Radio; Perot, H. Ross; Shock Jocks; Stern, Howard; Terkel, Studs.

Further Reading

Douglas, Susan J. "Letting the Boys Be Boys: Talk Radio, Male Hysteria, and Political Discourse in the 1980s." In *Radio Reader: Essays in the Cultural History of Radio*, ed. Michele Hilmes and Jason Loviglio, 485–503. New York: Routledge, 2002.

Godfrey, Donald G., and Frederic A. Leigh, eds. *Historical Dictionary of American Radio*. Westport, CT: Greenwood Press, 1998.

Hoyt, Mike. "Talk Radio: Turning Up the Volume." In *Taking Sides: Clashing Views on Controversial Issues in Mass Media and Society*, ed. Alison Alexander and Janice Hanson, 62–67. 2nd ed. Guilford, CT: Dushkin, 1995.

Pease, Edward C., and Everette E. Dennis, eds. *Radio: The Forgotten Medium*. New Brunswick, NJ: Transaction, 1995.

Tax Reform

Taxes have been the subject of political controversy in the United States since the founding of the nation. From 1776 to World War I, tariffs and excise taxes were the primary sources of revenue for the federal government. The income tax was unknown until the Civil War, when it was implemented briefly, then discontinued until 1894. President Grover Cleveland convinced Congress to lower tariffs and substitute a modest tax on incomes to recoup revenues, but in 1895 the Supreme Court ruled the income tax unconstitutional, at least if it was based on income derived from property (*Pollock v. Farmers' Loan & Trust Company*). As a reaction to the government's inability to balance the federal budget in the ensuing years, Congress proposed the Sixteenth Amendment, giving it the power to lay and collect taxes on any form of income; the amendment was ratified in 1913.

The modern tax reform movement is often said to have been launched in 1978 with the passage of Proposition 13 in California, a ballot referendum that dramatically lowered property taxes in the state. Proposition 13 was successful in part because there had been dramatic increases in the state property tax just prior to the ballot measure. The California government had not actually increased tax rates, but huge increases in property values had suddenly pushed property assessments much higher than they had been. Since property taxes are based on a proportion of assessed value, Californians were paying considerably more in property taxes even without an increase in the property tax rates.

Tax reduction referenda also succeeded in a number of other states, including Illinois, Massachusetts, and Michigan. Buoyed by the success of these state tax reform measures, conservatives sought to reduce taxes even further following the election of Ronald Reagan as president in 1980. The Reagan budget of 1981 represented a major ideological shift from the budgets over the previous half century and was one of the most significant presidential legislative initiatives in American history. The tax cuts in the 1981 federal budget were the largest to that time, representing over 2 percent of the gross domestic product (GDP).

Another significant change in policy during the Reagan years came with the Tax Reform Act of 1986, which made major changes in how income was taxed. The measure simplified the tax code, broadening the tax base and eliminating a number of tax shelters and other preferences. The top tax rate was lowered from 50 percent to 28 percent, and the bottom rate was raised from 11 percent to 15 percent—the only time in U.S. history that the income tax rate was reduced for the top tier while simultaneously increased in the bottom tier. The act also reduced the capital gains tax to the same rate for ordinary income, and it increased incentives to invest in owner-occupied housing rather than rental housing, thus raising the home mortgage interest deduction. The legislation, which was seen as revenue neutral, passed by a large bipartisan majority in Congress.

Deficit levels increased dramatically during the 1980s, and President George H.W. Bush was faced with record deficits. Despite having campaigned in 1988 on a pledge of "read my lips, no new taxes," Bush reluctantly agreed in a budget summit to a deficit reduction package in the Budget Enforcement Act of 1990. The law raised taxes and imposed new user fees in return for entitlements

cuts. Despite the measure's unpopularity, however, the 1990 budget laid the groundwork for a significant reduction in the deficit after Bush left office.

Early in the administration of President Bill Clinton, Congress passed the 1993 Budget Reconciliation Bill, which attempted to reduce the federal budget deficit through both tax increases and spending cuts. Clinton's call for a tax increase was a direct repudiation of the economic philosophies of his two Republican predecessors, suggesting that the tax policies of Ronald Reagan and George H.W. Bush came at the price of high deficits. Clinton raised most of the new revenue with an array of higher taxes on upper-income Americans and corporations, and more than half of the new taxes fell on families making more than $200,000 a year.

President George W. Bush made cutting taxes the top priority of his administration after he was inaugurated in 2001. His plan reduced all federal income tax rates, raised the child credit, gave a break to married couples, and repealed the federal tax on large estates. The largest portion of the cuts, however, came from lowering the income tax rates for all income groups—from 15 percent, 28 percent, 31 percent, and 36 and 39.6 percent to 10 percent, 15 percent, 25 percent, and 33 percent, respectively.

A controversial tax reform enacted in 2001 was a reduction in the federal estate tax. Since the estate tax is imposed on an estate only after someone has died, critics of the estate tax refer to it as the "death tax." Before the 2001 cuts, the estate tax was imposed on only those estates valued at more than $1 million. As of 2006, the figure was raised to $2 million, and as of 2009 to $3.5 million, with the tax scheduled to disappear completely in 2010 and then resume in 2011 at the 2001 level. Thus, under the legislation, the effective transfer tax rate fell from a peak of 55 percent in 2001 to 50 percent in 2002 and to 45 percent by 2007, but it would rise again to 55 percent in 2011. Proponents of the estate tax argue that it is an important source of revenue for the federal government and is necessary to a system of progressive taxation because it affects large estates only. Opponents of the legislation argued further that a higher effective transfer tax encourages the wealthy to make billions of dollars in charitable donations each year, since the donations substantially reduce taxes on large estates.

Patrick Fisher

See also: Bush Family; Clinton, Bill; Contract with America; Corporate Welfare; Norquist, Grover; Privatization; Reagan, Ronald; Social Security; Supply-Side Economics; *Wall Street Journal, The.*

Further Reading
Peters, B. Guy. *The Politics of Taxation*. Cambridge, MA: Blackwell, 1991.

Steinmo, Sven. *Taxation and Democracy.* New Haven, CT: Yale University Press, 1993.

Wildavsky, Aaron, and Naomi Caiden. *The New Politics of the Budgetary Process.* 4th ed. New York: Longman, 2001.

Televangelism

With ties to mid-nineteenth-century tent revivals, televangelism in contemporary America pursues new converts through the mass media. Widely associated with bombastic preaching, gospel revelry, and sometimes faith healing, the "electronic church" is not merely the business of evangelical Christians. As a particularly North American phenomenon, it also reflects social, cultural, and economic currents. At its core, televangelism is socially conservative, underscoring the traditional nuclear family in its anti-abortion, antigay, and antifeminist stances. Promoting the Religious Right's social and political agenda to a mostly lower-middle-class audience, televangelism plays a major role in mobilizing conservative Christians, ushering them into the political arena to press for legislated morality.

While liberal Protestants tend toward relativism, conservative evangelicals and fundamentalists believe in salvation only for those "born again" in accordance with their exacting interpretation of the Bible—a simple theological message conducive to broadcasting. In the 1920s, secular radio stations gave free airtime to religious programs; mainline Protestant and Catholic groups filled most of it, forcing evangelical and fundamentalist Christians to pay for their broadcasts. Frustrated, the National Association of Evangelicals (NAE) in 1944 formed the National Religious Broadcasters (NRB) to fight the radio monopoly held by liberal churches. This arrangement remained in place until 1960, when all airtime was made available for purchase. Stations tended to favor conservative Christian televangelists, who were eager to pay, and the situation quickly changed. Since that time, evangelicals have dominated the religious airwaves in America.

In the 1950s, evangelical preachers began a shift from radio to television. Among the first to do so was the Reverend Billy Graham, a Southern Baptist and the television preacher of choice for mainline evangelicals. In televising his "crusades," Graham showed that TV was a medium that could be used to stir up religious enthusiasm. Gaining celebrity status as the spiritual adviser to American presidents from Harry S. Truman to George W. Bush, Graham legitimized evangelicalism, on the wane since the Scopes "Monkey" Trial in 1925. During his Cold War crusades, Graham proselytized using American fears of nuclear annihilation, as evidenced by such sermon titles as "The End of the World" (1950) and "Will God Spare America?" (1953).

Graham proved to be a role model for other evange-lists hoping to use the airwaves to expand their flock. In 1960, Southern Baptist minister Pat Robertson purchased a television station in Virginia Beach, Virginia, and formed the Christian Broadcasting Network (CBN)—now the Family Channel and the largest religious network in America. During a 1963 telethon, Robertson asked for 700 people to pledge money to keep the station solvent. These designated saviors became the foundation of Robertson's show *The 700 Club*, which premiered in November 1966 with the Reverend Jim Bakker as host. Bakker, a Pentecostal, also co-hosted a CBN show with his singer-wife, Tammy Faye. The Bakkers left CBN for the Trinity Broadcasting Network, where they began the *PTL* (for Praise the Lord) *Club*, a variety show emulating the *Tonight Show.* The program and the Bakkers moved to their own PTL Network, founded in 1974. Also joining the ranks of televangelists in the 1960s were the Reverend Jerry Falwell, an independent Baptist, and his *Old-Time Gospel Hour,* as well as Jimmy Swaggart's Pentecostal show, the *Jimmy Swaggart Telecast.*

The 1980s ushered in an era of politically oriented televangelism. Initially against mixing politics and religion, Falwell changed his position with the founding of the Moral Majority in 1979. An evangelical political lobby group, the Moral Majority gained a pulpit for its views on Falwell's *Old-Time Gospel Hour.* Touting American exceptionalism and the wickedness of secular humanism, Falwell pushed for social and political change as the group's leader, making valuable connections with Republicans, especially President Ronald Reagan. Seeking the support of the Religious Right, Reagan hosted televangelists at the White House and gave his 1983 "evil empire" speech (applying that term to the Soviet Union) at an NAE meeting. Indeed, politically minded televangelists like Falwell took credit for Reagan's election victory in 1980. Fearing televangelists' political influence over their viewers, liberals responded by forming a progressive advocacy group, People for the American Way, to protest the blurring between church and state.

At the same time, the *700 Club* added Robertson's ultra-conservative political opinions on feminism, abortion, gay rights, and labor unions to his apocalyptic predictions. Robertson's first foray into politics came in April 1980 with "Washington for Jesus," a day of prayer and conservative political messages. In 1986, he began a grassroots campaign to become the Republican presidential candidate. With his "invisible army" of viewers, Robertson said he would run if 3 million people petitioned and offered monetary support for a campaign. In 1987, he formally announced his intentions to run, leaving CBN to his son. Controversy dogged Robertson's bid, as questions over his education and military service uncovered falsehoods, and it was clear by 1988 that victory was impossible. Robertson threw his support behind

George H.W. Bush, returned to CBN, and founded the Christian Coalition in 1989.

The late 1980s was a difficult time for televangelists, as Robertson's campaign was hurt by sex and money scandals surrounding televangelist superstars Jim Bakker and Jimmy Swaggart. In 1987, Bakker was accused of paying off a woman with whom he had had extramarital sex. The following year, he was indicted on charges of fraud and tax evasion for allegedly diverting millions of dollars through Heritage USA, PTL's investment arm. Convicted on twenty-four criminal counts, he was sentenced to forty-five years in prison (of which he served five). Also in 1988, Jimmy Swaggart, whose Pentecostal Assemblies of God ministry was said to have generated $150 million annually at its peak, became the object of another sex scandal, as photos of him with a prostitute surfaced. Swaggart resigned from his ministry after confessing an obsession with pornography during a tear-soaked telecast.

In the pursuit of "getting right with God," televangelists implore their viewers to contribute to their ministries so they can fulfill the tenets of the "health-and-wealth" gospel: faith in God will bring material rewards. For critics, televangelism and the gaudy lifestyle of its practitioners symbolize unadulterated greed—a view reflected in a significant decline in viewer ratings and lampooned in the Genesis hit single, "Jesus He Knows Me" (1991). The rock star and international humanitarian Bono, among others, has criticized televangelists for practicing a faith devoid of social justice.

Revived in the 1990s, televangelism remains very much alive and politically active in the United States. Both Robertson and Falwell were visible during the 1992, 1996, and 2000 national elections. The old guard may have given way to new televangelists, such as Joel Osteen and his "prosperity gospel," but liberals continue to warn of televangelism's influence over Christian voters and to criticize its narrow view of American society.

Anna Zuschlag

See also: American Exceptionalism; Christian Radio; Church and State; Evangelicalism; Falwell, Jerry; Fundamentalism, Religious; Graham, Billy; Reagan, Ronald; Religious Right; Robertson, Pat; Secular Humanism.

Further Reading

Alexander, Bobby C. *Televangelism Reconsidered: Ritual in the Search for Human Community.* Atlanta, GA: Scholars Press, 1994.

Bruce, Steve. *Pray TV: Televangelism in America.* New York: Routledge, 1990.

Frankl, Razelle. *Televangelism: The Marketing of Popular Religion.* Carbondale: Southern Illinois University Press, 1987.

Hadden, Jeffrey K. "The Rise and Fall of American Televangelism." *Annals of the American Academy of Political and Social Science* 527 (May 1993): 113–30.

Howley, Kevin. "Prey TV: Televangelism and Interpellation." *Journal of Film and Video* 53:2–3 (2001): 23–37.

Sine, Tom. *Cease Fire: Searching for Sanity in America's Culture Wars.* Grand Rapids, MI: Eerdmans, 1995.

Television

See Media Bias

Teller, Edward

A physicist whose work led to the development of the hydrogen bomb, Edward Teller was also a primary visionary of President Ronald Reagan's Strategic Defense Initiative (SDI). He is remembered by his detractors as "Dr. Strangelove"—the unstable presidential adviser in the Stanley Kubrick film of the same name (1964)—while admirers credit him with helping the United States win the Cold War.

Born on January 15, 1908, in Budapest, Hungary, Teller obtained his doctorate in theoretical physics at the University of Leipzig in Germany (1930) but left Germany for Denmark and then the United States with the rise of Adolf Hitler. He taught at George Washington University (1935–1941) and worked on the Manhattan Project during World War II to help develop the atomic bomb. He remained at the Los Alamos National Laboratory in New Mexico after the war, later moving to the University of California, Berkeley (1953–1970). A cofounder of the Lawrence Livermore National Laboratory in California, he served as its associate director (1954–1958, 1960–1975) and director (1958–1960).

Teller testified against physicist and former Manhattan Project director J. Robert Oppenheimer at a 1954 security board hearing, and Oppenheimer eventually lost his security clearance. Observers believed that Teller wished to topple Oppenheimer for not fully supporting his efforts to develop the hydrogen bomb. Oppenheimer had chaired the General Advisory Committee of the Atomic Energy Commission, which in 1949 advised against proceeding with the H-bomb, citing moral and technical concerns. In 1952, however, the United States detonated the world's first hydrogen bomb, based in part on Teller's design. Teller faced widespread condemnation for his testimony against Oppenheimer.

Known for opposing nuclear test bans, downplaying the effects of radioactive fallout, and designing submarine-launched nuclear bombs, Teller faced a hostile counterculture movement on the Berkeley campus. Student activist Jerry Rubin once threw a custard pie in his face. More serious was the student tribunal of November 23, 1970, which conducted a hearing, attended by hundreds, to discuss campus ties to the military-industrial complex. Teller was singled out as "a leading sparkplug . . . for an even greater nuclear arsenal," and police had to hold back a rowdy crowd that attempted an assault on the physicist's home.

In 1979, after an accident at the Three Mile Island nuclear power plant in Pennsylvania, Teller testified before Congress in defense of atomic energy and to counter statements by Jane Fonda and Ralph Nader against the nuclear industry. The next day, Teller suffered a heart attack, which he later blamed on Fonda in a two-page advertisement in the *Wall Street Journal* (July 1, 1979).

Equally controversial was Teller's lobbying for SDI, the nuclear defense system widely referred to as Star Wars. The system was to use laser devices stationed in outer space that would shoot down incoming missiles. Although many scientists regarded SDI as technically unfeasible, Teller was able to persuade Defense Department officials and President Reagan, who announced a long-term development program in March 1983. Teller died on September 9, 2003, in Stanford, California, just weeks after receiving the Presidential Medal of Freedom.

Roger Chapman

See also: Cold War; Counterculture; Fonda, Jane; Kubrick, Stanley; McCarthyism; Nader, Ralph; Nuclear Age; Oppenheimer, J. Robert; Reagan, Ronald; Science Wars; Strategic Defense Initiative; Three Mile Island Accident.

Further Reading

Goodchild, Peter. *Edward Teller: The Real Dr. Strangelove.* Cambridge, MA: Harvard University Press, 2004.

Teller, Edward, with Judith L. Shoolery. *Memoirs: A Twentieth-Century Journey in Science and Politics.* Cambridge, MA: Perseus, 2001.

Ten Commandments

The culture wars have brought an ongoing series of legal battles and public debates between the Religious Right and groups like the American Civil Liberties Union over the appropriateness and constitutionality of displaying the Ten Commandments on public property such as schools, courthouses, and capitol grounds.

According to the Hebrew Bible (or Christian Old Testament), the Ten Commandments—also known as the Decalogue (Greek for "ten words")—are part of the Law that Moses received on stone tablets from God on Mt. Sinai (Exodus 20:2–14; Deuteronomy 5:6–18). Since there are different ways of numbering the commandments (Roman Catholics and Lutherans have one system, while Jews and the Orthodox and Reformed churches have another), the way in which one displays the Decalogue may betray a religious preference. The Ten Commandments, all sides agree, specify duties toward God (prohibition of polytheism and the making of idols, the proper use of God's name, and observance of the Sabbath) and duties

Members of the Religious Right kneel in prayer at a monument to the Ten Commandments inside the state courthouse in Montgomery, Alabama, in 2003. Chief Justice Roy S. Moore was removed from office for defying a federal court order to remove the monument. *(Gary Tramontina/Getty Images)*

toward other humans (honoring parents and prohibitions against murder, adultery, stealing, giving false testimony, and coveting).

The Decalogue emerged as a potent symbol during the Cold War with the release of the Hollywood film *The Ten Commandments* (1956). The director of the film, Cecil B. DeMille, viewed the story of the Decalogue as a metaphor of American freedom in contrast to the Soviet Union. In the film's prologue, DeMille explains, "The theme of this picture is whether men ought to be ruled by God's law or whether they are to be ruled by the whims of a dictator. . . . Are men the property of the state or are they free souls under God? This same battle continues throughout the world today." In the meantime, with financial backing from DeMille, the Fraternal Order of the Eagles donated thousands of Decalogue statues across the country, including a six-foot (1.8-meter) granite monument that was placed on the grounds of the Texas State Capitol in Austin in 1961.

Although the New Testament deemphasizes the Hebrew Law, certain conservative Christians favor the Ten

Commandments. Some assert that the Decalogue inspired the Bill of Rights, and many argue that the Ten Commandments were the basis of common law and American jurisprudence—a view most legal scholars regard as an exaggeration at best. The Christian Reconstructionist Rousas J. Rushdoony, in his two-volume commentary on the Ten Commandments, *The Institutes of Biblical Law* (1973), argues that the Decalogue is foundational for establishing a Christian theocracy. The Religious Right, although influenced by Rushdoony, mainly sought to bolster its argument that America was founded as a Christian nation.

In *Stone v. Graham* (1980), the U.S. Supreme Court overturned a Kentucky law that required a copy of the Ten Commandments to be posted in every classroom of its public schools, with the notation: "the fundamental legal code of Western Civilization and the Common Law of the United States." The court ruled that such a requirement had no secular purpose and promoted religion rather than the teaching of history. That decision did not settle the matter, however, because it suggested that displaying the Decalogue in a different context might be permissible. Following the 1999 school shooting at Columbine High School in Littleton, Colorado, a number of states proposed the posting of the Ten Commandments in historical displays at public schools. In 2003, Alabama chief justice Roy S. Moore was removed from the bench for defying a higher court's order to remove a 2.5-ton (2,273-kilo) granite Decalogue monument inside his courthouse. Although Moore's appeal to the Supreme Court went unanswered, other Decalogue cases were later heard.

In *McCreary County, Kentucky et al. v. ACLU* (2005), the Supreme Court ruled 5–4 against two Kentucky county executives who ordered framed copies of the Ten Commandments, in the language of the King James Bible, displayed in two courthouses. Based on the wording of the enabling resolution, the majority of the justices saw this action as promoting religion. In contrast, the same Court in *Van Orden v. Perry* (2005) ruled 5–4 that the granite Decalogue memorial on the grounds of the state capitol in Austin is constitutionally permissible because the context of its placement was not religious. The fact that the Texas monument was installed by a private group and had been in place for over four decades without public objection contributed to the favorable ruling. Moreover, the Texas monument depicts a Jewish Star of David as well as a Christian symbol and features eleven, possibly twelve, commandments, all indicative of nonsectarianism.

Proponents of the public display of the Decalogue argue that the U.S. Supreme Court building in Washington, D.C., includes the Ten Commandments as part of its decor, making it appropriate as well for lower courts across the land. Opponents answer that nowhere does the ornamentation in the Supreme Court give prefer-

ence to Moses and his Law. The eastern pediment at the back outside of the building, they point out, features the three great lawgivers of ancient Eastern civilization: Confucius, Moses (holding a tablet without inscription), and Solon. The pediment also includes allegorical figures, all symbolic of law. The wooden doors of the courtroom have a design depicting two tablets, one engraved with the Roman numerals I through V and the other VI through X, otherwise without inscription. The marble frieze bordering the high ceiling inside the courtroom depicts eighteen lawgivers in history: Menes, Hammurabi, Moses, Solomon, Lycurgus, Solon, Draco, Confucius, and Octavian (the south wall); Justinian, Mohammed, Charlemagne, King John, Louis IX, Hugo Grotius, William Blackstone, John Marshall, and Napoleon (north wall). Directly above the seat of the chief justice on the east wall, there are two figures, one with tablets, whom proponents of the Decalogue say represents Moses with the Ten Commandments. According to a letter by the designer Adolph Weinman, dated October 31, 1932, the two figures represent "Majesty of the Law and the power of Government" and the "figure of Law, resting on the tablet of the ten amendments [sic] to the Constitution known as the 'Bill of Rights.'" Because of that letter, some suggest that the engravings on the wooden doors symbolize the Bill of Rights and not the Ten Commandments. Undaunted, Decalogue proponents have questioned the authenticity of the Weinman letter, which is on file in the Supreme Court archives.

Roger Chapman

See also: Christian Reconstructionism; Cold War; Moore, Roy S.; Religious Right.

Further Reading

Green, Steven K. "The Fount of Everything Just and Right? The Commandments as a Source of American Law." *Journal of Law and Religion* 14:2 (1999–2000): 525–58.

Nadel, Alan. "God's Law and the Wide Screen: The Ten Commandments as Cold War 'Epic.'" *PMLA* 108:3 (May 1993): 415–30.

Pollitt, Katha. "Stacked Decalogue." *Nation*, September 22, 2003.

Wright, Melanie J. *Moses in America: The Use of Biblical Narrative.* New York: Oxford University Press, 2003.

Terkel, Studs

Writer, journalist, and broadcaster Studs Terkel won popular and critical acclaim for his published interviews of ordinary Americans who shared their life experiences, reflecting on the Great Depression, World War II, race, working life, the American Dream, and death and dying. Many of his oral histories were the product of the *Studs Terkel Program* (1952–1997), a five-day-a-week radio show on station WFMT in Chicago. Terkel, who characterized his own ideology as "socialism with a human face," often used his interviews to draw out liberal themes. He liked to joke that he and Richard Nixon had one thing in common: recognition of the importance of the tape recorder. In October 2007, Terkel published an op-ed piece in the *New York Times* that criticized President George W. Bush's domestic surveillance program.

The son of Russian-Jewish immigrants, Louis Terkel was born in the Bronx, New York, on May 16, 1912, and he grew up in Chicago—where he would spend much of his life. As a young man, he was nicknamed after Studs Lonigan, a character in the trilogy of novels about life in that city by James Farrell. During the Great Depression, Terkel attended the University of Chicago (PhB, 1932; JD, 1934) and worked briefly with the Chicago Repertory Theater (1937) and the radio division of the Federal Writers' Project (1938). After overseas duty with the Red Cross during World War II, he hosted *Studs' Place* (1949–1953), a folksy current events show on the new medium of television. During the McCarthy era, he was briefly accused of past communist activities (because he had signed petitions against Jim Crow and the poll tax), but with no lasting impact on his career. In 1956 he published his first book, *Giants of Jazz*, a series of biographical sketches of jazz artists.

The collection of oral histories for which Terkel became best known began with *Division Street: America* (1967), presenting Chicago as a microcosm of contemporary American life. This was followed by *Hard Times: An Oral History of the Great Depression* (1970) and *Working: People Talk About What They Do and How They Feel About What They Do* (1974), which became controversial for its uncensored language and frank views. He returned to investigating Americans' views of their nation in *American Dreams: Lost and Found* (1980), focusing on the hopes and disillusionment that have come with the American Dream.

Terkel won a Pulitzer Prize for *"The Good War": An Oral History of World War II* (1984). Deeply critical of Presidents Ronald Reagan and George H.W. Bush for their opposition to labor causes and their contempt of New Deal legacies, he revisited the idea of American dreams in *The Great Divide: Second Thoughts on the American Dream* (1988), focusing on the effects of social division. He continued on the theme of American social divisions in *Race: How Blacks and Whites Think and Feel About the American Obsession* (1992). In the years since, he published *Coming of Age: The Story of Our Century by Those Who Lived It* (1995) and *Will the Circle Be Unbroken? Reflections on Death, Rebirth, and Hunger for Faith* (2001). He also conducted a post–September 11th investigation on how people respond to difficult times in *Hope Dies Last* (2004).

Terkel also turned the microphone on himself, publishing an oral history about his life's observations, *Talking to Myself: A Memoir of My Times* (1977). Years later this was followed by other self-reflections: *Touch and Go* (2007) and *P.S.: Further Thoughts from a Lifetime of Listening* (2008). In a revised edition of *Talking to Myself*, Terkel ends with "The Ultimate Fantasy: My First Inaugural Address." In this "speech," pretending to have been an independent candidate elected as the forty-first president of the United States, he promises: "I shall not at any time during this brief talk use the words Family, Flag, God, or Country. Nor shall I use the phrase Standing Tall. I am your President, not your Phys Ed instructor. I assume . . . that you believe in the faith and in those ideas that evoke the spirit of free thoughtful beings in a free, thoughtful society." Denigrating the Reagan administration, the period of which he characterizes as a time when the nation's intelligence was "assaulted," he goes on to attack the Cold War and the nuclear arms race. "May I add a personal note here?" he continues. "Mine will not be an Imperial Presidency." Terkel died at age ninety-six on October 31, 2008.

Rachel Donaldson and Roger Chapman

See also: Bush Family; Cold War; Labor Unions; McCarthyism; New Deal; Nixon, Richard; Nuclear Age; Reagan, Ronald; Watergate.

Further Reading

Baker, James T. *Studs Terkel.* New York: Twayne, 1992.

Barsamian, David. "Studs Terkel." *Progressive*, November 2004.

Chambers, Aaron. "History from the Bottom Up." *Illinois Issues*, December 2001.

Parker, Tony. *Studs Terkel: A Life in Words.* New York: Henry Holt, 1996.

Terkel, Studs. *Talking to Myself: A Memoir of My Times.* New York: Pantheon Books, 1984.

———. *Touch and Go: A Memoir.* New York: New Press, 2007.

Thanksgiving Day

An American national holiday observed annually on the fourth Thursday of November, Thanksgiving is typically a time in which families gather to partake of a large meal featuring roasted turkey with all of the trimmings. Since the history of Thanksgiving is rooted in different places and dates, culture warriors have debated its meaning. Presidents on occasion have politicized the holiday by associating it with their agendas, and Native Americans have used the occasion to offer revisionist history pertaining to the European conquest of North America.

Determining when and where the first American

Thanksgiving was held is a controversy that has divided red states and blue states. Traditionally most Americans associate the origins of Thanksgiving with the Pilgrims sharing a harvest feast with native peoples at Plymouth, Massachusetts, in 1621. In Virginia, officials point to an earlier date, December 4, 1619, as the first Thanksgiving; on that day, it is said, colonists at Berkeley Plantation, on the James River near current-day Charles City, offered prayers of thanks for their safe arrival in the New World. Multiculturalists suggest even older Thanksgivings, pointing to events that occurred by the French in Florida (1564) and the Spanish in Texas (1598). All agree that days of thanksgiving were observed at different times in many parts of the American colonies and early republic. George Washington announced official days of thanksgiving in 1789 and 1795. After some important Union victories during the Civil War, Abraham Lincoln proclaimed the fourth Thursday of November 1863 as a nationwide day of gratitude, although some southerners would thereafter refer to the national holiday as "a damned Yankee institution."

While social conservatives argue that Christianity and "family values" represent the true meaning of Thanksgiving, others insist that the holiday is strictly secular. In his painting *Freedom from Want*, part of a 1943 series on the Four Freedoms, Norman Rockwell presents a Thanksgiving scene of a family gathered around a table with a turkey platter. Although Rockwell does not offer any overt signs of religiosity, that aspect is readily apparent in Newell Conyers Wyeth's painting *The Thanksgiving Feast* (1945), a scene of the Pilgrim Thanksgiving with a Puritan elder holding a Bible. Religious conservatives emphasize the theistic wording of Thanksgiving proclamations issued over the years, including ones by Washington and Lincoln. Those who regard Thanksgiving as a secular holiday argue that harvest festivals were not generally viewed as sacred events. Some academics recognize Thanksgiving as a part of American civil religion with the turkey dinner symbolizing a sacramental meal.

In 1939, swayed by retailer lobbyists seeking to extend the Christmas shopping season, President Franklin Roosevelt moved up the date of Thanksgiving by one week. This prompted criticism from traditionalists, including the Reverend Norman Vincent Peale, who argued that the date for "a sacred religious day" should not be changed "on the specious excuse that it will help Christmas sales." Some state governors refused to comply with the calendar change, while pundits dubbed the competing dates "Democratic Thanksgiving" and "Republican Thanksgiving." After Roosevelt announced in 1941 that he would restore the traditional date, Congress made it law.

In the years since, the holiday occasionally became politicized by presidential speeches. In 1966, for example, President Lyndon B. Johnson made his Great Society program the theme for his Thanksgiving address,

prompting *Time* magazine to editorialize that it was "one of the most palpably political Thanksgiving messages." The following year, the liberal *Christian Century* refused for the first time to publish a presidential Thanksgiving address, objecting to Johnson's use of the occasion to promote the Vietnam War.

In 1970, Native American groups began the tradition of a Thanksgiving protest vigil at Plymouth, calling the holiday a "Day of Mourning." In 2005, members of the Wailkikie tribe met at San Francisco's Alcatraz Island to hold an "Unthanksgiving Day" ceremony. Bear Lincoln of the tribe stated, "It was a big mistake for us to help the Pilgrims survive that first winter. They betrayed us once they got their strength." In her essay on the meaning of Thanksgiving, the Rutgers University anthropologist Janet Siskind argues, "The stuffed turkey represents the Native Americans, sacrificed and consumed in order to bring civilization to the New World."

Roger Chapman

See also: American Civil Religion; Christmas; Columbus Day; Founding Fathers; Great Society; Red and Blue States; Rockwell, Norman.

Further Reading

Appelbaum, Diana Karter. *Thanksgiving: An American Holiday, An American History*. New York: Facts On File, 1984.

Sigal, Lillian. "Thanksgiving: Sacred or Profane Feast?" *Mythosphere* 1:4 (1999): 451–61.

Siskind, Janet. "The Invention of Thanksgiving: A Ritual of American Nationality." In *Food in the USA: A Reader*, ed. Carole M. Counihan, 41–58. New York: Routledge, 2002.

Think Tanks

A think tank is a nongovernmental, nonprofit organization that devotes a significant portion of its activities to public policy analysis. Think tanks identify policy issues, evaluate ideas, and design public policies.

As originally employed, the term "think tank" referred to secret locations where U.S. military planners and scientists met to discuss strategy during World War II. Use of the term in reference to organizations for the clandestine meeting of minds did not come into widespread use until the proliferation of such institutions in the mid-1970s. Until then, they were commonly referred to as policy-planning organizations, policy-planning groups, elite policy-planning networks, public policy institutes, government policy consultants, policy scientists, research institutes, research brokers, issue networks, civil society organizations, public interest groups, research centers, or public policy research organizations. Early think tanks in America that remain prominent to the present day include the Brookings Institution (1916), an independent social science and public policy research organization headquartered in Washington, D.C., and the Hoover Institution on War, Revolution and Peace (1919), founded by Herbert Hoover at Stanford University, his alma mater.

Orientation and Funding

Think tank independence is derived from the organizations' IRS classification—501(c)3—which forbids any nonprofit organization from engaging in partisan campaign activities, challenging political candidates, or influencing legislation as a significant part of its activities. At times they are originators of policy, at other times merely consultants to legislators. Still, many think tanks have an explicit ideological proclivity that orients their research. A case in point, the Manhattan Institute for Policy Research, founded in 1978, considers individual responsibility and a greater role for the private sector the impetus behind its policy positions for stronger criminal penalties; a corporation-friendly legal system; school vouchers; tax relief; and an end to welfare, disability benefits, and race- and gender-based affirmative action.

Ideologically oriented think tanks forge ties with funders who value a range of policy viewpoints. For example, the Economic Policy Institute (EPI), a liberal-oriented think tank of economic analysis, receives three-quarters of its revenues from foundations and unions that support a robust welfare state and equitable distribution of resources. The Heritage Foundation, a conservative counterpart of EPI, generates research in support of free-market principles, a limited welfare state, individual responsibility, and a strong national defense. Heritage's institutional funding from foundations and corporations represents 25 percent ($9 million) of its budget, but considerably more than EPI's $3.7 million annual budget.

Functions

Think tanks also function as repositories of policy expertise where analysts, based on their technical knowledge and experience, seek to inform, clarify, dissuade, and persuade policymakers and the public. They serve as a kind of revolving door for federal bureaucrats and politicians, who find a home there when their government careers are over. Former President Gerald Ford, Judge Robert Bork, Secretary of State Henry Kissinger, Ambassador Jeane Kirkpatrick, and Representative Newt Gingrich (R-GA) all have found second careers at conservative think tanks. Think tanks also train young minds for future careers as congressional staffers or appointed bureaucrats in the executive branch. Whether as training grounds for future public officials or institutional homes to former ones, think tanks succeed in extending their policy preferences when former staffers join or rejoin the federal government. Such senior of-

ficials and high-level advisers in the George W. Bush administration as Defense Secretary Donald Rumsfeld and Deputy Secretary of Defense Paul Wolfowitz had been members of the Project for the New American Century (PNAC), a think tank founded in 1997 that called for the overthrow of Iraqi leader Saddam Hussein. As members of the Bush administration, Rumsfeld and Wolfowitz were in a position to sway foreign policy.

Aside from ideology, think tanks differ in terms of their focus on local, national, or foreign policy issues. As of 2008, there were more than 3,500 think tanks located around the world, with more than half based in the United States. A majority of U.S. think tanks are located in academic communities, and about one-third—the most visible ones—are located in Washington, D.C.

An integral part of the "third sector" between government and the private (for-profit) sector, think tanks maintain an important relationship with the public. Their staff members are often perceived as third-party or neutral-policy spokespeople—intellectuals who are not beholden to partisan, industry, or special interests. They inform, educate, and at times advocate policy viewpoints, presumably with the public's interests in mind. Their ideological preferences, however, are mediated in large measure by their policy position vis-à-vis the economy. Conservative and libertarian think tanks advocate a limited welfare state and an unfettered market, with the idea that this is the kind of environment in which individual responsibility and success will flourish. Liberal and mainstream think tanks tend to be critical of the market's shortcomings, especially in regard to the distribution of resources (wealth, education, health care, etc.) and the federal government's role (or lack thereof) in facilitating their distribution.

Whether located in academic settings or not, think tanks engage in basic social science research similar to that done in universities. President Lyndon Johnson's War on Poverty, for example, was heavily influenced by government and think tank research. Two decades later, think tanks like the Manhattan Institute and the American Enterprise Institute (AEI) published research that questioned the legitimacy of the welfare state and general assistance in particular, leading to sweeping reforms.

Think tanks are differentiated from their academic research counterparts by several organizational features. Members of think tanks do not have teaching duties, and their writings and general performance are not scrutinized through the peer-evaluation system. Much of their uncomplicated research is aimed at policymakers, newspaper editors, and the public. The research methodology may be less than rigorous at times, but there is little to stop "think tankers" or journalists from reporting erroneous information or misleading conclusions. Moreover, media access and training place them in the spotlight more often than their academic counterparts. Thus, think tankers'

President Ronald Reagan addresses a meeting of the Heritage Foundation, a prominent conservative think tank based in Washington, D.C., in 1986. The policy research organization was founded in 1973 but rose to prominence during the Reagan administration. *(Diana Walker/Time & Life Pictures/ Getty Images)*

See also: Affirmative Action; Education Reform; Global Warming; Heritage Foundation; Immigration Policy; Privatization; School Vouchers; Social Security; Tax Reform; War on Poverty; Wealth Gap; Welfare Reform.

Further Reading

Abelson, Donald E. *Do Think Tanks Matter? Assessing the Impact of Public Policy Institutes.* Montreal: McGill-Queens University Press, 2002.

Burch, Philip H. *Reagan, Bush, and Right-Wing Politics: Elites, Think Tanks, Power, and Policy. Part A: The American Right Wing Takes Command: Key Executive Appointments.* Greenwich, CT: Jai Press, 1997.

McGann, James G., and R. Kent Weaver, eds. *Think Tanks and Civil Societies: Catalysts for Ideas and Action.* New Brunswick, NJ: Transaction, 2000.

Ricci, David M. *The Transformation of American Politics: The New Washington and the Rise of Think Tanks.* New Haven, CT: Yale University Press, 1993.

Stefancic, Jean, and Richard Delgado. *No Mercy: How Conservative Think Tanks and Foundations Changed America's Social Agenda.* Philadelphia: Temple University Press, 1996.

policy ideas have a distinct advantage over those of their academic counterparts.

Despite their media access, think tanks engage in a variety of other activities to disseminate their messages. They organize conferences, seminars, and policy briefings for media and policymakers alike, at which panels of experts comment on proposed or pending legislation. Many of these events are co-sponsored with similarly oriented think tanks, which cite each other's work in support of a particular viewpoint—though not always objectively or accurately. For example, a misleading claim by the Heritage Foundation that $5.4 billion had been spent on welfare since the War on Poverty was cited in the research of such like-minded think tanks as the CATO Institute and the National Center for Policy Analysis and repeated in many newspapers and television news broadcasts. Think tanks also promote their views and findings by submitting opinion pieces to newspaper editorial pages. And they also write succinct policy briefs with marketable messages for federal officials, intended to sway legislators and executive branch policymakers.

Among the many key issues on which think tanks have helped influence public perceptions, legislation, and policymakers are global warming (both concern and skepticism); incarceration rates; standardized educational testing; privatization of Social Security; economic inequality analysis; restrictive welfare reform; energy and telecommunications deregulation; regressive and progressive taxation; increased immigration restrictions; free-trade treaties; and foreign military intervention.

Sergio Romero

Third Parties

Third parties in American politics, also referred to as independent parties, are minority political organizations offered as alternatives to the Democrat and Republican mainstream. Although their candidates generally have little chance of winning a major election—in the entire history of American national elections, only eight third-party presidential candidates earned more than 10 percent of the popular vote—third parties field candidates to raise issues and perspectives that might otherwise go unaddressed in a political campaign. Controversially, third-party candidates can be "spoilers" in a close contest, handing victory to the party that would have otherwise placed second.

The culture wars, it can be argued, have been fostered by a two-party system that has represented the middle of the political spectrum with no serious competition from the far left or far right, creating conditions in which both Republicans and Democrats feel that it is imperative to elevate partisanship and exaggerate differences in order to attract voters. True or not, this has not prevented third parties in the post–World War II era from providing an outlet for fringe groups, dissenters, independents, and those whose ideology falls outside the political mainstream. Still, most postwar third parties have been ad hoc and short-lived, often dominated by a high-profile figure and passing from the scene with changing political circumstances.

In 1948, the Democratic Party, headed by incumbent President Harry Truman, experienced dissension in its ranks, leading to the creation of two independent parties:

the Progressive Party and the States' Rights Democratic Party (or "Dixiecrats"). The former, led by former Vice President Henry Wallace, took an anti-anticommunist position, opposing Truman's Cold War policies and his tough stance against the Soviet Union. The latter, headed by South Carolina governor Strom Thurmond, was a result of several southern Democrats walking out of that year's Democratic National Convention in protest over proposals to repeal Jim Crow. Polls and pundits predicted that Truman would lose the race against the Republican challenger, Thomas Dewey. Fortunately for Truman, the Progressive Party suffered the stigma of being supported by the Communist Party USA. As for the threat posed by Thurmond, it was strictly limited to the South and turned out to be less damaging than expected. Truman won with 49.5 percent of the popular vote. Thurmond, however, remained popular enough in his state to serve in the U.S. Senate from 1954 to 2003, first as a Democrat, then as a Republican.

In 1968, a new pro-segregationist party, the American Independent Party (later renamed the American Party), ran George Wallace for president, the frequent Democratic governor of Alabama. Wallace's strategy was to press the issue of racial segregation and prevent Democrat Hubert Humphrey or Republican Richard Nixon from attaining a majority of the Electoral College vote, forcing the election to be decided by the House of Representatives. Wallace won 46 Electoral College votes and 13.5 percent of the popular vote, essentially undermining Humphrey's support; Nixon won by about a half-million votes.

During the 1972 election, in which Nixon won re-election by a landslide, the American Party ran California congressman John Schmitz as its candidate, winning more than 1 million votes. The Libertarian Party, which would later become the largest third party in the United States, nominated California philosopher John Hospers as its candidate but would appear on the ballot in only two states. Although Hospers received only 3,700 votes, an elector from Virginia, Roger MacBride, cast his vote for Hospers and his running mate, Theodora Nathan. Also in the 1972 election, Gus Hall made his debut as Communist presidential candidate, receiving 25,595 votes; he would run for the office three more times (1976, 1980, and 1984).

In 1980, former House Republican chairman John Anderson, a U.S. representative from Illinois, garnered 6.6 percent of the popular vote as an independent presidential candidate, taking away votes primarily from the Republican Party; this barely detracted from Ronald Reagan's landslide victory over President Jimmy Carter, however. Libertarians, meanwhile, fared better than in the past, gaining just over 1 percent of the vote with candidate Ed Clark; and the Citizens Party, a liberal Democratic splinter group led by scientist and environmentalist Barry Commoner, gained 0.3 percent of the vote.

The 1992 presidential election marked a return for a large number of third-party candidates, particularly among conservatives. Independent Texas billionaire Ross Perot was a true "spoiler" in the election, winning almost 20 million popular votes, many of which would have gone to the incumbent George H.W. Bush, whose 39 million votes fell short of Bill Clinton's nearly 45 million. Perot, who ran a strong campaign against the federal budget deficit, global free trade, and Washington "insider" politics, actually led the pre-election polls at one point in the months leading up to the election. In the end, Perot did not win any Electoral College votes despite garnering 18.9 percent of the popular vote. Other third-party candidates taking Republican votes that year were Libertarian Andre Marrou, Populist Bo Gritz, and Howard Phillips of the U.S. Taxpayers Party (later renamed the Constitution Party).

In 1998, Ross Perot returned with a new third party, the Reform Party, this time pulling only slightly more than 8 million votes. Also emerging that year was Ralph Nader, the consumer advocate and former Democrat who was drafted by the liberal environmentalist Green Party, spent $5,000 on his campaign, and won just under 700,000 votes (or 0.7 percent). New Age scientist John Hagelin was nominated by the liberal Natural Law Party, winning 0.1 percent of the vote. Beyond the presidential election, the Reform Party that same year successfully ran professional wrestler Jesse Ventura for the governorship of Minnesota.

In the 2000 presidential election, third parties were a key factor in the outcome. Although losing the popular vote to Vice President Al Gore by 543,895 votes, Republican nominee George W. Bush won the Electoral College 271 to 266. Nader took 2.7 percent of the popular vote—a total of 2.8 million—for the Green Party, which many analysts believe tipped the election to Bush. The Reform Party, which was successful enough in 1996 to get federal funding for its campaign, split in two and nominated two different candidates at the same party convention. Republican Pat Buchanan, one Reform Party nominee, took 450,000 votes, and liberal Reform nominee John Hagelin took 83,700 votes. The Electoral College decision came down to the state of Florida, which was plagued by logistical problems. In the end, Bush was officially declared the winner in that state by 537 votes.

Christopher D. Rodkey

See also: Commoner, Barry; Communists and Communism; Democratic Party; Election of 2000; Hall, Gus; Nader, Ralph; Perot, H. Ross; Republican Party; Ventura, Jesse; Wallace, George.

Further Reading
Bibby, John F., and L. Sandy Maisel. *Two Parties—Or More? The American Party System.* 2nd ed. Boulder, CO: Westview Press, 2003.

Klobuchar, Lisa. *Third Parties: Influential Political Alternatives.* Minneapolis, MN: Compass Point Books, 2008.

Lentz, Jacob. *Electing Jesse Ventura: A Third-Party Success Story.* Boulder, CO: Lynne Reinner, 2002.

Reynolds, David. *Democracy Unbound: Progressive Challenges to the Two Party System.* Boston: South End Press, 1997.

Thomas, Clarence

The second African American appointed to the U.S. Supreme Court (1991), one of its most controversial nominees, and among its most conservative members, Clarence Thomas was born on June 23, 1948, in Pin Point, Georgia. Raised by his grandfather, he was taught to believe that hard work is the path to success. After a brief stint at a Catholic seminary in Missouri, Thomas earned a bachelor's degree (1971) from Holy Cross College in Worcester, Massachusetts, where he co-founded the Black Student Union. He earned a law degree from Yale Law School in 1974.

Following law school, Thomas was assistant attorney general in Missouri (1974–1977), corporate counsel for the Monsanto Company (1977–1979), legislative assistant for U.S. Senator John Danforth (1979–1981), assistant secretary for civil rights at the U.S. Department of Education (1981–1982), and chair of the U.S. Equal Employment Opportunity Commission (1982–1990). In 1990, President George H.W. Bush nominated him to the U.S. Court of Appeals for the District of Columbia Circuit.

With the retirement of Justice Thurgood Marshall—the first African American to serve on the Supreme Court—President Bush saw an opportunity to place a decidedly conservative jurist on the Court and nominated Thomas to fill the position in 1991. The move outraged many in the black community, who regarded it as a slight to have Thomas replace the man who, as an attorney for the NAACP, had won the landmark 1954 school segregation case *Brown v. Board of Education.*

Thomas's nomination was opposed by such organizations as the NAACP, Urban League, and National Bar Association because of his opposition to affirmative action and general fears that he would undermine the gains achieved by the civil rights movement. The National Organization for Women and other groups supporting women's access to abortion were concerned that Thomas would vote to overturn *Roe v. Wade.* The American Bar Association expressed reservations about his judicial ability, citing his lack of experience, and gave him a split rating between "qualified" and "not qualified."

During Thomas's confirmation proceedings, Democratic staffers leaked an FBI report to the press concerning sexual harassment charges filed against the nominee by a former employee at the Office of Civil Rights, Anita Hill. Television coverage of hearings by the Senate Judiciary Committee preempted daytime soap operas and competed with the World Series for viewers. The ensuing investigation, which drew national attention to the issue of sexual harassment, revealed a number of contradictory statements by both sides, resulting in a "he said, she said" situation. Years later, journalist David Brock dramatically confessed his role in a conservative disinformation campaign to smear Hill in support of Thomas. After the Judiciary Committee ended its investigation, Thomas's nomination was sent to the full Senate without a recommendation. On October 15, 1991, Thomas was confirmed by a 52-48 vote, the narrowest margin for a Supreme Court nominee in the twentieth century.

On the Court, Thomas applies a strict constructionist approach to interpreting the Constitution, believing that Court rulings should be based on what the Constitution literally states, rather than on inference. He argues that the intent of the drafters of the Constitution weighs more heavily than *stare decisis*, or the record of previous Court decisions. Some commentators have suggested that Thomas has no judicial philosophy of his own but merely follows the opinions of the rigorous conservative and textualist Justice Antonin Scalia. According to Scalia, Thomas "doesn't believe in *stare decisis*, period" but is very willing to reexamine precedent if he thinks the "line of authority is wrong." For this reason, critics view Thomas as a justice guided by ideology rather than by established case law.

Justice Thomas's voting record has been conservative, as he has ruled against race-based affirmative action programs, school busing, partial-birth abortion, prison reform, gay rights, and minority voting districts. He also tends to have a narrow interpretation of the Commerce Clause (Article I, section 8) but a broad interpretation of the Second Amendment. In *Kelso v. City of New London, Connecticut* (2005), he dissented from the majority who gave a broad interpretation of the eminent domain provision of the Fifth Amendment. In *Bush v. Gore* (2000), he voted with the majority in overruling Florida's electoral procedures, thereby throwing his support to the son of the man who had appointed him to the Supreme Court.

Thomas's jurisprudence does not prevent him from adopting a liberal position on very specific issues. He has been known to promote a broad interpretation of the First Amendment's free speech provision, except when it concerns cross burnings. In *U.S. v. Bajakajian* (1998), he joined the Court's four liberals in the first-ever decision to strike down a federal statute based on the Eighth Amendment's Excessive Fines Clause. He also believes in a broad interpretation of the Fifth Amendment's Self-Incrimination Clause. In *U.S. v. Hubbell* (2000), he argued that self-incrimination should be expanded to include revealing incriminating evidence.

James W. Stoutenborough

See also: Affirmative Action; Brock, David; Bush Family; Busing, School; Election of 2000; Gay Rights Movement; Hill, Anita; Judicial Wars; Lynching; National Association for the Advancement of Colored People; National Organization for Women; Prison Reform; School Vouchers.

Further Reading

Foskett, Ken. *Judging Thomas: The Life and Times of Clarence Thomas.* New York: Morrow, 2004.

Gerber, Scott Douglas. *First Principles: The Jurisprudence of Clarence Thomas.* New York: New York University Press, 2002.

Hill, Anita Faye, and Emma Coleman Jordan. *Race, Gender, and Power in America: The Legacy of the Hill-Thomas Hearings.* New York: Oxford University Press, 1995.

Merida, Kevin, and Michael Fletcher. *Supreme Discomfort: The Divided Soul of Clarence Thomas.* New York: Doubleday, 2007.

Thomas, Clarence. *My Grandfather's Son: A Memoir.* New York: Harper, 2007.

Thompson, Hunter S.

The eccentric and iconoclastic journalist Hunter S. Thompson emerged in the late 1960s as a voice of the counterculture with a unique and irreverent perspective on random subject matter—from the Hell's Angels and the Kentucky Derby to the Las Vegas gambling scene and presidential election campaigns—while inventing a genre of New Journalism known as "gonzo journalism." Thompson was a hard-drinking, drug-using free spirit who once ran for county sheriff in Colorado as the "Freak Party" candidate, maintained his membership in the National Rifle Association (NRA), and for years served as a board member of the National Organization for the Reform of Marijuana Laws (NORML).

The son of an insurance agent, Hunter Stockton Thompson was born in Louisville, Kentucky, on July 18, 1937. After a stint in the air force (1956–1958), he wrote for newspapers in New York and New Jersey. This was followed by work as a South American correspondent for the *National Observer* (1961–1963). Later, Thompson developed his journalism style as a contributor to alternative periodicals, chiefly *The Nation* (1964–1966) and *Rolling Stone* (1970–1999), and was also a syndicated columnist for the *San Francisco Examiner* (1985–1989). Thompson's magazine work was the basis for his many books—*Prince Jellyfish* (1960); *Hell's Angels* (1966); *Fear and Loathing in Las Vegas* (1972); *Fear and Loathing on the Campaign Trail '72* (1973); *The Great Shark Hunt* (with Ralph Steadman, 1979); *The Curse of Lono* (1983); *Generation of Swine* (1988); *Songs of the Doomed* (1999); *Screwjack* (1991); *Better Than Sex* (1993); *The Proud Highway* (1997); *The Rum Diary* (1998); *Fear and Loathing in America* (2000); and *Kingdom of Fear* (2002).

Thompson's career breakthrough came in 1966, when *The Nation* magazine published his gritty but conventional account of the Hell's Angels motorcycle gang. Gonzo journalism per se is said to have been born in 1970 when Thompson, on assignment for *Scanlan's Monthly*, submitted his raw notes for an essay on the Kentucky Derby and his editor deemed the manuscript brilliant. The same style, with the drunk or stoned author raging at the center of the narrative, became a staple of *Rolling Stone* magazine, which originally published the two "Fear and Loathing" works that came to be regarded as commentaries on the death of the American Dream. In the Las Vegas piece, which introduces the author as Raoul Duke, Thompson covers an antidrug conference while constantly stoned himself. In the latter piece, his coverage of the 1972 presidential campaign was primarily a satire on the homogenous mainstream media.

Although some have compared Thompson with Mark Twain, Jack Kerouac, and even F. Scott Fitzgerald, insisting that the raucous storyteller was an American original who provided an antidote to the inauthentic aspects of modern society, others characterize his writings as drug-induced egocentric outpourings. Thompson's public persona, featuring a cigarette holder, dark sunglasses, garish attire, and stoned demeanor, was satirized as the Uncle Duke character in the *Doonesbury* comic strip by Gary Trudeau. On February 20, 2005, Thompson shot himself to death in Woody Creek, Colorado; a few weeks later, his comic-strip counterpart did the same. The escapades of Hunter S. Thompson have been the subject of several films, including *Where the Buffalo Roam* (1980), starring Bill Murray as Thompson; a screen adaptation of *Fear and Loathing in Las Vegas* (1998), starring Johnny Depp; Alex Gibney's documentary *Gonzo: The Life and Work of Dr. Hunter S. Thompson* (2008); and another adaptation of a Thompson book, *The Rum Diary* (2010), again starring Depp.

Roger Chapman

See also: Comic Strips; Counterculture; McGovern, George; *Nation, The*; National Rifle Association; New Journalism; War on Drugs; Wolfe, Tom.

Further Reading

McKeen, William. *Outlaw Journalist: The Life and Times of Hunter S. Thompson.* New York: W.W. Norton, 2008.

Nocera, Joseph. "How Hunter Thompson Killed New Journalism." *Washington Monthly*, April 1981.

Perry, Paul. *Fear and Loathing: The Strange and Terrible Saga of Hunter S. Thompson.* New York: Thunder's Mouth Press, 2004.

Thompson, Anita. *The Gonzo Way.* Golden, CO: Fulcrum, 2007.

Wenner, Jann, and Corey Seymour. *Gonzo: The Life of Hunter S. Thompson: An Oral Biography.* New York: Little, Brown, 2007.

Three Mile Island Accident

The worst nuclear accident in U.S. history occurred in March 1979, at the Three Mile Island Nuclear Generating Station, Unit 2 (TMI-2), near Middletown, Pennsylvania, triggering vigorous public debate about the safety of nuclear power. Throughout the 1970s, prior to the accident, nuclear power had been widely hailed as a clean source of energy. Despite opposition by some antinuclear protest groups, the air of optimism was exemplified by the nation's seventy-two operating nuclear power plants and nearly a hundred others under construction.

Early in the morning of March 28, the steam generators of TMI-2, used to remove the intense heat created by nuclear reaction, broke down when an unidentified malfunction caused their water supply to stop. Pressure inside the nuclear reactor began to increase. Plant operators attempted to reduce the pressure by opening a valve at the top of the reactor, but afterward the valve failed to close promptly. Water that cooled the reactor's core began to leak out, causing the core to overheat and release an unknown quantity of radiation into the air.

Experts from state and federal agencies arrived within hours to monitor radiation levels and determine the cause of the accident. Two days later, as scientists from the U.S. Nuclear Regulatory Commission (NRC) researched the possibility of a hydrogen explosion inside the reactor, Governor Richard Thornburgh advised expectant mothers and young children to leave the area. Although it was determined the following day that a lack of oxygen within the reactor would prevent any explosion, thousands of people had already fled the area. On April 1, with the situation under control, President Jimmy Carter visited the site, inspiring confidence and relief among government officials and civilians alike.

In the aftermath of the accident, many Americans expressed a heightened fear of nuclear power and distrust of the government. The sentiments were reinforced by a recently released film, *The China Syndrome* (1979), starring Jane Fonda, about a near meltdown at a nuclear plant. Due in part to a wave of local activism, TMI-2 was permanently closed and by 1993 completely defueled. In the meantime, power companies experienced a decline in private investment across the board. Lobbyist groups and picket lines of local residents spearheaded a political movement that resulted in new legislation on nuclear regulation and modifications within the NRC. Citizens across the country organized campaigns to prevent the nuclear industry from entering their communities.

The effects of radiation around TMI-2 were carefully monitored in the years following the accident. Some area residents claimed to have suffered from skin irritation, nausea, and an increase in cancer rates. More than a dozen independent studies, however, supported the government's claim that health effects were minimal. Radiation exposure from the accident was said to be akin to receiving a full set of chest x-rays, while psychologists attributed the residents' physical symptoms to an increase in stress following the event. Although the medical effects of the accident were a matter of some dispute, the sociopolitical consequences were clearly felt in the farthest reaches of government, industry, and society.

Gwendolyn Laird

See also: Carter, Jimmy; Environmental Movement; Fonda, Jane; Nuclear Age; Teller, Edward.

Further Reading

Goldsteen, Raymond L., and John K. Schorr. *Demanding Democracy After Three Mile Island.* Gainesville: University of Florida Press, 1991.
Houts, Peter S., et al. *The Three Mile Island Crisis: Psychological, Social, and Economic Impacts on the Surrounding Population.* University Park: Pennsylvania State University Press, 1988.
U.S. Nuclear Regulatory Commission. *Fact Sheet: The Accident at Three Mile Island.* Washington, DC: Office of Public Affairs, 2004.

Thurmond, Strom

The Democratic governor of South Carolina from January 1947 to January 1951, a 1948 third-party presidential candidate, a U.S. senator for forty-eight years (from December 1954 to December 2002, except for nine months), first as a Democrat and then as a Republican, Strom Thurmond in 1997 became the longest-serving member in the U.S. Senate to that time. (His record was broken in 2006 by Robert C. Byrd of West Virginia.) Thurmond served in the Senate until shortly after his one-hundredth birthday. He was involved in many issues during his decades as a legislator, but as a central figure in southern politics during a period of sweeping change, he was best known for his opposition to desegregation.

James Strom Thurmond was born on December 5, 1902, in Edgefield, South Carolina, the son of a locally prominent Southern Baptist family. He graduated from Clemson College (BS, 1923), returned home to farm and teach school, was tutored in law by his father (an attorney and politician), and practiced law. He entered politics, resigned a judgeship to serve in World War II, and in 1946 was elected governor of South Carolina. He generally was progressive, even on race, but then opposed integration of the military. In 1948, he opposed the Democratic Party's strong civil rights plank and ran unsuccessfully for president as a member of the breakaway Dixiecrats (or States' Rights Democrats).

Thurmond was appointed to the U.S. Senate as a Democrat in 1954, completing the term of Charles E.

Opposing the anti–Jim Crow plank of the Democratic Party platform in 1948, South Carolina governor Strom Thurmond ran for president as a Dixiecrat. He went on to serve in the U.S. Senate from 1954 to 2002, eventually switching from Democrat to Republican. *(Tony Linck/Time & Life Pictures/ Getty Images)*

revealed that he had fathered a biracial daughter when he was in his early twenties—confirming a rumor that had been circulating for years. Essie Mae Washington-Williams announced that she had been born in 1925, the daughter of Thurmond and Carrie Butler, a young maid in the Thurmond household. Although she indicated receiving monetary support from the senator over the years, including payment of her college tuition, some observers speculated that the maid might have been raped. In 2007 it was revealed that the great-grandfather of the Reverend Al Sharpton, a black activist from New York, had been the slave of one of Thurmond's ancestors.

Abraham D. Lavender

See also: Byrd, Robert C.; Civil Rights Movement; Democratic Party; Goldwater, Barry; Johnson, Lyndon B.; Lott, Trent; Race; Republican Party; Sharpton, Al; Thomas, Clarence; Truman, Harry S.

Further Reading

Bass, Jack. *Strom: The Turbulent Political and Personal Life of Strom Thurmond.* New York: Public Affairs, 2006.

Cohodas, Nadine. *Strom Thurmond and the Politics of Southern Change.* Macon, GA: Mercer University Press, 1994.

Washington-Williams, Essie Mae. *Dear Senator: A Memoir by the Daughter of Strom Thurmond.* New York: Regan Books, 2005.

Daniel, who had resigned. Thurmond stepped down in April 1956 to fulfill a campaign promise, won reelection without opposition that November, and was returned to office every six years for the next seven terms. In 1964, as the civil rights movement swept the nation, Thurmond switched from Democratic to Republican, supported Barry Goldwater against Lyndon Johnson for president, and from that point forward played a major role in the "southern strategy" to maintain segregation. As African Americans became registered voters in increasing number, however, Thurmond gradually softened his position on race, hired black staff members, supported the Martin Luther King, Jr., holiday, voted in favor of Clarence Thomas's appointment to the Supreme Court in 1991, and provided dedicated constituent service equally to whites and blacks. Even so, some continued to remember the 1948 presidential race. In 2002, during the senator's one-hundredth birthday celebration, Republican senator Trent Lott of Mississippi publicly boasted that Thurmond had won Alabama in 1948, adding, "And if the rest of the country had followed our lead, we wouldn't have had all these problems over all these years, either." A media firestorm followed, with even President George W. Bush calling Lott's comments inappropriate.

Six months after retiring from the Senate, Thurmond died on June 26, 2003. In December of that year, it was

Till, Emmett

The death of Emmett Till, a fourteen-year-old African American who was brutally murdered on August 28, 1955, in Mississippi for speaking to a white woman, caused widespread outrage and gave impetus to the civil rights movement. The quick acquittal of the two accused murderers, both white men, made the case a symbol of southern injustice.

Born on July 25, 1941, Emmett Louis Till was raised by his Mississippi-born mother in the integrated suburbs of Chicago. When visiting his uncle's family in Money, Mississippi, he failed to take seriously the Jim Crow ways of the South. A few days after arriving in the summer of 1955, Till and some other teenagers visited a grocery store to buy candy. Exactly what happened inside the store is uncertain, but it was reported that Till either whistled at, flirted with, or physically grabbed the white woman behind the counter, Carolyn Bryant. When the woman's husband, Rob Bryant, returned from out of town a few days later, he and his half-brother, J.W. Milam, allegedly dragged Emmett out of bed at 2:30 in the morning, took him to a nearby farm, beat him brutally, and shot him to death. Three days later, Till's body, tied with barbed wire to a 70-pound (32-kilo) cotton-gin fan, was found in the Tallahatchie River.

The public funeral for Emmett Till, held back in Chicago, was attended by 50,000 mourners. His mother, Mamie Till, refused to have a closed casket because she wanted to "let the world see what I've seen." Her son's face had been beaten beyond recognition. A picture of the open casket was published in *Jet* magazine, searing the memory of all who viewed it. The murder, occurring one year after *Brown v. Board of Education* and a few months prior to the Montgomery bus boycott, contributed to the burgeoning sentiment in the African-American community to actively oppose institutionalized racism.

The trial of Bryant and Milam, which began on September 19 at the Tallahatchie County Courthouse, received national attention and was closely monitored by the NAACP and African-American journalists. An eighteen-year-old farm boy testified that he saw a pickup truck pull up to a shed; Bryant, Milam, and two other whites sat in the cab, with Emmett and two black men sitting in the back. Later, screams were heard coming from the shed. The boy's uncle identified Milam and Bryant as the kidnappers. An all-white jury heard the evidence and delivered its not-guilty verdict in a little over one hour. Four months afterward, Bryant and Milam, then safe from prosecution, admitted to the murder in a paid interview for *Look* magazine.

Nearly fifty years after the murder, based on new evidence in Keith Beauchamp's documentary film *The Untold Story of Emmett Louis Till* (2004), the federal government launched an investigation. According to the film, Bryant and Milam had accomplices, some of whom were still living. Although new criminal charges could not be filed under federal law because of the statute of limitations, they could be pursued at the state level. In March 2006, the FBI forwarded its updated findings to Mississippi officials for possible legal action, but the following year a state grand jury closed the case without issuing any new indictments.

E. Michael Young and Roger Chapman

See also: *Brown v. Board of Education* (1954); Civil Rights Movement; Hate Crimes; King, Martin Luther, Jr.; Lynching; Morrison, Toni; National Association for the Advancement of Colored People; Parks, Rosa; Philadelphia, Mississippi; Vigilantism.

Further Reading

Huie, William Bradford. "The Shocking Story of Approved Killing in Mississippi." *Look*, January 1956.

Metress, Christofer. *The Lynching of Emmett Till: A Documentary Narrative.* Charlottesville: University of Virginia Press, 2002.

Till-Mobley, Mamie, and Christopher Benson. *Death of Innocence: The Story of a Hate Crime That Changed America.* New York: One World Ballantine Books, 2003.

Tobacco Settlements

Faced with legal proceedings in the 1990s, major American cigarette manufacturers decided to settle out of court, paying state governments billions of dollars to offset the taxpayer cost of treating diseases related to smoking. These tobacco settlements raise philosophical questions about corporate responsibility and personal responsibility. Not only is there the ambiguity of counting the fiscal cost of smoking, but not all of the settlement money has been used for its intended purposes. Furthermore, the settlements have greatly benefited the major tobacco companies.

On March 23, 1994, in the first government lawsuit of its kind, Mississippi attorney general Mike Moore sued the major U.S. cigarette producers to recover costs incurred by his state in treating smoking-related diseases. The defendants were blamed for placing cigarettes into the "stream of commerce" despite knowing that they were hazardous even when used as intended, that some smoking-related health care costs would be shifted to the taxpayers, and "that the State itself thereby would be harmed." Prior to the Mississippi lawsuit, complaints seeking compensation for damages caused by exposure to harmful substances, such as asbestos, were brought as private class actions. By 1998, bolstered by damaging documents released after the cigarette manufacturer Liggett broke ranks in early 1996, Minnesota, Florida, and Texas had joined Mississippi in settling similar lawsuits. In November of that year, the attorneys general of the remaining forty-six states finalized the Master Settlement Agreement (MSA), resolving all of their outstanding claims against the tobacco companies.

The MSA had two related purposes: to reimburse the states for their past smoking-related health care costs, incurred mainly under the Medicaid program, and to fund programs aimed at reducing smoking in the future. Including the four separately negotiated settlements, the defendants agreed to pay out $246 billion to the states over twenty-five years. Other provisions of the MSA imposed restrictions on tobacco advertising and lobbying, required the tobacco companies to pay for tobacco education and smoking cessation and prevention programs, and granted compensation to tobacco farmers for lost sales caused by cigarette price increases—of forty to forty-five cents per pack—permitted to fund the settlement pool. In return, the states pledged not to seek recovery of smoking-attributable public health care costs incurred after 1998.

The tobacco settlements were negotiated against the backdrop of a broader culture war between smokers and nonsmokers, a war launched in 1964 when the surgeon general issued the first official report linking cigarette smoking to coronary and lung disease. While smokers argue that they have a right to consume a legal product, nonsmokers argue that they have a right to avoid exposure to tobacco smoke. But the key issue for public policymakers in the tobacco settlements was that smokers use taxpayer-financed health care services for which they do not fully pay.

The $246 billion payout was based on estimates of gross increases in public health care costs. The amounts the states recovered were not offset by savings they realized in the form of lower pension benefits for smokers or by the considerable public revenue generated by state sales and excise taxes on cigarettes. Nor were any adjustments made for the Medicaid program's matching provision, whereby the federal government pays at least half of the costs states incur in serving their eligible populations. Moreover, studies show that only 53 percent of the $39.4 billion dispersed by the tobacco companies through 2004 was allocated to state programs directly related to smoking and health—the remainder was spent elsewhere, either held in reserve or budgeted for other uses, such as teacher pay raises.

Perhaps the biggest winners were the tobacco companies. Because nonparticipating cigarette manufacturers must start contributing to the settlement pool if their market share exceeds a predetermined threshold, the MSA protects the major companies against expansion by competitors and new entry. In the meantime, cigarette price increases have more than offset the settlement costs.

William F. Shughart II

See also: Health Care; Smoking in Public; Tort Reform; Whistleblowers.

Further Reading

Dixon, Lee, and James Cox. *State Management and Allocation of Tobacco Settlement Revenue, 2002.* Washington, DC: National Conference of State Legislatures, 2002.

Gruber, Jonathan. "Tobacco at the Crossroads: The Past and Future of Smoking Regulation in the United States." *Journal of Economic Perspectives* 15:2 (2001): 193–212.

McKinley, Andrew, Lee Dixon, and Amanda Devore. *State Management and Allocation of Tobacco Settlement Revenue, 2003.* Washington, DC: National Conference of State Legislatures, 2003.

Stevenson, Taylor P., and William F. Shughart II. "Smoke and Mirrors: The Political Economy of the Tobacco Settlements." *Public Finance Review* 34:6 (2006): 712–30.

Viscusi, W. Kip. *Smoke-Filled Rooms: A Postmortem on the Tobacco Deal.* Chicago: University of Chicago Press, 2002.

Wilson, Joy Johnson. *Summary of the Attorneys General Master Tobacco Settlement Agreement.* Washington, DC: National Conference of State Legislatures, 1999.

Tort Reform

Tort reform refers to the trend toward limiting large monetary awards in liability cases concerning individuals and corporations. Traditionally, monetary punitive damages have a twofold purpose: to provide compensatory relief to the victim and, perhaps more important, to punish the guilty party severely enough to discourage a repeat of the infraction.

Beginning in the 1970s, tort reform has been promoted by political conservatives, backed by the lobbying of corporate interests, who argue that American society has been suffering a "litigation explosion" characterized by "fraudulent lawsuits." According to those in favor of limiting the punishment in tort cases, private enterprise (including the medical profession) is preyed upon by greedy trial lawyers, who collect on average 20 percent of the award, which leads to an overall increase in the price of goods and services. This perspective regards tort cases as "litigation tyranny." The other side, which argues that liability lawsuits are a means to hold injury-causing parties accountable, refers to tort as "corporate accountability." Consumer activist Ralph Nader, in fact, has characterized the "reform" of tort reform as a euphemism for "the perversion of justice" by corporations. In short, the controversy of tort reform pits economic interests against consumer interests.

The tort reform movement was formally launched in 1986 with the formation of the American Tort Reform Association (ATRA), which was backed by hundreds of manufacturers, trade associations, and insurance companies. In 1994, after Republicans gained control of the House of Representatives for the first time in decades, efforts for tort reform were pushed hard. In the Senate, however, filibustering in 1994, 1995, and 1998 prevented tort-reform legislation from going to the floor for a vote. In 1996, a tort-reform bill was passed by both houses, but it was vetoed by President Bill Clinton. Two years later a watered-down tort-reform bill was heading to passage, but it was ultimately defeated after Senator Trent Lott (R-AL) tried to quietly insert a handwritten provision that would have added further liability protection to Baxter Healthcare Corporation, a large biomedical company in his state.

The case that has often been cited as an example of why there needs to be tort reform is the $2.7 million verdict issued in 1994 in New Mexico to a woman who sued McDonald's after receiving third-degree burns from a spilt cup of coffee that had been served at the restaurant's drive-through window. Often left out of the telling of this story is the fact that the elderly woman (she was seventy-nine when the injury occurred) had initially sought $10,000 to pay for her medical bills (her injuries led to painful skin grafts on her thighs, groin, and buttocks, as well as eight days in the hospital), but McDonald's refused to settle. During the subsequent trial it was learned that over a ten-year period the restaurant chain had received 700 complaints about injuries pertaining to coffee that was served hotter than at most other restaurants. The jury decided on $2.7 million for punitive damages because that was the amount McDonald's takes in for two days' worth of coffee sales. Afterward, the judge reduced the amount to $640,000. In the end, the plaintiff and McDonald's settled out of court, probably for a lower amount.

Tort reform gained momentum during the George W. Bush administration, which asserted that limiting liability was necessary for decreasing the overall costs of medical care. It was argued that tort reform would lead to a more efficient health care system because doctors would not have to do extra procedures to "cover" themselves from possible liability and would not have to pay so much for malpractice insurance. Bush's call for capping awards at $5 million led to the passage of the Class Action Fairness Act of 2005, allowing federal oversight of certain kinds of class-action lawsuits.

The question of liability has been an ongoing controversy for years. Since cigarette packs dating back to 1965 have had health-warning labels, tobacco companies steadfastly maintained that smokers have only themselves to blame for ignoring the risks of smoking. Juries more often than not agreed, as from the 1950s to the early 1990s the tobacco companies won all but two of the 930 lung-cancer cases. Beginning in the 1980s, however, stricter liability standards were put in play. This led to the $246 billion Master Settlement Agreement (1998) between forty-six states and the major tobacco companies. States were to use the settlement funds to offset the medical costs of smoking-related diseases and to educate young citizens about the dire consequences of smoking.

Critics of the tobacco settlement noted the high fees the tort attorneys garnered from the deal—five attorneys involved with the Texas tobacco settlement, for example, collected $3.3 billion in fees. Similar criticism was aimed at John Edwards, the 2004 Democratic vice-presidential nominee and 2008 presidential candidate, who as a trial lawyer had earned millions of dollars trying product liability cases. Edwards was able to deflect criticisms of profiting on the suffering of others by relating personal stories of individuals harmed by faulty products or medical malpractice. Tort law, he insisted, was a way to hold corporations accountable. He thus framed tort reform as motivated by "corporate greed" and the desire not to be held accountable for misdeeds.

There are those who believe that tort law should be strengthened because the legal process, as currently practiced, allows corporations to lessen the sting of accountability. For instance, the large awards juries require corporations to pay are routinely reduced on appeal. In most cases the parties eventually agree to confidential out-of-court settlements. In addition, by forcing the silence of the plaintiff in these settlements, the corporation avoids being held publicly accountable, and hence its business practices are not held in question. Business interests have the advantage over the harmed individual as they use time and legal maneuverings to wear down the person, inducing individuals to accept a lower amount and agree to silence in order to bring the legal dispute to an end.

Anthony C. Gabrielli and Roger Chapman

See also: Medical Malpractice; Nader, Ralph; Tobacco Settlements.

Further Reading

Abraham, Kenneth. *The Liability Century: Insurance and Tort Law from the Progressive Era to 9/11.* Cambridge, MA: Harvard University Press, 2008.

Bogus, Carl T. *Why Lawsuits Are Good for America: Disciplined Democracy, Big Business, and the Common Law.* New York: New York University Press, 2001.

Levy, Robert. *Shakedown: How Corporations, Government, and Trial Lawyers Abuse the Judicial Process.* Washington, DC: Cato Institute, 2004.

Nader, Ralph. *No Contest: Corporate Lawyers and the Perversion of Justice in America.* New York: Random House, 1996.

Olson, Walter. *The Litigation Explosion: What Happened When America Unleashed the Lawsuit.* New York: Truman Talley Books, 1992.

Ruschmann, Paul. *Tort Reform.* Philadelphia: Chelsea House, 2006.

Transgender Movement

The umbrella term "transgender" refers to people who express their gender differently from the cultural norm. The transgendered include (1) cross-dressers and transvestites (sometimes known as drag queens and drag kings), individuals who adopt gender expressions culturally inconsistent with their gender (such as wearing apparel and accessories associated with the opposite sex); (2) transsexuals, those who have opted for hormone treatments and sex-reassignment surgery to physically alter their sex; (3) the intersexed, persons who were born with sexual anatomy that is both male and female (constituting one out of every 2,000 individuals); and (4) gay men and lesbians who identify themselves as transgendered. In the culture wars the transgender movement has campaigned to promote civil rights for people who do not fall into the traditional male/female dichotomy and to put a stop to what they call "transphobia" and "gender terrorism," the societal pressure (including violence) to enforce "gender normativity."

The transgender movement in the United States dates back to the 1966 riots at Compton's Cafeteria in San Francisco, involving some fifty protesters opposing perceived prejudice against the transgendered. Three years later there was a riot at the Stonewall Inn nightclub on Christopher Street in Greenwich Village, New

York, involving transgendered and homosexual patrons resisting a police raid of their social hangout. Prior to that, Christine Jorgensen's sex-reassignment surgery in 1952 was widely publicized, and she remained in the public spotlight with a nightclub act and the publication of her life story (1967), which was made into a movie in 1970. During the early 1970s Jorgensen spoke on many college campuses, telling of how she had been born a "female" in a male body (and initially named George). In the meantime, there was the debut of Virginia Prince's *Transvestia* magazine (1960). Further legitimating the transgendered were medical texts such as Harry Benjamin's *Transsexual Phenomenon* (1966) and John William Money and Richard Green's *Transexualism and Sex Reassignment* (1969).

The transgender movement did not coalesce politically until the 1980s and 1990s, even though people have been challenging gender stereotypes throughout history. Since then, some dozens of cities have enacted laws protecting the rights of the transgendered. In 1991, Minnesota was the first state to pass such an antidiscrimination measure. This was followed by Rhode Island, New Mexico, California, Illinois, Maine, Hawaii, Washington, the District of Columbia, New Jersey, Iowa, Vermont, Colorado, and Oregon. Some activists have pushed for hate crime legislation to punish those who violently target the transgendered. Transgender rights have been promoted by various organizations, including the International Foundation for Gender Education (founded in 1984), the Transgender Law and Policy Institute (founded in 2000), and the National Center for Transgender Equality (founded in 2003).

Ironically, the transgender movement has faced resistance from certain members of the lesbian, gay, and bisexual community. Whereas the transgender movement is about gender identity, the gay rights movement is about sexual orientation: although there are transgender people who identify as lesbian, gay, or bisexual, others see themselves as heterosexual. But by and large transgender rights have been part of the broader gay rights movement.

People who are physically transitioning and modifying their bodies through hormone treatments and/or surgical procedures can face difficult challenges such as employment and housing discrimination—for instance, in 2007 the City Commission of Largo, Florida, voted to dismiss its city manager after he announced plans to have sex-change surgery. There have also been cases in which the transgendered have been denied medical care or mistreated by health care professionals—the 2001 documentary film *Southern Comfort* tells the story of a female-to-male transsexual who had difficulty getting treatment for his cervical and ovarian cancer. The transgender movement has been dedicated to working with health care professionals, lawmakers, and public-service

sectors to educate people about transgender issues. The goal is to achieve dignity in public policies, court systems, media, literature, and corporations.

In their quest to remove any lingering stigma, activists have raised questions about the diagnostic term that the American Psychiatric Association continues to apply to transgender cases: "gender identity disorder." Health professionals view this heading, which is published in the *Diagnostic and Statistical Manual of Mental Disorders*, as necessary and positive, for it enables access to medical care, some of which is covered by health insurance. The transgender movement sees this appellation as implying that transgendered people are abnormal or pathological.

Jordon Johnson

See also: Androgyny; Gay Rights Movement; Jorgensen, Christine; Kinsey, Alfred; McCloskey, Deirdre; Rodman, Dennis; Stonewall Rebellion; Women's Studies.

Further Reading

Bornstein, Kate. *Gender Outlaw: On Men, Women, and the Rest of Us.* New York: Vintage Books, 1995.

Califia, Pat. *Sex Changes: The Politics of Transgenderism.* San Francisco: Cleis Press, 1997.

Currah, Paisley, Richard M. Juang, and Shannon Price Minter. *Transgender Rights.* Minneapolis: University of Minnesota Press, 2006.

Feinberg, Leslie. *Transgender Warrior: Making History from Joan of Arc to Dennis Rodman.* Boston: Beacon Press, 1997.

Stryker, Susan, and Stephen Whittle. *The Transgender Studies Reader.* New York: Routledge, 2006.

Truman, Harry S.

An unassuming Democratic senator from Missouri, compromise choice as President Franklin D. Roosevelt's running mate in 1944, and thirty-third president of the United States upon FDR's death the following year, Harry Truman proved to be a highly and enduringly controversial figure for several reasons, including his order to drop atomic bombs on Japan to end World War II and setting the United States on the course of the Cold War to "contain" the Soviet Union. Truman was deeply committed to the New Deal and argued for a continuation of domestic reform in the closely contested election of 1948, which he won against all odds.

The son of a livestock farmer, Harry S. Truman was born in Lamar, Missouri, on May 8, 1884. He did not attend college, but served in World War I as a commander of an artillery battalion in France. Upon returning to Missouri, he worked in banking, shared a haberdashery business, tended a farm, and entered politics as part of Tom Pendergast's Democratic machine in Kansas City. After serving as a Jackson County judge (1922–1924, 1926–

1934), he was elected to the U.S. Senate (1935–1945) as the candidate of the state Democratic machine.

Senator Truman made a mark during wartime mobilization as chairman of the Special Committee to Investigate the National Defense Program (widely known as the Truman Committee), which rooted out fraud and waste in government contracting, saving taxpayers an estimated $15 billion. During the 1944 presidential campaign, he was chosen as Roosevelt's running mate to replace the controversial vice president Henry A. Wallace. The Democrats easily won that election, but Roosevelt died of a massive stroke only five months later. On April 12, 1945, Truman was sworn in as president, having served a mere eighty-two days as vice president. He won the presidency in his own right in 1948, upsetting Republican Thomas E. Dewey. Truman died at age eighty-eight on December 26, 1972, in Kansas City.

Truman's first major decision as president was to use atomic weapons against Japan, ending World War II with the bombing of Hiroshima and Nagasaki in August 1945. Later, revisionist historians would question the morality of that decision and Truman's motives. In his memoirs, Truman argued that he authorized the bombings to save American lives by bringing the war to an end at the earliest possible time. Critics have questioned whether the cost in civilian lives—estimated in the hundreds of thousands—was justified, whether the Japanese populace should have been warned in advance of the attack, and whether the Japanese might have been close to surrendering anyway. Still others have posited that the ulterior motive for dropping the bombs was a show of force to the Soviet Union, seen as a prospective rival in the postwar era.

Indeed, as he served out the remainder of Roosevelt's term, President Truman took measures to "contain" the spread of communism. The Truman Doctrine, articulated by the president in a speech to Congress on March 12, 1947, argued for economic and military aid to nations struggling against communism so as to keep them out of the Soviet sphere of influence. Truman also helped create the modern U.S. military and intelligence communities with the National Security Act of 1947, which merged the various war departments into the Department of Defense and established both the National Security Council and the Central Intelligence Agency. Truman's containment doctrine garnered ongoing criticism in American society, especially during America's later involvement in the Vietnam War.

Despite public opinion polls and the predictions of virtually every political commentator, Truman defeated Dewey in the 1948 presidential contest by a margin of 49.5 percent to 45.1 percent, earning the nickname "Give 'em hell Harry" for his campaign style and tenacity. In his mind, the campaign was a mandate on the New Deal. In a cross-country "whistle stop" tour, he addressed crowds from the back of a railroad car, presenting himself as a fiery populist. Calling the GOP "the party of privilege," he characterized the Republican record from 1921 to 1933 as one of "depression, poverty, and despair" and blamed his own political woes on the "do-nothing" Republican-controlled Congress. Democrats, Truman argued, believe that "prosperity begins with looking after the little fellow." The day after the election, Truman was captured in a photograph that would become an icon of modern American politics: holding a copy of the *Chicago Tribune*, a conservative newspaper he loathed, Truman beamed at the erroneous front-page headline: "DEWEY DEFEATS TRUMAN."

Within two years, the United States would be bogged down in the unpopular Korean War, a conflict that would end in stalemate. "To err is Truman" was a common refrain during his last years in office. His decline in popularity was hastened by his firing of General Douglas MacArthur in April 1951 for persistently advocating more drastic measures against the Korean communists. In April of the following year, Truman nationalized the U.S. steel industry to avoid a strike and maintain production during the war; the U.S. Supreme Court declared the move unconstitutional. President Truman gained a reputation for sticking to his convictions through thick and thin; a sign on his desk in the Oval Office emphasized presidential responsibility: "The buck stops here."

Eric J. Morgan

See also: Central Intelligence Agency; Cold War; Democratic Party; *Enola Gay* Exhibit; Health Care; Hiroshima and Nagasaki; New Deal; New Left; Nuclear Age; Oppenheimer, J. Robert; Soviet Union and Russia; Third Parties; Vietnam War.

Further Reading

Alperovitz, Gar. *The Decision to Use the Atomic Bomb and the Architecture of an American Myth.* New York: Alfred A. Knopf, 1995.

Hamby, Alonzo. *Man of the People: A Life of Harry S. Truman.* New York: Oxford University Press, 1995.

McCullough, David. *Truman.* New York: Simon & Schuster, 1992.

Spalding, Elizabeth Edwards. *The First Cold Warrior: Harry Truman, Containment, and the Making of Liberal Internationalism.* Lexington: University of Kentucky Press, 2006.

Truman, Harry S. *Memoirs.* 2 vols. Garden City, NY: Doubleday, 1955–1956.

Turner, Ted

The place of media mogul Ted Turner in America's culture wars is difficult to categorize. As a rugged individualist and wealthy proponent of free enterprise, he is often identified with the conservative right. Through his generous philanthropy, directed largely at promoting world peace and environmentalism, he is also widely identified with left-leaning causes.

Robert Edward "Ted" Turner III was born on November 19, 1938, in Cincinnati, Ohio, and grew up in Savannah, Georgia, where his father ran a successful billboard-advertising company. He attended Brown University (1956–1959), but did not graduate. After his father's suicide in 1963, Turner took over the business and increased its profitability so much that he soon acquired three southern radio stations and an Atlanta television station (1968–1970). Taking advantage of emerging satellite and cable technologies, Turner turned his TV station into one of America's first national "superstations" (1976–1979), challenging the supremacy of the ABC, CBS, and NBC broadcast networks.

Turner took an even bolder step in 1980 by launching the Cable News Network, a 24-hour news channel that transformed television journalism. Since its founding, CNN has been accused of bias—both liberal and conservative—further complicating Turner's position in the culture wars. Based on CNN's success, the Turner Broadcasting System (TBS) established other news and entertainment outlets, including the Cartoon Network, Turner Network Television, Turner Classic Movies, and the Cable Music Channel (a short-lived attempt to counter what he regarded as the immorality of MTV). In 1995, when TBS merged with Time Warner, Inc., Turner became vice chairman of the latter company. He resigned the position in 2003, however, disenchanted with Time Warner's merger with America Online (AOL). Beginning in 2002, Turner has expanded his business interests to include solar energy and eco-friendly restaurants.

In addition to his success as a media mogul, Turner has also prospered as a sports entrepreneur. In 1976, he acquired the Atlanta Braves baseball team and the Atlanta Hawks basketball team—and later the Atlanta Thrashers hockey team—partly for his love of athletic competition and partly to provide programming for his media empire. In addition, Turner has long been a world-class yachtsman, captaining the yacht *Courageous* to victory in the 1977 America's Cup sailing championship.

Turner has been married and divorced three times: to Judy Nye (1960–1964), Jane Smith (1965–1988), and actress Jane Fonda (1991–2001). Turner's relationship with Fonda, the former leftist activist, raised additional questions about his political and cultural allegiances. Sometimes calling himself a conservative liberal and sometimes a liberal conservative, Turner has regularly defied convention and expectations. An avid hunter, he also strongly supports conservation and sustainability, particularly on the 2 million acres (809,000 hectares) he owns in six states and Argentina (making him the largest private landowner in North America). Turner surprised many observers in 1998 by pledging $1 billion to support the work and causes of the United Nations around the world. Other philanthropic causes he has supported include environmental education, protecting endangered species, and reducing nuclear proliferation. Known variously as "Captain Outrageous" and "The Mouth from the South" for speaking his mind, Turner seems to have enjoyed putting his money where his mouth is.

James I. Deutsch

See also: Endangered Species Act; Environmental Movement; Fonda, Jane; Media Bias; Nuclear Age; United Nations.

Further Reading

Auletta, Ken. *Media Man: Ted Turner's Improbable Empire.* New York: W.W. Norton, 2004.

Bibb, Porter. *It Ain't as Easy as It Looks: Ted Turner's Amazing Story.* New York: Crown, 1993.

Goldberg, Robert, and Gary Jay Goldberg. *Citizen Turner: The Wild Rise of an American Tycoon.* New York: Harcourt Brace, 1995.

Twenty-Second Amendment

The Twenty-Second Amendment to the U.S. Constitution, ratified on February 26, 1951, prohibits a president from being elected more than twice, or serving as chief executive beyond two full terms plus two years of an inherited term. It was the first constitutional amendment of the postwar era, in the aftermath of the presidency of Franklin D. Roosevelt, who was elected an unprecedented four times (1932, 1936, 1940, 1944).

Limiting a presidency to two terms was a priority of the 80th Congress (1947–1948), the first time since 1931 that Republicans controlled both houses. Democrats at the time accused the GOP of seeking revenge against Roosevelt and the legacy of the New Deal. The vote on House Joint Resolution 27, which later became the Twenty-Second Amendment, followed party lines—with Republicans unanimously in favor in both houses and Democrats overwhelmingly opposed. Of the forty-seven Democrats in the House who voted with the Republicans, all were southern opponents of the New Deal. Congressman Adolph Sabath (D-IL) characterized the vote as a "pitiful victory over a great man now sleeping on the banks of the Hudson." A combination of Republican-dominated and southern state legislatures ensured the necessary support from three-quarters of the states. After the amendment was ratified, Rep. Joseph Martin (R-MA) declared it "a victory for the people and . . . a defeat for totalitarianism and the enemies of freedom."

Proponents of presidential term limits argue that George Washington established a precedent by stepping aside after two terms as chief executive, an unwritten rule that was followed by all presidents until FDR. The Twenty-Second Amendment, they believe, corresponds with the intentions of the nation's founders to safeguard the presidency from becoming a dictatorship. Opponents of the amendment argue that it weakens the executive branch, reducing a president to lame-duck status immediately following reelection. Furthermore, they contend, such a restriction limits the power of the people to decide and may force an unwanted change of leadership during a time of national crisis.

Presidents of both parties have criticized the Twenty-Second Amendment, among them Harry Truman, Dwight D. Eisenhower, Ronald Reagan, and Bill Clinton. Truman and Eisenhower were in favor of term limits for members of Congress but not for the president.

Roger Chapman

See also: Clinton, Bill; Contract with America; Democratic Party; Eisenhower, Dwight D.; Founding Fathers; New Deal; Reagan, Ronald; Republican Party; Truman, Harry S.

Further Reading

Lemelin, Bernard. "Opposition to the 22nd Amendment: The National Committee Against Limiting the Presidency and Its Activities, 1949–1951." *Canadian Review of American Studies* 29 (1999): 133–48.

Neale, Thomas H. "Presidential and Vice Presidential Terms and Tenure." *Congressional Research Service Report*, February 26, 2001.

Reagan, Ronald, et al. *Restoring the Presidency: Reconsidering the Twenty-Second Amendment.* Washington, DC: National Legal Center for the Public Interest, 1990.

Unabomber

Dubbed the Unabomber after his early choice of targets (un = universities; a = airlines), recluse and former mathematics professor Ted Kaczynski killed three people and injured twenty-three others in a nationwide bombing spree that spanned nearly two decades (1978–1995). The rationale behind the attacks was an antitechnology ideology that Kaczynski outlined in a 35,000-word manifesto—"Industrial Society and Its Future"—as published by the *Washington Post* and *New York Times* in September 1995. In his treatise, the Unabomber argued that technology aids big government and big business and fosters tyranny, all of which must be opposed by revolutionaries advancing "WILD nature." He criticized both conservatives and liberals, the former for supporting technology that erodes traditional values and the latter for advocating social solutions dependent upon technology. Some have speculated that the Unabomber issued his manifesto to regain the spotlight after the media began focusing attention on the Oklahoma City bombing, but it led to his arrest in April 1996 after his younger brother, recognizing Kaczynski's writing style, tipped off authorities.

Theodore John Kaczynski, born in Chicago on May 22, 1942, was raised in an atheistic, blue-collar family in a Chicago suburb, where he graduated from high school at age sixteen as a National Merit Scholarship finalist; his IQ had been measured at 167. He went on to study mathematics at Harvard University (BS, 1962) and the University of Michigan at Ann Arbor (MS, 1965; PhD, 1967). After a short time teaching mathematics at the University of California at Berkeley (1967–1969), he surprised his colleagues by abruptly resigning. Kaczynski eventually took up residence in a small, primitive cabin near Lincoln, Montana. Even in this rustic setting he could not escape from the technological society, whether it was snowmobilers in the nearby woods or commercial airliners flying overhead. After a logging company built a road near his cabin, he turned violent.

Kaczynski's homemade bombs, most bearing the initials "FC" for Freedom Club, were packages either mailed or hand placed. They caused injuries on or near the campuses of Northwestern University (1978, 1979), Vanderbilt University (1982), the University of California at Berkeley (1982, 1985), the University of Michigan at Ann Arbor (1985), the University of California at San Francisco (1993), and Yale University (1993). A bomb ignited but did not explode inside the cargo hold of an American Airlines jet (Chicago–Washington, D.C., flight, 1979), while another exploded at the Chicago home of the president of that same airline company

(1980). Finally, Kaczynski was responsible for the deaths of a computer-store owner (Sacramento, California, 1985), an advertising executive who worked for a company that handled Exxon's public relations following the *Exxon Valdez* oil spill (New Jersey, 1994), and a timber lobbyist (Sacramento, 1995). Other bombs were defused or detonated without injury.

In January 22, 1998, after a federal judge refused to allow Kaczynski to act as his own counsel, he pleaded guilty to the bombings in order to thwart his attorneys, who planned to present a "mental defect" defense. He was subsequently sentenced to life in prison without parole. In March 2002, the U.S. Supreme Court rejected the Unabomber's appeal for a new trial.

Two competing views of Kaczynski have persisted in the public dialogue. According to one, he was an "evil genius" who reduced people to abstract figures and killed them for supporting the advancement of the technological society. Thus, he has been widely characterized as an anarchist, libertarian, eco-terrorist, "product of the sixties," and a man with views on the environment like those of Al Gore or Lewis Mumford. According to the other view, Kaczynski is mentally ill, a diagnosed paranoid schizophrenic who in childhood suffered as a social misfit, later suffered harm as a guinea pig in an extensive Harvard psychological experiment that may have been part of a CIA mind-control program (known as MKULTRA), and once considered having a sex-change operation to be able to get close to a woman, all of which reduced him to hate-filled rage.

Roger Chapman

See also: Central Intelligence Agency; Ecoterrorism; Gore, Al; McVeigh, Timothy.

Further Reading

Chase, Alston. *Harvard and the Unabomber: The Education of an American Terrorist.* New York: W.W. Norton, 2003.

Gibbs, Nancy, Richard Lacayo, Lance Morrow, Jill Smolowe, and David Van Biema. *Mad Genius: The Odyssey, Pursuit, and Capture of the Unabomber Suspect.* New York: Warner Books, 1996.

Kaczynski, Theodore John. *The Unabomber Manifesto: Industrial Society and Its Future.* Berkeley, CA: Jolly Roger Press, 1996.

Waits, Chris, and Dave Shors. *Unabomber: The Secret Life of Ted Kaczynski.* Helena, MT: Helena Independent Record/Montana Magazine, 1999.

United Nations

Founded in 1945 and headquartered in New York City, the United Nations (UN) is an international organization that promotes collective security, human rights, economic and cultural exchange, and humanitarian relief. The organization, with an annual operating budget of over $4 billion, is staffed by 8,900 civil servants and directed by a secretary general. From its inception through 2008, the UN grew from a body of 52 member states to 192. Each member state has one vote in the General Assembly, but the organization's power resides in the fifteen-seat Security Council, on which the United States, Great Britain, France, Russia, and China have permanent membership status that includes veto power. Over the years the United States has played a major role in the UN while providing on average 25 percent of its funding. In the culture wars, conservatives are generally critical of the UN, believing that it is too bureaucratic, sometimes corrupt, and a threat to American sovereignty. Liberals often emphasize multilateralism as opposed to unilateralism, arguing that the UN is the last best hope for world peace.

Most Americans, despite earlier tendencies toward isolation, initially regarded the establishment of the UN as a positive development. According to a 1947 Gallup poll, 65 percent wanted their country to "take an active part in world affairs." In 1949, the UN was regarded with either general or qualified approval by 61 percent. As the Cold War intensified, a 1950 poll indicated that half of Americans believed a reorganized UN minus the membership of the Soviet Union and its satellite nations would be better able to maintain world peace, but five years later only 35 percent clung to that position. Indeed, 59 percent of the public indicated in 1965 that without the UN there probably would have already been World War III. However, Cold War politics hampered the functionality of the UN as the Soviet Union exercised its veto power more than any other member of the Security Council—103 times during the organization's first two decades.

In the early 1960s the John Birch Society was stridently conducting its "Get the US out of the UN and the UN out of the US" campaign. According to group leader Robert Welch, communists had conceived the UN for the ultimate purpose of establishing a world government. Welch denigrated the UN as "The House That Hiss Built," a reference to Alger Hiss, a State Department official who had been a delegate at the founding of the UN in San Francisco and who five years later was convicted of falsely testifying that he had not passed classified information to the Soviet Union. In addition, G. Edward Griffin, a member of the John Birch Society, wrote of the "Communist infiltration" of the UN in *The Fearful Master: A Second Look at the United Nations* (1964).

Religious fundamentalists such as Billy Hargis and Carl McIntire also cast the United Nations as part of a communist conspiracy. They were later joined by Hal Lindsey, Tim and Beverly LaHaye, and Pat Robertson, all of whom framed the issue in an eschatological fashion, suggesting a link between Satan and the UN. The "one

world body" foretold in the Book of Revelation might signify the UN, they explained. Later, President George H.W. Bush unwittingly reinforced the suspicions of the Religious Right when he pronounced at the end of the Cold War a "new world order." Robertson's *New World Order* (1991) offered updated commentary. Meanwhile, a network of rural gun enthusiasts and conspiracy theorists, alarmed over the prospect of a world government perhaps ushered in by the UN, formed the militia movement for the purpose of preparing for battle.

The major opposition to the UN, however, has not been the radical right but mainstream conservatives and moderates. After 1962, with the UN's infusion of new member states from Africa, Asia, and the Middle East, the United States no longer had an automatic majority and often lost votes in the General Assembly. Reflecting a North-South split rather than the Cold War East-West split, the UN began voicing criticism of the superpowers (especially the United States) and multinational corporations. Under such circumstances, the General Assembly officially equated Zionism (Jewish self-determinism) with racism, and authoritarian countries such as Libya took turns chairing the human rights committee. Daniel Patrick Moynihan, who served a short stint as a U.S. representative to the UN, afterward wrote *A Dangerous Place* (1978) to tell what he thought of that world body. In 1984, denouncing the "tyranny of the Third World," Senator Nancy Kassebaum (R-KS) persuaded her colleagues to approve her amendment limiting the U.S. contribution to the UN and its agencies from 25 percent to 20 percent unless consensus-basis decision making were introduced. From 1966 to 1990, the United States exercised the veto seventy-two times, more than any other member of the Security Council. In 1992, Washington refused to sign the Kyoto Protocol, the UN initiative on global warming.

By the end of the Cold War, conservatives had reached a consensus that the UN needed to be either reformed or abandoned. During the 1990s, as chair of the Senate Foreign Relations Committee, Senator Jesse Helms (R-NC) began blocking the U.S. dues to the UN. In 1996, Helms wrote an article in *Foreign Affairs* arguing that the UN, a "quasi-sovereign entity" that "represents an obvious threat to U.S. interests," cannot be "radically overhauled . . . without the threat of American withdrawal." In contrast, the following year the broadcaster Ted Turner established the United Nations Foundation with a $1 billion personal contribution, the amount of membership payments the United States was in arrears. Turner indicated that the United Nations was one of his favorite organizations, and he credited it with helping the world survive the Cold War.

The 2003 U.S.-led invasion of Iraq renewed debate about the effectiveness of the United Nations. Supporters of the Bush administration argue that following the

Gulf War (1991), the Iraqi dictator Saddam Hussein had defied with impunity numerous UN resolutions. Moreover, the Oil for Food scandal, involving Iraqi bribery of UN officials, proved the extent of corruption in the UN bureaucracy. However, critics of Bush's unilateral action say it tragically diminished the authority of the UN. Iraqi weapons of mass destruction proved nonexistent, corroborating what UN inspectors had said all along.

John Calhoun and Roger Chapman

See also: Cold War; Hargis, Billy; Helms, Jesse; Hiss, Alger; Human Rights; Israel; John Birch Society; Kyoto Protocol; Militia Movement; Moynihan, Daniel Patrick; Premillennial Dispensationalism; Soviet Union and Russia; Turner, Ted.

Further Reading

Gold, Dore. *Tower of Babble: How the United Nations Has Fueled Global Chaos.* New York: Crown Forum, 2004.

Helms, Jesse. "Saving the UN: A Challenge to the Next Secretary-General." *Foreign Affairs* 75:5 (September–October 1996): 2–8.

Mingst, Karen A., and Margaret P. Karns. *The United Nations and the Post–Cold War Era.* Boulder, CO: Westview Press, 2005.

Montgomery, David. *New World Government Exposed!* Sultan, WA: Montgomery, 2002.

O'Sullivan, Christopher. *The United Nations: A Concise History.* Malabar, FL: Krieger, 2005.

Shawn, Eric. *The U.N. Exposed: How the United Nations Sabotages America's Security.* New York: Sentinel, 2006.

USA PATRIOT Act

In the wake of the terrorist attacks of September 11, 2001, Congress passed legislation referred to as the USA PATRIOT Act—Uniting and Strengthening America by Providing Appropriate Tools Required to Intercept and Obstruct Terrorism—precipitating a political clash over national security and civil liberties. While proponents of the measure emphasized the need for strong counterterrorism measures, critics warned of a wholesale expansion of domestic surveillance.

The PATRIOT Act, amending the Foreign Intelligence Surveillance Act (FISA), the Electronic Communications Privacy Act of 1986 (ECPA), the Computer Fraud and Abuse Act (CFAA), the Family Education Rights and Privacy Act (FERPA), and other federal statutes, was overwhelmingly passed by Congress—357–66 (House) and 98–1–1 (Senate)—and signed into law by President George W. Bush on October 26, 2001. Although there was no public hearing or congressional debate on the legislation, a sunset proviso was added due to concerns raised about civil liberties. In March 2006, the USA PATRIOT Improvement and Reauthorization Act was

The USA PATRIOT Act divides Americans between those who believe its surveillance provisions are an unacceptable violation of privacy rights—such as this protester at the 2004 Democratic Convention—and those who believe they are vital to national security. *(Michael Springer/Getty Images)*

passed—280–138 (House) and 89–10 (Senate)—making permanent all but two of the original sections of the law.

Under the PATRIOT Act's counterterrorism provisions, federal authorities (generally the FBI) are granted greater latitude to tap telephone calls (including voice mail) and Internet communications; search financial, tax, medical, library, and school records; monitor the activities of foreigners inside U.S. borders; and conduct "sneak and peek" searches of homes or businesses (including virtual networks). By issuing a National Security Letter (NSL), federal investigators may demand certain information from an institution without court approval. In addition, the new criminal designation of "domestic terrorism" was established, raising concern among civil libertarians that it could be used for inappropriate purposes against political activists (such as abortion protesters, environmental activists, and antiwar demonstrators).

The American Civil Liberties Union (ACLU) opposed the USA PATRIOT Act from its inception, raising particular concern about the monitoring of libraries, under Section 215, which allowed federal agents to access information on the reading activities of patrons. The ACLU also objected to Section 206, pertaining to "roving" wiretaps—under this provision, the government may obtain a warrant to monitor all communication devices used by a suspect (including those shared with others) with no safeguards to restrict the monitoring of actual communication activities.

Concerns about government surveillance were heightened on December 18, 2005, when the *New York Times* broke a story that the National Security Agency (NSA) had been conducting eavesdropping since early 2002, without search warrants, of international telephone calls and electronic mail originating from the United States. In response, Senator Russell Feingold (D-WI), the Senate's sole nay voter of the original PATRIOT Act, proposed a motion of censure against President Bush. Justifying his actions based on the 2001 congressional resolution authorizing him to carry out the War on Terror, Bush admitted to authorizing the NSA wiretaps. "Why did we bother debating the Patriot Act if President Bush could make up his own rules about spying on U.S. citizens?" the ACLU bristled in a full-page ad in the *New York Times* (January 5, 2006). According to a *Washington Post*–ABC opinion poll that week, two out of three Americans believed the government was violating privacy rights; 75 percent of Republicans considered it acceptable, while 61 percent of Democrats deemed it unacceptable.

Roger Chapman

See also: American Civil Liberties Union; *New York Times, The*; Privacy Rights; September 11.

Further Reading

Ball, Howard. *The USA PATRIOT Act of 2001: Balancing Civil Liberties and National Security: A Reference Handbook.* Santa Barbara, CA: ABC-CLIO, 2004.

Etzioni, Amitai. *How Patriotic Is the Patriot Act? Freedom Versus Security in the Age of Terrorism.* New York: Routledge, 2004.

Foerstel, Herbert N. *The Patriot Act: A Documentary and Reference Guide.* Westport, CT: Greenwood Press, 2008.

Gerdes, Louis I. *The Patriot Act: Opposing Viewpoints.* Detroit, MI: Greenhaven Press, 2005.

Ventura, Jesse

Jesse Ventura, a former professional wrestler and actor, was unexpectedly elected governor of Minnesota in 1998 as the Reform Party candidate.

Born James George Janos on July 15, 1951, the son of a steamfitter and a nurse, Ventura is a native of Minneapolis, Minnesota, where he attended public school. He served as a U.S. Navy Seal from 1969 to 1975, including active duty in Vietnam. He attended community college during the mid-1970s but dropped out after one year. It was around this time that he took up bodybuilding and, after a series of odd jobs (including a brief stint as bodyguard for the Rolling Stones) became a professional wrestler under the name Jesse "The Body" Ventura. By the early 1980s, he was one of the most popular "bad guys" in the World Wrestling Federation. After blood clots in his lungs ended his wrestling career, he appeared in several action films, including two with another future governor, Arnold Schwarzenegger.

Ventura began his political career as mayor of Brooklyn Park, Minnesota (1991–1995), and later worked as a radio talk show host. Running for Minnesota governor on a platform of fiscal conservatism and social liberalism, he won a stunning victory on election day. He served from 1999 to 2003 and did not seek a second term.

As governor, Ventura also found time to work as a commentator for pro wrestling and the XFL football league, and he wrote several books. When the Reform Party came under the influence of Pat Buchanan and drifted toward a more conservative platform, Ventura quit the party in 2000, ultimately aligning himself with the Independence Party of Minnesota.

Ventura's decisions as governor attracted bipartisan criticism, though mostly from the right for his support of medical marijuana, gay rights, and abortion rights, as well as his opposition to organized religion and the flag pledge. He stirred further controversy when he sharply criticized pundits on both sides who politicized the 2002 funeral for Minnesota senator Paul Wellstone. Ventura was the subject of a popular satire by Minnesota-based humorist Garrison Keillor, who released a book featuring a Ventura-like character named Jimmy "Big Boy" Valente who becomes a politician.

After leaving office, Ventura hosted a short-lived cable TV talk show called *Jesse Ventura's America*, and in 2004 he was recruited by a fellow navy veteran for a lecture series and study group at Harvard University. Ventura also served on the board for Operation Truth, a support organization for veterans of the Iraq War.

Benjamin W. Cramer

See also: Abortion; Buchanan, Pat; Christian Coalition; Gay Rights Movement; Humphrey, Hubert H.; Medical Marijuana; Schwarzenegger, Arnold; Third Parties; Wellstone, Paul.

Further Reading

Keillor, Garrison. *ME: By Jimmy (Big Boy) Valente*. New York: Viking, 1999.

Lentz, Jacob. *Electing Jesse Ventura: A Third-Party Success Story*. Boulder, CO: Lynne Rienner, 2002.

Ventura, Jesse. *Do I Stand Alone? Going to the Mat Against Political Pawns and Media Jackals*. New York: Pocket Books, 2000.

———. *I Ain't Got Time to Bleed: Reworking the Body Politic from the Bottom Up*. New York: Villard Books, 1999.

Ventura, Jesse, and Heron Marquez. *Jesse Ventura Tells It Like It Is: America's Most Outspoken Governor Speaks Out About Government*. Minneapolis, MN: Lerner, 2002.

Victimhood

Victimhood entails the experience of suffering, which sometimes serves as the basis of legal, political, and/or cultural claims. At least since the 1970s, recognizing a group's cultural distinctiveness, including the injuries it has sustained, has emerged as a central demand of social movements on the American left. Second-wave feminists declared that the "personal is political," calling on survivors of rape and incest to transform their private experiences into public speech. Other identity groupings followed suit: gays and lesbians "came out" en masse; families and friends who lost loved ones to AIDS created massive quilts to bear witness to their loss; and the descendants of African slaves invoked the legacy of the Middle Passage. In response to these developments, conservatives warned against a "culture of victimhood" overshadowing American national identify and turning the country into "a nation of victims."

In a society where identity politics has become increasingly central, victimhood offers moral authority, visibility, and, in some cases, political clout. It says to a public composed largely of strangers: "Attention must be paid to us. You must recognize and honor that which makes us different from you, and you must be acquainted with our culture and history, including our sufferings." Before the rise of the gay liberation movement, for example, the stories of gay and lesbian lives were private and personal; today, the "coming-out story" has become a master narrative of collective identity. Even so, not all individuals who have suffered have identified themselves as victims, such as the many victims of rape who never come forward to report their injuries for fear of stigma or retaliation.

The relationship between individual experiences of pain and suffering and claims to group victimhood is not straightforward. Being a member of a victimized group does not necessarily make that individual a victim. Some groups identify on the basis of past victimhood even though many members of those groups did not themselves endure pain or suffering. American-born Jews, for example, may identify with the victims of the Holocaust even though they did not personally experience the tragedy. Similarly, blacks who did not personally suffer from slavery argue that they are nonetheless victims of its legacies; for that reason many African-American leaders have called for reparations.

One important controversy surrounding the politics of victimhood has centered on the question of whether traumatic events can be forgotten and then remembered later in life. That debate has focused on memories of childhood sexual abuse, though it extends to other traumas as well. A "repressed memory" is a memory of an event, frequently traumatic, that is stored by the unconscious mind but outside conscious awareness. Some theorize that such memories may be "recovered" and integrated into consciousness years or decades after the event, often through therapy. The accused and their allies, on the other hand, have tried to demonstrate the relative ease with which "false memories" have been deliberately implanted by therapists and other authority figures.

Conservatives such as radio talk show host and writer Charles Sykes have been critical of victimhood status, believing it is used to justify irresponsible behavior. In *A Nation of Victims* (1992), Sykes argues that "I am not responsible; it's not my fault" is a common refrain employed by compulsive gamblers, co-dependents in dysfunctional relationships, and even obese people "oppressed" by narrow airline seats. Sykes and other conservatives excoriate the psychiatric profession for inventing new "disease" categories and creating a "therapeutic culture" that turns everyday difficulties into certified psychological problems. There are those on the left who find fault with victim-based politics as well. For example, the sociologist Frank Furedi has decried efforts relegating victimization as "a kind of disease" that can be passed on to the next generation; and the feminist/queer theorist Lauren Berlant has suggested that the pervasiveness of "victim-talk," and the personalization of political discourse in general, is impoverishing the public sphere.

Most liberals maintain, however, that the politicization of victimhood signals a democratization of culture. They argue, for example, that the Holocaust in American consciousness is a response to the earlier suppression of the subject—much like the suppression of talk of homosexuality, sexual abuse, and other previously taboo topics. Before victimhood was widely discussed in public, individual and group injuries were stigmatized and hidden. By highlighting victimization, identity groups turn stigma into honorable marks of difference. In a multicultural society, they contend, the distinctiveness of group identities, which may be linked to a history of injury or persecution, should be preserved. Moreover,

they maintain that it is society's ethical duty to recognize and even identify with the suffering of others.

Arlene Stein

See also: AIDS; Anti-Semitism; Civil Rights Movement; Feminism, Second-Wave; Feminism, Third-Wave; Gay Rights Movement; Holocaust; Multiculturalism and Ethnic Studies; Race; Sex Offenders; Sexual Assault.

Further Reading

Berlant, Lauren. *The Queen of America Goes to Washington City.* Durham, NC: Duke University Press, 1997.

Furedi, Frank. *Therapy Culture.* London: Routledge, 2003.

Novick, Peter. *The Holocaust in American Life.* New York: Houghton Mifflin, 1999.

Prager, Jeffrey. *Presenting the Past: Psychoanalysis and the Sociology of Misremembering.* Cambridge, MA: Harvard University Press, 1998.

Sykes, Charles. *A Nation of Victims.* New York: St. Martin's Press, 1992.

Vidal, Gore

The novelist, screenwriter, and essayist Gore Vidal has provoked considerable controversy as a public intellectual with iconoclastic views, including his major thesis that the United States has drifted from a republican form of government to an empire—specifically, "a garrison state." American aggression, Vidal maintains, provoked the Oklahoma City bombing of April 1995 and the terrorist attacks of September 11, 2001, actions he regards as justifiable. Openly homosexual, Vidal was one of the first American writers to treat same-sex preference as normal; other public figures scorned him for his sexual orientation.

The son of an airline executive and an actress, Eugene Luther Gore Vidal, Jr., was born on October 3, 1925, in West Point, New York. After graduating from the Phillips Exeter Academy (1943) and serving in the U.S. Army during World War II (1943–1946), he worked briefly as a book editor at E.P. Dutton while beginning a writing career in earnest. He ran unsuccessfully for Congress as a Democrat in New York (1960) and later for a Senate seat in California, losing the primary to Jerry Brown (1982). He served as a member of the President's Advisory Committee on the Arts (1961–1963), hosted the television program *Hot Line* (1964), and co-founded the New Party (1968–1971) and co-chaired the People's Party (1970–1972), both centered on opposition to the Vietnam War. Vidal is the grandson of the progressive Oklahoma senator Thomas P. Gore and is a distant cousin of Al Gore. The author of nearly fifty books, he has published two autobiographies, *Palimpsest* (1995) and *Point to Point Navigation* (2006).

An early public controversy Vidal faced was the brouhaha over *The City and the Pillar* (1948), one of the first novels that treated homosexuality as mainstream. Although it was a best-seller, most reviews were negative. For a time, Vidal's subsequent novels did not sell well, partly because literary critics refused to review any books by an author who would promote the gay lifestyle. Later, in the essay "Pink Triangle and Yellow Star," Vidal suggested that the persecution of homosexuals was on par with anti-Semitism. Vidal returned to the theme of homosexuality in the satirical novel *Myra Breckenridge* (1968), about a Hollywood homosexual male who has a sex-change operation. This was followed by its sequel, *Myron* (1974). In 1968, while on live television during the coverage of the Democratic National Convention in Chicago, Vidal and the conservative activist William F. Buckley, Jr., verbally clashed: Buckley, after being called a "pro-crypto-Nazi," denounced Vidal as a "queer." After writing a critical review on Norman Mailer's *The Prisoner of Sex* (1971), calling it "three days of menstrual flow," Vidal appeared on *The Dick Cavett Show*, where Mailer accused him on the air of ruining the Beat writer Jack Kerouac by going to bed with him.

Other than his essays—he won the National Book Award for *United States: Essays, 1952–1992* (1993)—Vidal's long-term reputation will most likely be staked on his "Narratives of Empire" series, consisting of seven historical novels that offer a revisionist perspective: *Washington, D.C.* (1967), *Burr* (1973), *1876* (1976), *Lincoln* (1984), *Empire* (1987), *Hollywood* (1997), and *The Golden Age* (2000). These works tell the story of two fictional American families across the generations while focusing on the development of the United States into an empire. In the essay collection *Inventing a Nation: Washington, Adams, Jefferson* (2003), Vidal demythologizes the founders. A recurring theme in his writing is political ambition and the acquisition of power. This was explored in the plays *The Best Man* (1960), based on his novel about the behind-the-scenes doings of a presidential nomination, and *An Evening with Richard Nixon* (1972). Likewise in the novel *Messiah* (1955), the author tells the story of a future American dictator who comes to power by the aid of an adoring media.

More recently, Vidal has stirred controversy with political essays on American foreign policy, domestic security, and terrorism. These anthologized writings, including *The Last Empire: Essays, 1992–2000* (2001), *Perpetual War for Perpetual Peace: How We Got to Be So Hated* (2002), and *Imperial America: Reflections on the United States of Amnesia* (2004), condemn neoconservatism and the expansion of federal domestic security. Vidal links the federal attacks at Ruby Ridge (1992) and Waco (1993) with Operation Desert Storm (1991) and U.S. foreign intervention in general. Waco, he argues, was "the largest massacre of Americans by their own government

since 1890, when a number of Native Americans were slaughtered at Wounded Knee, South Dakota." Timothy McVeigh's truck bombing of the federal building in Oklahoma City (1995) was a "revolutionary act" in revenge for Waco, maintains Vidal, who nonetheless thinks much of the real story has been suppressed. The attacks of September 11 he categorizes with the Oklahoma City bombing: just recompense. Some have criticized Vidal for promoting conspiracy theories in much of his analysis, including his assertion that President George W. Bush knew the attacks of September 11 were coming.

Roger Chapman

See also: Buckley, William F., Jr.; Conspiracy Theories; Gay Rights Movement; Kerouac, Jack; Mailer, Norman; McVeigh, Timothy; Revisionist History; Ruby Ridge Incident; September 11; Waco Siege; War Protesters; Wounded Knee Incident.

Further Reading

Altman, Dennis. *Gore Vidal's America.* Malden, MA: Polity, 2005.

Harris, Stephen. *Gore Vidal's Historical Novels and the Shaping of American Consciousness.* Lewistown, NY: Edwin Mellen Press, 2005.

Kaplan, Fred. *Gore Vidal: A Biography.* New York: Doubleday, 1999.

Vietnam Veterans Against the War

The organization Vietnam Veterans Against the War (VVAW), founded in 1967 by members of the U.S. armed forces returning home from the Vietnam War, opposed the continuation of American involvement in what it regarded as a civil war that posed no threat to U.S. security. Although most of its members had volunteered for military service, they became radicalized after concluding that the war was immoral and not winnable. They considered themselves "winter soldiers," in contrast to the "sunshine patriots" who offered bravado without confronting "the ugly truth" about the Vietnam War. The Oliver Stone film *Born on the Fourth of July* (1989) is based on the autobiography of Ron Kovic, a Vietnam "wheelchair" veteran, and concludes with the VVAW protest march during the 1972 Republican National Convention. The organization, which never disbanded, inspired the formation of the Iraq Veterans Against the War in 2004.

An antiwar advertisement in the February 1971 issue of *Playboy* helped double VVAW membership to 20,000; 10 percent were soldiers still deployed in Vietnam. Stories circulated of entire platoons belonging to the VVAW, with some soldiers wearing its insignia—an upside-down rifle with a helmet on top (the symbol of death)—on their uniforms. The group's membership peaked in 1972 at 25,000. Although they were latecomers to the antiwar movement, VVAW activists were generally more radical and angrier than student protesters.

U.S. attorney general John Mitchell, who served under President Richard M. Nixon during the height of the antiwar movement in the early 1970s, publicly denounced the VVAW as the most dangerous group in the United States. The FBI, through its controversial Counter-Intelligence Program (COINTELPRO), monitored the VVAW practically from its inception and over the years infiltrated many chapters with informants. In July 1972, eight VVAW leaders were indicted for conspiring to disrupt the upcoming Republican National Convention in Miami.

A week-long demonstration by the VVAW in the nation's capital in April 1971, culminating in a ceremony in which decorated veterans threw away their medals, came to be regarded as a pivotal protest event of the era. The incident was restored to public attention in 2004 when John Kerry, a former navy lieutenant and VVAW activist, ran as the Democratic candidate for president of the United States. In that election, a group calling itself Swift Boat Veterans for Truth raised questions about Kerry's war record and at the same time condemned him for his role as a VVAW spokesman, specifically his April 1971 testimony before the Senate Foreign Relations Committee, in which he raised the issue of American war crimes. The book *Unfit for Command* (2004) and film documentary *Stolen Honor* (2004) were part of this attack against Kerry.

Roger Chapman

See also: Bush Family; Cold War; Fonda, Jane; Kerry, John; My Lai Massacre; Nixon, Richard; Silent Majority; Stone, Oliver; Vietnam War; War Protesters; Watergate; Wayne, John.

Further Reading

Hunt, Andrew E. *The Turning: A History of Vietnam Veterans Against the War.* New York: New York University Press, 1999.
Kerry, John, and Vietnam Veterans Against the War. *The New Soldier.* New York: Collier, 1971.
Vietnam Veterans Against the War Web site. http://www.vvaw.org.

Vietnam Veterans Memorial

Located on the Washington Mall in the nation's capital, the Vietnam Veterans Memorial is a V-shaped, black granite wall, measuring 400 feet (122 meters) long, inscribed with the names of the more than 58,000 veterans who lost their lives in the Vietnam War, listed in the chronological order in which they died. Designed by Maya Lin, who at the time was an architectural student

at Yale University, the $8 million, privately financed monument was dedicated on November 13, 1982. The most visited memorial in Washington, D.C., the site was baptized by fire in the culture wars.

The memorial was the inspiration of Jan Scruggs, who had served in the war as a rifleman. He envisioned a memorial that listed by name every military person who died in the conflict, spanning the years 1957 to 1975. Eventually, a total of 650,000 individuals made monetary donations for the project. On July 1, 1980, President Jimmy Carter approved the allocation of two acres (0.81 hectares) on Constitution Gardens (located between the Washington Monument and the Lincoln Memorial) for the National Vietnam Veterans Memorial.

Although the idea for the memorial was widely favored, the unveiling of Lin's design led to acrimonious debate. Opponents argued that it reflected an attitude of shame toward the war. The design called for the wall to be set into an embankment, and critics argued that it should be built above ground, not below. They also contended that the color should be white, not black. Moreover, the austere monument was said to lack patriotic ambience. Those in favor of Lin's design—many of whom preferred a nonpolitical memorial, so as not to honor war—said that it reflected the nobility of sacrifice.

The *New York Times* praised the "extreme dignity and restraint" of Lin's vision, but industrialist and later presidential candidate H. Ross Perot, who donated $160,000 for the design competition, regarded the winning entry as a disgrace. Novelist Tom Wolfe denounced the design as "a tribute to Jane Fonda" and the committee that approved it the "Mullahs of Modernism." The conservative magazine *National Review* declared it "Orwellian glop" and called on the Reagan administration to halt the project. Others described it as "a black gash of shame."

James Watt, the secretary of the Department of Interior, resisted issuing a groundbreaking permit and did so only after demanding that an American flag and statue be added. In another compromise, two brief inscriptions, a prologue and epilogue, were added to the wall of names. After a three-day prayer vigil at the National Cathedral in which the names of all the war dead were read, the memorial was officially dedicated in a ceremony attended by more than 150,000 people.

The flag, on a sixty-foot (18.3-meter) staff, was added in 1983, and Frederick Hart's bronze sculpture of three American soldiers was installed the following year; both were placed to the side of the wall, rather than in front of it, as Watt had desired. After years of more debate, a sculpture honoring women veterans was added in 1993. A plaque was placed in the plaza area in 2004, stating, "We honor and remember their sacrifice." In 2006, an underground visitor center was approved, but some veterans denounced it as a reminder of Viet Cong tunnels. For most visitors over the years, however, the power of

Designer Maya Lin stands alongside the Vietnam Veterans Memorial shortly after its dedication in 1982. The innovative original design met with resistance, and several elements were added. *(James P. Blair/National Geographic/Getty Images)*

walking along the wall, finding the name of a loved one inscribed on the surface, and reaching out to touch it has triumphed over the design dispute.

Roger Chapman

See also: American Civil Religion; Anti-Intellectualism; Fonda, Jane; *National Review*; Perot, H. Ross; September 11 Memorial; Vietnam Veterans Against the War; Vietnam War; Watt, James; Wolfe, Tom; World War II Memorial.

Further Reading

Scruggs, Jan C., and Joel L. Swerdlow. *To Heal a Nation: The Vietnam Veterans Memorial.* New York: Harper and Row, 1985.

Vietnam War

Only one war over Vietnam ended when North Vietnamese forces captured Saigon in April 1975. Conflict over the meaning of U.S. involvement in Vietnam and the implications of it continued to be waged in American culture and politics for the rest of the twentieth century and into the early years of the twenty-first.

The U.S. military presence in Vietnam began in the 1950s, when the first aid and advisers were sent to support the Diem regime in Saigon, South Vietnam, in the struggle against communist North Vietnam. Combat troops arrived in 1965 and reached a peak of almost 550,000 in 1969. By the time U.S. troops were withdrawn after the Paris peace accords of 1973, almost 58,000 had died. The fact that the war was so long and so costly, ending essentially in American defeat, yielded historical interpretations that evolved very differently from those of other American wars. Initial journalistic and scholarly accounts in the aftermath of previous conflicts typically highlighted the nobility of U.S. interests, the bravery of U.S. armed forces, and the strength of national effort and support. The first reflections on the Vietnam War, by contrast, evinced a sense of disillusion and frustration.

Historical Interpretation and Conservative Revision

Even before the fighting was over, historian Arthur Schlesinger, Jr., wrote about the folly of Washington policymakers, who had an unreasonable confidence in America's ability to shape global affairs and little appreciation for how local issues affected the Third World. Such misperceptions were magnified by an unshaken belief that communist movements had to be fought everywhere and at all times. By 1979, with the publication of George Herring's *America's Longest War*, a standard historical interpretation of the Vietnam experience had formed: the war was wrong, the war was unwinnable, and U.S. policymakers pursued it out of a flawed commitment to contain global communism at all costs.

The conventional wisdom on the Vietnam War was challenged in the conservative ascendancy of the 1980s. Revisionist historians asserted that America had been morally obligated to support the South Vietnamese. They also argued that the U.S. military could have won the war had it not been hampered by civilian leadership, the antiwar protest movement, and the media's portrayal of the war on television.

No grand consensus has emerged between the two camps and the competing views of the war, though historians generally favor the standard interpretation. In any event, the place of the Vietnam War in America's culture wars is not entirely reflected in the evolution of scholarship and academic interpretation. During the early stages of U.S. involvement, it was generally expected that the outcome would be another in a long line of noble American victories. The ultimate failure of the U.S. military effort thus prompted a deep questioning of the nature of America itself.

In the years following the war, with the help of movies, television, novels, and public rhetoric, the nation created a set of evolving and competing collective memories of Vietnam and its lessons. Pundits and politicians on both sides of the culture wars began to draw very different conclusions about the nature of America's role in world affairs. For those on the left, one of the lessons of Vietnam was that U.S. military force should be used only sparingly and with a clear purpose in the world arena, lest the tragedy of Vietnam be repeated. For those on the right, the failure in Vietnam rested with those who protested U.S. involvement and failed to allow the armed forces to complete the job.

During the early years of the Vietnam War, presidential rhetoric called for Americans to unite and not to second-guess the decision of American intervention. In 1975, a few weeks before the final North Vietnamese victory, President Gerald Ford told Americans that the pre-Vietnam "sense of pride" could not be achieved by "refighting a war that is finished as far as America is concerned." President Jimmy Carter tended to avoid broad discussions of the legacy of Vietnam, focusing instead on the plight of veterans. In his final State of the Union address, Carter boasted about the nation's ability to "separate the war from the warrior" and provide Vietnam veterans with a proper, if deferred, homecoming.

The rhetoric of President Ronald Reagan urged a new slant on the meaning and public perception of the conflict. During the 1980 presidential campaign, he called the Vietnam War a "noble cause" and urged Americans not to submit to "feelings of guilt" about it. In 1985, President Reagan contended that America "did not lose the war" after all, arguing that the U.S. military had won

every engagement with the enemy. The media had been responsible for distorting the truth, he maintained, and the cause was not lost until the United States withdrew in 1973 and then failed to supply the South Vietnamese army. President George H.W. Bush, in his inaugural address in 1989, returned to Ford's theme, declaring that "the lesson of Vietnam is that no great nation can long afford to be sundered by a memory." President Bill Clinton affirmed that view when, during the announcement of the normalization of relations with Vietnam in 1995, he said: "Whatever divided us before let us consign to the past." President George W. Bush, however, returned to the idea that the United States had withdrawn from the war too soon.

Cinematic Interpretations and the Vietnam Syndrome

Many Americans have acquired their understanding of Vietnam from films made about the war. Cinematic representations of Vietnam, mediated through the eyes of screenwriters and directors, have mirrored and influenced the wider cultural and political memories. *The Green Berets* (1968) was John Wayne's effort to portray the honorable nature of America's role in Vietnam; this was a hard sell during the same year as the Tet Offensive, as American public opinion was turning rapidly against the war. It was not until the late 1970s that major studio productions about the war began to appear—among them such notable releases as *Coming Home* (1978), *The Deer Hunter* (1978), and *Apocalypse Now* (1979). Each of these films echoed the growing national sense that the war was a mistake. The first two focused on the treatment of veterans.

The *Rambo* series and *Red Dawn* exemplify the 1980s conservative challenge to the conventional wisdom about Vietnam. In *First Blood* (1982), the first of the Rambo movies, the lead character is a Vietnam veteran who complains that "somebody wouldn't let us win" and bristles over the lack of respect accorded to returning veterans. In the sequel, *Rambo: First Blood II* (1985), and a series of other mid-1980s movies, the heroes go back to Vietnam to rescue soldiers still held in Vietnamese prisons. *Red Dawn* (1984), depicting an invasion of America's heartland by Soviet, Cuban, and Nicaraguan forces after U.S. withdrawal from NATO and a communist takeover in Mexico, attempted to show the consequences of the left's reluctance to adopt an aggressive foreign policy after Vietnam.

The issues raised by the Vietnam movies of the 1980s corresponded with the ongoing political debate about the "Vietnam syndrome" and Reagan's foreign policy objectives. Conservative intellectuals led an assault on the Vietnam syndrome, shorthand for a collective sense of caution about America's involvement in the world. For the left, that sense of caution seems a positive legacy of the

Vietnam experience, helping avert other reckless military adventures, injecting a sense of realism into the choice of national interests, and focusing attention on the moral consequences of American foreign policies. For the right, the Vietnam syndrome fosters undue restraint on military and covert actions and impedes the pursuit of American interests in the world. During the 1980 presidential campaign, Reagan called on the nation to "rid ourselves of the Vietnam syndrome" in order for America to regain its rightful place as leader of the free world. His administration's failure to gain congressional or widespread public support for its actions in Central America suggests, however, that Reagan was unsuccessful in changing the national mood. By the end of his term, a national defense commission wrote that the loss in Vietnam "still casts a shadow over U.S. intervention anywhere."

Almost all public opinion polls since 1969 have shown that a majority of Americans believe the Vietnam War to have been a mistake. That belief, it has been suggested, has influenced the public's perception of most or all American military actions since 1975. But policymakers on the right, particularly the neoconservatives, have tried to reshape the lessons of the Vietnam War. Following the U.S. victory in the 1991 Persian Gulf War, President George H.W. Bush declared that America had "kicked the Vietnam syndrome once and for all." The caution that was a legacy of Vietnam resurfaced, however, after the collapse of the humanitarian mission to Somalia in 1993. And surprisingly, conservatives resisted President Bill Clinton's use of military action in Eastern Europe to stop ethnic cleansing in the civil wars that erupted as Yugoslavia disintegrated into independent nations.

In the run up to the U.S.-led invasion of Iraq in 2003, protestors again raised the specter of Vietnam, but a majority of Americans supported President George W. Bush's plan to invade a foreign country. The ensuing counterinsurgency and civil war in Iraq eventually turned public opinion against U.S. involvement there, and many Americans contemplated the possible parallels with the Vietnam War.

John Day Tully

See also: American Century; Carter, Jimmy; Cold War; Communists and Communism; Ford, Gerald; My Lai Massacre; Nixon, Richard; Reagan, Ronald; Revisionist History; Vietnam Veterans Against the War; Vietnam Veterans Memorial; War Powers Act; War Protesters.

Further Reading

Hellman, John. *American Myth and the Legacy of Vietnam.* New York: Columbia University Press, 1986.
Herring, George. *America's Longest War: The United States and Vietnam, 1950–1975.* 4th ed. New York: McGraw-Hill, 2001.
Martin, Andrew. *Receptions of War: Vietnam in American Culture.* Norman: University of Oklahoma Press, 1993.
McMahon, Robert. "Contested Memory: The Vietnam War and American Society, 1975–2001." *Diplomatic History* 26:2 (2002): 159–84.
Schlesinger, Arthur M., Jr. *The Bitter Heritage: Vietnam and American Democracy, 1941–1966.* Boston: Houghton Mifflin, 1967.
Summers, Harry G., Jr. *On Strategy: A Critical Analysis of the Vietnam War.* Novato, CA: Presidio, 1982.
Turner, Fred. *Echoes of Combat: The Vietnam War in American Memory.* New York: Anchor Books, 1996.

Vigilantism

In the United States, extralegal justice—or taking the law into one's own hands—has been associated with civil rights abuses such as lynching. But in the 1960s and 1970s, different vigilante activities were used to protest laws and practices that discriminated based on race, ethnicity, and gender. New forms of vigilantism that have emerged in recent years include cyber-vigilantism, in which the focus is online sexual predators, terrorists, and fraudulent activities on the Internet.

Members of the legal community view vigilantism as a social reaction to a perceived breakdown in law. Political scientists define it as violence aimed at changing the current political establishment. Psychologists tend to consider a vigilante's motive before judging whether the action is antisocial or in the interest of society. Nevertheless, several typical, shared characteristics generally define vigilantism. It is more often a group activity than an individual act, for the purpose of changing or maintaining the status quo, often through force or violence. Since the overall goal is to restore or preserve the social order rather than destroy it, vigilante organizations are not necessarily considered hate groups, gangs, or terrorists. Also, since vigilante activity typically ceases once its immediate goal is fulfilled, vigilantism is not regarded as a social movement.

A common target of vigilantes is perceived criminals. Many vigilantes seek to punish individuals they believe have broken the law but have not been brought to justice. These vigilantes believe that the criminal justice system fails to mete out appropriate punishments. This type of vigilantism is contradictory in nature because the vigilante responds to violence with violence. Crime-control vigilantes tend to favor capital punishment and oppose gun control laws, and some believe that self-defense is legally justified not only in response to direct threats to personal safety but also in response to minor trespassing on personal property.

Some vigilantes see themselves as moral crusaders. They might oppose abortion or deny civil rights for ethnic minorities or immigrants. For example, the activities of the Minuteman Movement, which has patrolled the U.S.-Mexican border to curtail the flow of illegal immigrants, was castigated by President George W. Bush as vigilantism. In 1998, New York governor George Pataki called the murder of an abortion doctor "an act of terrorism."

Vigilantism can be viewed as both constructive and destructive. It is destructive because it undercuts due process so that the targets of vigilantism are persecuted without being proven guilty in a court of law. Vigilantism is often violent. Unlike the use of force by police, which is subject to rules and regulations, vigilante violence is uncontrolled. Liberals who support a justice system that protects due process rights for the accused tend to regard vigilantism as unwarranted and destructive.

Others believe that vigilantes provide a necessary service to society. To some, vigilantes are victims of society who seek retribution for their suffering. Some view vigilantism as useful because it tries to correct societal and governmental flaws. Since the rise of television, movies, and comic books after World War II, cultural icons such as the Lone Ranger, Superman, Rambo, and Dirty Harry suggest that extralegal violence is a legitimate way to solve problems.

Political conservatives, especially those who favor harsh punishments for crime and oppose abortion and gun control, are more likely to see vigilantism as constructive. Some supporters of these causes see vigilantism as a legitimate way of addressing what the law does not currently criminalize. Some political analysts foresee an increase in vigilantism if more Americans favor personal responsibility for actions over ensuring the due process rights of those accused of crimes. While no hard data exist on the frequency of vigilantism, the increase in political polarization of citizens suggests a trend in support of vigilante activity.

Changes in public perception of crime may also increase support for vigilantism. While crime rates have decreased significantly in recent years, fear of crime among Americans has increased, with personal handgun sales rising as a result. In response to this increased fear of crime, harsher punishments for street crimes have been implemented, primarily based on demands by conservative politicians and their constituents. These harsh laws, including mandatory minimum sentences for drug offenses and "three strikes" laws, are seen as excessive by political liberals. Conservatives who support these laws may be more likely to support vigilantism that uses harsh punishments above those specified by law.

Definitions of vigilantism vary, but most scholars agree that vigilantism involves the extralegal use of force to either change or maintain the status quo. The debate regarding vigilantism is whether it is a constructive or destructive activity. Conservatives are more likely to see vigilantism as a useful way to supplement legal forms of social control, while liberals view vigilantism as a violation of the due process rights guaranteed by the U.S. Constitution. Vigilantism may become a more politically charged issue as conservative politicians continue to run on platforms that support harsh penalties for crime and the criminalization of illegal immigration and abortion.

Stephanie L. Kent and Candace Griffith

See also: Civil Rights Movement; Comic Books; Ecoterrorism; Gangs; Goetz, Bernhard; Guardian Angels; Hate Crimes; Illegal Immigrants; Lynching; Militia Movement; Operation Rescue; Philadelphia, Mississippi; Rudolph, Eric; Sex Offenders.

Further Reading

Culberson, William C. *Vigilantism: Political History of Private Power in America.* New York: Greenwood, 1990.

Hine, Kelly D. "Vigilantism Revisited: An Economic Analysis of the Law of Extra-Judicial Self-Help, or Why Can't Dick Shoot Henry for Stealing Jane's Truck?" *American University Law Review* 47 (1998): 1221–55.

Johnston, Les. "What Is Vigilantism?" *British Journal of Criminology* 36 (1996): 220–36.

Tucker, William. *Vigilante: The Backlash Against Crime in America.* New York: Stein and Day, 1985.

Voegelin, Eric

A political philosopher, Eric Voegelin specialized in the Western political and spiritual ideas that he called "the Mediterranean tradition." He contributed to the American culture wars by arguing that liberalism has links with totalitarianism. Born Eric Herman Wilhelm Voegelin on January 3, 1901, in Cologne, Germany, he studied and taught at the University of Vienna (PhD, 1922) before escaping from Nazi Austria in 1938. He became an American citizen in 1944 and held positions at Louisiana State University (1943–1958), the University of Munich (1958–1969), and the Hoover Institution (1969–1985).

Although many of Voegelin's writings, including the multivolume *Order and History* (1956–1987), are beyond the reach of general readers, conservative leaders such as William F. Buckley, Jr., succeeded in popularizing the philosopher's indictment of utopian schemes and, by extension, liberal politics. In his study of the relationship between Greek philosophy and Christianity, Voegelin concluded that Gnosticism (an early variant of Christianity) was the consequence of alienation resulting from the failed quest to find spiritual transcendence in the material world. He extended his conclusion to the modern era, suggesting that totalitarianism, or any other situation in which leaders of a state attempt to create an ideal society, is Gnostic in essence.

Conservative intellectuals, co-opting his ideas to advance their political undertakings, typically quote from chapter four of Voegelin's *The New Science of Politics* (1952), where he criticizes attempts to create heaven on earth: "The problem of an edios [form] in history . . . arises only when Christian transcendental fulfillment becomes immanentized [literalized]. Such an immanentist hypostasis of the eschaton [the fulfillment of end times], however, is a theoretical fallacy." Exploiting that reflection as a condemnation of liberalism, Buckley recast it in soundbite form: "Don't Immanentize the Eschaton!"

This Voegelin-inspired nugget was Buckley's campaign slogan in his 1965 bid to become mayor of New York, running against the Republican liberal candidate John Lindsay. Buckley, a candidate of the newly formed Conservative Party, received only 13 percent of the vote. The group Young Americans for Freedom, which Buckley helped form in 1961, also made use of the slogan. The twentieth-anniversary issue of Buckley's *National Review* credited Voegelin with helping to establish the philosophical foundations of the modern American conservative movement. Ironically, Voegelin, a rejecter of "isms," did not wish to be associated with conservatism.

Voegelin's assertion that the misappropriation of religious symbols constitutes the major error of modern times can serve as a critique against the conservative movement's embrace of the Religious Right. Christian conservatives have criticized Voegelin's writings for reflecting a negative bias against Christianity and failing to highlight its positive contributions to Western civilization.

Voegelin died on January 19, 1985, leaving political theorists with texts to ponder. It has been argued that his writings are actually radical and not conservative. Some have associated Voegelin with the political philosopher Leo Strauss, who also emigrated to America while fleeing from Nazism.

Roger Chapman

See also: American Civil Religion; Buckley, William F., Jr.; *National Review*; New Deal; Religious Right; Student Conservatives; Strauss, Leo.

Further Reading

Federici, Michael P. *Eric Voegelin: The Restoration of Order*. Wilmington, DE: ISI Books, 2002.

Jardine, Murray. "Eric Voegelin's Interpretation(s) of Modernity: A Reconstruction of the Spiritual and Political Implications of Voegelin's Therapeutic Analysis." *Review of Politics* 57 (1995): 581–605.

Voegelin, Eric. *The New Science of Politics: An Introduction*. Chicago: University of Chicago Press, 1952.

Voting Rights Act

On August 6, 1965, President Lyndon Johnson signed into law the Voting Rights Act (VRA), passed by Congress two days earlier to protect the rights of black voters. Although the Fifteenth Amendment to the U.S. Constitution, ratified in 1870, granted the right to vote without regard to "race, color, or previous condition of servitude," African Americans in the South were often denied this right, even after the passage of the Civil Rights Acts of 1957, 1960, and 1964. The VRA prohibited any voting requirements with a discriminatory purpose or effect, and gave the federal government unprecedented authority to reject any election practices that could keep minorities from voting. Since its initial passage, the VRA has been extended and amended in 1970, 1975, 1982, and 2006.

On March 7, 1965, millions of Americans watched on television as state troopers using tear gas, bullwhips, and billy clubs spurred their horses into a crowd of peaceful civil rights protestors marching on the Edmund Pettus Bridge in Selma, Alabama. The marchers had been demonstrating for black voter rights in the South. At a joint session of Congress eight days later, President Johnson adopted the refrain of the anthem of the civil rights movement, stating, "Their cause must be our cause, too. Because it's not just Negroes, but really it's all of us, who must overcome the crippling legacy of bigotry and injustice. And we shall overcome." The voting rights bill that Johnson sent to Congress on March 17 sought to reverse almost a century of opposition to the Fifteenth Amendment.

Critics of the VRA objected to the federal government's interference in the state and local election process. Further, southern whites knew that it represented the potential for a tremendous shift in political power. In Selma, for example, home to 15,000 blacks and 14,000 whites, the enfranchisement of minority voters gave African Americans new and real political opportunity. Almost immediately after being into signed into law, the VRA was challenged in federal court by several southern states. In the case of *South Carolina v. Katzenbach* (1966), the U.S. Supreme Court upheld the legislation, ruling that Congress did have the power to suspend literacy tests previously required of African-American voters, particularly since illiterate whites had never been denied the vote.

Passage of the VRA inspired creative political responses at the state level. Redistricting, for example, became a tactic used by politicians eager to control the outcome of statewide elections. Redrawn boundary lines sometimes created predominately white or African-American districts whose proponents were accused of gerrymandering. The city of Atlanta, Georgia, with a 52 percent African-American population, was split into three smaller, predominantly white districts that opponents argued gave whites an unfair number of congressional seats. When the U.S. Department of Justice intervened, the districts were redrawn yet again to give African Americans more representation. Critics have argued that the tendency to carve "minority" congressional districts results in political polarization based on race because, in the "majority" districts, the usually white elected members to Congress can safely ignore issues that are important to minority voters because they are not of equal concern to constituents.

Although Congress voted in July 2006 to reauthorize the VRA for another twenty-five years, some critics, mostly Republican, suggested that the law had outlived its usefulness. They contended that the provision requiring certain jurisdictions to seek permission from the U.S. Justice Department prior to making any change in local election laws was bureaucratic overkill. Certain critics also objected to the VRA's multilingual requirement for when there are many foreign-speaking voters, believing that ballots written in English should suffice. Despite the objections, President George W. Bush signed the extension on July 27.

In the meantime, states such as Indiana passed laws requiring voters to bring to the polls government-produced picture identification cards (e.g., a driver's license), arguing that such a measure would reduce voter fraud. Liberal critics believe that this trend goes against the spirit of the VRA, arguing that the true motive behind the requirement for ID cards is to place obstacles in the way of largely Democratic voters—minorities, the poor, and the elderly (people less likely to have a driver's license and naturally reluctant to spend money acquiring the necessary documentation). That concern was rebuffed 6–3 by the Supreme Court, which in April 2008 upheld the Indiana law.

Sara Hyde

See also: Civil Rights Movement; English as the Official Language; Great Society; Johnson, Lyndon B.

Further Reading

Epstein, David L., Richard H. Pildes, Rodolfo O. de la Garza, and Sharyn O'Halloran, eds. *The Future of the Voting Rights Act.* New York: Russell Sage Foundation, 2006.

Grofman, Bernard, and Chandler Davidson, eds. *Controversies in Minority Voting: The Voting Rights Act in Perspective.* Washington, DC: Brookings Institute, 1992.

Kotz, Nick. *Judgment Days: Lyndon Baines Johnson, Martin Luther King, Jr., and the Laws That Changed America.* Boston: Houghton Mifflin, 2005.

Waco Siege

The Waco siege of February–April 1993, a fifty-one-day standoff between federal agents and the Branch Davidians, a religious cult led by David Koresh, outside Waco, Texas, was one of the longest and largest police actions in U.S. history, involving nearly 700 local, state, and federal law enforcement personnel. The fiery end of the situation was viewed by many political conservatives, especially those of the militia movement, as the result of an unnecessary and inordinate use of government force.

The Branch Davidians, a sect of the Seventh Day Adventists dating to 1929, had come under federal scrutiny for alleged firearms violations. Taking a millennialist interpretation of the Bible, believing in a restoration of the Davidic Kingdom, Koresh and his followers lived in a secluded community they called Mount Carmel, about 15 miles (24 kilometers) east of Waco, where they awaited the fulfillment of biblical prophecy. Koresh, who became the group's leader in 1988, emphasized apocalyptic doctrines, focusing on the Book of Revelation and the meaning of its Seven Seals. Revelation predicts that a chosen one, identified as the "Lamb of God," will open the seals and initiate an apocalyptic confrontation with God. Koresh claimed to have had a vision in 1989 in which it was revealed that he was this chosen one and that God's confrontation would be with the United States.

On February 28, 1993, the U.S. Bureau of Alcohol, Tobacco, Firearms and Explosives (ATF) attempted to serve warrants to search the Davidian compound for illegally stockpiled weapons and to arrest Koresh for abusing children. As warrants were being served, however, gunfire from the compound was said to have resulted in the deaths of four ATF agents and the wounding of more than a dozen others. In addition, five Davidians were killed and four others, including Koresh, were injured in the exchange. The Federal Bureau of Investigation (FBI) took over as the lead law enforcement agency at the site. Negotiators tried to convince Koresh over the telephone to surrender peacefully while a hostage rescue team surrounded the compound with tanks.

The situation became a standoff when, on the second day of negotiations, Koresh reneged on an agreement that he come out of the compound in exchange for a one-hour airing of his teachings on the Seven Seals over the Christian Broadcasting Network. After the broadcast, minutes before he was to come out, Koresh claimed that God spoke to him and told him to wait. This brought the negotiations to an impasse and produced a conflicting view of the situation—as well as a kind of culture clash—between the cult members inside and federal agents outside. The FBI viewed it as a barricade situation, in which the Davidians were seen as perpetrators who shot and killed federal law enforcement officers, possessed hundreds of firearms and countless rounds of ammunition, and were led by a man whose mental stability was in question. The Davidians, on the other hand, saw themselves as standing on a moral and spiritual high ground against the earthly law of the U.S. government. For the Branch Davidians, surrendering meant either renouncing their beliefs or literally handing themselves over to Satan.

Twenty-two days into the standoff, federal agents began using tactics to coax the Davidians out, such as cutting the electricity and flooding the area at night with bright lights and annoying sounds to cause sleep deprivation. On the forty-fifth day, Koresh promised to come out after he had documented his understanding of the Seven Seals. By that time, however, U.S. attorney general Janet Reno had approved a plan to force the Davidians out with tear gas. During the raid on the morning of April 19, the compound caught fire. According to the FBI, thirty-five people left the compound during the standoff, nine survived the fire, five bodies were found freshly buried (from the gunfight on February 28), and seventy-five were found burned to death.

Several issues concerning the standoff were disputed in the aftermath, including the purpose of the Davidians's large inventory of weapons, which side shot first on February 28, and which side was responsible for the April 19 fire. The FBI initially denied charges that it had fired pyrotechnic grenades into the compound but later admitted that it had. The incident also generated sympathy for the Davidians among various members of the citizens' militia movement, including Timothy McVeigh, whose April 1995 truck bombing of the Alfred P. Murrah Federal Building in Oklahoma City was, in part, revenge for what happened at Waco.

Robert R. Agne

See also: Gun Control; Liddy, G. Gordon; McVeigh, Timothy; Militia Movement.

Further Reading

Docherty, Jayne Seminare. *Learning Lessons from Waco: When the Parties Bring Their Gods to the Table.* Syracuse, NY: Syracuse University Press, 2001.

Lewis, James R., ed. *From the Ashes: Making Sense of Waco.* Lanham, MD: Rowman & Littlefield, 1994.

Tabor, James D., and Eugene V. Gallagher. *Why Waco? Cults and the Battle for Religious Freedom in America.* Berkeley: University of California Press, 1995.

Wright, Stuart, ed. *Armageddon in Waco: Critical Perspectives on the Branch Davidian Conflict.* Chicago: University of Chicago Press, 1995.

Wall Street Journal, The

With an average daily paid circulation of more than 2 million, the *Wall Street Journal* is the second-widest-circulating newspaper in the United States (exceeded only by *USA Today*) and, with the *Financial Times* of London, the most influential financial daily in the English-speaking world. The New York–based paper was first published in 1889, converted from a stock and bond trade sheet called the *Customer's Afternoon Letter.* Over the course of the twentieth century, the *Journal*—published by Dow Jones & Company until December 2007, when it was acquired by Rupert Murdoch's News Corporation—emerged as one of the nation's most respected dailies, read and relied on by business leaders, government officials, and professionals. Although known for its rigidly neoconservative editorial page, the *Journal* over the years has enjoyed a sterling reputation among readers of all political stripes for its balanced and informative news and business articles, as well as long and sometimes whimsical feature pieces, all packaged in a gray and dull format without sports section, comics, or photographs.

The financial information and publishing firm Dow Jones & Company, of which the *Wall Street Journal* was the longtime flagship, was founded in 1882 by three journalists, Charles H. Dow, Edward D. Jones, and Charles M. Bergstresser. The company was purchased in 1902 by Clarence Walker Barron, who eventually left his publishing companies, including the *Journal*, to his adopted daughter, Jane Waldron Bancroft. In 2007, Australian-born media tycoon Rupert Murdoch—owner of the conservative Fox News Channel among many other holdings—acquired Dow Jones & Company for more than $5 billion (paying $60 per share for stock that had been trading for $36). Under the ownership of the Bancroft family, the *Journal* had been allowed to operate with a level of editorial independence cherished by the staff, which made the News Corporation takeover a source of concern to it. Before the deal was completed, therefore, the Bancroft family exacted an agreement from Murdoch that the *Journal*'s editorial page would retain its independence and that a wall would be maintained between the editorial and news departments. Some observers nevertheless predicted that it was only a matter of time before Murdoch would compromise the journalistic integrity of the paper, making it "more Wall Street, less journal."

The *Wall Street Journal* became a major American newspaper under the guidance of managing editor Bernard Kilgore (1942–1967), who broadened its focus from the traditional emphasis on business, stocks, and bonds to encompass domestic and international economics, politics, and society. Near the end of Kilgore's watch, the paper's circulation surpassed 1 million. Although typically conservative in its editorial pronouncements—supportive of tax cuts and supply-side economics and against welfare programs, communism, and tort attorneys—the *Journal* has at times gone against the grain of conservative thinking. In 1968, for example, the paper recommended an end to the Vietnam War. The *Journal* also supported the U.S. Supreme Court's decision in *Roe v. Wade* (1973) legalizing abortion.

Robert L. Bartley, chief of the *Journal*'s editorial page from 1972 to 2002, created controversy by putting his conservative stamp on the paper, once declaring, "Journalistically, my proudest boast is that I've run the only editorial page in the country that actually sells newspapers." Some African Americans, however, have charged that the *Journal*'s stance against major civil rights legislation, affirmative action programs, and the Martin Luther King, Jr., national holiday signifies long-running racism. The *Journal* has taken significant heat in recent years on the issue of immigration, supporting a "pathway to citizenship" for illegal aliens, which many conservatives regard as "amnesty" for lawbreakers.

Todd Scribner and Roger Chapman

The venerable *Wall Street Journal*, America's leading financial daily, is guided by unabashedly "free market and free people" principles. Here the paper reports on the takeover of its parent corporation, Dow Jones & Company, by media mogul Rupert Murdoch in 2007. *(Karen Bleier/AFP/Getty Images)*

See also: Affirmative Action; Civil Rights Movement; Immigration Policy; Media Bias; Murdoch, Rupert; Neoconservatism; *Roe v. Wade* (1973); Supply-Side Economics; Vietnam War.

588   Wallace, George

Further Reading

Dealy, Francis X. *The Power and the Money: Inside the* Wall Street Journal. Secaucus, NJ: Carol Publishing Group, 1993.

Rosenberg, Jerry Martin. *Inside the* Wall Street Journal: *The History and the Power of Dow Jones & Company and America's Most Influential Newspaper.* New York: Macmillan, 1982.

Scharff, Edward. *Worldly Power: The Making of the* Wall Street Journal. New York: A Plume Book, 1986.

"Waiting for Gigot: Blacks May Applaud the Changing of the Guard at the *Wall Street Journal.*" *Journal of Blacks in Higher Education* 36 (Summer 2002): 72–74.

Wall Street Journal Web site. www.online.wsj.com.

Wallace, George

One of the most controversial political figures of the 1960s and 1970s, George Wallace was a Democratic governor of Alabama notorious for his outspoken defiance of antisegregationist policies and court orders before settling on a more moderate conservative agenda. As a populist figure, he was one of the first politicians to resonate with white blue-collar voters, who lauded him as a southerner who stood up to federal encroachments on states' rights and rebuffed hippie hecklers in his campaign appearances. Others loathed him as a race-baiter and potential fascist. Some believe that Wallace's main role in the culture wars was as a harbinger of the conservative agenda of Richard Nixon, and later Ronald Reagan and Newt Gingrich.

Born George Corley Wallace in Clio, Alabama, on August 25, 1919, he studied law at the University of Alabama (LLB, 1942). A lawyer, part-time boxer, and flight engineer in the Pacific Theater during World War II (1942–1945), Wallace began his political career as a progressive Democrat. Returning to Alabama after the war, he served as assistant attorney general (1946–1947), representative in the state assembly (1947–1953), and judge in the third judicial district (1953–1959). His lifelong dream of becoming governor was shattered, if only temporarily, when John Patterson defeated him in the 1958 Democratic gubernatorial primary. Wallace attributed the defeat to his opponent's extreme views on race relations, which he copied in his successful 1962 bid for the governorship against "Big Jim" Folson. Wallace occupied the governor's office for a total of four terms (1963–1967, 1971–1979, and 1983–1987), while entering national politics as a presidential aspirant four times (1964, 1968, 1972, and 1976).

As governor, Wallace became a leading opponent of the civil rights movement. In his January 14, 1963, inaugural address, he famously pledged to uphold "segregation now, segregation tomorrow, and segregation forever." Another promise to oppose desegregation in schools, by standing at the schoolhouse door if necessary, led to a televised confrontation at the University of Alabama later that year in which he attempted to bar two black students from entering; he finally stepped aside at the behest of a federal attorney and the National Guard. Claiming that he was defending states' rights from federal judicial activism, Wallace was popular among white Alabamians, but two further incidents marred his reputation nationwide. In September 1963, four black girls died after white extremists bombed the Sixteenth Street Baptist Church in Birmingham; Wallace was accused of fanning the racial hatred that led to the incident. And in March 1965, demonstrators marching in support of black voting rights were violently dispersed by police as they crossed Edmund Pettus Bridge in Selma, Alabama; again, blame accrued to the state's segregationist governor.

Barred by the Alabama state constitution from running for a second term as governor in 1966 (a restriction later lifted), Wallace convinced his wife, Lurleen Burns Wallace, to run for the office, which she won. She died two years later, however, and George Wallace was reelected in his own right in 1970. After serving two more terms, and a hiatus in the early 1980s, Wallace put together an unlikely coalition of blacks and whites, recanted his segregationist past, and won a final term in 1982.

In national politics, meanwhile, Wallace had run for president in 1964 as a conservative defender of "law and order" and family values, and an opponent of welfare, communism, and the youth counterculture. He avoided the overtly racist rhetoric he had used as governor, but critics asserted that his attacks against "welfare queens" and inner-city riots were thinly veiled racial slurs. Still, Wallace's skill and wit on the campaign trail attracted significant support in his campaigns for president. In 1964, he made a surprisingly strong showing in the Wisconsin primary, but lost the Democratic nomination to Lyndon Johnson. Running as a third-party candidate in 1968, representing the American Independent Party, he came close to throwing the election to the House of Representatives when he carried five southern states despite vice-presidential running mate Curtis LeMay's unpopular stance on the use of nuclear weapons. Running as a Democrat again in 1972, he won the Florida primary but was felled in an assassination attempt while campaigning that May, leaving him partially paralyzed for life.

He became a born-again Christian in the late 1970s, and his racial views mellowed with age. In private encounters, he apologized to civil rights leaders Rosa Parks, John Lewis, Coretta Scott King, and Ralph Abernathy for his segregationist policies and rhetoric. Wallace died in Montgomery on September 13, 1998.

Philippe R. Girard

See also: Civil Rights Movement; Counterculture; Democratic Party; Gingrich, Newt; Johnson, Lyndon B.; LeMay, Curtis; McGovern, George; Parks, Rosa; Race; Reagan, Ronald; Republican Party.

Further Reading

Carter, Dan T. *The Politics of Rage: George Wallace, the Origins of the New Conservatism, and the Transformation of American Politics.* New York: Simon & Schuster, 1995.

Lesher, Stephen. *George Wallace: American Populist.* Reading, MA: Addison-Wesley, 1994.

Rohler, Lloyd. *George Wallace: Conservative Populist.* Westport, CT: Praeger, 2004.

Wallace, George C. *Stand Up for America.* Garden City, NY: Doubleday, 1976.

Wallis, Jim

Jim Wallis, founder of *Sojourners* magazine, is an evangelical pastor-activist whose work is devoted to applying biblical principles to causes of poverty and social justice. He is known for his prophetic style in addressing social problems.

Wallis was born into an evangelical family, affiliated with the Plymouth Brethren, on June 4, 1948, near Detroit, Michigan. Exposed to the 1960s counterculture during his youth, he quit the Boy Scouts, grew his hair long, and was profoundly unsettled by the Detroit race riots in 1967. He attended the University of Michigan (BS, 1970), where he joined the Students for a Democratic Society (SDS) and participated in the antiwar and civil rights movements. Sensing that evangelicalism was ignoring real-life concerns, Wallis turned to the Sermon on the Mount for his guide.

At Trinity Evangelical Divinity School in Illinois (1970–1972), he and other students formed a Christian community emphasizing radical discipleship and started the magazine *Post-American*, later renamed *Sojourners*. The group, called the Sojourners Community, eventually moved to the nation's capital to address injustice at local and national levels. Sojourners has devoted itself to concerns of the urban poor such as housing, food, tutoring children, and gentrification.

In 1995, Wallis helped form a national "Call to Renewal," uniting faith-based communities and leaders across the theological spectrum to overcome poverty. Based in evangelical Protestantism but with political commitments at the progressive end of the political spectrum, he has been consistently critical of the politics of the Religious Right. At the same time, he insists that Democrats must incorporate a concern for moral values. His double-edged sword approach to political criticism is evident in his best-selling book *God's Politics: Why the Right Gets It Wrong and the Left Doesn't Get It* (2004). Wallis's activism has aroused opposition in fundamentalist and conservative Christian circles; Jerry Falwell, for example, likened him to Hitler.

Sojourners in 2006 launched "The Covenant for a New America" campaign to address social responsibility for such recurring problems as the breakdown of the family, persistent poverty in the United States, and global poverty. Wallis has advocated on behalf of these causes through a nationwide lecture circuit in a town-meeting style to stimulate discussion about issues of faith and social justice. Many of his social concerns are shared by the evangelists Tony Campolo, Ron Sider, and Rick Warren.

Susan Pearce

See also: Boy Scouts of America; Campolo, Anthony "Tony"; Civil Rights Movement; Counterculture; Evangelicalism; Falwell, Jerry; Fundamentalism, Religious; Religious Right; Sider, Ron; Students for a Democratic Society; Vietnam War; Warren, Rick.

Further Reading

Mangu-Ward, K. "God's Democrat." *Weekly Standard*, April 11, 2005.

Wallis, Jim. *God's Politics: Why the Right Gets It Wrong and the Left Doesn't Get It.* New York: HarperCollins, 2004.

———. *Revive Us Again: A Sojourner's Story.* Nashville, TN: Abingdon, 1983.

———. *The Soul of Politics: A Practical and Prophetic Vision for Change.* New York: New Press, 1994.

———. *Who Speaks for God? An Alternative to the Religious Right—A New Politics of Compassion, Community, and Civility.* New York: Delacorte, 1996.

Wal-Mart

A retailer that sells consumer goods and groceries at low prices, Wal-Mart Stores, Inc., in 2008 operated more than 4,000 stores in fifty states with 1.4 million employees (while also maintaining 3,000 overseas stores with 620,000 employees), making it the world's largest company and private-sector employer. Known for its large, box-shaped stores—including Wal-Mart supercenters and discount stores, Neighborhood Markets, and Sam's Club warehouses—the company has for years been a source of controversy in the American culture wars.

Although designated the "most admired company" by *Fortune* magazine (2003 and 2004), hailed by investors for its eleven 100 percent stock splits (1971–1999), mentioned approvingly in Gretchen Wilson's debut hit single "Redneck Woman" (2004; with its lines, "Victoria's Secret, well their stuff's real nice / But I can buy the same damn thing on a Wal-Mart shelf half price"), and praised by conservative think tanks for saving the average American family $2,500 annually (2007), Wal-Mart has also been a subject of vilification. The company has been spoofed as "Stuff Mart" in the VeggieTales animation film *Madame Blueberry* (1998), portrayed as a mistrusting and ungenerous employer in Barbara Ehrenreich's book *Nickel and Dimed* (2001), criticized for lacking social responsibility in Robert Greenwald's "mockumentary" film *Wal-Mart: The High Cost of Low Price* (2005), and lampooned as an Orwellian nightmare in the musical satire *Walmartopia* (2007).

In the mid-2000s, the company began an effort to soften its public image by adding three women and two blacks to its board of directors; announcing improved health benefits for its employees; calling for an increase in the federal minimum wage; and promising major environmental initiatives, some of which provoked social conservatives to criticize Wal-Mart for capitulating to "political correctness."

Founded in 1962 by Sam Walton and based in Bentonville, Arkansas, Wal-Mart is a company operating with "red state" values, having originated in the South and originally restricting store openings to small towns with population sizes of 5,000 or less. From the onset, women employees were paid less than men and not considered for management positions because it was assumed that they were farm wives, not "bread winners" or careerists. The anti-union Walton designated his employees "associates" to promote management and store workers as a team. As he bought in bulk from producers (not wholesalers), he passed on the discount to consumers, realizing that it would lead to higher sales volume and greater profitability. Also, in terms of stocking its shelves, the company has relied on "family values" as a guide, following red-state sensibilities (media materials containing nudity and any recorded music with parental warning labels are banned; as was the "morning after" or Plan B contraceptive pill until courts overruled).

Soon after Walton retired as chief executive officer in 1988—he was succeeded by David Glass (1988–2000), H. Lee Scott, Jr. (2000–2009), and Michael T. Duke (2009–)—the company rose to higher levels, becoming the nation's number one retailer in 1990 and opening its first overseas store in Mexico City the following year. By 1995, Wal-Mart was present in all fifty states, operating 1,200 stores. In the 2000s, as Wal-Mart expanded in major urban centers of the Northeast, Upper Midwest, and West Coast, criticism of the company ramped up. Fostering the negative image of Wal-Mart has been the United Food and Commercial Workers Union, which in 2005 launched the Wake-Up Wal-Mart campaign. In 2000, the meat cutters at a Wal-Mart store in Jacksonville, Texas, had actually voted to join this union, but soon afterwards Wal-Mart headquarters announced that it no longer needed butchers since it would start buying prepackaged "case-ready" meat from wholesalers. (On the overseas side, Wal-Mart in 2005 closed a profitable store in Quebec, Canada, after employees voted to unionize, but in 2006 it reluctantly agreed to accept unionization of its stores in China.)

The debate concerning Wal-Mart is largely about American-style capitalism in the era of globalization and to what degree social responsibility is to be connected with it. Critics fault Wal-Mart for (1) price-squeezing its 56,000 suppliers and accelerating outsourcing for cheaper labor costs (sometimes using sweatshops) at the expense of American jobs (and consequently providing China an easy in-road to the U.S. market); (2) providing inadequate pay and benefits to its workers (wages often near the federal poverty level), encouraging them to rely on government social services (in 2008, only 52 percent of Wal-Mart employees were on company-sponsored health insurance), discriminating against female and minority employees (in 2001, a nationwide class-action lawsuit pertaining to gender discrimination was filed against Wal-Mart on behalf of 1.6 million past and present female employees), and sometimes cheating workers of pay that is due (in 2008, the company agreed to an out-of-court settlement of between $352 million and $640 million for violating wage and labor laws in forty-two states); (3) disrupting the social fabric of local communities by driving "mom-and-pop" stores out of business while exacting enormous tax breaks (about $4 million per site, according to a 2004 estimate); and (4) monopolizing retailing to the point that consumer choices are limited (dubbed "Wal-Martization") while policing American culture by refusing to carry items it finds objectionable.

Critics such as Wal-Mart Watch suggest that the consumer savings the company provides are undermined by the burden that is placed on taxpayers. From this perspective, Wal-Mart is not paying its fair share since it relies on government—federal, state, and local—to subsidize its operation through tax abatements (which are seldom granted to small businesses) and social services provided to Wal-Mart employees who are not receiving a living wage. According to *Everyday Low Wages: The Hidden Price We All Pay for Wal-Mart*, a February 2004 report prepared by the Democratic staff of the House Education and Workforce Committee, Wal-Mart employees that year possibly cost the federal government $2.5 billion in social services including Medicaid, food stamps, housing subsidies, and free school lunches. Defenders of Wal-Mart dispute the report, calling it partisan research, and emphasize the $4 billion the company paid in taxes that year. No matter, they say, Wal-Mart is not obligated to pay higher wages and benefits for unskilled labor. Some state governments, however, think Wal-Mart should be forced to pay for social services utilized by its employees if it refuses to upgrade benefits. In 2006, for example, Maryland, specifically targeting Wal-Mart, passed a law requiring any company with 10,000 or more employees to devote 8 percent of its payroll toward health insurance or else reimburse the state for medical services rendered; the measure was later overturned for violating federal law.

Roger Chapman

See also: Censorship; China; Environmental Movement; Family Values; Globalization; Health Care; Illegal Immigrants; Labor Unions; Red and Blue States; Wealth Gap.

Further Reading

Bianco, Anthony. *The Bully of Bentonville: How the Cost of Wal-Mart's Everyday Low Prices Is Hurting America.* New York: Thomas Dunne Books / St. Martin's Press, 2006.

Head, Simon. "Inside the Leviathan." *New York Review of Books*, December 16, 2004.

Vedder, Richard K., and Wendell Cox. *The Wal-Mart Revolution: How Big-Box Stores Benefit Consumers, Workers, and the Economy.* Washington, DC: AEI Press, 2006.

Wake-Up Wal-Mart Web site. www.wakeupwalmart.com.

Wal-Mart Stores, Inc., Web site. www.walmartstores.com.

Walt Disney Company

Synonymous with the best and worst of American culture, depending on who is being asked, the Walt Disney Company—originally called Walt Disney Productions—continues to flourish long after the death of its namesake in 1966. Launched in 1923 as a producer of silent cartoons, the company has gone on to produce and market motion pictures, television programs, theme parks, music, books, comics, and character merchandise under one internationally renowned brand name. Those businesses, combined with its ownership of the American Broadcasting Company (ABC), cable networks, film studios, sports franchises, and other leading brands and companies, have made Disney a leading "multimedia corporation" of the twenty-first century. As adored as its movies and theme parks remain for millions of consumers worldwide, however, the company has not escaped ridicule for its commercialism, pop-culture romanticism, and unfair labor practices. Beginning in 1996, Disney was boycotted for more than eight years by the conservative Southern Baptist Convention because of its support of gay rights and for permitting "Gay Days" at Disney World.

The first major breakthrough for the California-based company came in 1928 with the appearance of a scrappy little mouse named Mickey in the cartoon animation *Steamboat Willie.* Over the next decade, Mickey Mouse starred in almost a hundred films, ensuring economic stability for the company despite the Great Depression. Further success came with Disney's first full-length animated film, *Snow White and the Seven Dwarfs* (1937), which became the highest-grossing movie of its time and won a special Academy Award for "screen innovation." Profits from the film were used to build Disney Studios in Burbank, California.

One of the first major motion picture producers to go into television, Disney launched the series *Disneyland* on ABC in October 1954. An entertaining mix of cartoons and live-action features, the show unabashedly promoted upcoming Disney films and the new theme park Disneyland, which opened in 1955 in Anaheim, California. Family-oriented Disney films included *20,000 Leagues Under the Sea* (1954), *Old Yeller* (1957), *Toby Tyler* (1960), *The Absent-Minded Professor* (1961), *Son of Flubber* (1963), and *That Darn Cat!* (1965).

Disney and ABC tapped into the growing Baby Boom market by premiering the *Mickey Mouse Club,* an hour-long children's afternoon program that ran five days a week from 1955 to 1959. Not only did the *Club* help guarantee Mickey Mouse's place in popular culture, but it also proved to be a bonanza for advertisers, who used Disney characters to sell a myriad of kid-friendly products. Jack Gould, TV critic for the *New York Times*, groused that he had never seen "a children's program—or an adult's for that matter—that was quite as commercial as Mr. Disney's."

Almost everything associated with the Disney name became an instant success. In 1966 alone, some 240 million people watched a Disney movie, 100 million a week watched a Disney television show, 80 million read a Disney book, 50 million listened to Disney records, and 7 million visited Disneyland. The *New York Times* eulogized Walt Disney as "probably the only man to have been praised by both the American Legion and the Soviet Union." Indeed, one of the Soviet premier Nikita Khrushchev's disappointments about his 1959 visit to the United States was his inability to visit Disneyland due to security concerns.

Despite this popularity—or perhaps because of it—the company has consistently attracted critical scrutiny. In a 1965 letter to the *Los Angeles Times,* UCLA librarian and faculty member Frances Clarke Sayers famously accused Disney of debasing the "traditional literature of childhood." "Every story is sacrificed to the 'gimmick' . . . of animation," she argued, and called Disney's "cliché-ridden" books "laughable." Since then, the terms "Disneyfication" and "Disneyization" have been used as pejoratives to describe places and concepts that are overly simplified, sanitized, or blatantly romanticized. Disney theme parks, including Disney World in Orlando, Florida (which opened in 1971), have been especially maligned for presenting an unrealistically homogenized world in which everyone is happy. Disney World's EPCOT, the Experimental Prototype Community of Tomorrow, which opened in 1982, has been criticized for its uncritical promotion of "futuristic technologies," its excessively advertised corporate sponsorship of particular pavilions, and its sugar-coated "American Adventure" history lesson, which presents a national narrative void of controversy.

For many, "The Happiest Place on Earth" is actually a ruthless corporation that exploits its workers and goes to "greedy" lengths to enforce its copyright protections. In 1993, as Disney faced criticism for underpaying its lower-level workers and taking advantage of sweatshops in developing countries, corporate head Michael Eisner was the highest-paid CEO in the United States, receiving a $203 million salary-and-benefits package. Over the years, various nonprofits have called for a boycott of Disney products. In 2001, the company held the dubious distinction of being named "Sweatshop Retailer of the Year" by the Canadian Labour Congress. The National Labor Committee in New York, which tracks American corporate use of sweatshop labor, once called Disney one of the "greediest sweatshop abusers." Also generating negative publicity has been the company's aggressive approach in going after violators of Disney copyright. In 1989, for example, it threatened legal action against three day-care providers in Florida for having unauthorized murals with Disney characters. In 1997, the company demanded remuneration from the U.S. Postal Service for plans to print commemorative postage stamps with Disney characters; the stamps were never issued.

Christian groups, such as the American Family Association and the Catholic League for Religious and Civil Rights, have also attacked Disney for abandoning its "wholesome" image by releasing violent and controversial films, such as *Pulp Fiction* (1994) and *Priest* (1995), through its subsidiary production company Miramax. Controversy also centered on some the content of certain animated films—including *Who Framed Roger Rabbit?* (1988), in which Jessica Rabbit's dress blows up, revealing that she is not wearing underwear, and *Lion King* (1994), with its alleged homosexual characters and a dust cloud that spells "SEX." In 1996, the national convention of Southern Baptists voted to boycott all Disney theme parks and stores after the company agreed to offer health care coverage to the partners of gay employees and because of its unofficial hosting of "Gay Days" (every first Saturday in June since 1991) at Disney World. In 1997, when the company's TV network ballyhooed Ellen DeGeneres's coming out as a lesbian on the sitcom *Ellen*, the ban was expanded to include all Disney publications, movies, and radio and television shows. The boycott, which lasted until 2005, had no apparent impact on Disney, however, as the popularity of its products continued to soar.

Cindy Mediavilla

See also: Blackface; Family Values; Gay Capital; Labor Unions; Outing; Southern Baptist Convention; Wildmon, Donald.

Further Reading

Gabler, Neal. *Walt Disney: The Triumph of the American Imagination.* New York: Alfred A. Knopf, 2006.

Griffin, Sean. "Curiouser and Curiouser: Gay Days at Disney Theme Parks." *Rethinking Disney: Private Control, Public Dimensions,* ed. Mike Budd and Max H. Kirsch, 125–50. Middletown, CT: Wesleyan University Press, 2005.

Schweizer, Peter, and Rochelle Schweizer. *Disney: The Mouse Betrayed.* Washington, DC: Regnery, 1998.

Smoodin, Eric, ed. *Disney Discourse: Producing the Magic Kingdom.* New York: Routledge, 1994.

War on Drugs

As a much-debated culture wars issue, the U.S. war on drugs has engendered two opposing positions: generally speaking, conservatives emphasize law enforcement, while liberals emphasize rehabilitation treatment and education. For the first group, the drug problem is a criminal issue that necessitates a reduction in the supply of all illegal substances—tracking down and arresting distributors; seizing their supplies; and carrying out military interdiction wherever necessary, including foreign countries, to eliminate the source of drugs. For the second group, the drug problem is primarily a public health issue that is best solved by curbing the demand for drugs. Beyond issues of emphasis and ideology, the two sides have also debated vigorously over the very success or failure of the war on drugs: while one side points to the decline in drug abuse by young people, the other notes that Americans continued to lead the world in consumption of marijuana and cocaine in 2008.

Although federal regulation of illicit drugs dates to the early 1900s, when the Harrison Narcotics Act (1914) limited the manufacture, importation, and distribution of opiates and cocaine to medical and scientific uses, the modern war on drugs began during the administration of President Richard Nixon. A disdainer of the counterculture movement, in particular its permissiveness and irreverence toward authority, Nixon singled out drugs as "a serious national threat" during a speech to Congress on July 14, 1969. The following year, Congress passed the Comprehensive Drug Abuse Prevention and Control Act, consolidating the nation's drug laws and establishing five categories of illegal substances and the penalties for their distribution. On June 17, 1971, declaring illicit substances "public enemy No. 1," Nixon called for a "war on drugs." In 1973, he established by executive order the Drug Enforcement Administration (DEA) to head the federal effort in "an all-out global war on the drug menace."

During the 1980s, as cocaine use became more prevalent in American society, Congress passed the Comprehensive Crime Control Act (1984), establishing mandatory prison sentences for drug offenders and broadening the government's ability to seize the assets of drug dealers. The provision for stiffer federal penalties, following a trend introduced by New York in the 1970s, led to a lengthening of the average drug-related prison sentence from 48.1 months in 1980 to 84 months in 1990. Between 1985 and 1992, federal law enforcement agencies hauled in billions of dollars from seized assets, but not without complaints about violations of due process as agents confiscated money and vehicles often based on circumstantial evidence.

Following the fatal cocaine overdose of University of Maryland basketball star Len Bias in 1986, Congress, at the urging of House Speaker Thomas "Tip" O'Neill,

Jr. (D-MA), passed the Anti-Drug Abuse Act. Controversially, this new law brought race politics into the mix by making a legal distinction between crack cocaine and powder cocaine, establishing stiffer penalties for possession of the former, which was especially prominent among poor urban blacks. (Following years of acrimonious debate, federal mandatory sentencing guidelines for crack were reduced in 2007.)

The decade of the 1980s marked the beginning of a major effort to warn schoolchildren of the harm of drugs. In 1983, the Los Angeles Police Department began the D.A.R.E. (Drug Abuse Resistance Education) pilot program, aimed at fifth and sixth graders, to teach against substance abuse. The program would later expand to other grade levels and be adopted nationally as well as overseas. In 1984, First Lady Nancy Reagan introduced the slogan "Just Say No" as a public campaign to combat the peer pressure often associated with drug usage. Five years later, with heroin emerging as the new problem drug, President George H.W. Bush bolstered efforts at drug deterrence by creating the Office of National Drug Control Policy and appointing William J. Bennett as the nation's first "drug czar."

Skeptics over the years have characterized the various antidrug programs as alarmist and ineffectual. Others cite a University of Michigan survey titled Monitoring the Future, which indicated that while 54.2 percent of high school seniors used illicit drugs in 1979, the figure dropped to 38.5 percent in 1988 and 32.5 percent in 1990, rose to 42.4 percent in 1997, and then declined to 36 percent in 2007—all said to be the result of the war on drugs.

Some have argued that the war on drugs has been an inordinate economic burden. According to the *New York Times*, the federal government in 2007 spent $1.4 billion on foreign antidrug assistance, including aerial-spray eradication of coca crops in the Andes; $7 billion on drug enforcement overseas and at home; and $5 billion on education and treatment to curb American drug use. Although the annual budget of the DEA increased from less than $75 million in 1973 to $2.4 billion in 2008, and its manpower expanded from 1,470 special agents to 5,235 during that same period, cocaine, heroin, and other illicit substances continued to be smuggled into the country. (Many drugs also originate in the United States, including marijuana, PCP, mescaline, ecstasy, methamphetamine, and various prescription painkillers.) Meanwhile, the number of drug-related federal incarcerations increased from 40,000 in 1980 to nearly 500,000 in 2008. In the period from 1985 to 2000, nonviolent drug offenses accounted for 65 percent of the rise in the federal prison population. In 2008, federal and state governments spent nearly $55 billion keeping 2.3 million drug offenders behind bars. New York that year spent $500 million housing its drug-related convicts.

Staunch critics of the war on drugs regard it as a failure on par with Prohibition and recommend that marijuana, the most commonly used illicit drug, be decriminalized or legalized. According to the National Household Survey on Drug Use and Health, 20.4 million Americans (8.3 percent of the population) engaged in illegal drug use in 2006. Of those, 14.8 million people (representing 6 percent of the population) used marijuana, which accounted for nearly 44 percent of the total 1.8 million drug arrests. Since marijuana is officially considered a "gateway drug" that leads to the abuse of more dangerous substances—and since it is increasing in potency (between 1999 and 2006 the plant's active ingredient, THC or tetrahydrocannabinol, reportedly doubled from 4.6 percent to 8.8 percent)—calls for its legalization are met with sharp rejoinders.

Roger Chapman

See also: Bennett, William J.; Counterculture; Drug Testing; Hoffman, Abbie; Leary, Timothy; Medical Marijuana; Nixon, Richard; Prison Reform; Reagan, Ronald; Zero Tolerance.

Further Reading

Benavie, Arthur. *Drugs: America's Holy War.* New York: Haworth Press, 2006.

Bennett, William J., John J. Dilulio, and John P. Walters. *Body Count—and How to Win America's War Against Crime and Drugs.* New York: Simon & Schuster, 1996.

Jonnes, Jill. *Hep-Cats, Narcs, and Pipe Dreams: A History of America's Romance with Illegal Drugs.* New York: Scribner, 1996.

Miller, Joel. *Bad Trip: How the War Against Drugs Is Destroying America.* Nashville, TN: WND Books, 2004.

Provine, Doris Marie. *Unequal Under Law: Race in the War on Drugs.* Chicago: University of Chicago Press, 2007.

War on Poverty

The War on Poverty, an effort by President Lyndon Johnson to reverse what he regarded as a vicious cycle in American life, was part of the Great Society domestic agenda. In his first State of the Union address on January 8, 1964, Johnson announced, "This administration today, here and now, declares unconditional war on poverty in America." The war, he explained, would be fought "in city slums and small towns, in sharecropper shacks and in migrant labor camps, on Indian reservations, among whites as well as Negroes, among the young as well as the old, in the boom towns and in the depressed areas." At the time, an estimated one out of five American families—or nearly 35 million residents—was living in poverty.

In March 1964, the White House sent to Congress the Economic Opportunity Act, a $970 million measure,

President Lyndon Johnson beams with pride after signing the Economic Opportunity Act of 1964, a centerpiece of his War on Poverty and Great Society. The expansion of federal social programs in the 1960s gave way to a major ideological shift by the 1980s. *(Arnold Sachs/Consolidated News Pictures/ Getty Images)*

representing 1 percent of the total federal budget. Republican opponents of the bill advised southern Democrats that the antipoverty program was primarily a civil rights package tailored for blacks, hoping the issue of race would undermine Dixiecrat support. But Senator Robert F. Kennedy denied that blacks were the principal recipients, arguing, "After all, Negroes comprise only 20 percent of the poor in this country." The measure eventually passed.

In many respects, the War on Poverty was politically conservative in orientation. The program addressed poverty as the consequence of too many individuals without adequate job skills and/or proper work habits. Thus, the newly created Office of Economic Opportunity aimed to increase self-reliance by having local "community action" organizations train poor people. A more liberal program would have guaranteed citizens an annual income, strengthened the rights of labor unions, penalized businesses for shifting factories to regions of cheap labor, and addressed the problem of corporate downsizing due to automation. In fact, leftists generally regarded the War on Poverty as essentially an effort to stifle social unrest.

Statistics show that between 1965 and 1969, the official poverty rate in the United States dropped from 17.3 percent of the population to 12.1. It is estimated that only 10 percent of that reduction was due to rising employment and the overall improvement of the economy. On the other hand, the "manpower training" aspect of the program did not seem to help because some people were displaced from jobs as others were lifted to gainful employment. The financial costs of the Vietnam War ultimately undermined the War on Poverty, but many of the programs associated with it continued after Johnson left office.

In a diary entry when he was president, Ronald Reagan expressed his intention to undo Johnson's Great Society (rather than the New Deal). "LBJ's war on poverty," Reagan wrote, "led us to our present mess." Another conservative Republican icon, Barry Goldwater, likewise stated in a 1986 interview, "A lot of our present problems stem from what Lyndon Johnson had passed by the Congress." Reagan's remedy was to cut back on government social programs and allow supply-side economics, activated by tax cuts for the wealthy, to stimulate business growth and create jobs. According to Reagan conservatives, the War on Poverty expanded the welfare rolls, institutionalized poverty, and reinforced the "social pathology" of the ghetto.

Roger Chapman

See also: Compassionate Conservatism; Ehrenreich, Barbara; Goldwater, Barry; Great Society; Harrington, Michael; Johnson, Lyndon B.; Migrant Labor; New Deal; Reagan, Ronald; Supply-Side Economics; Tax Reform; Welfare Reform.

Further Reading

Collins, Sheila. *Let Them Eat Ketchup! The Politics of Poverty and Inequality.* New York: Monthly Review Press, 1996.

Gilder, George. *Wealth and Poverty.* New York: Basic Books, 1981.

Unger, Irwin. *The Best of Intentions: The Triumph and Failure of the Great Society Under Kennedy, Johnson and Nixon.* New York: Doubleday, 1996.

Witkin, Gordon. "Great Society: How Great Has It Been?" *U.S. News & World Report,* July 2, 1984.

War Powers Act

Introduced by Senator Jacob K. Javits (R-NY) after the 1970 U.S. invasion of Cambodia, the War Powers Act (or Resolution) of 1973 was an attempt by Congress to limit presidential war-making powers and to ensure greater congressional control of the nation's armed forces. In a larger context, the act represented a desire on the part of legislators to recoup some of its authority over the military that had been lost to the executive branch since the start of World War II in 1941. As scholars contend, the act was not just a reaction to the Vietnam War, but the fruition of an evolutionary debate on the war powers of Congress and the president that had been going on for decades.

The War Powers Act was passed over President Richard Nixon's veto on November 7, 1973, with the House of Representatives and the Senate voting 284–135 and 75–18, respectively. The law requires the president to consult Congress before military forces are sent into combat abroad or to areas where hostilities are likely. It also requires the president to report in writing forty-eight hours after troops are deployed. Under the act, the president must end the use of military force within sixty days, and for another thirty days beyond that if the president certifies to Congress in writing that the safety of the force so requires. Unless Congress authorizes a continuation of the deployment through a declaration of war, a concurrent resolution, or appropriate legislation, it cannot be continued beyond ninety days.

Nixon believed that the law could potentially harm the nation in times of crisis. He argued further that it granted Congress authority over troop deployments in violation of Article II of the Constitution, which explicitly grants such powers to the executive. Proponents of the measure regarded it as a check on the power of the president to commit the country to military action by exercising the constitutional authority of Congress to declare war under Article I.

In April 1975, President Gerald Ford became the first commander in chief to adhere to the act, submitting four reports to Congress that announced the use of armed forces to evacuate refugees and U.S. nationals from Cambodia and Vietnam. Again on May 15, 1975, President Ford reported to Congress that he ordered U.S. forces to rescue the crew of the ship *Mayagüez*, which had been seized by Cambodian navy patrol boats. All told, presidents have submitted approximately 120 such reports to Congress under the legislation.

Despite its flaws and controversies, the War Powers Act has not been amended since its passage. The constitutionality of the law, however, has been debated vigorously. Arguments range from the claim that it violates the separation of powers to the claim that a congressional declaration of war applies only to total war and not a military police action. Nevertheless, in every instance since passage of the act, presidents have been granted their requests for authorization to use force consistent with the provisions of the resolution without a formal declaration of war.

Michael A. Vieira

See also: Ford, Gerald; Nixon, Richard; Vietnam War.

Further Reading

Bobbitt, Philip. "War Powers: An Essay on John Hart Ely's *War and Responsibility: Constitutional Lessons of Vietnam and Its Aftermath.*" *Michigan Law Quarterly* 92:6 (May 1994): 1364–400.

Fisher, Louis. *Presidential War Powers.* Lawrence: University of Kansas, 1995.

Stern, Gary M., and Martin Halperin, eds. *The U.S. Constitution and the Power to Go to War: Historical and Current Perspectives.* Westport, CT: Greenwood Press, 1994.

War Protesters

In the aftermath of World War II, as the United States sought a return to normal life, the Cold War and nuclear arms race fractured the peace and created a growing fissure in American society. War protesters emerged to oppose the growing strategic reliance on atomic weaponry and then to oppose the Vietnam War (1964–1975). Between June 1963 and May 1968, a total of 104 antiwar demonstrations were held across the United States, involving 680,000 participants and 3,258 arrests. Later came protests against the Gulf War (1990–1991) and the Iraq War (2003–). Throughout the postwar era, the American peace movement itself has often been motley, with participants ranging from pacifists who oppose war in general to activists who simply oppose a particular war. In addition, solidarity has been strained when other "social justice" issues—such as civil rights, feminism, globalization, environmentalism, and animal rights—have been incorporated into the protest.

At the same time, to protest war while troops are deployed in combat is viewed by many as unpatriotic and unconscionable. On occasion, war protesters have been accused of bringing aid and comfort to the enemy—as in the actress Jane Fonda's July 1972 visit to North Vietnam, during which she met with North Vietcong officials and sang an antiwar song while posing for pictures in front of an anti-aircraft gun. War protesters insist that dissent is a privilege and an expression of democracy, and claim that they truly care for the soldiers because they seek their quick and safe return. Nevertheless, "Support the Troops" bumper stickers are widely understood as political statements against those who would voice antiwar sentiments.

Radioactive Fallout and the Rise of the New Left

The American antinuclear movement was spurred in the 1950s by the research of Washington University biologist Barry Commoner, who documented the ecological consequences of radioactive fallout from above-ground nuclear testing. In 1957, Norman Cousins (editor of the *Saturday Review*), A.J. Muste (formerly of the American Workers Party), and Benjamin Spock (the popular pediatrician and author) founded the Committee for a Sane Nuclear Policy (SANE) in opposition to atomic testing. SANE is credited with encouraging adoption of the Limited Test Ban Treaty in 1963 and went on to play an active role in the anti–Vietnam War effort. During the 1980s, SANE began its Nuclear Weapons Freeze Campaign, seeking to pressure the United States and the Soviet Union to stop producing and upgrading atomic weapons. SANE opposed the Gulf War in the early 1990s and changed its name to Peace Action in 1993.

Old Left groups such the War Resisters League

(WRL), founded in 1923, were the first to mobilize against the Vietnam War. In New York City on May 16, 1964, the WRL sponsored an antiwar demonstration involving a dozen young men who burned their draft cards. The major thrust of the Vietnam-era antiwar movement, however, was the rise of the New Left, specifically SDS (Students for a Democratic Society), founded by Tom Hayden in 1962; and the Yippies (Youth International Party), founded by David Dellinger and Jerry Rubin in 1967. The latter group was largely responsible for coordinating the National Mobilization to End the War in Vietnam (MOBE) and its massive three-day protest in Washington, D.C., in October 1967. Billed as "Stop the Draft Week," the event involved the burning of draft cards outside the U.S. Justice Department and a march from the steps of the Lincoln Memorial to the front of the Pentagon. This protest marked a militant, if peaceful, turn in the 1960s peace movement, with a stated purpose to "Confront the War Makers." According to various estimates, the protesters numbered between 70,000 and 200,000. In front of photographers who made the image famous, the protesters placed flowers in the barrels of the rifles held by soldiers guarding the complex. Signs bearing the face of President Lyndon B. Johnson read: "WAR CRIMINAL." More than 680 participants were arrested, including novelist Norman Mailer, who went on to write *Armies of the Night* (1968), a Pulitzer Prize–winning account of the demonstration.

"Rage" and Counterculture

In August 1968, Yippie and SDS leaders organized a major demonstration in Chicago in conjunction with the Democratic National Convention. Richard Daley, the Democratic mayor of Chicago, was also against the war but assured those attending the convention: "As long as I am mayor of this city, there's going to be law and order in Chicago." Approximately 6,000 National Guardsmen were mobilized, and there was violence in the street when the protesters violated the 11:00 P.M. curfew or ventured where they did not have a permit to demonstrate. At one point, a riotous confrontation outside the convention hall was captured by television news cameramen as municipal police clubbed protesters in the head and dragged them into paddy wagons. There were a total of 668 arrests during the week of protests. The following year, organizers of the demonstration, known as the Chicago Eight (later Chicago Seven), were put on trial for conspiracy and inciting riots. While the court trial was taking place, the Weathermen, a splinter of the SDS, launched the "Days of Rage" street protest in Chicago (October 8–11, 1969). "Bring the War Home" was their slogan as they resorted to violence and vandalism. Meanwhile, FBI director J. Edgar Hoover initiated a secret counterintelligence program called COINTELPRO to disrupt the Weathermen and other protest groups.

The counterculture movement in opposition to the Vietnam War and the draft was fueled as well by the songs of some of the most popular musicians of the day, from Bob Dylan's "Blowin' in the Wind" (1963), The Byrds' "Turn! Turn! Turn!" (1965), and Pete Seeger's "Knee Deep in the Big Muddy" (1967) to Arlo Guthrie's "Alice's Restaurant Massacree" (1967), The Doors' "Unknown Soldier" (1968), and Glen Campbell's "Galveston" (1969). A highlight at the Woodstock Music and Arts Festival in August 1969 was the electric-guitar rendition of the "Star Spangled Banner" performed by Jimi Hendrix (a former paratrooper), which mimicked the sounds of falling bombs and air raid sirens. Meanwhile, country singer Merle Haggard released "Okie from Muskogee" (1969), an antiprotest song featuring the lines, "We don't burn our draft cards down on Main Street."

In 1969, John Lennon of the Beatles and his wife, Yoko Ono, conducted a widely publicized "Bed-In for Peace" at hotels in Amsterdam and Montreal, dramatizing the popular antiwar slogan of the time "Make love, not war" and offering a new one: "All we are saying is give peace a chance." That same year, Lennon and Ono conducted a Christmastime antiwar billboard campaign across the United States as well as in Europe—the signs read "WAR IS OVER! / IF YOU WANT IT / Happy Christmas from John & Yoko"—and released a hit single titled "Give Peace a Chance." In 1971, Crosby, Stills, Nash & Young released the song "Ohio," with the somber lyrics "Tin soldiers and Nixon coming" and "four dead in Ohio," alluding to the National Guard shootings at Kent State University on May 4, 1970.

Gulf War and Iraq War

The Gulf War was over and done before peace activists had time to effectively mobilize. On January 12, 1991, Congress voted to authorize military action to remove Iraqi forces from Kuwait, and by February 27, 1991, the war was declared finished. Nevertheless, demonstrations against U.S. involvement were held in San Francisco and Washington, D.C. A number of soldiers who refused to go to war were given legal assistance by the WRL. The recognized "anthem" of the Gulf War was Bette Midler's Grammy-winning single "From a Distance" (1990), with the lines (written by Julie Gold), "From a distance / I just cannot comprehend / What all this fighting's for" and "God is watching us / From a distance."

Although the terrorist attacks of September 11, 2001, generally unified the country, an antiwar movement quickly got under way. The Washington, D.C.–based Act Now to Stop War and End Racism (ANSWER) was founded three days after the attacks. This group, designating itself anti-imperialist, led a number of peace rallies in Washington, D.C., and San Francisco. The progressive advocacy group MoveOn.org, founded in 1998, quickly launched the MoveOn Peace campaign, calling for a "restrained and multi-lateral response to the attacks." In November 2002, the California-based CODEPINK: Women for Peace was formed, launching its activist activities with a four-month, all-day vigil in front of the White House. As the George W. Bush administration mobilized for war against Iraq, protesters coined the slogan "No Blood for Oil." At that point, however, many Americans identified with the sentiments of county singer Toby Keith's post–September 11 fight song, "Courtesy of the Red, White, and Blue" (2002).

In 2003, ten days before the start of the Iraq War, country radio stations stopped playing the songs of the Dixie Chicks after band member Natalie Maines commented during a London concert that she was "ashamed" that President George W. Bush was from her state of Texas. Ted Koppel, the anchor of ABC's *Nightline*, found himself in controversy in 2004 when his program took forty minutes to read the names of the Americans who had so far died in the Iraq War; critics saw this as a thinly veiled antiwar message. In August 2005, Cindy Sheehan, who had lost a son in Iraq, camped outside Bush's ranch in Crawford, Texas, maintaining a twenty-six-day vigil with thousands of others. One newspaper columnist in the *Indianapolis Star* referred to the war demonstrations as "adolescent temper tantrums." Others called the protesters "anarchists." Sheehan was scorned by conservative radio talk show host Rush Limbaugh with the words "We all lose things."

Roger Chapman

See also: Chicago Seven; Commoner, Barry; Counterculture; Fonda, Jane; Hoffman, Abbie; My Lai Massacre; New Left; Rock and Roll; September 11; Students for a Democratic Society; Vietnam Veterans Against the War; Vietnam War.

Further Reading

CODEPINK Web site. www.codepink4peace.org.

DeBenedetti, Charles, and Charles Chatfield. *An American Ordeal: The Antiwar Movement of the Vietnam Era.* Syracuse, NY: Syracuse University Press, 1990.

Epstein, Barbara. "The Antiwar Movement During the Gulf War." *Social Justice* (1992): 115–37.

Garfinkle, Adam. *Telltale Hearts: The Origins and Impact of the Vietnam Antiwar Movement.* New York: St. Martin's Press, 1995.

Harris, Nancy, ed. *The Peace Movement.* Detroit, MI: Greenhaven Press, 2005.

Katz, Milton S. *Ban the Bomb: A History of SANE, the Committee for a SANE Nuclear Policy.* New York: Praeger, 1987.

Sheehan, Cindy. *Peace Mom: A Mother's Journey Through Heartache to Activism.* New York: Atria Books, 2006.

War Toys

During the 1950s, the widespread use of plastics enabled American toy manufactures to cheaply expand their line of products, including new designs of war toys. Although most boys have played with toy soldiers since ancient times, a debate on the appropriateness of war toys accelerated as the Vietnam War turned unpopular in the mid-1960s. The debate continues to the present, with opponents arguing that war toys glorify violence, manipulate patriotic symbols, and impose military socialization. Moreover, critics believe, they promote aggression and antisocial behavior in children. Defenders of war toys insist that they give children a healthy outlet for acting out good over evil and provide a healthy catharsis for violent impulses.

In 1964, which marked the debut of Parents for Responsibility in the Toy Industry and their annual protest at the American Toy Fair in New York, the toy manufacturer Hassenfeld Brothers (later renamed Hasbro) introduced what would become the most recognized war toy in American history: the GI Joe "action figure." An 11.5-inch (29-centimeter) boy's doll with twenty-one bendable joints, the masculine-looking polyvinyl GI Joe, featuring a facial scar, sported a U.S. military uniform (with elements from all four services) and could be outfitted with a variety of plastic war "accessories" (sold separately). Two years later, a group of mothers at the toy fair demonstrated in Mary Poppins costumes and brandished black umbrellas carrying the inscription, "Toy Fair or Warfare." Also in 1966, the Children's Peace Union, founded by a fifth grader, demonstrated in front of a department store on Fifth Avenue in New York City carrying signs that read, "War Toys Kill Minds" and "Constructive Toys, Not Destructive Toys." In 1969, Parents Against the Encouragement of Violence picketed the American Toy Fair, calling into question the social benefit of war toys. It was during this period that the Sears catalog stopped offering war toys.

As the news from Vietnam worsened, the GI Joes grew beards and were retooled into the "Adventure Team" to hunt wild animals or search for buried treasure. In 1971, California passed legislation, signed into law by Governor Ronald Reagan, that prohibited the manufacture or sale of "torture toys," including toy bombs and grenades. At the 1972 American Toy Fair, a group of Vietnam veterans joined Parents for Responsibility in the Toy Industry to discourage retailers from stocking their shelves with war toys. Although some observers thought war toys were making a comeback during the Christmas season of 1974, a spokesman for the Toy Manufacturers of America reported that there were fewer on the market then than in the mid-1960s. By 1978, GI Joe was temporarily pulled off of the market, unable to compete with Kenner's 4-inch- (10-centimeter-) tall Star Wars action figures, establishing the trend for smaller figures.

The decade of the 1980s witnessed the introduction of new lines of action figures, including Mattel's He-Man and Masters of the Universe (1981), Tonka's GoBots (1983), and Hasbro's Transformers (1984). Critics said they were even more violent than GI Joe. The War Resisters League, known for its logo of a broken rifle, picketed Coleco of Hartford, Connecticut, for introducing the Rambo doll, an action figure based on the main character of Sylvester Stallone's films *First Blood* (1982) and *Rambo: First Blood Part II* (1985). On the West Coat, the Eugene, Oregon–based Families for Survival began hosting Peace Toy Fairs to publicize alternatives to war toys, capping off events with a burial ceremony in which war toys are given last rites. In actuality, thanks to government deregulation pushed by President Ronald Reagan, changes in children's television programming made possible by the relaxation of content rules by the Federal Communications Commission (FCC) gave war toys a commercial resurrection. Although the Federal Trade Commission in 1977 concluded that some television advertising aimed at children is inherently unethical, the FCC permitted the airing of violent war cartoons featuring toy products as the main characters.

In 1982, a GI Joe cartoon commercial promoted the toy's rebirth (at 3.5 inches [9 centimenters]), and Marvel comics began publishing *G.I. Joe: A Real American Hero* (1982–1994). These were followed by two GI Joe cartoon mini-series on television, *A Real American Hero* (1983) and *The Revenge of Cobra* (1984); and later, five times a week, *The Pyramid of Darkness* (1985) and *Arise, Serpentor, Arise* (1986). In 1986, Hasbro enjoyed $185 million in sales for GI Joes, and the following year saw the release of *G.I. Joe: The Movie* (1987). The success of the GI Joe TV series inspired other war programs, including a cartoon promoting Transformers (1984–1987) that reportedly averaged eighty-three acts of violence per episode. The Illinois-based National Coalition on Television Violence reported a 350 percent increase in the sale of war toys from 1982 to 1985, noting that the five top-selling products of the mid-1980s all had their own violent cartoon program. In 1984 alone, some 214 million units of action figures were sold. In 1988, Congress passed the Children's Television Act to curb the involvement of toy manufacturers in children's programming, but President Reagan vetoed the legislation on First Amendment grounds.

Meanwhile, toy guns, some in the shape of military assault rifles, began to look so realistic that children waving them were occasionally shot by law enforcement officers who thought they were acting in self-defense. Thus, a number of states passed legislation during the 1980s aimed at regulating toy guns. New York, New Jersey, Connecticut, and California, as well as a number of municipalities, simply outlawed the manufacture or sale of toy guns. Congress approved the Federal Toy Gun Law (1988), requiring toy guns to feature a bright orange plug. Despite this remedy, police continued to mistake toy guns for real ones. In 1994, after a boy in Brooklyn, New York, was fatally shot by police who mistook his toy gun for a genuine weapon, Toys "R" Us announced that it would stop selling realistic toy guns.

After the terrorist attacks of September 11, 2001, and the start of the War on Terror, the debate on war toys continued afresh. CODEPINK, a women's peace movement founded in 2002 in opposition to the Iraq War, protested against retailers selling war toys, including violent video games. During the 2005 Christmas season, CODEPINK launched Operation "Stick It to 'Em" by encouraging its followers to place warning stickers on toys in stores: "Surgeon General's Warning: Violent Toys = Violent Boys." The group also recommended a "buy and return" tactic in order to register complaints to store managers about violent toys while creating longer lines in customer service departments.

Roger Chapman

See also: Barbie Doll; Comic Books; Federal Communications Commission; Vietnam War; War Protesters.

Further Reading

Chapman, Roger. "From Vietnam to the New World Order: The GI Joe Action Figure as Cold War Artifact." In *The Impact of the Cold War on American Popular Culture*, ed. Elaine McClarnand and Steve Goodson, 47–55. Carrollton: State University of West Georgia, 1999.

Clark, Eric. *The Real Toy Story: Inside the Ruthless Battles for America's Youngest Consumers.* New York: Free Press, 2007.

Paige-Carlsson, Nancy, and Diane E. Levin. *Who's Calling the Shots? How to Respond Effectively to Children's Fascination with War Play and War Toys.* Philadelphia: New Society, 1990.

Regan, Patrick. "War Toys, War Movies, and the Militarization of the United States, 1900–85." *Journal of Peace Studies* 31:1 (February 1994): 45–58.

Warhol, Andy

The painter, photographer, writer, and filmmaker Andy Warhol was a prominent figure in the Pop Art movement beginning in the 1960s. Determined to achieve fame and fortune through commercial art, Warhol mass-produced his works, which focused on food, money, sex, violence, and celebrity. Noted for his trademark silver wig and the observation that "In the future everyone will be famous for fifteen minutes," Warhol remains a controversial cultural figure.

The son of Czechoslovakian immigrants, he was born Andrew Warhola on August 6, 1928, in Pittsburgh, Pennsylvania. After obtaining a fine arts degree in 1949 at the Carnegie Institute of Technology (now Carnegie Mellon University) in Pittsburgh, he went to New York and earned a reputation for the blotted-line technique he used in commercial advertisements in *Glamour*, *Vogue*, and

Harper's Bazaar magazines. He won the Art Director's Club Medal for a shoe advertisement in 1957 and was later hailed by *Women's Wear Daily* as "the Leonardo da Vinci of the shoe trade."

From the 1960s onward, Warhol pursued his career as a pop artist and gained international acclaim for his canvases depicting popular consumer items such as Campbell's soup cans and Coca-Cola bottles, mocking the banality of commercial homogenization. In 1962, he founded a New York City studio called The Factory, where his "art workers" silk-screened hundreds of superstar images, including ones of Elizabeth Taylor and Marilyn Monroe. In 1968, having survived a gun blast from the radical feminist Valerie Solanas, founder of SCUM (Society for Cutting Up Men), Warhol turned to death-image art on race riots, car accidents, electrocutions, and the atomic bomb. Condemned by some critics as lifeless, nihilist, and even dangerous, his work was lauded by others as a powerful representation of a consumerist culture driven by mass advertising and obsessions with sex and violence.

A prolific film producer, Warhol made sixty-one underground movies from 1963 to 1972. Many of his projects, such as *Blow Job* (1963) and *Chelsea Girls* (1966), deal with pornographic and homoerotic themes (Warhol himself was gay). Although sometimes tedious and lacking a storyline, but with brilliant color photography and in-camera editing, his movies attracted a generation of experimental filmmakers, including Jean-Luc Godard and Norman Mailer. Warhol died on February 22, 1987, in New York City after gall bladder surgery.

Selina S.L. Lai

See also: Cold War; Counterculture; Feminism, Third-Wave; Gay Capital; Mailer, Norman; Nuclear Age; Pornography.

Further Reading

Bockris, Victor. *The Life and Death of Andy Warhol.* New York: Bantam Books, 1989.
Pratt, Alan R., ed. *The Critical Response to Andy Warhol.* Westport, CT: Greenwood, 1997.

Warren, Earl

The fourteenth chief justice of the United States (1953–1969), Earl Warren became a lightning rod in the culture wars for the controversial decisions issued by the Supreme Court during his tenure. The most notable cases, addressing issues of civil rights, individual freedom, separation of church and state, and voting rights, were seen as shifting the high court—and the nation—in a liberal direction, prompting conservative critics to deplore what they regarded as "judicial activism."

He was born on March 14, 1891, in Los Angeles to a Norwegian immigrant father and a Swedish immigrant mother. After studying law at the University of California, Berkeley (BA, 1912; JD, 1914), he worked for the Associated Oil Company and later a law firm. His career was interrupted by service in World War I (1917–1918), after which he entered politics in his home state, serving as district attorney (1925–1939), state attorney general (1939–1943), and governor (1943–1953). His election to the governorship followed his support of President Franklin Roosevelt's internment of Japanese Americans during World War II; he later expressed regret for that position in his autobiography, published after his death. In 1948, Warren ran as Thomas Dewey's vice-presidential nominee in the Republican Party. He sought the GOP nomination for president in 1952, but lost to Dwight Eisenhower, who appointed him to the Supreme Court because of his loyalty in delivering California's votes. Later, Eisenhower remarked that the Warren appointment was his greatest mistake as president.

The year after becoming chief justice, Warren presided over the landmark ruling in *Brown v. Board of Education* (1954), a unanimous decision that declared racial segregation in schools unconstitutional. The ruling, which Warren wrote, overturned the "separate but equal" doctrine on which institutional segregation had been legally based since the case of *Plessy v. Ferguson* (1896). Warren's interpersonal skills enabled the justices to reach unanimity in *Brown*, all the more remarkable considering the ideological divisions and personality conflicts that were represented on the bench. Associate justices Hugo Black and William Douglas initially favored a forceful ruling that would declare school segregation unconstitutional, while factional rivals Robert Jackson and Felix Frankfurter, though morally opposed to school segregation, were unsure as to whether or not the Constitution allowed the judiciary to outlaw it. Moderates on the court, including Harold Burton and Tom Clark, could have ruled either way on *Brown*.

Warren believed that the justices had to reach a unanimous decision in order for the ruling to carry weight. He knew that white southerners would fight any attempts by the federal government to desegregate schools, and he feared that any dissenting or even separate concurring opinions could spur greater resistance. Thus, Warren wrote a concise majority opinion that declared school segregation to be unconstitutional, but also allowed the South to desegregate its schools gradually. Years later, some liberals would criticize *Brown* for being too moderate and accommodating toward segregationists; others believed that the ruling spurred a white southern backlash more than it helped desegregate schools. Over time, most conservatives and liberals would concede that the decision was inherently correct.

The Warren Court issued several other important rulings that broadly interpreted the Constitution and

The U.S. Supreme Court under Chief Justice Earl Warren (front row, center)—posing here in 1953—is said to have marked a distinct shift toward liberal "judicial activism." Its historic ruling in *Brown v. Board of Education* (1954) ended school segregation. *(George Tames/New York Times Co./ Getty Images)*

increased the Supreme Court's power to protect minorities and individuals' rights. In *Engel v. Vitale* (1962), the justices held that the First Amendment's guarantee of the separation of church and state made even nondenominational school prayers unconstitutional—a ruling that many Americans criticize to the present day. Also in 1962, the Warren Court declared in *Baker v. Carr* that states must divide their electoral districts proportionally to ensure that every person's vote counts equally; this marked a departure from a 1946 ruling in which the high court stated that federal courts could not interfere with states' apportionment of districts. The Warren Court ruled in *Griswold v. Connecticut* (1965) that married couples can purchase contraceptives, a historic and far-reaching opinion that declared a constitutional right to personal privacy for the first time. And in *Miranda v. Arizona* (1966), the Court declared that the law requires police officers to inform suspects of their right to remain silent and have an attorney present during questioning.

Conservatives roundly criticized Warren for many of these decisions. They criticized the *Griswold* ruling for extrapolating a right to privacy not explicitly granted in the text of the Constitution. And the *Miranda* decision, they feared, would make it too difficult for police officers to fight crime. In these and other landmark rulings, they charged Warren with engaging in "judicial activism" and overstepping the limits of the Supreme Court's authority. In 1957, in fact, Senator William Jenner (R-IN) proposed legislation that would limit the appeals the Court could accept, so that some of the Supreme Court's power would be transferred to the executive and legislative branches.

Conservatives mounted a campaign to "Impeach Earl Warren," and Republican presidential candidate Richard Nixon in 1968 made the Warren Court and judicial activism an issue in his campaign.

In the meantime, Warren had also become associated with the commission he headed—which was named for him—under appointment by President Lyndon Johnson in 1963 to investigate the assassination of President John F. Kennedy that November. The commission's report, issued in September 1964, became ever controversial for its conclusion that Lee Harvey Oswald acted alone in carrying out the shooting.

Earl Warren retired from the U.S. Supreme Court in 1969, succeeded as chief justice by Warren Burger. To conservatives, he represented the wrongs of liberal America and pushed the country away from law and toward disorder. Liberals, on the other hand, applauded the major rulings of the Warren Court. While they recognized that Warren might not have been the outstanding legal scholar that some other justices were, they saw him as the first chief justice to take an active role in enforcing minority and individual rights, even if he had to issue unpopular verdicts to do so. Not long after Warren retired, Yale professor Joseph Bishop argued that few of the Warren Court's important decisions were "palatable to a large segment of the population, including a great many highly vocal politicians. . . . But in these areas it is my judgment . . . that (1) the Court was right, and (2) most people knew it was right." To Warren, the Constitution guaranteed certain basic rights for all Americans, and with the Supreme Court's verdicts in cases like *Brown, Engle, Baker, Griswold,* and *Miranda,* he helped grant them. Warren died on July 9, 1974.

Aaron Safane

See also: Birth Control; *Brown v. Board of Education* (1954); Church and State; Communists and Communism; Conspiracy Theories; Eisenhower, Dwight D.; John Birch Society; Judicial Wars; Kennedy Family; Miranda Rights; Nixon, Richard; Reparations, Japanese Internment; School Prayer.

Further Reading

Lewis, Frederick P. *The Context of Judicial Activism: The Endurance of the Warren Court Legacy in a Conservative Age.* Lanham, MD: Rowman & Littlefield, 1999.

Pollack, Jack Harrison. *Earl Warren: The Judge Who Changed America.* Englewood Cliffs, NJ: Prentice-Hall, 1979.

Powe, Lucas A., Jr. *The Warren Court and American Politics.* Cambridge, MA: Belknap Press of Harvard University Press, 2000.

Tushnet, Mark, ed. *The Warren Court in Historical and Political Perspective.* Charlottesville: University Press of Virginia, 1993.

Warren, Earl. *The Memoirs of Earl Warren.* New York: Doubleday, 1977.

Warren, Rick

A Southern Baptist pastor, popular evangelical preacher, and best-selling writer, Rick Warren is the founder of a West Coast megachurch called Saddleback and the author of *The Purpose-Driven Life: What on Earth Am I Here For?* (2002). A theological and political conservative, Warren is also widely viewed as an alternative voice to the Religious Right.

The son of a minister, Richard Duane "Rick" Warren was born on January 28, 1954, in San Jose, California. He was educated at California Baptist College (BA, 1977), Southwestern Baptist Theological Seminary (MA, 1979), and Fuller Theological Seminary (MDiv, 1989). In 1980, he founded the Saddleback Community Church in Lake Forest, California, near Los Angeles, which twenty-five years later had more than 80,000 members. Prior to establishing Saddleback, Warren served as youth evangelist at the California Southern Baptist Convention, Fresno (1970–1974); associate pastor at First Baptist Church of Norwalk, California (1974–1976); and assistant to the president at the International Evangelism Association in Fort Worth, Texas (1977–1979).

Warren has been viewed as an alternative to the Religious Right for a message perceived as more inclusive and less negative. *The Purpose-Driven Life*, which sold 22 million copies in its first two years of publication, has inspired Christians for its "can-do" message. Rather than focus primarily on abortion, same-sex marriage, stem-cell research, and liberal judges, Warren has spoken out on the plight of the poor, whom he says are mentioned some 2,000 times in the Bible. Interviewed by the *Philadelphia Inquirer* in 2006, Warren complained, "[T]he last 100 years . . . the church has just been a mouth. And mostly, it's been known for what it's against," adding, "I'm so tired of Christians being known for what they're against." Warren has launched a ministry to address the problem of poverty and AIDS in Africa, using 90 percent of his book royalties to fund such projects. To the disappointment of the Religious Right, he joined a handful of other evangelicals in petitioning President George W. Bush to address the problem of global warming and participated in a United Nations prayer event.

Earlier, Warren had gained notoriety for taking the Internal Revenue Service (IRS) to court and inadvertently jeopardizing federal tax exemptions for clergy housing (which costs the U.S. government as much as $500 million annually). After the IRS determined in 1996 that Warren's "parsonage exemption" exceeded the rental value of his new home, the pastor filed suit to protest the cap on the amount of the deduction. The U.S. Tax Court ruled in Warren's favor in 2000, but the IRS appealed to the U.S. Court of Appeals for the Ninth Circuit in San Francisco, which began questioning the constitutionality of the deduction itself. In the meantime, Congress unanimously passed the Clergy Housing Clarification Act of 2002, signed into law by President Bush. The legislation authorized the IRS to impose a "fair market rental" cap from that day forward, but to allow past excessive deductions to stand. Satisfied, the IRS withdrew its appeal of the Warren case, avoiding the issue of church-state constitutionality.

During the 2008 presidential election Warren hosted a forum at Saddleback in which he separately interviewed John McCain and Barack Obama. The questions largely pertained to social issues, such as when human life begins and the definition of marriage. Warren also asked each candidate to describe their greatest moral failings. Some observers criticized the event as imposing a "religious test" on presidential candidates. Later, Obama caused a furor among certain liberals, including gay activists, for choosing Warren to deliver the invocation during the inauguration. Warren's political visibility, some observers have suggested, casts him as the Billy Graham of the twenty-first century.

Roger Chapman

See also: Abortion; AIDS; Bush Family; Campolo, Anthony "Tony"; Church and State; Global Warming; Judicial Wars; Religious Right; Same-Sex Marriage; Southern Baptist Convention; Tax Reform; United Nations.

Further Reading
Darman, Jonathan. "An Inexact Analogy." *Newsweek*, January 12, 2009.
Gladwell, Malcolm. "The Cellular Church." *The New Yorker*, September 12, 2005.
Mair, George. *A Life with Purpose: Reverend Rick Warren, the Most Inspiring Pastor of Our Time.* New York: Berkeley Books, 2005.
Steptoe, Sonja. "The Man with the Purpose." *Time*, March 29, 2004.

Washington Times, The

The newspaper equivalent of the Fox News Channel in terms of conservative ideology, the *Washington Times* was founded in May 1982 by the Reverend Sun Myung Moon, head of the Unification Church, whose followers are sometimes referred to as Moonies. The previous year, the *Washington Star* ceased operations after 128 years of publication, giving the *Washington Post* a monopoly status in the nation's capital at a time when London and Paris had nine and thirteen daily newspapers, respectively. In founding the *Washington Times*, Moon sought to fill the void left by the *Star* and increase his church's political influence in American culture. The paper began publication one day after he was convicted of tax fraud, an offense that led to an eighteen-month prison sentence.

Known as the "Moonie paper" by its detractors,

the *Washington Times* has been a prominent voice in the culture wars, promoting the pro-life movement, sexual abstinence, and family values while criticizing political correctness, feminism, gay rights, rap music, and public schools. Its conservative editorials are mirrored by its op-ed columns, which are written by conservatives such as L. Brent Bozell, Georgie Anne Geyer, Nat Hentoff, John Leo, Oliver North, A.M. Rosenthal, Cal Thomas, and Thomas Sowell. In 1997, the paper began publishing a weekly section called "Family Times," providing a forum for, among others, James Dobson and his evangelical Christian group Focus on the Family. The Unification Church's interference in the newspaper's editorials led to the resignation of James Whalen, the paper's first editor, in 1984. Three years later, editorial page editor William Cheshire quit for the same reason, as have others.

The *Washington Times* was a strong voice against communism during the last decade of the Cold War, supporting President Ronald Reagan's Strategic Defense Initiative and launching a public fundraiser for the Contra fighters in Nicaragua after Congress ended federal support. "Read the Paper Moscow Hates" was one of its early advertisement slogans.

The paper also had a role in the events leading to the impeachment of President Bill Clinton. Its first article about Clinton's alleged extramarital affairs, written by Jerry Seper, appeared on July 30, 1991, seven years before the Monica Lewinsky story broke. The paper published nearly 400 articles about Whitewater, the Arkansas real estate deal with which the Clintons were associated prior to his presidency. The paper was also consistently critical of the Clinton administration's policies.

It is estimated that the Unification Church spent up to $1 billion in the *Washington Times*'s first decades to keep afloat a paper that never exceeded a circulation of 126,000, while the *Post* was enjoying profitability with 750,000 daily copies sold. Even so, the *Washington Times* has been influential by providing a forum for conservative agenda setters. President George W. Bush praised the paper, calling it "the conscience" of the nation's capital.

Roger Chapman

See also: Bush Family; Clinton, Hillary; Clinton Impeachment; Cold War; Dobson, James; Family Values; Fundamentalism, Religious; Iran-Contra Affair; North, Oliver; Sowell, Thomas; Strategic Defense Initiative.

Further Reading

Edwards, Lee, ed. *Our Times: The Washington Times 1982–2002.* Washington, DC: Regnery, 2002.

Gorenfeld, John. *Bad Moon Rising: How the Reverend Moon Created* The Washington Times, *Seduced the Religious Right.* Sausalito, CA: PoliPointPress, 2008.

Washington Times Web site. www.washtimes.com.

Watergate

Watergate is the popular designation for the dramatic political scandal and constitutional crisis that culminated in the resignation of Richard Nixon as president of the United States on August 9, 1974. The sequence of events got its name from the Watergate hotel and office complex in Washington, D.C., where five burglars were caught in June 1972 breaking into the headquarters of the Democratic National Committee (DNC). The break-in and White House cover-up that ensued led to a constitutional showdown between the executive branch and Congress in televised public hearings by a Senate investigating committee in spring and summer 1973 and a series of revelations, in both those hearings and the media, that deeply shook the American people's faith in government. The entire incident brought an intensification of the culture wars due to Nixon's lack of political transparency and the lasting bitterness of many Republicans toward the Democrats who demanded White House accountability.

The road to Watergate began in 1971 with the formation of the White House Plumbers, a secret investigative force tasked to prevent the disclosure of classified information to the media. The group was established in reaction to the leak of the top-secret Pentagon Papers to the *New York Times* by former Pentagon insider Daniel Ellsberg in June 1971. Members of the Plumbers group were enlisted during Nixon's 1972 reelection campaign to obtain sensitive campaign information from the Democratic opposition. It was later revealed that a plan to conduct electronic surveillance of DNC headquarters in the Watergate building was approved by U.S. attorney general John Mitchell, who also chaired the Committee to Re-Elect the President (CRP or "CREEP").

During the early morning of June 17, 1972, municipal police were called to the Watergate complex after a security guard noticed a piece of tape on a door latch that kept it unlocked. Upon entering the DNC offices, the police discovered five men hiding under desks, carrying fifty rolls of film and equipment used for electronic surveillance—unconventional gear for burglars. These men and two others were indicted by a grand jury for burglary and attempted interception of telecommunications.

One of the men arrested at the Watergate was James McCord, Jr., who had worked for the CIA and FBI, and was now officially employed as chief of security for CRP. A notebook he was carrying proved especially damaging, as it contained the telephone number of E. Howard Hunt, who directed the break-in and had direct ties to the White House. As was later revealed, the White House quickly began its cover-up of the incident by buying the silence of the Watergate burglars. The obstruction of justice continued in succeeding months, involving senior White House officials, including John Dean, counsel to the president; H.R. Haldeman, Nixon's chief of staff; John Ehrlichman, assistant to the president for domestic affairs; Jeb Magruder, deputy director of CRP; and, ultimately, President Nixon himself. The White House remained untouched into the fall and Nixon won a landslide reelection, but matters began to unravel in March 1973 after McCord sent a letter to Judge John J. Sirica, who was presiding over the case, stating that the Watergate defendants were under political pressure to plead guilty and that other unidentified persons were also involved in the break-in. Later McCord named names, including Dean and Magruder, exposing the depth of the political scandal.

After Dean was implicated in the scandal, he sought immunity in exchange for testimony before the Senate Watergate Committee. In dramatic televised testimony in June 1973, Dean directly implicated President Nixon in the cover-up and indicated that there was a secret tape-recording system in the Oval Office. The latter claim was verified by White House deputy assistant Alexander Butterfield, touching off a battle for the tapes between the Senate and the president, who refused to turn them over on grounds of executive privilege. The constitutional showdown climaxed in the so-called Saturday Night Massacre, in which Special Prosecutor Archibald Cox, who had issued a subpoena for the case, was fired and high-level Justice Department officials resigned. The White House did turn over transcripts of the tapes, albeit edited and with gaps. Both the Senate and the general public were outraged, leading to calls for Nixon's impeachment. In July 1974, the U.S. Supreme Court ordered Nixon to turn over all the pertinent tapes, which ultimately proved the president's involvement in a cover-up. Any lingering support the president had in the Senate evaporated, ensuring that he would be convicted under the articles of impeachment approved by the House Judiciary Committee on July 27, 1974. Nixon resigned on August 9, before the matter reached the full House.

President Gerald Ford, who succeeded to the presidency, promptly granted Nixon a blanket pardon for his involvement in the Watergate scandal, sparing him a possible prison sentence. By accepting the pardon, Nixon confirmed his guilt. The legacy of Watergate continues to cast a long shadow on American politics, leaving many citizens less trusting of government. Many people have continued to argue that Nixon was no different than most other politicians; he just happened to get caught. Indeed, that lack of trust has revealed itself during the course of subsequent political scandals involving the White House, whose very nomenclature evokes Watergate—Contragate (the Iran-Contra Affair), Koreagate, Travelgate, Monicagate, and others. With regard to the Monica Lewinsky scandal, it has been suggested that the impeachment proceedings against President Bill Clinton in 1998–1999 represented political retribution on the part

of a Republican-controlled Congress for the Democrats' handling of Watergate.

Maria T. Baldwin

See also: Clinton Impeachment; Colson, Chuck; Democratic Party; Felt, W. Mark; Ford, Gerald; Iran-Contra Affair; Liddy, G. Gordon; McGovern, George; Nixon, Richard; Presidential Pardons; Republican Party; Woodward, Bob.

Further Reading
Emery, Fred. *Watergate: The Corruption of American Politics and the Fall of Richard Nixon.* New York: Touchstone, 1995.
Genovese, Michael A. *The Watergate Crisis.* Westport CT: Greenwood Press, 1999.
Kutler, Stanley. *Abuse of Power: The New Nixon Tapes.* New York: Touchstone, 1998.
Lasky, Victor. *It Didn't Start with Watergate.* New York: Dell, 1977.
Olson, Keith W. *Watergate: The Presidential Scandal That Shook America.* Lawrence: University Press of Kansas, 2003.

Watt, James

As President Ronald Reagan's secretary of the interior (1981–1983), James Watt infuriated environmentalists for advocating the exploitation of natural resources, championing the development of federal land, and loosening environmental regulations. He once likened the philosophy of the environmental movement to that of Nazi Germany. During the first year of his tenure in the Interior Department, the Sierra Club wilderness advocacy group organized a "Dump Watt" campaign, gathering 1.1 million signatures on a petition calling for his dismissal. In the end, however, it was his controversial remarks about political correctness that led to Watt's abrupt resignation.

James Gaius Watt was born on January 31, 1938, in Lusk, Wyoming. After attending the University of Wyoming (BS, 1960; JD, 1962), he began his political career as a legislative assistant and later a speechwriter to U.S. Senator Milward L. Simpson (R-WY). Watts went on to various positions in the federal government, including deputy assistant secretary of the interior (1969–1972). He also directed the Denver-based Mountain States Legal Foundation (1977–1980), a property rights organization affiliated with the anti-environmental Wise Use Movement.

One of two members of the New Right in Reagan's first cabinet, Watt became a focus of controversy for opposing many of the environmental regulations that the Department of the Interior was bound to uphold. In 1982, the department announced plans for selling 35 million acres (14 million hectares) of federal land, but the ensuing storm of criticism from both liberals and conservatives forced him to withdraw the proposal. He also supported the removal of environmental restrictions on offshore oil drilling, attempted to open Alaska and other coastal and wilderness areas for energy exploration, curtailed the expansion of the national park system, and halted new additions to the endangered species list. Watt's policies grew out of his commitment to the commercial development of lands controlled by the federal government. In support of this outlook, he cited the Bible, saying it "calls on us to occupy the lands until Jesus returns."

Watt was also controversial for his socially conservative views, which were related to his Christian fundamentalism. He once declared that there were two types of people in the country, "liberals" and "Americans." He tried to ban female employees at his department from wearing pantsuits. In 1982, he invoked his authority over the National Mall in Washington in order to cancel a Beach Boys concert scheduled to take place there, arguing that the group did not represent American values. During a press conference on September 21, 1983, he sarcastically highlighted the diversity of an advisory panel that he had appointed, explaining, "We have every kind of mix you can have . . . a black . . . a woman, two Jews, and a cripple," adding, "And we have talent." Watt resigned on October 9 of that year, a consequence of the public backlash prompted by those remarks.

After leaving the government, Watt worked as a business consultant, only to be indicted in 1995 on eighteen felony counts of perjury and obstruction of justice related to an investigation of his lobbying practices. He eventually pleaded guilty to a single misdemeanor charge, for which he was fined $5,000 and sentenced to 500 hours of community service.

Charlotte Cahill

See also: Arnold, Ron; Endangered Species Act; Environmental Movement; Forests, Parklands, and Federal Wilderness; Fundamentalism, Religious; Multiculturalism and Ethnic Studies; Political Correctness; Reagan, Ronald; Vietnam Veterans Memorial.

Further Reading

Bratton, Susan Power. "The Ecotheology of James Watt." *Environmental Ethics* 5 (Fall 1983): 225–36.

"James Watt Lashes Back at Critics." *U.S. News & World Report*, June 14, 1982.

Short, C. Brant. *Ronald Reagan and the Public Lands: America's Conservation Debate, 1979–1984.* College Station: Texas A&M University Press, 1989.

Watt, James, and Doug Wead. *Courage of a Conservative.* New York: Simon & Schuster, 1985.

Watts and Los Angeles Riots, 1965 and 1992

For six days in August 1965, and again for six days in April and May 1992, violence erupted in the Watts neighborhood of south-central Los Angeles. The outbreaks sparked extensive debate among scholars, the media, and the general public. At the center were the issues of race and economic inequality in America.

The 1965 riots began with a routine traffic stop on the evening of August 11 that triggered violence between residents and the police. After five more days of street fighting, looting, burning, and other destruction, President Lyndon B. Johnson sent in some 16,000 National Guard troops to quell the rioting. The uprising officially left 34 people dead, more than 1,100 injured, and over $200 million in property damage.

President Johnson and California governor Edmund (Pat) Brown established commissions to determine the cause of the rioting. Their reports, as well as the studies of a number of scholars, pointed to several underlying issues. Police brutality was central to most explanations. The Los Angeles Police Department was regarded as perhaps the most violent and virulently racist in the United States; the city's African-American and Mexican-American communities had complained about city police for years. Inadequate, overcrowded, segregated housing, segregated schools, high unemployment and poverty, and the lack of effective antipoverty programs all contributed to the feelings of isolation and helplessness that led many blacks in Watts to participate in the violence.

One of the important social consequences of the Watts riots of 1965 was a white backlash. Days prior to the outbreak of violence, President Johnson had signed the Voting Rights Act of 1965. When the riots erupted, many whites retreated from support of further civil rights initiatives, and many of Johnson's Great Society programs, particularly those aimed at cities and racial minorities, faced increasing opposition. White flight from downtown urban centers to suburban neighborhoods gained momentum after Watts and subsequent rioting in Detroit, Newark, and elsewhere in 1966–1968.

In April 1992, Los Angeles again exploded in violence over issues of race and police brutality. The riots of 1992 were larger and broader in scope than those of 1965, resulting in 52 persons killed, some 2,300 injured, and over $1 billion in property damage. This time, however, more Latinos than blacks participated in the riots, and the violence took place throughout the city of Los Angeles, not just in Watts.

Despite some fundamental differences between the events, the similarities were clear to many observers—as noted in the film documentary *Straight from the Streets* (1999), produced by Keith O'Derek and Robert Corsini. The 1992 rioting was triggered by a not-guilty verdict against the police officers who had beaten black motorist Rodney King in an incident captured on videotape and viewed by the general public through media coverage. Issues of race and economic inequality once again outraged the city's poor minority communities. The rioters were primarily blacks and Latinos who felt left out of American society. The economy of south-central Los Angeles had been in steep decline, with unemployment and poverty chronically high and getting worse.

One of the strongest similarities between the 1965 and 1992 riots was that both set off a national debate over racial inequality, poverty, and the role of the federal government. President George H.W. Bush and other conservatives blamed the violence on the legacies of the Great Society and other federal attempts to aid residents of inner cities. In their view, the promises of federal programs created unrealistic expectations among inner-city residents, as well as a culture of dependency on government. Liberals blamed the federal retrenchment and abandonment of the cities in the 1980s, arguing that it was the reduction of Great Society programs by the Reagan administration, not the programs themselves, that had led to the frustrations and anger that boiled over again in Los Angeles.

The debates surrounding the riots reflected a political, cultural, and racial divide in the United States. In 1965, many whites, especially conservatives, responded to the events in Los Angeles by blaming blacks for their own conditions and urging a return to law and order. Blacks and liberal whites encouraged more economic aid to inner cities to improve the prospects for housing and employment. Twenty-seven years later, conservatives blamed black and Latino residents and liberal social programs for inner-city ills, while liberals blamed the lack of federal participation in those areas.

Robert Bauman

See also: Bush Family; Compassionate Conservatism; Great Society; Hispanic Americans; Johnson, Lyndon B.; King, Rodney; Police Abuse; Reagan, Ronald; War on Poverty; Welfare Reform.

Further Reading

Gooding-Williams, Robert, ed. *Reading Rodney King, Reading Urban Uprising.* New York: Routledge, 1993.

Horne, Gerald. *Fire This Time: The Watts Uprising and the 1960s.* Charlottesville: University of Virginia Press, 1995.

Viorst, Milton. *Fire in the Streets: America in the 1960s.* New York: Simon & Schuster, 1979.

Wayne, John

Born Marion Robert Morrison on May 26, 1907, in Winterset, Iowa, the film star John Wayne—popularly referred to as "the Duke"—was a cultural icon who appeared mostly in westerns and war movies. His rugged, masculine image and the heroic frontier individualism of many of his roles were said to epitomize the American spirit. In the culture wars, Wayne is remembered for his

Film icon John Wayne—seen in his Oscar-winning role as Rooster Cogburn in *True Grit* (1969)—was a staunch Republican and a larger-than-life symbol of patriotism, heroism, and traditional American values during the antiwar turbulence of the 1960s. *(Keystone/Getty Images)*

cinematic support of the Vietnam War, even though he had declined to serve in World War II.

Wayne began his career as a fill-in and stunt actor at local studios in California. He dropped out of college to pursue acting and had his first starring role in *The Big Trail* (1930). Appearing in more than 250 films—and starring in 142 of them—he, perhaps more than any other actor, tapped into the folklore of the American West and the imagery of a new frontier. Most often, he was a gun-wielding, whiskey-drinking hero who imposed his will in a quest for righteousness, whether on the frontier or the battlefront. His characters championed good over evil, overcame adversity at great odds, and gallantly opposed all foes in films that generally offered stereotyped portrayals of Indians, women, and others. Among his western classics are John Ford's *Stagecoach* (1939), *She Wore a Yellow Ribbon* (1949), and *The Searchers* (1956); Howard Hawks's *Red River* (1948) and *Rio Bravo* (1959); and Henry Hathaway's *True Grit* (1969), for which Wayne won the Academy Award for Best Actor.

Wayne was well on his way to establishing himself in Hollywood when World War II broke out in December 1941. Unlike other actors his age, such as Clark Gable and Henry Fonda, Wayne chose not to enlist in the armed forces, fearing that he would be too old to make a comeback in movies after the fighting. The decision elicited sharp criticism, which perhaps led him to cultivate the persona of a super patriot.

Wayne's staunch Republican and anticommunist views extended into his work. In 1951, he appeared in *Big Jim McLain*, which gave a favorable impression of the House Committee on Un-American Activities and its pursuit of communists. In 1968, Wayne co-directed and starred in *The Green Berets*, one of the few films of the time to openly support the Vietnam War. Critics thought the film too political, considering the high casualty rate of the war, but Wayne was intent on displaying his support for the troops with a film tribute. To right-wing supporters of the war and the U.S. government, Wayne was a hero once again. Others contended that his own patriotic role in the film, as well as in the public eye, attempted to deflect attention from the fact that he avoided wartime service. Wayne died of lung and stomach cancer on June 11, 1979.

Margaret Dykes

See also: Cold War; Communists and Communism; McCarthyism; Political Correctness; Republican Party; Vietnam War.

Further Reading

Roberts, Randy, and James Olson. *John Wayne: American.* New York: Free Press, 1995.

Wills, Gary. *John Wayne's America: The Politics of Celebrity.* New York: Simon & Schuster, 1997.

Wealth Gap

The term "wealth gap" refers to the economic disparity between the richest people in the United States—the top 10 percent—and the rest of the population. The wealth gap has widened considerably since the late 1970s, with each decade resulting in the rich having a larger percentage of the nation's total wealth. In the culture wars, this phenomenon has been the subject of vigorous debate and statistical interpretation.

Liberals argue that the widening wealth gap represents an unhealthy trend, entrenching privilege and power while retarding equal opportunity and social mobility. Those sharing this concern suggest that tax reform is necessary to narrow the wealth gap, since those who have benefited the most from society should be required to give more back. Long-term inequities should be addressed, some argue, by policies such as affirmative action to foster greater competition. Conservatives argue that since more wealth is being created, the ones responsible for making this happen should enjoy the direct benefit and not be punished with higher tax rates. Affirmative action, they contend, is reverse discrimination that inhibits competition and fails to address the behavioral and cultural differences that are the root cause of the wealth gap.

According to 2004 statistics issued by the U.S. Federal Reserve Board, the wealthiest 10 percent of American families owned 63 percent of the nation's total family assets. By other indicators, the wealthiest 10 percent of Americans in 2003 owned 85 percent of all outstanding stocks and financial securities and 90 percent of all business assets. At the same time, 10 percent of the least well off owned few or no assets.

A major contributing factor to the wealth gap is the income gap. According to 2005 federal tax data, the combined income of the top 300,000 Americans was nearly equivalent to the total income of the bottom 150 million of the nation. The top income group had earnings 440 times higher than the average individual of the bottom half; thus, the top 1 percent received nearly 20 percent of the total national income. Also in 2005, 12.6 percent of the population, representing 37 million people, was officially classified as poor (earning below $19,806 for a family of four). All told, the income gap in America nearly doubled between 1980 and 2005, a chasm wider than at any time since the late 1920s.

While it is universally agreed that free enterprise enriches more people than any other system of exchange, it is also argued that the capital used for investment purposes, which stimulates economic growth, is largely connected with income inequality and the related problem of "wage stagnation." Even more problematic than income inequality, however, is the intergenerational transmission of assets and liabilities, which results in concentrations of wealth for the few and debt for many. In the long run, critics argue, such entrenched disparity has the potential to undermine both capitalism and democracy because the "have nots" constituting the majority of the population will have fewer economic opportunities and less political influence. Bill Gates, Sr., executive director of the Bill and Melinda Gates Foundation and father of the richest man in America, contends that estate taxes are a "valuable tool of democracy" because they serve as an economic recalibration. During the presidency of George W. Bush, however, the federal estate tax was eliminated, allowing the wealthy to pass on more of their inheritance to their heirs and thus perpetuating the widening wealth gap.

Those who disagree with Gates emphasize individual liberty, arguing that personal life choices play a major role in economic affairs. For example, studies of Americans who have achieved millionaire status indicate that a stable marriage is an important factor of economic success; the poorest households, by contrast, are inordinately headed by single parents, usually female. Critics of Gates's "tool of democracy" argument, such as the late economist Milton Friedman, argue that increasing taxes serves only to increase the power of the central government and, therefore, the threat to personal liberty. In any event, the clear trend in America since the 1980s has been significant tax cuts on unearned income, such as inheritances and capital gains, and tax hikes on wage income. In the 1990s and 2000s, the Internal Revenue Service reported that a growing number of wealthy Americans avoid paying federal taxes by utilizing intricate tax shelters, exemption schemes not possible for people of lower incomes. From 1979 to 1997, the richest 1 percent of Americans enjoyed a more than 250 percent increase in after-tax income (from $263,700 to $677,900), while their share of all federal tax payments climbed from 15.5 percent to 23 percent.

Many argue that the wealth gap not only separates Americans by socioeconomic class, but also increases segregation among ethnic groups. In the early 2000s, an estimated 7 million Americans were living in "white" gated communities, while homelessness was on the rise—up 100 percent from the previous decade, according to some estimates. Residential segregation increases the exposure of poor and ethnic minorities to the problems that plague high-poverty neighborhoods. Declining public health, job prospects, and environmental conditions in urban areas where the poor and minorities are increasingly concentrated have cumulative effects that substantially impact all aspects of development, as well as the future income potential of the children being raised in those communities. Thus, poverty is passed on from generation to generation while at the top strata of society wealth concentration increases.

Indeed, the black-white wealth gap is the most persistent and well-documented cleavage in American society. According to New York University economist Edward Wolff in 2003, the average American black family takes in just 60 percent of the earnings and holds a mere 18 percent of the wealth of the average white family. And according to a 2005 study, black children make up 90 percent of the long-term poor in the United States and continue to be alienated from the experience of upward mobility within and across generations that is the privilege of white children. A child born in poverty has about a 7 percent chance of reaching the top fifth of income earners, while a child born to the top fifth of income earners has a 42 percent chance of being in the top fifth as an adult.

Holona LeAnne Ochs and Roger Chapman

See also: Affirmative Action; Bankruptcy Reform; Executive Compensation; Friedman, Milton; Great Society; Tax Reform; War on Poverty; Welfare Reform.

Further Reading

Bowles, Samuel, Herbert Gintis, and Melissa Osborne Groves. *Unequal Chances: Family Background and Economic Success.* Princeton, NJ: Princeton University Press, 2005.

Danziger, Sheldon, Peter Gottschalk, Russell Sage Foundation, and Population Reference Bureau. "Diverging Fortunes: Trends in Poverty and Inequality." In *The American People: Census 2000,* ed. Reynolds Farley and John Haaga, 449–72. New York: Russell Sage Foundation, 2005.

Lardner, James, and David A. Smith, eds. *Inequality Matters: The Growing Economic Divide in America and Its Poisonous Consequences.* New York: Free Press, 2005.

Munger, Frank. *Laboring Below the Line: The New Ethnography of Poverty, Low-Wage Work, and Survival in the Global Economy.* New York: Russell Sage Foundation, 2002.

Neckerman, Kathryn M. *Social Inequality.* New York: Russell Sage Foundation, 2004.

Weekly Standard, The

First published on September 18, 1995, the *Weekly Standard* is a neoconservative magazine with a circulation of about 55,000 and a reported annual deficit of $1 million or more. The magazine's debut was inspired by the 1994 federal elections, which for the first time in four decades gave the Republican Party control of Congress. Interpreting that result as a sea change in American politics—signaling a "lasting" political realignment—the neoconservative commentator William Kristol decided to start a magazine of "opinion journalism" for the primary purpose of influencing Washington policymakers to help set the nation on a new path. During the presidency of George W. Bush, the *Standard* was said to be the White House's magazine of choice.

Owned by Rupert Murdoch's News Corporation, the *Weekly Standard* is by its own definition an "iconoclastically conservative" counterpart to the "iconoclastically liberal" *New Republic.* Edited by Kristol and Fred Barnes, the *Standard* is primarily a neoconservative platform that promotes an aggressive U.S. foreign policy in harmony with Kristol's Project for a New American Century. Following the terrorist attacks of September 11, 2001, the magazine, which reportedly had been on the brink of folding, gained a renewed sense of purpose. The following September, conservative journalist and politician Pat Buchanan announced the start-up of his own magazine, the *American Conservative,* wishing to offer a competing conservative voice to the *Standard.* Buchanan complained, "The movement has been hijacked and turned into a globalist, interventionist, open-borders ideology, which is not the conservative movement I grew up with."

To mark the tenth anniversary of his magazine, Kristol edited a collection of what he deemed the best reflective political essays he had published to date, titled *The Weekly Standard: A Reader, 1995–2005* (2005). In the foreword, Kristol notes that numerous people speak of his magazine as if it were part of a sinister conspiracy, replete with articles published "in code . . . to advance a surreptitious agenda." Dismissing the conspiracy theorists, he writes, "Sometimes a magazine is really just a magazine."

Over the years, the magazine has advised the Republican Party to discard its anti-abortion plank (editorial, September 1995); castigated Hillary Clinton's book *It Takes a Village* (article by P.J. O'Rourke, February 1996); mocked and ridiculed President Bill Clinton throughout the Monica Lewinsky scandal (capped by David Tell's parody of an Italian opera, March 1999); urged regime change in Iraq as early as November 1997 ("Saddam Must Go" editorial by Kristol and Robert Kagan); articulated the importance of American protection of Israel (article by Charles Krauthammer, "At Last Zion," May 1998); and defended the torture of terrorism suspects (a cover article by Krauthammer, December 2005).

Roger Chapman

See also: Abortion; Abu Ghraib and Gitmo; American Century; Buchanan, Pat; Clinton Impeachment; Contract with America; Gingrich, Newt; Israel; Kristol, Irving, and Bill Kristol; Murdoch, Rupert; Neoconservatism; September 11.

Further Reading

Alterman, Eric. "Kristolizing the (Neoconservative) Movement." *Nation*, February 12, 2007.

Kristol, William, ed. *The Weekly Standard: A Reader, 1995–2005.* New York: HarperCollins, 2005.

McConnell, Scott. "The Weekly Standard's War." *American Conservative*, November 21, 2005.

Weekly Standard Web site. www.weeklystandard.com.

"What Is Bill Kristol Up To?" *Human Events*, December 21, 1995.

Welfare Reform

The debate over welfare in America for much of the twentieth century was characterized by variations of two opposing arguments: the progressive or liberal concern of collective responsibility versus the conservative resistance to individual dependency. These two positions on the topic of public assistance have continued to be debated in America's culture wars, despite evolving social understandings of motherhood, family, and the government's role in the economy.

Prior to the New Deal, state-sponsored pensions for mothers were largely premised on the idea of providing stable homes for children of widows. Yet even these popular programs, implemented in forty-four states by 1930, faced the criticism that cash assistance inevitably corrupts its recipients by destroying their work ethic and, in turn, their children's work ethic. Even during the Great Depression, cash relief was limited out of a concern, expressed even by President Franklin D. Roosevelt, that its fostering of dependency undermines individual integrity and self-sufficiency.

Aid to Dependent Children, created in 1935 under the Social Security Act, allowed substantial state control over the size of payments and eligibility rules in an effort not to violate local norms of deservedness. Despite the debate over deserving versus undeserving poor, a distinction that relied heavily on race and subjective evaluations of recipients' lifestyles, federally backed welfare continued

through the mid-twentieth century without dramatic changes. Welfare was tolerated by conservatives largely because of the preponderance of local control and the modest financial impact on local economies.

By the early 1960s, middle-class whites and Washington policymakers were influenced by Michael Harrington's best-selling book on poverty, *The Other America* (1962). President Lyndon B. Johnson declared a "War on Poverty" in 1964, and welfare came to be seen as an entitlement—something deserved by poor families that met formal eligibility requirements. With a significant push from community organizers and the U.S. Supreme Court, the status of welfare as a "property right" was cemented around 1970. By the early 1970s, however, disillusioned liberals, such as Daniel Patrick Moynihan, peeled away from the left, forming the neoconservative movement, in reaction to this new trend toward entitlements.

Neoconservatives thought the excesses of welfare had corrupted liberalism and that a new perspective was needed. They argued for greater personal responsibility and more reliance on market incentives. In time, this movement would lead conservatives such as George Gilder and Charles Murray to call for welfare's abolition, attacking what they took to be welfare's perverse incentives for nonwork and out-of-wedlock childbearing.

By the time Ronald Reagan ran for president in 1980, talk of "welfare queens" was common. And indeed, there would be poster children for the cause. Jacqueline Williams, a mother of fourteen children receiving welfare in the District of Columbia, engaged in a public spat with Washington Mayor Marion Barry. The mayor publicly criticized her fertility, but Williams claimed a God-given right to reproduce. In 1987, while pregnant with her fifteenth child, she commented to a *Washington Post* reporter, "I don't intend to stop until God stops me. . . . I don't want to mess up my body with birth control." Opponents of welfare could not have imagined a better case to bolster their argument. Although liberal scholars such as William J. Wilson have linked underlying social structures to persistent poverty and the emergence of an urban underclass, the general public seemed more persuaded by conservatives' explanations that focused instead on the counterproductive behaviors of poor people.

Never amounting to more than 1–1.5 percent of the federal budget, welfare garnered a disproportionate share of public attention through the 1980s and 1990s. President Bill Clinton's effort to govern from the center and his mantra of "ending welfare as we know it" represented an attempt to have it both ways. Welfare was to take on the trappings of reciprocal responsibility through work requirements and personal responsibility agreements, and there would be a sixty-month maximum lifetime limit. In a return to mid-twentieth-century practice, welfare authority was substantially transferred to the states, working within loose federal parameters. Devolution to the states facilitated a renewed role for local norms in determining welfare eligibility. Although this was not stepping back in time to the overtly discriminatory days of the 1940s and 1950s, it nonetheless put state policymakers in a position to tailor their welfare programs.

Liberals' concern that states would become much stingier in providing welfare was largely allayed by a provision in the law that required states to substantially maintain the level of investment they had been making in their respective welfare programs prior to 1996. In addition, robust economic growth through the end of the 1990s helped achieve a more than 50 percent reduction of the national welfare caseload by the end of that decade. Instead of crediting the economy, however, conservatives pointed to mandates in the law as the primary cause of the caseload reduction.

Studies of people leaving welfare show that post-welfare employment is sporadic for many, low-paying for nearly all, and often without health insurance. If liberals feel a sense of vindication by such findings, conservatives tend to claim that even low-level employment is better than a lifestyle of unemployment and welfare dependency.

Debates about welfare have moved largely off the public stage and into seminar rooms, where the outcomes of the 1996 legislation have been dissected by policy analysts. Media attention has faded, and much of the public assumes the problem has been fixed. This is reflected in a decline in the number of newspaper stories on the subject as well as in public opinion polls. In that respect, the waxing and waning public attention to the issue of welfare follows a well-known trajectory.

Greg M. Shaw

See also: Clinton, Bill; Compassionate Conservatism; Contract with America; Corporate Welfare; Faith-Based Programs; Harrington, Michael; Health Care; Johnson, Lyndon B.; Neoconservatism; New Deal; Reagan, Ronald; War on Poverty.

Further Reading

Gilder, George. *Wealth and Poverty.* New York: Basic Books, 1981.

Harrington, Michael. *The Other America: Poverty in the United States.* New York: Macmillan, 1962.

Kilty, Keith M., and Elizabeth A. Segal, eds. *The Promise of Welfare Reform: Political Rhetoric and Reality of Poverty in the Twenty-First Century.* New York: Haworth Press, 2006.

Murray, Charles. *Losing Ground: American Social Policy 1950–1980.* New York: Basic Books, 1986.

Wilson, William J. *The Truly Disadvantaged: The Inner City, the Underclass, and Public Policy.* Chicago: University of Chicago Press, 1987.

Wellstone, Paul

Considered the most liberal member of the U.S. Senate at the turn of the twenty-first century, Democrat Paul Wellstone of Minnesota represented the populist left until his tragic death in a plane crash on October 25, 2002. He spoke out for the working poor, backed universal health care, opposed oil drilling in the Arctic National Wildlife Refuge in Alaska, and twice voted against going to war in Iraq (1991, 2002). The controversy over his funeral reflected the intensity of the culture wars at the time.

Paul David Wellstone, the son of Jewish immigrants from Ukraine, was born on July 21, 1944, in Washington, D.C., and raised in northern Virginia. After receiving a BA (1965) and a PhD (1969) in political science from the University of North Carolina at Chapel Hill, he taught political science at Carleton College, a small liberal arts institution in Northfield, Minnesota (1969–1990).

In 1981, Wellstone co-authored *Powerline: The First Battle in America's Energy War*, presenting the viewpoint of farmers opposed to a power line crossing agricultural fields in west-central Minnesota. After running unsuccessfully for state auditor in 1982, Wellstone achieved his first electoral victory in the 1990 Senate race. Endorsed by the Democratic-Farmer-Labor Party (DFL), he defeated Rudy Boschwitz, a two-term Republican incumbent who had become increasingly conservative. Boschwitz committed a damaging tactical error during the campaign by issuing what came to be known as the "Jew letter," a mailing that went out to thousands of Jewish voters calling Wellstone a "bad Jew" for marrying a gentile and not raising his children as Jews. (Boschwitz was Jewish, too.) The letter is said to have had a negative effect.

Wellstone's very arrival in Washington, D.C., was rancorous, beginning with his refusal to shake hands with archconservative Senator Jesse Helms (R-NC). (During his college days in North Carolina, Wellstone had come to loathe Helms for his opposition to the civil rights movement.) In one of his most controversial moments, Wellstone held a press conference at the Vietnam Veterans Memorial to denounce U.S. participation in the Persian Gulf War. (Wellstone voted against the use of force before Operation Desert Storm in 1991 and before the Iraq War in 2002.) The memorial had never been used for a political purpose, and veterans' groups voiced disapproval.

Wellstone comfortably won reelection in 1996, again facing off with Boschwitz, who made an unsubstantiated charge that as a college student the incumbent had burned the American flag. Wellstone later ran an exploratory campaign for the presidency and published *The Conscience of a Liberal* (2001), an intentionally ironic play on Barry Goldwater's title, *The Conscience of a Conservative* (1960).

In his third run for the Senate, Wellstone was opposed by Norman Coleman, the former mayor of St.

Paul. In the midst of the campaign, while on the way to a funeral, Wellstone, his wife, daughter, and five others died in a plane crash in northern Minnesota. The memorial service, held in Minneapolis and nationally televised, was marred by politically charged eulogies and the booing of certain Republicans, prompting a walkout by Governor Jesse Ventura and others. Some linked the Democrat's subsequent loss of the Senate to that fracas. In the words of Garrison Keillor, host of the radio program *Prairie Home Companion*, "The Democrats stood up in raw grief and yelled and shook their fists and offended people." Coleman easily defeated former vice president Walter Mondale, the DFL's replacement candidate, for the Senate seat.

Tony L. Hill

See also: Civil Rights Movement; Conspiracy Theories; Democratic Party; Flag Desecration; Franken, Al; Goldwater, Barry; Health Care; Helms, Jesse; Mondale, Walter; Ventura, Jesse; Vietnam Veterans Memorial.

Further Reading

Lofy, Bill. *Paul Wellstone: The Life of a Passionate Progressive.* Ann Arbor: University of Michigan Press, 2005.

McGrath, Dennis J., and Dane Smith. *Professor Wellstone Goes to Washington: The Inside Story of a Grassroots U.S. Senate Campaign.* Minneapolis: University of Minnesota Press, 1995.

Wellstone, Paul David. *The Conscience of a Liberal: Reclaiming the Compassionate Agenda.* New York: Random House, 2001.

West, Cornel

Scholar and theologian Cornel West, a prominent African-American voice in the culture wars, advocates a progressive Christianity that incorporates some Marxist ideals, believing that the black community in particular has accepted a religious worldview that is too politically conservative. This has been the theme of many of his writings, including *Black Theology and Marxist Thought* (1979), *Prophesy Deliverance! An Afro-American Revolutionary Christianity* (1982), and *The Ethical Dimensions of Marxist Thought* (1991).

Cornel Ronald West was born on June 2, 1953, in Tulsa, Oklahoma, and raised in a Baptist household. He spent his teenage years in Sacramento, California, where he was attracted to the black nationalism of Malcolm X and participated in civil rights demonstrations. He later attended Harvard University (AB, 1973) and Princeton University (MA, 1975; PhD, 1980). West has taught philosophy of religion at Union Theological Seminary in New York (1977–1983, 1988), the Yale Divinity School (1984–1987), Princeton University (1988–1994, 2002–present), and Harvard University (1994–2002).

Race Matters (1993), West's best-known work, is

Professor and author Cornel West decries the "racist patriarchy" of American society and the negative stereotypes it has placed on the black community. West has referred to himself as a "non-Marxist socialist" and "radical democrat." *(Richard Alan Hannon/Getty Images)*

required reading on many college campuses. In it he argues that African Americans have accepted the negative stereotypes imposed on them by white Americans and have consequently suffered from a lack of self-worth and hope for the future that has descended into cultural nihilism. In his judgment, as articulated in *Beyond Eurocentrism and Multiculturalism* (1993), the solution depends on the revival of a "race-transcending" progressive political coalition.

West has criticized black churches for supporting gender inequality and for being hostile to homosexuals. He is also critical of whites, particularly Jews, for abandoning blacks after the heyday of the civil rights movement, a topic further discussed in a work he coauthored with Rabbi Michael Lerner, *Jews and Blacks: A Dialogue on Race, Religion, and Culture in America* (1995). In *Democracy Matters: Winning the Fight Against Imperialism* (2004), the sequel to *Race Matters*, West accuses and condemns American political leaders for participating in worldwide economic exploitation, state repression, and political imperialism.

Following the publication of *Race Matters*, West was invited to join the African and African American Studies program at Harvard. He left in 2002 after the newly installed university president, Lawrence Summers, criticized him for engaging in too many nonscholarly activities in the political and pop culture arenas. West had worked on the Million Man March in 1995, served as an adviser to Bill Bradley's 2000 presidential campaign, and recorded hip-hop CDs. Upon returning to the Princeton University faculty, he continued his outside pursuits, such as making a cameo appearance in the film *Matrix Reloaded* (2003) and supporting Al Sharpton's 2004 presidential bid.

Conservatives such as David Horowitz have charged West with publishing writings of poor quality and fostering relativism and political correctness on campus. In spite of such criticisms, West continues to receive numerous campus speaking invitations, furthering the view of conservatives that American academic life is dominated by the left.

Martin J. Plax

See also: Academic Freedom; Bradley, Bill; Horowitz, David; Malcolm X; Marxism; Million Man March; Multiculturalism and Ethnic Studies; Neoconservatism; Rap Music; Relativism, Moral; Sharpton, Al; Summers, Lawrence.

Further Reading

Cowan, Rosemary. *Cornel West: The Politics of Redemption.* Malden, MA: Polity, 2003.

Horowitz, David. "Cornel West: No Light in His Attic." *Salon,* October 11, 1999.

Johnson, Clarence Sholé. *Cornel West and Philosophy: The Quest for Social Justice.* New York: Routledge, 2003.

Kimball, Roger. "Dr. West and Mr. Summer." *National Review,* January 28, 2002.

West, Cornel. *The Cornel West Reader.* New York: Basic Civitas Books, 1999.

Weyrich, Paul M.

One of the architects of the New Right, social activist and political commentator Paul Weyrich was instrumental in shaping the message of American conservatives. A key figure in several organizations, including the Krieble Institute (a training ground for democratic reformers in Eastern Europe), and a variety of causes, such as tax reform, he was best known for his defense of social conservative values, including opposition to abortion and homosexuality. Weyrich viewed America as a cultural battleground where competing ideologies pit conservatives against liberals. Though Catholic, Weyrich was widely seen as an important strategist for the Religious Right.

Born Paul Michael Weyrich on October 7, 1942, in Racine, Wisconsin, he attended the University of Wisconsin at Parkside (AA, 1962) and began his career in journalism, reporting for the *Milwaukee Sentinel* and for radio station WAXO in Kenosha, Wisconsin. In 1973, Weyrich and Edwin Feulner—with financial backing by Joseph Coors of the beer-brewing family—created the Heritage Foundation, a public policy research institute in Washington, D.C. He followed this up with the Committee for the Survival of a Free Congress, an organization that explored the fundraising possibilities of direct mail and discovered a resource for political activism: the recruiting and training of evangelical Christians to campaign for conservative candidates and

causes. Weyrich continued to cultivate the Christian base among political conservatives, joining with the Reverend Jerry Falwell to create the Moral Majority in 1979.

Through the 1980s and 1990s, Weyrich also tapped into the power of mass media, writing for and co-publishing the *Conservative Digest* and hosting a daily television talk show called *Direct Line.* In 1993, to counter what many conservatives consider a liberal bias in media, he launched National Empowerment Television (NET), an issues-orientated cable network with a conservative perspective on politics. Weyrich later left the network, renamed America's Voice, when he clashed with network head Bob Sutton over a plan to include both liberal and conservative views on NET.

In February 1999, Weyrich issued an open letter to conservative leaders in which he called for a major shift in the focus of political efforts. American society could not be rescued from the corrupting influence of liberalism, he wrote, and social conservatives should therefore redirect their energies from reforming America to segregating themselves from society at large. They should create "a sort of quarantine," Weyrich said, creating their own schools and other institutions. His letter was precipitated by the Senate's failure to remove President Bill Clinton from office in 1999 following his impeachment in the House. If a "moral majority" truly existed, he lamented, then Clinton should have been driven out of office. Consequently, he continued, "I believe that we probably have lost the culture war."

In his latter years, Weyrich worked to influence public policy under the auspices of the Council for National Policy and the Free Congress Foundation, organizations that include some of the most powerful conservatives in the United States. He died on December 18, 2008.

Daniel Melendrez

See also: Abortion; Clinton Impeachment; Evangelicalism; Family Values; Fundamentalism, Religious; Gay Rights Movement; Heritage Foundation; Media Bias; Moral Majority; Religious Right.

Further Reading

Cromartie, Michael, ed. *No Longer Exiles: The Religious New Right in American Politics.* Washington, DC: Ethics and Public Policy Center, 1993.

Gizzi, John. "Weyrich's Back!" *Human Events,* November 10, 2000.

Utter, Glenn H., and James L. True. *Conservative Christians and Political Participation: A Reference Handbook.* Santa Barbara, CA: ABC-CLIO, 2004.

Weyrich, Paul M., and Connaught Marshner, eds. *Future 21: Directions for America in the 21st Century.* Greenwich, CT: Devin-Adair, 1984.

Whistleblowers

Individuals who report misdeeds involving fraud, waste, or abuse in government agencies and private corporations are known as whistleblowers. More formally identified as "ethical resisters" and often recognized as the political descendants of muckrakers, whistleblowers are generally credited for putting the good of society ahead of the organization that would benefit by wrongdoing. At the same time, however, whistleblowers are sometimes viewed as suspect characters (informants, traitors, or simply disgruntled employees) operating with ulterior motives (political partisanship, revenge against a supervisor, the desire to collect reward money, etc.). Laws have been passed to shield whistleblowers from employer retribution, but that has not always kept them from being harassed, transferred, demoted, or fired.

Prominent whistleblowers in the culture wars have included the medical researcher A. Dale Console, who in 1960 informed Congress of deceptive drug testing by the pharmaceutical industry; Daniel Ellsberg, who leaked the Pentagon Papers in 1971; New York City police officer Frank Serpico, who in the early 1970s exposed corruption in the department; W. Mark Felt, the Watergate informant known as Deep Throat; Karen Silkwood, the technician who documented safety violations at an Oklahoma nuclear power plant in 1974; Jeffrey Wigand, a former tobacco executive who in 1995 revealed the manipulation of nicotine levels in cigarettes; Coleen Rowley, the FBI agent who reported a failure of the bureau to investigate terrorist leads weeks prior to the attacks of September 11, 2001; and army captain Ian Fishback and specialist Joseph Darby, both of whom turned over information about detainee abuse at the Abu Ghraib prison in Iraq in 2003.

During the Civil War, whistleblowers were encouraged to report government contractors selling "shoddy" war supplies to the Union army. With that in mind, Congress passed the False Claims Act (1863), authorizing citizens and civil servants to sue fraudulent contractors for a portion of the recovered money. That law, in an updated form, remains in effect to the present day. In the wake of the Watergate scandal, Congress in 1978 passed the Civil Service Reform Act, giving protections to federal whistleblowers. In 1989, President George H.W. Bush approved a bill establishing an office of special counsel to investigate alleged incidents in which federal whistleblowers were punished for making disclosures. Whistleblower protection was added to the Sarbanes-Oxley Act of 2002 to protect private-sector employees who report violations of federal health, safety, and environmental laws.

In one dramatic episode of the mid-1960s, two former staffers of Senator Thomas Dodd (D-CT) copied incriminating documents from the files of their old boss and handed them over to syndicated newspaper columnist Jack Anderson. The records indicated that Dodd had spent more than $200,000 of campaign funds for personal use. When the story broke, much negative attention was focused on those who leaked the information, and the whistleblowers ultimately were criticized in a report by the Senate Ethics Committee for "a breach of the relationship of trust between a Senator and his staff." The evidence was so damaging, however, that on June 23, 1967, the Senate passed a motion of censure against Dodd.

The following year, A. Ernest Fitzgerald, a civilian financial analyst at the Pentagon, informed a congressional subcommittee headed by Senator William Proxmire (D-WI) that the Lockheed Corporation's development of the air force C-5A cargo plane was leading to cost overruns of some $2 billion. Fitzgerald's testimony came after his superiors had told Congress that there were no concrete figures to report on that project. This incident underscored the collusion that sometimes occurs between the Pentagon and defense contractors—officers who are not strict about reducing costs and addressing quality control are more likely to land a job with a private contractor following retirement from the military. Attempts were made to oust Fitzgerald, but he won in court with the help of the American Civil Liberties Union. In 1981, he and others formed the Project on Military Procurement to aid whistleblowers in reporting waste and inefficiency in defense contracting.

The consumer activist Ralph Nader, who had been assisted in the 1950s and 1960s by insiders of the automotive industry when he investigated car safety, was one of the first to defend whistleblowers. In January 1971, Nader promoted the cause of whistleblowers at the Conference on Professional Responsibility held in Washington, D.C. In his report, Nader hailed whistleblowers as society's "last line of defense . . . against . . . secretive and powerful institutions." Nader went on to establish the Coalition to Stop Government Waste, which was largely a support organization for whistleblowers. His call for the legitimization of whistleblowers also inspired the founding in 1977 of the Project on Official Illegality (later renamed the Government Accountability Project), which provided the legal defense for Daniel Ellsberg over his release of the top-secret Pentagon Papers.

The most controversial whistleblowers are those dealing with national security issues. In 1971, six months after Nader's endorsement of whistleblowers, Ellsberg became a cause célèbre for exposing government deceptions on the Vietnam War by turning over to the *New York Times* the Vietnam Study Task Force's secret history (1945–1967), otherwise known as the Pentagon Papers. The work, comprising forty-seven volumes, was written by thirty-six analysts and historians and revealed a behind-the-scenes analysis that the war was not going well and that—contrary to what the American public was being told at the time—it probably could not be won. In

2006, the *New York Times* reported an illicit eavesdropping program being carried out by the National Security Agency, while the *Washington Post* broke the story of a secret network of overseas CIA detention centers. In all three of these incidents, individuals without authorization provided secret information to the media for the purpose of exposing government abuse. From the perspective of officials within the executive branch of government, such individuals are engaging in sabotage. Others contend that on too many occasions the government uses security classification to avoid public accountability.

Much whistleblowing is a natural consequence of the increase in federal regulation of the business sector, beginning in the 1960s and 1970s with the establishment of new federal agencies (such as the Equal Employment Opportunity Commission, Environmental Protection Agency, Occupational Safety and Health Administration, Mining Enforcement and Safety Administration, and Consumer Product Safety Commission) to protect workers, consumers, the general public, and the natural environment. Often it has been whistleblowers who have reported violations of federal law—either workers in a firm that failed to follow regulations or bureaucrats whose federal agency was derelict in enforcement.

Roger Chapman

See also: Abu Ghraib and Gitmo; Central Intelligence Agency; Felt, W. Mark; Nader, Ralph; *New York Times, The*; Occupational Safety; Privatization; September 11; Tobacco Settlements; Tort Reform; Vietnam War; Watergate.

Further Reading

Alford, C. Fred. *Whistleblowers: Broken Lives and Organizational Power.* Ithaca, NY: Cornell University Press, 2001.

Devine, Thomas. "The Whistleblower Protection Act of 1989: Foundation for the Modern Law of Employment Dissent." *Administrative Law Review* 35 (1999): 531–79.

Glazer, Myron Peretz, and Penina Migdal Glazer. *The Whistleblowers: Exposing Corruption in Government and Industry.* New York: Basic Books, 1989.

Johnson, Robert Ann. *Whistleblowing: When It Works—and Why.* Boulder, CO: Lynne Rienner, 2003.

Katel, Peter. "Protecting Whistleblowers." *CQ Researcher*, March 31, 2006.

White, Reggie

One of professional football's greatest defensive players, Reggie White made headlines in the culture wars when he equated homosexuality with the nation's moral decline and said that he found offensive any comparison of the gay rights movement with the civil rights movement.

Reginald Howard White, an African American and an ordained Baptist minister, was born on December 19, 1961, in Chattanooga, Tennessee. During his collegiate playing days at the University of Tennessee, he earned the nickname "Minister of Defense" for his dual identity as a minister and hard-charging lineman. After a false start with the Memphis Showboats of the now defunct United States Football League, he played in the National Football League with the Philadelphia Eagles (1985–1992), Green Bay Packers (1993–1999), and Carolina Panthers (2000). He was elected to the Pro Bowl a record thirteen straight times (1986–1998) and twice was named NFL defensive player of year (1987 and 1998). He helped the Packers win Super Bowl XXXI (January 1997). Upon retirement, he held the NFL record for most career sacks. In 2006, he was elected to the Pro Football Hall of Fame.

Throughout his football career, White practiced his faith openly and with evangelical fervor. He initiated regular post-game prayer circles and, after tackling players on the field, would ask them, "Are you all right with Jesus?" Off the field, he devoted his time to inner-city religious charities and reaching out to gang members, drug addicts, and convicts. In 1992, he spoke at the Billy Graham Greater Philadelphia Crusade, urging racial unity and cooperation between urban and suburban churches. In reaction to the spate of arsonist attacks on black churches throughout the South during the 1990s, he challenged American society to address the nation's race problem and confront white supremacists.

His critics, emphasizing a side of White they regarded as bigoted and hateful, noted that in his March 1998 address to the Wisconsin state legislature, he listed the "gifts" of different races in what were perceived as primitive stereotypes. Gays and lesbians were especially offended by his statement, "Homosexuality is a decision; it's not a race." The Religious Right, in particular the Christian Coalition and Focus on the Family, rallied behind White, commending him for the courage to declare his biblical convictions and not fret over political correctness. Others, however, suggested that the largely white conservative groups exploited White to advance "pro-family" positions that otherwise smacked of bigotry. On December 26, 2004, at age forty-three, White suddenly died of pulmonary sarcoidosis, a respiratory disease.

Roger Chapman

See also: Censorship; Christian Coalition; Civil Rights Movement; Focus on the Family; Fundamentalism, Religious; Gay Rights Movement; Graham, Billy; Political Correctness; Religious Right; Speech Codes; Stern, Howard; White Supremacists.

Further Reading

White, Reggie, with Jim Denney. *Reggie White in the Trenches: The Autobiography.* Nashville, TN: Thomas Nelson, 1997.

White, Reggie, with Andrew Peyton Thomas. *Fighting the Good Fight: America's "Minister of Defense" Stands Firm on What It Takes to Win God's Way.* Nashville, TN: Thomas Nelson, 1999.

White Supremacists

Political groups based on the ideology that whites constitute a superior race are known as white supremacists, though they typically view themselves as white nationalists. Such movements comprise disparate elements, representing a complex array of racist positions. While some white supremacists advance their cause through peaceful means, utilizing free speech and seeking to appear mainstream (emphasizing that they are about "heritage" and not hate), many others overtly resort to violence against minorities and openly identify themselves as racist. According to the Southern Poverty Law Center (SPLC), a civil rights organization based in Montgomery, Alabama, which since 1971 has been monitoring "hate groups," there are six major categories of white supremacists in America today: Ku Klux Klan (KKK), white nationalist, neo-Confederate, neo-Nazi, racist skinhead, and Christian Identity.

Ku Klux Klan

An obvious player in the white supremacist movement is the KKK, which originated during post–Civil War Reconstruction and violently enforced Jim Crow segregation throughout the South. The Klan had an unexpected resurgence during the 1920s, as it spread into the Midwest as part of the "nativist movement," opposing blacks, Eastern European and Asian immigrants, Catholics, Jews, and even flappers. The third era of the Klan began largely in response to the Supreme Court decision in *Brown v. Board of Education* (1954), which overturned school segregation. In 1955, Eldon Lee Edwards in Georgia founded the Knights of the Ku Klux Klans (U.S. Klans). On September 29 of the following year, the U.S. Klans held a rally of 3,000 with a pageant cross-burning on Stone Mountain, Georgia, site of the 1915 rebirth of the KKK. By the late 1950s, the organization had spread to nine states, and its members were responsible for carrying out assaults, bombings, and cross-burnings.

The largest KKK organization in the 1960s and 1970s was the United Klans of America (UKA), headquartered in Tuscaloosa, Alabama, and led by imperial wizard Robert Shelton. At its peak in 1965, the UKA had an estimated membership of 30,000. In its violent opposition to the civil rights movement, the UKA beat up Freedom Riders and firebombed their buses in Anniston, Alabama (May 14, 1961); dynamited the 16th Street Baptist Church in Birmingham, Alabama, killing four girls and injuring over twenty others (September 15, 1963); and murdered civil rights worker Viola Liuzzo near Selma, Alabama (March 25, 1965). Operating independently of the UKA, the White Knights of the Ku Klux Klan, Mississippi, committed similar violence, including the slaying of three Congress of Racial Equality (CORE) activists in Philadelphia, Mississippi (June 21, 1964).

During the 1970s, the UKA was active in Michigan through the efforts of grand dragon Robert Miles, who ended up serving prison time for a plot to bomb empty school buses to thwart integration through busing.

The Louisiana-based Knights of the Ku Klux Klan, founded in 1974 by David Duke, attempted to bring the Klan above ground and mainstream ("from the cow pasture to hotel meeting rooms" was the theme) by emphasizing nonviolence and legal means for advancing white nationalism. Catholics were now deemed acceptable, though not Jews. Duke was more likely to be seen in a suit and tie than in a white robe and hood, but he also sold books denying the occurrence of the Holocaust. Duke's loose network included Bill Wilkinson's Louisiana Knights, Don Black's Alabama Knights, Louis Beam's Texas Knights, and Tom Metzger's California Knights. Dissension was the norm for these individuals. At odds with Duke's vision of a "moderate" KKK, Wilkinson in 1975 formed the Invisible Empire of the Ku Klux Klan, which committed itself to violently confronting civil rights marchers. In the early 1980s, Metzger left to form the neo-Nazi underground group the White Aryan Resistance (WAR), enlisting violent racist skinheads.

The 1970s marked the decline of the KKK, but not its disappearance. According to the SPLC, in 2008 there were 155 KKK groups in thirty-four states with a total membership of 5,000–8,000. The states with the most KKK chapters were Texas (20), Tennessee (12), Mississippi (11), Ohio (10), and Kentucky (8).

White Nationalist and Neo-Confederate Groups

In 1980, David Duke founded the National Association for the Advancement of White People (NAAWP), which he billed as a civil rights group for whites that was no more racist than the National Association for the Advancement of Colored People (NAACP). In contrast to Duke's outwardly peaceful approach, F. Glenn Miller of the North Carolina Knights founded in the same year the paramilitary organization the White Patriot Party, which would become unraveled by 1987 with its leader on the lam after violating his probation by declaring "total war" on Jews, African Americans, and the federal government. Meanwhile, in 1989, Duke was elected to the Louisiana House of Representatives as a Republican, despite the opposition of national party leaders. In 1990, he lost a race for a U.S. Senate seat. During that campaign, Duke said, "I believe the time has come for equal rights for everyone in this country, even for white people."

Calling for segregation of the races, Duke in 1984 produced a national map designating eight peripheral regions for "unassimilable minorities" and the remainder of the land (the vast majority) to be inhabited by whites. The proposed eight minority states were Francia (a tract of land near the Maine-Canada border for French Canadians); West Israel (Long Island and Manhattan for Jews); Minoria (the non-Jewish part of metropolitan New York for Puerto Ricans, southern Italians, Greeks, and people from the eastern and southern Mediterranean); New Cuba (Miami and Dade County, Florida, for Cuban Americans); New Africa (the southern half of Louisiana, Mississippi, Alabama, Georgia, and Florida for African Americans); Alta California (a sliver of the Southwest from California to the tip of Texas for "documented" Mexican Americans); Navahona (a portion of New Mexico for American Indians); and East Mongolia (Hawaii for Asian Americans).

Many whites over the years have joined the Council of Conservative Citizens (CCC), which is considered to be the largest white nationalist group. The St. Louis, Missouri–based organization was founded in 1985. The group's lineage, detractors note, is the former Citizens' Councils of America, which during the 1950s and 1960s opposed desegregation. CCC officials insist that their group is not racist, but the group's Web site does identify the United States as a "European country" and Americans as "a European people," an unmistakable expression of whiteness. According to the SPLC, in 2008 there were 125 white nationalist groups in thirty-four states plus the District of Columbia. Of the total white nationalist groups, about fifty were CCC chapters, operating in twenty-one states. Another white nationalist group with state chapters is the European-American Unity and Rights Organization (EURO), founded in 2000 by David Duke and initially called the National Organization for European-American Rights (NOFEAR).

The neo-Confederate groups, mostly centered in the South and largely represented by the League of the South (LOS), could be classified as espousing white regionalism. Founded in Tuscaloosa, Alabama, in 1994 by Michael Hill for the stated goal of "a free and independent southern republic," the LOS asserts that southern culture, due to its Anglo-Celtic heritage, is distinctive and superior to mainstream American culture. The LOS is a nonviolent organization, but critics suggest that white supremacy is its main agenda. In 2001, there were an estimated 9,000 members nationwide. In 2008, the SPLC counted 104 LOS chapters in eighteen states, including South Carolina (29), Florida (14), and Georgia (9).

Neo-Nazi, Racist Skinhead, and Christian Identity Groups

Anti-Semitism is the tie that binds neo-Nazi, racist skinhead, and Christian Identity adherents. The neo-Nazi movement champions the ideals of Adolf Hitler and Nazi Germany, expresses hatred of Jews, and warns of a worldwide Zionist conspiracy, even asserting that the United States federal government is a ZOG (Zionist Occupied Government). The European-inspired racist skinheads, who are known to physically attack minorities and homosexuals as well as desecrate synagogues, view themselves as the shock troops that will usher in the neo-Nazi revolution. Christian Identity is a religious ideology (a mutated version of British Israelism) that places whites (the Aryans) as the true children of Israel, Jews as the mixed-race children of Satan, and people of color as subhuman. Many adherents of Christian Identity belong to the militia network Posse Comitatus, which rejects state and federal authority, based on the notion that the county is the highest level of government and the sheriff the top law enforcement official—numerous Posse members, who refuse to pay federal income tax, have had shootouts with federal agents.

The early lineage of the radicalized right can be traced to William Dudley Pelley, founder of the Silver Legion (or Silver Shirts), centered in Asheville, North Carolina (1933); Gerald L.K. Smith, founder, among other things, of the Christian Nationalist Crusade, headquartered in St. Louis (1942); Willis Carto, founder of the Liberty Lobby, located in California (1955); Robert Welch, founder of the John Birch Society, established in Indianapolis (1958); and Robert DePugh, founder of the Minutemen, based in Norborne, Missouri (early 1960s). These groups embraced global conspiracy theories, with most linking communism to Jews. With such radicalism in mind, President John F. Kennedy gave a speech on November 18, 1961, in which he called critical attention to "those fringes of our society" that "sow the seeds of doubt and hate" and launch "crusades of suspicion."

Although the pro-Nazi Silver Shirts disbanded after the United States became involved in World War II (and Pelley in 1942 went to prison on sedition-related charges), its influence would continue with many of its former followers in California and the Pacific Northwest joining the Christian Identity movement. In addition, former Silver Shirts member Henry Beach in 1969 founded a Posse group in Portland, Oregon. During the 1950s and 1960s Wesley Swift, a former Klansman and associate of Smith, was the most influential Christian Identity preacher with his Church of Jesus Christ-Christian (CJCC) in California. Swift inspired Robert Butler, the one-time national director of the Christian Nationalist Crusade, to establish the Aryan Nations (1973), which was run as the political arm of the CJCC from a compound in Hayden Lake, Idaho. For years, prior to forfeiting its property after losing a lawsuit in 2000, the Aryan Nations annually hosted the largest gathering of white supremacists.

In 1959, George Lincoln Rockwell founded the American Nazi Movement in Arlington, Virginia, calling for the extermination of "Jewish traitors" and the expulsion of blacks to Africa. The group was renamed the National Socialist White People's Party, but it imploded following the assassination of Rockwell by a disgruntled member (August 25, 1967). In 1970, Frank

Collin founded the National Socialist Party of America, which made the news that same year by attempting a demonstration march in Skokie, Illinois, a largely Jewish suburb of Chicago. American television viewers got a glimpse of racist turbulence in November 1988 as it watched talk show host Geraldo Rivera get his nose broken while trying to break up an on-air brawl involving neo-Nazi skinheads of the American Front, antiracist skinheads, blacks, and Jews.

One of the most notorious neo-Nazis was William Pierce, a former physics professor and follower of Rockwell. In 1970, he joined the National Youth Alliance, originally Willis Carto's Youth for Wallace. Pierce, who envisioned a United States inhabited only by white people for the preservation of the race, led a faction in establishing the neo-Nazi group National Alliance (1974). Under the pseudonym Andrew Macdonald, he published the race-war novel, *The Turner Diaries* (1978). Five years later, the Order (or Silent Brotherhood) was formed by Robert Mathews in Metaline Falls, Washington, patterning itself on a cell by the same name featured in Pierce's novel. The Order went on to engage in robbery, counterfeiting, and murder, including the gunning down of Alan Berg (June 18, 1984), a Denver radio talk show host who criticized neo-Nazism. Later, Timothy McVeigh, inspired by a passage in *The Turner Diaries*, carried out the truck bombing of a federal office building in Oklahoma City, killing 168 people (April 19, 1995).

According to the SPLC, in 2008 there were 207 known neo-Nazi groups in forty-two states, with the most concentrated in California (13), Texas (12), and Michigan (11). There were also ninety racist skinhead groups in twenty-six states, including California (21), Pennsylvania (11), New Jersey (12), and Florida (6). Of the thirty-six Christian Identity groups scattered across twenty-five states, considerably weakened following the 2004 death of Robert Butler, some 20 percent were based in California (7).

Roger Chapman

See also: Anti-Semitism; Aryan Nations; Civil Rights Movement; Confederate Flag; Duke, David; Militia Movement; Montana Freemen; Philadelphia, Mississippi; Race; Rockwell, George Lincoln; Ruby Ridge Incident; Vigilantism.

Further Reading

Barkun, Michael. *Religion and the Racist Right: The Origins of the Christian Identity Movement.* Rev. ed. Chapel Hill: University of North Carolina Press, 1997.

Newton, Michael. *The Ku Klux Klan: History, Organization, Language, Influence and Activities of America's Most Notorious Secret Societies.* Jefferson, NC: McFarland, 2007.

Ridgeway, James. *Blood in the Face: The Ku Klux Klan, Aryan Nations, Nazi Skinheads, and the Rise of a New White Culture.* New York: Thunder's Mouth Press, 1990.

Schlatter, Evelyn A. *Aryan Cowboys: White Supremacists and the Search for a New Frontier, 1970–2000.* Austin: University of Texas Press, 2006.

Southern Poverty Law Center Web site. www.splcenter.org.

Young, Mitchell. *White Supremacy Groups.* Detroit, MI: Greenhaven Press, 2008.

Wildmon, Donald

The founder and executive director of the American Family Association (AFA), an evangelical Christian organization, the Reverend Donald E. Wildmon pioneered the use of boycotts by conservative Protestants and fundamentalists against advertisers on television programs with content identified as offensive to traditional Christian moral standards. He later expanded his watchdog activities to other entertainment and artistic media. In the culture wars, Wildmon's highest achievement was drawing public attention to the controversial art photos of Robert Mapplethorpe and Andres Serrano in the 1980s, which led to a national debate on the public funding of the arts by the National Endowment for the Arts. Wildmon has also called for eliminating government funding of the Public Broadcasting Service (PBS).

Donald Ellis Wildmon was born on January 18, 1938, in Dumas, Mississippi. He graduated from Millsap College in Jackson, Mississippi (BA, 1960) and Emory University in Atlanta (MDiv, 1965). After serving in the U.S. Army (1961–1963), he was ordained in the United Methodist Church (1964) and pastored at congregations in various Mississippi towns until 1977, when he established the National Federation for Decency, predecessor of the AFA.

Organizationally, the Tupelo-based AFA consists of a legal arm, the AFA Center for Law and Policy, and an advocacy arm, AFA Action. The nonprofit organization syndicates a half-hour radio program called *AFA Report*, aired by some 1,200 stations; and the AFA itself operates about 200 stations through noncommercial educational licenses controlled by the American Family Radio Network, launched in 1987. Wildmon has taken advantage of federal law to operate his stations at full power and broadcast over several of the "liberal and secular" National Public Radio (NPR) stations.

Wildmon has written more than eighteen books, primarily in the genre of Christian inspiration, including *Stand Up to Life! A Man's Reflection on Living* (1975) and *Following the Carpenter: Parables to Inspire Obedience in the Christian Life* (1997). His book *The Home Invaders* (1985) offers an analysis of television and the general media, which the jacket proclaims a "mind-polluting tide seeking to submerge us all!"

The People for the American Way, often in opposition to the AFA, suggests that Wildmon's definition of "indecent" means anything not in accordance with his Christian worldview and political preferences, including "television, the separation of church and state, pornography, 'the homosexual agenda,' premarital sex, legal abortion, the National Endowment for the Arts, gambling, unfiltered Internet access in libraries, and the removal of school-sponsored religious worship from public schools."

Over the years, Wildmon's boycott and decency campaigns have targeted such corporations as Allstate Insurance, American Airlines, Citigroup, Coca-Cola Company, Eastman Kodak, Ford Motor Company, Kraft Foods, PepsiCo., and Wal-Mart; such television shows as *Desperate Housewives*, *Ellen*, *Nightline*, *NYPD Blue*, *Rose-anne*, and *Saturday Night Live*; the film *Last Temptation of Christ* and others; and pop culture figures including radio "shock jock" Howard Stern and singer Madonna. Critics maintain that AFA boycotts are largely ineffective and serve primarily to generate publicity and funds for the organization.

Chip Berlet

See also: Censorship; Evangelicalism; Family Values; Fundamentalism, Religious; Mapplethorpe, Robert; Media Bias; National Endowment for the Arts; National Public Radio; Public Broadcasting Service; Religious Right; Serrano, Andres; Sexual Revolution.

Further Reading

AFA Online Web site. www.afa.net.

Boston, Rob. "In Don We Trust?" *Church & State*, May 2001.

Dedman, Bill. "Bible Belt Blowhard." *Mother Jones*, October 1992.

Wildmon, Donald, with Randall Nulton. *Don Wildmon: The Man the Networks Love to Hate.* Wilmore, KY: Bristol Books, 1989.

Will, George

An influential political commentator, George Will has provided a conservative perspective on American politics and culture as well as international affairs since the 1970s. His eloquent, self-confident style and strong opinions have generated criticism from both the left and the right.

George Frederick Will was born on May 4, 1941, in Champaign, Illinois. He received his education at Trinity College (BA, 1962), Oxford University (MA, 1964), and Princeton University (PhD, 1967). After teaching political philosophy at Michigan State University and the University of Toronto, he served from 1970 to 1972 on the staff of U.S. Senator Gordon Allott (R-CO). Will began his career in journalism as Washington editor for the conservative journal National Review from 1972 to 1975. As a member of the Washington Post Writers Groups beginning in 1974, his columns became syndicated in more than 450 newspapers across the United States. In 1976, he also became a weekly columnist for Newsweek. Expanding his commentary to television, he joined Agronsky and Company (1977–1984) and ABC's This Week (1981–present).

In addition to publishing several collections of his columns, Will has written several books on politics and world affairs, including *Statecraft as Soulcraft: What Government Does* (1983); *The New Season: A Spectator's Guide to the 1988 Election* (1987); *Restoration: Congress, Term Limits, and the Recovery of Deliberative Democracy* (1992); *The Woven Figure: Conservatism and America's Fabric: 1994–1997* (1997); *With a Happy Eye But . . . : America and the World, 1997–2002* (2002); and *One Man's America: The Pleasures and Provocations of Our Singular Nation* (2008). A committed Chicago Cubs fan who frequently makes references to baseball in his commentary, he also wrote about the sport in *Men at Work* (1992) and *Bunts* (1998). Will has won a number of journalism awards, including the Pulitzer Prize for commentary in 1977.

Strongly influenced by Aristotle, Edmund Burke, John Henry Newman, and Benjamin Disraeli, Will rejects the libertarian version of conservatism in favor of traditionalism, sometimes called "Tory conservatism." His emphasis on the public good over individual interest, and the values of justice and equality of opportunity, has led him to oppose uncontrolled free-market capitalism and support certain taxes, welfare programs, and civil rights laws. Will's desire to use government to achieve social ends has its limits, however, as evidenced by his opposition to efforts to bring about racial equality through affirmative action, busing, and quotas.

As a traditionalist, Will has sought to preserve historic practices, institutions, and values and promote individual virtue. Government, in his view, has the responsibility to regulate activities, such as pornography, drugs, abortion, and surrogate motherhood, that threaten these elements. He also argues for limitations on freedom of speech and states that some forms of sexual behavior should not be tolerated. Will carries these views of domestic affairs into his understanding of foreign policy, where he advocates a nationalist stance and the need for U.S. leaders to explain to Americans why and when the citizenry must sacrifice personal interests for the security of the larger community.

Libertarian conservatives have criticized Will's support of big government and rejection of the free market. Liberals have argued that he is inconsistent and has an inadequate concept of justice. He has also been accused of ethical lapses, particularly for his undisclosed participation in Ronald Reagan's preparation for the 1980 campaign debate with Jimmy Carter and his commentary on the 1996 presidential race while his wife served in the campaign of Republican nominee Robert Dole.

Gary Land

See also: Abortion; Affirmative Action; Carter, Jimmy; *National Review*; Reagan, Ronald; War on Drugs.

Further Reading

Burner, David, and Thomas R. West. *Column Right: Conservative Journalists in the Service of Nationalism.* New York: New York University Press, 1988.

Chappell, Larry W. *George F. Will.* New York: Twayne, 1997.

Francis, Samuel T. "The Case of George Will." *Modern Age* 30:2 (1986): 141–47.

Neuchterlein, James. "George Will and American Conservatism." *Commentary* 76 (1983): 35–43.

Rozell, Mark J. "George F. Will's 'Tory Conservatism.'" In *American Conservative Opinion Leaders,* ed. Mark J. Rozell and James F. Pontuso, 13–28. Boulder, CO: Westside, 1990.

Williams, William Appleman

Issuing a devastating—some said "un-American"—reinterpretation of U.S. foreign relations, William Appleman Williams became a leading figure in the "revisionist school" of American diplomatic history. As opposed to the standard depictions of the United States as a benevolent and benign Cold War power containing Soviet aggression, from Williams's pen came the chronicles of a conniving imperialist tyrant driven to global expansion by its own economic avarice.

Born on June 12, 1921, in Atlantic, Iowa, Williams seemed the quintessential patriotic young American, enrolling at the U.S. Naval Academy and late in World War II serving as an executive officer in the Pacific, where he earned a Purple Heart. His outlook began to change after the war, however, when the navy reassigned him to flight school in Corpus Christi, Texas, where he recognized the injustice of racial segregation and began to work with African Americans, Quakers, and communists to promote integration. For his efforts, his superiors reprimanded him, the FBI threatened him, and local officials physically assaulted him. After his military discharge, he earned a PhD in history at the University of Wisconsin at Madison (1950) and later served on its faculty (1957–1968). He taught history at a number of institutions, chiefly Oregon State University (1968–1988), from which he retired.

In most history books of the time, the United States unintentionally acquired global power as a consequence of World War II. Catapulted into power by the war, the story went, isolationist and peace-loving Americans had little choice but to develop a "realist" foreign policy and pragmatically wield power for good in the containment of the Soviet Union. Thus, global politics forced an unwilling and disinterested America to serve as the architect and enforcer of a new world order, a mission the United States never sought and often detested.

Williams, instead, described a long-term pursuit of empire. In *The Tragedy of American Diplomacy* (1959), he outlined late-nineteenth-century policies, such as the Open Door policy in China, that belied the image of a nation averse to global power. In *The Contours of American History* (1961), Williams expanded his critique, locating the designs of American imperialism in antebellum mercantilism and leaders such as Thomas Jefferson and Andrew Jackson. In *The Roots of the Modern American Empire* (1969), Williams attributed the nation's imperialism during the Gilded Age to agricultural interests rather than simply industrial concerns. Thus, he presented the United States as a nation with a history of voluntarily selling its democratic birthright for a mess of capitalist pottage. Once set on the path to empire, the American nation had little choice but to suppress national liberation movements—a betrayal of the ideals of the American Revolution.

Critics such as Arthur M. Schlesinger, Jr., have denounced Williams's interpretation of U.S. imperialism as dogmatic and poorly documented. Schlesinger and others have noted, for example, that Williams's research did not include manuscript collections outside the United States that might have challenged his unilateral depiction of U.S. imperialism.

The Organization of American Historians elected Williams president of the professional association in 1980. That same year, he published his retrospective, *Empire as a Way of Life: An Essay on the Causes and Character of America's Predicament Along with a Few Thoughts About an Alternative*, using it to challenge Reagan conservatism. He died two years after his retirement from teaching, on March 8, 1990.

Richard C. Goode

See also: American Exceptionalism; Chomsky, Noam; Cold War; Reagan, Roland; Revisionist History; Schlesinger, Arthur M., Jr.; Soviet Union and Russia.

Further Reading

Berger, Henry W. *A William Appleman Williams Reader.* Chicago: Ivan R. Dee, 1992.

Buhle, Paul M., and Edward Rice-Maximin. *William Appleman Williams: The Tragedy of Empire.* New York: Routledge, 1995.

Wilson, Edmund

Once praised by Gore Vidal as "America's best mind," Edmund Wilson was a widely respected literary critic and social commentator. His most commercially successful work, a collection of stories titled *Memoirs of Hecate County* (1946), was for a time banned as obscene. As a political progressive, Wilson participated in the culture wars as a critic of capitalism, the Cold War, and the increasing specialization of literary studies.

The bookish Wilson, whose ancestors enjoyed prominence in Puritan New England, was born on May 8, 1895, in Red Bank, New Jersey. After studying literature at Princeton University (AB, 1916), where he befriended F. Scott Fitzgerald, he served in World War I as a hospital orderly in France. After the war, he served as editor of *Vanity Fair* magazine (1920–1921) and later worked on the staffs of the *New Republic*, *The New Yorker*, and the *New York Review of Books*. His works of criticism, many of them collections of magazine articles, focused primarily on literature, politics, and culture, and earned him a reputation as the preeminent cultural critic of his time.

Fascinated with Marxism, Wilson wrote *To the Finland Station* (1940), tracing three centuries of socialist development, capped by Vladimir Lenin's arrival in Russia at the start of the Bolshevik Revolution. In *Patriotic Gore* (1962), he analyzes American literature of the Civil War era, concluding that the nation's desire for order is based largely on a hunger for power. In reaction to personal difficulties with the Internal Revenue Service—he refused to file tax returns from the mid-1940s to mid-1950s—he wrote *The Cold War and the Income Tax* (1963), complaining that high taxes were a consequence of the Vietnam War. In *The Fruits of the MLA* (1968), he scorns that organization's "hyphen-hunting" (emphasis on "ethnic" literature) and output of academic editions of unimportant literary works. His critique inspired the creation of the Library of America editions.

Wilson's cause célèbre was *Memoirs of Hecate County*, published by Doubleday in 1946. In it, the unnamed male narrator, while offering misogynistic stories that take place in a fictitious New York suburb, graphically recounts numerous sexual relations. During the obscenity trial initiated by the New York Society for the Improvement of Morals, literature professor Lionel Trilling argued that the book's redeeming value was its study of good and evil. Wilson lost the case on appeal in 1948, when the U.S. Supreme Court rendered a 4–4 decision, with one justice not participating. The book was therefore banned in New York State for several years. Wilson died at the age of seventy-seven on June 12, 1972.

Roger Chapman

See also: Book Banning; Censorship; Cold War; Great Books; Kubrick, Stanley; Marxism; Multiculturalism and Ethnic Studies; Pornography; Tax Reform; Vidal, Gore; Vietnam War.

Further Reading

Karolides, Nicholas J., Margaret Bald, and Dawn B. Sova. *100 Banned Books: Censorship History of World Literature.* New York: Checkmark Books, 1999.

Menand, Louis. "Missionary." *The New Yorker*, August 8 and 15, 2005.

Meyers, Jeffrey. *Edmund Wilson: An Autobiography.* Boston: Houghton Mifflin, 1995.

Winfrey, Oprah

Television superstar, magazine publisher, actress, and writer Oprah Winfrey, widely known by her first name alone, is said to be the highest-paid entertainer in the world, the first African-American billionaire (net worth exceeding $1.4 billion in 2006), and the most influential woman in the media industry. Although Winfrey's wealth and influence derive in large measure from ownership of her own multimedia production company, called Harpo, the foundation of her success is said to be the ability to connect on a personal level with audiences of her Emmy-winning daytime talk show and the readers of her magazine. At the same time, her emotion-centered approach and the ways in which she has used her influence have also made her the target of criticism in the culture wars.

Orpah (later spelled Oprah) Gail Winfrey was born on January 29, 1954, in Kosciusko, Mississippi. After studying speech communication and performing arts at Tennessee State University (BA, 1976), she spent several years in broadcasting and became the host of WLS-TV's *AM Chicago* in 1984. It soon became the highest-rated talk show in Chicago, and two years later, renamed the *Oprah Winfrey Show*, entered national syndication. Winfrey went on to star in film adaptations of Alice Walker's *The Color Purple* (1985) and Toni Morrison's *Beloved* (1998), which she co-produced. In 1996, she introduced a segment on her television show called Oprah's Book Club, which dramatically increased the sale of books she recommended (many of them the "great books"), a phenomenon that came to be called the "Oprah Effect." In 2000, she founded *O, The Oprah Magazine*, which reached a paid monthly circulation of 2.7 million copies within two years. In 2004, Winfrey became the first African American to be included in *BusinessWeek*'s list of the Fifty Most Generous Philanthropists. In 2006, she announced a three-year deal with XM Satellite Radio to launch a new channel called Oprah & Friends. And in 2008, she announced plans for a new cable TV network: OWN, the Oprah Winfrey Network.

The *Oprah Winfrey Show* began with a somewhat sensationalist bent, featuring such provocative guests as nudists, transsexuals, white supremacists, sex offenders, and the like. As the program found its niche and audience, it became less provocative, but nonetheless gained a reputation as a "group-therapy session." Oprah added a personal touch with frank confessions, talking about her weight problem and revealing that she had been sexually abused as a child and tried crack cocaine as a young adult.

In 1996, she was sued by a group of Texas cattle producers for airing a show on mad cow disease, after which beef sales declined significantly at grocery stores nationwide. Winfrey was accused of unfairly disparaging beef by having an animal rights activist on the program and raising public awareness of mad cow disease, which had infected millions of cows in Great Britain. Supporters argued that she was exercising her right to free speech; critics said she was guilty of making unreasonable and unsubstantiated claims regarding beef. The case was thrown out by the U.S. District Court in Amarillo, Texas.

In 2007, with Winfrey drawing 60 million viewers to her program every day, critics contended that she was not doing enough to effectuate progressive social change. Her unwillingness to address complex social issues, such as racism, sexism, and class warfare, earned her the label "Mammy" from cultural critics such as the University of Maryland sociologist Patricia Hill Collins. Rather than lead nuanced discussions on social and structural inequities in American society, Oprah focused on the promotion of "self healing" and "personal change." Such an approach, argued her critics, ignores the long-standing societal structures that enable social ills to continue and fails to promote the necessary social or political transformation. On the other hand, Winfrey's expressions of concern about sexual predators led to federal legislation in 1993. Meanwhile, an appearance on the *Oprah Winfrey Show* became a must for any candidate seeking success on the presidential campaign trail. The host rarely uttered a word regarding her own political preferences until 2007, when she publicly endorsed Barack Obama, the U.S. senator from Illinois. Her appearances with Obama during the Democratic primary campaign drew large crowds, and her support was regarded as especially influential among women voters.

Even Winfrey's philanthropic efforts have been the subject of debate. In 2007, she opened an all-girls school in South Africa to much fanfare, with skeptics disparaging the venture from the outset as a publicity stunt and public relations tactic. When allegations of physical and sexual abuse emerged shortly after the school's opening, critics charged that Oprah had failed by not properly screening and monitoring the staff. Her philanthropic efforts, meanwhile, had been far-reaching for years. Since its founding in 1998, Oprah's Angel Network alone had raised more than $50 million for international charity. In 2005, *BusinessWeek* estimated Oprah's philanthropic contributions at some $250 million.

Danielle R. Vitale and Valerie Palmer-Mehta

See also: Animal Rights; Blackface; Doctor Phil; Donahue, Phil; Great Books; Morrison, Toni; Obama, Barack; Sex Offenders; Transgender Movement; White Supremacists.

Further Reading

Garson, Helen. *Oprah Winfrey: A Biography.* Westport, CT: Greenwood Press, 2004.

Harris, Jennifer, and Elwood Watson. *The Oprah Phenomenon.* Lexington: University Press of Kentucky, 2007.

Illousz, Eva. *Oprah Winfrey and the Glamour of Misery: An Essay on Popular Culture.* New York: Columbia University Press.

Oprah.com: Live Your Best Life Web site. www.oprah .com.

Squire, Corrinne. "Empowering Women? *The Oprah Winfrey Show.*" In *Feminist Television Criticism: A Reader,* ed. Charlotte Brunsdon, Julie D'Acci, and Lynn Spigel, 98–113. New York: Clarendon Press, 1997.

Wolf, Naomi

Feminist author Naomi Wolf is known for her best-selling first book, *The Beauty Myth: How Images of Beauty Are Used Against Women* (1991), regarded as one of the central texts of third-wave feminism. The "beauty myth," she argues, is not about physical appearance but the conditioning of female behavior in order to maintain male dominance in society. Through an examination of the cosmetic industry, fashion magazines, eating disorders, diets, silicone breast implants, and cosmetic surgery, Wolf argues that such cultural controls make women subject to outside approval and censure, replacing traditional religious and sexual taboos with new forms of repression. Moreover, she sees the "beauty myth" as part of a backlash against the gains of the feminist movement. Wolf calls for a reinterpretation of beauty as "noncompetitive, nonhierarchical, and nonviolent."

Born on November 12, 1962, in San Francisco, Wolf studied English literature at Yale University (BA, 1984)

Third-wave feminist Naomi Wolf argues in her acclaimed 1991 book *The Beauty Myth* that "beauty" is a paternalistic social construct perpetuated by popular culture, industry, and the legal and medical communities to exploit and suppress women. *(Michael A. Smith/Time & Life Pictures/Getty Images)*

and was a Rhodes Scholar at Oxford (1984–1987). A prolific writer of both books and essays, Wolf has been interviewed extensively in print and on television. Her other writings include *Fire with Fire: The New Female Power and How It Will Change the Twenty-first Century* (1993), which examines the feminist movement and argues that "victim" feminism must be replaced by "power" feminism that "hates sexism without hating men"; *Promiscuities: The Secret Struggles of Womanhood* (1997), which decodes popular culture's mixed sexual messages that stigmatize girls and women; *Misconceptions: Truth, Lies, and the Unexpected on the Journey to Motherhood* (2001), which discusses how society simultaneously sentimentalizes pregnancy and fails to support mothers; *The Tree House: Eccentric Wisdom from My Father on How to Live, Love, and See* (2005), which recounts the advice of her father, writer Leonard Wolf, on living and creativity; and *The End of America: A Letter of Warning to a Young Patriot* (2007), which warns how America could slip into fascism.

Because her writings bridge journalism and academics, Wolf has been variously criticized for self-indulgent reflections, overstating statistics, and watering down feminism to make it more inclusive. Her stint as a paid consultant to Al Gore's 2000 presidential campaign raised eyebrows, and Gore received unfavorable publicity after *Time* magazine reported Wolf's advice to have the candidate dress as an "alpha male" to attract female voters. In 2004, Wolf accused the literary critic Harold Bloom of sexually inappropriate behavior when she was an undergraduate at Yale. Two years later the Jewish feminist was again in the news when she reported having a vision, under hypnosis, of Jesus Christ, a claim questioned by both the Religious Right and the Jewish community.

Rebecca Nicholson-Weir

See also: Beauty Pageants; Feminism, Second-Wave; Feminism, Third-Wave; Gore, Al; Paglia, Camille; Religious Right; Sexual Assault; Stay-at-Home Mothers; Victimhood.

Further Reading

Foster, Patricia. *Minding the Body: Women Writers on Body and Soul.* New York: Anchor Books, 1995.
Gotschall, Mary G. "Poisoned Apple." *National Review,* July 8, 1991.
Greene, Gayle. "The Empire Strikes Back." *Nation,* February 10, 1992.
Wolf, Naomi. "The Silent Treatment." *New York Magazine,* March 1, 2004.

Wolfe, Tom

A leading exponent of "New Journalism," and famous for wearing white suits at every public appearance, the flamboyant author Tom Wolfe has chronicled many aspects of American society, targeting some of its most enduring institutions while snubbing liberal orthodoxy. A social conservative, Wolfe famously dubbed the 1960s the "Me Decade."

Thomas Kennerly Wolfe, Jr., born on March 2, 1931, in Richmond, Virginia, earned a bachelor's degree from Washington and Lee University (1951) and a PhD in American Studies from Yale (1957); his doctoral dissertation focused on communist influences on American writers from 1929 to 1942. Wolfe worked as a journalist for various newspapers, but he is best known for his magazine articles, essays, nonfiction books, and novels; several of the latter were made into Hollywood films.

In 1963, Wolfe investigated Southern California's custom car culture for *Esquire* magazine but struggled to write an article. Facing a deadline, he wrote a long letter to his editor explaining what he had found, and the letter was subsequently printed almost verbatim, launching Wolfe on what he called "New Journalism," a style also used by writers such as Truman Capote, Hunter S. Thompson, and Norman Mailer. Unlike traditional journalism, in which the reporter remains an inconspicuous observer and objective nonentity, New Journalism interjects the writer's personality and subjective point of view. Wolfe took this approach in several books documenting the radical youth culture of the 1960s and 1970s.

The Kandy-Kolored Tangerine-Flake Streamlined Baby (1965), a collection of nonfiction pieces, was Wolfe's first longer work of New Journalism, though he gained greater notoriety with the publication of *The Electric Kool-Aid Acid Test* (1968) and *The Pump House Gang* (1968). Novelistic treatments of real events, these works provided a descriptive account of the lifestyle of the 1960s counterculture. *Mauve Gloves and Madmen, Clutter and Vine* (1976) included one of his most widely cited essays, or at least its catchphrase, "The Me Decade and the Third Great Awakening."

Wolfe addressed race relations in *Radical Chic and Mau-Mau-ing the Flak-Catchers* (1970) and *A Man in Full* (1998), sexual mores in *Hooking Up* (2000), modern art and architecture in *The Painted Word* (1975) and *From Bauhaus to Our House* (1981), and the hedonism of college campuses in the novel *I Am Charlotte Simmons* (2004). His portrayal of NASA and its fledgling space program, as well as the mores and exploits of the astronauts training for the moon missions, was the focus of *The Right Stuff* (1979), which won a National Book Award and was made into a popular movie. *The Bonfire of the Vanities* (1987), a fictional indictment of the greed of the 1980s, was also made into a film. The audiobook *Ambush at Fort Bragg* (1997), promoted as a negative critique of television newscasters, was a morality tale against gays in the military.

Wolfe has been frequently interviewed for his views on cultural issues. His opinions range from the humorous to the caustic, showing particular disdain for liberal academics, the New Left, anticapitalist pontifications, and political correctness. He once stated that Alexander Solzhenitsyn's *The Gulag Archipelago* will be regarded as one of the most important works of history because it unalterably linked socialism and concentration camps.

Kirk Richardson and Roger Chapman

See also: Civil Rights Movement; Communists and Communism; Counterculture; Gays in the Military; New Journalism; New Left; Political Correctness; Race; Sexual Revolution; Thompson, Hunter S.

Further Reading

Bloom, Harold. *Tom Wolfe*. Philadelphia: Chelsea House, 2001.
Ragen, Brian Abel. *Tom Wolfe: A Critical Companion*. Westport, CT: Greenwood, 2002.
Scurra, Dorothy, ed. *Conversations with Tom Wolfe*. Jackson: University Press of Mississippi, 1990.
Shomette, Doug, ed. *The Critical Response to Tom Wolfe*. Westport, CT: Greenwood, 1992.

Women in the Military

American women have been part of the nation's regular standing forces since passage of the Women's Armed Services Integration Act in 1948, but it was not until the abolition of the separate women's corps in each of the major service branches in the 1970s and the introduction of mixed-gender basic training by the air force (1976), navy (1992), and army (1993) that the U.S. armed forces have approached anything near gender integration. By 2000, women made up 20 percent of all military personnel.

Opponents of gender integration in the military have argued that the lowering of physical requirements necessary to accommodate women diminishes force strength and readiness, and that combat effectiveness is compromised by the complications of mixing men and women in the field. Proponents dismiss such arguments as antiquated, believing that proper tactics, training, and use of technology can more than compensate for female physical limitations. Men and women, they argue further, can effectively work together if that is the professional expectation communicated and enforced by all leaders. Proponents of women serving fully in all military roles, including combat, argue that commanders should not be restricted in how to deploy their troops.

Major changes were instituted during the 1970s, as Congress opened the federal service academies to women; the army, navy, and air force began admitting women to flight training; and several discriminatory regulations and policies were revised, including the practice of discharg-ing pregnant servicewomen. The number of women in the U.S. armed services more than doubled over the course of the decade. Despite the reforms, however, the movement toward gender equality stopped short of allowing women to hold combat positions. Moreover, until 1994, women could not be assigned anywhere there was even the threat of combat, hostile fire, or capture equal to that of a combat area, regardless of their vocations. Between 1992 and 1994, restrictions against women serving on combat aircraft and naval vessels were lifted (submarines excluded); such restrictions remained in place for direct ground combat, leaving women still ineligible for positions in infantry, armor, field artillery, and all special operations divisions.

Such exclusions have not kept American servicewomen out of harm's way, however, as eleven of the fifteen women who died in the Persian Gulf War (1991) fell in combat situations. And as the 2003 experiences of Pfc. Jessica Lynch in the Iraq War dramatically attest, keeping women out of combat occupations does not always shield them from direct ground combat. Captured in Iraq on March 23, 2003, the twenty-year-old Lynch was the only survivor of an insurgent attack on her Humvee in a maintenance convoy on the road near Nasiriyah. In releasing the video of her rescue, the Pentagon acknowledged the extraordinary interest the public had taken in Lynch's plight. The extensive coverage of her ordeal was seen by some as a reflection of public ambivalence about daughters serving in combat situations. Between 2003 and 2007, over 160,500 women served in Iraq and Afghanistan, meaning in those theatres of war one in seven soldiers were female. In Iraq during that period, seventy-one female soldiers died and another 450 were wounded.

The U.S. military has often been accused of holding its women to different standards of conduct than it does its men. Throughout the 1980s, for example, female service members were investigated and dismissed under suspicion of homosexuality at a much higher rate than their male counterparts. Lt. Kelly Flinn, the first bomber pilot in the Air Force, resigned in 1997 under threat of court-martial for adultery. Her defenders argued that while she had engaged in an affair with a married man, adultery was routinely ignored among male officers; thus, it was said, prosecuting Flinn for that offense was sexist and discriminatory. Flinn's critics countered that it was her failure to follow orders in continuing the affair that constituted an untenable breach of military order, and that such an offense was uniformly punished regardless of gender.

A series of scandals in the 1990s and early 2000s revealed the extent of sexual harassment and abuse of women in the services, and the consistent failure of their commanders to prosecute offenders. Dozens of women went public in June 1991 with accounts of sexual assault at the September 1990 convention of Tailhook, a popular private organization for naval aviators. Although many of these women had reported the incidents to their commanders, there had been no investigation. Public embarrassment over this failure was great enough to prompt the resignation of Secretary of the Navy H. Lawrence Garrett, but, according to a report issued by the inspector general in September of 1992, the navy's subsequent investigation of the allegations was poorly conducted and concealed evidence in an effort to avoid bad publicity. Four years later, the army suffered its own scandal when it was reported that male drill sergeants had demanded sex from female trainees at the Aberdeen Proving Ground in Maryland. Throughout the Iraq War, which began in 2003, there were reports numbering in the thousands of sexual harassment and rape of female soldiers by men in their units. In 2004, Spc. Suzanne Swift was court-martialed for desertion after she went AWOL from the army while home on leave from Iraq; she claimed she had been forced into sexual relations with a commanding officer and did not want to return to duty.

Critics of gender integration in the military, such as senators Rick Santorum (R-PA) and Charles Robb (D-VA) during the 1990s, blamed sexual misconduct on policies that place men and women in the same training situations. After the Tailhook and Aberdeen incidents, Representative Roscoe Bartlett (R-MD) introduced a bill to ban co-ed basic training, but the proposal was opposed by the heads of the major service branches. Proponents of integrated military training and units, such as Senator Olympia Snow (R-MA), argue that women will be treated with less respect if they are not subject to the same regime as their male counterparts.

Holly Alloway

See also: Gays in the Military; Sexual Harassment; Southern Baptist Convention.

Further Reading

Fenner, Lorry M., and Marie de Young. *Women in Combat: Civic Duty or Military Liability?* Washington, DC: Georgetown University Press, 2001.

Mitchell, Brian. *Women in the Military: Flirting with Disaster.* Washington, DC: Regency, 1998.

Nelson, T.S. *For Love of Country: Confronting Rape and Sexual Abuse in the U.S. Military.* New York: Hawthorn Maltreatment and Trauma Press, 2002.

Zeigler, Sara L., and Gregory G. Gunderson. *Moving Beyond G.I. Jane: Women and the U.S. Military.* Lanham, MD: University Press of America, 2005.

Women's Studies

Women's studies, with roots in the feminist and social movements of the 1960s and 1970s, is an interdisciplinary academic discipline that focuses on the lives and experiences of women, as well as theories about gender. More than 700 programs have been offered on college campuses nationwide in the three decades since the inception of the first women's studies program at San Diego State University in 1969. In the meantime, the National Women's Studies Association was founded in 1977 to promote women's studies at all levels of education, from preschool to doctorate programs. Proponents of women's studies cite inclusiveness and the expansion of knowledge as justification for the field, whereas critics suggest that such an approach fosters political correctness while unwittingly marginalizing the study of women by ghettoizing it as a narrow field of academe.

In the 1960s, as scholars and activists explored areas of interest and research that included female voices and perspectives, there was a demand to integrate these new findings in higher education. There was likewise a desire to create a formal space in the academic world, which had been largely dominated by male history, achievements, and perspectives, to include the study of women, gender, and women's achievements. At the same time, there was a sense that women's studies could boost female representation on college faculties. From these concerns and interests grew women's studies classes that dealt with international women's issues in history, literature, art, and feminist theory. Many colleges and universities now have women's studies programs and departments, and students are able to pursue a major, minor, or graduate degree in women's studies.

As American academia has come under attack by conservatives since the 1980s for being too liberal and overly concerned with the study of minorities and women, the field of women's studies—in particular its feminist content—has been widely criticized as radical. The negative stereotypes associated with feminists have often been directed at the faculty, students, and curriculum of women's studies. Critics argue, for example, that women's studies is largely antimale and against traditional values. "Why is there not men's studies?" they ask. Those who support the inclusion of women's studies in academia contend that mainstream classes generally focus on men and male culture, making them normative.

Another widely debated issue has to do with the balance between scholarship and activism. While the advent and growth of women's studies as an academic discipline has been influenced by the feminist movement, some individuals believe women's studies focuses unduly on social activism rather than intellectual advancement. On the other hand, many radical proponents feel that women's studies is too theoretical and elitist, minimizing its real-world effectiveness.

The designation "women's studies" itself has been the subject of debate. Some think the term is too limiting, considering that much of current theory and research has to do with broader issues of gender, femininity, and masculinity, thereby encompassing the experiences and identities of women, men, and transgendered persons rather than just women. To reflect this multifaceted approach, programs at some institutions have been renamed "women's and gender studies" or simply "gender studies." Those who prefer to keep "women" (or some form of it) in the designation are fearful that referring only to "gender studies" will diminish the emphasis on women, both in the program of study and in the academic space for them.

Alexandra DeMonte

See also: Academic Freedom; Feminism, Second-Wave; Feminism, Third-Wave; Men's Movement; Multiculturalism and Ethnic Studies; Transgender Movement.

Further Reading

Baumgardner, Jennifer, and Amy Richards. *Manifesta: Young Women, Feminism, and the Future.* New York: Farrar, Straus and Giroux, 2000.

Boxer, Marilyn. *When Women Ask the Questions: Creating Women's Studies in America.* Baltimore: Johns Hopkins University Press, 1998.

Grewal, Inderpal, and Caren Kaplan, eds. *An Introduction to Women's Studies: Gender in a Transnational World.* New York: McGraw-Hill Humanities, 2002.

Howe, Florence, ed. *The Politics of Women's Studies: Testimony from 30 Founding Mothers.* New York: Feminist, 2000.

Woodward, Bob

As a reporter for the *Washington Post*, Bob Woodward helped to break the story of the Watergate scandal, leading to President Richard M. Nixon's resignation and ushering in a new era of hard-charging investigative journalism. Woodward later evolved into an "insider journalist" known for his prolific output of books on powerful people and institutions in the nation's capital.

The son of a judge, Robert Upshur Woodward was born on March 26, 1943, in Geneva, Illinois, and grew up in nearby Wheaton. A graduate of Yale University (1965), he served in the U.S. Navy as a communications officer (1965–1970). After one year as a reporter for the *Montgomery Sentinel* in Rockville, Maryland, he joined the *Washington Post*. On June 17, 1972, ten months after being hired by the *Post*, Woodward began collaborating with fellow reporter Carl Bernstein on investigating the break-in at the headquarters of the Democratic National Committee in the Watergate hotel complex in Washington, D.C. Woodward and Bernstein's dogged pursuit of the details, after many other reporters lost interest, eventually revealed connections between the burglars and the White House. In 1973, the *Post* was awarded the Pulitzer Prize for its Watergate coverage. In August 1974, Nixon resigned from office to avoid impeachment.

The young investigative duo followed up their newspaper series with the best-selling book *All the President's Men* (1974), an overview of their Watergate investigation, and *The Final Days* (1976), an account of Nixon's resignation. In the movie version of *All the President's Men* (1976), Robert Redford plays Woodward. In 1990, the executive director of the Richard Nixon Library and Birthplace in Yorba Linda, California, called Woodward "not a responsible journalist" and indicated that he would be denied access to the library's holdings—a statement that was later retracted, but an indication of lasting bitterness. In 2003, Woodward and Bernstein sold their Watergate papers to the University of Texas at Austin for $5 million. In 2005, Watergate again became the focus of national debate when W. Mark Felt, the former associate director of the FBI, revealed himself as "Deep Throat," Woodward's secret inside source during the investigation.

After Watergate, Woodward became an editor at the *Post* and was allowed to pursue special projects. His embarrassment as an editor in overseeing Janet Cooke's 1980 coverage of a child heroin addict, a story that won a Pulitzer Prize but later turned out to be a fabrication, was later offset by his team coverage of the September 11 attacks that earned the *Post* a Pulitzer Prize in 2002. Most of his time as an editor has been spent writing books: *Wired: The Short and Fast Times of John Belushi* (1984); *Veil: The Secret Wars of the CIA, 1981–1987* (1987); *The Commanders* (1991); *The Agenda: Inside the Clinton White House* (1994); *The Choice: How Clinton Won* (1996); *Shadow: Five Presidents and the Legacy of Watergate* (1999); *Maestro: Greenspan's Fed and the American Boom* (2001); *Bush at War* (2002); *Plan of Attack* (2004); *The Secret Man: The Story of Watergate's Deep Throat* (2005); *State of Denial* (2006); and *The War Within: A Secret White House History 2006-2008* (2008). He also co-authored *The Brethren: Inside the Supreme Court* (1979) and *The Man Who Would Be President: Dan Quayle* (1992).

Woodward's books rely on anonymous "deep background" interviews with top officials. Critics, such as David Corn of the *Nation* magazine, contend that such an approach relegates Woodward to the role of a stenographer, and one who can be easily manipulated by political players who parcel out information and "spin" the story in accordance with a rehearsed message. In the introduction of *The Agenda*, Woodward maintains, "I believe there is a place for reporting that aspires to combine the thoroughness of history with the immediacy of journalism."

In *Bush at War* and *Plan of Attack*, Woodward provided laudatory accounts of the George W. Bush administration and its decision to invade Iraq in 2003, but *State of Denial* and *The War Within* were more hard-hitting books.

Woodward had been criticized for holding back information from the public. For example, he did not expose the illegal sale of arms to the Contras in the 1980s until after a congressional investigation was launched. And he did not reveal Colin Powell's opposition to Operation Desert Storm, the name for the 1991 attack on Iraq, until after Congress voted approval. When Bush administration officials wanted to leak the identity of CIA operative Valerie Plame to retaliate against her husband, Joseph Wilson, for his criticism of their rationale for invading Iraq in 2003, Woodward was one of the first reporters to receive the information, although he did not make use of it. He did not reveal his knowledge of the leak until well after Plame's identity became public, but his critics saw it as confirming his chumminess with the Bush administration.

Roger Chapman

See also: Bush Family; Central Intelligence Agency; Felt, W. Mark; Iran-Contra Affair; Liddy, G. Gordon; Media Bias; Nixon, Richard; September 11; Watergate; Whistleblowers.

Further Reading

Corn, David. "Who's in Charge?" *Nation*, March 3, 2003.
———. "Woodward Revised." *Nation*, October 2, 2006.
Evan, Thomas, Rich Wolffe, and John Barry. "The Woodward War." *Newsweek*, October 9, 2006.
Havill, Adrian. *Deep Truth: The Lives of Bob Woodward and Carl Bernstein.* Secaucus, NJ: Carol, 1993.
Jensen, Carl. *Stories That Changed America: Muckrakers of the 20th Century.* New York: Seven Stories Press, 2000.

World

World magazine, established in 1986, is a national weekly news magazine that serves as a conservative Christian counterpart to *Time* and *Newsweek*. Its editor, Marvin Olasky, popularized the phrase "compassionate conservatism," served as an adviser to Texas gubernatorial candidate George W. Bush in the mid-1990s, and later became the provost of King's College, an evangelical school in Manhattan. The magazine has been controversial in the culture wars for its rigid stance on family values, abortion, and homosexuality.

World describes itself as striving for "factual accuracy and biblical objectivity, trying to see the world as best we can the way the Bible depicts it," and notes: "Journalistic humility for us means trying to give God's perspective." In 1999, the publishers of *World* founded the World Journalism Institute with the aim of training its reporters; it has since expanded its mission to "recruit, equip, place and encourage journalists who are Christians in the mainstream newsrooms of America." The institute has been criticized for teaching "directed reporting," or skewing objectivity with religious beliefs. For example,

factual coverage of same-sex marriages might be combined with the position that such marriages are inherently wrong and ungodly.

Conservative Christians who subscribe to *World* regard it as a spiritual alternative to the secular news media that ignores the Bible. Liberal readers, both Christian and non-Christian, argue that such a religious focus can lead to reporting that is biased and inaccurate.

Nevertheless, *World* continues to interpret the news in its unique fashion, offering many readers conservative Christian guidance in their understanding of current affairs.

Joseph Gelfer

See also: Bush Family; Compassionate Conservatism; Evangelicalism; Family Values; Fundamentalism, Religious; Media Bias; Religious Right; Same-Sex Marriage; Secular Humanism; *Washington Times, The.*

Further Reading

Beckerman, Gal. "God Is My Co-Author." *Columbia Journalism Review*, September/October 2004.
Moll, Rob. "World Journalism Institute Changes Its Focus." *Christianity Today*, June 7, 2004.
Olasky, Marvin. *Telling the Truth: How to Revitalize Christian Journalism.* Wheaton, IL: Crossway Books, 1996.
World Magazine Web site. www.worldmag.com.

World Council of Churches

The World Council of Churches (WCC) is an international ecumenical organization dedicated to many social justice issues, including pacifism and peaceful conflict resolution, the eradication of poverty, the rights of oppressed peoples, and environmental preservation. The stated goal of the WCC is to promote Christian unity, which it advances through ecumenism, an effort to bring all churches into a visible unity in one faith and one eucharistic fellowship. Critics, however, characterize it as a leftist organization masking a radical socialist or communist agenda behind acts of faith.

Founded in August 1948, the World Council of Churches now represents approximately 550 million Christians in 340 churches, denominations, and fellowships from 100 countries and territories worldwide—including most orthodox churches, and many Anglican, Baptist, Lutheran, Methodist, and Protestant Reformation denominations. The Roman Catholic Church, although it shares a relationship with the WCC through a joint working group, is not a member.

An assembly and 158-member central council whose officers make up an executive committee govern the WCC, which has no legislative power over its member organizations. The WCC is intended to facilitate dialogue among internal member and other external organizations.

To this end, the WCC has convened the Programme to Combat Racism and many convocations bringing together various religions, all aimed at providing a theological response to pluralism. Though the bulk of the WCC's membership resides in developing nations in the Southern Hemisphere, its primary donors are European Protestant churches.

Due in part to its membership constituency and active political advocacy, the WCC often adopts positions counter to those of the United States and other Western developed nations. The WCC has increasingly become involved in international public policy matters, taking many controversial positions. During the 1970s, for example, it received criticism for its Programme to Combat Racism and alleged funding of liberation movements, guerrillas, and terrorist groups, including the Patriotic Front of Zimbabwe. In recent years, the WCC has urged divestment from Israel; called for a relaxation of U.S., British, and European Union sanctions on the Hamas government in Palestine; apologized for the 2003 invasion of Iraq, calling it a violation of norms of justice and human rights; criticized the U.S. position on global warming; registered disapproval of United Nations' reforms backed by the United States; deplored global economic disparities, calling on developed nations to forgive foreign debt; and blamed racism for the half-hearted response to the global HIV/AIDS crisis and the Hurricane Katrina disaster on the U.S. Gulf Coast in 2005.

Traci L. Nelson

See also: AIDS; Catholic Church; Global Warming; Hurricane Katrina; Israel; McIntire, Carl; Multiculturalism and Ethnic Studies; United Nations.

Further Reading

Lefever, Ernest W. *Nairobi to Vancouver: The World Council of Churches and the World, 1975–1987.* Lanham, MD: University Press of America, 1987.

Vermaat, J.A. Emerson. *The World Council of Churches and Politics.* New York: Freedom House, 1989.

World Council of Churches Web site. www.wcc-coe.org.

World War II Memorial

After years of debate, the National World War II Memorial, located in the heart of the National Mall in Washington, D.C., was dedicated on Memorial Day in 2004. Designed by Friedrich St. Florian, the $195 million memorial has been criticized for its imperial grandiosity (some suggest reminiscent of Nazi architecture) and for crowding the civic space between the Lincoln Memorial and the Washington Monument, a perceived desecration of the American core values the vista has traditionally venerated. Others argue that the memorial is appropriately designed and positioned, affirming the nation's values by paying homage to the men and women who fought in the war to preserve freedom.

Inspiration for the memorial is credited to Roger Durbin, a World War II army veteran who in 1987 complained to U.S. representative Marcy Kaptur (D-OH) that the Marine Corps Iwo Jima statue, the sole "good war" monument in Washington, D.C., does not adequately honor all of those who fought in the war. On May 25, 1993, President Bill Clinton signed legislation authorizing a national World War II monument; two years later, he dedicated the mall site for the project. The design, site selection, and fundraising process prompted a number of lawsuits and twenty-two rounds of acrimonious public hearings. Tom Brokaw's best-selling book *The Greatest Generation* (1998), a tribute to World War II veterans, gave a timely boost to the memorial's backers.

A sunken granite and bronze complex in the classical architectural style, the memorial is situated on 7.4 acres (3.0 hectares) adjacent to the Rainbow Pool on the eastern end of the Reflecting Pool. It features two five-story arches with 10-foot-wide (3-meter) bronze laurel wreaths overhead (representing the Atlantic and Pacific theaters); fifty-six pillars adorned with oak and wheat wreaths (for the industrial and agricultural war output of each state, territory, and the District of Columbia); 4,000 gold stars on the Freedom Wall (each representing 100 war dead); twenty-four bas relief panels (depicting Americans during the war, overseas and at home); four bronze eagles; a victory medal inlayed on the floors; Americans flags on poles; and various fountains and inscriptions. A majority of the funding was provided by corporations and private individuals, the result of a drive spearheaded by Senator Robert Dole (R-KS), himself a decorated veteran of the war.

Opposition to the memorial was mounted by the National Coalition to Save Our Mall, World War II Veterans to Save the Mall, conservation groups, architects, and civil rights activists. These groups wanted the memorial located off to the side, in Constitution Gardens, arguing that the space between the shrines honoring the two greatest presidents—the founder of the nation (Washington) and the emancipator of the slaves (Lincoln)—should not be disrupted by a massive structure having nothing to do with national development. As a compromise, St. Florian modified the memorial's silhouette by lowering the plaza and fountains six feet (1.8 meters) below ground level. Regarding World War II as the pivotal event that ushered in the American Century, establishing the United States as a redeemer nation to the world, proponents countered that the center of the mall was a perfectly appropriate site for the memorial.

Roger Chapman

See also: American Century; American Civil Religion; Brokaw, Tom; Clinton, Bill; Generations and Generational Conflict; September 11 Memorial; Vietnam Veterans Memorial.

Further Reading

Goldberger, Paul. "Down at the Mall." *The New Yorker*, May 31, 2004.

Mills, Nicolaus. *Their Last Battle: The Fight for the National World War II Memorial.* New York: Basic Books, 2004.

National WWII Memorial Web site. www.wwiimemorial. com.

Tolson, Jay. "Scenes from the Mall." *U.S. News & World Report*, September 18, 2000.

Wounded Knee Incident

During the early months of 1973, the village of Wounded Knee, located on the Pine Ridge Reservation in South Dakota, was the scene of a seventy-one-day armed rebellion against the federal government by militants of the American Indian Movement (AIM) led by activist Russell Means. A highly charged site for Native Americans, Wounded Knee was the scene of an 1890 bloody standoff between a group of the Oglala Sioux and the U.S. Army's Seventh Calvary in which between 150 and 200 Indian men, women, and children were killed (along with about 25 soldiers)—an incident variously referred to as the Wounded Knee Massacre and the Battle of Wounded Knee, depending on who is recounting the episode. The 1973 incident drew international attention, exposing the lingering tension between American Indians and the federal government as well as rifts among Indian peoples themselves.

On February 28, 1973, between 200 and 300 Indian activists, primarily armed with deer-hunting rifles, seized Wounded Knee to protest the poor living conditions on Indian reservations and the perceived corruption of reservation officials. One of the first acts of the protesters was to visit and pray over the mass grave of 1890. Others raided the reservation's trading post and museum, destroying artifacts such as a nineteenth-century government ledger of cattle receipts in which Indian recipients were listed by made-up vulgar names.

AIM members believed that the Wounded Knee tribal chairman Richard (Dick) Wilson and his supporting Sioux council represented an illegitimate puppet regime, which they referred to as "white Wounded Knee." Protest leaders presented three demands to the U.S. government: (1) restore and honor 371 broken treaties; (2) reform the Bureau of Indian Affairs (BIA); and (3) conduct an investigation of the corruption at Wounded Knee. The ultimate goal of AIM was to secure self-government for Native Americans, apart from federal rule, in order to reestablish a traditional tribal organization centered on the chiefs and spiritual leaders.

The senior U.S. senator of South Dakota, Democrat George McGovern, freshly defeated in the 1972 presidential election, arrived at the scene of conflict only to be largely rebuffed by AIM. McGovern was remembered for having stated that past wrongs against Native Americans should be forgotten. "It is ridiculous to talk about treaties abrogated by an act of Congress over a hundred years ago," he had complained. During the standoff with federal authorities, AIM declared the independence of the Oglala Sioux Nation and specified that its boundaries were in accordance with the Treaty of Laramie (1868).

The government side of the standoff was being handled by the Department of Justice. Because the occupiers were armed, President Richard Nixon chose to deploy hundreds of Federal Bureau of Investigation (FBI) and U.S. Marshals Service agents. However, being acutely aware of public empathy with the activists, he sought to resolve the situation peacefully; despite those intentions, two AIM members were killed during the siege. As the negotiations ensued, federal agents carried out a series of paramilitary operations designed to exhaust the occupiers. The protesters finally surrendered on May 8, accomplishing little more than publicizing their grievances. Nixon's supporters praised the federal government's patience and restraint throughout the ordeal. In the aftermath of the incident, 185 activists were indicted by federal grand juries for their part in the rebellion, Wilson's government remained intact, hostility between AIM and the FBI continued, and Indians disagreed over the tactics employed by AIM.

Gwendolyn Laird and Roger Chapman

See also: American Indian Movement; Deloria, Vine, Jr.; McGovern, George; Nixon, Richard.

Further Reading

Dewing, Rolland. *Wounded Knee: The Meaning and Significance of the Second Incident.* New York: Irvington, 1985.

Hendricks, Steve. *The Unquiet Grave: The FBI and the Struggle for the Soul of Indian Country.* New York: Thunder's Mouth Press, 2006.

O'Neal, Floyd A., June K. Lyman, and Susan McKay, eds. *Wounded Knee 1973: A Personal Account by Stanley David Lyman.* Lincoln: University of Nebraska Press, 1991.

Young, Neil

Since his debut in the mid-1960s, the Canadian-born singer, songwriter, and guitarist Neil Young has been known for some of the most powerful social protest songs in rock music, targeting with his unmistakable high, warbly voice everything from commercialism to war to racism to drug abuse. His artistic output includes almost five dozen albums, as well as song videos and films. Regarded as one of the premier rock guitarists of all time, nominated for an Oscar, a member of the board of directors of Farm Aid (an organization that helps small, family-owned farms survive in an era of factory farming), and a part owner of the model-train company Lionel, Young is considered the godfather of grunge music. Throughout his eclectic career, he has participated in the culture wars while offering commentary in his original way.

He was born Neil Percival Young on November 12, 1945, in Toronto, Canada. By the time he was in high school, he was a fixture on the music scene of Winnipeg, where he became friends with future band mate Stephen Stills and the folksinger Joni Mitchell. In 1966, Young's band Buffalo Springfield, playing out of Los Angeles, scored a hit with "For What It's Worth," one of the most acclaimed antiwar songs of the 1960s. In 1970, as part of Crosby, Stills, Nash, and Young, he wrote "Ohio" in response to the Kent State shootings of May 4, 1970. The song was banned on many radio stations because of its harsh stance against the Vietnam War and open contempt for President Richard M. Nixon. Years later, in concert, Young dedicated "Ohio" to the Chinese students who died in the June 1989 Tiananmen Square massacre.

Young's songs "Southern Man"—from the album *After the Gold Rush* (1970)—and "Alabama"—from *Harvest* (1972)—painted the picture of a South filled with ignorance and racial prejudice. In rebuttal, the southern band Lynyrd Skynyrd produced the rock classic "Sweet Home Alabama" (1974). Young also spoke out against the drug scene, as in his recording "The Needle and the Damage Done" (1972). "I am not a preacher," he explained, "but drugs killed a lot of great men."

MTV banned the music video of Young's "This Note's for You" (1988) because it lampooned artists shilling goods for money. He produced "Let's Roll" (2001) as a tribute to the passengers of Flight 93 who tried to retake the plane from the terrorists who had hijacked it on September 11, 2001. And on his album *Living with War* (2006), he recorded "Let's Impeach the President" in response to President George W. Bush's policies and the war in Iraq.

Kirk Richardson

See also: Bush Family; Canada; Censorship; China; Dylan, Bob; Factory Farms; Nelson, Willie; Rock and Roll; September 11; Vietnam War; War on Drugs; War Protesters.

Further Reading

McDonough, Jimmy. *Shakey: Neil Young's Biography*. New York: Anchor Books, 2002.

Petridis, Alexis. *Neil Young*. New York: Thunder's Mouth Press, 2000.

Rogan, Johnny. *Neil Young: The Complete Guide to His Music*. London: Omnibus, 2006.

Williamson, Nigel. *Journey Through the Past: The Stories Behind the Classic Songs of Neil Young*. San Francisco: Backbeat Books, 2002.

Zappa, Frank

A politically active, highly prolific, internationally acclaimed rock musician and composer, Frank Zappa, founder of the "freak rock" band Mothers of Invention (1966–1969) and a longtime solo performer, produced more than sixty albums, including *Freak Out!* (1966), the first double rock album; *Absolutely Free* (1967); *We're Only in It for the Money* (1968); *Lumpy Gravy* (1968); *Sheik Yerbouti* (1979); *Tinsel Town Rebellion* (1981); and *Jazz from Hell* (1986). His two biggest hits were "Don't Eat the Yellow Snow" (1974) and "Valley Girl" (1982). Zappa's output was characterized by an eclectic blend of rock, rhythm and blues, jazz, doo-wop, classical music, and avant-garde music, as well as irreverent and satirically smutty lyrics. His songs offered satirical commentary on everything from police states, human sexuality, televangelists, Catholics, "Jewish princesses," hippies, and cocaine users to commercialism, suburbia, war protesters, the Beatles, and anything else he considered hypocritical or banal.

Born Frank Vincent Zappa into a Catholic Italian-American family on December 21, 1940, in Baltimore, Maryland, he spent his formative years in California, where he became interested in musical composition, arrangement, and recording production. In 1962, still a struggling artist, he was set up by a San Bernardino undercover police detective to produce an audio-only sex tape, leading to ten days in jail for "conspiracy to commit pornography." That run-in with the law made Zappa a lifelong cynic toward authority and a champion of free speech. Fear of arrest made him militantly intolerant of drug use in his band.

In the culture wars, Zappa opposed the Parents' Music Resource Center (PMRC), founded in 1985 by Tipper Gore, the wife of then senator Al Gore, and other concerned mothers to lobby against "porn rock"; the PMRC called for warning labels with "decency" ratings to appear on record covers. Zappa spent $70,000 on a personal campaign against PMRC, viewing it as a threat to free speech. In September 1985, he testified before the Senate Commerce, Technology, and Transportation Committee, denouncing PMRC for imposing the values of religious fundamentalism; he later referred to PMRC and its supporters as "cultural terrorists." In the months after his testimony, he released the album *Frank Zappa Meets the Mothers of Prevention*, which features "Porn Wars," a twelve-minute track of sound bites from the hearing, juxtaposed in a way to make his opponents sound ridiculous.

During the late 1980s, Zappa, who was strongly anticommunist, took an interest in the political changes taking place in Eastern Europe and visited the Soviet Union for the first time. In 1990, he was especially welcomed in Czechoslovakia, where he enjoyed cult status and befriended Václav Havel, the leader of the Velvet Revolution. When the country was under Soviet control, Zappa's antitotalitarian song "Plastic People" (1967) had inspired the first underground Czech band, the Plastic People of the Universe. Havel briefly appointed Zappa the country's Special Ambassador to the West on Trade, Culture, and Tourism, a mission that ended abruptly after Zappa publicly referred to U.S. Vice President Dan Quayle as "stupid," triggering a protest from U.S. secretary of state James Baker (whose wife was a co-founder of PMRC). Zappa died of prostate cancer on December 6, 1993, and was posthumously inducted into the Rock and Roll Hall of Fame in 1995.

Roger Chapman

See also: Catholic Church; Censorship; Counterculture; Fundamentalism, Religious; Pornography; Quayle, Dan; Record Warning Labels; Rock and Roll; Soviet Union and Russia.

Further Reading

Miles, Barry. *Zappa: A Biography*. New York: Grove, 2004.

Zero Tolerance

Zero tolerance indicates a strict enforcement of rules or laws and that behaviors such as drug use, sexual harassment, or academic cheating will not be acceptable under any circumstance. Such "get tough" policies are implemented in a wide range of settings, from schools to courts to the workplace. Zero tolerance may be formally codified in rules or laws, but the term is also used informally to imply that certain behaviors are completely forbidden.

Schools are a primary site of zero tolerance policies, due to the passage of the Safe and Drug-Free Schools Act of 1994, which requires all schools receiving federal funding to expel any student who brings a weapon or drugs to school. By 1998, three out of four of the nation's schools had zero tolerance policies in place. In response, suspension and expulsion rates rose nationwide. However, actual rates of school crime remained flat during the 1990s, leading critics to question whether increasing punishment was really the appropriate policy change. Stories emerged of students suspended for drawing pictures of weapons, pointing fingers like guns, or bringing over-the-counter medications to school.

Many school administrators, parents, and the general public tend to support strict policies in the name of school safety and protecting children. High-profile school shootings, such as the one at Columbine High School in Littleton, Colorado, in 1999, created the impression that schools across the country were no longer safe, even in communities with little violence. Such incidents encourage the public to favor tough penalties for minor offenses in hopes of preventing similar tragedies.

The American Bar Association has opposed zero tolerance policies, charging that the "one size fits all" punishments deprive people of their basic due process rights. Zero tolerance, whether in schools, courts, or other settings, ignores the critical factor of context. Without careful examination of circumstances, civil liberties advocates contend, uniform punishments may be applied unfairly.

In addition to education scholars and civil liberties groups, zero tolerance has conservative critics. A *National Review* article charges that zero tolerance is an outgrowth of "political correctness," noting that a Kansas student was suspended for drawing a Confederate flag and his parents' licensed gun was confiscated. Some critics from the right have suggested that zero tolerance policies exist so that people of color cannot complain that they are being punished unfairly, and thus everyone receives severe punishments. While supporters of zero tolerance policies argue that they promote fairness, people from privileged backgrounds are more likely to use legal recourse to challenge rigid applications of rules or laws.

Karen Sternheimer

See also: American Civil Liberties Union; Confederate Flag; Drug Testing; *National Review*; Political Correctness; School Shootings; War on Drugs.

Further Reading

Derbyshire, John. "The Problem with 'Zero.'" *National Review*, May 28, 2001.

Halloway, John H. "The Dilemma of Zero Tolerance." *Educational Leadership* 59 (2001): 85.

Skiba, Russel J., and Reece L. Peterson. "The Dark Side of Zero Tolerance: Can Punishment Lead to Safe Schools?" *Phi Delta Kappan* 80 (1999): 372–76.

Sternheimer, Karen. *Kids These Days: Facts and Fictions About Today's Youth*. Lanham, MD: Rowman and Littlefield, 2006.

Zinn, Howard

Since the early 1960s, Howard Zinn has been an activist intellectual, practitioner of civil disobedience, and America's foremost radical historian. More so than even Eric Foner or Noam Chomsky, Zinn has been the oracle of the left in the realm of historical interpretation. He has played a prominent role in the civil rights movement, antiwar movements, and other social causes.

Born on August 24, 1922, to an immigrant working-class family in Brooklyn, New York, Zinn was a shipyard worker as a young adult. World War II altered the direction of his life, however, as he enlisted in the U.S. Air Force as a bombardier. His service included the devastating napalm bombing of Royan, France, shortly before the war's end, an experience that lastingly informed his view of war. Taking advantage of the postwar GI Bill, Zinn earned a PhD in history from Columbia University in 1958. Shortly before finishing his degree requirements, Zinn accepted a teaching position at Spelman College in Atlanta, Georgia. He eventually became chair of the history department.

Living in the South during the early stages of the civil rights era, Zinn quickly immersed himself in the movement. When young activists launched the Student Nonviolent Coordinating Committee (SNCC) in 1960, they invited Zinn to serve on the advisory executive board. He chronicled the organization's early work in *SNCC: The New Abolitionists* (1964). One year before that book appeared, however, Zinn's involvement in regional and campus activism led the Spelman administration to fire him for "insubordination." He then taught political science at Boston University. Continuing his involvement in the struggle for civil rights, he participated in the Mississippi Freedom Summer (1964) and the Selma March (1965). With the escalation of the Vietnam conflict, Zinn added antiwar protest to his activism, writing *Vietnam: The Logic of Withdrawal* (1967). More than thirty years and twenty books later, still highly active, Zinn was a leading critic of President George W. Bush's "War on Terror."

Zinn's magnum opus is *A People's History of the United States* (1980), which retells the nation's history from the perspective of oppressed and disenfranchised groups—from Native Americans and slaves to immigrant laborers and women—rather than the ruling elites. In it, Zinn eschews any pretense of "objectivity" or "neutrality," instead striving to reintroduce voices long concealed from cultural consciousness by orthodox histories. The mission of the historian, he believes, is to take sides, giving voice to the racially, economically, and philosophically disinherited of America's past.

To counteract the stultifying effects of conventional and militaristic history, Zinn celebrates the life and deeds of rebels and dissidents. These marginal and "unimportant" individuals can be seen as the real heroes who gave life to authentic democracy. Far from being a pessimistic rant against injustice, Zinn's work is decidedly optimistic about the future. Critics, of whom there are many, regard *A People's History* as overly simplified revisionist history. They say that in Zinn's book, economic avarice explains nearly every U.S. war, and that most of the civil rights movements are presented without appreciation for their theological vision. Despite its detractors, however, the work remains required reading in many college history programs and has appeared in numerous revised editions and reprints.

Richard C. Goode

See also: Academic Freedom; Civil Rights Movement; Revisionist History; September 11; Vietnam War; War Protesters.

Further Reading

Joyce, Davis. *Howard Zinn: A Radical American Vision.* Amherst, MA: Prometheus Books, 2003.

Kazin, Michael. "Howard Zinn's History Lessons." *Dissent,* Spring 2004.

Zinn, Howard. *The Zinn Reader: Writings on Disobedience and Democracy.* New York: Seven Stories Press, 1997.

Bibliography

Books

Abbey, Edward. *The Monkey Wrench Gang*. Philadelphia: Lippincott, 1975.

Abelson, Donald E. *Do Think Tanks Matter? Assessing the Impact of Public Policy Institutes*. Montreal: McGill-Queens University Press, 2002.

Abraham, Kenneth. *The Liability Century: Insurance and Tort Law from the Progressive Era to 9/11*. Cambridge, MA: Harvard University Press, 2008.

Abrams, Richard. *America Transformed: Sixty Years of Revolutionary Change, 1941–2000*. Cambridge, MA: Cambridge University Press, 2006.

Aby, Stephen H. *The Academic Bill of Rights Debate: A Handbook*. Westport, CT: Praeger, 2007.

Ackerman, Bruce, ed. Bush v. Gore: *The Question of Legitimacy*. New Haven, CT: Yale University Press, 2002.

Acosta, Oscar Zeta. *The Revolt of the Cockroach People*. New York: Vintage Books, 1989.

Acuña, Rodolfo. *Occupied America: A History of Chicanos*. 5th ed. New York: Longman, 2004.

Adams, Cheryl. *Gay Liberation Today: An Exchange of Views*. New York: Pathfinder, 1977.

Adler, Margot. *Drawing Down the Moon: Witches, Druids, Goddess-Worshippers, and Other Pagans in America Today*. Boston: Beacon, 1986.

Adler, Mortimer J. *Philosopher at Large: An Intellectual Autobiography, 1902–1976*. New York: Macmillan, 1977.

———. *A Second Look in the Rearview Mirror*. New York: Macmillan, 1992.

Adler, Richard. *All in the Family: A Critical Appraisal*. New York: Praeger, 1979.

Agins, Donna Brown. *Maya Angelou: "Diversity Makes for a Rich Tapestry."* Berkeley Heights, NJ: Enslow, 2006.

Agnew, Jean-Christopher, and Roy Rosenzweig, eds. *A Companion to Post-1945 America*. Malden, MA: Blackwell, 2002.

Agnew, Spiro. *Go Quietly . . . Or Else*. New York: Morrow, 1980.

Aitken, Jonathan. *Charles W. Colson: A Life Redeemed*. Colorado Springs, CO: Waterbrook, 2005.

Albaum, Martin. *Safety Sells*. Arlington, VA: Insurance Institute for Highway Safety, 2005.

Alexander, Alison, and Janice Hanson, eds. *Taking Sides: Clashing Views on Controversial Issues in Mass Media and Society*. 2nd ed. Guilford, CT: Dushkin, 1995.

Alexander, Bobby C. *Televangelism Reconsidered: Ritual in the Search for Human Community*. Atlanta, GA: Scholars Press, 1994.

Alexander, Jane. *Command Performance: An Actress in the Theater of Politics*. New York: PublicAffairs, 2000.

Alexander, Paul. *Boulevard of Broken Dreams: The Life, Times, and Legend of James Dean*. New York: Viking, 1994.

———. *Machiavelli's Shadow: The Rise and Fall of Karl Rove*. New York: Modern Times/Macmillan, 2008.

———. *Man of the People: The Life of John McCain*. Hoboken, NJ: John Wiley & Sons, 2003.

Alexander-Moegerle, Gil. *James Dobson's War on America*. Amherst, NY: Prometheus Books, 1997.

Alex-Assensoh, Yvette M., and Lawrence J. Hanks, eds. *Black and Multiracial Politics in America*. New York: New York University Press, 2000.

Alford, C. Fred. *Whistleblowers: Broken Lives and Organizational Power*. Ithaca, NY: Cornell University Press, 2001.

Ali, Muhammad. *The Greatest: My Own Story*. New York: Random House, 1975.

Ali, Muhammad, and Thomas Hauser. *Muhammad Ali in Perspective*. San Francisco: Collins, 1996.

Allen, James, ed. *Without Sanctuary: Lynching Photography in America*. Santa Fe, NM: Twin Palms, 2000.

Allen, Steve. *Vulgarians at the Gate: Trash TV and Raunch Radio—Raising the Standards of Popular Culture*. Amherst, NY: Prometheus Books, 2001.

Allyn, David. *Make Love, Not War: The Sexual Revolution—An Unfettered History*. New York: Little, Brown, 2000.

Alperovitz, Gar. *Atomic Diplomacy: Hiroshima and Potsdam: The Use of the Atomic Bomb and the American Confrontation with Soviet Power*. New York: Penguin, 1985.

———. *The Decision to Use the Atomic Bomb and the Architecture of an American Myth*. New York: Alfred A. Knopf, 1995.

Al-Suwaidi, Jamal S., ed. *Biotechnology and the Future of Society: Challenges and Opportunities*. South Court, UK: Ithaca Press, 2004.

Alterman, Eric. *What Liberal Media? The Truth About Bias and the News*. New York: Basic Books, 2004.

Altman, Dennis. *Gore Vidal's America*. Malden, MA: Polity, 2005.

Altman, Nancy J. *The Battle for Social Security: From FDR's Vision to Bush's Gamble*. Hoboken, NJ: John Wiley & Sons, 2005.

Altschuler, Glenn C. *All Shook Up: How Rock 'n' Roll Changed America*. New York: Oxford University Press, 2003.

Ambrose, Stephen E. *Nixon*. 3 vols. New York: Simon & Schuster, 1987–1991.

Amburn, Ellis. *Subterranean Kerouac: The Hidden Life of Jack Kerouac*. New York: St. Martin's Press, 1998.

American Association of University Professors. *Policy Documents and Reports* (Redbook). 10th ed. Baltimore: Johns Hopkins University Press, 2006.

Ammerman, Nancy. *Baptist Battles: Social Change and Religious Conflict in the Southern Baptist Convention.* New Brunswick, NJ: Rutgers University Press, 1990.

Andersen, Alfred F. *Challenging Newt Gingrich.* Eugene, OR: Tom Paine Institute, 1996.

Andersen, Chris. *Citizen Jane: The Turbulent Life of Jane Fonda.* New York: Henry Holt, 1990.

Andersen, Robin. *A Century of Media, A Century of War.* New York: Peter Lang, 2006.

Anderson, David C. *Crime and the Politics of Hysteria: How the Willie Horton Story Changed American Justice.* New York: Times Books, 1995.

Anderson, Terry H. *The Pursuit of Fairness: A History of Affirmative Action.* New York: Oxford University Press, 2004.

Andrew, John A., III. *Lyndon Johnson and the Great Society.* Chicago: I.R. Dee, 1998.

———. *The Other Side of the Sixties: Young Americans for Freedom and the Rise of Conservative Politics.* New Brunswick, NJ: Rutgers University Press, 1997.

———. *Power to Destroy: The Political Uses of the IRS from Kennedy to Nixon.* Chicago: Ivan R. Dee, 2002.

Andrews, David L., and Steven J. Jackson, eds. *Sports Stars: The Cultural Politics of Sporting Celebrity.* London: Routledge, 2001.

Angelou, Maya. *On the Pulse of Morning.* New York: Random House, 1993.

Anson, Robert Sam. *McGovern: A Biography.* New York: Holt, Rinehart & Winston, 1972.

Antonio, Gene. *The AIDS Cover-Up.* San Francisco: Ignatius Press, 1986.

Appelbaum, Diana Karter. *Thanksgiving: An American Holiday, An American History.* New York: Facts On File, 1984.

Armstrong, Karen. *The Battle for God: A History of Fundamentalism.* New York: Ballantine Books, 2001.

Arnold, Ron, and Alan Gottlieb. *Trashing the Economy: How Runaway Environmentalism Is Wrecking America.* Bellevue, WA: Free Enterprise Press, 1989, 1993.

Arquilla, John. *The Reagan Imprint: Ideas in American Foreign Policy from the Collapse of Communism to the War on Terror.* New York: Ivan R. Dee, 2006.

Asante, Molefi Kete. *The Afrocentric Idea.* Philadelphia: Temple University Press, 1998.

Ashmore, Harry S. *Unseasonable Truths: The Life of Robert Maynard Hutchins.* Boston: Little, Brown, 1989.

Asim, Jabari. *What Obama Means—For Our Culture, Our Politics, Our Future.* New York: William Morrow, 2009.

Assayas, Michka. *Bono: In Conversation with Michka Assayas.* New York: Riverhead Books, 2005.

Atkins, Robert. *Censoring Culture: Contemporary Threats to Free Expression.* New York: New Press, 2006.

Attorney General's Commission on Pornography: Final Report. Vols. I and II. Washington, DC: U.S. Department of Justice, 1986.

Auerbach, Jerold S. *Labor and Liberty: The La Follette Committee and the New Deal.* Indianapolis: Bobbs-Merrill, 1996.

Auletta, Ken. *Media Man: Ted Turner's Improbable Empire.* New York: W.W. Norton, 2004.

———. *World War 3.0 and Its Enemies.* New York: Random House, 2001.

Babcox, Peter, and Deborah Babcox, eds. *The Conspiracy: The Chicago Eight Speak Out!* New York: Dell, 1969.

Baer, Kenneth S. *Reinventing the Democrats: The Politics of Liberalism from Reagan to Clinton.* Lawrence: University Press of Kansas, 2000.

Baer, Robert. *Sleeping with the Devil: How Washington Sold Our Soul for Saudi Crude.* New York: Crown, 2003.

Baez, Joan. *And a Voice to Sing With: A Memoir.* New York: Summit Books, 1987.

Baird, Eleanor, and Patricia Baird-Windle. *Targets of Hatred: Anti-Abortion Terrorism.* New York: Palgrave-MacMillan, 2001.

Baker, James T. *Studs Terkel.* New York: Twayne, 1992.

Baker, Paul (Frank Edmondson). *Contemporary Christian Music: Where It Came From, What It Is, Where It's Going.* Westchester, IL: Crossway, 1985.

Baker, Tom. *The Medical Malpractice Myth.* Chicago: University of Chicago Press, 2005.

Balak, Benjamin. *McCloskey's Rhetoric: Discourse Ethics in Economics.* New York: Routledge, 2006.

Ball, Howard. *The Bakke Case: Race, Education, and Affirmative Action.* Lawrence: University Press of Kansas, 2000.

———. *Justice in Mississippi: The Murder Trial of Edgar Ray Killen.* Lawrence: University Press of Kansas, 2006.

———. *The USA PATRIOT Act of 2001: Balancing Civil Liberties and National Security: A Reference Handbook.* Santa Barbara, CA: ABC-CLIO, 2004.

Balmer, Randall. *Mine Eyes Have Seen the Glory: A Journey into the Evangelical Subculture in America.* 4th ed. New York: Oxford University Press, 2006.

———. *Thy Kingdom Come: How the Religious Right Distorts the Faith and Threatens America.* New York: Basic Books, 2006.

Balsam, Steven. *An Introduction to Executive Compensation.* San Diego, CA: Academic Press, 2001.

Banet-Weiser, Sarah. *The Most Beautiful Girl in the World: Beauty Pageants and National Identity.* Berkeley: University of California Press, 1999.

Banner, Stuart. *The Death Penalty: An American History.* Cambridge, MA: Harvard University Press, 2003.

Banting, Keith, George Hoberg, and Richard Simeon, eds. *Degrees of Freedom: Canada and the United States in a Changing World.* Montreal: McGill-Queen's University Press, 1997.

Bardach, Ann Louise. *Cuba Confidential: Love and Vengeance in Miami and Havana.* New York: Random House, 2002.

Barker, Rocky. *Saving All the Parts: Reconciling Economics and the Endangered Species Act.* Washington, DC: Island Press, 1993.

Barkun, Michael. *Religion and the Racist Right: The Origins of the Christian Identity Movement.* Rev. ed. Chapel Hill: University of North Carolina Press, 1997.

Barnett, James H. *The American Christmas: A Study in National Culture.* New York: Macmillan, 1954.

Baron, Dennis. *The English-Only Question: An Official Language for Americans?* New Haven, CT: Yale University Press, 1990.

Barone, Michael. *Our Country: The Shaping of America from Roosevelt to Reagan.* New York: Free Press, 1990.

Barrett, Paul M. *American Islam: The Struggle for the Soul of a Religion.* New York: Farrar, Straus, and Giroux, 2007.

Barsky, Robert F. *Noam Chomsky: A Life of Dissent.* Cambridge, MA: MIT Press, 1997.

Bartkowski, John P. *The Promise Keepers: Servants, Soldiers, and Godly Men.* Piscataway, NJ: Rutgers University Press, 2004.

Bartlett, Bruce, and Timothy P. Roth, eds. *The Supply-Side Solution.* Chatham, NJ: Chatham House, 1983.

Bartlett, Donald L., and James B. Steele. *America: Who Really Pays the Taxes?* New York: Simon and Schuster, 1994.

Bass, Jack. *Strom: The Turbulent Political and Personal Life of Strom Thurmond.* New York: Public Affairs, 2006.

Bast, William. *Surviving James Dean.* Fort Lee, NJ: Barricade Books, 2006.

Bate, Roger, and Julian Morris. *Global Warming: Apocalypse or Hot Air?* Philadelphia: Coronet Books, 1994.

Baum, Bruce. *The Rise and Fall of the Caucasian Race: A Political History of Racial Identity.* New York: New York University Press, 2006.

Baumgardner, Jennifer, and Amy Richards. *Manifesta: Young Women, Feminism, and the Future.* New York: Farrar, Straus and Giroux, 2000.

Bayer, Ronald. *Homosexuality and American Psychiatry: The Politics of Diagnosis.* New York: Basic Books, 1981.

Bazyler, Michael J., ed. *Holocaust Restitution: Perspectives on the Litigation and Its Legacy.* New York: New York University Press, 2006.

Beck, Roy. *The Case Against Immigration.* New York: W.W. Norton, 1996.

Becker, Cynthia S. *Immigration and Illegal Aliens: Burden or Blessing?* Detroit, MI: Gale Group, 2006.

Bedau, Hugo Adam, and Paul G. Cassel. *Debating the Death Penalty: Should Americans Have Capital Punishment? The Experts on Both Sides Make Their Case.* New York: Oxford University Press, 2004.

Bego, Mark. *Madonna: Blonde Ambition.* New York: Harmony Books, 1992.

Belkin, Aaron, and Geoffrey Bateman, eds. *Don't Ask, Don't Tell: Debating the Gay Ban in the Military.* Boulder, CO: Lynne Rienner, 2003.

Bell, Derrick. *Silent Covenants:* Brown v. Board of Education *and the Unfulfilled Hopes for Racial Reform.* New York: Oxford University Press, 2005.

Belzer, Michael H. *Sweatshops on Wheels: Winners and Losers in Trucking Deregulation.* New York: Oxford University Press, 2000.

Benavie, Arthur. *Drugs: America's Holy War.* New York: Haworth Press, 2006.

Benedict, Jeff. *Without Reservation: The Making of America's Most Powerful Indian Tribe and Foxwoods, the World's Largest Casino.* New York: HarperCollins, 2000.

Bennett, Andy. *Cultures of Popular Music.* Philadelphia: Open University, 2001.

Bennett, W. Lance. *News: The Politics of Illusion.* 5th ed. New York: Longman, 2003.

Bennett, William J. *The Death of Outrage: Bill Clinton and the Assault on American Ideals.* New York: Free Press, 1998.

———. *The De-Valuing of America: The Fight for Our Culture and Our Children.* New York: Touchstone, 1992.

———. *Why We Fight: Moral Clarity and the War on Terrorism.* New York: Doubleday, 2002.

Bennett, William J., John J. Dilulio, and John P. Walters. *Body Count—and How to Win America's War Against Crime and Drugs.* New York: Simon & Schuster, 1996.

Benokraitis, Nijole, and Joe Feagin. *Modern Sexism: Blatant, Subtle, and Covert Discrimination.* 2nd ed. Englewood Cliffs, NJ: Prentice Hall, 1995.

Benson, Carol, and Allan Metz, eds. *The Madonna Companion: Two Decades of Commentary.* New York: Shirmer Books, 1999.

Benson, Jackson J. *The True Adventures of John Steinbeck, Writer: A Biography.* New York: Penguin, 1990.

Berg, Manfred. *"The Ticket to Freedom": The NAACP and the Struggle for Black Political Participation.* Gainesville: University Press of Florida, 2005.

Berger, Henry W. *A William Appleman Williams Reader.* Chicago: Ivan R. Dee, 1992.

Berkowitz, Edward D. *America's Welfare State: From Roosevelt to Reagan.* Baltimore: Johns Hopkins University Press, 1991.

Berlant, Lauren. *The Queen of America Goes to Washington City.* Durham, NC: Duke University Press, 1997.

Berlet, Chip, and Joel Bellman. *Lyndon LaRouche: Fascism Wrapped in an American Flag.* Cambridge, MA: Political Research Associates, 1989.

Berlinerblau, Jacques. *Heresy in the University: The Black Athena Controversy and the Responsibilities of American Intellectuals.* Piscataway, NJ: Rutgers University Press, 1999.

Berman, Paul, ed. *Debating P.C.: The Controversy over Political Correctness on College Campuses.* New York: Dell, 1992.

Berman, William C. *America's Right Turn: From Nixon to Clinton.* Baltimore: Johns Hopkins University Press, 1998.

———. *From the Center to the Edge: The Politics and Policies of the Clinton Presidency.* Lanham, MD: Rowman and Littlefield, 2001.

Bernal, Martin. *Black Athena: The Afroasiatic Roots of Classical Civilization.* Volumes 1–3. New Brunswick, NJ: Rutgers University Press, 1987–2006.

Bernstein, Amy, and Peter W. Bernstein, eds. *Quotations from Speaker Newt: The Little Red, White and Blue Book of the Republican Revolution.* New York: Workman, 1995.

Bernstein, Carl. *A Woman in Charge: The Life of Hillary Rodham Clinton.* New York: Alfred A. Knopf, 2007.

Bernstein, Carl, and Bob Woodward. *All the President's Men.* New York: Simon and Schuster, 1974.

Bernstein, Jeremy. *Oppenheimer: Portrait of an Enigma.* Chicago: Ivan R. Dee, 2004.

Bernstein, Matthew. *Controlling Hollywood: Censorship and Regulation in the Studio Era.* New Brunswick, NJ: Rutgers University Press, 1999.

Bernstein, Richard. *Dictatorship of Virtue: Multiculturalism and the Battle of America's Future.* New York: Alfred A. Knopf, 1994.

Bernstein, Richard, and Ross H. Munro. *China: The Coming Conflict with America.* New York: Vintage Books, 1997.

Berry, Mary Frances. *Why ERA Failed: Politics, Women's Rights, and the Amending Process of the Constitution.* Bloomington: Indiana University Press, 1986.

Bertlet, Chip, and Matthew N. Lyons. *Right-Wing Populism in America: Too Close for Comfort.* New York: Guilford, 2000.

Berube, Alan. *Coming Out Under Fire: The History of Gay Men and Women in World War II.* New York: The Free Press, 2000.

Bérubé, Michael. *Rhetorical Occasions: Essays on Humans and the Humanities.* Chapel Hill: University of North Carolina Press, 2006.

Best, Steven, and Anthony J. Nocella II, eds. *Terrorists or Freedom Fighters? Reflections on the Liberation of Animals.* New York: Lantern Books, 2004.

Betzold, Michael. *Appointment with Doctor Death.* Troy, MI: Momentum Books, 1993.

Biafra, Jello. *High Priest of Harmful Matter.* San Francisco: Alternative Tentacles, 1989.

————. *I Blow Minds for a Living*. San Francisco: Alternative Tentacles, 1991.

————. *Machine Gun in the Clown's Hand*. San Francisco: Alternative Tentacles, 2002.

Bianco, Anthony. *The Bully of Bentonville: How the Cost of Wal-Mart's Everyday Low Prices Is Hurting America*. New York: Thomas Dunne Books/St. Martin's Press, 2006.

Bibb, Porter. *It Ain't as Easy as It Looks: Ted Turner's Amazing Story*. New York: Crown, 1993.

Bibby, John F., and L. Sandy Maisel. *Two Parties—Or More? The American Party System*. 2nd ed. Boulder, CO: Westview Press, 2003.

Bilosi, Thomas, and Larry J. Zimmerman, eds. *Indians and Anthropologists: Vine Deloria, Jr., and the Critique of Anthropology*. Tucson: University of Arizona Press, 1977.

Bilton, Michael, and Kevin Sim. *Four Hours in My Lai*. New York: Viking, 1992.

Bily, Cynthia A., ed. *Global Warming: Opposing Viewpoints*. Farmington Hills, MA: Greenhaven Press/Thomson Gale, 2006.

Binkiewicz, Donna M. *Federalizing the Muse: United States Arts Policy and the National Endowment for the Arts 1965–1980*. Chapel Hill: University of North Carolina Press, 2004.

Biondi, Martha. *To Stand and Fight: The Struggle for Civil Rights in Postwar New York City*. Cambridge, MA: Harvard University Press, 2003.

Bird, Kai, and Lawrence Lifschultz, eds. *Hiroshima's Shadow*. Stony Creek, CT: Pamphleteer's Press, 1998.

Bird, Kai, and Martin J. Sherwin. *American Prometheus: The Triumph and Tragedy of J. Robert Oppenheimer*. New York: Alfred A. Knopf, 2005.

Biskupic, Joan. *Sandra Day O'Connor: How the First Woman on the Supreme Court Became Its Most Influential Justice*. New York: Ecco, 2005.

Black, Conrad. *Richard M. Nixon: A Life in Full*. New York: PublicAffairs, 2007.

Black, Edwin. *IBM and the Holocaust: The Strategic Alliance Between Nazi Germany and America's Most Powerful Corp*. New York: Three Rivers Press, 2002.

Black, Gregory D. *The Catholic Crusade Against the Movies, 1940–1975*. Cambridge, UK: Cambridge University Press, 1998.

Blake, R. Roy. *The Gary Hart Set-Up*. Aurora, CO: Laramide, 1992.

Blanchard, Dallas. *The Anti-Abortion Movement and the Rise of the Religious Right: From Polite to Fiery Protest*. New York: Twayne, 1994.

Bloom, Harold. *Tom Wolfe*. Philadelphia: Chelsea House, 2001.

————. *Toni Morrison*. Broomall, PA: Chelsea House, 2000.

Bloom, Lynn Z. *Doctor Spock: Biography of a Conservative Radical*. Indianapolis, IN: Bobbs-Merrill, 1972.

Blum, Elizabeth. *Love Canal Revisited: Race, Class, and Gender in Environmental Activism*. Lawrence: University of Kansas Press, 2008.

Blum, Lawrence N. *Stoning the Keepers at the Gate: Society's Relationship with Law Enforcement*. Brooklyn, NY: Lantern Books, 2002.

Bockris, Victor. *The Life and Death of Andy Warhol*. New York: Bantam Books, 1989.

Boggs, Carl. *Imperial Delusions: American Militarism and Endless War*. Lanham, MD: Rowman and Littlefield, 2005.

Bogus, Carl T. *Why Lawsuits Are Good for America: Disciplined Democracy, Big Business, and the Common Law*. New York: New York University Press, 2001.

Bollen, Peter. *Frank Talk: The Wit and Wisdom of Barney Frank*. Lincoln, NE: iUniverse, 2006.

Bolton, Michelle K. *The Third Shift: Managing Hard Choices in Our Careers, Homes, and Lives as Women*. San Francisco: Jossey-Bass, 2000.

Bonner, Robert E. *Colors and Blood: Flag Passions of the Confederate South*. Princeton, NJ: Princeton University Press, 2002.

Bordowitz, Hank, ed. *The U2 Reader: A Quarter Century of Commentary, Criticism, and Reviews*. Milwaukee, WI: Hal Leonard, 2003.

Bork, Robert H. *The Tempting of America: The Political Seduction of the Law*. New York: Free Press, 1990.

Bornstein, Kate. *Gender Outlaw: On Men, Women, and the Rest of Us*. New York: Vintage Books, 1995.

Bosco, Joseph. *A Problem of Evidence: How the Prosecution Freed O.J. Simpson*. New York: William Morrow, 1996.

Boston, Rob. *The Most Dangerous Man in America? Pat Robertson and the Rise of the Christian Right*. Amherst, NY: Prometheus Books, 1996.

Bowe, Frank. *Equal Rights for Americans with Disabilities*. New York: Franklin Watts, 1992.

Bowles, Samuel, Herbert Gintis, and Melissa Osborne Groves. *Unequal Chances: Family Background and Economic Success*. Princeton, NJ: Princeton University Press, 2005.

Bowman, Robert M., Jr. *Understanding Jehovah's Witnesses: Why They Read the Bible the Way They Do*. Grand Rapids, MI: Baker, 1991.

Boxer, Marilyn. *When Women Ask the Questions: Creating Women's Studies in America*. Baltimore: Johns Hopkins University Press, 1998.

Boy Scouts of America. *Fieldbook*. Irving, TX: Boy Scouts of America, 2004.

Boyer, Paul S. *Fallout: A Historian Reflects on America's Half-Century Encounter with Nuclear Weapons*. Columbus: Ohio State University Press, 1994.

————. *Purity in Print: Book Censorship in America from the Gilded Age to the Computer Age*. Madison: University of Wisconsin Press, 2002.

————. *When Time Shall Be No More: Prophecy Belief in Modern American Culture*. Cambridge, MA: Belknap Press of Harvard University Press, 1992.

Boykoff, Julius, and Kaia Sands. *Landscapes of Dissent: Guerilla Poetry and Public Space*. Long Beach, CA: Palm Press, 2008.

Bracey, Gerald W. *What You Should Know About the War Against America's Public Schools*. Boston: Pearson Education, 2003.

Bradley, Richard. *Harvard Rues: Lawrence Summers and the Battle for the World's Most Powerful University*. New York: HarperCollins, 2005.

Brady, Frank. *Hefner*. New York: Macmillan, 1974.

Brady, John. *Bad Boy: The Life and Politics of Lee Atwater*. New York: Addison-Wesley, 1997.

Brainard, Lori A. *Television: The Limits of Deregulation*. Boulder, CO: Lynne Rienner, 2004.

Branch, Taylor. *At Canaan's Edge: America in the King Years 1965–68*. New York: Simon and Schuster, 2006.

————. *Parting the Waters: America in the King Years 1954–63*. New York: Simon and Schuster; Touchstone, 1989.

————. *Pillar of Fire: America in the King Years, 1963–65*. New York: Simon and Schuster, 1998; Touchstone, 1999.

Brant, Clare, and Yun Lee Too, eds. *Rethinking Sexual Harassment*. Boulder, CO: Pluto Press, 1994.

Branwyn, Gareth. *Jamming the Media*. San Francisco: Chronicle Books, 1997.

Brennan, Mary C. *Turning Right in the Sixties: The Conservative Capture of the GOP*. Chapel Hill: University of North Carolina Press, 1995.

Brenson, Michael. *Visionaries and Outcasts: The NEA, Congress, and the Place of Visual Arts in America*. New York: New Press, 2001.

Breslin, Rosemary, and John Hammer. *Gerry! A Woman Making History*. New York: Pinnacle Books, 1984.

Bridges, Linda, and John R. Coyne, Jr. *Strictly Right: William F. Buckley and the Conservative Movement*. New York: John Wiley & Sons, 2007.

Bridges, Tyler. *The Rise of David Duke*. Jackson: University Press of Mississippi, 1994.

Brinkley, Alan. *The End of Reform: New Deal Liberalism in Recession and War*. New York: Alfred A. Knopf, 1995.

Brinkley, Douglas. *The Great Deluge: Hurricane Katrina, New Orleans, and the Mississippi Gulf Coast*. New York: William Morrow, 2006.

———. *Rosa Parks*. New York: Penguin, 2005.

Brinson, Susan L. *The Red Scare, Politics, and the Federal Communications Commission, 1941–1960*. Westport, CT: Praeger, 2004.

Broad, William J. *Star Warriors: A Penetrating Look into the Lives of the Young Scientists Behind Our Space Age Weaponry*. New York: Simon & Schuster, 1985.

Broadwater, Jeff. *Eisenhower and the Anti-Communist Crusade*. Chapel Hill: University of North Carolina Press, 1992.

Broder, David C., and Bob Woodward. *The Man Who Would Be President: Dan Quayle*. New York: Simon & Schuster, 1992.

Brokaw, Tom. *The Greatest Generation*. New York: Random House, 1998.

———. *A Long Way from Home: Growing Up in the American Heartland in the Forties and Fifties*. New York: Random House, 2003.

Bronner, Ethan. *Battle for Justice: How the Bork Nomination Shook America*. New York: Union Square Press, 2007.

Bronski, Michael. *The Pleasure Principle: Sex, Backlash, and the Struggle for Gay Freedom*. New York: St. Martin's Press, 1998.

Bronson, Rachel. *Thicker Than Oil: America's Uneasy Partnership with Saudi Arabia*. New York: Oxford University Press, 2006.

Brown, Charles C. *Niebuhr and His Age: Reinhold Niebuhr's Prophetic Role in the Twentieth Century*. Philadelphia: Trinity Press International, 1992.

Brown, D.M. *Hurricane Katrina: The First Seven Days of America's Worst Natural Disaster*. Napa, CA: Lulu, 2005.

Brown, Helen Gurley. *I'm Wild Again: Snippets from My Life and a Few Brazen Thoughts*. New York: St. Martin's Press, 2000.

Brownell, Kelly D., and Katherine Battle Horgan. *Food Fight: The Inside Story of the Food Industry, America's Obesity Crisis, and What We Can Do About It*. New York: McGraw-Hill, 2003.

Bruce, Steve. *Pray TV: Televangelism in America*. New York: Routledge, 1990.

Brunsdon, Charlotte, Julie D'Acci, and Lynn Spigel, eds. *Feminist Television Criticism: A Reader*. New York: Clarendon Press, 1997.

Bryant, Anita. *The Anita Bryant Story: The Survival of Our Nation's Families and the Threat of Militant Homosexuality*. Old Tappan, NJ: Revell, 1977.

———. *A New Day*. Nashville, TN: Broadman, 1992.

Brzezinski, Zbigniew. *The Grand Failure: The Birth and Death of Communism in the Twentieth Century*. New York: Collier, 1989.

Buchanan, Patrick J. *The Death of the West: How Dying Populations and Immigrant Invasions Imperil Our Country and Civilization*. New York: Thomas Dunne Books, 2002.

Buchwald, Art. *I'll Always Have Paris*. New York: G.P. Putnam, 1996.

Buchwald, Emilie, Pamela Fletcher, and Martha Roth. *Transforming a Rape Culture*. rev. ed. Minneapolis, MN: Milkweed Editions, 2005.

Buckley, Jack, and Mark Schneider. *Charter Schools: Hope or Hype?* Princeton, NJ: Princeton University Press, 2007.

Buckley, William F., Jr. *Let Us Talk of Many Things: The Collected Speeches with New Commentary by the Author*. Roseville, CA: Forum, 2000.

———. *Miles Gone By: A Literary Autobiography*. Washington, DC: Regnery, 2004.

Budd, Mike, and Max H. Kirsch, eds. *Rethinking Disney: Private Control, Public Dimensions*. Middletown, CT: Wesleyan University Press, 2005.

Budenz, Louis F. *The Bolshevik Invasion of the West*. Linden, NJ: Bookmailer, 1966.

———. *This Is My Story*. New York: McGraw-Hill, 1947.

Budenz, Margaret. *Streets*. Huntington, IN: Our Sunday Visitor, 1979.

Bufwack, Mary A., and Robert K. Oermann. *Finding Her Voice: The Saga of Women in Country Music*. New York: Crown, 1993.

Bugliosi, Vincent. *The Betrayal of America: How the Supreme Court Undermined the Constitution and Chose Our President*. New York: Thunder's Mouth Press, 2001.

———. *Outrage: The Five Reasons Why O.J. Simpson Got Away with Murder*. New York: W.W. Norton, 1996.

Buhle, Paul. *Taking Care of Business: Samuel Gompers, George Meany, Lane Kirkland, and the Tragedy of American Labor*. New York: Monthly Review Press, 1999.

Buhle, Paul M., and Edward Rice-Maximin. *William Appleman Williams: The Tragedy of Empire*. New York: Routledge, 1995.

Bullard, Robert D. *Confronting Environmental Racism: Voices from the Grassroots*. Boston: South End Press, 1993.

———. *Dumping in Dixie: Race, Class, and Environmental Quality*. Boulder, CO: Westview Press, 1990.

———. *The Quest for Environmental Justice: Human Rights and the Politics of Pollution*. San Francisco: Sierra Club Books, 2005.

Bullert, B.J. *Public Television: Politics and the Battle over Documentary Film*. New Brunswick, NJ: Rutgers University Press, 1997.

Burch, Philip H. *Reagan, Bush, and Right-Wing Politics: Elites, Think Tanks, Power, and Policy. Part A: The American Right Wing Takes Command: Key Executive Appointments*. Greenwich, CT: Jai Press, 1997.

Burke, Carole. *Camp All-American: Hanoi Jane and the High and Tight*. Boston: Beacon, 2004.

Burlein, Ann. *Lift High the Cross: Where White Supremacy and the Christian Right Converge*. Durham, NC: Duke University Press, 2002.

Burner, David, and Thomas R. West. *Column Right: Conservative Journalists in the Service of Nationalism*. New York: New York University Press, 1988.

Burns, Gene. *The Moral Veto: Framing Conception, Abortion, and Cultural Pluralism in the United States.* New York: Cambridge University Press, 2005.

Burns, Stewart, ed. *Daybreak of Freedom: The Montgomery Bus Boycott.* Chapel Hill: University of North Carolina Press, 1997.

Burt, Dan M. *Abuse of Trust: A Report on Ralph Nader's Network.* Washington, DC: Regnery Gateway, 1982.

Busch, Andrew H. *Reagan's Victory: The Presidential Election of 1980 and the Rise of the Right.* Lawrence: University Press of Kansas, 2005.

Buss, Dale. *Family Man: The Biography of Dr. James Dobson.* Wheaton, IL: Tyndale House, 2005.

Button, James W., Barbara A. Rienzo, and Kenneth D. Wald. *Private Lives, Public Conflicts: Battles over Gay Rights in American Communities.* Washington, DC: CQ Press, 1997.

Byrd, Robert C. *Losing America: Confronting a Reckless and Arrogant Presidency.* New York: W.W. Norton, 2004.

———. *Robert C. Byrd: Child of the Appalachian Coalfields.* Morgantown: West Virginia University Press, 2005.

Byrnes, Timothy A. *Catholic Bishops in American Politics.* Princeton, NJ: Princeton University Press, 1991.

Cadman, Chris, and Halstead Craig. *Michael Jackson: The Early Years.* Hertford, UK: Authors on Line, 2002.

Caesar, James W., and Andrew E. Busch. *The Perfect Tie: The True Story of the 2000 Presidential Election.* Lanham, MD: Rowman & Littlefield, 2001.

Califano, Joseph A., Jr. *The Triumph and Tragedy of Lyndon Johnson.* New York: Simon and Schuster, 1991.

Califia, Pat. *Public Sex: The Culture of Radical Sex.* Pittsburgh, PA: Cleis Press, 1994, 2000.

———. *Sex Changes: The Politics of Transgenderism.* San Francisco: Cleis Press, 1997, 2003.

Campbell, James T. *Middle Passages: African American Journeys to Africa, 1787–2005.* New York: Penguin Press, 2006.

Campbell, Joseph. *The Hero with a Thousand Faces.* Novato, CA: New World Library, 2008.

Campolo, Tony. *Can Mainline Denominations Make a Comeback?* Valley Forge, PA: Judson Press, 1995.

———. *Is Jesus a Republican or a Democrat?* Dallas: World Books, 1995.

———. *Speaking My Mind.* Nashville, TN: W. Publishing Group, 2004.

Campos, David. *Sex, Youth, and Sex Education: A Reference Handbook.* Santa Barbara, CA: ABC-CLIO, 2002.

Campos, Paul. *The Obesity Myth: Why America's Obsession with Weight Is Hazardous to Your Health.* New York: Penguin, 2004.

Cannon, James M. *Time and Chance: Gerald Ford's Appointment with History.* New York: HarperCollins, 1994.

Cannon, Lou. *Official Negligence: How Rodney King and the Riots Changed Los Angeles and the LAPD.* New York: Times Books, 1997.

———. *Reagan.* New York: G.P. Putnam's Sons, 1982.

Carbaugh, Donald A. *Talking American: Cultural Discourses on Donahue.* Norwood, NJ: Ablex Publishing, 1988.

Carlson, Allan. *The "American Way": Family and Community in the Shaping of American Identity.* Wilmington, DE: ISI Books, 2003.

Carmichael, Virginia. *Framing History: The Rosenberg Story and the Cold War.* Minneapolis: University of Minnesota Press, 1993.

Carnegie Commission on the Future of Public Broadcasting. *A Public Trust.* New York: Bantam, 1979.

Carnoy, Martin, Rebecca Jacobsen, Lawrence Mishel, and Richard Rothstein. *The Charter School Dust-Up: Examining the Evidence on Enrollment and Achievement.* Washington, DC: Economic Policy Institute, 2005.

Carruthers, Bruce G., and Terence C. Halliday. *Rescuing Business: The Making of Corporate Bankruptcy Law in England and the United States.* New York: Oxford University Press, 1998.

Carson, D.A. *The Inclusive-Language Debate: A Plea for Realism.* Grand Rapids, MI: Baker Books, 1998.

Carson, Rachel. *Silent Spring.* Boston: Houghton Mifflin, 1962.

Carter, Dan T. *The Politics of Rage: George Wallace, the Origins of the New Conservatism, and the Transformation of American Politics.* New York: Simon & Schuster, 1995.

Carter, Jimmy. *Keeping Faith: Memoirs of a President.* New York: Bantam Books, 1982.

Cegielski, Jim. *The Howard Stern Book: An Unauthorized, Unabashed, Uncensored Fan's Guide.* Secaucus, NJ: Carol, 1994.

Chadwick, Andrew. *Internet Politics: States, Citizens, and New Communication Technologies.* New York: Oxford University Press, 2006.

Chafe, William H., ed. *The Achievement of American Liberalism: The New Deal and Its Legacies.* New York: Columbia University Press, 2003.

Chamberlain, John. *Freedom and Independence: The Hillsdale Story.* Forewords by William F. Buckley and William E. Simon. Hillsdale, MI: Hillsdale College Press, 1979.

Chandler, Raymond. *All That Glitters: The Crime and the Cover-Up.* Las Vegas, NV: Windsong Press, 2004.

Chandler, Russell. *Understanding the New Age.* Dallas, TX: Word, 1988.

Chang, Jeff. *Can't Stop Won't Stop: A History of the Hip-Hop Generation.* New York: Picador/St. Martin's Press, 2005.

Chappell, Larry W. *George F. Will.* New York: Twayne, 1997.

Charen, Mona. *Useful Idiots: How Liberals Got It Wrong in the Cold War and Still Blame America First.* Washington, DC: Regnery, 2003.

Chase, Alston. *Harvard and the Unabomber: The Education of an American Terrorist.* New York: W.W. Norton, 2003.

———. *Playing God in Yellowstone: The Destruction of America's First National Park.* San Diego, CA: Harvest Books, 1987.

Chatterjee, Dean K., ed. *Democracy in a Global World: Human Rights and Political Participation in the 21st Century.* Lanham, MD: Rowman & Littlefield, 2008.

Cheney, Lynne V. *Telling the Truth.* New York: Simon & Schuster, 1995.

Cheney, Mary. *Now It's My Turn: A Daughter's Chronicle of Political Life.* New York: Threshold Editions, 2006.

Chenoweth, Neil. *Rupert Murdoch: The Untold Story of the World's Greatest Media Wizard.* New York: Crown Business, 2001.

Chermak, Steven M. *Searching for a Demon: The Media Construction of the Militia Movement.* Boston: Northeastern University Press, 2002.

Chilton, David. *Productive Christians in an Age of Guilt Manipulators: A Biblical Response to Ron Sider.* Tyler, TX: Institute for Christian Economics, 1981.

Chisholm, Shirley. *The Good Fight.* New York: Harper and Row, 1973.

———. *Unbought and Unbossed.* Boston: Houghton Mifflin, 1970.

Chomsky, Noam. *9–11.* New York: Seven Stories Press, 2001.

Chomsky, Noam, and Edward S. Herman. *Manufacturing Consent: The Political Economy of the Mass Media.* New York: Pantheon Books, 1988.

Christe, Ian. *Sound of the Beast: The Complete Headbanging History of Heavy Metal.* New York: HarperCollins, 2003.

Christensen, Bryce J. *Utopia Against the Family: Problems and Politics of the American Family.* San Francisco: Ignatius Press, 1990.

Christensen, Thomas. *Useful Adversaries: Grand Strategy, Domestic Mobilization, and Sino-American Conflicts, 1947–1958.* Princeton, NJ: Princeton University Press, 1996.

Christofferson, Bill. *The Man from Clear Lake: Earth Day Founder Senator Gaylord Nelson.* Madison: University of Wisconsin Press, 2004.

Churchill, Ward. *Acts of Rebellion: The Ward Churchill Reader.* New York: Routledge, 2003.

———. *On the Justice of Roosting Chickens: Reflections on the Consequences of U.S. Imperial Arrogance and Criminality.* Oakland, CA: AK Press, 2003.

Clapham, Andrew. *Human Rights: A Very Short Introduction.* New York: Oxford University Press, 2007.

Claridge, Laura. *Norman Rockwell: A Life.* New York: Random House, 2001.

Clark, Eric. *The Real Toy Story: Inside the Ruthless Battles for America's Youngest Consumers.* New York: Free Press, 2007.

Clark, Victoria. *Allies for Armageddon: The Rise of Christian Zionism.* New Haven, CT: Yale University Press, 2007.

Clarke, Richard. *Against All Enemies: Inside America's War on Terror.* New York: Free Press, 2004.

Clatterbaugh, Kenneth C. *Contemporary Perspectives on Masculinity: Men, Women, and Politics in Modern Society.* Boulder, CO: Westview Press, 1997.

Claussen, Dane S. *Anti-Intellectualism in American Media: Magazines and Higher Education.* New York: Peter Lang, 2004.

———, ed. *The Promise Keepers: Essays on Masculinity and Christianity.* Jefferson, NC: McFarland, 2000.

Cleary, Edward J. *Beyond Burning the Cross: The First Amendment and the Landmark* R.A.V. *Case.* New York: Random House, 1994.

Cleaver, Kathleen, and George Katsiaficas. *Liberation, Imagination, and the Black Panther Party.* New York: Routledge, 2001.

Clendinen, Dudley, and Adam Nagourney. *Out for Good: The Struggle to Build a Gay Rights Movement in America.* New York: Simon & Schuster, 1999.

Clinton, Bill. *My Life.* New York: Alfred A. Knopf, 2004.

Clinton, Hillary Rodham. *It Takes a Village, and Other Lessons Children Teach Us.* New York: Simon & Schuster, 1996.

———. *Living History.* New York: Simon & Schuster, 2003.

Clotfelter, Charles. *After* Brown: *The Rise and Retreat of School Desegregation.* Princeton, NJ: Princeton University Press, 2006.

Clymer, Adam. *Edward M. Kennedy: A Biography.* Boston: Houghton Mifflin, 1999.

Coates, Patricia Walsh. *Margaret Sanger and the Origin of the Birth Control Movement, 1910–1930: The Concept of Women's Sexual Autonomy.* Lewiston, NY: Edwin Mellen, 2008.

Coats, David. *Old MacDonald's Factory Farm: The Myth of the Traditional Farm and the Shocking Truth About Animal Suffering in Today's Agribusiness.* New York: Continuum, 1991.

Cobb, James C. *Away Down South: A History of Southern Identity.* New York: Oxford University Press, 2005.

Cobb, John B., Jr., ed. *Progressive Christians Speak: A Different Voice on Faith and Politics.* Louisville, KY: Westminster John Knox Press, 2003.

Cockburn, Alexander, and Jeffrey St. Clair. *Al Gore: A User's Manual.* New York: Verso, 2000.

Cocks, Geoffrey. *The Wolf at the Door: Stanley Kubrick, History, and the Holocaust.* New York: Peter Lang, 2004.

Coffey, Thomas M. *Iron Eagle: The Turbulent Life of General Curtis LeMay.* New York: Crown, 1986.

Cohen, Richard M., and Jules Witcover. *A Heartbeat Away: The Investigation and Resignation of Vice President Spiro T. Agnew.* New York: Viking, 1974.

Cohen, Stephen. *Failed Crusade: America and the Tragedy of Post-Communist Russia.* New York: W.W. Norton, 2001.

Cohn, Jonathan. *Sick: The Untold Story of America's Health Care Crisis—And the People Who Pay the Price.* New York: HarperCollins, 2007.

Cohodas, Nadine. *Strom Thurmond and the Politics of Southern Change.* Macon, GA: Mercer University Press, 1994.

Cole, David. *No Equal Justice: Race and Class in the American Criminal Justice System.* New York: New Press, 1999.

Cole, Luke W., and Sheila R. Foster. *From the Ground Up: Environmental Racism and the Rise of the Environmental Justice Movement.* New York: New York University Press, 2001.

Colford, Paul D. *Howard Stern: King of All Media—The Unauthorized Biography.* New York: St. Martin's, 1996.

———. *The Rush Limbaugh Story: Talent on Loan from God: An Unauthorized Biography.* New York: St. Martin's Press, 1993.

Colker, Ruth. *Abortion & Dialogue: Pro-Choice, Pro-Life, and American Law.* Bloomington: Indiana University Press, 1992.

Collier, Peter, and David Horowitz. *Destructive Generation: Second Thoughts About the '60s.* New York: Free Press, 1996.

———. *The Kennedys: An American Drama.* New York: Summit Books, 1984.

———, eds. *The Anti-Chomsky Reader.* San Francisco: Encounter Books, 2004.

Collins, Robert M. *Transforming America: Politics and Culture During the Reagan Years.* New York: Columbia University Press, 2006.

Collins, Rodnell, and Ella Coll. *Malcolm X: The Man Behind the Myth.* New York: HarperCollins, 1997.

Collins, Sheila. *Let Them Eat Ketchup! The Politics of Poverty and Inequality.* New York: Monthly Review Press, 1996.

Colson, Charles, with Jack Eckerd. *Why America Doesn't Work.* Dallas: Word, 1992.

Colson, Charles, with Richard John Neuhaus, eds. *Evangelicals and Catholics Together: Toward a Common Mission.* Nashville, TN: Thomas Nelson, 1995.

Commins, David. *The Wahhabi Mission and Saudi Arabia.* New York: I.B. Tauris, 2006.

Commission on Obscenity and Pornography (1967) Report. Washington, DC: U.S. Government Printing Office, 1970.

Conason, Joe. *Big Lies: The Right-Wing Propaganda Machine and How It Distorts the Truth.* New York: St. Martin's Griffin Press, 2004.

Conroy, W.J. *Challenging the Boundaries of Reform: Socialism in Burlington.* Philadelphia: Temple University Press, 1990.

Continetti, Matthew. *The K Street Gang: The Rise and Fall of the Republican Machine.* New York: Doubleday, 2006.

Conyers, James L., and Andrew P. Smallwood. *Malcolm X: A Historical Reader.* Durham, NC: Carolina Academic Press, 2008.

Cooper, Bruce S., ed. *Home Schooling in Full View: A Reader.* Greenwich, CT: Information Age Publishing, 2005.

Cooper, Terry L., and N. Dale Wright, eds. *Exemplary Public Administrators: Character and Leadership in Government.* San Francisco: Jossey-Bass, 1992.

Corrado, Anthony. *Campaign Finance Reform: Beyond the Basics.* New York: Century Foundation Press, 2002.

Corsi, Jerome. *The Obama Nation: Leftist Politics and the Cult of Personality.* New York: Threshold Editions/Simon & Schuster, 2008.

Cortner, Richard C. *A Mob Intent on Death: The NAACP and the Arkansas Riot Cases.* Middletown, CT: Wesleyan University Press, 1988.

Coulter, Ann. *Treason: Liberal Treachery from the Cold War to the War on Terrorism.* New York: Crown Forum, 2003.

Counihan, Carole M., ed. *Food in the USA: A Reader.* New York: Routledge, 2002.

Covington, Sally. *Moving a Public Policy Agenda: The Strategic Philanthropy of Conservative Foundations.* Washington, DC: National Committee for Responsive Philanthropy, 1997.

Cowan, Rosemary. *Cornel West: The Politics of Redemption.* Malden, MA: Polity, 2003.

Craig, Maxine Leeds. *Ain't I a Beauty Queen? Black Women, Beauty, and the Politics of Culture.* New York: Oxford University Press, 2002.

Crawford, James, ed. *Language Loyalties: A Source Book on the Official English Controversy.* Chicago: University of Chicago Press, 1992.

Cray, Ed. *Ramblin' Man: The Life and Times of Woody Guthrie.* New York: W.W. Norton, 2004.

Cremin, Lawrence. *The Transformation of the School: Progressivism in American Education, 1876–1957.* New York: Alfred A. Knopf, 1961.

Crigler, Ann N., Marion R. Just, and Edward J. McCaffery, eds. *Rethinking the Vote: The Politics and Prospects of Election Reform.* New York: Oxford University Press, 2004.

Cristol, A. Jay. *The Liberty Incident: The 1967 Israeli Attack on the U.S. Navy Spy Ship.* Washington, D.C.: Brassey's, 2002.

Critchlow, Donald T. *Intended Consequences: Birth Control, Abortion, and the Federal Government in Modern America.* New York: Oxford University Press, 1999.

———. *Phyllis Schlafly and Grassroots Conservatism: A Woman's Crusade.* Princeton, NJ: Princeton University Press, 2005.

———. *The Politics of Abortion and Birth Control in Historical Perspective.* University Park: Pennsylvania State University Press, 1996.

Critser, Greg. *Fat Land: How Americans Became the Fattest People in the World.* Boston: Houghton Mifflin, 2003.

Cromartie, Michael, ed. *No Longer Exiles: The Religious New Right in American Politics.* Washington, DC: Ethics and Public Policy Center, 1993.

Cronkite, Walter. *A Reporter's Life.* New York: Alfred A. Knopf, 1996.

Crothers, Lane. *Rage on the Right: The American Militia Movement from Ruby Ridge to Homeland Security.* New York: Rowman and Littlefield, 2003.

Crow, Barbara A., ed. *Radical Feminism: A Documentary Reader.* New York: New York University Press, 2000.

Culberson, William C. *Vigilantism: Political History of Private Power in America.* New York: Greenwood, 1990.

Cullen, Lisa. *A Job to Die For: Why So Many Americans Are Killed, Injured or Made Ill at Work and What to Do About It.* Monroe, ME: Common Courage Press, 2002.

Cunningham, Jesse G., and Laura K. Egendorf, eds. *The McCarthy Hearings.* San Diego, CA: Greenhaven Press, 2003.

Currah, Paisley, Richard M. Juang, and Shannon Price Minter. *Transgender Rights.* Minneapolis: University of Minnesota Press, 2006.

Curran, Charles E. *Catholic Higher Education, Theology, and Academic Freedom.* Notre Dame, IN: University of Notre Dame Press, 1990.

Curt, Gentry. *J. Edgar Hoover: The Man and the Secrets.* New York: W.W. Norton, 1991.

Curtis, Edward, ed. *The Columbia Sourcebook of Muslims in the United States.* New York: Columbia University Press, 2008.

D'Souza, Dinesh. *Illiberal Education: The Politics of Race and Sex on Campus.* New York: Macmillan, 1991.

Daffron, Carolyn. *Gloria Steinem.* New York: Chelsea House, 1988.

Dalhouse, Mark Taylor. *An Island in the Lake of Fire: Bob Jones University, Fundamentalism, and the Separatist Movement.* Athens: University of Georgia Press, 1996.

Dallek, Robert. *Lone Star Rising.* New York: Oxford University Press, 1991.

———. *An Unfinished Life: John F. Kennedy, 1917–1963.* Boston: Little, Brown, 2003.

Daniels, Roger. *Prisoners Without Trial: Japanese Americans in World War II.* New York: Hill and Wang, 1993.

Danner, Mark. *Torture and Truth: America, Abu Ghraib, and the War on Terror.* New York: New York Review of Books, 2004.

Danzon, Patricia A. *Medical Malpractice: Theory, Evidence, and Public Policy.* Cambridge, MA: Harvard University Press, 1985.

Davies, Gareth. *From Opportunity to Entitlement: The Transformation and Decline of Great Society Liberalism.* Lawrence: University Press of Kansas, 1996.

Davis, Charles N., and Sigman L. Splichal, eds. *Access Denied: Freedom of Information in the Information Age.* Ames: Iowa State University Press, 2000.

Davis, Flora. *Moving the Mountain: The Women's Movement in America Since 1960.* New York: Touchstone Books, 1991.

Dawidowicz, Lucy S. *War Against the Jews, 1933–1945.* New York: Holt, Rinehart and Winston, 1975.

Day, James. *The Vanishing Vision: The Inside Story of Public Television.* Berkeley: University of California Press, 1995.

De Grazia, Edward. *Girls Lean Back Everywhere: The Law of Obscenity and the Assault on Genius.* New York: Random House, 1992.

Dealy, Francis X. *The Power and the Money: Inside the Wall Street Journal.* Secaucus, NJ: Carol Publishing Group, 1993.

Dean, Howard, with Judith Warner. *You Have the Power: How to Take Back Our Country and Restore Democracy in America.* New York: Simon & Schuster, 2004.

Dean, Jodi. *Aliens in America: Conspiracy Culture from Outerspace to Cyberspace.* Ithaca, NY: Cornell University Press, 1998.

Dean, John, and Jean-Paul Gabilliet, eds. *European Readings of American Popular Culture.* Westport, CT: Greenwood Press, 1996.

DeAngelis, Michael. *Gay Fandom and Crossover Stardom: James Dean, Mel Gibson, and Keanu Reeves.* Durham, NC: Duke University Press, 2001.

Dearborn, Mary V. *Mailer: A Biography*. Boston: Houghton Mifflin, 1999.

DeBenedetti, Charles, and Charles Chatfield. *An American Ordeal: The Antiwar Movement of the Vietnam Era*. Syracuse, NY: Syracuse University Press, 1990.

Deckman, Melissa M. *School Board Battles: The Christian Right in Local Politics*. Washington, DC: Georgetown University Press, 2004.

Dees, Morris. *Gathering Storm: America's Militia Threat*. New York: HarperCollins, 1996.

Dees, Morris, with James Corcoran. *Gathering Storm: America's Militia Threat*. New York: HarperCollins, 1996.

DeFreitas, Gregory. *Inequality at Work: Hispanics in the U.S. Labor Force*. New York: Oxford University Press, 1991.

DeGroot, Gerard J. *The Atomic Bomb: A Life*. Cambridge, MA: Harvard University Press, 2005.

———. *The Bomb: A History*. Cambridge: Harvard University Press, 2005.

DeLay, Tom, with Stephen Mansfield. *No Retreat, No Surrender: One American's Fight*. New York: Sentinel, 2007.

Delgado, Richard, and Jean Stefancic. *Understanding Words That Wound*. Boulder, CO: Westview Press, 2004.

Dellinger, David. *From Yale to Jail*. New York: Pantheon Books, 1993.

Deloria, Vine, Jr. *Custer Died for Your Sins: An Indian Manifesto*. New York: Macmillan, 1969.

Delves, Donald P. *Stock Options and the New Corporate Accountability*. New York: McGraw-Hill, 2004.

Dembling, Sophia, and Lisa Gutierrez. *The Making of Dr. Phil: The Straight-Talking True Story of Everyone's Favorite Therapist*. Hoboken, NJ: John Wiley & Sons, 2004.

Depoe, Stephen P. *Arthur M. Schlesinger, Jr., and the Ideological History of American Liberalism*. Tuscaloosa: University of Alabama Press, 1994.

Derickson, Alan. *Health Security for All: Dreams of Universal Health Care in America*. Baltimore: Johns Hopkins University Press, 2005.

Dershowitz, Alan. *The Case for Israel*. Hoboken, NJ: John Wiley & Sons, 2003.

Dewing, Rolland. *Wounded Knee: The Meaning and Significance of the Second Incident*. New York: Irvington, 1985.

Di Sabatino, David. *The Jesus People: An Annotated Bibliography and General Resource*. 2nd ed. Lake Forest, CA: Jester Media, 2004.

Diamond, Peter A., and Peter R. Orszag. *Saving Social Security: A Balanced Approach*. Washington, DC: Brookings Institution, 2004.

Diamond, Sara. *Roads to Dominion: Right-Wing Movements and Political Power in the United States*. New York: Guilford, 1995.

———. *Spiritual Warfare: The Politics of the Christian Right*. Boston: South End Press, 1989.

Diaz, Tom. *Making a Killing: The Business of Guns in America*. New York: New Press, 1999.

Dierenfield, Bruce J. *The Battle over School Prayer: How* Engel v. Vitale *Changed America*. Lawrence: University Press of Kansas, 2007.

Digby, Tom, ed. *Men Doing Feminism*. New York: Routledge, 1998.

Diggins, John Patrick. *Ronald Reagan: Fate, Freedom, and the Making of History*. New York: W.W. Norton, 2007.

———, ed. *The Liberal Persuasion: Arthur Schlesinger, Jr., and the Challenge of the American Past*. Princeton, NJ: Princeton University Press, 1997.

Dillard, Angela D. *Guess Who's Coming to Dinner Now? Multicultural Conservatism in America*. New York: New York University Press, 2001.

Dillon, Michele. *Catholic Identity: Balancing Reason, Faith, and Power*. New York: Cambridge University Press, 1999.

Dimond, Diane. *Be Careful Who You Love: Inside the Michael Jackson Case*. New York: Atria, 2005.

Dinnerstein, Leonard. *Antisemitism in America*. New York: Oxford University Press, 1994.

Dionne, E.J., and Ming Hsu Chen, eds. *Sacred Places, Civic Purposes: Should Government Help Faith-Based Charity?* Washington, DC: Brookings Institution Press, 2001.

Dixon, Lee, and James Cox. *State Management and Allocation of Tobacco Settlement Revenue, 2002*. Washington, DC: National Conference of State Legislatures, 2002.

Dobratz, Betty A., and Stephanie L. Shanks-Meile. *"White Power, White Pride!": The White Separatist Movement in the United States*. Baltimore: Johns Hopkins University Press, 2000.

Docherty, Jayne Seminare. *Learning Lessons from Waco: When the Parties Bring Their Gods to the Table*. Syracuse, NY: Syracuse University Press, 2001.

Dockery, David S., ed. *Southern Baptists and American Evangelicals: The Conversation Continues*. Nashville, TN: Broadman & Holman, 1993.

Dodd, John, with David Tyson. *And the World Came His Way: Jesse Helms' Contributions to Freedom*. Wingate, NC: Jesse Helms Center Foundation, 2002.

Domiguez, Jorge I., and Rafael Fernandez de Castro. *United States and Mexico: Between Partnership and Conflict*. New York: Routledge, 2001.

Donahue, Phil. *Donahue: My Own Story*. New York: Fawcett Crest, 1981.

Donahue, Sean, ed. *Gangs: Stories of Life and Death from the Streets*. New York: Thunder Mouth, 2002.

Donavan, John B. *Pat Robertson: The Authorized Biography*. New York: Macmillan, 1988.

Donohue, William A. *Twilight of Liberty: The Legacy of the ACLU*. New Brunswick, NJ: Transaction, 1994.

Donziger, Steven R. *The Real War on Crime: The Report of the National Criminal Justice Commission*. New York: HarperPerennial, 1996.

Dorgan, Byron L. *Take This Job and Ship It: How Corporate Greed and Brain-Dead Politics Are Selling Out America*. New York: Thomas Dunne Books/St. Martin's Press, 2006.

Dougherty, Richard. *Goodbye, Mr. Christian: A Personal Account of McGovern's Rise and Fall*. Garden City, NJ: Doubleday, 1973.

Douglas, Susan J. *Where the Girls Are: Growing Up Female with the Mass Media*. New York: Times Books, 1994.

Doumani, Beshara, ed. *Academic Freedom After September 11*. New York: Zone Books, 2006.

Downing, David. *Robert Redford*. New York: St. Martin's Press, 1982.

Dracos, Ted. *Ungodly: The Passions, Torrents, and Murder of Atheist Madalyn Murray O'Hair*. New York: Free Press, 2003.

Drake, Frances. *Global Warming: The Science of Climate Change*. New York: Oxford University Press, 2000.

Draper, Theodore. *A Very Thin Line: The Iran-Contra Affairs*. New York: Hill and Wang, 1991.

Dray, Phillip. *At the Hands of Persons Unknown*. New York: Random House, 2002.

Dreisbach, Daniel L. *The Founders on God and Government.* Lanham, MD: Rowman & Littlefield, 2004.

Drew, Elizabeth. *Citizen McCain.* New York: Simon & Schuster, 2002.

———. *Showdown: The Struggle Between the Gingrich Congress and the Clinton White House.* New York: Simon and Schuster, 1996.

Drudge, Matt. *The Drudge Manifesto.* New York: NAL, 2001.

Drury, Shadia B. *Leo Strauss and the American Right.* New York: St. Martin's, 1997.

Duberman, Martin. *Stonewall.* New York: Plume, 1994.

Dubose, Lou. *Vice: Dick Cheney and the Hijacking of the American Presidency.* New York: Random House, 2006.

Dubose, Lou, and Jan Reid. *The Hammer: God, Money, and the Rise of the Republican Congress.* New York: Public Affairs, 2004.

Dudley, Mark. E. *Gideon v. Wainwright (1963): Right to Counsel.* New York: Twenty-First Century Books, 1995.

Dunaway, David King. *How Can I Keep from Singing: Pete Seeger.* New York: McGraw-Hill, 1981.

Dunbar, David, and Brad Regan, eds. *Debunking 9/11 Myths: Why Conspiracy Theories Can't Stand Up to the Facts.* New York: Hearst Books, 2006.

Duncan, Paul. *Stanley Kubrick: The Complete Films.* Los Angeles: Taschen, 2003.

Dunne, John Gregory. *Delano: The Story of the California Grape Strike.* Berkeley: University of California Press, 2008.

Dunphy, Eamon. *Unforgettable Fire: The Definitive Biography of U2.* New York: Warner, 1987.

Dupré, Judith. *Monuments: America's History in Art and Memory.* New York: Random House, 2007.

Duram, James C. *A Moderate Among Extremists.* Chicago: Nelson-Hall, 1981.

Duriez, Colin. *Francis Schaeffer: An Authentic Life.* Wheaton, IL: Crossway Books, 2008.

Dworkin, Andrea. *Heartbreak: The Political Memoir of a Feminist Militant.* New York: Basic Books, 2002.

Dworkin, Ronald. *Life's Dominion: An Argument About Abortion, Euthanasia, and Individual Freedom.* New York: Vintage Books, 1994.

Dylan, Bob. *Chronicles.* Vol. 1. New York: Simon & Schuster, 2004.

Dyson, Michael Eric. *Come Hell or High Water: Hurricane Katrina and the Color of Disaster.* New York: Perseus, 2006.

Eagleton, Terry. *The Idea of Culture.* Malden, MA: Blackwell, 2000.

———. *Literary Theory: An Introduction.* Minneapolis: University of Minnesota Press, 1996.

Easton, Nina J. *Gang of Five: Leaders at the Center of the Conservative Crusade.* New York: Simon & Schuster, 2000.

Ebenstein, Alan O. *Milton Friedman: A Biography.* New York: Palgrave Macmillan, 2007.

Eberly, Don, ed. *Building a Healthy Culture: Strategies for an American Renaissance.* Grand Rapids, MI: William B. Eerdmans, 2001.

Eberstadt, Mary, ed. *Why I Turned Right: Leading Baby Boom Conservatives Chronicle Their Political Journeys.* New York: Threshold Editions, 2007.

Echeverria, John, and Raymond Booth Eby, eds. *Let the People Judge: Wise Use and the Private Property Rights Movement.* Washington, DC: Island Press, 1995.

Echols, Alice. *Daring to Be Bad: Radical Feminism in America, 1967–1975.* Minneapolis: University of Minnesota Press, 1989.

Editors of *Lingua Franca*. *The Sokal Hoax: The Sham That Shook the Academy.* Lincoln, NE: Bison Books, 2000.

Edsall, Thomas Byrne, and Mary D. Edsall. *Chain Reaction: The Impact of Race, Rights, and Taxes on American Politics.* New York: W.W. Norton, 1991, 1992.

Edwards, Bob. *Edward R. Murrow and the Birth of Broadcast Journalism.* Hoboken, NJ: John Wiley & Sons, 2004.

Edwards, Lee. *Goldwater: The Man Who Made a Revolution.* Washington, DC: Regnery, 1995.

———. *Our Times:* The Washington Times *1982–2002.* Washington, DC: Regnery, 2002.

Egan, Michael. *Barry Commoner and the Science of Survival: The Remaking of American Environmentalism.* Cambridge, MA: MIT Press, 2007.

Ehrenreich, Barbara. *Nickel and Dimed: On (Not) Getting By in America.* New York: Henry Holt, 2001.

Ehrman, John. *The Rise of Neoconservatism: Intellectuals and Foreign Affairs, 1945–1994.* New Haven, CT: Yale University Press, 1995.

Einstein, Mara. *Media Diversity: Economics, Ownership, and the FCC.* Mahwah, NJ: Lawrence Erlbaum, 2004.

Eisenstat, Stuart E. *Imperfect Justice: Looted Assets, Slave Labor, and the Unfinished Business of World War II.* New York: Perseus, 2003.

Eitzen, D. Stanley, and Maxine Baca Zinn. *Globalization: The Transformation of Social Worlds.* Belmont, CA: Thompson Wadsworth, 2006.

Eksterowicz, Anthony J., and Glenn P. Hastedt, eds. *The Presidencies of George Herbert Walker Bush and George Walker Bush: Like Father Like Son?* New York: Nova Science Publishers, 2008.

Eldredge, Niles. *The Triumph of Evolution and the Failure of Creationism.* New York: W.H. Freeman, 2001.

Ellwood, Robert S., Jr. *One Way: The Jesus People Movement and Its Meaning.* Englewood Cliffs, NJ: Prentice-Hall, 1973.

Elster, Jon. *Making Sense of Marx.* Cambridge, MA: Cambridge University Press, 1985.

Emberley, Julia B. *The Cultural Politics of Fur.* Ithaca, NY: Cornell University Press, 1997.

Emery, Fred. *Watergate: The Corruption of American Politics and the Fall of Richard Nixon.* New York: Touchstone, 1995.

Emirates Center for Strategic Studies and Research. *Biotechnology and the Future of Society: Challenges and Opportunities.* London: I.B. Tauris, 2004.

Engelhardt, Tom. *The End of Victory Culture: Cold War America and the Disillusioning of a Generation.* New York: Basic Books, 1995.

Engelman, Ralph. *Public Radio and Television in America: A Political History.* Thousand Oaks, CA: Sage, 1996.

Epstein, Benjamin R., and Arnold Forster. *The Radical Right: Report on the John Birch Society and Its Allies.* New York: Random House, 1967.

Epstein, David L., Richard H. Pildes, Rodolfo O. de la Garza, and Sharyn O'Halloran, eds. *The Future of the Voting Rights Act.* New York: Russell Sage Foundation, 2006.

Epstein, Jason. *The Great Conspiracy Trial: An Essay on Law, Liberty, and the Constitution.* New York: Random House, 1970.

Epstein, Lee, and Jeffrey Segal. *Advice and Consent: The Politics of Judicial Appointments.* New York: Oxford University Press, 2007.

Eribon, Didier. *Michel Foucault.* Translated by Betsy Wing. Cambridge, MA: Harvard University Press, 1991.

Erzen, Tanya. *Straight to Jesus: Sexual and Christian Conversion in the Ex-Gay Movement.* Berkeley: University of California Press, 2006.

Esbensen, Finn-Aage, Stephen G. Tibbets, and Larry Gaines, eds. *American Youth Gangs at the Millennium.* Long Grove, IL: Waveland, 2004.

Escoffier, Jeffrey, ed. *Sexual Revolution.* New York: Thunder's Mouth, 2003.

Eskridge, William N., Jr. *Dishonorable Passions: Sodomy Laws in America, 1861–2003.* New York: Viking, 2008.

Eskridge, William N., Jr., and Darren R. Spedale. *Gay Marriage: For Better or for Worse? What We've Learned from the Evidence.* New York: Oxford University Press, 2006.

Estrich, Susan. *Soulless: Ann Coulter and the Right-Wing Church of Hate.* New York: HarperCollins, 2006.

Etzioni, Amitai. *How Patriotic Is the Patriot Act? Freedom Versus Security in the Age of Terrorism.* New York: Routledge, 2004.

Evans, M. Stanton. *Blacklisted by History: The Untold Story of Joseph McCarthy and His Fight Against America's Enemies.* New York: Crown Forum, 2007.

———. *The Theme Is Freedom: Religion, Politics, and the American Tradition.* Washington, DC: Regnery Publishing, 1994.

Evans, Sara. *Personal Politics: The Roots of Women's Liberation in the Civil Rights Movement and the New Left.* New York: Vintage, 1980.

Faderman, Lillian. *Odd Girls and Twilight Lovers: A History of Lesbian Life in Twentieth-Century America.* New York: Columbia University Press, 1991.

Fager, Charles. *Selma 1965: The March That Changed the South.* Boston: Beacon, 1985.

Falsetto, Mario. *Stanley Kubrick: A Narrative and Stylistic Analysis.* 2nd ed. Westport, CT: Praeger, 2001.

Falwell, Jerry. *America Can Be Saved!* Murfreesboro, TN: Sword of the Lord, 1979.

———. *Falwell: An Autobiography.* Lynchburg, VA: Liberty House, 1997.

Farber, Stephen. *The Movie Ratings Game.* Washington, DC: Public Affairs Press, 1972.

Farley, Reynolds and John Haaga, eds. *The American People: Census 2000.* New York: Russell Sage Foundation, 2005.

Farrell, Amy Erdman. *Yours in Sisterhood: Ms. Magazine and the Promise of Popular Feminism.* Chapel Hill: University of North Carolina Press, 1998.

Farris, Michael. *The Future of Homeschooling: A New Direction for Home Education.* Washington, DC: Regnery, 1997.

Faux, Marian. *Roe v. Wade: The Untold Story of the Landmark Supreme Court Decision That Made Abortion Legal.* New York: Macmillan, 1988.

Federici, Michael P. *Eric Voegelin: The Restoration of Order.* Wilmington, DE: ISI Books, 2002.

Fehrenbach, T.R. *Lone Star: A History of Texas and the Texans.* New York: Da Capo Press, 2000.

Feinberg, Leslie. *Transgender Warrior: Making History from Joan of Arc to Dennis Rodman.* Boston: Beacon Press, 1997.

Felsenthal, Carol. *The Sweetheart of the Silent Majority: The Biography of Phyllis Schlafly.* New York: Doubleday, 1981.

Felt, Mark, and John D. O'Connor. *A G-Man's Life: The FBI, Being "Deep Throat," and the Struggle for Honor in Washington.* Washington, DC: PublicAffairs, 2006.

Fenner, Lorry M., and Marie de Young. *Women in Combat: Civic Duty or Military Liability?* Washington, DC: Georgetown University Press, 2001.

Fenno, Richard F., Jr. *The Making of a Senator: Dan Quayle.* Washington, DC: CQ Press, 1998.

Fenster, Mark. *Conspiracy Theories: Secrecy and Power in American Culture.* Minneapolis: University of Minnesota Press, 1999.

Ferrara, Peter J., and Michael Tanner. *A New Deal for Social Security.* Washington, DC: Cato Institute, 1998.

Ferraro, Geraldine A., with Linda Bird Francke. *Ferraro: My Story.* Evanston, IL: Northwestern University Press, 2004.

Ferraro, Geraldine A., with Catherine Whitney. *Framing a Life: A Family Memoir.* New York: Scribner, 1998.

Ferriss, Susan, and Ricardo Sandoval. *The Fight in the Fields: César Chávez and the Farmworkers' Movement.* New York: Harcourt Brace, 1997.

Finley, Laura L., and Peter Finley. *Piss Off! How Drug Testing and Other Privacy Violations Are Alienating America's Youth.* Monroe, ME: Common Courage, 2005.

Fiorina, Morris P., with Samuel J. Abrams and Jeremy C. Pope. *Culture War? The Myth of a Polarized America.* New York: Pearson Education, 2004, 2005.

Fischer, Claude S., et al. *Inequality by Design: Cracking the Bell Curve Myth.* Princeton, NJ: Princeton University Press, 1996.

Fisher, James. *The Theater of Tony Kushner: Living Past Hope.* New York: Routledge, 2001.

Fisher, Louis. *Presidential War Powers.* Lawrence: University of Kansas, 1995.

Fisher, Patrick. *Congressional Budgeting: A Representational Perspective.* Lanham, MD: University Press of America, 2005.

Fishman, Ethan M. *The Prudential Presidency: An Aristotelian Approach to Presidential Leadership.* Westport, CT: Praeger, 2001.

FitzGerald, Dawn. *Julia Butterfly Hill: Saving the Redwoods.* Brookfield, CT: Millbrook Press, 2002.

Fitzgerald, Deborah. *Every Farm a Factory: The Industrial Ideal in American Agriculture.* New Haven, CT: Yale University Press, 2003.

Fitzgerald, Frances. *Cities on a Hill.* New York: Touchstone, 1987.

———. *Way Out There in the Blue: Reagan, Star Wars, and the End of the Cold War.* New York: Simon & Schuster, 2000.

Fleischer, Doris Zames, and Freida Fleischer. *The Disability Rights Movement: From Charity to Confrontation.* Philadelphia: Temple University Press, 2001.

Fleiss, Heidi. *Pandering.* Los Angeles: One Hour Entertainment, 2002.

Fletcher, George. *A Crime of Self-Defense: Bernhard Goetz and the Law on Trial.* Chicago: University of Chicago Press, 1990.

Florence, Namulundah. *bell hooks' Engaged Pedagogy: A Transgressive Education for Critical Consciousness.* Westport, CT: Bergin & Garvey, 1998.

Flynt, Larry. *Sex, Lies, and Politics: The Naked Truth.* New York: Kensington, 2004.

———. *An Unseemly Man: My Life as a Pornographer, Pundit, and Social Outcast.* Los Angeles: Dove Books, 1996.

Foege, Alec. *The Empire God Built: Inside Pat Robertson's Media Machine.* New York: John Wiley & Sons, 1996.

Foerstel, Herbert N. *Banned in the U.S.A.: A Reference Guide to Book Censorship in Schools and Public Libraries.* Westport, CT: Greenwood, 2002.

———. *The Patriot Act: A Documentary and Reference Guide*. Westport, CT: Greenwood Press, 2008.

Fonda, Jane. *My Life So Far*. New York: Random House, 2005.

Foner, Eric. *Free Soil, Free Labor, Free Men: The Ideology of the Republican Party Before the Civil War*. New York: Oxford University Press, 1970.

Ford, Gerald R. *A Time to Heal: The Autobiography of Gerald R. Ford*. New York: Harper and Row, 1979.

Foreman, Dave. *Confessions of an Eco-Warrior*. New York: Harmony Books, 1991.

Forrest, Barbara, and Paul R. Gross. *Creationism's Trojan Horse: The Wedge of Intelligent Design*. New York: Oxford University Press, 2004.

Forster, Arnold, and Benjamin R. Epstein. *Danger on the Right: The Attitudes, Personnel and Influence of the Radical Right and Extreme Conservatives*. New York: Random House, 1964.

Foskett, Ken. *Judging Thomas: The Life and Times of Clarence Thomas*. New York: Morrow, 2004.

Foster, Lawrence, and Patricia Susan Herzog. *Defending Diversity: Contemporary Philosophical Perspectives on Pluralism and Multiculturalism*. Amherst: University of Massachusetts Press, 1994.

Foster, Patricia. *Minding the Body: Women Writers on Body and Soul*. New York: Anchor Books, 1995.

Foubert, John D. *The Men's Program: A Peer Education Guide to Rape Prevention*. 3rd ed. New York: Routledge, 2005.

Fowler, Robert. *The World of Chick?* San Francisco: Last Gasp, 2001.

Fox, Michael W. *Superpigs and Wondercorn: The Brave New World of Biotechnology and Where It May Lead*. New York: Lyons & Burford, 1992.

Fox, Richard Wightman. *Reinhold Niebuhr: A Biography*. New York: Pantheon Books, 1985.

Foxman, Abraham H. *The Deadliest Lies: The Israel Lobby and the Myth of Jewish Control*. New York: Palgrave Macmillan, 2007.

Frady, Marshall. *Billy Graham: A Parable of American Righteousness*. Boston: Little, Brown, 1979.

———. *The Life and Pilgrimage of Jesse Jackson*. New York: Simon & Schuster, 2006.

Francione, Gary L. *Animals, Property, and the Law*. Philadelphia: Temple University Press, 1995.

Frank, Barney. *Speaking Frankly: What's Wrong with the Democrats and How to Fix It*. New York: Crown, 1992.

Frank, Francine Wattman, and Paula A. Treichler. *Language, Gender, and Professional Writing: Theoretical Approaches and Guidelines for Nonsexist Usage*. New York: Modern Language Association of America, 1989.

Frank, Thomas. *The Conquest of Cool: Business Culture, Counterculture, and the Rise of Hip Consumerism*. Chicago: University of Chicago Press, 1998.

———. *What's the Matter with Kansas? How Conservatives Won the Heart of America*. New York: Metropolitan Books, 2004.

Franken, Al. *Lies (And the Lying Liars Who Tell Them): A Fair and Balanced Look at the Right*. New York: Dutton, 2003.

———. *Rush Limbaugh Is a Big Fat Idiot and Other Observations*. New York: Delacorte Press, 1996.

Frankl, Razelle. *Televangelism: The Marketing of Popular Religion*. Carbondale: Southern Illinois University Press, 1987.

Fraser, Steve, and Gary Gerstle, eds. *The Rise and Fall of the New Deal Order, 1930–1980*. Princeton, NJ: Princeton University Press, 1989, 1990.

Fraser, Steven, ed. *The Bell Curve Wars: Race, Intelligence, and the Future of America*. New York: Basic Books, 1995.

Freeman, Derek. *The Fateful Hoaxing of Margaret Mead: A Historical Analysis of Her Samoan Researches*. Boulder, CO: Westview Press, 1999.

Freeman, Steven F. *Was the 2004 Presidential Election Stolen? Exit Polls, Election Fraud, and the Official Count*. New York: Seven Stories Press, 2006.

Fried, Amy. *Muffled Echoes: Oliver North and the Politics of Public Opinion*. New York: Columbia University Press, 1997.

Fried, Richard M. *Nightmare in Red: The McCarthy Era in Perspective*. New York: Oxford University Press, 1990.

———. *The Russians Are Coming! The Russians Are Coming! Pageantry and Patriotism in Cold War America*. New York: Oxford University Press, 1998.

Friedan, Betty. *Life So Far*. New York: Simon and Schuster, 2000.

Friedlander, Paul. *Rock & Roll: A Social History*. 2nd ed. Cambridge, MA: Westview Press, 2006.

Friedman, Leon, ed. *Brown v. Board: The Landmark Oral Arguments Before the Supreme Court*. New York: New Press, 2004.

Friedman, Lester D., ed. *Unspeakable Images: Ethnicity and the American Cinema*. Chicago: University of Illinois Press, 1991.

Friedman, Milton, and Rose Friedman. *Free to Choose: A Personal Statement*. New York: Harcourt Brace Jovanovich, 1980.

Friedman, Thomas. *The World Is Flat: A Brief History of the Twenty-First Century*. New York: Farrar, Straus, and Giroux, 2005.

Friel, Howard, and Richard A. Falk. *The Record of the Paper: How the New York Times Misreports US Foreign Policy*. New York: Verso, 2004.

Frost, David. *Billy Graham: Personal Thoughts of a Public Man*. Colorado Springs, CO: Chariot Victor, 1997.

Frykholm, Amy Johnson. *Rapture Culture: "Left Behind" in Evangelical America*. New York: Oxford University Press, 2004.

Fukuyama, Francis. *America at the Crossroads: Democracy, Power, and the Neoconservative Legacy*. New Haven, CT: Yale University Press, 2006.

———. *Our Posthuman Future: Consequences of the Biotechnology Revolution*. New York: Farrar, Straus and Giroux, 2002.

Fulz, Lucille P. *Toni Morrison: Playing with Difference*. Urbana: University of Illinois Press, 2003.

Furedi, Frank. *Therapy Culture*. London: Routledge, 2003.

Furgurson, Ernest B. *Hard Right: The Rise of Jesse Helms*. New York: W.W. Norton, 1986.

Gabarino, James. *Lost Boys: Why Our Sons Turn Violent and How We Can Save Them*. New York: Free Press, 1999.

Gabler, Neal. *Walt Disney: The Triumph of the American Imagination*. New York: Alfred A. Knopf, 2006.

Gaddis, John Lewis. *The Cold War: A New History*. New York: Penguin Press, 2005.

———. *The United States and the Origins of the Cold War, 1941–1947*. New York: Columbia University Press, 1972, 2000.

Gaines, Richard, and Michael Segal. *Dukakis: The Man Who Would Be President*. New York: Avon, 1988.

Galbraith, John Kenneth, and Andrea D. Williams, eds. *The Essential Galbraith*. Boston: Houghton Mifflin, 2001.

Gallaher, Carolyn. *On the Fault Line: Race, Class, and the American Patriot Movement*. Lanham, MD: Rowman & Littlefield, 2003.

Gamboa, Erasmo. *Mexican Labor and World War II: Braceros in the Pacific Northwest, 1942–1947*. Austin: University of Texas Press, 1990.

Ganz, Nicholas, and Tristan Manco. *Graffiti World: Street Art from Five Continents*. New York: Harry N. Abrams, 2004.

Garcia, Juan Ramon. *Operation Wetback: The Mass Deportation of Mexican Undocumented Workers in 1954*. Westport, CT: Greenwood Press, 1980.

Gardell, Mattias. *In the Name of Elijah Muhammad: Louis Farrakhan and the Nation of Islam*. Durham, NC: Duke University Press, 1996.

Garfinkle, Adam. *Telltale Hearts: The Origins and Impact of the Vietnam Antiwar Movement*. New York: St. Martin's Press, 1995.

Garman, Bryan. *A Race of Singers: Whitman's Working-Class Hero from Guthrie to Springsteen*. Chapel Hill: University of North Carolina Press, 2000.

Garrow, David J. *Bearing the Cross: Martin Luther King, Jr., and the Southern Christian Leadership Conference*. New York: Vintage, 1986.

———. *Liberty and Sexuality: The Right to Privacy and the Making of Roe v. Wade*. Berkeley: University of California Press, 1998.

Garson, Helen. *Oprah Winfrey: A Biography*. Westport, CT: Greenwood Press, 2004.

Gates, Henry Louis, Jr. *Loose Canons: Notes on the Culture Wars*. New York: Oxford University Press, 1992.

Gathorne-Hardy, Jonathan. *Sex–The Measure of All Things: A Life of Alfred C. Kinsey*. Bloomington: Indiana University Press, 2004.

Geller, William A., and Hans Toch. *Police Violence: Understanding and Controlling Police Abuse of Force*. New Haven, CT: Yale University Press, 2005.

Gelman, Andrew. *Red State, Blue State, Rich State, Poor State: Why Americans Vote the Way They Do*. Princeton, NJ: Princeton University Press, 2008.

Genovese, Michael A. *The Nixon Presidency: Power and Politics in Turbulent Times*. Westport, CT: Greenwood, 1990.

———. *The Watergate Crisis*. Westport CT: Greenwood Press, 1999.

Geoghegan, Thomas. *Which Side Are You On? Trying to Be for Labor When It's Flat on Its Back*. New York: Farrar, Straus and Giroux, 1991.

George, Nelson. *Hip Hop America*. New York: Penguin, 2005.

Gerber, David, ed. *Anti-Semitism in American History*. Urbana: University of Illinois Press, 1986.

Gerber, Scott Douglas. *First Principles: The Jurisprudence of Clarence Thomas*. New York: New York University Press, 2002.

Gerdes, Louis I. *The Patriot Act: Opposing Viewpoints*. Detroit, MI: Greenhaven Press, 2005.

Gerring, John. *Party Ideologies in America, 1828–1996*. New York: Cambridge University Press, 1998.

Gerson, Mark. *The Neoconservative Vision: From the Cold War to the Culture Wars*. Lanham, MD: Madison Books, 1997.

Gerstenfeld, Phyllis B. *Hate Crimes: Causes, Controls, and Controversies*. Thousand Oaks, CA: Sage, 2004.

Gever, Martha. *Entertaining Lesbians: Celebrity, Sexuality, and Self-Invention*. New York: Routledge, 2003.

Gibbs, Jewelle Taylor. *Race and Justice: Rodney King and O.J. Simpson in a House Divided*. San Francisco: Jossey-Bass, 1996.

Gibbs, Lois Marie, with Murray Levine. *Love Canal: My Story*. Albany: State University of New York Press, 1982.

Gibbs, Nancy, Richard Lacayo, Lance Morrow, Jill Smolowe, and David Van Biema. *Mad Genius: The Odyssey, Pursuit, and Capture of the Unabomber Suspect*. New York: Warner Books, 1996.

Gilder, George. *Wealth and Poverty*. New York: Basic Books, 1981.

Gill, Leslie. *The School of the Americas: Military Training and Political Violence in the Americas*. Durham, NC: Duke University Press, 2004.

Gillespie, Carmen. *Critical Companion to Toni Morrison: A Literary Reference to Her Life and Work*. New York: Facts On File, 2008.

Gillon, Steven M. *The Democrats' Dilemma: Walter F. Mondale and the Liberal Legacy*. New York: Columbia University Press, 1992.

Gilmore, Mikal. *Shot in the Heart*. New York: Anchor Books, 1994.

Gingrich, Newt. *Rediscovering God in America: Reflections on the Role of Faith in Our Nation's History and Future*. Nashville, TN: Integrity House, 2006.

Gingrich, Newt, et al. *Contract with America: The Bold Plan by Rep. Newt Gingrich, Rep. Dick Armey, and the House Republicans to Change the Nation*. New York: Times Books, 1994.

Gingrich, Newt, Vince Haley, and Rick Tyler. *Real Change: From the World That Fails to the World That Works*. Washington, DC: Regnery, 2008.

Ginsberg, Allen. *Collected Poems, 1947–1980*. New York: Harper and Row, 1984.

Gitlin, Todd. *The Sixties: Years of Hope, Days of Rage*. New York: Bantam Books, 1987, 1993.

———. *The Twilight of Common Dreams: Why America Is Wracked by Culture Wars*. New York: Metropolitan Books, 1995.

Glantz, Stanton A., John Slade, Lisa A. Bero, Peter Hanauer, and Deborah E. Barnes, eds. *The Cigarette Papers*. Berkeley: University of California Press, 1998.

Glazer, Myron Peretz, and Penina Migdal Glazer. *The Whistleblowers: Exposing Corruption in Government and Industry*. New York: Basic Books, 1989.

Glazer, Nathan, and Daniel Patrick Moynihan. *Beyond the Melting Pot: The Negroes, Puerto Ricans, Jews, Italians, and Irish of New York City*. Cambridge, MA: MIT Press, 1963.

Gluckman, Amy, and Betsy Reed. *Homo Economics: Capitalism, Community, and Lesbian and Gay Life*. New York: Routledge, 1997.

Goad, Jim. *The Redneck Manifesto*. New York: Simon & Schuster, 1997.

Goble, Dale D., J. Michael Scott, and Frank W. Davis, eds. *The Endangered Species Act at Thirty, Volume 1: Renewing the Conservation Promise*. Washington, DC: Island Press, 2005.

Godfrey, Donald G., and Frederic A. Leigh, eds. *Historical Dictionary of American Radio*. Westport, CT: Greenwood Press, 1998.

Goings, Kenneth W. *Mammy and Uncle Mose: Collectibles and American Stereotyping*. Bloomington: Indiana University Press, 1994.

Gold, Dore. *Tower of Babble: How the United Nations Has Fueled Global Chaos*. New York: Crown Forum, 2004.

Goldberg, Bernard. *Arrogance: Rescuing America from the Media Elite*. New York: Warner Books, 2003.

———. *Bias: A CBS Insider Exposes How the Media Distort the News*. Washington, DC: Regnery, 2002.

Goldberg, David Theo. *Multiculturalism: A Critical Reader.* Cambridge, MA: Blackwell, 1994.

Goldberg, Robert Alan. *Enemies Within: The Culture of Conspiracy in Modern America.* New Haven, CT: Yale University Press, 2001.

Goldberg, Robert, and Gerald Jay Goldberg. *Anchors: Brokaw, Jennings, Rather, and the Evening News.* New York: Birch Lane, 1990.

———. *Citizen Turner: The Wild Rise of an American Tycoon.* New York: Harcourt Brace, 1995.

Goldberg-Hiller, Jonathan. *The Limits to Union: Same-Sex Marriage and the Politics of Civil Rights.* Ann Arbor: University of Michigan Press, 2002.

Golden, Jane, Robin Rice, and Monica Yant Kinney. *Philadelphia Murals and the Stories They Tell.* Philadelphia: Temple University Press, 2002.

Goldgeier, James M., and Michael McFaul. *Power and Purpose: U.S. Policy Toward Russia After the Cold War.* Washington, DC: Brookings Institution Press, 2003.

Goldsteen, Raymond L., and John K. Schorr. *Demanding Democracy After Three Mile Island.* Gainesville: University of Florida Press, 1991.

Goldstein, Robert Justin. *Flag Burning and Free Speech: The Case of* Texas v. Johnson. Kent, OH: Kent State University Press, 2000.

Goldwater, Barry. *With No Apologies.* New York: William Morrow, 1979.

Gómez-Quiñones, Juan. *Chicano Politics: Reality and Promise, 1940–1990.* Albuquerque: University of New Mexico Press, 1990.

Gonzalez, Doreen. *Alex Haley: Author of Roots.* Hillside, NJ: Enslow, 1994.

Gonzalez, Juan. *Harvest of Empire: A History of Latinos in America.* New York: Viking Penguin, 2000.

Goodchild, Peter. *Edward Teller: The Real Dr. Strangelove.* Cambridge, MA: Harvard University Press, 2004.

Gooding-Williams, Robert, ed. *Reading Rodney King, Reading Urban Uprising.* New York: Routledge, 1993.

Goodman, Allan E., and Bruce D. Berkowitz. *The Need to Know: The Report of the Twentieth Century Fund Task Force on Covert Action and American Democracy.* New York: Twentieth Century Fund Press, 1992.

Goodwin, Doris Kearns. *Lyndon Johnson and the American Dream.* New York: Signet, 1976.

Gordon, Avery, and Christopher Newfield, eds. *Mapping Multiculturalism.* Minneapolis: University of Minnesota Press, 1996.

Gordon, Linda. *The Moral Property of Women: A History of Birth Control Politics in America.* Urbana: University of Illinois Press, 2002.

———. *Woman's Body, Woman's Choice.* New York: Penguin Books, 1990.

Gore, Al. *An Inconvenient Truth: The Planetary Emergency of Global Warming and What We Can Do About It.* Emmaus, PA: Rodale Press, 2006.

Gore, Tipper. *Raising PG Kids in an X-Rated Society.* Nashville, TN: Abingdon, 1987.

Gorenfeld, John. *Bad Moon Rising: How the Reverend Moon Created* The Washington Times, *Seduced the Religious Right.* Sausalito, CA: PoliPointPress, 2008.

Gorman, Robert A. *Michael Harrington: Speaking American.* New York: Routledge, 1995.

Gorn, Elliott J., ed. *Muhammad Ali, the People's Champ.* Urbana: University of Illinois Press, 1995.

Gosse, Van. *Rethinking the New Left: An Interpretive History.* New York: Palgrave Macmillan, 2005.

Gostin, Lawrence O. *The AIDS Pandemic: Complacency, Injustice, and Unfulfilled Expectations.* Chapel Hill: University of North Carolina Press, 2004.

Gott, Richard. *Cuba: A New History.* New Haven, CT: Yale University Press, 2005.

Gottlieb, Alan M. *The Wise Use Agenda: The Citizen's Policy Guide to Environmental Resource Issues.* Bellevue, WA: Free Enterprise Press, 1989.

Gottlieb, Robert. *Forcing the Spring: The Transformation of the American Environmental Movement.* Rev. ed. Washington, DC: Island Press, 2005.

Gould, Jon B. *Speak No Evil: The Triumph of Hate Speech Regulation.* Chicago: University of Chicago Press, 2005.

Grabb, Edward, and James Curtis, eds. *Regions Apart: The Four Societies of Canada and the United States.* New York: Oxford University Press, 2005.

Graebner, William. *Patty's Got a Gun: Patricia Hearst in 1970s America.* Chicago: University of Chicago Press, 2008.

Graham, Billy. *Just As I Am: The Autobiography of Billy Graham.* New York: HarperCollins, 1997.

Graham, Hugh Davis. *The Civil Rights Era: Origins and Development of National Policy, 1960–1972.* New York: Oxford University Press, 1990.

Grant, George. *Buchanan: Caught in the Crossfire.* Nashville, TN: Thomas Nelson, 1996.

———. *Immaculate Deception: The Shifting Agenda of Planned Parenthood.* Chicago: Northfield, 1996.

Greeley, Andrew. *The Catholic Imagination.* Berkeley: University of California Press, 2000.

Greenberg, David. *Nixon's Shadow: The History of an Image.* New York: W.W. Norton, 2003.

Greenberg, Jack. *Crusaders in the Courts: How a Dedicated Band of Lawyers Fought for the Civil Rights Revolution.* New York: Basic Books, 1994.

Greenberg, Judith, ed. *Trauma at Home After 9/11.* Lincoln and London: University of Nebraska Press, 2003.

Greenburg, Jan Crawford. *Supreme Conflict: The Inside Story of the Struggle for Control of the United States Supreme Court.* New York: Penguin Press, 2007.

Greene, John Robert. *The Presidency of Gerald R. Ford.* Lawrence: University Press of Kansas, 1995.

Gregory, Raymond F. *Age Discrimination in the American Workplace: Old at a Young Age.* New Brunswick, NJ: Rutgers University Press, 2001.

Grewal, Inderpal, and Caren Kaplan, eds. *An Introduction to Women's Studies: Gender in a Transnational World.* New York: McGraw-Hill Humanities, 2002.

Grey, Richard. *A History of American Literature.* Malden, MA: Blackwell, 2004.

Griswold del Castillo, Richard, and Richard A. Garcia. *César Chávez: A Triumph of Spirit.* Norman: University of Oklahoma Press, 1995.

Griswold, Robert L. *Fatherhood in America: A History.* New York: Basic Books, 1993.

Groening, Matt. *The Simpsons: A Complete Guide to Our Favorite Family.* New York: HarperPerennial, 1997.

Grofman, Bernard, and Chandler Davidson, eds. *Controversies in*

Minority Voting: The Voting Rights Act in Perspective. Washington, DC: Brookings Institute, 1992.

Gross, Larry. *Contested Closets: The Politics and Ethics of Outing.* Minneapolis: University of Minnesota Press, 1993.

Grossberg, Lawrence, and Nelson Cary, and Paula A. Treichler, eds. *Cultural Studies.* New York: Routledge, 1992.

Guilbert, Georges-Claude. *Madonna as Postmodern Myth: How One Star's Self-Construction Rewrites Sex, Gender, Hollywood, and the American Dream.* Jefferson, NC: McFarland, 2002.

Guillermo, Kathy Snow. *Monkey Business: The Disturbing Case That Launched the Animal Rights Movement.* Washington, DC: National Press Books, 1993.

Guither, Harold D. *Animals Rights: History and Scope of a Radical Social Movement.* Carbondale: Southern Illinois University Press, 1997.

Gullette, Margaret Morganroth. *Aged by Culture.* Chicago: University of Chicago Press, 2004.

Gushee, David P., ed. *Christians and Politics Beyond the Culture Wars: An Agenda for Engagement.* Grand Rapids, MI: Baker Books, 2000.

Guterson, David. *Family Matters: Why Homeschooling Makes Sense.* New York: Harcourt Brace Jovanovich, 1992.

Gutiérrez, José Angel. *The Making of a Chicano Militant: Lessons from Cristal.* Madison: University of Wisconsin Press, 1998.

Guttenplan, D.D. *The Holocaust on Trial.* New York: W.W. Norton, 2002.

Habermas, Jürgen. *The Future of Human Nature.* Cambridge, MA: Polity Press, 2003.

Hackney, Sheldon. *One America Indivisible: A National Conversation on American Pluralism and Identity.* Washington, DC: National Endowment for the Humanities, 1997.

Haddad, Yvonne Yazbeck, ed. *Muslims of America.* New York: Oxford University Press, 1993.

Haerens, Margaret, ed. *Illegal Immigration.* Detroit, MI: Greenhaven Press, 2006.

Hagan, Kay Leigh, ed. *Women Respond to the Men's Movement.* San Francisco: Pandora, 1992.

Hajdu, David. *Positively 4th Street: The Lives and Times of Joan Baez, Bob Dylan, Mimi Baez Fariña, and Richard Fariña.* New York: Farrar, Straus and Giroux, 2001.

Halberstam, David. *The Fifties.* New York: Villard Books, 1993.

Haley, Alex. *Roots: The Saga of an American Family.* Garden City, NY: Doubleday, 1976.

Hall, Ivan P. *Bamboozled! How America Loses the Intellectual Game with Japan and Its Implications for Our Future in Asia.* Armonk, NY: M.E. Sharpe, 2002.

Hall, Kermit L., and John J. Patrick. *The Pursuit of Justice: Supreme Court Decisions That Shaped America.* New York: Oxford University Press, 2006.

Halperin, David. *Saint Foucault: Towards a Gay Hagiography.* New York: Oxford University Press, 1995.

Halprin, Lawrence. *The Franklin Delano Roosevelt Memorial.* San Francisco: Chronicle Books, 1997.

Hamburger, Philip. *Separation of Church and State.* Cambridge, MA: Harvard University Press, 2002.

Hamby, Alonzo. *Man of the People: A Life of Harry S. Truman.* New York: Oxford University Press, 1995.

Hamilton, Marci A. *God vs. the Gavel: Religion and the Rule of Law.* New York: Cambridge University Press, 2005.

Hampton, Wayne. *Guerrilla Minstrels: John Lennon, Joe Hill, Woody Guthrie, and Bob Dylan.* Knoxville: University of Tennessee Press, 1986.

Hangen, Tona J. *Redeeming the Dial: Radio, Religion, and Popular Culture in America.* Chapel Hill: University of North Carolina Press, 2002.

Hannaford, Ivan. *Race: The History of an Idea in the West.* Baltimore: Johns Hopkins University Press, 1996.

Harding, Susan Friend. *The Book of Jerry Falwell: Fundamentalist Language and Politics.* Princeton, NJ: Princeton University Press, 2000.

Hardisty, Jean V. *Mobilizing Resentment: Conservative Resurgence from the John Birch Society to the Promise Keepers.* Boston: Beacon, 1999.

Harer, John B., and Jeanne Harrell. *People For and Against Restricted or Unrestricted Expression.* Westport, CT: Greenwood Press, 2002.

Hargreaves, Tracy. *Androgyny in Modern Literature.* New York: Palgrave Macmillan, 2005.

Harrell, David Edwin, Jr. *Pat Robertson: A Personal, Religious, and Political Portrait.* New York: HarperCollins, 1988.

Harrington, Michael. *The Next Left: The History of a Future.* New York: Henry Holt, 1986.

———. *The Other America: Poverty in the United States.* New York: Macmillan, 1962.

Harris, David A. *Profiles in Injustice: Why Racial Profiling Cannot Work.* New York: New Press, 2002.

Harris, Jennifer, and Elwood Watson. *The Oprah Phenomenon.* Lexington: University Press of Kentucky, 2007.

Harris, John F. *The Survivor: Bill Clinton in the White House.* New York: Random House, 2005.

Harris, Nancy, ed. *The Peace Movement.* Detroit, MI: Greenhaven Press, 2005.

Harris, Stephen. *Gore Vidal's Historical Novels and the Shaping of American Consciousness.* Lewistown, NY: Edwin Mellen Press, 2005.

Hart, Gary. *The Good Fight: The Education of an American Reformer.* New York: Random House, 1993.

———. *Right from the Start: A Chronicle of the McGovern Campaign.* New York: Quadrangle, 1973.

Hart, Jeffrey. *The Making of the American Conservative Mind: National Review and Its Times.* Wilmington, DE: ISI Books, 2005.

Hart, Peter, and Fairness and Accuracy in Reporting (FAIR). *The Oh Really? Factor: Unspinning Fox News Channel's Bill O'Reilly.* New York: Seven Stories Press, 2003.

Hartmann, Robert T. *Palace Politics: An Inside Account of the Ford Years.* New York: McGraw-Hill, 1980.

Harvey, David. *The New Imperialism.* New York: Oxford University Press, 2005.

Harvey, Paul, Jr., ed. *Paul Harvey's For What It's Worth.* New York: Bantam Books, 1991.

Hauerwas, Stanley. *The Hauerwas Reader.* Durham, NC: Duke University Press, 2001.

———. *With the Grain of the Universe: The Church's Witness and Natural Theology.* Grand Rapids, MI: Brazos, 2001.

Hauerwas, Stanley, and William Willimon. *Resident Aliens: Life in the Christian Colony.* Nashville, TN: Abingdon, 1989.

Havill, Adrian. *Deep Truth: The Lives of Bob Woodward and Carl Bernstein.* Secaucus, NJ: Carol, 1993.

Hawthorne, Fran. *Inside the FDA: The Business and Politics Behind the Drugs We Take and the Food We Eat.* Hoboken, NJ: John Wiley & Sons, 2005.

Hay, Harry. *Radically Gay: Gay Liberation in the Words of Its Founder.* Boston: Beacon Press, 1996.

Hayashi, Brian Masaru. *Democratizing the Enemy: The Japanese-American Internment.* Princeton, NJ: Princeton University Press, 2004.

Hayden, Tom. *Reunion: A Memoir.* New York: Random House, 1988.

———. *Trial.* New York: Holt, Rinehart & Winston, 1970.

———. *Writings for a Democratic Society: The Tom Hayden Reader.* San Francisco: City Lights, 2008.

Hayes, Stephen F. *Cheney: The Untold Story of America's Most Powerful and Controversial Vice President.* New York: HarperCollins, 2007.

Hayford, Jack, et al. *Seven Promises of a Promise Keeper.* Nashville, TN: W Publishing, 1999.

Haynes, John Earl, and Harvey Klehr. *In Denial: Historians, Communism, and Espionage.* San Francisco: Encounter Books, 2005.

———. *Venona: Decoding Soviet Espionage in America.* New Haven, CT: Yale University Press, 1990.

Hays, Samuel P. *A History of Environmental Politics Since 1945.* Pittsburgh: University of Pittsburgh Press, 2000.

Heale, M.J. *McCarthy's Americans: Red Scare Politics in State and Nation, 1935–1965.* Athens: University of Georgia Press, 1998.

Hearst, Patricia, with Alvin Moscow. *Every Secret Thing.* Garden City, NY: Doubleday, 1982.

Heath, Joseph, and Andrew Potter. *Nation of Rebels: Why Counterculture Became Consumer Culture.* New York: HarperBusiness, 2004.

Heelas, Paul. *The New Age Movement: The Celebration of the Self and the Sacralization of Modernity.* Oxford, UK: Blackwell, 1996.

Heer, Jeet, and Kent Worcester. *Arguing Comics: Literary Masters on a Popular Medium.* Jackson: University Press of Mississippi, 2004.

Hefner, Hugh M., ed. *The New Bedside* Playboy: *A Half Century of Amusement, Diversion & Entertainment.* Chicago: Playboy Press, 2006.

Heidenry, John. *What Wild Ecstasy: The Rise and Fall of the Sexual Revolution.* New York: Simon & Schuster, 1997.

Heilbrun, Carolyn G. *Toward a Recognition of Androgyny.* New York: Knopf, 1973.

Heilemann, John. *Pride Before the Fall: The Trials of Bill Gates and the End of the Microsoft Era.* New York: HarperCollins, 2001.

Heller, Joseph. *Conversations with Joseph Heller.* Jackson: University Press of Mississippi, 1993.

———. *Now and Then: From Coney Island to Here.* New York: Alfred A. Knopf, 1998.

Hellman, John. *American Myth and the Legacy of Vietnam.* New York: Columbia University Press, 1986.

Helms, Jesse. *Here's Where I Stand: A Memoir.* New York: Random House, 2005.

Helvarg, David. *The War Against the Greens: The "Wise-Use" Movement, the New Right, and Anti-Environmental Violence.* San Francisco: Sierra Club Books, 1997.

Hemenway, David. *Private Guns, Public Health.* Ann Arbor: University of Michigan Press, 2004.

Hemphill, Hellen, and Ray Haines. *Discrimination, Harassment, and the Failure of Diversity Training: What to Do Now.* Westport, CT: Quorum Books, 1997.

Hendershot, Heather. *Shaking the World for Jesus: Media and Conservative Evangelical Culture.* Chicago: University of Chicago Press, 2004.

Hendricks, Steve. *The Unquiet Grave: The FBI and the Struggle for the Soul of Indian Country.* New York: Thunder's Mouth Press, 2006.

Hennessee, Judith. *Betty Friedan: Her Life.* New York: Random House, 1999.

Henningfield, Diane Andrews. *Charter Schools.* Detroit, MI: Greenhaven Press, 2008.

Henry, Astrid. *Not My Mother's Sister: Generational Conflict and Third-Wave Feminism.* Bloomington: Indiana University Press, 2004.

Henry, Charles P. *Ralph Bunche: Model Negro or American Other?* New York: New York University Press, 1999.

Herbert, Anthony B., with James T. Wooten. *Soldier.* New York: Dell, 1973.

Herda, D.J. *Sandra Day O'Connor: Independent Thinker.* Springfield, NJ: Enslow, 1995.

Herman, Arthur. *Joseph McCarthy: Reexamining the Life and Legacy of America's Most Hated Senator.* New York: Free Press, 2000.

Herold, Eve. *Stem Cell Wars: Inside Stories from the Frontlines.* New York: Palgrave Macmillan, 2006.

Herring, George. *America's Longest War: The United States and Vietnam, 1950–1975.* 4th ed. New York: McGraw-Hill, 2001.

Herrnstein, Richard J., and Charles Murray. *The Bell Curve.* New York: Free Press, 1994.

Hersberger, Mary. *Jane Fonda's War: A Political Biography of an American Icon.* New York: New Press, 2005.

Hersh, Seymour M. *Chain of Command: The Road from 9/11 to Abu Ghraib.* New York: HarperCollins, 2005.

Hersh, Seymour M. *Cover-Up.* New York: Vintage Books, 1973.

———. *The Dark Side of Camelot.* Boston: Little, Brown, 1997.

Herzog, Lawrence A. *Where North Meets South: Cities, Space, and Politics on the U.S.-Mexico Border.* Austin: University of Texas, Center for Mexican American Studies, 1990.

Hesse-Biber, Sharlene, and Greg Lee Carter. *Working Women in America: Split Dreams.* New York: Oxford University Press, 2000.

Hession, Charles H. *John Kenneth Galbraith and His Critics.* New York: New American Library, 1972.

Heumann, Milton, and Lance Cassak. *Good Cop, Bad Cop: Racial Profiling and Competing Views of Justice.* New York: Peter Lang, 2003.

Heywood, Leslie, and Jennifer Drake, eds. *Third Wave Agenda.* Minneapolis: University of Minnesota Press, 1997.

Hill, Anita F. *Speaking Truth to Power.* New York: Doubleday, 1997.

Hill, Anita Faye, and Emma Coleman Jordan. *Race, Gender, and Power in America: The Legacy of the Hill-Thomas Hearings.* New York: Oxford University Press, 1995.

Hill, Julia Butterfly. *The Legacy of Luna: The Story of a Woman, a Tree, and the Struggle to Save the Redwoods.* San Francisco: HarperCollins, 2000.

———. *One Makes the Difference: Inspiring Actions That Change Our World.* San Francisco: HarperCollins, 2002.

Hilley, Joseph H. *Sarah Palin: A New Kind of Leader.* Grand Rapids, MI: Zondervan, 2008.

Hilliard, Robert, and Michael C. Keith. *Dirty Discourse: Sex and Indecency in American Radio.* Ames: Iowa State Press, 2003.

Hilmes, Michele, and Jason Loviglio, eds. *Radio Reader: Essays in the Cultural History of Radio.* New York: Routledge, 2002.

Hilts, Philip J. *Protecting America's Health: FDA, Business, and One Hundred Years of Regulation.* New York: Alfred A. Knopf, 2003.

———. *Smokescreen: The Truth Behind the Tobacco Industry Cover-up.* Reading, MA: Addison-Wesley, 1996.

Himmelfarb, Gertrude. *The De-Moralization of Society: From Victorian Virtues to Modern Values.* New York: Alfred A. Knopf, 1995.

Hirsch, E.D., Jr. *Cultural Literacy: What Every American Needs to Know.* Boston: Houghton Mifflin, 1987.

Hiss, Alger. *Recollections of a Life.* New York: Henry Holt, 1988.

Hiss, Tony. *The View from Alger's Window: A Son's Memoir.* New York: Alfred A. Knopf, 1999.

Hoffman, Abbie. *The Best of Abbie Hoffman.* Ed. Daniel Simon. New York: Four Walls Eight Windows, 1989.

Hoffman, David. *The Oklahoma City Bombing and the Politics of Terror.* Venice, CA: Feral House, 1998.

Hoff-Wilson, Joan, ed. *Rights of Passage: The Past and Future of the ERA.* Bloomington: Indiana University Press, 1986.

Hofstadter, Richard. *Anti-Intellectualism in American Life.* New York: Vintage, 1963.

Hofstadter, Richard, and Walter P. Metzger. *The Development of Academic Freedom in the United States.* New York: Columbia University Press, 1955.

Hofstede, David. *James Dean: A Bio-Bibliography.* Westport, CT: Greenwood, 1996.

Hogan, Neal C. *Unhealed Wounds: Medical Malpractice in the Twentieth Century.* New York: LFB Scholarly, 2003.

Holden, Andrew. *Jehovah's Witnesses: Portrait of a Contemporary Religious Movement.* London: Routledge, 2002.

Homer, Christopher C. *The Politically Incorrect Guide to Global Warming and Environmentalism.* Washington, DC: Regnery, 2007.

hooks, bell. *Ain't I a Woman: Black Women and Feminism.* Boston: South End Press, 1981.

———. *Wounds of Passion: A Writing Life.* New York: Henry Holt, 1997.

Horne, Gerald. *Fire This Time: The Watts Uprising and the 1960s.* Charlottesville: University of Virginia Press, 1995.

Horowitz, Daniel. *Betty Friedan and the Making of "The Feminine Mystique": The American Left, the Cold War, and Modern Feminism.* Boston: University of Massachusetts Press, 1998.

Horowitz, David. *Indoctrination U.: The Left's War Against Academic Freedom.* New York: Encounter Books, 2007.

———. *Left Illusions: An Intellectual Odyssey.* Dallas: Spence, 2003.

———. *The Professors: The 101 Most Dangerous Academics in America.* Washington, DC: Regnery, 2006.

———. *Radical Son: A Generational Odyssey.* New York: Simon & Schuster, 1997.

Horwitz, Tony. *Confederates in the Attic: Dispatches from the Unfinished Civil War.* New York: Vintage Books, 1998.

House, H. Wayne, Thomas Ice, and Rodney L. Morris, eds. *Dominion Theology: Blessing or Curse? An Analysis of Christian Reconstructionism.* Portland, OR: Multnomah Press, 1988.

Houts, Peter S., et al. *The Three Mile Island Crisis: Psychological, Social, and Economic Impacts on the Surrounding Population.* University Park: Pennsylvania State University Press, 1988.

Howard, Jay R., and John M. Streck. *Apostles of Rock: The Splintered World of Contemporary Christian Music.* Lexington: University Press of Kentucky, 1999.

Howard, Philip. *New Media Campaigns and the Managed Citizen.* New York: Cambridge University Press, 2006.

Howe, Florence, ed. *The Politics of Women's Studies: Testimony from 30 Founding Mothers.* New York: Feminist, 2000.

Howe, Neil, and William Strauss. *Millennials Rising: The Next Great Generation.* New York: Vintage Books, 2000.

Hoy, David Couzens, ed. *Foucault: A Critical Reader.* New York: Basil Blackwell, 1986.

Hoyt, Edwin Palmer. *William O. Douglas: A Biography.* Middlebury, VT: Eriksson, 1979.

Huber, Peter. *Hard Green: Saving the Environment from the Environmentalists: A Conservative Manifesto.* New York: Basic Books, 1999.

Hughes, Jeff. *The Manhattan Project: Big Science and the Atomic Bomb.* New York: Columbia University Press, 2002.

Huie, William Bradford. *Three Lives for Mississippi.* Introduction by Martin Luther King, Jr. New York: New American Library, 1968.

Hull, N.E.H., and Peter Charles Hoffer. *Roe v. Wade: The Abortion Rights Controversy in American History.* Lawrence: University Press of Kansas, 2001.

Humber, James M., and Robert F. Almeder, eds. *Stem Cell Research.* Totawa, NJ: Humana Press, 2004.

Humphrey, Hubert H. *The Education of a Public Man: My Life and Politics.* Garden City, NJ: Doubleday, 1976.

Hunt, Andrew E. *The Turning: A History of Vietnam Veterans Against the War.* New York: New York University Press, 1999.

Hunt, Lynn. *Inventing Human Rights: A History.* New York: W.W. Norton, 2007.

Hunter, James Davison. *Before the Shooting Begins: Searching for Democracy in America's Culture Wars.* New York: Macmillan, 1994.

———. *Culture Wars: The Struggle to Define America.* New York: Basic Books, 1991.

Huntington, Samuel P. *The Clash of Civilizations and the Remaking of World Order.* New York: Simon & Schuster, 1996.

———. *Who Are We? The Challenges to America's National Identity.* New York: Simon & Schuster, 2004.

Hursley, Timothy. *Brothels of Nevada: Candid Views of America's Legal Sex Industry.* New York: Princeton Architectural Press, 2004.

Hutchins, Robert Maynard. *The Higher Learning in America.* New Haven, CT: Yale University Press, 1936.

Ifill, Gwen. *The Breakthrough: Politics and Race in the Age of Obama.* New York: Doubleday, 2009.

Iganski, Paul. *The Hate Debate: Should Hate Be Punished as a Crime?* London: Profile Books, 2002.

Illegal Incidents Report: A 25-Year History of Illegal Activities by Eco and Animal Extremists. Washington, DC: Foundation for Biomedical Research, February 2006.

Illousz, Eva. *Oprah Winfrey and the Glamour of Misery: An Essay on Popular Culture.* New York: Columbia University Press.

Inge, M. Thomas. *Comics as Culture.* Jackson: University Press of Mississippi, 1990.

Inglis, Fred. *The Cruel Peace: Everyday Life in the Cold War.* New York: Basic Books, 1991.

Ippolito, Dennis S. *Why Budgets Matter: Budget Policy and American Politics.* University Park: Pennsylvania State University Press, 2003.

Irvine, Janice. *Talk About Sex: The Battles over Sex Education in the United States.* Berkeley: University of California Press, 2003.

Irvine, Reed. *Media Mischief and Misdeeds.* Chicago: Regnery Gateway, 1984.

Irvine, Reed, and Cliff Kincaid. *How the News Media Are Deceiving the American People.* Smithtown, NY: Book Distributors, 1990.

Irwin, William, Mark T. Conrad, and Aeon J. Skoble, eds. *The Simpsons and Philosophy: The D'Oh of Homer.* Chicago: Open Court, 2001.

Isbister, John. *The Immigration Debate: Remaking America.* West Hartford, CT: Kumarian, 1996.

Isikoff, Michael. *Uncovering Clinton: A Reporter's Story.* New York: Random House Press, 1999.

Isserman, Maurice. *If I Had a Hammer: The Death of the Old Left and the Birth of the New Left.* New York: Basic Books, 1997.

———. *The Other American: The Life of Michael Harrington.* New York: Public Affairs, 2000.

Isserman, Maurice, and Michael Kazin. *America Divided: The Civil War of the 1960s.* New York: Oxford University Press, 2000.

Iverson, Peter. *Barry Goldwater: Native Arizonian.* Norman: University of Oklahoma Press, 1997.

Jackson, Jesse L., Jr., with Frank E. Watkins. *A More Perfect Union: Advancing New American Rights.* New York: Welcome Rain, 2001.

Jacobs, James B. *Drunk Driving: An American Dilemma.* Chicago: University of Chicago Press, 1989, 1992.

Jacobs, James B., and Kimberly Potter. *Hate Crimes: Criminal Law and Identity Politics.* New York: Cambridge University Press, 1998.

Jacoby, Russell, and Naomi Glauberman, eds. *The Bell Curve Debate.* New York: Three Rivers Press, 1995.

Jakes, Dale, Connie Jakes, and Clint Richmond. *False Prophets: The Firsthand Account of a Husband-Wife Team Working for the FBI and Living in Deepest Cover with the Montana Freemen.* Los Angeles: Dove Books, 1998.

James, Doug. *Cronkite: His Life and Times.* Brentwood, TN: J.N. Press, 1991.

Jameson, Fredric. *Postmodernism, or The Cultural Logic of Late Capitalism.* Durham, NC: Duke University Press, 1991.

Jamieson, Kathleen Hall. *Dirty Politics: Deception, Distraction, and Democracy.* New York: Oxford University Press, 1992.

Jaspersohn, William. *Senator: A Profile of Bill Bradley in the U.S. Senate.* San Diego, CA: Harcourt Brace Jovanovich, 1992.

Jay, Karla, and Allen Young, eds. *Out of the Closets: Voices of Gay Liberation.* New York: New York University Press, 1992.

Jeffers, Thomas L., ed. *The Norman Podhoretz Reader: A Selection of His Writings from the 1950s Through the 1990s.* New York: Free Press, 2004.

Jefferson, Margo. *On Michael Jackson.* New York: Pantheon, 2006.

Jeffrey, Douglas A. *Educating for Liberty: The Best of Imprimis, 1972–2002.* Hillsdale, MI: Hillsdale College Press, 2002.

Jeffreys, Sheila. *Anticlimax: A Feminist Perspective on the Sexual Revolution.* New York: New York University Press, 1990.

Jeffreys-Jones, Rhodri. *The CIA and American Democracy.* New Haven, CT: Yale University Press, 1989.

Jelen, Ted, ed. *Ross for Boss: The Perot Phenomenon and Beyond.* Albany: State University of New York Press, 2001.

Jenkins, Philip. *Moral Panic: Changing Concepts of the Child Molester in America.* New Haven, CT: Yale University Press, 1998.

Jenness, Valerie, and Ryken Grattet. *Making Hate a Crime: From Social Movement to Law Enforcement.* New York: Russell Sage Foundation, 2001.

Jensen, Carl. *Stories That Changed America: Muckrakers of the 20th Century.* New York: Seven Stories Press, 2000.

Johansson, Warren, and William A. Percy. *Outing: Shattering the Conspiracy of Silence.* New York: Haworth Press, 1994.

Johnson, Chalmers. *The Sorrows of Empire: Militarism, Secrecy, and the End of the Republic.* New York: Owl Books, 2004.

Johnson, Clarence Sholé. *Cornel West and Philosophy: The Quest for Social Justice.* New York: Routledge, 2003.

Johnson, John W. *Griswold v. Connecticut: Birth Control and the Constitutional Right of Privacy.* Lawrence: University Press of Kansas, 2005.

Johnson, Kaylene. *Sarah: How a Hockey Mom Turned the Political Establishment Upside Down.* Kenmore, WA: Epicenter Press, 2008.

Johnson, Kevin R., ed. *Mixed Race America and the Law: A Reader.* New York: New York University Press, 2003.

Johnson, Mary. *Make Them Go Away: Clint Eastwood, Christopher Reeve, and the Case Against Disability Rights.* Louisville, KY: Avocado, 2003.

Johnson, Robert Ann. *Whistleblowing: When It Works—and Why.* Boulder, CO: Lynne Rienner, 2003.

Johnson, Troy, Joane Nagel, and Duane Champagne, eds. *American Indian Activism: Alcatraz to the Long Walk.* Urbana: University of Illinois Press, 1997.

Johnston, Jill. *Lesbian Nation: The Feminist Solution.* New York: Simon & Schuster, 1973.

Jones, Charles E., ed. *The Black Panther Party Reconsidered.* Baltimore: Black Classic Press, 1998.

Jones, James H. *Kinsey: A Life.* New York: W.W. Norton, 2004.

Jonnes, Jill. *Hep-Cats, Narcs, and Pipe Dreams: A History of America's Romance with Illegal Drugs.* New York: Scribner, 1996.

Jordan, Hamilton. *Crisis: The Last Year of the Carter Presidency.* New York: G.P. Putnam's Sons, 1982.

Jorstad, Erling. *The Politics of Doomsday: Fundamentalists of the Far Right.* Nashville and New York: Abingdon Press, 1970.

Joseph, Jonathan. *Marxism and Social Theory.* New York: Palgrave Macmillan, 2006.

Josephy, Alvin M., Jr., ed. *Red Power: The American Indians' Fight for Freedom.* New York: McGraw-Hill, 1971.

Joyce, Davis. *Howard Zinn: A Radical American Vision.* Amherst, MA: Prometheus Books, 2003.

Judis, John B. *William F. Buckley Jr.: Patron Saint of the Conservatives.* New York: Simon & Schuster, 1988.

Jumonville, Neil. *Henry Steele Commager: Midcentury Liberalism and the History of the Present.* Chapel Hill: University of North Carolina Press, 1999.

Kaczynski, Theodore John. *The Unabomber Manifesto: Industrial Society and Its Future.* Berkeley, CA: Jolly Roger Press, 1996.

Kahn, Si. *Fox in the Henhouse: How Privatization Threatens Democracy.* San Francisco: Berrett-Koehler, 2005.

Kallen, Stuart A., ed. *Media Bias.* San Diego, CA: Greenhaven Press, 2004.

Kanellos, Nicolas. *Thirty Million Strong: Reclaiming the Hispanic Image in American Culture.* New York: Fulcrum, 1998.

Kaplan, Amy, and Donald E. Pease, eds. *Cultures of United States Imperialism.* Durham, NC: Duke University Press, 1993.

Kaplan, Fred. *Gore Vidal: A Biography.* New York: Doubleday, 1999.

Karolides, Nicholas J., Margaret Bald, and Dawn B. Sova. *100 Banned Books: Censorship History of World Literature.* New York: Checkmark Books, 1999.

Katz, Lee Michael. *My Name Is Geraldine Ferraro: An Unauthorized Biography.* New York: New American Library, 1984.

Katz, Milton S. *Ban the Bomb: A History of SANE, the Committee for a SANE Nuclear Policy.* New York: Praeger, 1987.

Katzmann, Robert A., ed. *Daniel Patrick Moynihan: The Intellectual in Public Life.* Baltimore: Johns Hopkins University Press, 2004.

Kauffman, Bill. *America First! Its History, Culture, and Politics.* Amherst, NY: Prometheus Books, 1995.

Kaufman, Burton I. *The Presidency of James Earl Carter, Jr.* Lawrence: University of Kansas Press, 1993.

Kaufman, Michael T. *Soros: The Life and Times of a Messianic Billionaire.* New York: Alfred A. Knopf, 2002.

Keck, Thomas M. *The Most Activist Supreme Court in History: The Road to Modern Judicial Conservatism.* Chicago: University of Chicago Press, 2004.

Kecskemeti, Paul, ed. *Essays on the Sociology of Knowledge.* London: Routledge and Kegan Paul, 1952.

Keillor, Garrison. *ME: By Jimmy (Big Boy) Valente.* New York: Viking, 1999.

Kelling, George L., and Catherine Coles. *Fixing Broken Windows.* New York: Free Press, 1996.

Kellogg, Charles F. *NAACP: A History of the National Association for the Advancement of Colored People.* Baltimore: Johns Hopkins University Press, 1967.

Kelly, Charles M. *The Great Limbaugh Con: And Other Right-Wing Assaults on Common Sense.* Santa Barbara, CA: Fithian Press, 1993.

Kelly, Richard T. *Sean Penn: His Life and Times.* New York: Canongate U.S., 2005.

Kelly, William W. *The Liberals and J. Edgar Hoover: Rise and Fall of a Domestic Intelligence State.* Princeton, NJ: Princeton University Press, 1989.

Kendrick, Alexander. *Prime Time: The Life of Edward R. Murrow.* Boston: Little, Brown, 1969.

Kengor, Paul. *The Crusader: Ronald Reagan and the Fall of Communism.* New York: Regan Books, 2006.

Kennedy, David. *Birth Control in America: The Career of Margaret Sanger.* New Haven, CT: Yale University Press, 1970.

Keown, John. *Euthanasia, Ethics, and Public Policy: An Argument Against Legalisation.* Cambridge, MA: Cambridge University Press, 2002.

Kerry, John, and Vietnam Veterans Against the War. *The New Soldier.* New York: Collier, 1971.

Kessler-Harris, Alice. *A Woman's Wage: Historical Meanings and Social Consequences.* Lexington: University of Kentucky Press, 1990.

Kettl, Donald F. *Deficit Politics.* New York: Longman, 2003.

Kevorkian, Jack. *Prescription-Medicide: The Goodness of a Planned Death.* Buffalo, NY: Prometheus Books, 1991.

Keyes, Alan L. *Masters of the Dream: The Strength and Betrayal of Black America.* New York: William Morrow, 1995.

———. *Our Character, Our Future: Reclaiming America's Moral Destiny.* Grand Rapids, MI: Zondervan, 1996.

Kilner, John F., Arlene B. Miller, and Edmund D. Pellegrino, eds. *Dignity and Dying: A Christian Appraisal.* Grand Rapids, MI: Eerdmans, 1996.

Kilty, Keith M., and Elizabeth A. Segal, eds. *The Promise of Welfare Reform: Political Rhetoric and Reality of Poverty in the Twenty-First Century.* New York: Haworth Press, 2006.

Kimball, Roger. *The Long March: How the Cultural Revolution of the 1960s Changed America.* San Francisco: Encounter, 2001.

———. *Tenured Radicals: How Politics Has Corrupted Our Higher Education.* Rev. ed. Chicago: Ivan R. Dee, 1998.

Kimmel, Michael. *Manhood in America: A Cultural History.* New York: Free Press, 1996.

Kindred, Dave. *Sound and Fury: Two Powerful Lives, One Fateful Friendship.* New York: Free Press, 2006.

King, Billie Jean, and Frank Deford. *Billie Jean.* New York: Viking, 1982.

King, C. Richard, and Charles Fruehling Springwood. *Beyond the Cheers: Race as Spectacle in College Sports.* Albany: State University of New York Press, 2001.

———, eds. *Team Spirits: The Native American Mascot Controversy.* Lincoln: University of Nebraska Press, 2001.

King, Dennis. *Lyndon LaRouche and the New American Fascism.* New York: Doubleday, 1989.

Kipnis, Laura. *Bound and Gagged: Pornography and the Politics of Fantasy in America.* New York: Grove Press, 1996.

Kirchmeir, Mark. *Packwood: The Public and Private Life from Acclaim to Outrage.* New York: HarperCollins, 1994.

Kirk, Russell, and James McClellan. *The Political Principles of Robert A. Taft.* New York: Fleet, 1967.

Kitman, Marvin. *The Man Who Would Not Shut Up: The Rise of Bill O'Reilly.* New York: St. Martin's Press, 2007.

Kitty, Alexandra. *Outfoxed: Rupert Murdoch's War on Journalism.* New York: Disinformation, 2005.

Klein, Joe. *The Natural: The Misunderstood Presidency of Bill Clinton.* New York: Doubleday, 2002.

———. *Woody Guthrie: A Life.* New York: Alfred A. Knopf, 1980.

Klein, Malcolm. *American Street Gangs.* Oxford, UK: Oxford University Press, 1997.

Klein, Malcolm, and Cheryl Maxson. *Street Gangs: Patterns and Processes.* Oxford, UK: Oxford University Press, 2006.

Klein, Michael. *Man Behind the Sound Bite: The Real Story of the Rev. Al Sharpton.* New York: Castillo International, 1991.

Klinger, David. *Into the Kill Zone: A Cop's Eye View of Deadly Force.* San Francisco: Jossey-Bass, 2004.

Klobuchar, Lisa. *Third Parties: Influential Political Alternatives.* Minneapolis, MN: Compass Point Books, 2008.

Kluger, Richard. *Simple Justice: The History of* Brown v. Board of Education *and Black America's Struggle for Equality.* New York: Vintage, 2004.

Knight, Peter, ed. *Conspiracy Nation: The Politics of Paranoia in Postwar America.* New York: New York University Press, 2002.

Knight, Richard L., and Suzanne Riedel, eds. *Aldo Leopold and the Ecological Conscience.* New York: Oxford University Press, 2002.

Kohl, Herbert R. *She Would Not Be Moved: How We Tell the Story of Rosa Parks and the Montgomery Bus Boycott.* New York: New Press/W.W. Norton, 2005.

Kolakowski, Leszek. *Main Currents of Marxism: The Founders, the Golden Age, the Breakdown.* New York: W.W. Norton, 2008.

Koon, Stacey C., with Robert Deitz. *Presumed Guilty: The Tragedy of the Rodney King Affair.* Washington, DC: Regnery Gateway, 1992.

Koop, C. Everett. *Koop: The Memoirs of America's Family Doctor.* New York: Random House, 1991.

———. *The Right to Live, the Right to Die.* Wheaton, IL: Tyndale House, 1976.

Kotz, Nick. *Judgment Days: Lyndon Baines Johnson, Martin Luther King, Jr., and the Laws That Changed America.* Boston: Houghton Mifflin, 2005.

Kovler, Peter B., ed. *Democrats and the American Idea: A Bicentennial Appraisal.* Washington, DC: Center for National Policy Press, 1992.

Kramer, Jane. *Allen Ginsberg in America.* New York: Random House, 1969.

Kramer, Rita. *Ed School Follies: The Miseducation of America's Teachers.* New York: Free Press, 1991.

Kramnick, Isaac, and R. Laurence Moore. *The Godless Constitution: The Case Against Religious Correctness.* New York: W.W. Norton, 1997.

Kranish, Michael, Brian C. Mooney, and Nina J. Easton. *John F. Kerry: The Complete Biography by the* Boston Globe *Reporters Who Know Him Best.* New York: Public Affairs, 2004.

Krannawitter, Thomas L., and Daniel C. Palm. *One Nation Under God? The ACLU and Religion in American Politics.* Lanham, MD: Rowman & Littlefield, 2005.

Krasner, David, ed. *A Companion to Twentieth-Century American Drama.* Malden, MA: Blackwell, 2005.

Krent, Harold J. *Presidential Powers.* New York: New York University Press, 2005.

Kriebel, David, ed. *Barry Commoner's Contribution to the Environmental Movement: Science and Social Action.* Amityville, NY: Baywood, 2002.

Krieger, Linda Hamilton. *Backlash Against the ADA: Reinterpreting Disability Rights.* Ann Arbor: University of Michigan Press, 2003.

Kristol, Irving. *Neoconservatism: The Autobiography of an Idea.* New York: Free Press, 1995.

Kristol, William, ed. The Weekly Standard: *A Reader, 1995–2005.* New York: HarperCollins, 2005.

Krugman, Paul. *The Conscience of a Liberal: Reclaiming the Compassionate Agenda.* New York: W.W. Norton, 2007.

———. *The Great Unraveling: Losing Our Way in the New Century.* New York: W.W. Norton, 2003.

———. *Peddling Prosperity: Economic Sense and Nonsense in the Age of Diminished Expectations.* New York: W.W. Norton, 1994.

Kubrick, Christine. *Stanley Kubrick: A Life in Pictures.* New York: Little, Brown, 2002.

Kuersteiner, Kurt. *The Unofficial Guide to the Art of Jack T. Chick: Chick Tracts, Crusader Comics, and Battle Cry Newspapers.* Atglen, PA: Schiffer, 2004.

Kukathas, Uma. *Death Penalty.* Detroit, MI: Greenhaven Press, 2008.

Kukis, Mark. *"My Heart Became Attached": The Strange Journey of John Walker Lindh.* Washington, DC: Brassey's, 2003.

Kurtz, Howard. *Hot Air: All Talk, All the Time.* New York: Times Books, 1996.

Kurtz, Paul. *In Defense of Secular Humanism.* Buffalo, NY: Prometheus Books, 1983.

Kurzweil, Ray. *The Singularity Is Near: When Human Beings Transcend Biology.* New York: Viking, 2005.

Kutler, Stanley. *Abuse of Power: The New Nixon Tapes.* New York: Touchstone, 1998.

Kutulas, Judy. *The American Civil Liberties Union and the Making of Modern Liberalism, 1930–1960.* Chapel Hill: University of North Carolina Press, 2006.

Kuypers, Jim A. *Press Bias and Politics: How the Media Frame Controversial Issues.* Westport, CT: Praeger, 2002.

Kuzenski, John C., Charles S. Bullock III, and Ronald Keith Gaddie, eds. *David Duke and the Politics of Race in the South.* Nashville, TN: Vanderbilt University Press, 1995.

Kwoka, John E., Jr., and Lawrence J. White, eds. *The Antitrust Revolution: Economics, Competition, and Policy.* 4th ed. New York: Oxford University Press, 2004.

Laarman, Peter, ed. *Getting on Message: Challenging the Christian Right from the Heart of the Gospel.* Boston: Beacon, 2005.

LaFeber, Walter. *America, Russia, and the Cold War, 1945–2006.* Boston: McGraw-Hill, 2008.

———. *The Deadly Bet: LBJ, Vietnam, and the 1968 Election.* Lanham, MD: Rowman and Littlefield, 2005.

Lakoff, George. *Moral Politics: How Liberals and Conservatives Think.* Chicago: University of Chicago Press, 2002.

Lakoff, Sanford, and Herbert F. York. *A Shield in Space? Technology, Politics, and the Strategic Defense Initiative.* Berkeley: University of California Press, 1989.

Lampton, David M. *Same Bed, Different Dreams: Managing U.S.-China Relations, 1989–2000.* Berkeley: University of California Press, 2001.

Landis, Dan, Janet M. Bennett, and Milton J. Bennett, eds. *Handbook of Intercultural Training.* Thousand Oaks, CA: Sage, 2004.

Langalan, Martha. *Back Off: How to Stop and Confront Sexual Harassers.* New York: Simon & Schuster/Fireside, 1993.

Langley, Winston E., and Vivian C. Fox, eds. *Women's Rights in the United States: A Documentary History.* Westport, CT: Greenwood Press, 1994.

LaPierre, Wayne. *The Global War on Your Guns: Inside the U.N. Plan to Destroy the Bill of Rights.* Nashville, TN: Thomas Nelson, 2006.

Lapin, Daniel. *America's Real War.* Sisters, OR: Multnomah, 2000.

———. *Thou Shall Prosper: Ten Commandments for Making Money.* Indianapolis: John Wiley & Sons, 2002.

Lardner, James, and David A. Smith, eds. *Inequality Matters: The Growing Economic Divide in America and Its Poisonous Consequences.* New York: Free Press, 2005.

Larner, Jeremy. *Nobody Knows: Reflections on the McCarthy Campaign of 1968.* New York: Macmillan, 1969.

Larner, Jesse. *Forgive Us Our Sins: Michael Moore and the Future of the Left.* Hoboken, NJ: John Wiley & Sons, 2006.

LaRouche, Lyndon H., Jr. *The Power of Reason: A Kind of an Autobiography.* New York: New Benjamin Franklin House, 1979.

Larson, Arthur. *Eisenhower: The President Nobody Knew.* New York: Charles Scribner's Sons, 1968.

Larson, Edward J. *Summer for the Gods: The Scopes Trial and America's Continuing Debate over Science and Religion.* New York: Basic Books, 1997.

———. *Trial and Error: The American Controversy over Creation and Evolution.* 3rd ed. New York: Oxford University Press, 2003.

Lasky, Victor. *It Didn't Start with Watergate.* New York: Dell, 1977.

Latell, Brian. *After Fidel: The Inside Story of Castro's Regime and Cuba's Next Leader.* New York: Palgrave Macmillan, 2005.

Lawrence, David G. *The Collapse of the Democratic Presidential Majority: Realignment, Disalignment, and Electoral Change from Franklin Roosevelt to Bill Clinton.* Boulder, CO: Westview, 1996.

Lawson, Steven F. *Civil Rights Crossroads: Nation, Community, and the Black Freedom Struggle.* Lexington: University Press of Kentucky, 2003.

Le Beau, Bryan. *The Atheist: Madalyn Murray O'Hair.* New York: New York University Press, 2003.

Leamer, Laurence. *Fantastic: The Life of Arnold Schwarzenegger.* New York: St. Martin's Press, 2005.

Leary, Timothy. *Flashbacks.* New York: Putnam, 1990.

Lebrun, Marcel. *Books, Blackboards, and Bullets: School Shootings and Violence in America.* Lanham, MD: Rowman & Littlefield Education, 2009.

Lee, Martin A., and Bruce Shalin. *Acid Dreams: The Complete Social History of LSD.* New York: Grove, 1985.

Lee, Spike, with Lisa Jones. *Do The Right Thing.* New York: Simon & Schuster, 1989.

Leebaert, Derek. *The Fifty-Year Wound: How America's Cold War Victory Shapes Our World.* Boston: Little, Brown, 2002.

Lefever, Ernest W. *Nairobi to Vancouver: The World Council of Churches and the World, 1975–1987.* Lanham, MD: University Press of America, 1987.

Lefkowitz, Mary. *Not Out of Africa: How Afrocentrism Became an Excuse to Teach Myths as History.* New York: Basic Books, 1996.

Lehne, Richard. *Government and Business.* Washington, DC: CQ Press, 2006.

Lehring, Gary L. *Officially Gay: The Political Construction of Sexuality by the U.S. Military.* Philadelphia: Temple University Press, 2003.

Lennon, J. Michael. *Conversations with Norman Mailer.* Oxford: University Press of Mississippi, 1988.

———. *Critical Essays on Norman Mailer.* Boston: G.K. Hall, 1986.

Lentz, Jacob. *Electing Jesse Ventura: A Third-Party Success Story.* Boulder, CO: Lynne Reinner, 2002.

Leopold, Aldo. *A Sand County Almanac, and Sketches Here and There.* New York: Oxford University Press, 1949.

Lesher, Stephen. *George Wallace: American Populist.* Reading, MA: Addison-Wesley, 1994.

Lesley, Mark, and Charles Shuttleworth. *Subway Gunman: A Juror's Account of the Bernhard Goetz Trial.* Latham, NY: British American, 1988.

Levenstein, Harvey. *We'll Always Have Paris: American Tourists in France Since 1930.* Chicago: University of Chicago Press, 2004.

Levering, Ralph B. *The Cold War: A Post–Cold War History.* 2nd ed. Wheeling, IL: Harlan Davidson, 2005.

Levine, Ellen. *Rachel Carson: A Twentieth-Century Life.* New York: Viking, 2007.

Levine, Judith. *Harmful to Minors: The Perils of Protecting Children from Sex.* Minneapolis: University of Minnesota Press, 2003.

Levine, Lawrence. *The Opening of the American Mind.* Boston: Beacon Press, 1996.

Lévi-Strauss, Claude. *The Elementary Structure of Kinship.* Boston: Beacon Press, 1971.

Levitas, Daniel. *The Terrorist Next Door: The Militia Movement and the Radical Right.* New York: St. Martin's Press, 2002.

Levy, Leonard. *The Establishment Clause: Religion and the First Amendment.* New York: Macmillan, 1986.

Levy, Robert. *Shakedown: How Corporations, Government, and Trial Lawyers Abuse the Judicial Process.* Washington, DC: Cato Institute, 2004.

Lewis, Bernard. *The Crisis of Islam: Holy War and Unholy Terror.* New York: Modern Library, 2003.

Lewis, David Levering. *W.E.B. Du Bois: The Fight for Equality and the American Century, 1919–1963.* New York: Henry Holt, 2000.

Lewis, Finlay. *Mondale: Portrait of an American Politician.* New York: Harper and Row, 1980.

Lewis, Frederick P. *The Context of Judicial Activism: The Endurance of the Warren Court Legacy in a Conservative Age.* Lanham, MD: Rowman & Littlefield, 1999.

Lewis, George. *The White South and the Red Menace: Segregationists, Anticommunism, and Massive Resistance, 1945–1965.* Gainesville: University Press of Florida, 2004.

Lewis, Harry. *Excellence Without a Soul: How a Great University Forgot Education.* New York: Public Affairs, 2006.

Lewis, James R., ed. *From the Ashes: Making Sense of Waco.* Lanham, MD: Rowman & Littlefield, 1994.

Lewis, Jon. *Hollywood v. Hard Core: How the Struggle over Censorship Saved the Modern Film Industry.* New York: New York University Press, 2000.

Lewis, Michael L., ed. *American Wilderness: A New History.* New York: Oxford University Press, 2007.

Lewis, Robert. *Real Family Values: Leading Your Family into the 21st Century with Clarity and Conviction.* Portland, OR: Multnomah, 2000.

Lhamon, W.T., Jr. *Raising Cain: Blackface Performance from Jim Crow to Hip Hop.* Cambridge, MA: Harvard University Press, 1998.

Lichtenstein, Nelson. *State of the Union: A Century of American Labor.* Princeton, NJ: Princeton University Press, 2002.

Liebowitz, Stan J., and Stephen E. Margolis. *Winners, Losers, and Microsoft: Competition and Antitrust in High Technology.* Oakland, CA: Independent Institute, 1999.

Lieven, Anatol. *America Right or Wrong: An Anatomy of American Nationalism.* New York: Oxford University Press, 2004.

Light, Alan, ed. *The Vibe History of Hip Hop.* New York: Random House, 1999.

Light, Steven Andrew, and Kathryn R.L. Rand. *Indian Gaming and Tribal Sovereignty: The Casino Compromise.* Lawrence: University Press of Kansas, 2005.

Lim, Elvin T. *The Anti-Intellectual Presidency: From George Washington to George W. Bush.* New York: Oxford University Press, 2008.

Limbaugh, Rush H., III. *See, I Told You So.* New York: Pocket Books, 1993.

———. *The Way Things Ought to Be.* New York: Pocket Books, 1992.

Lindemann, Barbara. *Age Discrimination in Employment Law.* Washington, DC: Bureau of National Affairs, 2003.

Linenthal, Edward T. *Symbolic Defense: The Cultural Significance of the Strategic Defense Initiative.* Urbana: University of Illinois Press, 1989.

Link, Michael. *The Social Philosophy of Reinhold Niebuhr.* Chicago: Adams Press, 1975.

Link, William A. *Righteous Warrior: Jesse Helms and the Rise of Modern Conservatism.* New York: St. Martin's Press, 2008.

Linn, Susan. *Consuming Kids: The Hostile Takeover of Childhood.* New York: The New Press, 2004.

Lippman, Theodore, Jr. *Spiro Agnew's America*. New York: W.W. Norton, 1972.

Lipset, Seymour Martin. *American Exceptionalism: A Double-Edged Sword*. New York: W.W. Norton, 1996.

———. *Continental Divide: The Values and Institutions of the United States and Canada*. New York: Routledge, 1990.

Lipset, Seymour Martin, and Gary Marks. *It Didn't Happen Here: Why Socialism Failed in the United States*. New York: W.W. Norton, 2000.

Lipstadt, Deborah E. *History on Trial: My Day in Court with a Holocaust Denier*. New York: Harper Perennial, 2005.

Loffreda, Beth. *Losing Matt Shepard: Life and Politics in the Aftermath of Anti-Gay Murder*. New York: Columbia University Press, 2000.

Lofy, Bill. *Paul Wellstone: The Life of a Passionate Progressive*. Ann Arbor: University of Michigan Press, 2005.

Lomborg, Bjørn. *The Skeptical Environmentalist: Measuring the Real State of the World*. New York: Cambridge University Press, 2001.

Long, Douglas. *Ecoterrorism*. New York: Facts On File, 2004.

Long, Kristi S., and Matthew Nadelhaft, eds. *America Under Construction: Boundaries and Identities in Popular Culture*. New York: Garland, 1997.

Lord, M.J. *Forever Barbie: The Unauthorized Biography of a Real Doll*. New York: William Morrow, 1994.

Lott, Trent. *Herding Cats: A Life in Politics*. New York: Regan-Books, 2005.

Lowry, Richard. *Legacy: Paying the Price for the Clinton Years*. Washington, DC: Regnery, 2003.

Lubin, Alex. *Romance and Rights: The Politics of Interracial Intimacy, 1945–1954*. Jackson: University of Mississippi Press, 2005.

Lucaire, Luigi. *Howard Stern, A to Z: The Stern Fanatic's Guide to the King of All Media*. New York: St. Martin's, 1997.

Lucas, Peter. *Luke on Duke: Snapshots in Time*. Boston: Quinlan, 1988.

Lukas, Anthony. *Common Ground: A Turbulent Decade in the Lives of Three American Families*. New York: Knopf, 1985.

Luker, Kristin. *Abortion and the Politics of Motherhood*. Berkeley: University of California Press, 1984.

———. *When Sex Goes to School: Warring Views on Sex—and Sex Education—Since the Sixties*. New York: W.W. Norton, 2006.

Lupton, Mary Jane. *Maya Angelou: A Critical Companion*. Westport, CT: Greenwood, 1998.

Lynch, Frederick R. *The Diversity Machine: The Drive to Change the "White Male Workplace."* New York: Free Press, 1997.

Lynn, Barry W. *Polluting the Censorship Debate: A Summary and Critique of the Final Report of the Attorney General's Commission on Pornography*. Washington, DC: American Civil Liberties Union, 1986.

Lyon, David. *Postmodernity*. 2nd ed. Minneapolis: University of Minnesota Press, 1999.

Lyotard, Jean-François. *The Postmodern Condition: A Report on Knowledge*. Trans. Geoff Bennington and Brian Massumi. Minneapolis: University of Minnesota Press, 1984.

Lytle, Mark H. *The Gentile Subversive: Rachel Carson, Silent Spring, and the Rise of the Environmental Movement*. New York: Oxford University Press, 2007.

MacDonald, Heather. *Are Cops Racist?* Chicago: Ivan R. Dee, 2003.

Macey, David. *The Lives of Michel Foucault*. New York: Pantheon Books, 1994.

MacKinnon, Catharine A., and Andrea Dworkin, eds. *In Harm's Way: The Pornography Civil Rights Hearings*. Cambridge, MA: Harvard University Press, 1998.

MacKinnon, Catharine A., and Reva B. Spiegel, eds. *Directions in Sexual Harassment Law*. New Haven, CT: Yale University Press, 2004.

MacMillan, Margaret. *The Week That Changed the World*. New York: Random House, 2007.

Madhubati, Haki R., and Maulana Karenga. *Million Man March/Day of Absence: A Commemorative Anthology*. Chicago: Third World Press, 1996.

Madsden, Deborah L. *American Exceptionalism*. Jackson: University Press of Mississippi, 1998.

Magida, Arthur J. *Prophet of Rage: A Life of Louis Farrakhan and His Nation*. New York: Basic Books, 1996.

Magnet, Myron. *The Dream and the Nightmare: The Sixties' Legacy of the Underclass*. San Francisco: Encounter, 2000.

Magnuson, Eric Paul. *Changing Men, Transforming Culture: Inside the Men's Movement*. Boulder, CO: Paradigm Publishers, 2007.

Maher, Paul, Jr. *Kerouac: The Definitive Biography*. Lanham, MD: Taylor Trade, 2004.

Maier, Thomas. *Dr. Spock: An American Life*. New York: Harcourt Brace, 1998.

Mailer, Norman. *The Executioner's Song*. Boston: Little, Brown, 1979.

Mair, George. *A Life with Purpose: Reverend Rick Warren, the Most Inspiring Pastor of Our Time*. New York: Berkeley Books, 2005.

Malcolm X, with Alex Haley. *The Autobiography of Malcolm X*. New York: Ballantine Books, 1965, 1992.

Malkin, Michelle. *In Defense of Internment: The Case for "Racial Profiling" in World War II and the War on Terror*. Washington, DC: Regnery, 2004.

Malone, Bill C. *Country Music, U.S.A*. 2nd rev. ed. Austin: University of Texas Press, 2002.

———. *Don't Get Above Your Raisin': Country Music and the Southern Working Class*. Urbana: University of Illinois Press, 2002.

Maney, Patrick J. *"Young Bob" La Follette: A Biography of Robert M. La Follette, Jr., 1895–1953*. 2nd ed. Madison: Wisconsin Historical Society Press, 2003.

Mann, James. *About Face: A History of America's Curious Relationship with China, from Nixon to Clinton*. New York: Vintage Books, 1998.

Manring, M.M. *Slave in a Box: The Strange Career of Aunt Jemima*. Charlottesville: University Press of Virginia, 1998.

Mansbridge, Jane J. *Why We Lost the ERA*. Chicago: University of Chicago Press, 1986.

Manson, Marilyn, and Neil Strauss. *The Long Hard Road Out of Hell*. New York: Regan Books, 1999.

Mapplethorpe, Robert. *Mapplethorpe*. New York: Random House, 1992.

Maraniss, David, and Ellen Nakashima. *The Prince of Tennessee: The Rise of Al Gore*. New York: Simon & Schuster, 2000.

Marc, David. *Comic Visions: Television Comedy and American Culture*. Boston: Unwin Hyman, 1989.

Marcello, Patricia Cronin. *Ralph Nader: A Biography*. Westport, CT: Greenwood Press, 2004.

Marcus, Eric. *Making History: The Struggle for Gay and Lesbian Equal Rights, 1945–1990*. New York: HarperCollins, 1992.

Marijuana Policy Project. *State-by-State Medical Marijuana Laws: How to Remove the Threat of Arrest.* Washington, DC: Marijuana Policy Project, 2007.

Mark, Joan T. *Margaret Mead, Anthropologist: Coming of Age in America.* New York: Oxford University Press, 1998.

Marker, Sheery. *Norman Rockwell: Unabridged.* New York: World, 2004.

Marks, Laura V. *Sexual Chemistry: A History of the Contraceptive Pill.* New Haven, CT: Yale University Press, 2001.

Marks, Robbin. *Cesspools of Shame: How Factory Farm Lagoons and Sprayfields Threaten Environmental and Public Health.* Washington, DC: Natural Resources Defense Council and the Clean Water Network, 2001.

Marotta, Toby. *The Politics of Homosexuality.* New York: Twayne, 1995.

Mars, Florence. *Witness in Philadelphia.* Baton Rouge: Louisiana State University Press, 1977.

Marsden, George M. *Fundamentalism and American Culture.* 2nd ed. New York: Oxford University Press, 2006.

————. *Understanding Fundamentalism and Evangelicalism.* Grand Rapids, MI: Eerdmans, 1991.

Marsh, Clifton E. *From Black Muslims to Muslims: The Resurrection, Transformation, and Change of the Lost-Found Nation of Islam in America, 1930–1995.* Lanham, MD: Scarecrow Press, 1996.

Marsh, Dave. *Bruce Springsteen: Two Hearts.* New York: Routledge, 2004.

Martin, Andrew. *Receptions of War: Vietnam in American Culture.* Norman: University of Oklahoma Press, 1993.

Martin, Justin. *Nader: Crusader, Spoiler, Icon.* Cambridge, MA: Perseus, 2002.

Martin, Linda, and Kerry Segrave. *Anti-Rock: The Opposition to Rock 'n' Roll.* New York: DaCapo Press, 1993.

Martin, William. *A Prophet with Honor: The Billy Graham Story.* New York: William Morrow, 1991.

————. *With God on Our Side: The Rise of the Religious Right in America.* New York: Broadway Books, 1996.

Mason, Todd. *Perot: An Unauthorized Biography.* Homewood, IL: Dow Jones–Irwin, 1990.

Mason, W. Dale. *Indian Gaming: Tribal Sovereignty and American Politics.* Norman: University of Oklahoma Press, 2000.

Mathy, Jean-Philippe. *French Resistance: The French-American Culture Wars.* Minneapolis: University of Minnesota Press, 2000.

Matthiessen, Peter. *Sal Si Puedes (Escape If You Can): César Chávez and the New American Revolution.* Berkeley: University of California Press, 2000.

Matthiessen, Peter, ed. *Courage for the Earth: Writers, Scientists, and Activists Celebrate the Life and Writing of Rachel Carson.* Boston: Houghton Mifflin, 2007.

Mauer, Marc. *Race to Incarcerate.* New York: New Press, 2006.

Maxwell, J.C. *Pro-Life Activists in America: Meaning, Motivation, and Direct Action.* Cambridge, MA: Cambridge University Press, 2002.

May, Ernest R. *The 9/11 Commission Report with Related Documents.* Boston: Bedford/St. Martin's, 2007.

————, ed. *American Cold War Strategy: Interpreting NSC 68.* Boston: Bedford/St. Martin's, 1993.

Mayer, George H. *The Republican Party, 1854–1966.* New York: Oxford University Press, 1967.

Mayer, Jane. *Dark Side: The Inside Story of How the War on Terror Turned into a War on American Ideals.* New York: Doubleday, 2008.

Mayer, Jane, and Jill Abrahamson. *Strange Justice: The Selling of Clarence Thomas.* Boston: Houghton Mifflin, 1994.

McAllister, Matthew P., Edward H. Sewell, Jr., and Ian Gordon, eds. *Comics and Ideology.* New York: Peter Lang, 2001.

McCain, John, with Mark Salter. *Faith of My Fathers: A Family Memoir.* New York: Random House, 2008.

————. *Worth the Fighting For: A Memoir.* New York: Random House, 2002.

McCarthy, Eugene J. *First Things First: New Priorities for America.* New York: New American Library, 1968.

McCarthy, Timothy Patrick, and John McMillan, eds. *The Radical Reader.* New York: The New Press, 2003.

McCauley, Michael. *NPR: The Trials and Triumphs of National Public Radio.* New York: Columbia University Press, 2005.

McClarnand, Elaine, and Steve Goodson, eds. *The Impact of the Cold War on American Popular Culture.* Carrollton: State University of West Georgia, 1999.

McCloskey, Deirdre. *Crossing: A Memoir.* Chicago: University of Chicago Press, 1999.

McCourt, Thomas. *Conflicting Communication Interests in America: The Case of National Public Radio.* Westport, CT: Praeger, 1999.

McCullough, David. *Truman.* New York: Simon & Schuster, 1992.

McDonough, Jimmy. *Shakey: Neil Young's Biography.* New York: Anchor Books, 2002.

McFarland, Andrew S. *Common Cause: Lobbying in the Public Interest.* Chatham, NJ: Chatham House, 1984.

McGann, James G., and R. Kent Weaver, eds. *Think Tanks and Civil Societies: Catalysts for Ideas and Action.* New Brunswick, NJ: Transaction, 2000.

McGilvray, James, ed. *The Cambridge Companion to Chomsky.* Cambridge, UK: Cambridge University Press, 2005.

McGovern, George S. *Grassroots: The Autobiography of George McGovern.* New York: Random House, 1977.

McGrath, Dennis J., and Dane Smith. *Professor Wellstone Goes to Washington: The Inside Story of a Grassroots U.S. Senate Campaign.* Minneapolis: University of Minnesota Press, 1995.

McGreevy, John T. *Catholicism and American Freedom.* New York: W.W. Norton, 2003.

McKeen, William. *Outlaw Journalist: The Life and Times of Hunter S. Thompson.* New York: W.W. Norton, 2008.

McKeever, James. *The AIDS Plague.* Medford, OR: Omega, 1986.

McKenna, Elizabeth Perle. *When Work Doesn't Work Anymore: Women, Work, and Identity.* New York: Dell, 1998.

McKinley, Andrew, Lee Dixon, and Amanda Devore. *State Management and Allocation of Tobacco Settlement Revenue, 2003.* Washington, DC: National Conference of State Legislatures, 2003.

McLoughlin, William G., and Robert N Bellah, eds. *Religion in America.* Boston: Houghton Mifflin, 1968.

McLuhan, Eric, and Frank Zingrone, eds. *Essential McLuhan.* New York: BasicBooks/HarperCollins, 1995.

McMillan, Patricia J. *The Ruin of J. Robert Oppenheimer and the Birth of the Modern Arms Race.* New York: Viking, 2005.

McNamara, Robert S. *In Retrospect: The Tragedy and Lessons of Vietnam.* New York: Times Books, 1995.

McNeil, William H. *Hutchins' University: A Memoir of the University of Chicago, 1929–1950.* Chicago: University of Chicago Press, 1991.

McShane, Larry. *Cops Under Fire: The Reign of Terror Against Hero Cops*. Washington, DC: Regnery, 1999.

McWilliams, Carey. *The Education of Carey McWilliams*. New York: Simon & Schuster, 1979.

Means, Russell. *Where White Men Fear to Tread: The Autobiography of Russell Means*. New York: St. Martin's Press, 1995.

Meara, Ellen, Meredith Rosenthal, and Anna Sinaiko. *Comparing the Effects of Health Insurance Proposals: Employer Mandates, Medicaid Expansions, and Tax Credits*. Washington, DC: Employment Policies Institute, February 2007.

Mearsheimer, John J., and Stephen M. Walt. *The Israel Lobby and U.S. Foreign Policy*. New York: Farrar, Straus and Giroux, 2007.

Mechanic, David. *Policy Challenges in Modern Health Care*. New Brunswick, NJ: Rutgers University Press, 2004.

Mechling, Jay. *On My Honor: Boy Scouts and the Making of American Youth*. Chicago: University of Chicago Press, 2001.

Medved, Michael. *Hollywood vs. America: Popular Culture and the War on Traditional Values*. New York: HarperCollins, 1992.

Meeks, Kenneth. *Driving While Black: Highways, Shopping Malls, Taxicabs, Sidewalks: How to Fight Back if You Are a Victim of Racial Profiling*. New York: Broadway Books, 2000.

Meeropol, Robert. *An Execution in the Family: One Son's Journey*. New York: St. Martin's Press, 2003.

Meine, Curt. *Aldo Leopold: His Life and Work*. Madison: University of Wisconsin Press, 1988.

Mello, Michael. *Legalizing Gay Marriage*. Philadelphia: Temple University Press, 2004.

Menell, Jeff. *Howard Stern: Big Mouth*. New York: Windsor, 1993.

Menendez, Albert J. *Three Voices of Extremism: Charles Colson, James Dobson, D. James Kennedy*. Silver Spring, MD: Americans for Religious Liberty, 1997.

Merida, Kevin, and Michael Fletcher. *Supreme Discomfort: The Divided Soul of Clarence Thomas*. New York: Doubleday, 2007.

Merrifield, John. *The School Choice Wars*. London: Scarecrow, 2001.

Messner, Michael A. *Politics of Masculinities: Men in Movements*. Thousand Oaks, CA: Sage, 1997.

Metcalf, Tom, and Gena Metcalf. *Obesity*. Detroit, MI: Thomson/Gale, 2008.

Metress, Christofer. *The Lynching of Emmett Till: A Documentary Narrative*. Charlottesville: University of Virginia Press, 2002.

Meyer, Peter. *Defiant Patriot: The Life and Exploits of Lt. Colonel Oliver L. North*. New York: St. Martin's Press, 1987.

Meyerowitz, Joanne. *How Sex Changed: A History of Transsexuality in the United States*. Cambridge, MA: Harvard University Press, 2002.

Meyers, Jeffrey. *Edmund Wilson: An Autobiography*. Boston: Houghton Mifflin, 1995.

Meyrowitz, Joshua. *No Sense of Place: The Impact of Electronic Media on Social Behavior*. New York: Oxford University Press, 1985.

Meyssan, Thierry. *9/11: The Big Lie*. London: Carnot USA Books, 2002.

Michael, George. *Confronting Right-Wing Extremism in the U.S.A.* New York: Routledge, 2003.

Michaels, Patrick J. *Meltdown: The Predictable Distortion of Global Warming by Scientists, Politicians, and the Media*. Washington, DC: CATO Institute, 2004.

Michel, Lou, and Dan Herbeck. *American Terrorist: Timothy McVeigh and the Oklahoma City Bombing*. New York: Regan Books, 2001.

Micklethwait, John, and Adrian Wooldridge. *The Right Nation: Conservative Power in America*. New York: Penguin Books, 2004.

Mieczkowski, Yanek. *Gerald Ford and the Challenges of the 1970s*. Lexington: University of Kentucky Press, 2005.

Milbank, Dana. *Smashmouth: Two Years in the Gutter with Al Gore and George W. Bush*. New York: Basic Books, 2001.

Miles, Barry. *Ginsberg: A Biography*. London: Virgin, 2000.

———. *Zappa: A Biography*. New York: Grove, 2004.

Mileur, Jerome M. *The Great Society and the High Tide of Liberalism*. Amherst: University of Massachusetts Press, 2005.

Milkis, Sidney M., and Jerome M. Mileur. *The New Deal and the Triumph of Liberalism*. Amherst: University of Massachusetts Press, 2002.

Miller, Donald L., ed. *The Lewis Mumford Reader*. Athens: University of Georgia Press, 1995.

Miller, Elliot. *A Crash Course on the New Age Movement*. Grand Rapids, MI: Baker Book House, 1989.

Miller, James. *Democracy in the Streets: From Port Huron to the Siege of Chicago*. Cambridge, MA: Harvard University Press, 1994.

———. *The Passion of Michel Foucault*. New York: Simon & Schuster, 1993.

Miller, Joel. *Bad Trip: How the War Against Drugs Is Destroying America*. Nashville, TN: WND Books, 2004.

Miller, Kenneth R. *Finding Darwin's God: A Scientist's Search for Common Ground Between God and Evolution*. New York: Harper, 1999.

Miller, Stephen. *Excellence and Equity: The National Endowment for the Humanities*. Lexington: University Press of Kentucky, 1984.

Miller, Timothy. *The 60s Communes: Hippies and Beyond*. Syracuse, NY: Syracuse University Press, 2000.

Millett, Kate. *Sexual Politics*. Urbana: University of Illinois Press, 2000.

Mills, Nicolaus. *Their Last Battle: The Fight for the National World War II Memorial*. New York: Basic Books, 2004.

Milton-Edwards, Beverley. *Islamic Fundamentalism Since 1945*. New York: Routledge, 2005.

Minamide, Elaine. *Medical Marijuana*. Detroit, MI: Greenhaven Press, 2007.

Mingst, Karen A., and Margaret P. Karns. *The United Nations and the Post–Cold War Era*. Boulder, CO: Westview Press, 2005.

Mink, Gwendolyn. *Hostile Environment: The Political Betrayal of Sexually Harassed Women*. Ithaca, NY: Cornell University Press, 2000.

Mintz, Benjamin W. *OSHA: History, Law, and Policy*. Washington, DC: Bureau of National Affairs, 1984.

Minutaglio, Bill. *First Son: George W. Bush and the Bush Family Dynasty*. New York: Times Books, 1999.

Mitchell, Brian. *Women in the Military: Flirting with Disaster*. Washington, DC: Regency, 1998.

Mitchell, Greg. *Tricky Dick and the Pink Lady: Richard Nixon vs. Helen Gahagan Douglas—Sexual Politics and the Red Scare, 1950*. New York: Random House, 1998.

Mitchell, Jack W. *Listener Supported: The Culture and History of Public Radio*. Westport, CT: Praeger, 2005.

Mittleman, Alan, and Robert Licht, eds. *Jews and the Public Square*. Lanham, MD: Rowman and Littlefield, 2002.

Mohr, Richard D. *Gay Ideas: Outing and Other Controversies.* Boston: Beacon Press, 1992.

Moi, Toril. *Sexual Textual Politics: Feminist Literary Theory.* New York: Routledge, 1985.

Montagu, Ashley, ed. *The Concept of Race.* Westport, CT: Greenwood Press, 1980.

Montgomery, David. *New World Government Exposed!* Sultan, WA: Montgomery, 2002.

Moody, Kim. *Labor in a Lean World: Unions in the International Economy.* New York: Verso, 1997.

Mooney, Chris. *The Republican War on Science.* New York: Basic Books, 2005.

Moore, James. *The Architect: Karl Rove and the Master Plan for Absolute Power.* New York: Crown, 2006.

Moore, Kathleen Dean. *Pardons: Justice, Mercy, and the Public Interest.* New York: Oxford University Press, 1989.

Moore, Mark Harrison. *Deadly Lessons: Understanding School Violence.* Washington, DC: National Academy Press, 2003.

Moore, Roy, with John Perry. *So Help Me God: The Ten Commandments, Judicial Tyranny, and the Battle for Religious Freedom.* Nashville, TN: Broadman and Holman, 2005.

Moran, Jeffery P. *Teaching Sex: The Shaping of Adolescence in the 20th Century.* Cambridge, MA: Harvard University Press, 2000.

Moran, Rachel F. *Interracial Intimacy: The Regulation of Race and Romance.* Chicago: University of Chicago Press, 2001.

Morgan Steiner, Leslie. *Mommy Wars: Stay-at-Home and Career-Moms Face Off on Their Choices, Their Lives, Their Families.* New York: Random House, 2006.

Morgan, Robin, ed. *Sisterhood Is Powerful: An Anthology of Writings from the Women's Liberation Movement.* New York: Random House, 1970.

Morris, Aldon D. *The Origins of the Civil Rights Movement.* New York: Free Press, 1984.

Morris, Dick. *Off with Their Heads: Traitors, Crooks & Obstructionists in American Politics, Media & Business.* New York: Regan Books, 2003.

Morris, Dick, and Eileen McGann. *Because He Could.* New York: Regan Books, 2004.

Morris, Henry M. *A History of Modern Creationism.* San Diego, CA: Master Books, 1984.

Morrison, Susan, ed. *Thirty Ways of Looking at Hillary: Reflections of Women Writers.* New York: Harper, 2008.

Morrisroe, Patricia. *Robert Mapplethorpe: A Biography.* New York: Papermac, 1995.

Moser, Paul K., and Thomas L. Carson. *Moral Relativism: A Reader.* New York: Oxford University Press, 2001.

Moskowitz, Eva S. *In Therapy We Trust: America's Obsession with Self-Fulfillment.* Baltimore: Johns Hopkins University Press, 2001.

Moss, George, and Linda M. Morra. *At the Speed of Light There Is Only Illumination: A Reappraisal of Marshall McLuhan.* Ottawa: University of Ottawa Press, 2004.

Mullis, Angela, and David Kamper. *Indian Gaming: Who Wins?* Los Angeles: UCLA American Indian Studies Center, 2000.

Mulloy, D.J. *American Extremism: History, Politics, and the Militia Movement.* New York: Routledge, 2004.

Mumford, Lewis. *Sketches from Life: The Autobiography of Lewis Mumford.* New York: Dial Press, 1982.

Munger, Frank. *Laboring Below the Line: The New Ethnography of Poverty, Low-Wage Work, and Survival in the Global Economy.* New York: Russell Sage Foundation, 2002.

Murphy, Bruce Allen. *Wild Bill: The Legend and Life of William O. Douglas.* New York: Random House, 2003.

Murphy, Priscilla Cort. *What a Book Can Do: The Public Reception of Silent Spring.* Amherst: University of Massachusetts Press, 2005.

Murray, Charles. *Losing Ground: American Social Policy 1950–1980.* New York: Basic Books, 1986.

Nader, Ralph. *Crashing the Party: Taking on the Corporate Government in an Age of Surrender.* New York: Thomas Dunne Books/St. Martin's Press, 2002.

———. *No Contest: Corporate Lawyers and the Perversion of Justice in America.* New York: Random House, 1996.

———. *The Ralph Nader Reader.* New York: Seven Stories Press, 2000.

Nadine, Corrine J., and Rose Blue. *Maya Angelou.* Chicago: Raintree, 2006.

Nash, Gary B. *History on Trial: Culture Wars and the Teaching of the Past.* New York: Vintage Books, 2000.

Nash, Gary B., Charlotte Crabtree, and Ross E. Dunn. *History on Trial: The Struggle for National Standards in American Classrooms.* New York: Alfred A. Knopf, 1997.

Nash, Roderick Frazier. *The Rights of Nature: A History of Environmental Ethics.* Madison: University of Wisconsin Press, 1989.

National Research Council. *Science and the Endangered Species Act.* Washington, DC: National Academies Press, 1995.

Navasky, Victor. *A Matter of Opinion.* New York: Farrar, Straus, and Giroux, 2005.

Navasky, Victor, and Katrina vanden Heuvel, eds. *The Best of the Nation: Selections From the Independent Magazine of Politics and Culture.* New York: Thunder's Mouth Press, 2000.

Neckerman, Kathryn M. *Social Inequality.* New York: Russell Sage Foundation, 2004.

Neely, William E., ed. *Public Lands: Use and Misuse.* New York: Nova Science Publishers, 2007.

Nelson, Daniel. *Shifting Fortunes: The Rise and Decline of American Labor, from the 1820s to the Present.* Chicago: Ivan R. Dee, 1997.

Nelson, Gaylord, with Susan Campbell and Paul Wozniak. *Beyond Earth Day: Fulfilling the Promise.* Madison: University of Wisconsin Press, 2002.

Nelson, T.S. *For Love of Country: Confronting Rape and Sexual Abuse in the U.S. Military.* New York: Hawthorn Maltreatment and Trauma Press, 2002.

Nelson, Todd D., ed. *Ageism: Stereotyping and Prejudice Against Older Persons.* Cambridge, MA: MIT Press, 2004.

Nelson, Willie, with Bud Shrake. *Willie: An Autobiography.* New York: Simon & Schuster, 1988.

Nelson-Pallmeyer, Jack. *School of Assassins: Guns, Greed, and Globalization.* Maryknoll, NY: Orbis Books, 2001.

Nestle, Marion. *Food Politics: How the Food Industry Influences Nutrition and Health.* Berkeley: University of California Press, 2002.

Neuhaus, Richard John. *The Naked Public Square: Religion and Democracy in America.* Grand Rapids, MI: W.B. Eerdmans, 1984.

Neuhaus, Richard John, and Michael Cromartie, eds. *Piety and Politics: Evangelicals and Fundamentalists Confront the World.* Washington, DC: Ethics and Public Policy Center/University Press of America, 1987.

Neve, Brian. *Film and Politics in America: A Social Tradition.* London: Routledge, 1992.

Newbeck, Phyl. *Virginia Hasn't Always Been for Lovers: Interracial Marriage Bans and the Case of Richard and Mildred Loving.* Carbondale: Southern Illinois University Press, 2004.

Newkirk, Ingrid. *Free the Animals: The Story of the Animal Liberation Front.* New York: Lantern Books, 2000.

Newman, Katharine S., Cybelle Fox, David Harding, Jal Mehta, and Wendy Roth. *Rampage: The Social Roots of School Shootings.* New York: Basic Books, 2004.

Newman, Mark. *The Civil Rights Movement.* Westport, CT: Praeger, 2004.

Newton, David E. *Nuclear Power.* New York: Facts On File, 2006.

Newton, Michael. *The Ku Klux Klan: History, Organization, Language, Influence and Activities of America's Most Notorious Secret Societies.* Jefferson, NC: McFarland, 2007.

Nicole, Neal, and Harry Wylie. *Between the Dying and the Dead: Dr. Jack Kevorkian's Life and the Battle to Legalize Euthanasia.* Madison: University of Wisconsin Press/Terrace Books, 2006.

Nicosia, Gerald. *Memory Babe: A Critical Biography of Jack Kerouac.* Berkeley: University of California Press, 1983.

Nissenbaum, Stephen. *The Battle for Christmas.* New York: Knopf, 1996.

Nixon, Richard. *RN: The Memoirs of Richard Nixon.* New York: Grosset & Dunlap, 1978.

Noll, Mark A. *American Evangelical Christianity: An Introduction.* Malden, MA: Blackwell, 2001.

———*The Scandal of the Evangelical Mind.* Grand Rapids, MI: Eerdmans, 1994.

Nomani, Asra Q. *Standing Alone in Mecca: An American Woman's Struggle for the Soul of Islam.* New York: HarperSanFrancisco, 2005.

Noonan, Peggy. *The Case Against Hillary Clinton.* New York: ReganBooks, 2000.

Norquist, Grover. *Leave Us Alone: Getting the Government's Hands Off of Our Money, Our Guns, Our Lives.* New York: W. Morrow, 2008.

Norris, Christopher. *Deconstruction: Theory and Practice.* 3rd ed. New York: Routledge, 2002.

North, Oliver. *Under Fire: An American Story.* New York: HarperCollins, 1991.

Norton, Anne. *Leo Strauss and the Politics of American Empire.* New Haven, CT: Yale University Press, 2004.

Novick, Peter. *The Holocaust in American Life.* New York: Houghton Mifflin, 1999.

Numbers, Ronald. *The Creationists: From Scientific Creationism to Intelligent Design.* Expanded ed. Cambridge, MA: Harvard University Press, 2006.

Nuzum, Eric. *Parental Advisory: Music Censorship in America.* New York: HarperCollins, 2001.

Nyberg, Amy Kiste. *Seal of Approval: The History of the Comics Code.* Jackson: University Press of Mississippi, 1998.

Oates, Stephen B. *Let the Trumpet Sound: The Life of Martin Luther King, Jr.* New York: Harper and Row, 1982.

Obama, Barack. *The Audacity of Hope: Thoughts on Reclaiming the American Dream.* New York: Crown Publishers, 2006.

———. *Dreams from My Father: A Story of Race and Inheritance.* New York: Three Rivers Press, 1995.

Oboler, Suzanne. *Ethnic Labels, Latino Lives: Identity and the Politics of (Re)Presentation in the U.S.* Minneapolis: University of Minnesota Press, 1995.

O'Brien, David M. *Privacy, Law and Public Policy.* New York: Praeger, 1979.

O'Connor, Roy. *Shock Jocks: Hate Speech and Talk Radio.* San Francisco: AlterNet Books, 2008.

O'Connor, Sandra Day. *The Majesty of the Law: Reflections of a Supreme Court Justice.* New York: Random House, 2003.

Ogbar, Jeffrey O.G. *Black Power: Radical Politics and African American Identity.* Baltimore: Johns Hopkins University Press, 2004.

Ogletree, Charles J., and Austin Sarat. *From Lynch Mobs to the Killing State: Race and the Death Penalty in America.* New York: New York University Press, 2006.

Olasky, Marvin. *Compassionate Conservatism: What It Is, What It Does, and How It Can Transform America.* New York: Free Press, 2000.

———. *Telling the Truth: How to Revitalize Christian Journalism.* Wheaton, IL: Crossway Books, 1996.

Oliver, Susan. *Betty Freidan: The Personal Is Political.* New York: Pearson Longman, 2008.

Olson, James S., and Randy Roberts. *My Lai: A Brief History with Documents.* Boston and New York: Bedford/St. Martin's, 1998.

Olson, Keith W. *Watergate: The Presidential Scandal That Shook America.* Lawrence: University Press of Kansas, 2003.

Olson, Walter. *The Litigation Explosion: What Happened When America Unleashed the Lawsuit.* New York: Truman Talley Books, 1992.

O'Neal, Floyd A., June K. Lyman, and Susan McKay, eds. *Wounded Knee 1973: A Personal Account by Stanley David Lyman.* Lincoln: University of Nebraska Press, 1991.

O'Neill, John E., and Jerome L. Corsi. *Unfit for Command: Swift Boat Veterans Speak Out Against John Kerry.* Washington, DC: Regnery, 2004.

Oram, James. *Reluctant Star: The Mel Gibson Story.* London: Fontana, 1991.

O'Reilly, Bill. *Culture Warrior.* New York: Broadway Books, 2006.

O'Reilly, Charles T., and William A. Rooney. *The Enola Gay and the Smithsonian Institution.* Jefferson, NC: McFarland, 2005.

O'Reilly, James T. *Federal Information Disclosure.* St. Paul, MN: West Group, 2000.

———. *Police Traffic Stops and Racial Profiling: Resolving Management, Labor and Civil Rights Conflicts.* Springfield, IL: Charles C. Thomas, 2002.

O'Reilly, Kenneth. *Hoover and the Un-Americans: The FBI, HUAC, and the Red Menace.* Philadelphia: Temple University Press, 1983.

Oshinsky, David M. *A Conspiracy So Immense: The World of Joe McCarthy.* New York: Oxford University Press, 2005.

O'Sullivan, Christopher. *The United Nations: A Concise History.* Malabar, FL: Krieger, 2005.

Packer, Herbert L. *Ex-Communist Witnesses: Four Studies in Fact Finding.* Palo Alto, CA: Stanford University Press, 1962.

Page, Bruce. *The Murdoch Archipelago.* New York: Simon & Schuster, 2003.

Paglia, Camille. *Sexual Personae: Art and Decadence from Nefertiti to Emily Dickinson.* New Haven, CT: Yale University Press, 1990.

———. *Vamps and Tramps: New Essays.* New York: Vintage, 1994.

Paige-Carlsson, Nancy, and Diane E. Levin. *Who's Calling the Shots? How to Respond Effectively to Children's Fascination with War Play and War Toys*. Philadelphia: New Society, 1990.

Palash, Dave, and Christopher Hitchens. *The Real Michael Moore: A Critical Biography*. New York: Touchstone Books, 2008.

Palermo, Joseph A. *Robert F. Kennedy and the Death of American Idealism*. New York: Pearson Longman, 2008.

Pampel, Fred C. *Threats to Food Safety*. New York: Facts On File, 2006.

Parker, Richard. *John Kenneth Galbraith: His Life, His Politics, His Economics*. New York: Farrar, Straus and Giroux, 2005.

Parker, Tony. *Studs Terkel: A Life in Words*. New York: Henry Holt, 1996.

Parks, Rosa, with Jim Haskins. *Rosa Parks: My Story*. New York: Puffin Books, 1999.

Parmet, Herbert. *George Bush: The Life of a Lone Star Yankee*. New York: Scribner, 1997.

Parson, Ann B. *The Proteus Effect: Stem Cells and Their Promise for Medicine*. Washington, DC: Joseph Henry Press, 2004.

Patterson, James T. *Mr. Republican: A Biography of Robert A. Taft*. Boston: Houghton Mifflin, 1972.

Patterson, Robert "Buzz." *Dereliction of Duty: The Eyewitness Account of How Bill Clinton Compromised America's National Security*. Washington, DC: Regnery, 2003.

Patterson, Romaine, and Patrick Hinds. *The Whole World Was Watching: Living in the Light of Matthew Shepard*. New York: Advocate Books, 2005.

Pauley, Garth E. *The Modern Presidency and Civil Rights: Rhetoric on Race from Roosevelt to Nixon*. College Station: Texas A&M University Press, 2001.

Pavlik, Steve, and Daniel R. Wildcat, eds. *Destroying Dogma: Vine Deloria, Jr. and His Influence on American Society*. Golden, CO: Fulcrum, 2006.

Peach, Linden. *Toni Morrison*. New York: St. Martin's Press, 2000.

Pearsall, Robert Brainard, ed. *The Symbionese Liberation Army: Documents and Communications*. Amsterdam: Rodopi N.V., 1974.

Pease, Edward C., and Everette E. Dennis, eds. *Radio: The Forgotten Medium*. New Brunswick, NJ: Transaction, 1995.

Penenberg, Adam. *Tragic Indifference: One Man's Battle with the Auto Industry over the Dangers of SUVs*. New York: HarperCollins, 2003.

Pennell, Susan, Christine Curtis, and Joel Henderson. *Guardian Angels: An Assessment of Citizen Response to Crime*. Vols. 1 and 2. San Diego, CA: San Diego Association of Government, 1985.

Penner, Lucille. *Celebration: The Story of American Holidays*. New York: Macmillan, 1993.

Pennock, Roger T., ed. *Philosophical, Theological, and Scientific Perspectives*. Cambridge, MA: MIT Press, 2001.

Penton, M. James. *Apocalypse Delayed: The Story of Jehovah's Witnesses*. 2nd ed. Toronto: University of Toronto Press, 1997.

Perez, Louis A., Jr. *Cuba: Between Reform and Revolution*. New York: Oxford University Press, 1995.

Perlstein, Rick. *Before the Storm: Barry Goldwater and the Unmaking of the American Consensus*. New York: Hill and Wang, 2002.

Perot, H. Ross. *My Life & the Principles of Success*. Fort Worth, TX: Summit Group, 1996.

Perry, Michael J. *Toward a Theory of Human Rights: Religion, Law, Courts*. New York: Cambridge University Press, 2007.

Perry, Paul. *Fear and Loathing: The Strange and Terrible Saga of Hunter S. Thompson*. New York: Thunder's Mouth Press, 2004.

Personal Justice Denied: Report of the Commission on Wartime Relocation and Internment of Civilians. Seattle: University of Washington Press, 1997.

Peskowitz, Miriam. *The Truth Behind the Mommy Wars: Who Decides What Makes a Good Mother?* Emeryville, CA: Seal, 2005.

Petchesky, Rosalind. *Abortion and Women's Choice: The State, Sexuality, and Reproductive Freedom*. Boston: Northeastern University Press, 1990.

Peters, B. Guy. *The Politics of Taxation*. Cambridge, MA: Blackwell, 1991.

Peterson, Peter G. *Running on Empty*. New York: Farrar, Straus and Giroux, 2004.

Petridis, Alexis. *Neil Young*. New York: Thunder's Mouth Press, 2000.

Phillips, Gene D., ed. *Stanley Kubrick: Interviews*. Jackson: University of Mississippi Press, 1999.

Phillips, Kevin. *American Dynasty: Aristocracy, Fortune, and the Politics of Deceit in the House of Bush*. New York: Viking Penguin, 2004.

———. *American Theocracy*. New York: Viking, 2006.

Phillips-Fein, Kim. *Invisible Hands: The Making of the Conservative Movement from the New Deal to Reagan*. New York: W.W. Norton, 2009.

Pieterse, Jan Nederveen. *Ethnicities and Global Multiculture: Pants for an Octopus*. Lanham, MD: Rowman and Littlefield, 2007.

Pike, Sarah M. *New Age and Neopagan Religions in America*. New York: Columbia University Press, 2004.

Pines, Wayne L., ed. *FDA: A Century of Consumer Protection*. Washington, DC: Food and Drug Law Institute, 2006.

Pinsky, Mark, and Tony Campolo. *The Gospel According to the Simpsons: The Spiritual Life of the World's Most Animated Family*. Louisville, KY: Westminster John Knox Press, 2001.

Pipes, Daniel. *Militant Islam Reaches America*. New York: W.W. Norton, 2002.

Pipes, Richard. *Vixi: Memoirs of a Non-Belonger*. New Haven, CT: Yale University Press, 2003.

Podhoretz, Norman. *Ex-Friends: Falling Out with Allen Ginsberg, Lionel and Diana Trilling, Lillian Hellman, Hannah Arendt, and Norman Mailer*. New York: Free Press, 1999.

Pollack, Jack Harrison. *Earl Warren: The Judge Who Changed America*. Englewood Cliffs, NJ: Prentice-Hall, 1979.

Posner, Gerald. *Citizen Perot: His Life and Times*. New York: Random House, 1996.

———. *Secrets of the Kingdom: The Inside Story of the Saudi-U.S. Connection*. New York: Random House, 2005.

Posner, Richard. *Breaking the Deadlock: The 2000 Election, the Constitution, and the Courts*. Princeton, NJ: Princeton University Press, 2001.

———. *Overcoming Law*. Cambridge, MA: Harvard University Press, 1995.

Postman, Neil. *Amusing Ourselves to Death: Public Discourse in the Age of Show Business*. New York: Penguin, 1985.

Potts, Stephen W. *From Here to Absurdity: The Moral Battlefields of Joseph Heller*. San Bernardino, CA: Borgo Press, 1995.

Powe, Lucas A., Jr. *The Warren Court and American Politics*. Cambridge, MA: Belknap Press of Harvard University Press, 2000.

Powell, Jim. *Deconstruction for Beginners*. New York: Readers and Writers, 2005.

———. *Postmodernism for Beginners.* New York: Writers and Readers Publishing, 1998.

Powers, Richard Gid. *Secrecy and Power: The Life of J. Edgar Hoover.* New York: Free Press, 1987.

Prager, Jeffrey. *Presenting the Past: Psychoanalysis and the Sociology of Misremembering.* Cambridge, MA: Harvard University Press, 1998.

Prasad, Pushkala, et al., eds. *Managing the Organizational Melting Pot: Dilemmas of Workplace Diversity.* Thousand Oaks, CA: Sage, 1997.

Pratt, Alan R., ed. *The Critical Response to Andy Warhol.* Westport, CT: Greenwood, 1997.

Preston, Julia, and Samuel Dillon. *Opening Mexico: The Making of a Democracy.* New York: Farrar, Straus, and Giroux, 2004.

Provine, Doris Marie. *Unequal Under Law: Race in the War on Drugs.* Chicago: University of Chicago Press, 2007.

Purcell, Natalie J. *Death Metal Music: The Passion and Politics of a Subculture.* Jefferson, NC: McFarland, 2003.

Pycior, Julie Leininger. *LBJ and Mexican Americans: The Paradox of Power.* Austin: University of Texas Press, 1997.

Quadagno, Jill S. *One Nation Uninsured: Why the U.S. Has No National Health Insurance.* New York: Oxford University Press, 2005.

Quaratiello, Arlene R. *Rachel Carson: A Biography.* Westport, CT: Greenwood Press, 2004.

Quayle, Dan. *Standing Firm: A Vice Presidential Memoir.* New York: HarperCollins, 1994.

Quayle, Dan, and Diane Medved. *The American Family: Discovering the Values That Make Us Strong.* New York: HarperCollins, 1996.

Queenan, Joe. *Imperial Caddy: The Rise of Dan Quayle and the Decline and Fall of Practically Everything Else.* New York: Hyperion Books, 1992.

Quirk, Lawrence J., and William Schoell. *The Sundance Kid: An Unauthorized Biography of Robert Redford.* Lanham, MD: Taylor Trade, 2006.

Radosh, Ronald, and Joyce Milton. *The Rosenberg File: A Search for the Truth.* 2nd ed. New Haven, CT: Yale University Press, 1997.

Ragen, Brian Abel. *Tom Wolfe: A Critical Companion.* Westport, CT: Greenwood, 2002.

Rainwater, Lee, and William L. Yancey. *The Moynihan Report and the Politics of Controversy.* Cambridge, MA: MIT Press, 1967.

Ranville, Michael. *To Strike a King: The Turning Point in the McCarthy Witch-Hunts.* Troy, MI: Momentum Books, 1997.

Rapley, John. *Globalization and Inequality: Neoliberalism's Downward Spiral.* Boulder, CO: Lynne Rienner, 2004.

Rapoport, Roger. *Citizen Moore: The Life and Times of an American Iconoclast.* Muskegon, MI: RDR Books, 2007.

Raskin, Jonah. *American Scream: Allen Ginsberg's "Howl" and the Making of the Beat Generation.* Berkeley: University of California Press, 2004.

———. *For the Hell of It: The Life and Times of Abbie Hoffman.* Berkeley: University of California Press, 1996.

Rasor, Dina. *Betraying Our Troops: The Destructive Results of Privatizing War.* New York: Palgrave Macmillan, 2007.

Rather, Dan. *The Camera Never Blinks: Adventures of a TV Journalist.* New York: William Morrow, 1977.

———. *The Camera Never Blinks Twice: The Further Adventures of a Television Journalist.* New York: William Morrow, 1994.

———. *Deadlines and Datelines: Essays at the Turn of the Century.* New York: William Morrow, 1999.

Ravitch, Diane. *The Language Police: How Pressure Groups Restrict What Students Learn.* New York: Alfred A. Knopf, 2003.

———. *Left Back: A Century of Failed School Reforms.* New York: Simon & Schuster, 2000.

Ravitch, Diane, and Maris A. Vinovskis, eds. *Learning from the Past: What History Teaches Us About School Reform.* Baltimore: Johns Hopkins University Press, 1995.

Reagan, Ronald, et al. *Restoring the Presidency: Reconsidering the Twenty-Second Amendment.* Washington, DC: National Legal Center for the Public Interest, 1990.

Redekop, John Harold. *The American Far Right: A Case Study of Billy James Hargis and Christian Crusade.* Grand Rapids, MI: Erdmans, 1968.

Rediscovering America: Thirty-Five Years of the National Endowment for the Humanities. Washington, DC: National Endowment for the Humanities, 2000.

Reed, Ralph. *Active Faith: How Christians Are Changing the Soul of American Politics.* New York: Free Press, 1996.

———. *Politically Incorrect: The Emerging Faith Factor in American Politics.* Dallas, TX: World, 1994.

Reeves, Thomas C. *America's Bishop: The Life and Times of Fulton J. Sheen.* San Francisco: Encounter Books, 2001.

Regan, Tom. *The Case for Animal Rights.* Berkeley: University of California Press, 2004.

Reid, Jan. *The Improbable Rise of Redneck Rock.* Austin: University of Texas Press, 2004.

Reid, Mark A. *Redefining Black Film.* Berkeley: University of California Press, 1993.

Remnick, David. *The Devil Problem and Other True Stores.* New York: Random House, 1996.

———. *King of the World: Muhammad Ali and the Rise of an American Hero.* New York: Random House, 1998.

Renshon, Stanley A. *America's Second Civil War: Dispatches from the Political Center.* New Brunswick, NJ: Transaction, 2002.

Reston, James, Jr. *The Conviction of Richard Nixon: The Untold Story of the Frost/Nixon Interviews.* New York: Harmony Books, 2007.

Reumann, Miriam G. *American Sexual Character: Sex, Gender, and National Identity in the Kinsey Reports.* Berkeley: University of California Press, 2005.

Reynolds, David. *Democracy Unbound: Progressive Challenges to the Two Party System.* Boston: South End Press, 1997.

Rhoads, Steven E. *Incomparable Worth: Pay Equity Meets the Market.* Cambridge, MA: Cambridge University Press, 1993.

Ricci, David M. *The Transformation of American Politics: The New Washington and the Rise of Think Tanks.* New Haven, CT: Yale University Press, 1993.

Riccio, Thomas J. *Busted! The Inside Story of the World of Sports Memorabilia, O.J. Simpson, and the Vegas Arrests.* Beverly Hills, CA: Phoenix Books, 2008.

Richburg, Keith B. *Out of America: A Black Man Confronts Africa.* New York: Basic Books, 1997.

Ricketts, Cliff, and Omri Rawlins. *Introduction to Agribusiness.* Albany, NY: Delmar Thompson Learning, 2001.

Ridgeway, James. *Blood in the Face: The Ku Klux Klan, Aryan Nations, Nazi Skinheads, and the Rise of a New White Culture.* New York: Thunder's Mouth, 1995.

Riley, Dorothy Winbush. *The Complete Kwanzaa: Celebrating Our Cultural Harvest.* New York: HarperCollins, 1995.

Riley, Kathleen L. *Fulton J. Sheen: An American Catholic Response to the Twentieth Century*. Staten Island, NY: St. Paul's/Alba House, 2004.

Rimmerman, Craig. *From Identity to Politics: The Lesbian and Gay Movements in the United States*. Philadelphia: Temple University Press, 2002.

Rimmerman, Craig A., Kenneth D. Wald, and Clyde Wilcox, eds. *The Politics of Gay Rights*. Chicago: University of Chicago Press, 2000.

Riordan, James. *Stone: The Controversies, Excesses, and Exploits of a Radical Filmmaker*. New York: Hyperion, 1995.

Risen, James, and Judy L. Thomas. *Wrath of Angels: The American Abortion War*. New York: Basic Books, 1998.

Rising, George. *Clean for Gene: Eugene McCarthy's 1968 Presidential Campaign*. Westport, CT: Greenwood, 1997.

Ritzer, George. *The McDonaldization of Society*. Thousand Oaks, CA: Pine Forge Press, 1993.

Riverol, Armando. *Live from Atlantic City: The History of the Miss America Pageant Before, After and in Spite of Television*. Bowling Green, OH: Bowling Green State University Popular Press, 1992.

Roberts, Kelly, and Michael Reid. *White Supremacy: Behind the Eyes of Hate*. Victoria, BC: Trafford, 2004.

Roberts, Randy, and James Olson. *John Wayne: American*. New York: Free Press, 1995.

Roberts, Sam. *The Brother: The Untold Story of Atomic Spy David Greenglass and How He Sent His Sister, Ethel Rosenberg, to the Electric Chair*. New York: Random House, 2001.

Roberts, Selena. *A Necessary Spectacle: Billie Jean King, Bobby Riggs, and the Tennis Match That Leveled the Game*. New York: Crown, 2005.

Robinson, Phyllis. *Robert A. Taft: Boy and Man*. Cambridge, MA: Dresser, Chapman and Grimes, 1963.

Rockwell, Norman, as told to Tom Rockwell. *Norman Rockwell: My Adventures as an Illustrator*. New York: Harry M. Abrams, 1994.

Rodriguez, Joseph A. *City Against Suburb: The Culture Wars in an American Metropolis*. Westport, CT: Praeger, 1999.

Rogan, Johnny. *Neil Young: The Complete Guide to His Music*. London: Omnibus, 2006.

Rogers, Kalen. *Marilyn Manson: The Unauthorized Biography*. New York: Omnibus, 1997.

Rohler, Lloyd. *George Wallace: Conservative Populist*. Westport, CT: Praeger, 2004.

Roland, Gérard. *Privatization: Successes and Failures*. New York: Columbia University Press, 2008.

Roosevelt, Kermit, III. *The Myth of Judicial Activism: Making Sense of Supreme Court Decisions*. New Haven, CT: Yale University Press, 2006.

Root, Maria P.P., ed. *Racially Mixed People in America*. Newbury Park, CA: Sage, 1992.

Rose, David. *Guantánamo: The War on Human Rights*. New York: New Press, 2004.

Rose, Douglas D., ed. *The Emergence of David Duke and the Politics of Race*. Chapel Hill: University of North Carolina Press, 1992.

Rose, Melody. *Safe, Legal, and Unavailable? Abortion Politics in the United States*. Washington, DC: CQ Press, 2007.

Rose, Tricia. *Black Noise: Rap Music and Black Culture in Contemporary America*. Hanover, NH: Wesleyan University Press/University Press of New England, 1994.

Rosen, Ruth. *The World Split Open: How the Modern Women's Movement Changed America*. New York: Viking, 2000.

Rosenberg, Jerry Martin. *Inside the* Wall Street Journal: *The History and the Power of Dow Jones & Company and America's Most Influential Newspaper*. New York: Macmillan, 1982.

Rosenfeld, Steven. *Making History in Vermont: The Election of a Socialist to Congress*. Wakefield, NH: Hollowbrook, 1992.

Rosenthal, Beth, ed. *Gun Control*. Farmington Hills, MI: Greenhaven Press, 2007.

Rosin, Hanna. *God's Harvard: A Christian College on a Mission to Save America*. New York: Harcourt, 2007.

Ross, Kirsten. *Fast Cars, Clean Bodies: Decolonization and the Reordering of French Culture*. Cambridge, MA: MIT Press, 2005.

Rossell, Christine. *The Carrot or the Stick for School Desegregation Policy: Magnet Schools or Forced Busing*. Philadelphia: Temple University Press, 1992.

Rosteck, Thomas. *See It Now Confronts McCarthyism: Television Documentary and the Politics of Representation*. Tuscaloosa: University of Alabama Press, 1994.

Roszak, Theodore. *The Making of a Counter Culture: Reflections on the Technocratic Society and Its Youthful Opposition*. Garden City, NY: Anchor Books, 1968.

Rothenberg, Lawrence S. *Linking Citizens to Government: Interest Group Politics at Common Cause*. New York: Cambridge University Press, 1992.

Rothman, Hal. *The Greening of a Nation? Environmentalism in the United States Since 1945*. Fort Worth: Harcourt Brace, 1998.

Rouche, George C., III *The Fall of the Ivory Tower*. Washington, DC: Regnery, 1994.

Rouverol, Jean. *Refugees from Hollywood: A Journal of the Blacklist Years*. Albuquerque: University of New Mexico Press, 2000.

Rozell, Mark J., and James F. Pontuso, eds. *American Conservative Opinion Leaders*. Boulder, CO: Westside, 1990.

Rubin, Eva R. *The Abortion Controversy: A Documentary History*. Westport, CT: Greenwood Press, 1994.

Ruddiman, William. *Plows, Plagues, and Petroleum: How Humans Took Control of Climate*. Princeton, NJ: Princeton University Press, 2005.

Ruddy, T. Michael. *The Alger Hiss Espionage Case*. Belmont, CA: Wadsworth, 2005.

Ruderman, Judith. *Joseph Heller*. New York: Continuum, 1991.

Ruegsegger, Ronald W., ed. *Reflections on Francis Schaeffer*. Grand Rapids, MI: Academie Books, 1986.

Ruland, Richard. *From Puritanism to Postmodernism: A History of American Literature*. New York: Viking, 1991.

Runte, Alfred. *National Parks: The American Experience*. Lincoln: University of Nebraska Press, 1987.

Ruschmann, Paul. *Tort Reform*. Philadelphia: Chelsea House, 2006.

Ruse, Michael. *Darwin and Design: Does Evolution Have a Purpose?* Cambridge, MA: Harvard University Press, 2003.

Ruse, Michael, and William A. Dembski, eds. *Debating Design: From Darwin to DNA*. New York: Cambridge University Press, 2004.

Rushdoony, Rousas J. *The Nature of the American System*. Vallecito, CA: Ross House Books, 2002.

———. *Roots of Reconstruction*. Vallecito, CA: Ross House Books, 1991.

Ryan, James G. *Earl Browder: The Failure of American Communism*. Tuscaloosa: The University of Alabama Press, 1997.

Rymph, Catherine. *Republican Women: Feminism and Conservatism from Suffrage Through the Rise of the New Right*. Chapel Hill: University of North Carolina Press, 2006.

Sabato, Larry J., ed. *Divided States of America: The Slash and Burn Politics of the 2004 Presidential Election*. New York: Pearson Longman, 2006.

Sadoff, Mickey. *Get MADD Again, America!* Irving, TX: Mothers Against Drunk Driving, 1991.

Safire, William. *Before the Fall: An Inside View of the Pre-Watergate White House*. New York: Doubleday, 1975.

Sagan, Carl. *The Demon-Haunted World: Science as a Candle in the Dark*. New York: Random House, 1995.

Said, Edward W. *Out of Place: A Memoir*. New York: Alfred A. Knopf, 1999.

Sale, Kirkpatrick. *SDS*. New York: Random House, 1973.

Salisbury, Harrison E. *Without Fear or Favor: The New York Times and Its Times*. New York: Times Book, 1980.

Saltman, Kenneth J. *The Edison Schools: Corporate Schooling and the Assault on Public Education*. New York: Routledge, 2005.

Samaha, Joel. *Criminal Procedure*. 4th ed. Belmont, CA: Wadsworth, 1999.

Sandbrook, Dominic. *Eugene McCarthy: The Rise and Fall of Postwar American Liberalism*. New York: Alfred A. Knopf, 2004.

Sanders, Bernie, and Huck Gutman. *Outsider in the House*. New York: Verso, 1997.

Santelli, Robert, and Emily Davidson, eds. *Hard Travelin': The Life and Legacy of Woody Guthrie*. Hanover, NH: Wesleyan University Press, 1999.

Santorum, Rick. *It Takes a Family: Conservatism and the Common Good*. Wilmington, DE: ISI Books, 2005.

Sarat, Austin. *Mercy on Trial: What It Takes to Stop an Execution*. Princeton, NJ: Princeton University Press, 2005.

Saunders, Frances Stonor. *The Cultural Cold War: The CIA and the World of Arts and Letters*. New York: New Press, 2001.

Saunders, Kevin W. *Saving Our Children from the First Amendment*. New York: New York University Press, 2003.

Saussure, Ferdinand de. *Course in General Linguistics*. LaSalle, IL: Open Court, 1998.

Savas, E.S. *Privatization and Public Private Partnerships*. New York: Chatham House, 2000.

Scanlon, Jennifer. *Bad Girls Go Everywhere: The Life of Helen Gurley Brown*. New York: Oxford University Press, 2009.

Scatamburlo, Valerie L. *Soldiers of Misfortune: The New Right's Culture War and the Politics of Political Correctness*. New York: Peter Lang, 1998.

Schaeffer, Francis A. *The Complete Works of Francis A. Schaeffer: A Christian Worldview*. 5 vols. Westchester, IL: Crossway Books, 1985.

Schaler, Jeffrey A., and Magda E. Schaler, eds. *Smoking: Who Has the Right?* Amherst, NY: Prometheus Books, 1998.

Schaller, Michael, and George Rising. *The Republican Ascendancy: American Politics, 1968–2001*. Wheeling, IL: Harlan Davidson, 2002.

Scharff, Edward. *Worldly Power: The Making of the Wall Street Journal*. New York: A Plume Book, 1986.

Scheader, Catherine. *Shirley Chisholm: Teacher and Congresswoman*. Berkeley Heights, NJ: Enslow, 1990.

Schecter, Cliff. *The Real McCain: Why Conservatives Don't Trust Him—and Why Independents Shouldn't*. Sausalito, CA: PoliPointPress, 2008.

Schiavo, Michael. *Terri: The Truth*. New York: Dutton, 2006.

Schick, Allen. *The Capacity to Budget*. Washington, DC: Urban Press, 1990.

Schier, Steven E. *Panorama of a Presidency: How George W. Bush Acquired and Spent His Political Capital*. Armonk, NY: M.E. Sharpe, 2009.

Schindler, Mary, and Robert Schindler. *A Life That Matters: The Legacy of Terri Schiavo—A Lesson for Us All*. New York: Warner Books, 2006.

Schippers, David. *Sellout: The Inside Story of President Clinton's Impeachment*. Washington, DC: Regnery, 2000.

Schlatter, Evelyn A. *Aryan Cowboys: White Supremacists and the Search for a New Frontier, 1970–2000*. Austin: University of Texas Press, 2006.

Schlesinger, Arthur M., Jr. *The Bitter Heritage: Vietnam and American Democracy, 1941–1966*. Boston: Houghton Mifflin, 1967.

———. *The Disuniting of America: Reflections on a Multicultural Society*. New York: W.W. Norton, 1998.

———. *A Life in the Twentieth Century: Innocent Beginnings, 1917–1950*. Boston: Houghton Mifflin, 2000.

Schmaltz, William H. *Hate: George Lincoln Rockwell and the American Nazi Party*. Washington, DC: Brassey's, 1999.

Schmidt, Susan, and Michael Weisskopf. *Truth at Any Cost: Ken Starr and the Unmaking of Bill Clinton*. New York: HarperCollins, 2000.

Schneider, Gregory. *Cadres for Conservatism: Young Americans for Freedom and the Rise of the Contemporary Right*. New York: New York University Press, 1999.

Schodt, Frederick L. *America and the Four Japans: Friend, Foe, Model, Mirror*. Berkeley, CA: Stone Bridge, 1994.

Schoem, David Louis. *Multicultural Teaching in the University*. Westport, CT: Praeger, 1993.

Schoen, Douglas. *Pat*. New York: Harper and Row, 1979.

Schoenwald, Jonathan M. *A Time for Choosing: The Rise of Modern American Conservatism*. Oxford: Oxford University Press, 2001.

Schomp, Gerald. *Birchism Was My Business*. New York: Macmillan, 1970.

Schrecker, Ellen. *The Age of McCarthyism: A Brief History with Documents*. 2nd ed. New York: Bedford Books, 2002.

———. *Many Are the Crimes: McCarthyism in America*. New York: Little, Brown, 1998.

Schulman, Bruce J. *Lyndon B. Johnson and American Liberalism*. New York: St. Martin's Press, 1995.

———. *The Seventies: The Great Shift in American Culture, Society, and Politics*. Cambridge, MA: Da Capo Press, 2001.

Schultze, Quentin J. *Christianity and the Mass Media in America: Toward a Democratic Accommodation*. East Lansing: Michigan State University Press, 2003.

Schuster, Henry, with Charles Stone. *Hunting Eric Rudolph*. New York: Berkeley Books, 2005.

Schwartz, John E. *America's Hidden Success*. New York: W.W. Norton, 1983.

Schwartz, Stephen. *Atomic Audit: The Costs and Consequences of U.S. Nuclear Weapons Since 1940*. Washington, DC: Brookings Institution Press, 1998.

———. *Is It Good for the Jews? The Crisis of America's Israel Lobby*. New York: Doubleday, 2006.

Schwarz, Ted. *Joseph P. Kennedy: The Mogul, the Mob, the Statesman, and the Making of an American Myth*. Hoboken, NJ: John Wiley & Sons, 2003.

Schweizer, Peter. *Do As I Say (Not As I Do): Profiles in Liberal Hypocrisy*. New York: Doubleday, 2005.

———. *Disney: The Mouse Betrayed*. Washington, DC: Regnery, 1998.

Schweizer, Peter, and Rochelle Schweizer. *The Bushes: Portrait of a Dynasty*. New York: Doubleday, 2004.

Sciabarra, Chris Matthew. *Ayn Rand: The Russian Radical*. University Park: Pennsylvania State University Press, 1995.

Scott, Nathan A., Jr., ed. *The Legacy of Reinhold Niebuhr*. Chicago: University of Chicago Press, 1975.

Scruggs, Jan C., and Joel L. Swerdlow. *To Heal a Nation: The Vietnam Veterans Memorial*. New York: Harper and Row, 1985.

Scurra, Dorothy, ed. *Conversations with Tom Wolfe*. Jackson: University Press of Mississippi, 1990.

Seale, Bobby. *Seize the Time*. Baltimore: Black Classic Press, 1970.

Seaman, Ann Rowe. *America's Most Hated Woman: The Life and Gruesome Death of Madalyn Murray O'Hair*. Harrisburg, PA: Continuum International, 2005.

Seeger, Pete. *Where Have All the Flowers Gone: A Singer's Stories, Songs, Seeds, Robberies*. Bethlehem, PA: Sing Out, 1993.

Segerston, Paul Stephen. *Naomi Klein and the Anti-Globalization Movement*. London: Centre for Economic Policy Research, 2003.

Seib, Philip M. *Broadcasts from the Blitz: How Edward R. Murrow Helped Lead America into War*. Washington, DC: Potomac, 2007.

Sen, Amartya Kumar. *Inequality Reexamined*. New York: Russell Sage Foundation, 1992.

Serrano, Andres. *Andres Serrano, Works 1983–1993*. Curated by Patrick T. Murphy. Essays by Robert Hobbs, Wendy Steiner, and Marcia Tucker. Philadelphia: Institute of Contemporary Art, University of Pennsylvania, 1994.

Serrin, Judith, and William Serrin, eds. *Muckraking! The Journalism That Changed America*. New York: New Press, 2002.

Shafer, Byron E., ed. *Is America Different? A Look at American Exceptionalism*. New York: Oxford University Press, 1991.

Shafer-Landau, Russ. *Whatever Happened to Good and Evil?* New York: Oxford University Press, 2004.

Shannan, J. Patrick. *The Montana Freemen: The Untold Story*. Jackson, MS: Center for Historical Analysis, 1996.

Sharp, Elaine B., ed. *Culture Wars and Local Politics*. Lawrence: University Press of Kansas, 1999.

Sharpton, Al, and Anthony Walton. *Go and Tell Pharaoh: The Autobiography of the Reverend Al Sharpton*. New York: Doubleday, 1996.

Sharpton, Al, and Karen Hunter. *Al on America*. New York: Dafina Books, 2002.

Shawn, Eric. *The U.N. Exposed: How the United Nations Sabotages America's Security*. New York: Sentinel, 2006.

Sheehan, Cindy. *Peace Mom: A Mother's Journey Through Heartache to Activism*. New York: Atria Books, 2006.

Sheehan, Jack. *Skin City: Uncovering the Las Vegas Sex Industry*. Las Vegas, NV: Stephens Press, 2004.

Shelton, Robert. *No Direction Home: The Life and Music of Bob Dylan*. New York: Da Capo Press, 1997.

Sherman, Janann, ed. *Interviews with Betty Friedan*. Jackson: University of Mississippi, 2002.

Sherrow, Victoria. *Love Canal: Toxic Waste Tragedy*. Berkeley Heights, NJ: Enslow, 2001.

Shichor, David. *Punishment for Profit: Private Prisons/Public Concerns*. Thousand Oaks, CA: Sage, 1995.

Shiell, Timothy C. *Campus Hate Speech on Trial*. Lawrence: University Press of Kansas, 1998.

Shiftel, Yoram. *Defending "Ivan the Terrible": The Conspiracy to Convict John Demjanjuk*. Washington, DC: Regnery Books, 2005.

Shilts, Randy. *The Mayor of Castro Street: The Life and Times of Harvey Milk*. New York: St. Martin's Press, 1982.

Shirley, David. *Alex Haley*. New York: Chelsea House, 1994.

Shomette, Doug, ed. *The Critical Response to Tom Wolfe*. Westport, CT: Greenwood, 1992.

Shorris, Earl. *Latinos: A Biography of the People*. New York: W.W. Norton, 1992.

Short, C. Brant. *Ronald Reagan and the Public Lands: America's Conservation Debate, 1979–1984*. College Station: Texas A&M University Press, 1989.

Sider, Ron. *Just Generosity: A New Vision for Overcoming Poverty in America*. Grand Rapids, MI: Baker, 1999.

———. *Rich Christians in an Age of Hunger: A Biblical Study*. Downers Grove, IL: InterVarsity Press, 1977.

Sifton, Elisabeth. *The Serenity Prayer: Faith and Politics in Times of Peace and War*. New York: W.W. Norton, 2003.

Signorile, Michelangelo. *Queer in America: Sex, the Media, and the Closets of Power*. New York: Random House, 1993.

Silet, Charles P., ed. *Oliver Stone: Interviews*. Jackson: University Press of Mississippi, 2001.

Simon, Merrill. *Jerry Falwell and the Jews*. New York: Jonathan David, 1984.

Simonelli, Frederick J. *American Fuehrer: George Lincoln Rockwell and the American Nazi Party*. Urbana: University of Illinois Press, 1999.

Simpson, David. *9/11: The Culture of Commemoration*. Chicago and London: University of Chicago Press, 2006.

Simpson, John Warfield. *Dam! Water, Politics, and Preservation in Hetch Hetchy and Yosemite National Park*. New York: Pantheon, 2005.

Sine, Tom. *Cease Fire: Searching for Sanity in America's Culture Wars*. Grand Rapids, MI: Eerdmans, 1995.

Singer, June. *Androgyny: The Opposites Within*. York Beach, ME: Nicolas-Hays, 2000.

Singer, Peter. *Animal Liberation*. New York: HarperCollins, 2001.

Singer, S. Fred. *Hot Talk, Cold Science: Global Warming's Unfinished Debate*. Oakland: Independent Institute, 1998.

Singh, Amritjit. *Interviews with Edward W. Said*. Jackson: University Press of Mississippi, 2004.

Singh, Robert. *The Farrakhan Phenomenon: Race, Reaction, and the Paranoid Style in American Politics*. Washington, DC: Georgetown University Press, 1997.

Skinner, Kiron K., Annelise Anderson, and Martin Anderson, eds. *Reagan: A Life in Letters*. New York: Free Press, 2003.

Skorsi, Alan. *Pants on Fire: How Al Franken Lies, Smears, and Deceives*. Nashville, TN: WMD Books, 2005.

Slater, David, and Peter J. Taylor, eds. *The American Century: Consensus and Coercion in the Projection of American Power*. Walden, MA: Blackwell, 1999.

Sloan, Frank A., et al. *Suing for Medical Malpractice*. Chicago: University of Chicago Press, 1993.

Smith, Bradley A. *Unfree Speech: The Folly of Campaign Finance Reform*. Princeton, NJ: Princeton University Press, 2001.

Smith, Christian, and Michael Emerson. *American Evangelicalism: Embattled and Thriving*. Chicago: University of Chicago Press, 1998.

———. *Divided by Faith: Evangelical Religion and the Problem of Race in America*. New York: Oxford University Press, 2001.

Smith, Christopher E. *The Rehnquist Court and Criminal Punishment*. New York: Garland, 1997.

Smith, F. LaGard. *ACLU—The Devil's Advocate*. Colorado Springs, CO: Marcon, 1996.

Smith, Paul Chatt, and Robert Allen Warrior. *Like a Hurricane: The Indian Movement from Alcatraz to Wounded Knee*. New York: New Press, 1996.

Smitherman, Geneva, ed. *African American Women Speak Out on Anita Hill–Clarence Thomas*. Detroit, MI: Wayne State University Press, 1995.

Smolla, Rodney A. *Jerry Falwell v. Larry Flynt: The First Amendment on Trial*. New York: St. Martin's Press, 1988.

Smoodin, Eric, ed. *Disney Discourse: Producing the Magic Kingdom*. New York: Routledge, 1994.

Snowball, David. *Continuity and Change in the Rhetoric of the Moral Majority*. New York: Praeger, 1991.

Sokal, Alan, and Jean Bricmont. *Fashionable Nonsense: Postmodern Intellectuals' Abuse of Science*. New York: Picador, 1998.

Soley, Lawrence. *Censorship, Inc: The Corporate Threat to Free Speech in the United States*. New York: Monthly Review Press, 2002.

Solinger, Rickie, eds. *Abortion Wars: A Half Century of Struggle, 1950–2000*. Berkeley: University of California Press, 1998.

Solomon, Stephen D. *Ellery's Protest: How One Young Man Defied Tradition and Sparked the Battle over School Prayer*. Ann Arbor: University of Michigan Press, 2007.

Sowell, Thomas. *A Personal Odyssey*. New York: Free Press, 2000.

Spada, James. *The Films of Robert Redford*. Secaucus, NJ: Citadel Press, 1977.

Spaeth, Harold J., and Jeffrey A. Segal. *The Supreme Court and the Attitudinal Model*. New York: Cambridge University Press, 1993.

Spalding, Elizabeth Edwards. *The First Cold Warrior: Harry Truman, Containment, and the Making of Liberal Internationalism*. Lexington: University of Kentucky Press, 2006.

Spence, Gerry. *O.J.: The Last Word*. New York: St. Martin's Press, 1997.

Sperling, John, Suzanne Helburn, Samuel George, John Morris, and Carl Hunt. *The Great Divide: Retro vs. Metro America*. Sausalito, CA: PoliPoint Press, 2004.

Spindel, Carol. *Dancing at Halftime: Sports and the Controversy over American Indian Mascots*. New York: New York University Press, 2000.

Spock, Benjamin, and Mary Morgan. *Spock on Spock: A Memoir of Growing Up with the Century*. New York: Pantheon Books, 1985.

Spoto, Donald. *Rebel: The Life and Legend of James Dean*. New York: HarperCollins, 1996.

Staggenborg, Suzanne. *The Pro-Choice Movement: Organization and Activism in the Abortion Conflict*. New York: Oxford University Press, 1994.

Stamper, Norm. *Breaking Rank: A Top Cop's Exposé of the Dark Side of American Policing*. New York: Nation Books, 2005.

Standaert, Michael. *Skipping Towards Armageddon: The Politics and Propaganda of the Left Behind Novels and the LaHaye Empire*. Brooklyn, NY: Soft Skull Press, 2006.

Stanfield, J. Ron. *John Kenneth Galbraith*. New York: St. Martin's Press, 1996.

Steel, Ronald. *Pax Americana*. New York: Viking, 1967.

Steely, Mel. *The Gentleman from Georgia: The Biography of Newt Gingrich*. Macon, GA: Mercer University Press, 2000.

Stefancic, Jean, and Richard Delgado. *No Mercy: How Conservative Think Tanks and Foundations Changed America's Social Agenda*. Philadelphia: Temple University Press, 1996.

Steger, Manfred N. *Globalism: The New Market Ideology*. Lanham, MD: Rowman & Littlefield, 2002.

Steinhorn, Leonard. *The Greater Generation: In Defense of the Baby Boom Legacy*. New York: St. Martin's Press, 2006.

Steinmo, Sven. *Taxation and Democracy*. New Haven, CT: Yale University Press, 1993.

Stern, Gary M., and Martin Halperin, eds. *The U.S. Constitution and the Power to Go to War: Historical and Current Perspectives*. Westport, CT: Greenwood Press, 1994.

Stern, Howard. *Miss America*. New York: Regan Books, 1995.

———. *Private Parts*. New York: Simon & Schuster, 1993.

Stern, Kenneth. *Antisemitism Today: How It Is the Same, How It Is Different, and How to Fight It*. New York: American Jewish Committee, 2006.

Stern, Sydney Landensohn. *Gloria Steinem: Her Passions, Politics and Mystique*. Secaucus, NJ: Carol, 1997.

Sternheimer, Karen. *Kids These Days: Facts and Fictions About Today's Youth*. Lanham, MD: Rowman and Littlefield, 2006.

Sternlicht, Sanford. *A Reader's Guide to Modern American Drama*. Syracuse, NY: Syracuse University Press, 2002.

Stevens, Jay. *Storming Heaven: LSD and the American Dream*. New York: Grove, 1987.

Stewart, David. *The PBS Companion: A History of Public Television*. New York: TV Books, 1999.

Stewart, Gary L. *Miranda: The Story of America's Right to Remain Silent*. Tuscon: University of Arizona Press, 2004.

Stiglitz, Joseph E. *Globalization and Its Discontents*. New York: W.W. Norton, 2002.

Stockman, David. *The Triumph of Politics: Why the Reagan Revolution Failed*. New York: Harper and Row, 1986.

Strausbaugh, John. *Black Like You: Blackface, Whiteface, Insult & Imitation in American Popular Culture*. New York: Penguin, 2006.

Strauss, Steven D. *The Complete Idiot's Guide to the Kennedys*. Indianapolis, IN: Macmillan USA, 2000.

Strauss, William, and Neil Howe. *Generations: The History of America's Future, 1584 to 2069*. New York: William Morrow, 1991.

Streissguth, Thomas. *Media Bias*. New York: Marshall Cavendish Benchmark, 2007.

Strout, Cushing, ed. *Conscience, Science, and Security: The Case of Dr. J. Robert Oppenheimer*. Chicago: Rand McNally, 1963.

Strum, Philippa. *When the Nazis Came to Skokie: Freedom for Speech We Hate*. Lawrence: University Press of Kansas, 1999.

Stryker, Susan, and Stephen Whittle. *The Transgender Studies Reader*. New York: Routledge, 2006.

Stunkel, Kenneth R. *Understanding Lewis Mumford: A Guide for the Perplexed*. Lewistown, NY: Edwin Mellen Press, 2004.

Sugarmann, Josh. *Every Handgun Is Aimed at You: The Case for Banning Handguns*. New York: New Press, 2001.

————. *National Rifle Association: Money, Power and Fear*. Washington, DC: National Press, 1992.

Sullum, Jacob. *For Your Own Good: The Anti-Smoking Crusade and the Tyranny of Public Health*. New York: Free Press, 1998.

Summers, Harry G., Jr. *On Strategy: A Critical Analysis of the Vietnam War*. Novato, CA: Presidio, 1982.

Sunstein, Cass R. *Animal Rights: Current Debates and New Directions*. New York: Oxford University Press, 2004.

Sussman, Barry. *The Great Coverup: Nixon and the Scandal of Watergate*. New York: Crowell, 1974.

Swan, Patrick, ed. *Alger Hiss, Whittaker Chambers, and the Schism in the American Soul*. Wilmington, DE: Intercollegiate Studies Institute, 2003.

Swirski, Peter. *From Lowbrow to Nobrow*. Montreal: McGill-Queen's University Press, 2005.

Sykes, Charles. *A Nation of Victims*. New York: St. Martin's Press, 1992.

Szatmary, David P. *Rockin' in Time: A Social History of Rock-and-Roll*. Upper Saddle River, NJ: Prentice Hall, 2000.

Tabor, James D., and Eugene V. Gallagher. *Why Waco? Cults and the Battle for Religious Freedom in America*. Berkeley: University of California Press, 1995.

Takaki, Ronald. *A Different Mirror: A History of Multicultural America*. Boston: Little, Brown, 1993.

————. *Hiroshima: Why America Dropped the Atomic Bomb*. Boston: Little, Brown, 1995.

Talese, Gay. *The Kingdom and the Power. Behind the Scenes at the* New York Times: *The Institution That Influences the World*. New York: Random House Trade Paperbacks, 2007.

Tancredo, Thomas G. *In Mortal Danger: The Battle for America's Border and Security*. Nashville, TN: WND Books, 2006.

Tatalovich, Raymond. *The Politics of Abortion in the United States and Canada: A Comparative Study*. Armonk, NY: M.E. Sharpe, 1997.

Taylor, John B. *The Right to Counsel and the Privilege Against Self-Incrimination: Rights and Liberties Under the Law*. Santa Barbara, CA: ABC-CLIO, 2004.

Teal, Donn. *The Gay Militants*. New York: Stein and Day, 1971.

Teller, Edward, with Judith L. Shoolery. *Memoirs: A Twentieth-Century Journey in Science and Politics*. Cambridge, MA: Perseus, 2001.

Terkel, Studs. *Talking to Myself: A Memoir of My Times*. New York: Pantheon Books, 1984.

————. *Touch and Go: A Memoir*. New York: New Press, 2007.

Terry, Karen J. *Sexual Offenses and Offenders: Theory, Practice, and Policy*. Belmont, CA: Wadsworth, 2006.

Theoharis, Athan, with Richard Immerman, Loch Johnson, Kathryn Olmsted, and John Prados, eds. *The Central Intelligence Agency: Security Under Scrutiny*. Understanding Our Government Series. Westport, CT: Greenwood Press, 2006.

Thomas, Cal, and Bob Beckel. *Common Ground: How to Stop the Partisan War That Is Destroying America*. New York: William Morrow, 2007.

Thomas, Clarence. *My Grandfather's Son: A Memoir*. New York: Harper, 2007.

Thomas, Evan. *"A Long Time Coming": The Inspiring, Combative 2008 Campaign and the Historic Election of Barack Obama*. New York: PublicAffairs, 2009.

Thompson, Anita. *The Gonzo Way*. Golden, CO: Fulcrum, 2007.

Thornhill, Randy, and Craig T. Palmer. *A Natural History of Rape: Biological Bases of Sexual Coercion*. 3rd ed. Cambridge, MA: MIT Press, 2000.

Thurber, Timothy N. *The Politics of Equality: Hubert H. Humphrey and the African American Freedom Struggle*. New York: Columbia University Press, 1999.

Tifft, Susan E., and Alex S. Jones. *The Trust: The Private and Powerful Family Behind the* New York Times. Boston: Little, Brown, 1999.

Till-Mobley, Mamie, and Christopher Benson. *Death of Innocence: The Story of a Hate Crime That Changed America*. New York: One World Ballantine Books, 2003.

Timberg, Bernard M. *Television Talk: A History of the TV Talk Show*. Austin: University of Texas Press, 2002.

Timmerman, Kenneth. *Shakedown! Exposing the Real Jesse Jackson*. Washington, DC: Regnery, 2002.

Timmons, Stuart. *The Trouble with Harry Hay: Founder of the Modern Gay Movement*. Boston: Allyson, 1996.

Tinsley, E.J., ed. *Reinhold Niebuhr, 1892–1971*. London: Epworth Press, 1973.

Todd, Chuck, and Sheldon Gawiser. *How Barack Obama Won: A State-by-State Guide to the Historic 2008 Election*. New York: Vintage Books, 2009.

Toeplitz, Jerzy. *Hollywood and After*. London: Allen and Unwin, 1974.

Toke, Dave. *The Politics of GM Food: A Comparative Study of the UK, USA and EU*. New York: Routledge, 2004.

Toobin, Jeffrey. *The Run of His Life: The People v. O.J. Simpson*. New York: Random House, 1996.

————. *Too Close to Call: The Thirty-Six-Day Battle to Decide the 2000 Election*. New York: Random House, 2001.

————. *Vast Conspiracy: The Real Story of the Sex Scandal That Brought Down a President*. New York: Random House, 1999.

Toplin, Robert Brent. *Michael Moore's Fahrenheit 9/11: How One Film Divided a Nation*. Lawrence: University Press of Kansas, 2006.

————. *Oliver Stone's USA: Film, History, and Controversy*. Lawrence: University Press of Kansas, 2000.

Torgoff, Martin. *Can't Find My Way Home: America in the Great Stoned Age, 1945–2000*. New York: Simon & Schuster, 2004.

Treichler, Paula. *How to Have Theory in an Epidemic: Cultural Chronicles of AIDS*. Durham, NC: Duke University Press, 1999.

Tribe, Laurence H. *Abortion: The Clash of Absolutes*. New York: W.W. Norton, 1990.

Trippi, Joe. *The Revolution Will Not Be Televised: Democracy, the Internet, and the Overthrow of Everything*. New York: Regan Books, 2004.

Troy, Gil. *Hillary Rodham Clinton: Polarizing First Lady*. Lawrence: University Press of Kansas, 2006.

————. *Morning in America: How Ronald Reagan Invented the 1980s*. Princeton, NJ: Princeton University Press, 2005.

Truman, Harry S. *Memoirs*. 2 vols. Garden City, NY: Doubleday, 1955–1956.

Tsang, Steve. *Intelligence and Human Rights in the Era of Global Terrorism*. Westport, CT: Praeger Security International, 2007.

Tuccille, Jerome. *Rupert Murdoch: Creator of a Worldwide Media Empire*. Washington, DC: Beard Books, 2003.

Tucker, William. *Vigilante: The Backlash Against Crime in America*. New York: Stein and Day, 1985.

Tunnell, Kenneth D. *Pissing on Demand: Workplace Drug Testing and the Rise of the Detox Society*. New York: New York University Press, 2004.

Turner, Daniel L. *Standing Without Apology: The History of Bob Jones University*. Greenville, SC: Bob Jones University Press, 1997.

Turner, Fred. *Echoes of Combat: The Vietnam War in American Memory*. New York: Anchor Books, 1996.

Turner, Richard Brent. *Islam in the African-American Experience*. Bloomington: Indiana University Press, 2003.

Turque, Bill. *Inventing Al Gore*. Boston: Houghton Mifflin, 2000.

Tushnet, Mark V. *The NAACP's Legal Strategy Against Segregated Education, 1925–1950*. Chapel Hill: University of North Carolina Press, 1987.

———, ed. *The Warren Court in Historical and Political Perspective*. Charlottesville: University Press of Virginia, 1993.

Tyner, James A. *The Geography of Malcolm X: Black Radicalism and the Remaking of American Space*. New York: Routledge, 2006.

U.S. Congress. House of Representatives. *In the Matter of Representative Newt Gingrich: Report on the Select Committee on Ethics*. Washington, DC: U.S. GPO, 1997.

U.S. Congress. *U.S. Relations with Saudi Arabia: Oil, Anxiety, and Ambivalence: Hearings before the Subcommittee on the Middle East and South Asia of the Committee on Foreign Affairs*. Washington, DC: US GPO, 2008.

U.S. Department of Education. *A Nation at Risk: The Imperative for Educational Reform: A Report to the Nation and the Secretary by the National Commission on Higher Education*. Washington, DC: U.S. Government Printing Office, 1983.

U.S. Environmental Protection Agency. *Respiratory Health Effects of Passive Smoking: Lung Cancer and Other Disorders*. Bethesda, MD: National Institutes of Health, 1993.

U.S. Nuclear Regulatory Commission. *Fact Sheet: The Accident at Three Mile Island*. Washington, DC: Office of Public Affairs, 2004.

U.S. Senate. "Tributes to the Honorable Robert C. Byrd in the Senate." Washington, DC: U.S. Government Printing Office, 1990.

U.S. Surgeon General. *The Health Consequences of Involuntary Smoking*. Rockville, MD: U.S. Department of Health and Human Services, 1986.

Unger, Irwin. *The Best of Intentions: The Triumph and Failure of the Great Society Under Kennedy, Johnson and Nixon*. New York: Doubleday, 1996.

Urofsky, Melvin I. *Money and Free Speech: Campaign Finance Reform and the Courts*. Lawrence: University of Kansas Press, 2005.

Urofsky, Melvin I., and Martha May, eds. *The New Christian Right: Political and Social Issues*. New York: Garland, 1996.

Urquhart, Brian. *Ralph Bunche: An American Life*. New York: W.W. Norton, 1993.

Utter, Glenn H., and James L. True. *Conservative Christians and Political Participation: A Reference Handbook*. Santa Barbara, CA: ABC-CLIO, 2004.

Vagacs, Robert. *Religious Nuts, Political Fanatics: U2 in Theological Perspective*. Eugene, OR: Cascade, 2005.

Vaid, Urvashi. *Virtual Equality: The Mainstreaming of Gay and Lesbian Liberation*. New York: Anchor Books, 1995.

Valley, David J., and Diana Lindsay. *Jackpot Trail: Indian Gaming in Southern California*. San Diego, CA: Sunbelt, 2003.

Van Alstyne, William W., ed. *Freedom and Tenure in the Academy*. Durham, NC: Duke University Press, 1993.

Van Heerden, Ivor, and Mike Bryan. *The Storm: What Went Wrong and Why During Hurricane Katrina*. New York: Viking, 2006.

Vance, Carole, ed. *Pleasure and Danger: Exploring Female Sexuality*. Boston: Routledge, 1984.

Vaughn, Jacqueline. *Disabled Rights: American Disability Policy and the Fight for Equality*. Washington, DC: Georgetown University Press, 2003.

Vaughn, Stephen. *Freedom and Entertainment*. New York: Cambridge University Press, 2006.

Vedder, Richard K., and Wendell Cox. *The Wal-Mart Revolution: How Big-Box Stores Benefit Consumers, Workers, and the Economy*. Washington, DC: AEI Press, 2006.

Ventura, Jesse. *Do I Stand Alone? Going to the Mat Against Political Pawns and Media Jackals*. New York: Pocket Books, 2000.

———. *I Ain't Got Time to Bleed: Reworking the Body Politic from the Bottom Up*. New York: Villard Books, 1999.

Ventura, Jesse, and Heron Marquez. *Jesse Ventura Tells It Like It Is: America's Most Outspoken Governor Speaks Out About Government*. Minneapolis, MN: Lerner, 2002.

Vermaat, J.A. Emerson. *The World Council of Churches and Politics*. New York: Freedom House, 1989.

Victor, David G. *The Collapse of the Kyoto Protocol and the Struggle to Slow Global Warming*. Princeton, NJ: Princeton University Press, 2004.

Vidal, Gore. *Perpetual War for Perpetual Peace: How We Got to Be So Hated*. New York: Thunder's Mouth Press/Nation Books, 2002.

Viguerie, Richard A. *The New Right: We're Ready to Lead*. Falls Church, VA: Viguerie, 1981.

Viorst, Milton. *Fire in the Streets: America in the 1960s*. New York: Simon & Schuster, 1979.

Virilio, Paul, and Sylvère Lotringer. *Crepuscular Dawn*. Los Angeles: Semiotext(e), 2002.

Viscusi, W. Kip. *Smoke-Filled Rooms: A Postmortem on the Tobacco Deal*. Chicago: University of Chicago Press, 2002.

Voegelin, Eric. *The New Science of Politics: An Introduction*. Chicago: University of Chicago Press, 1952.

Vollers, Maryanne. *Eric Rudolph: Murder, Myth, and the Pursuit of an American Outlaw*. New York: HarperCollins, 2006.

Vorlicky, Robert, ed. *Tony Kushner in Conversation*. Ann Arbor: University of Michigan Press, 1998.

Vose, Clement E. *Caucasians Only: The Supreme Court, the NAACP, and the Restrictive Covenant Cases*. Berkeley: University of California Press, 1959.

Wagner, David. *Blacklisted: The Film Lover's Guide to the Hollywood Blacklist*. New York: Palgrave Macmillan, 2003.

Waits, Chris, and Dave Shors. *Unabomber: The Secret Life of Ted Kaczynski*. Helena, MT: Helena Independent Record/Montana Magazine, 1999.

Walker, Clarence E. *We Can't Go Home Again: An Argument About Afrocentrism*. New York: Oxford University Press, 2001.

Walker, David M., and Daniel Gray. *Historical Dictionary of Marxism*. Lanham, MD: Scarecrow Press, 2007.

Walker, Dennis. *Islam and the Search for African-American Nationhood: Elijah Muhammad, Louis Farrakhan, and the Nation of Islam*. Atlanta, GA: Clarity Press, 2005.

Walker, Jeff. *The Ayn Rand Cult.* Chicago: Open Court, 1999.

Walker, Rebecca, ed. *To Be Real: Telling the Truth and Changing the Face of Feminism.* New York: Anchor Books, 1995.

Walker, Samuel. *In Defense of American Liberties: A History of the ACLU.* New York: Oxford University Press, 1990.

———. *Sense and Nonsense about Crime and Drugs.* Belmont, CA: Wadsworth, 1998.

Wallace, George C. *Stand Up for America.* Garden City, NY: Doubleday, 1976.

Wallace, Jonathan, and Mark Mangan. *Sex, Laws, and Cyberspace.* New York: Henry Holt, 1997.

Wallach, Lori, and Michelle Sforza. *The WTO: Five Years of Reasons to Stop Corporate Globalization.* New York: Seven Stories Press, 1999.

Wallis, Jim. *God's Politics: Why the Right Gets It Wrong and the Left Doesn't Get It.* New York: HarperCollins, 2005.

———. *Revive Us Again: A Sojourner's Story.* Nashville, TN: Abingdon, 1983.

———. *The Soul of Politics: A Practical and Prophetic Vision for Change.* New York: New Press, 1994.

———. *Who Speaks for God? An Alternative to the Religious Right—A New Politics of Compassion, Community, and Civility.* New York: Delacorte Press, 1996.

Walser, Robert. *Running with the Devil: Power, Gender, and Madness in Heavy Metal Music.* Hanover, NH: University Press of New England, 1995.

Walsh, Lawrence. *Firewall: The Iran-Contra Conspiracy and Cover-Up.* New York: W.W. Norton, 1997.

Walter, Jess. *Ruby Ridge: The Truth and Tragedy of the Randy Weaver Family.* New York: ReganBooks, 2002.

Walters, Suzanna Danuta. *All the Rage: The Story of Gay Visibility in America.* Chicago: University of Chicago Press, 2001.

Wanniski, Jude. *The Way the World Works: How Economies Fail and Succeed.* New York: Basic Books, 1978.

Ward, Mark, Sr. *Air of Salvation: The Story of Christian Broadcasting.* Grand Rapids, MI: Baker Books, 1994.

Wardle, Lynn, ed. *Marriage and Same-Sex Unions: A Debate.* New York: Praeger, 2003.

Warner, Michael. *The Trouble with Normal: Sex, Politics, and the Ethics of Queer Life.* New York: Free Press, 1999.

Warren, Earl. *The Memoirs of Earl Warren.* New York: Doubleday, 1977.

Wartzman, Rick. *Obscene in the Extreme: The Burning and Banning of John Steinbeck's* The Grapes of Wrath. New York: PublicAffairs, 2008.

Washington, James Melvin, ed. *A Testament of Hope: The Essential Writings of Martin Luther King, Jr.* San Francisco: Harper San Francisco, 1991.

Washington-Williams, Essie Mae. *Dear Senator: A Memoir by the Daughter of Strom Thurmond.* New York: Regan Books, 2005.

Watkins, Elizabeth Siegel. *On the Pill: A Social History of Oral Contraceptives, 1950–1970.* Baltimore: Johns Hopkins University Press, 1998.

Watkins, S. Craig. *Hip Hop Matters: Politics, Pop Culture, and the Struggle for the Soul of a Movement.* Boston: Beacon Press, 2006.

Watson, Elwood, and Darcy Martin, eds. *"Here She Is, Miss America": The Politics of Sex, Beauty, and Race in America's Most Famous Pageant.* New York: Palgrave Macmillan, 2004.

Watson, Justin. *The Christian Coalition: Dreams of Restoration, Demands for Recognition.* New York: St. Martin's Press, 1997.

Watt, James, and Doug Wead. *Courage of a Conservative.* New York: Simon & Schuster, 1985.

Watts, Rebecca Bridges. *Contemporary Southern Identity: Community Through Controversy.* Jackson: University of Mississippi, 2008.

Wattenberg, Martin P. *The Decline of American Political Parties, 1952–1996.* Cambridge, MA: Harvard University Press, 1998.

Webber, Robert E. *The Moral Majority: Right or Wrong?* Westchester, IL: Cornerstone Books, 1981.

———. *Secular Humanism: Threat and Challenge.* Grand Rapids, MI: Zondervan, 1982.

Weil, Kari. *Androgyny and the Denial of Difference.* Charlottesville: University Press of Virginia, 1992.

Weiler, Paul C. *Medical Malpractice on Trial.* Cambridge, MA: Harvard University Press, 1991.

Weingarten, Marc. *The Gang That Wouldn't Write Straight: Wolfe, Thompson, Didion, and the New Journalism Revolution.* New York: Crown, 2006.

Weinstein, Allen. *Perjury: The Hiss-Chambers Case.* New York: Random House, 1997.

Weinstein, Allen, and Alexander Vassiliev. *The Haunted Wood: Soviet Espionage in America—The Stalin Era.* New York: Modern Library, 2000.

Weinstein, Deena. *Heavy Metal: The Music and Its Culture.* Rev. ed. New York: Da Capo Press, 2000.

Weisberg, Jacob. *The Bush Tragedy.* New York: Random House, 2008.

Weisman, Alan. *Lone Star: The Extraordinary Life and Times of Dan Rather.* Hoboken, NJ: John Wiley & Sons, 2006.

Weitzer, Ronald John, and Steven A. Tuch. *Race and Policing in America: Conflict and Reform.* New York: Cambridge University Press, 2006.

Welch, Matt. *McCain: The Myth of a Maverick.* New York: Palgrave Macmillan, 2007.

Welch, Michael R. *Flag Burning: Moral Panic and the Criminalization of Protest.* Edison, NJ: Aldine Transaction, 2000.

Welch, Robert H.W., Jr. *The Blue Book of the John Birch Society.* Belmont, MA: John Birch Society, 1961.

———. *The Life of John Birch.* Boston: Western Islands, 1965.

Wellman, Sam. *Francis and Edith Schaeffer: Defenders of the Faith.* Uhrichsville, OH: Barbour, 2000.

Wellstone, Paul David. *The Conscience of a Liberal: Reclaiming the Compassionate Agenda.* New York: Random House, 2001.

Wenke, Joseph. *Mailer's America.* Hanover, NH: University Press of New England, 1987.

Wenner, Jann, and Corey Seymour. *Gonzo: The Life of Hunter S. Thompson: An Oral Biography.* New York: Little, Brown, 2007.

West, Cornel. *The Cornel West Reader.* New York: Basic Civitas Books, 1999.

———. *Race Matters.* Boston: Beacon Press, 1993.

Weyrich, Paul M., and Connaught Marshner, eds. *Future 21: Directions for America in the 21st Century.* Greenwich, CT: Devin-Adair, 1984.

White, John Kenneth. *The Values Divide: American Politics and Culture in Transition.* New York: Chatham House, 2003.

White, Joseph, and Aaron Wildavsky. *The Deficit and the Public Interest.* Berkeley: University of California Press, 1989.

White, Kenneth John. *The Values Divide: American Politics and Culture in Transition*. New York: Chatham House, 2003.

White, Reggie, with Andrew Peyton Thomas. *Fighting the Good Fight: America's "Minister of Defense" Stands Firm on What It Takes to Win God's Way*. Nashville, TN: Thomas Nelson, 1999.

White, Reggie, with Jim Denney. *Reggie White in the Trenches: The Autobiography*. Nashville, TN: Thomas Nelson, 1997.

White, Theodore H. *The Making of the President, 1968*. New York: Atheneum, 1969.

Whitfield, Dexter. *Public Services or Corporate Welfare: Rethinking the Nation State in the Global Economy*. Sterling, VA: Pluto, 2001.

Whitten, Mark Weldon. *The Myth of Christian America: What You Need to Know About the Separation of Church and State*. New York: Smith and Helwys, 1999.

Wildavsky, Aaron, and Naomi Caiden. *The New Politics of the Budgetary Process*. 4th ed. New York: Longman, 2001.

Wildmon, Donald, with Randall Nulton. *Don Wildmon: The Man the Networks Love to Hate*. Wilmore, KY: Bristol Books, 1989.

Wilentz, Amy. *I Feel Earthquakes More Often Than They Happen: Coming to California in an Age of Schwarzenegger*. New York: Simon & Schuster, 2006.

Williams, Juan. *Eyes on the Prize: America's Civil Rights Years, 1954–1965*. New York: Penguin, 1988.

———. *Thurgood Marshall: American Revolutionary*. New York: Three Rivers Press, 2000.

Williams, Mary E., ed. *Culture Wars: Opposing Viewpoints*. Farmington Hills, MA: Greenhaven Press, 2003.

Williams, Patrick, ed. *Edward Said*. 4 vols. Thousand Oaks, CA: Sage, 2004.

Williams, Rhys H., ed. *Cultural Wars in American Politics: Critical Reviews of a Popular Myth*. New York: Aldine de Gruyter, 1997.

———, ed. *Promise Keepers and the New Masculinity: Private Lives and Public Morality*. Lanham, MD: Lexington Books, 2001.

Williamson, Nigel. *Journey Through the Past: The Stories Behind the Classic Songs of Neil Young*. San Francisco: Backbeat Books, 2002.

Willman, Chris. *Rednecks and Bluenecks: The Politics of Country Music*. New York: New Press, 2005.

Wills, Gary. *John Wayne's America: The Politics of Celebrity*. New York: Simon & Schuster, 1997.

Wilson, Harry L. *Guns, Gun Control, and Elections: The Politics and Policy of Firearms*. Lanham, MD: Rowman and Littlefield, 2007.

Wilson, John. *The Myth of Political Correctness: The Conservative Attack on High Education*. Durham, NC: Duke University Press, 1995.

———. *Patriotic Correctness: Academic Freedom and Its Enemies*. Boulder, CO: Paradigm, 2007.

Wilson, Joy Johnson. *Summary of the Attorneys General Master Tobacco Settlement Agreement*. Washington, DC: National Conference of State Legislatures, 1999.

Wilson, William J. *The Truly Disadvantaged: The Inner City, the Underclass, and Public Policy*. Chicago: University of Chicago Press, 1987.

Winchell, Mark Royden. *Neoconservative Criticism: Norman Podhoretz, Kenneth S. Lynn, and Joseph Epstein*. Boston: Twayne, 1991.

———. *William F. Buckley, Jr.* Boston: Twayne, 1984.

Winkler, Alan M. *"To Everything There Is a Season": Pete Seeger and the Power of Song*. New York: Oxford University Press, 2009.

Witcover, Jules. *Party of the People: A History of the Democrats*. New York: Random House, 2003.

———. *White Knight: The Rise of Spiro Agnew*. New York: Random House, 1972.

Wittes, Benjamin. *Confirmation Wars: Preserving Independent Courts in Angry Times*. Lanham, MD: Rowman & Littlefield, 2006.

Wojtowicz, Robert. *Sidewalk Critic: Lewis Mumford's Writings on New York*. Princeton, NJ: Princeton Architectural Press, 2000.

Wolfe, Alan. *One Nation After All: What Middle-Class Americans Really Think About God, Country, Family, Racism, Welfare, Immigration, Homosexuality, Work, the Right, the Left, and Each Other*. New York: Viking, 1998.

Wolfe, Christopher, and Richard John Neuhaus. *The Naked Public Square Reconsidered: Religion and Politics in the Twenty-first Century*. Wilmington, DE: ISI Books, 2009.

Wolfe, Tom. *Ambush at Fort Bragg*. New York: Bantam Doubleday Dell Audio, 1997. Originally published in *Rolling Stone*, December 12 and 26, 1996.

Wolfe, Tom, and E.W. Johnson, eds. *The New Journalism*. New York: Harper and Row, 1973.

Wolff, Michael. *The Man Who Owns the News: Inside the Secret World of Rupert Murdoch*. New York: Doubleday, 2008.

Wolfson, Evan. *Why Marriage Matters: America, Equality, and Gay People's Right to Marry*. New York: Simon & Schuster, 2004.

Wood, John Cunningham, and Ronald W. Woods, eds. *Milton Friedman: A Critical Assessment*. New York: Routledge, 1990.

Wood, Peter. *Diversity: The Invention of a Concept*. San Francisco: Encounter Books, 2003.

Woodward, Bob. *The Secret Man: The Story of Watergate's Deep Throat*. New York: Simon and Schuster, 2005.

Woodward, Bob, and Carl Bernstein. *All the President's Men*. New York: Simon and Schuster, 1994.

———. *The Final Days*. New York: Simon and Schuster, 1976.

Workman, Dave. *PETA Files: The Dark Side of the Animal Rights Movement*. Bellevue, WA: Merril, 2003.

Worthington, Andy. *The Guantánamo Files: The Stories of the 774 Detainees in America's Illegal Prison*. Ann Arbor, MI: Pluto Press, 2007.

Wright, Bradford W. *Comic Book Nation: The Transformation of Youth Culture in America*. Baltimore: Johns Hopkins University Press, 2003.

Wright, Melanie J. *Moses in America: The Use of Biblical Narrative*. New York: Oxford University Press, 2003.

Wright, Stuart, ed. *Armageddon in Waco: Critical Perspectives on the Branch Davidian Conflict*. Chicago: University of Chicago Press, 1995.

Wuthnow, Robert. *The Restructuring of American Religion: Society and Faith Since World War II*. Princeton, NJ: Princeton University Press, 1988.

———. *Saving America? Faith-Based Services and the Future of Civil Society*. Princeton, NJ: Princeton University Press, 2004.

———. *The Struggle for America's Soul: Evangelicals, Liberals, and Secularism*. Grand Rapids, MI: W.B. Eerdmans, 1989.

Yannuzi, Della A. *Aldo Leopold: A Protector of the Wild*. Brookfield, CT: Millbrook Press, 2002.

Yarbrough, Slayden A. *Southern Baptists: A Historical, Ecclesiological, and Theological Heritage of a Confessional People.* Brentwood, TN: Southern Baptist Historical Society, 2000.

Yates, Michael D. *Why Unions Matter.* New York: Monthly Review Press, 1998.

Yeun, Eddie, George Katsiaficas, and Daniel Burton-Rose. *Battle of Seattle: The New Challenge to Capitalist Globalization.* New York: Soft Skull Press, 2001.

Young, Jonathan M. *Equality of Opportunity: The Making of the Americans with Disabilities Act.* Washington, DC: National Council on Disability, 1997.

Young, Mitchell. *White Supremacy Groups.* Detroit, MI: Green-haven Press, 2008.

Young, Mitchell, ed. *Culture Wars.* Detroit, MI: Greenhaven Press, 2008.

Zakin, Susan. *Coyotes and Town Dogs: Earth First! and the Environmental Movement.* New York: Viking, 1993.

Zangrando, Robert L. *The NAACP Crusade Against Lynching, 1909–1950.* Philadelphia: Temple University Press, 1980.

Zarkin, Kimberly A., and Michael J. Zarkin. *The Federal Communications Commission: Front Line in the Culture and Regulation Wars.* Westport, CT: Greenwood Press, 2006.

Zeiger, Hans. *Get Off My Honor: The Assault on the Boy Scouts of America.* Nashville, TN: Broadman and Holman, 2005.

Zeigler, Joseph Wesley. *Arts in Crisis: The National Endowment for the Arts Versus America.* Chicago: A Capella Books, 1994.

Zeigler, Sara L., and Gregory G. Gunderson. *Moving Beyond G.I. Jane: Women and the U.S. Military.* Lanham, MD: University Press of America, 2005.

Zelnick, Bob. *Gore: A Political Life.* Washington, DC: Regnery, 1999.

Zeman, Scott C., and Michael A. Amundson. *Atomic Culture: How We Learned to Stop Worrying and Love the Bomb.* Boulder: University Press of Colorado, 2004.

Zimmerman, Jean. *Tailspin: Women at War in the Wake of Tailhook.* New York: Doubleday, 1995.

Zimmerman, Jonathan. *Whose America? Culture Wars in the Public Schools.* Cambridge, MA: Harvard University Press, 2002.

Zinn, Howard. *A People's History of the United States.* New York: Harper & Row, 1980.

———. *The Zinn Reader: Writings on Disobedience and Democracy.* New York: Seven Stories Press, 1997.

Zoba, Wendy Murray. *Day of Reckoning: Columbine and the Search for America's Soul.* Grand Rapids, MI: Brazos Press, 2000.

Zucker, Marjorie B., ed. *The Right to Die Debate: A Documentary History.* Westport, CT: Greenwood, 1999.

Web Sites

Adbusters: Culture Jammers Headquarters Web site. www.adbusters.org.
AFA Online Web site. www.afa.net.
American Civil Liberties Union Web site. www.aclu.org.
American Indian Movement Web site. www.aimovement.org.
Americans for Tax Reform Web site. www.atr.org.
Answers in Genesis Web site. www.answersingenesis.org.
Ayn Rand Institute Web site. www.aynrand.org.
Black Radical Congress Web site. www.blackradicalcongress.org.
Bob Dylan Official Web site. www.bobdylan.com.
Bob Jones University Web site. www.bju.edu.
Boy Scouts of America Web site. www.scouting.org.
Bulletin of Atomic Scientists Web site. www.thebulletin.org.
The Carter Center Web site. www.cartercenter.org.
Center for the Defense of Free Enterprise Web site. www.cdfe.org.
Central Intelligence Agency Web site. www.cia.gov.
The Chalcedon Foundation Web site. www.chalcedon.edu.
Christian Coalition of America Web site. www.cc.org.
Circle of Life Web site. www.circleoflifefoundation.org.
CODEPINK Web site. www.codepink4peace.org.
Common Cause Web site. www.commoncause.org.
Death Penalty Information Center Web site. www.deathpenaltyinfo.org.
Federal Communications Commission Web site. www.fcc.gov.
FIRE—Foundation for Individual Rights in Education Web site. www.thefire.org.
Focus on the Family Web site. www.family.org.
Franklin Delano Roosevelt Memorial Web site, National Park Service. www.nps.gov/fdrm.
Freedom Center Web site. www.horowitzfreedomcenter.org.
G. Gordon Liddy's Official Web site. www.liddyshow.com.
GodHatesFags Web site. www.godhatesfags.com.
Guardian Angels Web site. www.guardianangels.org.
Heritage Foundation Web site. www.heritage.org.
Institute for Media Education Web site. www.drjudithreisman.com.
Jim Crow Museum of Racist Memorabilia Web site. www.ferris.edu/jimcrow.
John Birch Society Web site. www.jbs.org.
Kinsey Institute for Research in Sex, Gender, and Reproduction Web site. www.indiana.edu/~kinsey.
Lower Manhattan Development Corporation Web site. www.renewnyc.com.
Madonna Official Web site. www.madonna.com.
Marilyn Manson Web site. www.marilynmanson.com.
Matthew Shepard Society Web site. www.matthewshepard.org.
Media Matters Web site. www.mediamatters.org.
Michael Medved Web site. www.michaelmedved.com.
Mothers Against Drunk Driving Web site. www.madd.org.
Motion Picture Association of America Web site. www.mpaa.org.
Nation Web site. www.thenation.com.
National Endowment for the Arts Web site. www.nea.gov.
National Endowment for the Humanities Web site. www.neh.gov.
National Organization for Women Web site. www.now.org.
National Park Service Web site. www.nps.gov.
National Public Radio Web site. www.npr.org.
National Review Web site. www.nationalreview.com.
National Rifle Association Web site. www.nra.org.
National WWII Memorial Web site. www.wwiimemorial.com.
New York Times Web site. www.nytimes.com.
Newt Gingrich Web site. www.newt.org.
NoLogo Web site. www.nologo.org.
Norman Lear Web site. www.normanlear.com.
Occupational Safety and Health Administration Web site. www.osha.gov.
Official Al Franken Web site. www.al-franken.com.
Official Kwanzaa Web site. www.officialkwanzaawebsite.org.
Open Society Institute Web site. www.soros.org.

Oprah.com: Live Your Best Life Web site. www.oprah.com.

Panda's Thumb Web site. www.pandasthumb.org.

PBS Web site. www.pbs.org.

People for the American Way Web site. www.pfaw.org.

People for the Ethical Treatment of Animals (PETA) Web site. www.peta.org.

Perverted Justice Web site. www.Perverted-Justice.com.

Planned Parenthood Federation of America Web site. www.plannedparenthood.org.

ProEnglish Web site. www.proenglish.org.

Progressive Christians Uniting Web site. www.progressivechristiansuniting.org.

Project for the New American Century Web site. www.newamericancentury.org.

Promise Keepers Web site. www.promisekeepers.org.

Rainbow PUSH Coalition Web site. www.rainbowpush.org.

Reason Foundation Web site. www.reason.org.

Recording Industry Association of America (RIAA) Web site. www.riaa.com.

School of the Americas Watch Web site. www.soaw.org.

Social Security Administration Web site. www.socialsecurity.gov.

Southern Baptist Convention official Web site. www.sbc.net.

Southern Poverty Law Center Web site. www.splcenter.org.

TimesWatch Web site. www.timeswatch.org.

Tom DeLay Web site. www.tomdelay.com.

Toward Tradition Web site. www.towardtradition.org.

U.S. English, Inc., Web site. www.us-english.org.

U.S. Food and Drug Administration Web site. www.fda.gov.

Vermont Progressive Party Web site. www.answers.com.

Vietnam Veterans Against the War Web site. www.vvaw.org.

Wake-Up Wal-Mart Web site. www.wakeupwalmart.com.

Wall Street Journal Web site. www.online.wsj.com.

Wal-Mart Stores, Inc., Web site. www.walmartstores.com.

Washington Times Web site. www.washtimes.com.

Weekly Standard Web site. www.weeklystandard.com.

Western Hemisphere Institute for Security Cooperation Web site. www.benning.army.mil/whinsec.

Willie Nelson Official Web site. www.willienelson.com.

World Council of Churches Web site. www.wcc-coe.org.

World Magazine Web site. www.worldmag.com.

Index